NORMAN A. POLANSKY, PhD.
PARKWAY OFFICE BUILDING
ASHEVILLE, N. C. 28801

Dec. 1966

SOCIAL PSYCHOLOGY *Issues and Insights*

●

The Lippincott College Psychology Series
under the editorship of
Dr. Carl P. Duncan
Northwestern University
and
Dr. Julius Wishner
University of Pennsylvania

SOCIAL PSYCHOLOGY
ISSUES AND INSIGHTS

GOODWIN WATSON

J. B. Lippincott Company
Philadelphia & New York

FOR
B., D., J., and R.

Preface

Forty years of experience in teaching social psychology to college undergraduates, to graduate students, and to doctoral candidates experimenting with theses have developed the viewpoints underlying this text.

Foremost is our conviction that social psychology, in the years ahead, should contribute far more than it has in the past to enrichment of personal understanding and to a constructive attack on major social problems. Too many academic disciplines are taught only to prepare students to follow the methodological traditions of their mentors. Techniques, in the saddle, ride both teachers and students. "Scholarship" becomes a game in which the achievement of merit badges has no clear connection with any other concerns of humanity. Knowledge for its own sake has value, but, for most students of any subject, information is more valuable if it speaks to their existential concerns. From among the hundreds of thousands of published research studies which might have some bearing on social psychology, this book includes the selected hundreds which help to form fundamental concepts or which illuminate important issues. A basic text in social psychology should not attempt to cultivate the methodological sophistication required for doctoral and post-doctoral research. Only a few of the students taking this course will make their careers in laboratories of social psychology. Those few need far more understanding of experimental design and of the statistical operations than is suitable for the great majority who are to use what they learn of social psychology in their careers as homemakers, businessmen, professional practitioners, or citizens, and in their interpersonal relationships every day.

The emphasis on applying social psychology to vital activities in which most people are engaged does not diminish our concern about maintaining high standards of scientific method. Social psychology is here defined as the *scientific* study of human interaction and thus is differentiated from the contributions which come from ordinary observation, literary creations, historical or philosophical study. In almost every chapter some "Abstracts" are presented; each abstract states a problem, describes briefly the method of investigation, and summarizes some of the findings. On every topic scores of other studies are cited, with the expectation that interested students will want to look up some of these other investigations to see how the research was actually done. Some teachers may ask students to look up, report on, and make critical evaluations of some of the research here mentioned only in. a sentence with the name of the experimenter and the date serving as keys to the full reference in the bibliography. The author has found it useful, further, to ask students to replicate—perhaps on a small scale and with a few subjects—some of the studies which interest them. Students, in this way, come to realize that the findings of social psychology are not simply the prejudices of social scientists with which one may disagree at will.

Psychological research, like that in other sciences, has accelerated. As the numbers of psychologists and psychological journals have multiplied, work has become more specialized. When the American Psychological Association was founded, its members were generalists in the field. Today there are twenty-five Divisions in the Association, and members of one may have little awareness of what is being done in some of the other subdivisions of the discipline. This book has been written with a purpose and endeavor to avoid a narrow specialization and to encompass other areas of psychological research. While social psychology remains central, its relationships to educational psychology, clinical psychology, personality, developmental psychology, counseling psychology, psychotherapy, industrial psychology, and engineering psychology are kept in view. The perspective is even broader than that of psychology, for sociology, anthropology, psychiatry, and political science are also engaged in the scientific study of human interaction. More than most other texts in the field, this presentation recognizes and includes contributions from the related behavioral sciences.

Another feature of this text is that the research is viewed in historic depth. The author has the impression that some of his younger colleagues may have become too exclusively preoccupied with the most recent journals. For their own research this may be appropriate, although even here it might be true that there were insights and seminal beginnings more than a generation ago. Some of these may have been forgotten and lost. Sometimes they are rediscovered generations later. The student of this text is likely to find, on any topic, some references which reach back to the turn of the century and some from subsequent decades. Most references come from the last ten years because the volume of research has been mounting so rapidly, but the earlier, pioneer work is not ignored.

Distinguishing this text from any other known to the author is the central notion of the Structure-Process-Attitude (S-P-A) sequence, as set forth in Chapter 6. Later chapters apply the approach to the understanding of social class, race relations, business organizations, new roles for women, and the effort to harmonize international relations.

The author is aware of having explored further than many of his colleagues in earlier texts the implications of social psychological truths for the evaluation of personal and social values. Whenever one ventures beyond facts to seek their meaning for life, his thinking becomes controversial. The viewpoints here expressed are not intended as propaganda. They are intended to stimulate thoughtful inquiry. Disagreement, for good reasons, with the author's conclusions may often represent a higher level of achievement than would docile acceptance of them. We all share a common quest for truth; each of us needs corrective encounters with those who see things differently. In the grand dialectic, theses must be stated if there are to be antitheses and emerging syntheses. In this sense, the text offers many springboards to thought, rather than final conclusions.

It is reported that one professor when asked to recommend a certain student said: "I think he may be quite capable, but I have been disappointed that I have been unable to learn much from him." The author has been highly favored by opportunity to learn abundantly from a long line of highly gifted graduate assistants. Notable among these have been Carl R. Rogers, Theodore M. Newcomb, Ernest G. Osborne, Ruth E. Hartley, J. M. Stephens, Edward M. Glaser, John C. Sullivan, Joseph E. Dellen, Arnold Bernstein, James and Betty Tipton, Alan M. Thomas, Jr., Earl L. Jandron, Peggy Cook Marquis, Francine Lang, Lindy Geis, and F. Coit Johnson, II. This book would lack much of its value without their challenges and contributions to the writer's thinking. Debts to his instructors and colleagues are innumerable and immeasurable. One of the joys of work in any science or other intellectual discipline is the experience of moving within a stream composed almost entirely of contributions from others.

October, 1965   G. W.

Contents

CHAPTER ONE

What is social psychology?

Definition

Social psychology is the scientific study of human interaction. It is a relatively new branch of science concerned with the experience and behavior of persons in social situations in which each responds in some way to the behavior of others.

Social stimuli

Human beings respond, of course, to many impersonal stimuli: to a rain drop, a flash of lightning, a clap of thunder, a glass of milk, a book. The rain drop does not seek to hit or to avoid our upturned face; the lightning takes no account of our closed eyes; the thunder rolls and echoes in total disregard of our covered ears or quaking fears; the milk does not protest if spilled rather than drunk; the book cannot alter its contents to suit the wandering thoughts of the reader. Social psychology focuses upon the more fascinating and complex situations in which people adapt their responses to one another: each person in achieving his own purposes needs to take into consideration the activities and presumed purposes of the other persons involved. A good social conversation, for example, is a flow in which one speaker proceeds from the ideas expressed by another person, adding his bit, and listening as later speakers react to his contribution.

Social psychology differs from the other areas of psychological study because of the special qualities of persons as we perceive them. Persons differ from the other objects in our environment, in being more mobile, more capricious and therefore unpredictable, more truly a locus of causation and power, and, above all, responsive. We must pay special attention to other "persons"—in contrast to "things"—because they are livelier, harder to understand or control, and more likely to initiate welcome or unwelcome events.

Interaction at a distance

Social interaction can be clearly recognized in all immediate face-to-face relationships, but human beings also respond continually to persons who are more remote in place and time. For example, when we watch television, or read what someone has written in a magazine, or vote for our candidate in an election, or cash a check, or salute the flag, we are still responding to what other human beings have done. Some people, however far away from us, have written, edited, printed, and distributed the magazine we are reading. In voting, we interact not only with our candidate, but also with the opposition and the innumerable others who have contributed in some way to the campaign and to the underlying issues and policies. Cashing a check is one small act in a long chain of social interaction which includes our earning the money, depositing it, the bank accounting systems, and anything we do with the money that may directly or indirectly affect other people. Even the existence of private property, a money system, banks, and stores, is due to the behavior, past and present, of other human beings. The salute to the flag is a response, not just to that piece of colored cloth, but to our country—its heroes, history, institutions, traditions, culture, ideals, and all that our fellow citizens have done or are doing to sustain a national state.

In each of these examples, we respond to what others have done in the past, but our action also becomes a stimulus to many future activities of other persons. Television programs and magazine features survive or perish, depending on how many of us watch or read them. Depending upon our votes, in a democracy, candidates and policies come or go. We are the makers as well as the inheritors of history. We have become the kinds of persons we are, largely in response to the setting left to us by our forefathers. We speak the language, eat the food, work at jobs, play at games, live, love, and worship in accord with the culture formed by our predecessors, but we do not transmit that culture unchanged. Future generations will be a little different because of the way we have lived, our interests, our choices, our words, and our work. The story of mankind describes an immense flow of social interaction across the ages from the first act of the first man to the last thought of the last expiring human being.

Scientific study

Our definition began with emphasis on "scientific study" and perhaps this, too, needs some explanation. Everyone is interested in human interaction. Most magazine stories and television serials depend on human relations for their themes. Careful study of human interaction is the proper business of historians, novelists, dramatists, poets, moralists, and politicians, as well as social scientists. Psychologists differ from all these other observers of life not in their subject matter but in their techniques. Social psychologists operate within the norms of science, making their observations with care and avoiding the distortions of prejudice. Special instruments and techniques have been devised for seeing more than is apparent to the casual observer. As each topic in social psychology is presented in this book, we shall describe one or more investigations, undertaken in the scientific spirit. A question is raised or a hypothesis formed for testing. Procedures are devised which anyone concerned with the problem may repeat if he wishes to verify that the obtained results derive from nature and not from some idiosyncrasy of the investigator.

The task of the scientist requires more than careful, unbiased empirical investigation. He must think hard about the findings which turn up in his own experiments and those of other scientists and must try to see how these findings fit together. He proposes *constructs* which fit together into a kind of explanatory system. The atom and the electron are constructs of the physicist; so are gravity, voltage, and temperature. Physics is an "old" science, with many widely accepted constructs, but even in physics well-established theories occasionally have to give way to new evidence and better-fitting constructs. Social psychology is a very "young" science and its constructs and systems are more tentative and fragile. A consensus among social psychologists on what concepts are most helpful in leading to a systematic understanding of human interaction is slowly being built. In social psychology, as in all sciences, theories and factual knowledge are advancing together, an advance in one stimulating advance in the other.

Importance

Everything that people care very deeply about can profitably be studied as a form of social interaction. Love is certainly an interacting response to others; so are money, power, truth, beauty, and goodness. The most desperate failures in life can be seen as inappropriate social interaction. Failure on the job has been found in several studies to arise many times as often from poor interpersonal relations as from lack of technical skills.

Not infrequently a person who is a failure in one situation is successful in a different one. One love affair may not work out happily, but the same two persons may each achieve happiness with someone else. The difficulty, then, was not *in* each personality; it was in their particular kind of *interaction*. A man may fail on one job, but become highly successful at exactly the same kind of work in another setting where he is interacting with a different group of co-workers. The success or failure lies more in the interaction than in the individual.

The traditional, individualistic patterns of our thought have left many people unaware of the extent to which their lives are mingled with groups. Breakfast with a family, travel to work in a car pool, conferences and committees, luncheon clubs, factory teams, sales contacts, classrooms, court sessions, hospital wards, after-work cocktails or golf or community activities or social visits or family life—from morning to night the individual moves from group to group. A science which can improve social interaction will contribute to almost every hour of everyone's day.

Social problems

The problems of our broader society arise from complexes of interaction in which institutional structure (itself an accretion of past interactions which constrain present behavior), shared opinions and feelings (social norms), and activities of cooperation or conflict play a major part. The gravest and deepest concerns of our age lead us directly to problems of social interaction. The threat of a war of mass destruction is one immense, involved pattern of interactions. The recurring cycles of economic inflation and deflation, prosperity and depression, are forms of interaction among large numbers of people. Prejudice and discrimination, segregation and desegregation, are names for interaction patterns. Juvenile delinquency, political corruption, factional struggles, and totalitarian governments are better understood when analyzed as forms of interaction. It requires at least two persons, different in behavior but interacting, to make a criminal, a bribe, a fight or a tyranny. The aesthetic limitations of our society—the level of taste in popular entertainers; the prevailing ugliness of many communities, large or small; the garish offensiveness of much expensive advertising; the neglect of the creative artist and poet—these, too, can profitably be translated into processes of social interaction. It appears that our "American way of life," justly extolled for its virtues, also sustains rates of ulcers, alcoholism, insanity, murder, and suicide that are among the highest in the world. Something often goes wrong in human interaction. It is the task of social psychology to shed some light on all these problems.

It would be unreasonable to expect any science—particularly one so young as social psychology—to have the complete answer to all the grave problems that have beset mankind. Solutions will be worked out—if the problems are ever solved—on the basis of contributions from the study of history, economics, sociology, political science, anthropology, physiology, engineering, the arts, philosophy, and plain common sense, as well as from social psychology.

Methods

Interaction of concerns and techniques

Progress in social psychology comes at points where concern over social needs coincides with the discovery or development of appropriate methods of inquiry. Men may have desired for centuries to explore outer space, but fulfillment of such hopes had to await advances in technology to the point where giant rockets could be launched. Technical advances are of special interest to the scientist. Their application to practical concerns may be remote; they may never lead directly to solving major problems. But gradually, as methods of scientific discovery are improved and refined, our competence in dealing with human problems also advances. Problems persist, and it is progress in *methods* that eventually yields solutions.

Natural history

Most sciences have begun with a "natural history" approach. Men watched the behavior of ants and bees before there was any systematic zoology. Experiments are impossible in astronomy. We cannot bring the stars into our laboratories. Increasing knowledge of the universe comes through extending our observations, making measurements more precise, and analyzing mathematical relationships.

A natural history approach has many advantages in social psychology. One, of course, is that we can see social interaction taking place all around us at all times. Nothing is more open to observation. The natural history method has the further merit of interfering very little with the process observed. If a social group is brought into the laboratory, given special tests, and subjected to strange conditions, the behavior of members will certainly be unlike their behavior in an ordinary setting. The natural history method can often be applied in such a way that the people who are interacting are not aware that they are being observed. For example, in an office, it is possible most unobtrusively to record who talks to whom and for how long. Such simple records have been found (Chapple, Arensberg, 1940) to give a fairly good basis for estimating subtle and elusive variables like personal feelings or opinions, and communication difficulties in the organization. A group of three social psychologists (J. Watson, et al., 1948) made an interesting contribution simply by listening to conversations that could be easily overheard on the street, in parks, and in buses. They summarized 1001 conversations, reporting that most of what they overheard was about day-to-day affairs, with little reference to what historians might regard as the great public events of the time. The most common category was something about "myself and another." Men talked to other men most often about vocation, sports, and politics. Women talked to other women more about friends, clothes, shopping, love, and marriage.

An observer of a group discussion, to choose another illustration, can sit quietly on the sidelines and record who speaks, to whom he speaks, and the type of remark he contributes. Much of our knowledge about small groups comes from such records (Bales, 1950).

Among the most important sources of social psychological insight today are the anthropologists and ethnologists who have brought to us accurate accounts of the folkways of other cultures. Their observations have been disturbed as little as possible by the observer's presence. Two famous studies of an American city, *Middletown* and *Middletown in Transition* (Lynd, Lynd, 1929; 1937) and two of a smaller town, *Plainville* (West, 1945) and *Democracy in Jonesville* (Lloyd Warner, 1949) use methods and concepts rather like those employed by anthropologists in pre-industrial cultures. Almost every town has some peculiarities in its traditions, economic life, religious institutions, recreation, cliques, politics, leadership, and media of communication with neighboring communities which would furnish material for stimulating observations on social interaction.

The results of simple observation of a natural social act, process, or institutions may be written up as a social case history. Some of the classic observations used in social psychology are social case histories. For example, in later chapters of this text will be found:

William F. Whyte's observation of gangs in "Street Corner Society" (Chapter 3) and Bruno Bettelheim's account of life in Nazi concentration camps (Chapter 6).

Participant observation

A related method of studying social psychology uses the participant-observer. A student, while carrying out all his normal responsibilities as a member of a class, may also be observing interactions between himself and the instructor or with his fellow students. One enterprising student in one of the author's classes tabulated, quite unknown to the rest of us, all the laughter during class sessions and analyzed its causes. A committee member, while engaged in the committee tasks, may at the same time be observing factors making for cohesion or disintegration among his co-workers. Probably the best study of a street-corner gang that has ever been made was carried out by a young sociologist (Whyte, 1943) who managed to become accepted as an associate in all the activities of the group over a period of several years.

The special asset of the participant observer is that he is really on the inside. One who observes a football team from the sidelines has the advantage of giving all his attention to observing. A player cannot do that. But a player, as participant observer, can know some things which no bystander can see. He knows how it feels to be a team member; to make a crucial error or to snatch victory from apparent defeat.

Description only the first step

The data resulting from natural history methods, whether described by a participant or by a more detached observer, represent only the first step toward a science. Different observers attend to different parts of the scene and their reports are not strictly comparable. Subjective reactions distort the observations, even when reporters try to be fair and accurate. Any unique case may be vivid and impressive, but it does not justify generalizations or support a theoretical system.

Careful accounts of events can provide a starting point for formulation of some concepts and some hypotheses about the nature of the interaction process. The record of student laughter during class sessions has no scientific significance unless the data can be related to some sort of theory about the persons, situations, and attitudes involved. Reflection might, perhaps, suggest that students prefer class sessions when laughter is frequent, but learn more in sessions when laughter is infrequent. To test this interpretation would require supplementing the simple frequency count with a synchronized record of student enjoyment and student learning. The confirmation of such a hypothesis would constitute a meaningful connection but would still fall short of what would be needed for generalization. Are the observed correlations (positive for enjoyment; negative for learning) equally true for all ages and classes of students in all situations, with all teachers and all types of content? In further pursuit of scientific understanding, we might need to use more refined categories of observation. *Laughter*—when we think about it—is not a single phenomenon. There are several kinds of laughter: the kind set off, for example, by telling jokes; by witty remarks; by situations of embarrassment; by buffoonery; or by generally relaxed and enjoyable conversation. What does it mean to *enjoy* a class session? Are some responses based on a concept that only the amusing is enjoyable, while other responses proceed from the concept that class sessions are enjoyable only when something new and challenging is learned? Next, we might examine *learning*—another complex variable. Is something "learned" if it can be recognized in an objective test a few days later? Or are we interested in the kind of learning which goes deeper, has a lasting impact, and modifies subsequent behavior in noticeable ways?

We need not pursue this or other illustrations. The point is to recognize that social psychology begins to emerge only when the steps essential in every science have been followed: observation, comparison and classification, concept formation, generation of hypotheses, testing of hypotheses, generalization, fitting of generalizations into a scheme or system built slowly out of many scientifically established truths.

Instruments

Just as astronomers need telescopes and bacteriologists microscopes, to supplement observation by the unaided eye, so social psychologists have developed instruments for obtaining more detail and precision. Among these are interviews, questionnaires, rating scales, opinion polls, content analyses, attitude tests, and indirect or projective tests. These may help in field studies. In one natural setting, for example, interviews and ratings were used (Deutsch, Collins, 1951) to determine how attitudes of tenants changed as they moved into an interracial housing project. Questionnaires or tests are often given to classes and to larger groups in the community to discover what people are thinking or to identify extreme groups for special study. One large project attempted to discover how far the average American citizen of the mid-century thought our tradition of freedom and civil liberties should be restricted because of the danger of Communism (Stouffer, 1955). The same project pointed out differences in attitude between the average person and the typical community leader. The authors of "The Authoritarian Personality" (Adorno *et al.*, 1950), in studies to be discussed in a later chapter, were not trying to discover by their tests the distribution of opinion throughout the population, but rather to identify a certain type of person who seemed prone to adopt fascistic attitudes.

Experiments

Most sciences have progressed from natural history accounts and observation with instruments to a higher stage of carefully designed laboratory experimentation. Observation and surveys in life situations may yield many important facts, but a higher degree of precision and control can be achieved in experiments expressly designed to test particular hypotheses. It is much easier, of course, to set up controlled experiments in physics, where we deal with inanimate objects, or in those biological sciences which experiment on plants and lower animals, than it is in social psychology. It is neither ethical nor possible to manipulate people like fruit flies. Yet, in the literature of social psychology today there are records of hundreds, perhaps thousands, of significant controlled experiments with human beings.

For a simple illustration of a laboratory experiment in social psychology we go back more than a generation to some work by the German industrial psychologist, W. Moede (1920). He measured strength of pull in a tug of war with one person on each side, then two on each side, then three, four, and so on up to eight pulling together on each side. He found that when people work together at a task of this kind, a law of diminishing returns operates. One person pulled 63 kg; a second of equal strength on each side gave a total pull, not of twice 63 but of only 118. Thus the second, even when just as strong, added only 55 kg. Two were certainly stronger than one, but not twice as strong. A third added only 42 kg. When seven were pulling, an eighth man added very little to the total pull already being made by his seven teammates. A team of eight turned out to be only four times as strong as its average member. It is not hard to conceive why this may be so. Although each man adds something, he does not add his total strength because not all the members exert their maximum pull at the same time. Each may also relax a little, relying on the help of his teammates. There may be, as a further factor, some interference among the men pulling together; each has to accommodate his position somewhat to the others.

In the effort to conceptualize, to interpret, and to generalize the observed results, we raise new questions pertinent to social psychology as a science. Is it consistently true that when people cooperate, each contributes less than he would if he were working alone? Or, are there situations in which the stimulation of co-workers brings out more than the members would have achieved in the sum of their separate efforts? If so, how can the pattern of the two different kinds of situation be generalized and fitted into a system which takes account of other knowledge about human behavior?

Mathematical aids

Rigorous application of theory and critical examination of data, are facilitated by the use of mathematics. Standard statistical procedures enable social psychologists to test whether differences revealed by two procedures are so small that they could easily be obtained by chance, or are large enough to be "significant." In experimental studies, the size of the difference is related to statistical symbols, its standard deviation (S. D. or Sigma), and the ratio expressed in other statistical symbols such as "z" or "t." Another symbol often used in this connection is "p"— the probability that a difference of this size would be obtained by chance variation alone, in a series of similar comparisons. The symbols $p < .05$ or $p < .01$ or $p < .001$ mean that the probability of a difference as large as that found in the study, being due to the random or chance factors which affect any measure, is, respectively less than 5 in 100; or less than 1 in 100, or less than 1 in 1,000.

Another symbol frequently found in our summaries is "r," the coefficient of correlation. In general, an r shows the extent to which two measures are closely related. An r of 1.00 would mean perfect correspondence between the two; e.g., two competent persons measuring the height of 20 children, no two of whom are very much alike in stature. There is no reason why there should not be perfect agreement in such a task. On the other hand, if all 20 were close to 4′6″ tall, slight variations in the reading of the yardstick might bring discrepancies between the measures noted by Observer A and Observer B. The correlation (r) might drop to .90 or .70 or even to .50. A purely chance relationship is expressed by an r of .00. The half-way point of agreement between .00 and 1.00 is an r of about .70. A negative r means that one measure rises as the other falls. Thus we might expect a negative coefficient of correlation between a good test of racial prejudice, and the number of friends of other races which a student can name. Those high in prejudice will be low in friends of other races; those low in prejudice will more probably have a number of such friends. But this would not lead to a high negative correlation (-1.00) since many other factors would influence participation in cross-racial friendships. A higher negative r might be found between the intelligence of high school students and the number of mistakes they would make on tests of reading or arithmetic. The lower the I.Q. the more the mistakes, and vice versa. In general, an r of $.80 - 1.00$ is regarded as high and showing a close correspondence of two measures. One of $.50 - .80$ is substantial and indicates a relationship with some significance. One of $.20 - .50$ is fairly low, but still above chance. If r is below .20 the two measures can be regarded as largely independent.

This course does not always require statistics as a prerequisite, and no attempt is made in this book to teach the derivation or calculation of statistical measures. Rather, we attempt to make them clear and meaningful even to the reader who has not mastered the techniques. In other words, this volume aids the *consumer*; it does not attempt to train the producer of statistics. Our objective is to enable the reader to grasp the general meaning of a result, even if he is unable himself to perform the essential operations. The first time any statistical measure appears in a résumé of a study, a footnote explains what that symbol stands for.

Another kind of mathematical symbol was introduced into social psychology by Kurt Lewin (1936). He used "topological" concepts to describe "psychological space" (the situation in the mind of the person).

Thus, in Figure 1, the barrier AB is given a minus sign to indicate that it keeps the subject (S) away from the goal (G) which has a positive

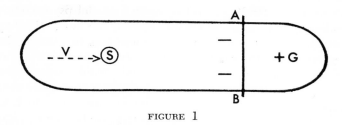

FIGURE 1

(+) attraction for him and toward which he is driven by a force represented by the vector (V). The interaction of two persons X and Y can be represented as in Figure 2. They are separated by various factors

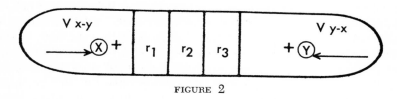

FIGURE 2

indicated as regions r_1, r_2 and r_3. Apparently the vector V_{y-x} is longer and stronger than the vector V_{x-y}, indicating that person Y will do a great deal to get closer to person X, but X only mildly reciprocates. X is unlikely to make much effort to overcome any barriers separating him from Y. Topological representation is helpful in picturing relationships, but it has proved disappointing in generating predictions.

Another kind of mathematical model is "stochastic." In a series of events which can turn out one way (A) or the opposite (Not A) the probability of an event far along in the series turning out as A can be estimated from the pattern of earlier responses. In a typical learning experiment, where A is the correct response, it may occur rarely at first, but more and more often as the learning is acquired, until it becomes almost 100 percent certain. If all the relevant parameters have been properly included, the observed result should be close to that which has been predicted.

Particularly in the European traditions, a distinction has been made between a form of analysis which describes social behavior (*wissenschaftliche*) and one which attempts to give understanding of the meaning of that behavior (*verstehende*). To predict that a child who has been burned will probably show avoidance behavior in a situation where there is fire and heat, is to describe objectively and scientifically and maybe in mathematical frequency what occurs. To realize just how a child once burned dreads the fire, is to enter into his experience with empathy and understanding. Most research in social psychology aims at scientific description, but in this book some of the illustrations and case studies are directed at conceiving the experiences in a more vivid way than is expressed by the mathematics.

Participation

The student beginning work in social psychology is urged to supplement his reading by first-hand observation, testing, and experiment. Natural-history methods can be applied to group processes on the campus or back in the student's home town. Participant-observer techniques can be utilized in classes, committees, fraternities, and other social groups. Attitudes on vital current issues can be explored through polls of a carefully chosen sample of students or other citizens. Relationships between attitude scores and sex, social class or other basic variables can be explored with a test constructed by a small group of students working together. Other students may organize groups to discuss the lectures, text or supplementary readings, and they may study their own processes as well as the subject matter. Still other groups may act out human-relations situations in which the members wish to develop more skill. These are sometimes called role-playing groups or psychodrama projects. If a student group tries to carry out, on a small scale and perhaps with some modifications, experiments like those reported in the textbook, they will learn far more about the scientific study of social interaction than reading alone could contribute. As later chapters turn attention to race relations, sex roles, propaganda, mass media, public opinion, business management, international tensions, and processes of social change, students should be able to review their own experiences in relation to the topic, re-examine prejudices, propose some theories of their own, and work out ways of collecting evidence which would test some theories. A course in social psychology—or any other science—which is limited to memorizing what previous investigators have found omits the most stimulating and exciting aspect of the work of the investigator. A student's first observations, hunches, explorations, tests, and experiments may lack the technical finesse of the experienced research worker, but this is not too serious a limitation. What is vitally important at the beginning is the excitement of venturing a little out into the frontier of the unknown, using one's own mind, asking a real question in such a way that observation, tests or experiment can discover an answer. Every student of this text can share, intellectually and emotionally, in the great adventure of scientific research in human interaction.

Students are urged also to use a critical approach in thinking about the research reports and the conclusions presented in subsequent chapters. In each chapter, a few important studies have been summarized to illustrate research characteristics of the topic or area. Each summary presents: the purpose; the subjects; the procedures; and some of the findings. The summary does not make explicit the recurring pertinent scientific questions: "How valid are these findings? How far can they be generalized? What refinements would purify the variables? How do the underlying concepts and generalizations fit into the structure of our developing science?" It is hoped that students and instructors will continually raise and explore thoughtfully the questions which move knowledge from simple facts to meaningful laws and principles.

It is recognized, of course, that most students of this book do not intend to make a career of research. Only a few will dedicate their lives to scientific investigation. Hence, attention is also given to the bearing of social psychological facts and theories on the practical concerns and puzzling issues of life. Each chapter will include suggestions about ways in which students, teachers, parents, managers, citizens, lawmakers, or other leaders can utilize some of the emerging insights.

CHAPTER TWO

Dyads

Definition

The simplest unit in which social interaction is possible consists of two members. Such a unit could be called a couple or a pair, but the more technical term *dyad* is preferable because it does not have those special associations with love and mating which we sometimes attach to "couple" or "pair." Scientists often have to use strange words, not because they enjoy impressive terms, but in order to keep their meaning precise and uncluttered. Any two persons interacting constitute a dyad. A husband and wife, a mother and baby, a couple dancing, two competing tennis players, a teacher and pupil, a plumber and his assistant, a policeman and a criminal, two doctors consulting, a nurse and patient, a foreign ambassador and the President—the range of dyads extends across the whole human race.

Dyadic interaction requires that the actions of one partner serve as stimuli to which the other is responding; ordinarily both are adapting to each other. George Herbert Mead (1934), one of America's first writers on social psychology, describes a dog fight as a model of one kind of dyadic interaction. Each dog continually adjusts his position to the other; each shifts, sways, lowers or raises his head, advances or retreats, even before any fighting actually begins.

Frequently dyadic interaction is directed toward some common goal. Woodworth (1925) has pointed out that the individual psychology of each partner does not properly describe a dyadic interaction.

> Two boys, between them, lift and carry a log which neither could move alone. You cannot speak of either boy as carrying half the log, in any concrete sense, for the log is not in halves. Nor can you speak of either boy as half carrying the log, for there is no such concrete fact as half carrying the log. The two boys, co-ordinating their efforts upon the log, perform a joint action and achieve a result which is not divisible between the numbers of this elementary group. To insist that the pair of boys consists simply of the two individuals is to commit an abstraction. It leaves out the log. By acting together upon the same object, the individuals composing the group co-ordinate their behavior, and the total behavior consequently possesses a unity analogous to that of a group of muscles in a co-ordinated movement.

The study of dyads provides the opportunity to become acquainted with many fundamental and elementary processes of social psychology. We shall see the problem of communication first in the dyad, later in groups and networks extending to millions. How one person influences another is at the heart of more complex processes of teaching and propaganda. We shall note cohesive and disruptive forces in dyads first, but later we shall see similar forces making for in-group unity and out-group hostility on a worldwide scale. We can study what happens when two persons try to solve problems together, and as we do so we shall become aware of elements which enter into the work of all committees and conferences. One vital social phenomenon—love—reaches its highest development in the dyad.

Dyads are held together by interpersonal attraction or by some kind of interdependence in meeting the needs of life. Even dyads in which the members are hostile rivals are still bound together in some way—otherwise each partner would go his own monadic way.

At the heart of dyadic interaction is some awareness by each person of the experience of the other, and this presents some psychological difficulties.

How we understand one another

Communication
Scientists are often intrigued by what more naïve observers take for granted. The child is certain that he can be aware of the feelings and thoughts of others and that he can communicate to others, unfailingly,

his own thoughts and feelings. Yet, upon more mature reflection, we know that we can never be *inside* the consciousness of another person. All we can see or hear of him is his behavior. He can never enter into the stream of our consciousness; he must comprehend us as best he can from the sounds we make and the movements of our face, hands, and body. We seem permanently barred from visiting the mind of another person, except by the inferences we might draw from his actions.[1] How then can we feel so confident that two persons really communicate?

Consider a simple dyadic interaction. John, crossing the campus, calls "Hi!" to his friend Jeanne, who waves back. This little incident contains eleven stages:

John's greeting
1. recognizes Jeanne
2. wants to greet her
3. calls out, "Hi!"

Transmission
4. sound waves with possible interference from other noise

Jeanne's experience
5. the greeting
6. from voice or a look, recognizes John
7. decides how cordial she wants to be
8. waves her hand

Transmission
9. light waves, with possible interference

John's experience
10. sees the gesture
11. interprets Jeanne's response to him

Jeanne surmised something about John's feeling from his tone of voice; he surmised something about hers from her gesture. In one experience (Davitz, 1959), subjects tried to express emotions as they recited the alphabet. An actress, for example, was able, as she recited A-B-C, etc., to convey the prescribed emotion so that it was correctly interpreted by listeners 53 percent of the time as against only a 10 percent probability by chance. Anger, nervousness, and happiness were the emotions most often correctly identified.

Gestures and facial or postural expressions may say more than is expressed by words. Helen Keller, completely blind and deaf, by holding her mother's hand could sense at once when something in the street excited her mother or aroused fear. There is an interesting example of contagion by muscular communication in Helen Keller's story of her life. She was walking with her mother when a boy threw a Fourth-of-July-firecracker which startled the mother. Helen, unable to hear or to see,

---

[1]Later, in this chapter we shall consider an apparent exception in such phenomena as telepathy.

at once asked, "what are we afraid of?" With her mother, the child even responded with appropriate smile and turn of her head to noises and the speech of others; if her hands were put on a table she gave no sign of response to similar stimuli (Keller, 1903). Yet did Helen Keller, in any sense, *know* what her mother was experiencing?

> We are all serving life sentences of confinement within our own bodies; like prisoners, we have, as it were, to tap in awkward code to our fellow men in their neighboring cells. Further, when A and B converse, there take part in their dialogue not two characters, as they suppose, but six. For there is A's real self—call it A_1; there is also A's picture of himself—A_2; there is also B's picture of A—A_3. And there are three corresponding personalities of B. With six characters involved even in a simple tete-a-tete, no wonder we fall into muddles and misunderstandings. (Lucas, 1960)

Some subtle distinctions

A German psychologist, Scheler (1954), has distinguished several forms of what may popularly be called "sympathy." One is *compathy* when two persons respond alike to the same situation (e.g., a scene in a movie), whether or not they are aware of this shared feeling. Another is *mimpathy* in which one is vicariously aware of what the other is feeling. He does not "sympathize" in this case, but he does actually live the feeling.

It is possible also to distinguish between *empathy* in which I may reproduce in myself a certain limited and temporary feeling of another and *mimpathy* in which I feel so completely identified with another, as in love, that whatever affects her has a parallel effect upon me. "I no longer live in myself, but only in her." In empathy we retain our sense of being a distinct and separate person even as we enter temporarily into the life of another; in mimpathy the boundaries of the personality dissolve. A typical instance of empathy is the psychotherapist's insight into the feelings of his disturbed patient.

A fourth form is *transpathy*, or simple contagion of an emotional state. Members of a mob may rage or panic together without any real attention to the feelings of others.

A fifth form is implied by the term "pity" and (we seem to have no one word for the positive) by rejoicing in another's good fortune. These experiences have been called *propathy*.

Social perception

Before we can sympathize with another we must be aware in some way of feelings within his self-perceived world or life-space. It is probably true that while babies at an early stage can experience compathy (being startled at the same thunderclap which upsets brother) or transpathy by contagion from the tension of the person holding them, real empathy or mimpathy would have to be learned. Hebb (1949) has summarized evidence that apes and people who have been blind from birth and later have their sight restored find it very difficult to differentiate the face of one person from another, even though they have seen the same person many times and have been cared for by him. The normal child develops recognition of some faces within the first year of life.

In watching a motion picture at normal speed we do not first see a series of still frames which we put together into an inferred movement; rather, we see the movement directly. A similar experience is our perception of intentions and motives behind the behavior of other persons. Some intriguing laboratory studies (Heider and Simmel, 1944), (Michotte, 1946, 1963) have shown that movement of two simple geometric figures on a screen is likely to be interpreted by observers in anthropomorphic terms. One triangle may be seen as pushing the circle, or chasing and catching the second as it tries to escape, or the two may be seen as drawn to one another, dancing, or fighting. Apparently there is a basic pattern underlying the movement of the simple geometric figures which reminds observers of similar patterns experienced in human relations. Asch (1952, p. 156) summarizes the conclusion from this line of evidence: "When we perceive a given act issuing from a person it is represented phenomenally as a motive, need, or intention. Just as we perceive certain happenings as swift or turbulent, so we perceive others as aggressive, gentle, reckless or uneasy." The flow of interpersonal interaction usually proceeds effectively because at every stage: from A's feeling, to A's expression of that feeling to B's perception of A's expression, and B's awareness of A's feeling, parallel patterns or *Gestalten* are operating.

Some types of personality seem especially likely to be mistaken in their impressions of what is going on in others. Katz (1963) lists among those deficient in empathy: (a) those too well socialized and hence very conformist; (b) persons concerned mainly with power and manipulation—the autocrats and authoritarians; (c) those dependent on a limited range of stereotypes for perceiving others.

Checking

The main basis upon which we test and revise our interpretations of the experience of another person is continued interaction. Maybe Jeanne underestimated how much emotion John was putting into his "Hi!", but time—and continuing interaction—will tell. John may have thought the return wave of greeting expressed pleasure equal to his own at seeing Jeanne, but a telephone call for a date may force him to revise his interpretation. We form quick impressions of what others mean by what they say and do. These impressions are the starting point of our next operations. Usually the impressions are correct, but occasionally we become aware that something is wrong; some misunderstanding has arisen. My friend does not look, talk, or act as I would have expected. A process of investigation and correction takes place.

How much we rely on feedback from the other person becomes apparent in a distressing telephone conversation in which we speak our piece but against so much noise that we cannot quite comprehend the replies. One social psychologist experimented with limiting the feedback during problem solving (Bavelas, 1957). The psychologist gave one partner a diagram for the arrangement of dominoes; the other, connected by telephone, had the dominoes and tried to follow directions. With one-way communication only, and no feedback, no dyad succeeded. The person receiving instructions soon found himself bewildered and frustrated. When the second man could react, even when limited to a push-button signal for "Yes" or "No," the task could be accomplished. Restriction on the communication brought about rejection of each partner by the other. Each viewed his co-worker as stupid and lacking in understanding. Later, we shall see also that some hierarchical structures in social institutions have a similarly restricting effect upon communication and similarly generate hostility within the organization. We proceed next to examine a familiar dyadic relationship which not only comes first in time but is among the most influential in life.

The mother—infant dyad

Psychological interaction between mothers and their babies begins before the baby's birth. It is affected sometimes by an imaginary interaction which may have gone on in the play or fantasy of the mother since she was a little girl. When the pregnancy is recognized, the fantasy merges with an urgent reality. Conception may be welcome or resisted, but it cannot well be ignored. Physiological interaction goes on within the maternal organism from the moment of conception, but this complicated process of development is largely unconscious for both mother and child. Only the byproducts are felt. When the mother first feels the stirring of the child within, psychological interaction comes closer. She may talk to her baby long before the child is born, in much the same way as she does later, but this remains a one-way process with very little immediate effect on the child.

The psychological significance of the birth experience is uncertain. One psychoanalyst (Rank, 1929) has suggested on the basis of clinical observation that the experience of the first separation of the baby from the mother influences reaction to later separations. This hypothesis sounds plausible but there is no substantial evidence that babies experiencing easy or difficult birth differ in their subsequent personalities. Other theories concern the mother. Some advocates of "natural" childbirth, in which the mother learns to control and bear the pain of labor with a minimum of anaesthesia, maintain that her more complete awareness during the whole process of birth lays a firmer foundation for her feeling that the child is her own. Again, the evidence is not impressive.

Babies find security in the sensations of contact with the warm, soft, smooth skin of the mother. Harlow (1958) has studied the reactions of baby chimpanzees to two types of substitute mother. One, of cold hard wire, held the bottle and so was associated with all the satisfactions of food. The other, of smooth cloth-covered foam rubber, provided a resilient surface to which the baby chimp could and did cling. When threatened and anxious, the little animal would consistently retreat to the safety and comfort of the cloth mother. The wire mother was not found reassuring, despite her provision of food. If the chimpanzee could not get to the soft pneumatic surface of the cloth mother, he gave easily recognized signs of deprivation and distress. Disturbance in the maternal-infant pattern of these apes was reflected in later behavior. Their socialization was defective, as compared with animals brought up under normal conditions, and their sexual adjustment was impaired (Seay, et al., 1964).

A human mother, holding a baby, provides surface contact and also other forms of reassurance in the way she holds it. While the mother holds her baby, a social interaction can be observed. If the mother is too timid or rejecting, the baby often senses the awkwardness and rigidity and responds by crying. This makes the mother more frightened, tense or hostile and creates a vicious circle. A warm, loving, tender, accepting mother as she talks to and holds her baby creates a sense of security which operates in a "virtuous circle" to make both happier.

Evidence on the interaction between mother and infant has been reported by a psychologist in a penal institution for women. The study is summarized in Abstract 1 in a form which we shall follow throughout the text as we describe other examples of psychological research. Dr. Escalona brings out a relationship between a mother's feelings about her baby's behavior in eating.

Margaret Mead (1946) has reported an interesting observation of a baby in Bali who had usually been quite happy in the arms of an adolescent girl responsible for its care, but who on this day seemed to cry from fear. In the arms of another nurse the infant seemed contented again. The significant fact is that the first girl had just quarreled with her guardian and been expelled from the Temple Society of unmarried girls. Apparently the tension of the nurse was communicated kinesthetically, or at least, without depending on words.

An important factor in the mother-child dyad is the set of unconscious expectations which the mother holds for the child. These determine many of her reactions of pleasure or annoyance with the baby's

Abstract 1

TITLE   Feeding Disturbances in Very Young Children

AUTHOR   Sibylle K. Escalona

PROBLEM   Why are some babies feeding problems although no physiological cause can be found? Is it related to the behavior
of the adult taking care of the baby?

SUBJECTS AND   At a reformatory for women some 50–60 babies under two
PROCEDURE   years of age were observed.

SOME FINDINGS   1. During 20 months of observations, there were ten instances where infants refused the breast although no
physical cause could be found. Eight of the ten mothers
were exceptionally high strung, nervous, and irritable.
2. In 15 instances babies rejected either orange juice or tomato juice; the
baby's preference, in each case, agreed with the preferences of the student
feeding that child.

SOURCE: *Amer. J. Orthopsychiat.*, 1945, XV, 76–80.

behavior. Richter, a German psychiatrist (1963), has proposed, on the
basis of longitudinal study of many disturbed children, that the parental
fantasies, wishes, anxieties and expectancies furnish the background for
neurotic behavior in the offspring. He observes children as caught in a
kind of trap or maze or spider-web of these implicit demands which
are not easy to understand. Explicit parental demands, on the other
hand, can be coped with by the child. His emotional disturbance, therefore, is more apt to be related to pressures which are not so obvious
and rational. Richter supports his thesis with numerous case histories
focusing on the continuous "dialogue" between unconscious needs of the
parent and the responses of the child.

We have been speaking of the child's response to the mother-figure,
but it should be remembered that interaction is continuous and moves
in both directions. When the Bali baby fussed, the adolescent girl doubtless grew more tense and this response increased the infant's discomfort.
As a famous psychiatrist has expressed it (Sullivan, 1947):

It is biological for the infant when nursing to show certain expressive
movements which are called the satisfaction response, and it is probably
biological for the parent concerned to see these things. Due to the empathic
linkage, this, the reaction of the parent to the satisfaction-response of the
infant, communicates good feeling to the infant and thus he learns that
this response has power.

The importance of this first dyad for love experiences throughout life is underlined by some striking observations of animals. Lorenz (1952) reports that a Muscovy duck egg was hatched by a Greylag goose. For six weeks the baby drake lived with the goose mother; then was reared with other little ducklings by a mother duck. Ten months later, at sexual maturation, the young drake pursued only Greylag geese. Lorenz calls this early conditioning "imprinting." Another report tells of doves reared by human care in isolation from other doves; at maturity their ideal of a mate was the hand of their keeper. J. P. Scott (1945) fed a lamb from a bottle; the lamb was not attracted by other sheep but tagged along with humans.

Clinical studies of humans have not shown such definite "imprinting," but agree on the importance of the early mother-child relationship as a foundation for personality. "The first demonstration of social trust in the baby is the ease of his feeding, the depth of his sleep, the relaxation of his bowels," writes Erikson (1950). Whether a child enters later life experiences with a basic trust and confidence which makes it easy to learn cooperation, or with a basic mistrust and expectation of trouble, depends on the quality of this earliest dyadic interaction.

Disruption at too early an age of the mother-child nursing pattern creates frustration which may have lasting consequences. A test of optimism-pessimism was given to 100 adults (ages 18 to 35) and the scores of those who had been weaned from the mother's breast before four months of age were compared with those who had been given five months or more of breast feeding (Goldman-Eisler, 1953). There proved to be a real difference (correlation coefficient was .30)[2] in present outlook on such questions as trust in people, faith that justice would prevail, and belief that atomic energy would prove more of a boon than a menace to mankind. A possible interpretation is that longer nursing of the baby tended to produce a good, secure, confident feeling about life in general. The findings are far from conclusive. Many other factors must have been influential and might account for the observed relationship.

Further evidence of the importance of a secure and satisfying social relationship to the growth of the infant is found in studies of maternal deprivation. Physical care is not all that babies need. At the turn of the century, the mortality rate among foundlings brought to New York City's Municipal Infant's Hospital on Randall's Island was over 90 percent; similar data were reported from other cities. The basic difficulty was not lack of food or sanitation but lack of what hospitals have since

[2] An "r" or correlation coefficient of .30 indicates only a fairly low degree of agreement between the data on nursing and that on adult optimism. If it were zero, we would conclude that the two measures were unrelated. Only about 10% of the variance in the adult attitude could be correctly predicted on the basis of the nursing factor.

come to call "TLC" (tender, loving care). Spitz (1945) studied babies in an institution that gave adequate physical care but, for lack of help, left babies all day (except for feedings) to lie in cubicles which screened them from all surrounding activity, with nothing to do but look at the ceiling. Each nurse cared for eight children. Mortality was much higher than in control studies; physical, intellectual, and emotional development, although normal at the beginning, became increasingly retarded. Among 26 two-year-olds, at which age most children can walk and say words, only two were able to speak a few words and the same two were the only ones who walked.

During the latter half of the first year of life, babies in a good hospital were observed by Spitz (1946) to suffer from a certain emotional disorder. They wept, became irritable, lost interest in food, and in extreme cases, deteriorated in mind and body. Such a "disease" has been named "marasmus." One remedy restored each of them to health and happiness: return to care by their own mother. This specific social interaction experience had become so important for them that deprivation seemed to mean loss of interest in living.

The pioneer observations by Spitz led to a spate of studies, some in agreement with him and others finding no such effects. Bowlby (1951, 1961) has concluded, after reviewing the literature on maternal deprivation and separation anxiety, that mental health is gravely injured by disruption of the infant's normal interaction with the mother. Stone (1954) in another critical review urges more careful delineation of what specific kinds of stimulation are given or missing, with what specific consequences. Dennis (1960) in some studies of institutionalized children in other countries, agrees. A report from Australia (Lyle, 1964) shows that adverse experiences of children with their mothers, prior to institutionalization, continued to depress verbal intelligence; and even those institution children who had relatively adequate mothers prior to entry, were retarded as compared with similar children who lived at home.

Observations on children brought up in institutions like hospitals and orphanages, also show retardation after the first few months (Fischer, 1953; Bowlby, Cantab, 1953). Schaffer (1958) studied 76 infants hospitalized during the first year of life. Before seven months of age, they developed a blank, bewildered facial expression like that described by Spitz; if older, they showed excessive dependence on the mother, manifested by clinging, crying, and aversion to strangers. Data reviewed by Greene and Miller (1958) indicated that separation from the mother in early childhood seemed to be associated with increased susceptibility to leukemia. Rheingold (1956, 1959) demonstrated rather clearly that eight hours a day of "mothering" did improve personality development in institutional babies as compared with controls in the same environment. "Multiple mothering" by several adults was as good as the single mother, except that speech was developed sooner and better in relation to one mother figure.

Provence and Lipton (1962) followed 75 infants in an institution and compared their experiences and development with those of a control group living at home. Institutional babies became cumulatively more and more deficient in imaginative play, coordinated movement, pleasure and zest in activity. Baldwin (1956) summarizes the general conclusion: "By now, we can be reasonably sure that something about institutionalization has a deleterious effect upon personality development" (p. 263).

Stendler (1952) hypothesizes that there are two periods in early childhood in which relations to the mother are of critical importance: one, around 8 months of age, vital for good ego-development and a later one, around 30 months of age, which greatly affects the development of conscience and character (super-ego). The most serious effects of deprivation of the normal dyadic relationship of mother and infant have usually been reported when babies were between the ages of six months and two years. Earlier, a baby can accept various kinds of substitute mothering, but after a strong attachment has been formed to a particular person—her face, voice, and ways of handling—replacements seem unacceptable. Later, children become less dependent on *the one* mother figure. If deprived at home, they can seek a substitute elsewhere. Sears (1963) has found that children of nursery school age, if frustrated in their dependent demands at home, will show increased dependence on the teacher.

Some studies of animals indicate that impaired relations with others of all ages may be as significant as depriving them of mothers. Seay (1964) working with Harlow, found that two rhesus monkeys who were separated at birth from their mothers, but who had normal peer interaction, became adequate mothers; seven others deprived of both peer and mother relationships became grossly inadequate mothers.

Seitz (1959) found that kittens, separated from their mothers at the age of two weeks, showed more anxiety than did controls; were less successful in learning, adaptation, and competition; and some of them developed somatic symptoms resembling asthma. Pfaffenberger and Scott (1959) found that puppies deprived at about three months of age of normal opportunity to be socialized in play with other dogs (including mother deprivation) could not be trained later to behave responsibly as guide dogs.

In the next chapter we shall be concerned further with the effects of social isolation vs. normal participation.

Self and others

The first dyad is especially important for the life of the child because out of it emerges the child's primary feelings about himself and others.

In the early days of infancy the baby has not yet discovered himself. He experiences the pleasant or the unpleasant, but there are no characters in this drama—things just occur. He has no clear notion of his mother or of himself. "Self" and "other" are combined in an undifferentiated blur. The first sorting out comes with awareness of activities the baby can control. He can change the view by moving his eyes, or he can move a hand or foot. This feels different from changes of experience he does not control. Touching his own skin gives a (double) sensation unlike touching mother's breast. He can't by himself make that nice mother-face appear. Gradually, then, he finds that part of his little world belongs to himself.

He separates "self" from "other"—usually mother. Yet each of the two has come from the same matrix of experience, previously recognized as satisfying or unsatisfying. If experiences prior to self-awareness were on the whole "good," so are both self and other when distinguished. Each part carries the tone of the former vague unity. If the earlier experience was frustrating and annoying, this, too, carries over to feelings about mother and about self. Consequently, acceptance of others goes with acceptance of self, and self-rejection accompanies hostility or disparaging attitudes toward others.

One of America's first social psychologists, James M. Baldwin (1897), saw and expressed clearly the close interdependence of "self" and "other." "See . . . how inextricably interwoven the ego and the alter really are! The development of the child's personality could not go on at all without the constant modification of his sense of himself by suggestions from others. So he himself, at every stage, is really in part someone else, even in his own thought of himself."

It was Charles H. Cooley (1902), a sociologist contemporary with Baldwin, who developed an idea from William James and formulated the famous theory of the "looking-glass self." Our feeling about ourselves is much influenced by what we imagine certain other people to see in us. "A self-idea of this sort (the looking-glass self) seems to have three principal elements: the imagination of our appearance to the other person; the imagination of his judgment of that appearance; and some sort of self-feeling, such as pride or mortification. The comparison with a looking-glass hardly suggests the second element, the imagined judgment, which is quite essential. . . . The character and weight of that other, in whose mind we see ourselves, makes all the difference with our feeling. . . . A man will boast to one person of an action—say some sharp transaction in trade—which he would be ashamed to own to another."

A careful statistical analysis of all statements made by ten patients in psychotherapy indicating their feeling about themselves and all statements indicating feeling about other persons, showed that as treatment succeeded, there was a reliable increase in self-acceptance and self-respect and also, along with this, increase in acceptance of, and respect for, others (Sheerer, 1949). We cannot identify which is cause and which is effect, because the two are so intimately related. Whatever makes it easier for a person to accept certain limitations in himself, and unnecessary for him to be defensive about these characteristics, at the same time reduces his hostility toward other persons with similar characteristics. Or the sequence can be equally well followed in the other direction. Whatever reduces the sense of threat which an individual experiences in his interaction with other persons at the same time relaxes his need to condemn himself. As Rogers (1951) puts it: "When there is no need to defend, there is no need to attack." More positively, we love our neighbors *as* we love ourselves.

Transference—parataxis

The parent-child dyad not only molds a general attitude of acceptance or rejection toward others, but also leaves the child with a predisposition to respond in certain specific ways to people whom he perceives as resembling one or the other parent. This is the phenomenon which Freud called *transference*. A boy who has usually felt that his father was remote, cold, and dominating is likely to expect the same kind of behavior from other men who have authority over him, for example his professor, his commanding officer, or his boss. The girl who, when four, easily "twists her father around her little finger" is likely at the age of 24 to prefer a man for a boss; she feels she knows how to get him to do what she wants.

Case 1, that of Albert, illustrates a common form of transference.

Case 1: Albert—The Silver Cord

Albert, a stocky man of 37, with quick intelligence and bright brown eyes, sought a woman psychoanalyst. His second marriage was on the rocks. His first marriage, to a woman ten years his senior, ended because Albert quickly lost interest in sex relations with her, but wanted to play around with several girl friends as he had done before marriage. The wife objected and, after Albert had tried several times in vain to reform, she got a divorce. Albert was lonesome, hated having to get his own meals, to care for his own laundry, and come home at night to an empty apartment. When he remarried after some months, he did not choose one of the younger girls he had been dating, but again turned to a woman more than five years his senior. Albert gave up his business, which was not going well, and went back to graduate study. His wife worked to support them. When she was ill, or indisposed by pregnancy, Albert found himself vaguely angry, resentful, and even hating the sight of her. When children came, Albert's wife gave up her job but bought a boarding house and still provided the family support. Albert dabbled vocationally in this and that, but couldn't settle into the husband role of being family provider. His wife was getting "fed up" with his "irresponsibility" and he was getting angry at his wife's "nagging." Analysis opened Albert's eyes to the fact—astonishing to him, although not so surprising to his friends—that his feeling for both wives had been more like that which, as a boy, he had felt toward his mother. He wanted to be cared for, and yet free to live his own life. He was not really seeing the actual qualities and needs of the women he married; he was mentally fitting over them his mother's house dress. He saw them as bringing him reliable loving care. His was a "transference" neurosis.

Freud discovered the transference when he observed that patients during treatment, were re-enacting with him their earlier dyadic relationships. Some were acting as though he were a loving mother; others as though he were a stern and authoritarian father, although he had actually done nothing to justify either view. Gradually it became apparent that these colored expectations were not limited to the doctor-patient dyad but were active all through life. Harry Stack Sullivan, an American psychiatrist, suggested that a better name for the phenomenon would be *parataxis*, denoting a tendency to see another form or order or meaning alongside (or inside) that which is objectively present to the senses.

Each member of a dyad, on first meeting the other, gets some impression. This first reaction is largely parataxic. It grows out of previous experience with persons who have seemed in some way like the new acquaintance. Some people are inclined to take this first impression of others too seriously. They think of it as "intuition" and imagine that they have the gift of almost magical insight into the character of one they have just met for the first time. This is an untrustworthy impression. Any reader can verify this for himself by writing down and filing away the first impression of several persons when he first meets them; then comparing this with his feeling about them after months of friendship or working together. He must be careful, however, not to let his first impression prejudice his later contacts. If we have a hunch that someone is untrustworthy, we are likely to act toward him in a way which makes him suspicious of us and far from frank. If, on the other hand, we start with a feeling that the other is a warm, friendly person, and act in accord with this impression, he is very likely to respond to us with warmth. Hence we tend to make our first impressions come true. Wisdom in human relations counsels that we discount our first impressions and let our estimate of another person emerge slowly from his actual behavior in many situations over a period of time. Even "love at first sight," as we shall note later, is not to be trusted.

An unusually good opportunity to study parataxis is provided by groups meeting for psychotherapy. Each is encouraged to express frankly his reactions to the other members. At a first meeting of several strangers, even before anyone has spoken, each member has an impression of the way he is likely to feel about each of the others. Sometimes this impression is very clear and sharp. Usually it can be connected with some previous interpersonal relationship charged with feeling. One man in the group, for example, may feel that another, older man is going to antagonize him by being dictatorial in manner, as the subject's father was (or seemed). He may feel also that he is going to like a certain girl whose brown eyes recall to him an adolescent sweetheart. Toward another man about his own age he may feel a budding envy and rivalry, recalling competition with his brother. A woman in the group he dislikes at once; she talks too fast, very much as his grandmother used to. Often, the same group member is seen at first by one neighbor as kind and indulgent, by another as stern and forbidding, and by a third as secretly seductive and lustful.

The danger of trusting first, intuitive impressions is well illustrated in a true story reported by a young professor. He had been invited to sit in as a member of the committee on the final oral examination of a candidate for the doctoral degree. He was new to the university faculty and had not met the candidate. As soon as the professor entered the room he experienced a sudden wave of distrust of the candidate, who was seated at the end of the table. He felt he would have no confidence in what the man would say. Fortunately, the professor had been through enough psychoanalysis to have learned to recognize and to mistrust such quick "intuition." Persistent effort to recall association enabled him to recognize that the candidate had disappointed him, years before, in an experience he had forgotten. A more naive man might have taken his feeling as evidence of keen insight into character—an ability to judge others on sight. That naive expectation might easily have seemed "confirmed" because the tone and nature of the examiner's questions could easily have brought out some shortcoming in the candidate.

We move on now, from first impressions to the influence that two members of a dyad have upon one another as they interact over a period of time.

Mutual influence

Convergence

Two people interacting adjust in many ways to each other. They speed up or slow down their rate of walking to keep pace together. One or both may put aside his own interests to talk about something of mutual interest. They may compete. A half century ago, a psychologist (Moede, 1914) showed that a young man, in competition with a weak rival who could pull only 16 kg., himself pulled 22 kg.; the same young man, competing with someone who was his equal, pulled 27 kg. A runner makes better time if paced by someone who is faster than he is.

Abstract 2

TITLE A Study of Some Social Factors in Perception

AUTHOR M. Sherif

PROBLEM How people influence one another in deciding what is correct when other criteria are lacking.

SUBJECTS Eight pairs of male college students; also eight groups of three students each. A second series of seven pairs.

PROCEDURES Subjects in a dark room looked for two seconds at a fixed point of light which appeared to move. (This is called the *auto-kinetic effect*). The difficulty is to judge the extent of such movements.

Some subjects gave their guesses first alone; later in pairs or groups; others began in groups and were later tested alone. The pairs in the second series contained one "planted" member who consistently made estimates within pre-arranged limits.

SOME FINDINGS Individuals modified the judgments they had made alone to come closer to estimates made by their partners. Those who began in pairs converged even more quickly. For example: one student alone averaged 8½ inches; his partner averaged only 3 inches when he made his estimates in individual sessions. In the first session together, giving their estimates aloud, the former student averaged only 5½ inches and his partner 4½. In the next session together they came even closer, averaging 5¼ and 4¾ inches, respectively.

Students in groups which had converged about a given figure (e.g. 3 or 6″) when tested alone later, continued to make the same size of estimate they had learned to make in the group.

Most students seemed unaware of the influence of partners on their estimates; they thought they were responding as they *saw* the movement.

SOURCE: *Arch. Psychol.*, N.Y., 1935. No. 187.

People adjust their expressions of attitude to the person to whom they are talking and sometimes the attitude itself is adapted. Dorothy Parker once wrote:

In youth, it was a way I had
To do my best to please,
And change with every passing lad,
To suit his theories. (1926)

The tendency to orient oneself to the other and to try to see through his eyes is particularly evident when one's own orientation is confused and mistrusted. Thus adolescents are particularly prone to talk and think and feel one way with one companion and quite otherwise with a different partner. They do not yet have stable moorings for their own outlook.

Imagine two persons, both lost in a forest. On meeting, each hopes the other can show him the right path out. They turn to one another for guidance. They compare notes and probably agree to try some direction which grows out of the experience and judgment of both combined.

A laboratory experiment, with a psychological structure very much like the two persons lost in the woods, has become one of the classical examples in social psychology and is reported in Abstract 2.

It is typical of the progress of science that the results of one experiment, like that of Sherif's, become the starting point for future experimenters who carry the original idea further or introduce new distinctions. Other researchers have repeated the Sherif experiment but delayed the re-testing of subjects alone for weeks or months after their experience together. One (Bovard, 1948) tried a delay of 28 days and found the influence still persisting; another team tried re-tests after a year and found the dyad norms still determining individual estimates (Rohrer et al., 1954).

Differences in confidence

Sherif showed that each student was influenced, in his estimates, by his partner. But the influence was not always equal. Why did some converge toward the partner's judgment more readily than others? Why did some stick to their own standard? Participants who, after a series of laboratory exercises, felt that they had performed poorly were much more likely to conform to the judgment of a strange partner than were other students who had survived the preliminiary experiments with a high confidence in their skill at performing (Mausner, 1953).

Differences in prestige

If there is a real basis for trusting one partner more than the other, this, too, makes for conformity toward the more authoritative member. Sherif, for example, introduced as one partner a laboratory assistant who was known to have prestige in the department. The following quotation comes from her verbatim report.

Miss X and I (Assistant in Psychology, Columbia University) were subjects for Dr. Sherif. I was well acquainted with the experiment but Miss X knew nothing whatsoever about it. Since she was a close friend of mine, and I carried some prestige with her, Dr. Sherif suggested that it would be interesting to see if we could predetermine her judgments. It was agreed beforehand that I was to give no judgments until she had set her own standard. After a few stimulations it was quite clear that her judgments were going to vary around five inches. At the next appropriate stimulation, I made a judgment of twelve inches. Miss X's next judgment was eight inches. I varied my judgments around twelve inches and she did the same. Then I changed my judgment to three inches, suggesting to Dr. Sherif that he had changed it. She gradually came down to my standard, but not without some apparent resistance (Sherif, 1956).

Another study required students to judge which of two paintings was better art. Actually one was a masterpiece, the other inferior. Students worked in two types of experimental pairs and in control pairs. The experimental pairs were formed by introducing to each student as his partner a confederate of the experimenter. One set of experiments (ten pairs) was designed to emphasize the prestige of the co-worker; he was introduced as art director of an important advertising agency. By prearrangement, this "art director" chose the poorer painting in each comparative judgment and called it better. Half of the time he gave his judgment before the naive student expressed his; half of the time the student spoke first. Influenced by the prestige of the supposed art director, the average student's errors on the test rose from 10.9 to 19.6—nearly doubled. In another set of pairs, the same confederate, introduced simply as another student, made the same prearranged wrong choices. In this case errors rose only from 13.3 to 17.0 (Mausner, 1953). The average student was influenced by his partner, even when the partner was wrong. This was true, especially, if the partner was assumed to have prestige.

In a later study (Willis, Hollander, 1964) some subjects were led to believe that their partner had had 18 of 20 responses correct in a pretest; others believed that their partner had only 3 of 20 correct. Both impressions were false and arbitrarily set by the experimenter. Those who thought their partner highly competent had a mean conformity of .54; those who thought him incompetent disagreed more often than they conformed, giving a mean of —.14.

Another piece of research (Turnure, Zigler, 1964) has shown that children became more imitative of an adult after they had experienced failure in several games. Normal children imitated less than did mentally retarded youngsters.

A further experiment compared the relative influence of self-indulgent behavior by a peer, and similar behavior by an adult, on imitative self-indulgence in a child. During a miniature bowling game, subjects were permitted to reward themselves (with chocolate candies) whenever they wished to do so. If a (control) child-partner held to a high standard, and rewarded himself only when he made scores of 20 or more (scores were reported in an arbitrary, predetermined sequence), 75 percent of the partners followed suit. If the pair consisted of an adult stooge and a child, the adult behavior was modeled by more than 90 percent of the younger partners (Bandura, Kupers, 1964).

Patients in psychotherapy converge toward the views of their therapist more than he, ordinarily, accepts their outlook. The tendency to agree may extend to many issues beyond those actually discussed together. In one study (Graham, 1960) the Rorschach test responses of patients of five therapists, all of whom made more than twice as many "movement" as "color" interpretations (presumably indicative of a lively, introversive, inner life), evidenced, after eight months of treatment, a movement in the same direction. In contrast, the patients of five therapists who made more color interpretations, tended to change in that direction.

Liking

Liking for a partner can have much the same influence as respect for prestige in bringing about convergence with his judgment. One experiment (Zeaman, 1956), again using the auto-kinetic effect, paired a male student first with a young woman he liked, and then with a young man whom he regarded as a rival in both academic and social affairs. Convergence with the young woman's judgment was marked— a drop from earlier estimates (alone) of 5.9 inches in the post-dyadic testing. But when paired with his rival, the same subject was only slightly affected; and that little was in a direction *away from* his partner's estimates.

A special case of attraction between partners often occurs when they are of opposite sex. Male students respond differently when paired with an older man and with an attractive co-ed, even though both have similar competence and prestige. Stevenson and Allen (1964), to cite only one of many examples, found that young men and young women both were willing to work longer and harder at a repetitive task when the supervisor directing their work (they worked in dyads—one supervisor for each worker) was of the opposite sex.

Consonance

Fondness for another person affects our judgment of his actions. Or, conversely, liking of his behavior affects our estimate of the person. We seem to operate on the assumption that if something is done by a good person, it should be a good act. If done by a bad person, it should be a bad act. When faced with a conflict—an apparently bad act done by a good person, or a good act done by a bad person—we try to resolve the inconsistency by saying: "I don't believe he did it. He couldn't!" or "It really wasn't his intention."

Several social psychologists have developed theories based on this tendency to harmonize our experience and expectations about persons and their attitudes. Heider (1946) formulated it as *cognitive harmony* and later (1958) as *balance.* Newcomb (1953) describes efforts to increase "similarity" or "congruence" in "co-orientation." Festinger's (1957) key phrase is "cognitive dissonance;" he sees the attempt to achieve *consonance* as a major motive. Deutsch and Solomon (1959) state the law as follows: "Whenever a state of imbalance exists or impends, a tendency will be produced in the individual to engage in behavior which will change the perceived entities in such a way as to remove or prevent imbalance." For the dyad, this rule implies convergence in the attitudes of partners who like each other, but a force toward maintaining distinctions and differences if the individuals do not like one another. It implies liking for new acquaintances who seem to share our values and rejection of those who do not.

The pressure toward balance may lead toward distorted perception of the attitudes of others. If P likes O, he tends to see O as sharing P's own values.

In one experiment (Berkowitz, Goranson, 1964) college girls first expressed their own attitude toward college fraternities. Then they were given a statement on this issue presumed to have been written by the partner with whom they were paired in the study. Half of the pairs had been induced to like each other ("a very good match"); the remaining half had low liking ("very different; may dislike her"). Although the pair statements deviated objectively by the same number of steps, the girls who expected to like their partner minimized the actual difference when they later were asked to estimate agreement or disagreement. The low-liking group was fairly objective.

In an auto-kinetic experiment, rather like Sherif's, the degree of liking of one subject for the other was manipulated in a series of pre-tests. A student who liked his partner and whose initial estimates were dissimilar, changed in the direction which brought his judgments closer to the stooge-partner. If the student had developed a dislike for his co-worker, and his estimates had been quite similiar, the difference became larger (Sampson, Insko, 1964). The effect was particularly pronounced in this research because the experimenters had explained to subjects that similarity in estimate of light movements signified, psychologically, basic similarity in personality. (This, of course, is not actually true, but was said to sharpen the meaning of the experiment.)

Another piece of research related to the balance or cognitive consistency theory reported how husbands and wives erred in reporting each other's attitudes. Each spouse filled out a test of left-right political opinions (Rokeach, 1960). Then each estimated what he thought his mate would say in response to each item. The correlation between actual attitudes of husband and wife on this test was represented by a coefficient

(r) of .35—only a modest degree of agreement. But their estimates of what the spouse would say agreed with their own responses to an extent represented by a correlation of .71 (husbands predicting wives) or .84 (wives predicting husbands). Clearly they both expected more agreement than actually existed (Byrne, Blaylock, 1963).

Interaction increases liking

The balance theory leads to the prediction that two strangers who hold similar attitudes will tend to develop a liking for each other when they do become acquainted. This has been confirmed in several studies (e.g., Newcomb, 1956; Byrne, 1961). But there is evidence to support a further thesis, that, usually, the more often two people interact, the better they will come to like one another. The relationship tends to be circular. We interact more frequently with people we know we like, but, as a rule, when we are led to interact extensively with a person who has been a relative stranger, we develop friendship.

We referred earlier to a simple experiment by Bavelas, in which two strangers, connected by telephone, tried to solve a problem. When the feedback from the second to the first was limited to a "Yes" or "No" push button, the pair managed to solve the problem, but 39 of 40 subjects spontaneously made derogatory remarks about his partner. When two-way, interactive communication was possible, each typically regarded his partner as intelligent and probably likeable.

It is usually true that people who frequently interact become friends. Most of our friends are found among those who are (or have been) our neighbors, fellow students, co-workers, or partners in golf or tennis or other recreational activities. If we move apart and discontinue the interaction friendship may persist for a time but then it wanes.

It is possible, however, for intimacy to become annoying. We do not yet know what turns the interaction experience from positive to negative. An unusually clear report of a case is given by a French anthropologist, Poincins (1943), who is writing of his attitude toward Paddy Gibson, a trader with whom he spent most of an Arctic winter.

> I liked Gibson as soon as I saw him, and from the moment of my arrival we got on exceedingly well. He was a man of poise and order; he took life calmly and philosophically; he had an endless budget of stories. In the beginning we would sit for hours . . . discussing with warmth and friendliness every topic that suggested itself, and I soon felt a real affection for him.
>
> Now as winter closed in round us, and week after week our world narrowed until it was reduced—in mind, at any rate—to the dimensions of a trap, I went from impatience to restlessness, and from restlessness finally to monomania. I began to rage inwardly and the very traits in my friend . . . which had struck me at the beginning as admirable, ultimately seemed to me detestable.

The time came when I could no longer bear the sight of this man who was unfailingly kind to me.

Suggestion

In a dyad, each member responds to the behavior of the other. He does things he would not do otherwise, or as he would not otherwise do them. Suggestion is continuous. A satiated hen, if placed with a hungry hen busily pecking at grain, starts eating again (Katz, 1937). A bored child who sees his partner quit work and start playing is likely to follow suit (Grosser, Polansky, Lippeth, 1951). A man with eyes closed, informed that he is leaning more and more forward, usually does so, although in some cases he reacts against the suggestion by leaning backward (Hull, 1933). Told that his outstretched arm is getting lighter and rising, a blindfolded subject usually lifts the arm slightly; in a small minority of cases he responds by a counteraction and lowers it (Aveling, Hargreaves, 1921). This pattern of general conformity, with a minority in protest reaction, will be confronted again on a larger scale when we study response to advertising and other public propaganda. The term "suggestion" can denote all degrees of influence, from the slightest to full surrender to direction by another. It is common for individuals to underestimate the extent to which they are influenced by their associates. We cherish the illusion that our attitudes are self-generated. There is probably a sound psychological basis for the concern which most parents feel when their child begins to associate closely with a friend of whom they do not approve. Each child will surely have some influence on the values, standards, and behavior of his friend. The stronger, more confident, more settled, more prestigious partner will probably be imitated more extensively.

Hypnosis

The influence of one personality over another is most marked in the fascinating phenomenon of hypnosis. Aided by special conditions, such as bodily relaxation of the subject and concentrated attention, one person may achieve an extraordinary degree of influence over another. The submissive member of the hypnotic dyad may, in some cases, be led to believe himself asleep or awake, happy or depressed, fed or hungry (hunger contractions in the stomach have sometimes been observed to stop at the suggestion, under hypnosis, that a meal has been eaten); in pain or free from pain (hypnotic anesthesia sometimes works), or induced to act the part of a young child, an old man, or even a dog or cat. The influence of suggestion made during trance may persist after the hypnotized subject has returned to an apparently normal condition of self-direction. He may carry out a silly instruction hours later, and offer some rationalization when asked to account for his behavior (Hull,

1933). Erickson (1941) reports one case of a suggestion offered under hypnosis and carried out five years later. In another case (Erickson, 1943) a person who had acquired a strong aversion to orange flavors (as a result of taking castor oil in orange juice) and who had been unable to free himself from this complex, relived the experience under hypnosis and emerged free once again to enjoy orange juice.

Can a hypnotized person be made to commit crimes revolting to his conscience? Usually there are limits, even in the deepest hypnosis, beyond which the subject refuses to follow the suggestion of his hypnotist. Evidence of conflict and disturbance appears instead of compliance and the trance may terminate. On the other hand, subjects in hypnosis have been induced to regard a rattlesnake as a coiled hose, or to throw acid (Rowland, 1939), and in an exceptional case have been known to do something repugnant to their waking self. Watkins (1947) reported a soldier who attacked his superior officer with a knife, acting under the hypnotic delusion that the victim was a Japanese soldier.

Thinking together

Proverbially, "two heads are better than one." Facing a critical problem of diagnosis, a highly competent doctor or lawyer may welcome a consultation. One psychologist (Almack, 1930) tested some 200 college students working, part of the time alone, and part of the time in pairs. The tasks included intelligence test items, crossword puzzles, and practical planning. He found the product of pairs superior to that of either member working alone. Two able students, of course, produced better results than did two average or two poor students, but a bright student, even when working with a poor student, produced a better result than he did when he worked alone. This is an instructive finding, for some people have supposed that cooperative work in some way levels off abilities to something like the average of the two partners. Actually each adds something to the other and neither prevents the other from doing his best. We shall return to this problem when we discuss group thinking in Chapter 4. Another study, in which college students worked alone or in pairs at five different kinds of tasks, is summarized in Abstract 3. Most problems were solved more quickly when two worked together, but two were not twice as fast as one.

In another study, grade school children were given arithmetic reasoning problems to solve alone or were allowed to work in pairs and instructed to talk the question over until both believed the answer correct. In this study, as in Husband's arithmetic exercises, the dyad took slightly longer than the single individual (20½ minutes as compared with 19 minutes when tested alone). But the pair produced more correct answers (7.29 as compared with 6.18). The difference was about as

Abstract 3

TITLE   Cooperative vs. Solitary Problem-Solving

AUTHOR   Richard W. Husband

PROBLEM   Working in pairs, do people solve problems faster than working alone?

SUBJECTS   120 college students; 40 working alone and 80 in 40 pairs.

PROCEDURE   Individuals and pairs were given a test consisting of:
1. a code to be deciphered;
2. a jigsaw puzzle to be assembled; and
3. five arithmetic problems (about Seventh-grade level).
Each was required to complete the task and time was the measure of efficiency.

SOME FINDINGS   The average student working alone took 12 minutes to decipher the code, but two working together did it in 9. (From one point of view, it took 18 man-minutes.) The jigsaw puzzle was completed by one person in 17 minutes; by a pair in 12 minutes. On the arithmetic tests, pairs were no faster than individuals.

SOURCE: *J. soc. Psychol.*, 1940, XI: 405–409.

great as that from one grade's average score to the average in the next grade. That is, two fifth-graders would get about the same number of right answers as one sixth-grader (Klugman, 1944).

In Chapter 4 we shall study in more detail some factors which facilitate or hamper problem solving when undertaken by groups thinking together. For the present we may conclude that two heads are usually better than one, but not twice as efficient.

Rivalry and conflict

Rivalry

We have discussed dyads in which one member depends on the other, influences the other, or helps the other. Almost as common is a dyadic pattern in which one or both try to surpass or to get the better of the other. Some unhappy people have been brought up to view life as a perpetual contest. Every dyadic relationship challenges them to compete. They can accept dependence of others upon them but find it hard to receive help because they feel it so urgent to demonstrate their superiority. Even friendship and love relations are distorted into rivalry situations in which the satisfaction comes only through overt or secret mastery of the partner. The chronic rival, confronting life as an endless series of contests, faces bitter defeats. There will always be someone better than he at something; no one can excel at everything. Many years ago a wise teacher told the writer: "I have never met another person who was not my superior in some respects."

Rivalry, in moderation, can be stimulating. A tennis player is likely to play a better game against someone worthy of his mettle. Such a game is also more fun. When the rivalry becomes too intense, however, the pressure may be demoralizing. Some children get so annoyed when they are losing at checkers that they upset the board.

A number of studies of subjects tested working alone and then in competition lead to the conclusion that rivalry usually brings some increase in effort and output, but may have a detrimental effect upon quality of work (Dashiell, 1935).

One experimenter (Shaw, 1958) contrasted cooperative and competitive pairs in a motor task (following an erratic, moving target) and a memory-reasoning task (working out the correct sequence among four switches to turn on a light). He found that while the college students usually enjoyed the competition, they performed most efficiently in the cooperatively structural task; next best when acting alone; and most poorly when competing. He concluded that the stimulating motives aroused by competition disrupted quality of performance. The same result was obtained in another study (Jones, Vroom, 1964) comparing jigsaw puzzle solutions achieved by two subjects working in a situation where each could observe the progress of the other. When told they were cooperating, they achieved a higher total level of performance (number of pieces correctly placed) and gave more evidence of division of labor (less duplication of a portion on which the other was working) than they did when they were instructed to compete with each other.

Conflict

It takes two to make a quarrel. Conflict arises typically from a situation in which both principals have a chance to win, but if one wins the other must lose. Competition for a girl, or to win a game, or to get a certain job, takes this form. So does a fist fight or an argument. Feeling may become so intense that each person would like to kill the other; historically, of course, many conflicts have led to homicide.

Resolution of an intense conflict may occur through: (1) victory of one and submission of the other to his fate; (2) a compromise in which each receives part of what he wants; (3) a genuine integration in which a way is found to meet the full demands of both parties; or (4) loss of interest by one or both in the object of dispute. Participants in a conflict usually narrow their view to the first of the four possible patterns of resolution. Part of the art of the mediator or diplomat or the

Abstract 4

TITLE Domination and Integration in the Social Behavior of Kindergarten Children in an Experimental Play Situation

AUTHOR Harold H. Anderson

PROBLEM Is a child consistently dominating or cooperative in his relationships with another child of his own age?

SUBJECTS 21 boys; 28 girls in three kindergartens.

PROCEDURE Each child was paired with another and taken to a play room with a sand box, a toy sand pail, a toy shovel, a sieve, two toy autos, and three toy animals of rubber. Concealed observers watched five minutes of play. Behavior was scored as "Domination" if the child: (a) made verbal demands for certain toys or play opportunities; (b) seized these by force; (c) defended or snatched back materials taken from him; (d) issued verbal commands to direct his partner's behavior; (e) used force to try to bring compliance; (f) blamed, reproved or made unfavorable comparisons. "Integration" was shown by: (a) attempts to share, to cooperate, to take turns; to volunteer help; requests for cooperation or help; suggestions for conversation or other activity in the form of "Let's"—or "Shall we?"—; (c) compliance with requests and suggestions; or (d) imitative play.

Two independent observers agreed very well on their ratings ($r = .90$).

SOME FINDINGS 1. A child who makes a dominating approach arouses dominating responses in his partner.

2. A child who makes an integrative approach arouses integrative responses in his partner.

3. Integrative behavior with other children increases from age three to six.

4. Kindergarten children are more integrative than dominating in their contacts with one another (ratio of I to D = 10:1), but teacher-child contacts are mainly dominating (ratio 1:2).

5. Child behavior with child of opposite sex is not significantly different from behavior with child of same sex and girls did not differ from boys in I:D ratio.

6. No children were always dominating or always integrative; the observed behavior depended on the dyad, as well as on the individual personality.

SOURCE: *Genet. Psychol. Monogr.*, 1939, XXI, 357–385.

parent or teacher who must untangle many quarrels, is to direct attention to a possible integration or to distract one or both combatants by suggesting other interests. One mother, finding herself frustrated in an effort to get her child to eat some cooked vegetables because the child wanted only bread and butter, hit on the happy integrative idea of a sandwich with the vegetables inside the bread and butter. Wise parents avoid getting involved in the dispute over who started it, and find ways instead to move children out of their combat postures into other activities.

Integrative approach and response

Whether a person sees his relationship with another as competitive or cooperative depends partly on the person himself and partly on the attitude the other one takes. An individual who usually plays tennis for the fun of it, may find himself responding to an apparent demand of his opponent to win by becoming just as competitive as the other player.

The study summarized in Abstract 4 shows that young children become counter-dominative in response to a partner who is dominating. If the partner's approach is integrative, the response is likely to be similarly cooperative.

Anderson's observation that a dominating approach calls forth counter-domination is related to a more general experience. A person who meets a stranger in a warm and friendly manner is likely to evoke a friendly response. (Hyde and Erichorn, in Sorokin, 1950, found this true in 73 percent of their cases.) If the approach was unfriendly, the response was likely also to be unfriendly (70 percent of the cases).

Anderson's finding that, sometimes, a dominating child may be compatible with a submissive partner, each reinforcing the characteristic behavior of the other, supports the observations of many parents of their own children. Beginning students of child psychology sometimes ask: "How can two children who have grown up in the same environment, with the same parents, become such different personalities?" While inherited tendencies cannot be ignored, we can find a large part of the answer in dyadic interaction. A mother once commented: "I have noticed that whenever virtue wanes in one of my sons, it waxes in the other!" Siblings are constantly interacting with one another; sometimes they join in activities that enhance their similarity, but often they react against one another. When one wins approval for his piano lesson or his reading, the other may regard this as the last conceivable realm in which to seek satisfaction. Interaction may increase convergence or divergence.

Another finding of the Anderson study, that teachers were much more dominating than integrative in their contacts with pupils, directs our attention to the psychology of the teacher-learner relationship.

The teacher-learner dyad

Only a small part of the teaching that goes on in the world takes place in schools. Everyone learns more outside of the classroom than within it. And most of what he learns comes not from books, but from other people. The teacher-learner dyad is even more ubiquitous than that of parent and child. Who have been our teachers? Our mothers and fathers, of course, but also our brothers and sisters, our playmates, our friends and lovers, our employers, and co-workers, our doctors and nurses and dentists, merchants from whom we have asked casual advice, the people who have shown us how to use new pieces of equipment, our ministers, our household helpers, our neighbors, athletic coaches, innumerable advertisers, writers for newspapers, magazines, posters, and bulletins as well as books, newscasters, political orators, critics, commentators and other speakers on radio and television. The novelists, dramatists, and actors who have given us heroes and villains to emulate or to despise, and who have given us new ways of looking at life's recurring pre-dicaments have been especially important teachers.

The forms of teacher-learner interaction are protean. Sometimes teachers have no awareness that they are teaching; learners may not realize that they are learning. What is actually learned may be quite different from what a teacher intends to convey. Charles Kingsley once admonished: "Let not the sour-faced teach morals, lest they create a distaste for virtue!" (His warning illustrates the principle of balance or consonance presented earlier in this chapter.)

Some learners adore their teachers; some give respect but not affec-tion; some hate their teachers but still learn from them. In Chapter 5, we shall develop more systematically the relationship of teacher and the taught.

The teacher-learner dyad, like the parent-child or therapist-patient dyads, is one which makes very unequal demands upon its two mem-bers. Teachers exist for the sake of the learners, not vice versa. Parents, whether their children be small or grown, properly weigh their children's needs above their own preferences. A good psychotherapist does not rely upon his patients for his emotional satisfaction. If a teacher comes to need too much affection, respect or gratitude of learners for his own satisfaction, this may actually cripple his effectiveness. Prolonged de-pendence on a teacher is not evidence of his excellence. When a learner asks a question, a prompt and correct answer from the teacher may be ego-satisfying, but it may not help the learner as much as a restrained pause while the learner thinks things out for himself. A good teacher is interested in the growth of the learner: the pupil's increasing capacity to meet situations without outside help. Teacher, therapist, and parent all should aim at making themselves dispensable. John Dewey, the first psychologist to direct his presidential address before the American Psychological Association to *social* psychology (entitled *Psychology and Social Practice*, 1899) well expressed the responsibility of anyone who tries to guide the life of another:

> To make others happy except through liberating their powers and engaging them in activities that enlarge the meaning of life is to harm them and to indulge ourselves under cover of exercising a special virtue. (Dewey, 1922)

One of the main skills of the teacher (or parent, or therapist) is to understand what he himself means, at any given time, in the life of the learner. This capacity to project oneself imaginatively into the life-space of another, and to see the world through his eyes, is also fundamental whenever two people converse.

Conversation

Children at age two or three often regard other children as fascinating toys. They "experiment" with these others, pushing or hitting or smiling, with no sure knowledge of what will happen as a result. They speak *to,* but not *with* their companions.

A Swiss psychologist, Jean Piaget, has studied the way in which young children "explain" things to one another. Their thinking is more "egocentric" or "autistic" than most adults; they leap to intuitive conclusions which are emotionally satisfying but are difficult to justify by logic or to explain to others. Their speech expresses a personal and private view, which does not communicate very fully. A child of six, for example, may understand 80 percent of a story told to him, but is able to convey only about 50 percent of this story to another child. "Conversation between children is therefore not sufficient at first to take the speakers out of their egocentrism, because each child, whether he is trying to explain his own thoughts or to understand those of others, is shut up in his own point of view" (Piaget, 1926). The child's one-sided kind of conversation is not yet mature interaction.

Sometimes autism persists even to adult levels. A distinguished professor once started to tell his companions at the Faculty Club a humorous anecdote that another member of the group had just finished telling. Apparently he had been reminded of the funny story, but had retired into his own thoughts and paid no further attention while the others were speaking. He returned mentally to the group only when he was free to perform. He was as egocentric as the children observed by Piaget and hence not really free to interact with others.

Buber (1947) distinguishes genuine dialogue, "where each of the participants has in mind the other or others in their present and particular being and turns to them with the intention of establishing a living mutual relation between himself and them," from "monologue disguised as dialogue." The latter is "a conversation characterized by the need neither to communicate something, nor to learn something, nor to influence someone, nor to come into connection with someone, but solely by the desire to have one's self-reliance confirmed by marking the impression that is made; . . . a friendly chat in which each regards himself as absolute and legitimate and the other as relativized and questionable; a lover's talk in which both partners alike enjoy their own glorious soul and their precious experience—what an underworld of faceless spectres of dialogue!"

Good conversationalists do more for one another than just to empathize successfully. They stimulate one another, each awakening memories or ideas or problems which both can develop further. Also, in a good conversation, each feels valued by the other. The two may not agree, but in the conversation they examine their disagreement in a way which respects the other as a person. There is a basic unity beneath the immediate disunity. If this be lacking, one or both will feel that further conversation is useless.

Ralph Waldo Emerson felt that good conversation was limited to dyads. He wrote in *Friendship* (1841):

> "Two is company; three is a crowd," runs an old proverb. I find this law of one to one peremptory for conversation, which is the practice and consummation of friendship. Do not mix waters too much. The best mix as ill as good and bad. You shall have very useful and cheering discourse at several times with two several men, but let all three of you come together, and you shall not have one new and hearty word. Two may talk and one may hear, but three cannot take part in a conversation of the most sincere and searching sort. In good company there is never such discourse between two, across the table, as takes place when you leave them alone.

Friendship

One of the most common forms of dyad is that of friends, cronies, or confidants. No one questions the value of friendship in human life—for many persons the bond with a friend gives meaning and worth to all other experience. Yet friendship is difficult to study scientifically, partly because it is hard to define. There are all degrees of friendship; the word may be applied to a casual acquaintance or to a deep, long-standing confidential relationship which means more than most love affairs. Friendships are as complex and varied as the personalities of various friends.

Dozens of psychologists have explored the best-friend choices of children. Moreno (1934) has invented a technique called *sociometry* for investigating the extent to which members of a group are chosen by one another. Pupils in a class may be asked to choose a partner to share a desk, to help out on a project, or to be invited to a party. Choices differ, depending on the proposed activity, but the technique brings out some important patterns. About one child in five turns out—in a typical class—to be an *isolate*. None of his classmates choose him. Personality problems usually accompany such isolation, both as cause and as effect of the rejection. At the other extreme, most groups have a few "stars," chosen by many of their classmates. In the next chapter, sociometric analysis will be discussed further. In the present connection, our interest is mainly in *pairs*, each member of which chooses the other.

Earlier we stated that frequency of interaction is highly correlated with liking. It follows that friendships are most often formed where circumstances have facilitated interaction. Among children and adolescents, friendship dyads have been found to depend heavily upon residential propinquity, closeness in age, socio-economic class, and interests. Best friends in the lower grades of elementary school commonly live very near one another. Choices are seldom made outside the same school class. Similarity in size and intelligence is less important than similarity of age, school grade, and special hobbies. From age 5 to 12, most best friends are of the same sex.

It would be unwise to extrapolate from these studies of children to adult friendships. Strong and genuine friendships frequently arise between men and women, contradicting a popular adolescent view that any cross-sex tie must involve romantic or sexual love. Friendships may endure over years of separation with wide variation in interests. Friendships between the young and old are not unknown.

A lively debate can be organized on whether our friends and marital partners are chosen because they are similar to us or because they are different from and complementary to us. Data can be found on both sides. Similarity in social class, education, and intelligence is the rule. One study (Izard, 1960) is based on results from the Edwards Personal Preference Schedule given to 200 students in a middle- or upper-class high school and college. Students named their best friends and 30 pairs were found, each of whom chose the other. These pairs were considerably more alike than were random pairs in four of the 15 traits measured by the test: need for achievement; deferential attitudes; orderliness; desire to be the center of attention; and perseverance. In no traits did one friend appear high and the other low. An earlier study (Newcomb, 1956) among college men showed preference for others who were perceived as more like oneself. Consonance would require that one also like himself.

A study of personality characteristics which individuals think apply to them, to their friends, and to an ideal person, revealed that friends are more alike in their ideals than in their self-image. There was also a marked resemblance between a person's ideal and his impression of his friend (Thompson, Nishimura, 1951), again illustrating consonance.

One of the best empirical studies of friendship was made in Puerto Rico by Dr. Sanchez-Hidalgo (1951), who interviewed each member of 40 same-sex pairs of college-age friends. Responses to the question, "What does a best friend do for me?" emphasized ego-support through such activities as: "I am important to him," "Recognizes my abilities," "Seeks my advice," "Thinks my ideas important," "Praises me," and "Remembers me." Almost equal in frequency of mention were activities that protected the friend's ego: "Keeps me from loneliness," "Defends me if someone gossips or criticizes," "Calms me when I'm excited or worried," "Shares my depressions," "Does not criticize me," "Does not brag," "Keeps up my courage," "Makes me feel secure." Activities of helpfulness, such as: "Does me a good turn," "Lends a hand," "Cooperates," "Assists," and so forth, came third and were more important for dyads of men than for women. Sanchez-Hidalgo characterized friendship dyads in general as *symbiotic,* meaning that each friend found some of his important life needs met by the other. One friend may obtain a sense of relaxation and peace of mind from his friend, while the other member of the pair values more the stimulation of new ideas and broader experience he finds in the relationship. The wider the range of needs met by one friend for the other, and the deeper and more essential these satisfactions, the stronger the bonds of the friendship. It is doubtful whether a one-sided contribution that meets needs for one friend but not for the other, will prove viable. In symbiosis, there is value for both partners.

A study (Watson, Riesman, 1964) of grouping and conversation at 26 parties showed that dyads differed significantly from larger social systems. Conversation was more intimate, especially between comparative strangers who frequently began their relationship by more thoughtful, self-revelatory, and appreciative expressions than were used by those already well acquainted. In dyads, *achievement* (meaning appreciation of individual effort as valuable and productive) was a more common theme than it was in larger groups; larger groups tended more toward *nihilism* (cynical derogation of conventional institutions or values). The authors present as a tentative hypothesis that the more optimistic themes of the dyad are related to the fact that each member has more power to influence what goes on in a small group of two.

There is a marked difference in self-confidence and feeling of adequacy between a person alone and a person accompanied by his friend. In a study of responses of young children to frustration occasioned by separating them from new toys they have just begun to enjoy, it was found that if the dyad were composed of two children who were close friends, they were more aggressive in their attacks upon the adult

experimenter than was true of dyads composed of more casual acquaintances (Wright, 1943). At times of emergency, danger, and bereavement, when we are particularly vulnerable to the human predicament,
nothing else helps so much as the quiet, sustaining presence of a friend.

Can one make a friend of another person whom he has previously
disliked? In accordance with the principle of consonance, most people
do not engage in this experiment. Yet it can be done. Thompson (reported by Sorokin) found that when college students deliberately tried
to treat companions they had disliked as if they were friends, it usually
brought an unexpectedly friendly response, making the next act of
friendliness much easier than the first one. As a counter-balance to this
benign approach, we may refer to another study (also reported by
Sorokin) in which relationships between a nurse and a patient improved
following a flare-up—an aggressive interchange. What happened, apparently, was that the mutual dislike had been carefully concealed beneath
polite formalities. The breakthrough of an honest, spontaneous personal
response was welcomed and laid the foundation for more genuine interaction and hence for better liking of each other.

Most commentators on friendship, whether amateur or professional
psychologists, stress the importance of sincerity and straightforwardness.
It is implicitly recognized that there is much that is false in most human
relationships. We exert ourselves to obtain certain ends—striving to get
the task done or to be a good employer or to please the customer. In
school we want to be liked by other students and approved by the
teachers. Thus we are constantly putting our best foot forward, concealing negative or hostile feelings, and wearing whatever mask seems
appropriate. Some people, constantly living for the approval of others,
become as superficial as the various masks they wear. One feels that
there is no real identity behind the endless succession of masks. One of
the virtues of good friendship is that masks can be laid aside. A person
feels secure with his friend: His friend knows and accepts his real self,
with all its limitations and weaknesses. Therefore he need not pretend
or cover up. The assurance that the friend will understand and accept
adds to his own self-acceptance and confidence. One may be even freer
to be oneself in the presence of an accepting friend than one is when
alone.

Rifts in friendship often occur when it has been assumed that the
friend understands, but he does not; or that he accepts what it turns out
he is unable to accept. It takes a long period of acquaintance, with
many testings, to build a solid friendship. The intuitive feeling that
someone we have recently met is a perfect friend is usually an illusion.
To quote Emerson again: "Our friendships hurry to short and poor conclusions, because we have made them a texture of wine and dreams,
instead of the tough fibre of the human heart. The laws of friendship

are austere and eternal, of one web with the laws of nature and of morals. But we have aimed at a swift and petty benefit, to suck a sudden sweetness. We snatch at the slowest fruit in the whole garden of God, which many summers and many winters must ripen."

Sex, love, and marriage

Despite the evident human concern with the dyadic relationships of sex, love, and marriage, social psychologists have done relatively little research in these areas. Alfred Kinsey (1948) aptly refers to "man's absorbing interest in sex and his astounding ignorance of it; his desire to know and his unwillingness to face the facts."

The usual criteria for defining an instinct: (1) having a physiological, biochemical basis in the organism; (2) appearing in all human cultures; (3) being difficult to suppress; and (4) being found also in other mammals—all apply clearly to mating. Yet anthropologists report that social norms in differing cultures lead to very different sex attitudes and behaviors. (More on this in Chapter 9). Children in some societies freely play at sexual intercourse; in other cultures any evidence of sex interest by children is taboo.

Neither sex interest nor love appears suddenly and fully developed at adolescence. Both form during childhood years. We noted earlier that imprinting of certain animals during the first days or weeks of life can affect their sexual behavior at maturity. Freud's observations on the Oedipus complex in human males (and its parallel, the Electra complex in females) postulates a connection between the unconscious attachment of a child about four years old to the parent of opposite sex, and the love objects in the child's later life. Hamilton (1929) found a considerable correlation between the terms men used to describe the personality of their mothers and those they used to describe the personality of their wives. Psychoanalytic observations are often unconvincing to those who have not had the special and unusual opportunity of the analyst to study intensively the fantasies and recollections of patients during hundreds of hours and under conditions fostering frankness and intimacy. But no psychoanalytic sophistication is required to make it seem plausible that small children, when they think of growing up and living with someone of the opposite sex, should first choose the person they have already learned to live with and to love.

In our society, initiative in a male-female sexual relationship is expected from the male. Kinsey's data indicate that boys and men at every age level are sexually more active than girls and women. The social psychologist asks whether such differences are innate or the product of social norms. The evidence supports both factors. Generally, in animals (Ford, Beach, 1951) and in men, the male is more quickly aroused to sexual excitement and is more easily conditioned to respond to a variety of associated stimuli: sights, sounds, odors, portions of the anatomy (genital and other). Most "perversions" and "fetishisms" have been observed among males. Yet there are times in most dyadic sexual relationships when the female is more aroused and demanding than is the male, and, as we shall report in Chapter 9, there are cultures in which the initiative is customarily assigned to the female.

Although sex drive and love are associated, there are important differences between them (Reik, 1945). Sex is stimulated quite directly by glandular secretions; love is integral to the whole personality. Sex goes through a cycle of tension and satisfaction; love remains constant. Erotic drives may be rather indiscriminate and are stimulated by novelty; love is highly discriminating and cherishes exclusiveness and continuity. There has been some controversy among psychologists about whether sex and love motivations have the same roots. Freud saw affection as derived from erotic pleasure. Fromm (1956) argues that desire for intercourse is only one manifestation of the larger and more inclusive impulse toward human brotherhood. We have seen that in the child the two kinds of experience are usually kept separate. The child's playmates in sex exploration are not the human beings he most loves (Bühler, 1935). One of the functions of adolescent caresses, kisses, and petting is to weld together these two strands of development as they unite in a good marriage.

Both sex and love may sometimes find expression in dyads of the same sex. Adolescents segregated in boarding schools or penal institutions frequently develop homosexual attachments, mostly temporary, but often involving strong affection (Kosotsky, Ellis, 1958; Halleck, Hersko, 1962).

A social psychological model for marriage would include: (1) the unity of love and sex; (2) frequent, close interaction with increasing and almost continuous liking for each other; (3) joint responsibility, deliberately undertaken, to carry out the social role of building and nurturing a family. The first two can exist in love affairs outside marriage; the unique factor in marriage is the public and private commitment to the family project. All societies recognize this important step with some kinds of ceremony and legal and status differentials.

The motivation for sex relations and for marriage includes more than the sexual impulses. Mating behavior, whether in or outside marriage, may satisfy needs for economic security, for "proving" one's masculinity or feminity, to dominate and control the other person, to revenge oneself upon another (the jilted lover rebounds), to win acceptance in a certain circle, or to achieve status in the society. These supplementary or secondary gains often become the primary factors in a decision to marry.

Abstract 5

TITLE Mate Selection

AUTHOR Robert F. Winch

PROBLEM Do we marry persons similar or opposite in personality traits?

SUBJECTS 25 married couples, all undergraduates at Northwestern University; white, non-Jewish.

PROCEDURE Interviews designed to bring out the kind of needs defined by H. A. Murray (1938). The interview included case history, early memories, developmental stages, and was supplemented by Thematic Apperception Test (stories made up about ambiguous pictures). Each person was rated on the basis of all available information.

SOME FINDINGS One relationship accounted for most of the positive results: Whenever one spouse was high in dominance the other was more deferential and self-effacing.

Case studies illustrate four types of complementariness: mother-son; "Ibsenian" (in which the husband dominates but provides, protection nurturance to a dependent wife); master-servant girl in which the husband dominates and the wife serves his needs; and the "Thurberian" in which the wife is dominant but expects to be cared for; the man is submissive but nurturant.

SOURCE: New York: Harper and Brothers, 1958.

Selection

Contemporary American culture places great stress on finding the one right partner. Other cultures in which marriages are arranged by parents or elders recognize that a "suitable" mate is desirable, but foster no illusion of the "one and only."

Historically, we know that the glorification of romantic love is characteristic of only a few cultures and of our own only since the twelfth century. In ancient Greece and Rome, amorous attachment was not the foundation for marriage; men experienced it more often with courtesans or with attractive boys. The anthropologist, Linton (1936), implies that even in modern man, the passionate spouse is usually consciously or unconsciously acting a prescribed role and trying to feel something which may not be genuinely moving. The hero of the modern American movie is always a romantic lover just as the hero of the old Arab epic is commonly an epileptic. A cynic might suspect that in any ordinary population the percentage of people capable of romantic love of the Hollywood type is about as large as that of persons able to throw genuine epileptic fits. However, given a little social encouragement, either situation can be adequately simulated without the performer's admitting even to himself that the performance is not genuine.

In the section on friendship, we found some studies emphasizing similarity and others the complementarity of friendship dyads. What is the pattern with love? Winch's book summarized in Abstract 5 points to a common pattern: if one partner is strongly dominant, it is better for the other to be submissive.

A subsequent study (Kerckhoff, Davis, 1962) integrates two generalizations about mate selection as characterizing phases of the relationship. Investigating 94 couples at six-month intervals, the authors found that those who moved toward closer relationships had begun with greater consensus in values. They postulate the following sequence:

1. First, interest in one another. This stage (homogamy) characterized by suitable similarily in age, socio-economic status, nationality, religion, education, etc.

2. Developing friendship. This stage characterized by increasing interaction and value consensus.

3. Interdependence: more complementarity of needs.

An essayist, under the title: *The Romantic Route to Divorce* (de-Rougemont, 1948) criticizes the prevailing emphasis on trying to find the one, ordained-by-Heaven ideal lover:

> The type of love on which a great majority of Western marriages is founded is a fever, generally light and considered infinitely interesting to contract. . . .
> . . . We are in the act of trying out—and failing miserably at it—one of the most pathological experiments that a civilized society has ever imagined, namely, the basing of marriage, which is lasting, upon romance, which is a passing fancy. . . .

Successful marriages are carefully built, not found by happy chance. Love is a vital ingredient and certain similarities, as shown in the study summarized in Abstract 6, are likely to be helpful. While some of the data are more sociological than psychological, they often point to psychological correlates. For example "number of same-sex friends before marriage" can be regarded as an index to general amiability and that capacity for brotherly love which Fromm finds fundamental. Age at time of marriage is a census item, but it has implications for the amount of previous experience and the readiness to be "tied down" to child-care.

The marriages studied by Burgess and Cottrell were more likely to be

Abstract 6

TITLE   Predicting Success Or Failure in Marriage

AUTHORS   E. W. Burgess and L. S. Cottrell, Jr.

PROBLEM   What factors are related to successful marriage?

SUBJECTS   526 couples (of 7,000 queried), in Illinois, all married from one to 6 years. Over 90 percent had finished high school; 60 percent had had some college. Husbands averaged 27 years of age; wives, twenty-three.

PROCEDURES   Questionnaire responses related to self-rating on happiness, and a 26 item index of marital adjustment. Reliability, .88.

SOME FINDINGS   1. Most were happy in their marriage (21 percent "happy," 43 percent "very happy."

2. Happier couples were better educated; had known one another five years or more; were over 28 at time of marriage; came from homes with good cultural background; felt closely attached to their parents; had numerous friends of their sex before marriage.

3. Unhappy couples were more apt to live in cities than in the country; had more financial difficulties; and entered marriages despite parental disapproval.

4. Differences in age, education, and religion did not prevent normal happiness.

SOURCE: New York: Prentice-Hall, 1939.

happy if the couple were well educated, mature (the younger at marriage the greater the probability of distress), acquainted for years, warmly attached to the family of origin and to other friends. Although a big point is often made of difficulties caused by difference in age, education, or formal religious affiliation, these differences had no effect upon chances for happiness among the 526 couples in the study. Other investigators have found confirmation of some of these conclusions. A Gallup poll showed 83 percent of marriages between college graduates rated as successful, but only 71 percent for those whose education stopped at high school graduation, and 62 percent for the couples who never went to high school. A sociologist reported that if either partner were under 20, chances for an unhappy marriage were five times as great as if both were 25 or older (Hart, 1939). A psychiatrist reported that the happiness of a marriage showed a fair measure of correlation ($r = .40$) with happiness of the parents' marriage (Hamilton, 1929). Among 200 successful adults, the best indication of probable marital happiness was that each thought his spouse had a personality like the parent of opposite sex whom the individual had loved in childhood. He found, although cases were few, that if the wife were a little older than her husband, the chances of happiness were improved. Among Terman's (1938) 792 couples, difference in age or schooling or religious training was not a variable related to happiness. Happiness seemed to relate more to the harmony of the parents' marriage and good relations in the family of origin. Each of these is a statistical comparison; it deals with proportions and probabilities. For the couple deciding on marriage, their relationship is unique. Despite any of the factors which seem statistically to be a handicap, the particular marriage may work out very well.

Two psychological facts about sex seem difficult to assimilate within our standard marriage pattern. One is that teen-age boys have a powerful sex drive years before they are ready to assume the mature responsibilities of marriage. Masturbation, prostitution, and premarital liaisons afford some outlets but each raises other problems. A second is that most men and some women are poly-erotic and, after a period of marital fidelity, are likely to be attracted by a novel partner. Kinsey reports that about half of all married men in America have had extra-marital adventures. This indulgence is likely if the concept of marriage over-emphasizes sexual attraction and under-emphasizes responsible commitment and the cultivation of a unique dyad with abundant sources of satisfaction in shared living.

Mutuality

Counselors report that one of the factors which commonly wreck a marriage is that the couple have virtually ceased to communicate. They sit opposite one another at meals, beside one another in the car they may sleep contentedly together, but they have almost ceased to communicate. Each carries on his own monologue, and neither quite hears the other. They may exchange enough signals to keep their engagement calendar, get the shopping done and the bills paid, but they do not experience the other as a living, aspiring person. A study of complaints of married persons about their mate showed that, for both sexes alike, the three most frequent ones were something like:

1. Is careless, thoughtless
2. Selfish. Thinks only of self
3. Takes me for granted

Two who are deeply in love transcend self, loving the other as themselves. What hurts the beloved or brings joy to the beloved, affects the lover as if it were really he that is hurt or gladdened. In Martin Buber's

words, "They experience (the beloved's) particular life in simple presence—not as a thing seen and touched, but from the innervations of his
movements, from the 'inner' to his 'outer'." In contrast, Buber describes
the varied "Eros of monologue" in which a partner is aware mainly of
his own delightful sensations:

> There a lover stamps around and is in love only with his passion. There
> one is wearing his differentiated feelings like medal-ribbons. There one is
> enjoying the adventures of his own fascinating effect. There one is gazing
> enraptured at the spectacle of his own supposed surrender. There one is
> collecting excitement. There one is displaying his "power." There one is
> preening himself with borrowed vitality. There one is delighting to exist
> simultaneously as himself and as an idol very unlike himself. . . . There one
> is experimenting. And so on and on—all the manifold monologists with
> their mirrors. (1947)

In contrast to this self-absorption is what Cyril Connolly (1945) has
aptly called "The Eternal Duologue" in which a couple, genuinely married for many years, continue to share so much of their experience
together that mere mention of a name, a time or a place, is sufficient to
arouse a whole bubbling spring of the memories in which both always
actively participate. Each becomes so accustomed to interaction with the
other, in relation to countless daily details, that the death of either
leaves the other as handicapped in mental life as he would be in loco-
motion if he lost one leg.

Telepathy
In this chapter, we have assumed that all the various dyads communicate only by speech, gestures, expressions, and contact. There is another
hypothesis: that underlying all of these and in some instances operating
without them, there is some kind of direct communication between mind
and mind. Telepathy is one form of extrasensory perception. Does it
exist? Under what conditions can it be demonstrated?

The largest body of evidence is summarized by Rhine (1937, 1940,
1947). He used an experimental setup which carefully screened out
possible cues from sight or sound. One partner in a dyad looked at a
card while the other tried to guess which of five symbols his partner
was then seeing. Most participants could do little, if any, better than
they would by chance. Yet, one psychologist reported that in 74 runs
of a series of 25 guesses, where the average, by chance, would be only
5 correct, one subject averaged 18.24 correct, and scored over 20 right
in 9 successive runs. (Riess, 1937, 1939). The odds against such a per-

formance by chance alone are staggeringly large. In 2,100 trials, the critical ratio was 53.57, while a critical ratio as large as 3.00 would occur only once in a thousand times by chance. Rhine has reported data from more than 900,000 properly controlled trials, with a critical ratio of 39.9.

Critics have been understandably reluctant to accept a phenomenon which seems so contrary to most of our assumptions about matter and mind. The experimental controls have been carefully scrutinized and the mathematics of probability re-examined. It would probably be correct to say that today most psychologists are uncomfortable because they cannot wholly accept nor clearly disprove the results.

The other kind of evidence comes from several hundred incidents which have been investigated by the Society for Psychical Research. Gardner Murphy recently reported a few of these (1961). A woman awoke with a start and the impression of a sharp blow on her mouth. Later she learned that her husband, out for an early sail, had been hit on the mouth at that moment by the tiller of the boat. Several teeth were knocked out. In another case, a businessman was on a trip to Rochester, New York. He felt an urgent message that he must go on to Buffalo. He went, against all his better judgment, and at a hotel in Buffalo where he had never stayed before, found a message from his wife, desperate because their small daughter was dying. In his book, *Mental Radio* (1936), Upton Sinclair reported his wife Craig's extraordinary success in hundreds of instances receiving and drawing an image approximately correctly from the mind of Mr. Sinclair or other relatives or friends. The "radio" analogy breaks down because distance does not seem to have any clear effect.

Rhine (1940) reports from informants he trusts incidents involving: a woman wakened by a nightmare about her brother shooting himself in the haymow and later discovering that the event had occurred as portrayed in the dream; two professors writing to each other the same day because each had dreamed of the other the preceding night; a mother impelled to leave a bridge game and call home at the moment her daughter met with an accident; a banker moved to unaccustomed tears while reading about a man's death in a novel associated the experience with his father, then in another continent, and later found the unexpected death confirmed. Most of the accounts could be supported by independent witnesses. Will coincidence suffice to explain them? Whenever a discussion of such events arises in a class or an informal gathering, one or two persons present are likely to contribute similar incidents from their own experience. It is conceivable that laws governing this special kind of non-physical communication will some day be discovered, and man may bring under deliberate control a process the evidence for which is still fragile and sporadic.

Transition

We turn now from dyads to the study of larger social units. We shall discover that many of the categories used in studying dyads are needed again as we investigate groups. Individuals enjoy belonging in groups in somewhat the same way as they enjoy acceptance in dyadic friendship and love. They turn to "reference groups" for guidance as we have seen individuals turn to a respected or desired partner. They "converge" in larger groups even more than in dyads. Problems of communication and ability really to empathize with others become more acute as the group increases in size. In the following chapter we shall be concerned mainly with the emotional aspect of group participation. In Chapter 4, we shall focus on the task-centered group and the process of group thinking.

CHAPTER THREE

Belonging in a group

Definition

What is a group?

Several people are sitting quietly in the waiting room of a small railroad station. Are they a group? Although each intends to board the same train, and although each can see and hear the others, they are not psychologically or sociologically a *group*. Three essential features of a group are missing. One is *interaction*. Each is concerned only with his own thoughts. They are not stimulating one another or responding to one another. A second is *satisfaction*. The existence of a group satisfies some need in each member. The need met may be different for different members. No one in that waiting room would mind if one or several other persons left. If they were a group, the absence of any member would be felt as something of a change. A group is sometimes defined by the fact that any member is missed. The third factor not present in the aggregation is intellectual recognition of their group unity by the members. Self-awareness of the group as a group, and of who belongs and who is outside the membership, is another feature of a genuine group.

All members must exist as a group in the psychological field of each member.

We would therefore define a group as an aggregate of persons in face-to-face interaction, each aware of his own membership in the group, each aware of the others who belong in the group, and each obtaining some satisfactions from his participation with the others. Sociologists distinguish primary groups like the family from secondary groups like the political party to which one belongs. In this chapter we shall be concerned with the psychological experience of belonging to and participating in primary groups.

Charles H. Cooley, a pioneer sociologist described "primary groups" and their psychological impact as follows:

> By primary groups I mean those characterized by intimate face-to-face association and cooperation. They are primary in several senses, but chiefly in that they are fundamental in forming the social nature and ideals of the individual. The result of intimate association, psychologically, is a certain fusion of individualities in a common whole, so that one's very self, for many purposes at least, is the common life and purpose of the group. Perhaps the simplest way of describing this wholeness is by saying that it is a "we"; it involves the sort of sympathy and mutual identification for which "we" is the natural expression (1912).

Size of Group

The requirement of face-to-face participation limits the effective size of a group. A dyad meets the requirements of this definition. It is a group in which ties of affection may reach unusual intensity, but one capable of disruption by the withdrawal of either member.

A triad—with three members—is an unstable sort of group. Any two may form a dyad excluding the third member. One experienced group therapist has reported: "Our triad groups in general did not do well. Problems of rivalry and jealousy consumed a great deal of time and actively interfered with the therapeutic process" (Loeser, 1957). Simmel, back at the turn of the century, pointed out that "there is no relationship so complete between three that each individual may not, under certain circumstances, be regarded by the other two as an intruder" (1902). He recognized, however, that when two disagree, the third member can mediate and reconcile. "There is no community of threes, from the conversation for an hour up to family life, in which there does not presently occur dissension, now between this pair, now between that, harmless or acute, momentary or permanent, of theoretical or practical nature, and in which the third does not exercise a mediatorial function. . . . Such mediations need not occur in words: a gesture, a way of listening, the quality of feeling which proceeds from a person, suffices to give to this dissent between two others a direction toward consensus."

When two members of a triad are hostile toward one another, the third holds the balance of power. Here is the simplest case of the political maxim: "Divide and rule."

As a group increases in size to four, five, six or more members, participation becomes less and less equally shared. After observing a large number of group sessions in the Harvard laboratory, Bales found that, on the average, in a dyad, one member talked 58 percent of the time, the other 42 percent (Bales, 1957). For a triad, the percentages were 42 for the most voluble, 34 for the mid-member and 24 for the least talkative. In a tetrad, the percentages ran 37, 27, 21, and 16. Five members increased the gap between the most and least loquacious: 39 percent for the most and only 9 percent for the least. This discrepancy increased steadily with increase in size of group. With 8–10 members, the most talkative made on the average 50–51 percent of the contributions, the least outspoken only 2–3 percent. This begins to resemble a speaker addressing a passive audience rather than the free social interaction of conversation and discussion. If there is to be enough interaction to make a good cohesive group of ten or more members, there will have to be a skilled leader, and probably also some accepted rules to control participation rates. In a free social situation, as at a party, when more than about half-a-dozen guests have gathered, conversation usually breaks up into subgroups.

In another study (Bales, et al., 1951) observers counted each act of initiation by each member in groups of varying size. In groups of three or four members, initiation was spread more evenly than might normally have been expected: The more aggressive were a little subdued and the more retiring were encouraged to participate. When group size reached five to eight members, the more aggressive dominated and the quiet ones participated less than the normal curve of expectation. Dominance by the most aggressive initiator increased with further increase in the size of the group.

Gregariousness

Need to belong

Man was not made to live alone; he is a social animal. Most other animals are also social. Allee (1938), reviewing the habits of living creatures from simple one-celled animals to the higher apes, finds that "the growing weight of evidence indicates that animals are rarely solitary, that they are almost necessarily members of loosely integrated . . . communities." One-celled animals which would be unable, alone, to tolerate certain unfavorable environmental conditions like a dilute poison in the water or freezing cold, cohering in clusters, are able to survive. An amoeba separated from the group moves back toward the others. Köhler, who spent the years of World War I on the island of Teneriffe observing a colony of chimpanzees, noted that if one were removed from the colony, the others would miss the absent member for a short time but would then forget him and go about their business. Not so for the one removed, however. He would press along the barrier to try to rejoin the others and would mourn and languish in apparent loneliness.

We can observe the need to belong at every stage of human life. Children are normally born into families, and in the preceding chapter we reported that separation from the mother can threaten a baby's development. The importance of group belonging for a boy is indicated in one member's report:

> The fellows in the gang were fast guys and good pals. We were like brothers and would stick by each other through thick and thin. We cheered each other in our troubles and loaned each other dough. Nothing could break our confidence in each other (Shaw, 1938).

When Alexis de Tocqueville visited America, early in the nineteenth century, he was astonished at the multitude of groups in which almost all people were active. He judged that participation in these numerous organizations was a necessary training for democracy.

> Americans of all ages, all conditions, and all dispositions constantly form associations. They have not only commercial and manufacturing companies, in which all take part, but associations of a thousand other kinds, religious, moral, serious, futile, general or restricted, enormous or diminutive . . . In democratic countries the science of association is the mother of science: the progress of all the rest depends upon the progress it has made (1945 edition).

Recent concern for aged and retired citizens has drawn attention to their loneliness and has resulted in clubs of numerous types which may help restore a sense of belonging in the social community.

The need to belong is so evident that when psychologists thought of "instincts" as a useful category, the "gregarious instinct" was always prominent.

More recent studies have abandoned the instinct terminology but have introduced the phrase *need for affiliation*. Schachter (1959) found that the desire to be with a group is stronger when anxiety has been aroused. Variations in experimental conditions led him to conclude that subjects wished social confirmation that their behavior in a threatening situation was appropriate. They were assured by findings that others shared their feelings.

In a later experiment resembling the second phase of Schachter's, Rabbie (1964) corroborated the desire of anxious subjects to talk with someone in a similar situation, but added one qualification. The girls concerned did not want to talk with a companion who was described as very frightened by the prospective experiment. Apparently they wanted not so much to share experience as to find a model that would reassure them. Further work (Wrightsman, 1960; Radloff, 1961; and Schachter and Singer, 1962) has shown that people seek affiliation in order to assimilate not only anxiety, but also differences of opinion and a variety of other emotions.

Related to Schachter's point on anxiety and affiliation is Dollard's (1943) finding that the feeling of solidarity with his unit was the soldier's principal aid in control of fear during battle.

> You know the men in your outfit. You have to be loyal to them. The men get close-knit together. They like each other—quit their bickering and having enemies. They depend on each other—wouldn't do anything to let the rest of them down. They'd rather be killed than do that. They begin to think the world of each other. It's the main thing that keeps a guy from going haywire. (Stouffer, et al., 1949)

The craving to belong has been studied experimentally in students who had been led to believe that others in their group thought of them as more of a liability than an asset (Jackson, Snock, 1959). Those who were told that they were regarded as likely to detract from the performance of their group, naturally felt ill at ease, but developed some surprising defenses. They overestimated their acceptance by the group, were more emphatic about wanting to remain in the group, and expressed more concern for other members. It seemed as though strong rejection made it difficult for the member to adopt an aggressive counter-rejection; instead he comforted himself with a kind of fantasy of acceptance.

First-born children

Schachter's finding that first-born children have a greater need for social reassurance has generated several subsequent studies generally confirming the point (Wrightsman, 1960; Staples, Walters, 1961; Becker, Carroll, 1962). The greater the threat and anxiety, the more marked is the tendency of older children to seek social reassurance (Singer, Shockley, 1965). A related finding is that the oldest child is more likely to be dependent (Haeberle, 1958) and less likely to be popular with peers (Schachter, 1964). Other studies show that, in response to a teacher's request for volunteers in a "cooperative task" (Capra, Dittes, 1962) or to undergo an experiment in sensory deprivation (Suedfeld, 1964), about 75 percent of the respondents were first-born. In stories made up in response to picture (Thematic Apperception Test, usually abbreviated to TAT) 18 of 22 first-born subjects scored high in need for affiliation while only 5 of 22 later-born respondents scored notably in this category (Dember, 1964). This accords with other observations that oldest children are more likely to be conscientious students and able to take responsibility. One theory is that having been displaced by younger siblings, they are eager to win back parental (or parent substitute) favor. Another is that they are used to being entrusted with much responsibility to help at home. Neither theory quite accounts for Schachter's finding that an only child is just as anxious, dependent, and eager for social reassurance as is the oldest. A more probable explanation is that parents are over-concerned with the upbringing of their first child. They watch every behavior and respond with more tension and anxiety than they would feel with later offspring. They lack confidence in themselves and in the child's own resources. This gets reflected in the child's image of himself, and produces the need to win approval, which is never fully satisfied.

Isolation

It is impossible for a child, even if he could survive physically in isolation, to develop normal human attributes except through social interaction. Extreme cases are the "wolf-children" reported from India (Gesell, 1940; Singh and Singh, 1942). Without fully accepting the notion that these abandoned children had been nourished by a pack of wolves, one does know that Kamala, when first seen by other human beings since her abandonment, was about eight years old (1920). She ran on all fours, howled at night, drank liquids by lapping them up, stole dead chickens and ate them raw. She never learned to run on two legs; when she died, at age 17, after nine years of care and training her vocabulary was only about 50 words.

Alfred Adler (1931) was led by his observation of disturbed personalities to conclude that the main trouble with most of them was that they had come to feel isolated from their fellows. He concluded:

> Since every human being has at one time been the youngest and weakest of mankind, and since mankind without cooperation would be completely at the mercy of its environment, we can understand how inescapably a child which has not trained itself in cooperation will be driven toward pessimism and a fixed inferiority complex.

The strength of inferiority or superiority feelings is one measure of lack of social integration. Where we feel fully accepted for ourselves alone, we feel no need to make anxious comparisons of our powers or contributions. Feeling alone, hostile toward his fellows and expecting only hostility from them, the neurotic builds his extraordinary defenses. So does the criminal. Adler goes on to say:

> We have found that the greatest common denominator among all the greatest variety of criminals and among all failures of very kind is this lack of cooperation, lack of interest in other people.

Adler's original term was *Gemeinschaftsgefühl*, which is often translated as "social interest" but implies something more like "communal feeling" or "sense of social solidarity."

"All failures—neurotics, psychotics, criminals, drunkards, problem children, suicides, perverts, and prostitutes," says Adler, "are failures because they are lacking in *Gemeinschaftsgefühl*. They approach the problems of occupation, friendship and sex without the confidence that they can be solved by cooperation."

Observations on job satisfaction frequently refer to enjoyment of the friendly contacts with other workers. One of the sources of dissatisfaction among mothers of young children is that they are confined all day to the house and feel isolated from adults outside their own family. When work was redistributed in a British factory, some men found themselves removed from their former associates and working in relative isolation. They appealed, through their union for "loneliness money" to compensate for the deprivation (Mann, Neff, 1961, p. 27).

Some years ago (1930) the writer asked about 400 graduate students to rate their general level of happiness in comparison with others of about the same age. Those who rated their happiness highest gave many evidences of better integration with groups of their fellows. Their self-descriptions differed from those of the unhappy students in such items as:

1. Not shy, timid, or unduly self-conscious
2. Able to administer a large group of workers
3. Prefer responsible job rather than one with great individual freedom
4. Able to lead in effective group discussion
5. Able to make a good impression at a tea
6. Good at telling a joke
7. More offices held in organizations
8. Believe clubs important for their happiness

It is simple to prescribe "socialization" for the deviate who is isolated, but such persons cannot use the normal channels of participation. They are too afraid, too hurt, too resentful, and too disagreeable. A teacher who discovers an isolate in the classroom cannot accomplish much by urging the class to accept him. A better technique is to discover

and cultivate some skill or talent which the other pupils will spontaneously admire. In one study (Johnson, 1939) an isolate sponsored by one
of the peer group was better received than an isolate sponsored by the
adult leader.

A goal in all psychotherapy—and group psychotherapy has many advantages in this respect—is to make it possible for the individual to
restore or to achieve his sense of social solidarity. Only being together
with other people will make the neurotic's fears, protective rituals, and
evasions unnecessary. The presence of even one good friend, as we
pointed out earlier, enables a nursery school child to assert himself
against a troublesome adult. But friends must be met part way.

Among the most drastic punishments known is enforced separation
from others. Many would prefer death to solitary confinement or banishment. Statistical analysis of suicides, reported by the French sociologist
Durkheim (1897) showed that a sense of separation, isolation, and
unrelatedness prevailed in those populations in which suicide rates were
high. A sense that one belongs, is wanted and needed by others is a
powerful tie to life.

Parties

It is curious that social gatherings which people attend only for
pleasure have been so little studied by social psychologists. They have
been considered too frivolous for serious attention by most social scientists. Recreational get-togethers have been analyzed in one major project
by participant observers (Riesman, *et al.*, 1960; J. Watson, 1958, 1962,
1964). They conclude that unlike a work group, which is goal oriented,
the party is "open-ended," cherishing freedom and spontaneity. Conversation moves where it will. In most instances—most obviously in stranger
dyads—it flows through mutual exploration toward real or pseudo-
intimacy. The norms of social life provide rituals for arrival, greeting
newcomers, serving refreshments and taking leave. Three types of party
episodes account for most of what goes on: (1) relational (two or more
persons developing new ties or sustaining old ones); (2) festive (when
all are dancing or involved in a game or enjoying refreshments or being
generally convivial); and (3) dramatic (performer before an audience).

Among the motives which may find satisfaction at a party are: desire
to escape monotony and enjoy stimulation; enjoyment of dilute or substitute impulse satisfaction (a "safe" measure of gratification of sex,
self-indulgence, or violation of taboos); enhancement of self-esteem
(compliments abound; criticism is suppressed); and some expansion of
awareness through meeting new people and learning new items of interest.

In party conversation manifest content can be distinguished from
latent content. People may appear to be talking about clothes, books,

politics or even the weather, when, beneath the surface, each is saying, "I like you." "Catty" remarks may seem innocent enough, apart from the hidden meaning.

One pattern of social activity among the wealthier families of a Southern city has been described in a sociological study (Davis *et al.,* 1941) as centered on drinking, talking, and flirting. Around 8:30 p.m. the cars begin to gather at someone's house, often without prearrangement. All members of the clique are on a first-name or nickname basis. Sometimes the men get off by themselves to chat about business, politics, or sports, but soon, as they go to the kitchen to mix drinks, dancing may begin and pairs form. Kisses are exchanged in the dusk of the garden or in a quiet hallway. Couples may carry on an affair for one evening only or over years. Groups form, dissolve and re-form, telling stories, or talking spontaneously about the past or planned activities of their social circle. Hard liquor, "on the rocks," with water or a mixer, is the only refreshment.

In middle-class groups of the same city, the men talk more with other men; the women more about housekeeping, clothes, children. They do not gather so casually, but at organized "parties." Women's gatherings are often for card playing or sewing; men may play poker and drink, but mixed-group drinking is less frequent. Flirtations by the married are frowned upon. Considerable effort is spent by hostesses on competitive preparation of food, decorations, or "party ideas."

Social comparison

Schachter proposed that one component of the drive to interact with others is the need to find some standards for self-evaluation. How can one know whether he is tall or short, fat or thin, pretty or homely, witty or dull except by some comparison with others? Is his pessimistic feeling that the world is blindly tumbling down a chute to hell a mere personal idiosyncrasy or is it supported and confirmed by what others are also feeling? Festinger (1954) has described this as a search for yardsticks in others by which we can interpret our own views and attitudes. It is difficult to attain a concept of oneself except in the processes of interaction. In Schachter's observation, people under conditions of anxiety and uncertainty are apt to want to be with others; they seek some reassurance that what they are feeling is no cause for concern—that it is what one ought to feel because others also feel it. Later we shall discuss the particular reference groups used for social comparison.

Therapeutic values in belonging

One of the most promising settings for the study of emotional aspects of social interaction is the psychotherapeutic group. Here participants are encouraged to speak about their feelings with unusual frankness.

While the presence of fellow group members may be threatening in part, it is in many ways reassuring. The disturbed individual comes to feel—after his initial hesitation and resistance—that he is accepted and *belongs* in his group. He gradually discovers that problems he had imagined were uniquely his own are actually experienced by many other people. He realizes that he is not so strange and different as he had fancied. He discovers, in the group, that he can say whatever he pleases and that this will not bring banishment. His spontaneous self-expression is more highly appreciated than is the carefully put-on mask which has been his defense in other social situations. He does not have to pretend any more in order to find affiliation. Most neuroses have arisen as a kind of defense for the person who feels that he lacks worth and that others look down on him. The countervailing social climate is one of respect for and full acceptance of the dignity of each individual.

The well-defined therapy group directed by a competent professional leader, usually a psychologist, psychiatrist or psychiatric social worker, is by no means the only kind of group which has therapeutic value. Many religious organizations teach their members the importance of practicing authenticity, self-exploration, brotherly love, and respect for each personality as a child of God. Many clubs and fraternities give members a sense of acceptance and belonging. Schools sometimes offer what Driver (1958) has called "multiple counseling." Groups have been assembled as "human relations clubs," as aids to failing students, projects in learning about group dynamics, aids to predelinquents, supplements to psychology courses, for parent education, creative dramatics, vocational guidance, and the correction of disciplinary problems. Teacher groups have been used to deepen insight into self and others, without aspiring to the deeper levels of emotional change implied by psychotherapy.

In group psychotherapy we observe a strong tendency among members when they first meet, not only to try to make a good impression on the others but also to think well of fellow members. In the early phases of association in any group, whether the members be avowed neurotics or only "normal neurotic," there are noticeable efforts to build cohesion. People tend to be unusually polite and friendly; they avoid saying anything which would seem controversial or critical of the others. First sessions of small discussion groups are often reported by students with great enthusiasm and high expectations. Disillusionment about some of their fellow members arises later. After a period of restraint and blocked movement there may be an outburst of negative feelings. If the group still stays together, the hostile period is usually brief and is followed by a much more relaxed and genuine accord, in which members are surprised at their growing liking for those who once irritated them.

Reviewing her experience with 121 members in fifteen such groups,

Driver reports that group members almost (but not quite) unanimously agreed that they enjoyed the experiences, felt support from fellow members, obtained some release by talking out their problems, attained a more objective view of themselves, improved in understanding others, and felt they had clarified some of the things which had been causing difficulty.

Group formation

Genetic development

Social feeling, the *we* experience, begins, for better or for worse, in the mother-child dyad. "The *We-collapse,* or, in other words, the phenomenon of unkindness between parents and children really provides the starting point of almost all the faulty developments and the countless sufferings in the history of man," wrote one experienced psychotherapist (Künkel). As the child learns to walk and to talk his social world expands. He may have brothers and sisters; if so, he early learns to balance the fun of playing with another against the cost of not always having his own way. Unhappy the child for whom the game is not worth this candle! In most pre-industrial societies, as in this country a century or two ago, the child's immediate environment includes a large family of relatives. He grows up in association with numerous cousins, uncles, and aunts as well as with his siblings and parents. He early acquires a sense of belonging in the larger kinship group. In typical communities of the United States today, families live apart from their close relatives. The sense of belonging in the larger family is weak. This is one of several social changes which underlie the rootless feeling of many moderns. Observation of young children in nursery schools (Ames, 1952) has shown that at 18 months of age most of the toddler's remarks are comments to himself on his own activities. At two years of age more remarks are directed to the teacher or are concerned with getting and keeping toys he wants. By three, he has begun to talk more with other children and to use the pronoun "we." His play relationships are still largely dyadic, with one other child at a time. There is a simple rule of thumb which says that the number of children at a birthday party during early childhood should be about the same as the child's years of age. Not until age four or five or six do most children enjoy playing in groups that large.

First playmates are selected largely by closeness in age and residence. Indeed, friendship studies throughout the elementary school age show "best friends" usually living only a few doors away. In crowded city areas, whole gangs may be made up entirely of children living within one block of one street. Attendance at the same school and church makes for closer ties.

Gangs

At around ten years of age, boys and girls form clubs or gangs which are usually ephemeral. For a week or two there is great excitement—a name, a secret hide-away, a password—and much ado over who is admitted and who is excluded. Then the enterprise usually dies. A few months later, with some changes in membership, another club takes form. The children may elect officers—commonly as many officers as there are members. A badge may be worn; if an interested father is a lawyer, there may be some bylaws. This, too, passes.

In the underprivileged areas of large cities, gang life becomes the center of interest for most boys. Thrasher (1927) studying 1,313 gangs in Chicago in the 1920's found that most of them had begun as spontaneous play groups in a limited neighborhood. The setting was usually a deteriorated residential area in between a business or manufacturing center and the good residential sections. Size of gang varied from less than six to more than 100 members. Age varied from six to adult, with most in the age group 11 to 17. About half engaged definitely in delinquent or criminal activities while most of the others sometimes carried on projects which were morally questionable. Thrasher believes that a key factor is the first expression of outside social disapproval which then unites the in-group members in conspiratorial solidarity. He reports:

> It does not become a gang . . . until it begins to excite disapproval and opposition . . . It discovers a rival or an enemy in the gang in the next block; . . . parents and neighbors look upon it with suspicion or hostility; 'the old man around the corner,' the storekeepers, or the 'cops,' begin to give it 'shags' (chase it): or some representative of the community steps in and tries to break it up. This is the real beginning of the gang, for now it starts to draw itself more closely together. Gangs represent the spontaneous effort of boys to create a society for themselves where none adequate to their needs exists.

Abstract 7 summarizes some of the observations made by William F. Whyte during his several years as a participant-observer of street-corner organizations in "Eastern City." The gangs in Street Corner Society served only the purpose of making life more satisfying by giving a structure which ensured the gratifications of reliable companionship.

In another study, Thrasher reports on Intervale, a crowded area of New York City. "The large number of boys who by choice or necessity play in the streets, creates a situation in which social interaction is intense, constant, and ubiquitous. There comes into being, as a result, a community of children and youths which continues and develops from year to year, independently of adult groups and institutions. . . . It is the real world of the boy and the young man, and as informal education it probably represents the most powerful set of social and moral forces which function in the development of youthful behavior patterns and

Abstract 7

TITLE Street Corner Society

AUTHOR William Foote Whyte

PROBLEM To present the natural history of one or two gangs of boys in a city slum.

SUBJECTS The Nortons, a dozen young fellows, led by Doc; the Italian Community Club, made up of college boys, led by Chick; all living in "Cornerville," a deteriorated area of "Eastern City."

PROCEDURE Bill Whyte took a room in the area, struck up a street-corner acquaintance with the boys, won the confidence of the leaders, posed as a writer of a history of the old customs of the area, learned Italian, was a participant observer for 3½ years.

SOME FINDINGS Gang association began in early boyhood, based on living in close proximity. The boys continued to meet in their particular area until their late twenties, continuing even after marriage. Activities fall into accepted routines; certain nights for bowling; certain seats in a certain restaurant; appearance at a certain corner at an expected time. "Fellows around here don't know what to do except within a radius of about three hundred yards."

Although outsiders might regard the social life of Cornerville as "disorganized," it has a sharply defined structure. Gang members recognize a hierarchy of leadership and systems of mutual rights and obligations. Doc, who fought his way to the top, is obligated to spend or lend whatever he had for his boys. Each member is required to help others whenever possible; the higher the status of the member the more obligated he is. Activity in the gang usually awaits the leader's appearance. The leader is supposed to have the best ideas, to be fair to all, to be pretty good at skills valued by the group, and to represent group members in dealing with the "outside." The leader works through his lieutenants; when his power is challenged it will probably be by one of his lieutenants. A follower may initiate action when he and the leader are the only ones involved (a dyad or "pair event"); when others are also concerned (a "set event"), the leader initiates. Decisions are usually made by simple consensus; as Doc put it: "As soon as you begin deciding questions by taking a vote, you'll see that some fellows are for you and some are against you, and in that way factions develop. It's best to get everybody to agree first and then you don't have to vote." Chick's gang, more middle class in outlook, fitted into the local Settlement House; Doc's boys gave it a try but moved out: "They consider us scum!" Limited experience and rigid patterns of interaction make any change and readjustment difficult for these boys. The gang was tied in, by personal friendship of its leaders, to a larger hierarchy of racketeers leading up to really "big shots," who sometimes included police officials.

SOURCE: Chicago: University of Chicago Press, 1943.

personalities in this district" (1934). Gang life is frequently thrilling as well as socially satisfying. "It is in such casual contacts and informal group association that the boy in the street often becomes inured to excitement," according to Thrasher, "so that it is very difficult for the school, the playground, the boys club, or the scout troop to compete with the excitement to which he has become habituated."

At one time social workers tried to lure promising individuals away from the gang to join in substitute activities at a settlement house or church. Then, since this usually failed, group workers capitalized on the solidarity of the gang and tried to bring the whole "natural group" into the neighborhood recreational center. This was more successful, but many gangs found middle-class respectability (as represented by Scouts, YMCA's, etc.) dull and alien. The next step was to send trained workers out into the neighborhood to be a friend to the gang. Most gangs want some sort of meeting place. Old basements were rented, renovated, and became "cellar clubs." Many gangs prefer this kind of headquarters to either a street corner or a well equipped recreational center. A skillful adult can become sufficiently accepted by the gang to be able to help the members achieve some of their more constructive goals without impairing the social fabric in which the boys are most comfortable.

Type of gang varies with social class, a variable to which we later devote a whole chapter. Upper-class cliques form junior sets at the country club. Middle-class cliques go to high school dances and the social affairs of young people's societies in churches. Lower-class youngsters lead more of their social life at roller skating rinks, dance halls, and pool room or candy store hangouts.

Most gang studies report on boys. A few gangs of girls are found, but these are often imitative and short-lived. Occasionally one or more girls associate with a gang of boys. Later the dances run by the boys include a fairly well recognized clique of neighborhood girls. The European tradition of a sheltered life for adolescent girls plays a part in keeping many of them off the streets in neighborhoods of foreign-born parents. In middle-class areas, girls congregate in pairs and often in larger groups, form cliques, share common hero-ideals, imitate certain heroines, and develop rituals. Boys and girls also join in co-ed groups, planning dances, hikes, staging plays or discussions, with or without formal organization.

Carney (1927) reported on 42 groups of girls. Most were between 8 and 14 years of age. Most met daily during summer vacation. All had "rules," including a demand for loyalty to the group. All engaged in running games and fighting. More than half included "plaguing people" in their informal program. Half paid dues. Most had one or more officers. Few had a regular meeting place or had developed any initiation ceremony.

Joining by adults

Studies of social participation by adults commonly show only a limited amount of membership in formal organizations, but beneath the surface an extensive, pervasive, informal organization of social life. Among 2,223 adults in New York City in 1934, 52 percent belonged to no organization except a church (Komarovsky, 1946). In Springfield, Mass., in 1939, a sample of 100,000 adults showed 61 percent with no organizational affiliation (Kaplan, 1943). In Erie County, Ohio, in 1940, about half the voters did not belong to any club or institution or association (Lazersfeld *et al.*, 1944). In Boulder, Colorado, 29 percent belonged to no organization and 48 percent to none except a church (Busbee, 1954). A study of farm families in rural New York showed that in 11 percent, no member of the family belonged to any organization, while in 41 percent of the families at least one grown member claimed no membership. In 25 percent of the families, no member had attended any meeting of any organization during the past year (Anderson, Plambeck, 1943). A survey in Cincinnati reported 41 percent in some group or organization; 59 percent in none.

If we look more closely at the social life of the community, we discover that most of these unorganized individuals are not isolates. They have their friends, their patterns of meeting and talking together. Lundberg's study of a New England village (1938) provides typical examples of the informal social pattern which lie beneath the formal organization of the community. He inquired about friendship ties and frequency of visiting among the 1,500 residents. One "constellation" of 25 to 30 people related often to a single matriarch—a widow from an old established upper-class family. Another 40 persons, mainly factory workers, shared a connection with a worker's wife who was also a dressmaker. Almost all residents were linked in one or another of eight cliques.

Psychological factors in participation

Members come into groups for many different reasons. Some are *extrinsic*—they may hope for certain advantages from association with a high-prestige fraternity, or a club which provides good business contacts. Others are *intrinsic*—they want to be with the particular people or to work toward the organizational goal. They may strive to be admitted or they may have to be almost dragged in. The pressure may have its value. One study (Jacobson, 1956) of the effectiveness of 100 local committees of a nationwide voluntary organization found that the probability that a committee member will be active increases with the social pressure applied during the process of getting him to serve. The greater the pressure the greater the sense of obligation. Minimal pressure is represented by a mail invitation; it is easy to decline or ignore. If accepted, the member may prove uninterested. More pressure is felt when an invitation has been extended in a personal conversation. If the appointment takes place in a meeting of citizens assembled on behalf of the cause, the social pressure and sense of obligation in someone selected for an office is still stronger. The study showed that those reached by mail were less active in their posts; those enlisted under pressure at a meeting were the most active.

Another study (Schachter, Hall, 1952) asked for volunteers for a psychological experiment. When it was made very easy to join—a show of hands when a majority of the class were apparently also volunteering —more students volunteered but a larger proportion failed at a later date to carry out their commitment. If the barrier to participation were too high, few volunteers were obtained. Moderate encouragement with moderate difficulties won the strongest cooperation.

Members in any group feel contradictory impulses toward, on the one hand, immersing themselves in "groupness," and on the other, escape to autonomy. It is as though centrifugal and centripetal forces were constantly active. If the centripetal and cohesive pressures are stronger, members stay with the group. When the centrifugal, escapist pressures are dominant, members drop out, offering one excuse or another.

There are subtle ways in which members remain apparently in the group but find subjective escape. Stock and Thelen (1958) describe five typical patterns of emotional task-avoidance behavior by group members: (1) *fight*—expressions of anger, aggression, and hostility; (2) *flight*—avoidance, tardiness, early departure, irrelevant talk, or withdrawal; (3) *dependency*—following the footsteps of another member, (or the leader) looking to him for clues; (4) *counter-dependency*— rebelliously acting the opposite of what some other member (or the leader) is seen as desiring or approving; and (5) *pairing*, which refers to efforts to deepen intimacy with other group members. When groups were composed of members, some of whom tended toward flight and some toward pairing, the incompatible tendencies appeared to make for difficulty, lack of rapport, and considerable frustration.

Preferred groups

Sociometry

The technique used to map social ties in Lundberg's survey of a New England village is known as *sociometry*. We introduced the term earlier in our discussion of friendship. Sociometric techniques record the attraction or repulsion which persons feel for one another. Moreno used the term *tele* to cover all forms of interpersonal feeling—liking, indifference, or rejection. The concept is a little like that of *valence* in chemistry.

The questions used in sociometric investigations vary. Moreno, who was then employed on the staff of an institution for delinquent girls, asked each member which other girls she would choose to have as cottage mates. Sometimes the question is: Which pupils would you like to sit next to in the classroom?", or "Whom would you choose to work on a committee with you?" or "What children would you like to invite to your party?"

When each member of a social aggregate has registered sociometrically his degree of liking or his dislike for the others, the results can be studied in many ways. A sociogram is a graphic record of these interpersonal feelings. Each individual, as in Figure 3, is represented by

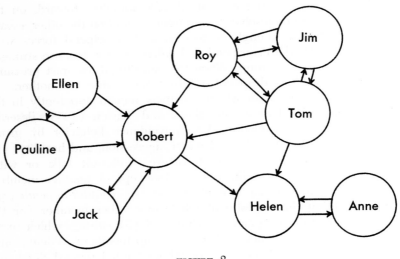

FIGURE 3

a circle. A choice for another is represented by an arrow from the chooser to the chosen. Mutual choices are connected by a double arrow —one in each direction. In the simple sociogram of a group of nine junior high school pupils in Figure 3, Robert and Jack form a mutual pair; so do Helen and Anne. Jim, Tom, and Roy form a sociometric triangle, each member choosing the other two. Robert is a "star"—he receives five choices from the eight other members of the group. Yet even a star is sometimes disappointed—Robert chooses Helen, but she chooses only her girl friend Anne. Ellen is the unhappy isolate. No one chooses her. Experience indicates that an isolate may have—both as a cause and as a result of the isolation—extraordinary problems of emotional adjustment. A sociogram of a club, a class, an office, a factory unit, a group of nurses or a neighborhood will usually show some stars, some pairs, perhaps a few triangles or chains, and almost always some isolates who are or will become personnel problems. If the group measured is fairly large, several cliques may be observed, as in Lundberg's study of the New England village, with relatively few ties to outsiders.

If persons indicate not only their choices but also their most pronounced rejections, it is possible to note additional forces in the group. Aversions may also be paired or organized by cliques. A "black star" is a target for many rejections.

Moreno found that choice of companions in a given group remained fairly stable; after three months 92 percent of the choices were the same. Mutual choices—pairs—increase from less than 10 percent at kindergarten age to over 25 percent by fifth grade.

Sociometric studies serve many purposes. They may sensitize a leader or supervisor to the inter-personal ties and tensions in his group. They may indicate real leaders. In one study of an institutional population, the girls more often chosen as preferred companions were (in 90 percent of the cases) the same as the girls receiving the highest votes for membership on the House Council (Jennings, 1947).

Moreno reported that the spread of rumors could be predicted from knowledge of the sociometric network. One day after a certain girl had been caught stealing, only the others in her clique knew about it; after a week the information was more widely known. An epidemic of runaway's (14 within 14 days) was found located within one network of close sociometric ties.

Sociometric techniques may be used to explore barriers such as those created in certain cultures by differences in sex, race, or age. Moreno found cross-sex choices by kindergarten children composing 25 percent of all selections. As boys and girls grew older they rejected one another's company. This reached its peak, in fourth grade, with only 3 percent of the choices across the gulf of sex difference. Then there was a gradual increase up to 8 percent in eighth grade, but even in high school cross-sex choices (to sit near, to serve on a committee with, to lunch with, to have as companion on a hike, to invite to a party) fell well below 50 percent.

It is sometimes charged that certain ethnic groups are too clannish. In a study (Watson, Harris, 1946) of fifth and sixth grade children in a school where one-third of the pupils were Jewish and two-thirds gentile, sociometric instruments checked the friendship choices. In-group choices made within the class were 78 percent for the gentiles and 24 percent for the Jews; among friends outside, gentiles chose 94 percent gentiles and Jews 72 percent Jews. By both indices the Jewish children were less clannish than their classmates.

Personality problems can often be identified by means of sociometric measures. A study (Kuhlen, Bretsh, 1947) of 700 high school pupils was accompanied by a check list of personality problems. Adolescents less well accepted (bottom 25 percent) by their peers showed more frequent problems such as: "being unhappy," "feeling that nobody understands me," "bashfulness," "feelings easily hurt," "getting tired very easily," "losing temper," and "headaches."

Leadership has been studied sociometrically. One study asked men to choose which of nine other colleagues in a ten-man group they would choose to work with, which they would choose to spend leisure time with, and which person's removal from the group would most change the group. The first two questions correlated about .40 with observer-rating on "leadership," but the third showed a correlation with observed leadership as high as .80 (Gibb, 1950).

In another study, using members of an Officer Candidate School, a variety of measures was tried: ratings by staff, personality test scores, achievement test scores, as well as choice by fellow platoon members for leadership. Tested against a criterion of "all-around ability as a combat officer," the sociometric measure proved better than any of the others (Williams, Leavitt, 1947). Another study, also on officer candidates, showed that "buddy ratings" were better measures of leadership than were intelligence tests, academic grades, or ratings by tactical officers (Wherry, Fryer, 1949).

Moreno and Jennings found that when girls were actually re-grouped to correspond as closely as possible with their choices, morale and discipline improved. When pupils in school were re-grouped according to their sociometric choices to maximize mutual acceptance, the morale of the classes rose (Zeleny, 1939). Thrasher (1947) refers to this as "assignment therapy." In another project (Kerstetter and Sargent, 1940), assignment therapy was used to separate members of a clique which had grown troublesome. Another application was made in youth work camps, and again it appeared that assigning congenial team mates made for better spirit all around (Faunce, Beegle, 1948).

Sociometric study of relationships among people who have just met one another for the first time has special value for understanding social perception. The transference—or parataxis—discussed earlier, appears distinctly. Later, these first impressions may be considerably revised on the basis of real experience. Sociometric ratings in a group in which the members have shared considerable experience and know one another quite well remain highly constant. In group psychotherapy, the feeling each member has about his fellow members is of major importance. Changes in these feelings are especially significant. The writer has found it helpful from time to time to ask patients in a psychotherapy group to make their own diagram of the group. In this experiment patients place themselves as a small circle in the center of the page, and place the circle for each other member of the group close to themselves if they feel strongly drawn to that person, but far away if they feel inclined to reject any association with that person. In one group, one patient drew a large circle for himself at the center, a small one in a far corner for the leader, and announced that so far as he was concerned the other members did not exist at all in his life space.

A refinement of the sociometric method asks members not only to rate or choose among the others, but also to report which others they expect will choose or reject them. This *relational analysis*, as it is sometimes termed, provides a basis for studying insight into the feelings of others. It is usually true that members with good insight are the over-chosen and those who are not well liked by their fellows are not very clearly aware of this rejection. Perhaps, in emotional self-defense they need to believe that others do accept them. It is important also to distinguish between acceptance in a particular group and general acceptability. An individual may be quite congenial in one group but find himself out of place in a different one. Later we shall return to a discussion of factors which make some members more popular than others.

Interaction and liking

In the preceding chapter we presented briefly the generalization that *frequency of interaction is closely related to degree of liking for one another.* The relationship between interaction and attraction under conditions of free social mobility is circular. The more A, B, and C associate, the better they like one another; conversely, the better they like each other, the more they will associate.

If the correlation depended wholly upon free choice of companions, the principle would seem obvious and banal. The important fact is that if strangers are brought into some kind of cooperative activity, and are not free to withdraw, they usually become friendly.

The evidence supporting this conclusion comes both from everyday observations and from psychological research. We often see the familiar become the favored. Children who are frequently served a certain kind of food grow up to like it; the old home town for most people has a quality of warmth and charm unlike that of any strange city; the stories and music we heard repeatedly in childhood have a special appeal; old acquaintances have a special place in our lives. A typical research finding is that intimacy among college students can well be predicted from extent of contact (Fischer, 1953).

The writer once encountered the force of liking engendered by interaction in a way which almost upset a projected experiment. A large class was divided into small discussion groups. An observer in each group noted the frequency with which each member spoke. Our plan was, after five sessions, to re-constitute the groups, so that students who were quite articulate would be put in a group with others who talked fluently, while the silent members would join a group made up of others as reticent as they were. Our hypothesis followed Charles Beard's famous generalization of one thing he had learned from history: "When the sun goes down the stars come out!" We wanted to give the stars a chance. We did not want to bias the results by telling the students this; we explained that we were reshuffling groups in order to give everyone a chance to become acquainted with a different group of associates who would contribute different experiences and viewpoints. This seemed reasonable, since the purpose of the small groups was mainly to broaden the experience of the student by sharing and comparing views. What surprised us and almost wrecked the experiment was the protest of the students against being shifted away from their accustomed associates. Although they had met as strangers and had had only five 50-minute sessions together, already interaction had created bonds not lightly severed. We insisted on the change and after another month, bonds were just as strong in the new groups. Incidentally, the level of participation of the quiet members did rise, and strong competition reduced the excessive loquacity of the talkers, but there remained an important difference in activity level between the two types of groups.

A corollary of the general relationship between interaction and liking is that those members within a group who interact more will like one another better. In a study of three small discussion groups made up of British students, the most talkative member proved to be also the most popular member in two groups and ranked second in popularity in the third group. Those who talked least were least popular (Klein, 1956). Again the relationship is probably circular; a sense of being well accepted by the group makes it easy to speak; a sense of rejection curbs participation.

High *activity* by a member does not always mean maximum *interaction* with others. One who talks too much in a group may be regarded as a nuisance and other members may cease to listen to him. Sometimes the member who makes most suggestions, particularly if the group task or situation is somewhat frustrating, becomes a target for resentment. Other members restrict their contact with him as much as possible. This relationship may also become circular; the over-talkative or rejected individual, feeling the barrier, talks louder, longer, and faster to try to break through.

If school classes are teacher-dominated, there is relatively less interaction among the students and correspondingly less friendship develops. Bovard (1951) showed that a group-centered method developed more liking for one another among the students than did a formal lecture method.

A study (Cogan, Shapiro, 1959) of sociometric reactions of group members at 10 intervals during a series of 47 meetings showed relatively high agreement within the group on which persons were most admired and most influential; much less agreement on the persons toward which members felt most warm and whom they liked best. Agreement on which members were disliked or made others angry, decreased as the sessions progressed. Agreement on the person one would most wish to be like (the ego-ideal) increased over time, as did also agreement on whose contributions to the group most deserved attention. A general summary of the study would be that, as interaction continued, members came to considerable agreement on the achievement characteristics of their fellows; moderate agreement on the persons toward whom they felt warmth and liking; and very little agreement on the infrequent negative reactions.

The Army provides an unusually good setting in which to study the effect of interaction during enforced association among men of widely different characteristics. One investigator (Maisel, 1960) reported that of 1,156 men named as among the "three best friends" of each soldier after his first few days of training, 54 percent came from the same squad. (Only 25 percent would have been from the same squad if chance selection had operated.) After seven weeks of training, 61 percent of best friends came from the same squad. Men asked (by secret ballot) to name the fellow they would want to have *least* contact with, named someone in their own squad in only 16 percent of the cases.

A study during World War II (Stouffer, *et al.*, 1949) showed that "pride in one's outfit" was about twice as strong among veterans who had seen combat as it was among troops who had trained together but had not yet shared the intense emotions of battle. Interaction during stress seemed to affect feelings about one another more than did more peripheral and superficial relationships.

One of the classics of social psychology is the series of experiments at the Hawthorne plant of Western Electric Company. In one of these investigations, a group of about a dozen men, engaged in wiring and soldering a complicated telephone bank, was removed from the larger factory work room to a special observation room. They were instructed to work as usual, but their behavior at work and leisure was unobtrusively recorded. Homans (1950), under the heading "Mutual Dependence of Interaction and Sentiment" reports one of the findings:

> Just as all the members of the group, thrown together in the room, were to some extent friendly, with the exception of Mazmanian, so individuals within the group, thrown together by the geography of the room, the nature of their work, and common membership in soldering and inspection units, were friendly to an ever greater extent. Winkowski, Taylor, Donovan, Steinhardt, and Allen, all working at the front of the room and in the same

inspection unit, were all linked by friendships, and the same was true of soldering unit 3, but only one strong friendship, that of Hasulak for Steinhardt linked members of two different cliques.

Homans sums up the relationship between interaction and sentiment by reiterating that the more frequently and freely persons interact with one another, the stronger their sentiments of friendship for one another are apt to become.

Another impressive study was carried out in a new student housing project in Cambridge. Most people liked their new neighbors; satisfaction was probably unusually high because of the homogeneity in a community of graduate students. Yet it is striking that none was dissatisfied, and three out of four felt no need for friends outside their immediate neighbors. The most impressive fact is the concentration of choice on the people who happen to live next door, or those whose apartment door one frequently passes. Propinquity brought increased interactions and interaction facilitated friendship (Festinger, Schachter, Back, 1950).

In stating the general principle and in summarizing the evidence, we have consistently left room for exceptions. "Closely related," "usually," "probably," "often," "for most people," has been our form of statement. In a minority of cases, frequent interaction intensifies the antagonism and rejection. Some people hate their families, some despise their home town, some are glad to be rid of old neighbors and old co-workers. This is particularly likely to be true if the circumstances of association were annoying and frustrating—a quarrelsome family, a neighborhood of poverty and filth, an unpleasant job. Yet even in the most distressing circumstance, human association usually creates positive ties. Boys sent to a model institution or good foster homes because of the impossibly bad situation at home will sometimes run away to get back to the familiar filth. People who have worked together in great emergencies—floods, fires, wartime bombing, concentration camps—frequently feel a bond which comes from their shared suffering. A married couple may feel closer when they have to meet the challenge of poverty or the tragedy of disaster and bereavement, than they ever did in conditions of ease and comfort.

Association and interaction with other persons has both gratifying and annoying consequences. Inter-personal attraction is inevitably somewhat ambivalent. Learning theory indicates that satisfying experiences with another person or a group will reinforce tendencies to be with them and to do more things with them. Unpleasant and hurtful experiences with others reinforce avoidance tendencies. Even in the warm intimacy of a happy family, some experiences are frustrating and there are some impulses to resent, to hate, and to escape. When one is ill or lonely he may welcome association with another person whom he would not ordinarily want as a friend. Yet generally, and as a rule, most of our gratifications come from other persons—those who love us, feed us, clothe us, play with us, enlighten us, compliment us, or challenge us. Despite occasional irritation, the great majority of inter-personal encounters bring some satisfaction to our basic human needs for security, acceptance, mastery, intimate response, and new experience. No toy or plaything has the satisfaction potential of other persons; even the arts are more likely to pall.

Freud interprets the cohesive power of a group as another of the many manifestations of love. Customarily we use the word "love" to describe ties ranging from those that bind us in the most intimate and intense sexual union to the vague and diffuse feelings represented by love of country or of all our fellow men. Freud's observations led him to approve this inclusive usage. "A group is clearly held together by a power of some kind: and to what power could this feat better be ascribed than to Eros, who holds together everything in the world? . . . If an individual gives up his distinctiveness in a group and lets its other members influence him by suggestion, it gives one the feeling that he does it because he feels the need of being in harmony with them rather than in opposition to them, so that perhaps after all he does it 'for love of them'" (1951).

Cohesion

The attractiveness of a group for its members depends upon the extent to which they think it will satisfy their needs. Among the basic needs which individuals hope to satisfy by group participation are (this listing follows Schutz, 1959): (1) *inclusion*—being with the people you want to be with; (2) *affection*—getting and giving love; (3) and *control*—opportunity to exercise power and to run things as seems best. These are intrinsic to participation. A group may also be valued extrinsically because members can gain certain advantages of wealth or status or privilege from belonging. Members so motivated will be fair-weather participants and what during the American Revolution Thomas Paine called "summer soldiers." They can be counted upon only so long as it suits their convenience. If the demands on time, money or effort increase or the prospect of reward decreases, they will drop out.

Groups that wish to retain their members often succeed by special efforts to make each individual feel that he is wanted, needed, and appreciated. If he is absent, the others get in touch with him to tell him what happened and to urge him to attend next time. This approach may combine all three of Schutz's motives—the member feels more inclusion, more affection, and more sense of power and importance.

Expressions of good feeling toward other members during a group session are likely to raise the general level of satisfaction and to strengthen cohesion. One study (Bales, 1952) analyzed the typical forms of participation by members which led to a summary rating of meetings as "highly satisfactory." In these sessions, 33 percent of all statements expressed solidarity or feeling at ease in the group; in "unsatisfactory" sessions such expressions were only half (17 percent) as frequent. Expressions of tension and antagonism were more frequent in the sessions rated as unsatisfactory.

Even one disaffected member can damage the morale of the whole group. In one experiment a single member planted in a group of five college students who were supposed to achieve a certain high norm in dart throwing performed as well as the others but verbally indicated that he was not interested, thought the task trivial and the proposed goal unattainable. These groups had lower aspiration levels for their group score than those of control groups with no disaffected member (Rosenthal, Cofer, 1948).

Among the characteristics of groups which increase intrinsic enjoyment and cohesion are those which make for freer and fuller interaction. If anything impedes the flow of communication, satisfaction is reduced. In the Bavelas (1957) experiment reported earlier, the dyad in which one member was limited to "yes" and "no" felt frustration and no desire to continue the contact. A study (Mann, Baumgartel, 1952) of crews working on electric power lines showed that those where there was more group discussion and group decision were more cohesive and actually had fewer absences.

One of the classics of social psychology is a study of the response of boys to club leaders who were autocratic, democratic, or laissez faire in their planning and direction of the club program (Lippitt, 1940). In the climate created by democratic discussion and planning together, boys more commonly used first person pronouns in the plural; they talked of "we," "our," and "us" rather than "I," "my," and "me." They also chatted in more friendly fashion about matters outside the work in hand.

An example of norms that impede free communication was reported by Riecken (1952). A work camp operated by the Society of Friends was characterized by an atmosphere of calm friendliness and gentle persuasion. Both verbal and physical aggression were condemned. When difficulties arose, members were careful to express only good will and reasonableness. Consequently the problems never really came into the open; members were only dimly aware of the feelings of others; and the annoyance and irritation continued beneath the surface. The total effect became extremely unpleasant. A similar state is sometimes reached in therapy groups in which members are so afraid of their own hostility or that of other members that they avoid and evade any possible controversies. They remain polite but the negative emotions rise to the point where members leave the group ("It was a waste of time. We weren't getting anywhere!"), or where an explosion takes place, all the accumulated resentments come out and the air is cleared for franker communication.

The introduction of a new member into a cohesive group presents difficulties. People show some of the hostility to newcomers which Kohler observed in apes which would attack any newcomer added to their colony, even if he or she were small and timid (1922). In some clubs and fraternities great importance is attached to the process of selection and initiation designed to guarantee suitability in the candidate for admission. Some research (Ziller, Behringer, 1960) indicates that groups which regard themselves as successful are less cordial to newcomers than groups that believe their previous performance has been inadequate. Even a person who was far more competent at a new task than were the members of the original group, was not welcomed or appreciated in a group highly pleased with its previous performance.

Differences in freedom of expression among members are related to their satisfaction in the group. Leavitt's study, which has become another classic in group dynamics and which is reported in Abstract 8, showed that the "central" members, who sent and received more messages than others, most enjoyed their job. The peripheral members, who could communicate back and forth with only one other person in the network, were most dissatisfied. The network of communication which was most efficient (the wheel) was least satisfying to the average worker.

Equal status

In Leavitt's experiment, the highest level of member satisfaction was achieved by the circle, in which every member had the same freedom of interaction which every other member was given. Spontaneous communication is most readily achieved in peer groups, where members feel that they are all on the same level. The presence of a lower-status participant is less inhibiting than would be the presence of some higher-status authority figure. One study (Harvey, 1953) has shown that the abilities of persons in high-status positions are overestimated by subordinates who look up to them. This overestimation is gradually internalized by the important personage and he comes to think of himself as more superior than he really is. This is an occupational hazard of prestige positions, affecting teachers whose pupils often (but not always) are less knowledgeable, clergymen who preach, judges who pass sentence, managers who direct the work of others, and other officials, in or

Abstract 8

TITLE   Some Effects of Certain Communication Patterns on Group Performance

AUTHOR   Harold J. Leavitt

PROBLEM   How does the structure of a network of communication in a task-centered group affect the performance and feelings of members?

SUBJECTS   100 male undergraduates at M.I.T. working in 20 groups of five men each.

PROCEDURE   Subjects sat around a circular table, with partitions separating each member from every other. Communication was written messages passed through slots. Groups tried to solve the problem of finding which of a number of symbols was common to the different cards held by all members of the group. Four communication patterns were set up as follows:

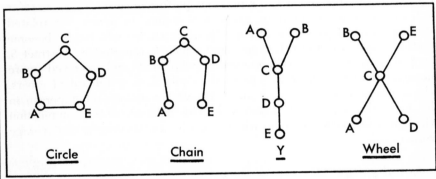

FIGURE 4

SOME FINDINGS   Persons in the most *central* positions, such as C in the Y or Wheel, most enjoyed their group experience. Persons in the most peripheral positions, such as A and E on the Chain or A, B, and E on the Y, were more frustrated and dissatisfied. On the whole, the circle, with freest interaction was most enjoyed by its members; the wheel, while quite as efficient in solving the problem, was disliked by four of its five members.

The time required, on the average, to solve the problems, did not differ significantly among patterns, although the wheel had a slight advantage.

SOURCE: *J. abnorm. soc. Psychol.*, 1951, XLV, 38–50.

out of government, who are vested with authority. The wiser among them learn to deprecate their own powers and talents, giving subordinates genuine respect and appreciation.

A study (Foshay, 1951) of the frequency with which children showed considerate behavior toward classmates demonstrated that those children who rated *low* on the classroom Social Distance Scale because few children wanted to associate with them were inconsiderately treated both by the high-acceptance pupils and by other low-acceptance youngsters. Those who had high social status were usually given considerate treatment by fellow pupils at all social levels.

Status differences within any group tend to restrict communication. People commonly feel obliged to watch what they say to their superiors. When committees or discussion groups bring together people of different rank—military officers, for example, or doctors and nurses, or supervisors and workers—a deliberate effort is sometimes made to minimize the status differentials. "Whatever you may be outside the group, here you are to be plain Tom, Dick or Harry—no rank, no degrees, no prestige beyond that of every other member!" A similar rule—unspoken—often prevails at informal, off-duty, social gatherings.

A strong pressure toward equality arises from the need to make everyone feel at ease. When students are asked to grade one another, almost everyone is awarded an A; when asked to grade themselves the requirements of modesty may lead to a B, but a B for everyone. In one college department where democratic policies allowed every member to vote on promotion, all members not yet full professors were recommended each year for advancement. To promote good feeling and reduce rivalry, in many establishments waiters pool their tips and divide them evenly; and during hard times salesmen have been known voluntarily to pool and divide commissions. In factories where piecework pay would permit great variation in earnings, it often turns out that all remain close to an acceptable group norm. Helen, a new employee in a plant where 50 units was the usual day's output, soon passed that level. She was subjected to hints and direct warnings which led her to ease her pace. Separated from her fellow workers, she demonstrated that she could easily produce 70, 80, then 90 units. Back in the group, however, she felt she had better be content with an undistinguished 55.

Children, in one laboratory experiment, worked in groups of four, each child building one wall with toy bricks. Under highly competitive motivation, the fastest worker received all the candy, the others none. Under semi-competitive motivation, the child who laid the most bricks got the most candy; the second got less; the third still less; and the slowest only a little, but everyone got something. Under equalitarian rewards, each child received the same amount however fast or slow his work. The highly competitive motivation resulted in rapid but slipshod work by the fastest workers with poor coordination at corners where the walls joined. Those who knew they were losing ceased to make an effort. Equalitarian motivation led all the children to do a better quality of work, especially at the points at which cooperation was necessary. It was especially interesting that every child—even the ones who had won the top prizes—when given a choice, preferred the situation with equal rewards (Tseng, 1952).

Even as this is being written, several small boys differing in maturity are playing a complex parlor game in the next room. One older boy, especially skilled in social leadership, is carefully managing the contest to keep anyone (including himself) from getting too far ahead or too far behind. He seems to sense that if the group is to stay together and have fun, the game must remain fun for all.

A news report (*New York World Telegram and Sun,* June 30, 1952) on a famous Spanish orchestra breaking records at the Starlight Roof of the Waldorf Astoria Hotel revealed that their excellent harmony and discipline arose from an unusual egalitarian social structure. They had no permanent leader, but elected one to serve for a limited period of time as *el jefe.*

European universities have not, as a rule, had a permanent president. They remained in the tradition of a company of scholars, equal in status, one of whom was persuaded for a brief time to take on the onerous duties of the rectorship.

The Zuni Indian culture is one that has fostered solidarity by disparaging any effort on the part of individuals to try to rise higher in status. A man who aspires to be a leader is criticized, laughed to scorn, and perhaps accused of sorcery. A young man who consistently outruns his competitors in foot-races, is debarred from further competition. The ideal Zuni citizen is seen as one who has his own dignity but has never endeavored to be better than his fellows. This culture, while highly cohesive, has some difficulty in filling necessary executive offices. During elections, the door of the hall is barred so that no one may escape, while pressure is exerted on one reluctant candidate after another until eventually someone yields and accepts the unwelcome responsibility.

Consonance

The greater the accord among the attitudes and values of group members the greater the satisfaction. In the preceding chapter we mentioned Heider's principle of consistency or, as we shall term it, *consonance,* which leads us to expect to like the people who like what we do, and to dislike those whose acts or opinions we dislike. In one group, after a discussion, members made sociometric ratings of the others. Members who held the same opinion as the rater were generally preferred; those who had disagreed were rejected (Schachter, 1951). Only rarely do we genuinely feel: "I disagree with you on this issue, but that doesn't change my affection for you."

Disagreement is an obstacle to communication and continued interaction. It often leads to a change of subject to something quite superficial or to discontinuance of the conversation. Decreased interaction means less liking for the opponents and for the group.

Groups, protecting their own existence, develop techniques for minimizing the effects of disagreement. One is to avoid controversial issues. When real differences begin to emerge in a discussion some "harmonizer" is likely to try to show that both really agree on the more vital points. The writer once observed a discussion in a church group on the topic of race relations. There were sharp divergencies on willingness to accept Negro neighbors—the group members were all white—and on the wisdom of desegregation. Finally the "harmonizer" said: "Anyway, we all agree on accepting Christian principles and trying to apply them in our daily lives!" Everyone nodded happily. A blanket of apparent agreement had been laid over the real differences. This method for dealing with disharmony reminds one of the slogan advertising a brand of paint: "Save the surface and you save all!"

One of the most important kinds of opinion is self-evaluation. Usually we like to have others approve and commend us; it raises our self-esteem. It accords with the principle of consonance that, if we think favorably of ourselves but some other person disparages us, we reject that person. What about the opposite case? Suppose a subject himself feels he has done poorly on a task. How will he react to favorable or unfavorable comments? Deutsch (1959) found that those who had been led to a personal conviction of poor performance evaluated favorably a person who agreed with this view and criticized their work.

Within groups and among groups, the principle of consonance requires that there be congruence or balance. The people we like should like one another. If we are favorable toward one group and find that it is closely allied with an organization new to us, we expect to approve that organization.

During the Truman-MacArthur controversy of 1951, Newcomb (1953) found that none of 48 students who sided with Truman thought that any of their close friends would disagree. These students generally (67 percent) believed that a rejected group ("uninformed people") would side with MacArthur.

A most pertinent observation on consonance was made years ago (Zillig, 1928) in a physical education class in Germany. Two small groups were organized, one of them containing pupils popular with their classmates; the other, pupils rather disliked. The latter were given secret coaching to enable them to perform certain calisthenic exercises faultlessly. The popular students had had only a limited amount of practice and naturally made a number of mistakes. When the rest of the class were questioned after they had observed both groups perform, errors made by the popular classmates were overlooked and were attributed to the ones who had been disliked, despite the unpopular pupils' perfect performance.

In another study (Muraskin, Iverson, 1958) New York students rated their acceptance or rejection of a number of nationality, racial, religious or ethnic groups. The same students were asked two weeks later to indicate how they thought members of these groups would rate the others. Groups which the students rejected (e.g., atheist, communist, mulatto, Puerto Rican) were seen as in disagreement with the students themselves and with what an "ideal American" would say. The more students disliked a given group, the more widely divergent was the attitude attributed to them.

Convergence

Conformity

Interaction increases both liking for one another and similarity among persons who interact. The fact of resemblance among those who see one another and who talk together was among the first to attract the attention of social psychologists. Walter Bagehot, writing in 1873, noted "the necessity which rules all but the strongest men to imitate what is before their eyes." *Imitation* was the first concept widely used in social psychology. It was used to explain the mimicry of children, the acquisition of language and customs, the relative uniformity within each culture group. A French political scientist, Tardé (1890), developed "laws" of imitation. One, for example, which he called the "law of descent" was based on observation that people lower in social status tried to imitate those whom they saw as their superiors. Subject nations imitate their conquerors. He noted also that innovations begin in cities and are imitated by people in rural regions. Tardé did not distinguish the several different processes which he grouped under the one term. They ranged from unconscious, compulsive, irrational repetition of the responses others are making, to deliberate copying with ulterior motives. Thorndike (1913) with his strong devotion to empiricism was not content to accept the inevitability of imitation, even in young children. He reviewed all the available evidence and found that it amounted to little more than one baby's sticking out its tongue when an adult did so. He himself tried in vain to get several youngsters spontaneously to imitate simple movements. They stared in some bewilderment. Murphy (1931), in one of the first attempts at an experimental social psychology, showed how a theory of learning by conditioning could well account for katydid responses to one another and for a child's repetition of sounds he has previously made when he hears them made by another. He describes an extreme form of compulsive imitation (echopraxia) under conditions of severe deprivation.

A vivid illustration is offered in Novakovsky's (1924) account of Arctic hysteria. The population of northern Siberia, no matter what its racial composition, suffers every winter from the combined effect of prolonged starvation, cold and uninterrupted darkness. The result is to reduce a large proportion, frequently nearly all the inhabitants of a village, to this curious condition: the patient involuntarily performs what he sees done by another.

The result is reminiscent of the children's taunt: "Monkey see, monkey do!"

More recently, experiments on small groups have focused on the tendency among members to arrive at similar views. In the dyad, discussed earlier, interaction led to convergence. Similar processes operate in larger groups, but "imitation" is too loose and general a term to describe what happens. In some instances, a new or low-status individual is eager for acceptance and ardently tries to do whatever he thinks the others will approve. We might call this *ingratiation conformity*. In others, when the situation is vague or ambiguous and members are uncertain, they may turn to one another for clues, asking, in effect: "This baffles me; what do you make of it?" Deutsch and Gerard (1955) have called this reaction *informational conformity*. Sherif's autokinetic phenomenon was highly ambiguous and led to this kind of convergence. A third type of agreement is submission to direct pressure. "If you are to work for ABC company, you will wear a clean white shirt every morning!" This has been called *normative conformity*.

The classic experiment in this connection, the one by Asch, summarized in Abstract 9, represents a large measure of informational conformity. There is no group purpose to be served by one student's bringing the estimates of length of lines into agreement with the estimates of other judges. The student, noticing that he and others are apparently reaching different conclusions, may decide to continue to call the decisions as he sees them, despite the discrepancy. About two-thirds of Asch's experimental subjects did so. Or he may decide that when he is in disagreement with everyone else, it must be he who is out of step. The one-third who conformed did so, apparently, mainly because they accepted a correction from the consensus. Yet the fact

Abstract 9

TITLE   Effects of Group Pressure upon the Modification and Distortion of Judgments

AUTHOR   S. E. Asch

PROBLEM   Will people trust their own judgment when a majority of others disagree?

SUBJECTS   Fifty male college students

PROCEDURE   Subjects tried to choose which of several lines came closest in length to a line they had just seen. Each naïve subject found himself in a group (3 to 15 members) most or all of whom agreed on an answer different from his own. The student thus faced a conflict between accepting the evidence of his own eyes and going along with the group.

SOME FINDINGS   Sixty-eight percent of the individual estimates remained independent despite difference from the unanimous confederates; 32 percent were deflected part or all of the way to the unanimous judgment of their associates. One-fourth of the subjects made no concessions to the unanimous majority; one-third conformed in half or more of the trials. Whether the majority consisted, in absolute size, of 3 or 15 members made little difference, so long as it was unanimous. If one other member agreed with the naïve subject, the tendency to err in the direction of the majority estimate dropped from 32 percent to 10 percent.

If the subject reported his results secretly, the pro-majority errors were fewer.

SOURCE: H. Guetzkow (ed.), *Groups, Leadership, and Men.* Pittsburgh: Carnegie Press, 1951.

that a private report made it easier to remain independent indicates that one important motive in the conformity was not to appear incompetent in the eyes of others.

Another good example of informational conformity is an experiment by Back (1951) in which two partners talked over the stories they had made up to interpret a picture. They were specifically instructed not to try to agree on any common story, but that each would write his own. Yet, even in the dyads which had been warned that they might not get on very easily together, as well as in those which expected to like one another, there were marked changes of story in the direction suggested by the partner.

When groups discuss issues, the members tend to converge toward what is perceived as the common standard. The same effect may be found if group members, without any discussion, are told the views of their peers. In one study (Wheeler, Jordan, 1929) students answered a questionnaire on campus affairs and economic and political issues. A week later it was given again with no information added in class. Apparently, the students had talked a little with one another, because there was a 22 percent change in the direction of the majority opinion and only an 8 percent change away from the still undisclosed group consensus. The third time the test was given, after another week, students were informed about how the majority of their classmates had voted. This time changes toward the group norm were 60 percent of possible such changes; those away from the group norm were only 14 percent of the possible changes. Information about what others thought proved quite potent in influencing answers. In our next chapter we shall see that this is not a foolish attitude. The individual who disagrees with the majority will usually—but not always—be wrong.

In subsequent research Asch (1956) showed that subjects who judged independently in the first test usually remained confident of their own estimates, despite cumulating disagreement from the paid participants. Gerard (1964) has shown the importance of public commitment in the tendency of both yielders and nonconformists to continue whichever type of response they made in the first trial. He found that when subjects could respond anonymously they were less consistent. Fewer made no conforming errors and fewer made five or more. Direct confrontation made for a kind of face-saving continuation of whichever response had been made the first time.

Other investigators have been concerned about identifying the characteristics of those group members to whom the others are most prone to turn for guidance. Attitude tests on current controversial issues were given to 168 college girls before and after four periods of group discussion. Those who were most influential (by both tests and ratings) in bringing others during discussion toward their position were found somewhat superior ($r = .45$) on the Scholastic Aptitude test of verbal ability. The more influential talked considerably more than other students. Tests devised to measure such personality traits as neurotic tendency, self-sufficiency, introversion, dominance, self-consciousness, sociability, and radicalism showed no distinct relationship to ability to influence others. Those who were most influenced—who moved farthest from their initial view—could not be identified by any of the tests. A suggestive finding was that rating on likeability as a personal friend was negatively related ($r = -.29$) to change. Apparently the less pliable were more valued as friends. One surprising finding was that amount of shift was not related to extremeness of initial position. Those who were "far out" were no more influenced than were the middle-of-the-roaders (Simpson, 1938). The observation that those who conform in an effort to win social approval defeat their own ends accords with a finding on first-born children reported earlier in this chapter. Although the first-born took special pains to win approval, they were less popular than were later-born, more secure and more independent children.

Ingratiating conformity implies an effort by the conformer to win approval from some reference group. Adolescents, uncertain of themselves and eager for acceptance, are notoriously prone to copy their peers, even to the latest fad in dress, hair-do, or slang phrases. The most frequent explanation given by addicts for beginning cigarette smoking, drinking, or sexual promiscuity is that it is done in their social set and they do not want to feel left out. The marginal member or the newcomer is especially prone to follow the group standards (Ziller, et al., 1960).

The third kind of conformity, in which deviates are conscious of some pressure, is commonly observed when mores are being enforced or when a jury must reach a unanimous decision.

The experiment reported in Abstract 10 gives evidence that when there is conscious group pressure to agree, communication is concentrated on the deviates, and usually they move into line with the rest. In a variation of the experiment, another investigator introduced paid stooges who consistently agreed with, disagreed with, or gradually conformed ("sliders") to the modal group opinion (Schachter, 1951). In almost all cases the persistent deviates were rejected—they were given low ratings for desirability in a club; they were not chosen for important committees. Individual members who did not reject the deviate addressed more communications to him, and more during the last half of the (45 min.) discussion period than during the first half. A fairly typical pattern was to begin with a normal amount of communication to the deviate; to step this up to a high point of persuasion in mid-discussion, then to give him up as "hopeless" and direct remarks thereafter to others as though the deviate no longer merited any consideration.

The subjects used by Asch and many who have replicated his research have been of college age. There is some question about the age at which children begin to turn to one another to get social verification. One study (Hunt, Synnderdahl, 1959) with ten kindergarten children showed four of them completely uninfluenced by the disagreement with peers, and no child who always conformed. One of the children tried helpfully to point out the errors of the three stooges.

A study of three factors in conformity (Blake, Helson, and Mouton, 1957) illustrates differentiation and refinement in scientific progress. Asch did not separate the influence of task-difficulty from that of social pressure. Blake and his associates found that on easy arithmetic problems there was little conformity; subjects felt sure of their

Abstract 10

TITLE   Interpersonal Communication in Small Groups

AUTHORS   Leon Festinger and John Thibaut

PROBLEM   How much pressure does a group exert on those who oppose the prevailing opinion?

SUBJECTS   41 groups of college students; 6–14 members in each group

PROCEDURES   Group members using a 7-point scale, reported their opinion on a controversial issue: one was in football strategy, another concerned the best type of foster home for a delinquent boy. Groups varied in range of opinion and in instruction: some were told to try to reach a unanimous opinion; others that "experts" had unanimously agreed on a correct solution and the group score would depend on the proportion of members selecting the correct answer; others to try to have a plurality for the best answer; still others only to discuss the question. All communication took place by written messages, which enabled identification of sender and addressee. This written discussion continued for 20 minutes.

SOME FINDINGS   In all groups the person whose opinion deviated furthest from the rest of the group received the most communication. The stronger the pressure toward uniformity, the greater the proportion directed to extremes. If minority reports were permitted by the instructions, there was less tendency to concentrate communication on extreme deviates. Instead, subgroups formed. On the foster home problem, students originally had stronger feelings and fewer changed to agree with the majority. The higher the pressure toward uniformity, the greater the agreement reached in the group.

SOURCE: *J. abnorm. soc. Psychol.*, 1951, XLVI, 92–99.

own answers. On more difficult problems, the students were less confident and more apt to believe others correct. These investigators found more conformity on attitude tests than on factual problems, and more when the deviation of the group norm from the student's own opinion was relatively slight.

An important variable in conformity studies is the opportunity to evade direct confrontation. In one study, partners judged the merit of Chagall paintings (Argyle, 1957). After subjects had made a rating, the stooge-partner disagreed, saying: "What you say is trivial because the painting as a whole is so ('meaningful' or 'meaningless,' whichever opposed the earlier rating.)" Sometimes subjects made their final decision on a confidential secret ballot; at other times, they had to state their conclusion aloud in the face of the partner's disagreement. In this latter condition, 54 percent converged toward the partner; on the secret ballot, only 23 percent converged.

Conformity to the group was found to be higher among subjects who wanted to belong, who felt accepted by the others, and who judged the activity to be important, than it was among non-members, the rejected, or the indifferent (Jackson, Saltzstein, 1956).

Tendency to conform increases with the group's need for unanimity, with the individual's desire to be accepted by the group, and with lack of confidence by the individual in his own independent judgment. This last characteristic may be specific to a certain task or kind of task or may be a general need of the individual. A questionnaire (Moeller, Applezweig, 1957) in which subjects selected the reason why a person behaved as reported in each of a series of different situations included as one alternative for each case the motive of seeking social approval. It was found that students who chose this kind of explanation, rather than emphasizing other motives such as security or self-consistency, were themselves on the average, twice as likely to be swayed by their fellow members into conforming with an erroneous judgment. Both group-situational and persisting personality characteristics enter into conformity.

One of the personality correlates of excessive conformity seems to be a harsh and punitive parent-image. Mussen and Kagan (1958) found that eight out of nine high conformers (among 27 male undergraduates) reflected parental punishment themes in making up stories about pictures (TAT). Only four of 11 independents expressed such themes in their stories.

Popularization of the idea of conformity, as in Riesman's (1950) "other-directed" personality type, and in Whyte's (1956) study *The Organization Man,* has led to an oversimplified idea reminiscent of the earlier loose application of the term "imitation." Both imitation and conformity are complex processes dependent upon numerous variables. Among these (as analyzed by Jahoda, 1959) are: (1) the *inducing agent,* who may be high or low in prestige, in attractiveness, or in credibility; (2) the *content of the issue,* which may be trivial or vital in the immediate conforming situation; (3) the *reference group* which may be more or less salient for the individual; (4) the *personality predisposition,* which may differ in emotional normality, self-esteem, hostility toward others, need for autonomy or approval; (5) *ambiguity of the stimulus issue;* and (6) whether the response is seen as *public or private.*

How far will a person deviate from his own convictions in response to social pressure? After all, most of the laboratory data concern actions near the "trivial" end of Jahoda's second dimension. Does it matter much whether, in an experiment, one calls line A longer or shorter than line B? Milgrim (1964) in a widely discussed experiment tried to induce normal male adults to give another person, known to have a mild heart condition, electric shocks so severe as to be painful, agonizing, and dangerous. The situation was supposed to be a learning experiment; whenever the "Learner" made an error he was to be punished. The degree of shock punishment could vary in 30 stages from one described as "slight," "15 volts" through "very strong" "195–240 volts;" "intense," "extreme intensity," "danger," and "XXX" "435–450 volts." The person being tested was the one who (called Teacher) decided how much shock the Learner should be given. The controls (N=40), left to their own judgment usually gave the Learner only slight or moderate shocks, although in one instance one Teacher administered a "375 volt," "danger" level shock; and one went the whole drastic way and gave the most extreme on the scale. In the experimental condition, there were supposed to be three Teachers voting on how much shock the Learner should get; the shock to be administered would be the *lowest* proposed by any of the three. Teachers 1 and 2 were confederates who by prearrangement both called for a one-step increase after each error—rising to stage 20 after 20 errors and reaching the top of the danger scale after 30 errors. The Control subjects, using their own judgment, went above level 8 (moderate shock) in only 15 percent of the cases; the experimental subjects, conforming to their two severe partners, went above this level in 85 percent of their decisions. Ten (or 25 percent) of their votes went all the way up to the level labeled "danger: severe shock" "375 volts" or more. This was in spite of groans, cries of pain, complaints of heart disturbance, screams of agony, and refusal to answer any more test questions from the "Learner." (The situation was acted; no shocks actually occurred.) The fact that normal men, under no pressure except the evidence that other men were apparently willing to inflict cruel punishment on a stranger, would go way beyond what their own judgment would sanction, is powerful evidence that conformity is not limited to trivial acts.

Mass hysteria

A special kind of conformity is evident in the behavior of a mob rioting in anger or surging in panic to escape from a building on fire. The French sociologist, Le Bon, in his influential book *The Crowd* (1895), described the member of a crowd as in a state like hypnosis: "Having lost all his conscious personality, he obeys all the suggestions of the operator (leader) . . . and commits acts in utter contradiction with his character and habits." Another factor is that "the individual forming part of a crowd acquires, solely from numerical considerations, a feeling of invincible power which allows him to yield to instincts which, had he been alone, he would perforce have kept under restraint. He will be the less disposed to restrain himself from the consideration that, a crowd being anonymous, and in consequence irresponsible, the sentiment of responsibility which always controls individuals disappears entirely." Then "contagion" controls. Le Bon says, "In a crowd, every sentiment and act is contagious, and contagious to such a degree that an individual readily sacrifices his personal interest to the collective interest."

Freud (1921) observed that Le Bon's view of the crowd corresponded to the psychoanalytic concept of the *Id*. "The mass mind, as it has been outlined by Le Bon, shows not a single feature which a psychoanalyst would find any difficulty in placing. . . . A mass is impulsive, changeable and irritable. It is led almost exclusively by the unconscious. . . . It cannot tolerate any delay between its desire and the fulfillment of what it desires. It has a sense of omnipotence. . . . (It) is extraordinarily credulous . . . it has no critical faculty . . . It thinks in images . . . It wants to be ruled and oppressed and to fear its masters . . . Masses demand illusions and cannot do without them. They constantly give what is unreal precedence over what is real. . . ."

Almost everyone has at some time been caught up in the passions and activities of an irrational crowd. After a football victory, a stampede of college students in one Midwestern town tore down goalposts, then fences around the field, paraded down Main Street, and finally broke into the local movie theatre. Evangelists in some communities have almost hypnotized audiences in tents with oratory, singing, rhythmic chanting, clapping, and sometimes dancing. The sect called Holy Rollers is one of many in which spiritual ecstasy has been associated with involuntary physical spasms. Political leaders have stirred mobs into frantic activity; primitive war dances worked up to frenzied attack; lynch mobs have transformed normally friendly, law-abiding citizens into screaming, bloodthirsty maniacs.

Using a broad range of incidents from history, Smelser (1963) has sorted "collective behavior" into five categories: (1) panics; (2) crazes; (3) hostile outbursts; (4) norm-oriented movements; and (5) value-oriented movements. One of the conditions common to all of these is the absence of institutionalized means for reorganizing the social situation as desired.

One emotional effect of the group is likely to be reduction in an individual's sense of responsibility and caution. Contrary to what some would have predicted, group decisions frequently involve more readiness to take a risk than would have been true of the same persons acting individually. In an experiment in which prudence might lead to small financial gains with little risk, but recklessness might bring large gains or large losses, individuals were more apt to be prudent, groups more willing to venture rashly or daringly (Wallach, Kogan, Bem, 1962; also 1964). There was more risk taking by group consensus than when individuals decided for themselves or for the group. In the next chapter, this factor will be examined further.

Anyone in panic may act irrationally, but in a maddened crowd, the control of reason may be still further reduced. An ill-considered act by one person may stimulate or sanction something even more extreme in others. Orson Welles, in a radio broadcast, "Invasion from Mars," created so realistic a drama that hundreds of people took it seriously and started to flee (Cantril, 1940).

Race riots have taken place in recent years in a number of American communities, large and small, in the North as well as in the South. Lynch mobs appeared, especially but not exclusively in the Southern states, with peak fervor in the late nineteenth century. The modal pattern contained the following elements:

1. A ground of frustration and insecurity. Correlation of number of lynchings (1882–1930) with price of cotton was −.67. Participants were most apt to come from "poor white" sections.
2. An exciting rumor as the catalyst, frequently exploiting the sexual theme: Negro attacks white girl. Rape, in fact, was alleged in only about 25 percent of the recorded attempts at lynching. The race riots in Detroit, on a hot Sunday afternoon in June, 1943, were touched off by a rumor in Negro circles that white hoodlums had thrown a Negro baby off the bridge over the Detroit river; among whites the rumor was that Negroes had thrown a white baby off the bridge.
3. Action initiated by some less-inhibited "leaders." Intolerance of calmer counsel.
4. Unthinking participation by the mob, with individuals swept off their feet and carried along in blind conformity.
5. An outbreak of general violence—window-smashing, looting, arson. Persons with criminal records are unusually active at this stage.
6. Closing of ranks afterward; solidarity; no tattling. Punishment has been very rare.

Attacks on alleged pro-Germans in the Midwest during World War I; on Jews in Eastern Europe and in Hitler Germany; and on alleged "Reds" or "subversives" in the United States have shown many similarities. Deprivation, contagious excitement, inhibition of self-criticism, and blind conformity have led to outrageous acts.

An instance in which newspapers fanned the flames of mass hysteria has been reported by Johnson (1945) under the striking title: "The

'Phantom Anaesthetist' of Mattoon." A woman in an Illinois city of 16,000 reported to the police that someone had opened her bedroom window and sprayed her with a sickening, sweet-smelling gas which partially paralyzed her. The paper headlined next day: *"Anesthetic Prowler on Loose."* The account led two other families to report that they had recently become mysteriously ill or upset during the night. During the next week 22 new cases reported attacks; only four of them were seen by physicians and all were diagnosed as hysteria. Just before the peak of the attacks the following story was carried in the Chicago *Herald American:*

> Groggy as Londoners, under protracted aerial blitzing, this town's bewildered citizens reeled today under the repeated attacks of a mad anaesthetist who has sprayed a deadly nerve gas into 13 homes and has knocked out 27 victims. Seventy others dashing to the area in response to the alarm, fell under the influence of the gas last night. All skepticism has vanished and Mattoon grimly concedes it must fight haphazardly against a demented phantom adversary who has been seen only fleetingly and so far has evaded traps laid by city and state police and posses of townsmen.
>
> (Page 1, Sept. 8, 1944)

A comparison of the "yielders," who thought they suffered attacks, with the total population of the city, showed that the suggestible were: more often women than men; over 20 years of age; had less education and came from lower economic levels.

Still another kind of hysterical conformity can be seen in meetings of such religious sects as have acquired names like Holy Rollers and Holy Jumpers. A sociologist (Hoult, 1958) reports that he once attended a religious celebration of the Church of Self-Realization of All Religions, where, after repeating the Hindu syllable *Om* over and over again for five minutes or more, he found himself making a weaving motion with the other participants and losing sense of time, place and distinctive self.

A dramatic account of "The Funeral of 'Sister President'" has been given by Douglass (1939). So many tried to attend the services in the little church that the building cracked and the crowd rushed over to the school. In excitement during the preaching and chanting, the audience stamped, shouted, screamed, and several fell prostrate. During the fifteenth century in Europe, whole communities joined in enthralling manias of religious dancing (Hecker).

In any mob or crowd, members show uniform behavior because they are moved by a common impulse. The distinctive features of individual personalities are submerged in the surge of emotional action. These are highly dramatic but exceptional circumstances. We return to the kind of convergence which characterizes all groups under more usual or normal conditions.

Norms

Members of a group share certain attitudes, values, understandings, frames of reference, and codes of behavior. These are called *norms.* Norms arise partly by selection. "Birds of a feather flock together." People who agree with the norms prevailing in a group find it congenial and are glad to join it. In accordance with the principle of consonance, they expect that such right-thinking people will also be likeable.

Norms are strengthened by all the forces in group interaction which make for harmony and agreement. We may summarize them as already presented in this chapter:

1. Interaction engenders liking.
2. Agreement makes groups more enjoyable.
3. Individuals rely on their fellows for cues
   (informational conformity).
4. Individuals seek to make themselves acceptable
   (ingratiating conformity).
5. Deviates experience pressure to agree
   (normative conformity).

We may speak of the norms of a family or small group, the norms of a subculture (e.g., upper middle-class suburbs in eastern U.S.A.) or of an entire culture (e.g., Apache Indians; Bali).

In the Westgate housing project surveyed by Festinger, Schachter, and Back (1950) a tenant organization was formed. In the course of the survey, it was discovered that attitudes toward the new organization, although ostensibly it served all alike, varied from one court to another. Of 13 residents whose apartments were grouped together around Tolman court, for example, 11 were favorable in their comments on the agency and 12 were active in it. The norm for this group was to support the organization. The 13 surrounding Carson Court developed a very different norm. None was favorable, six were neutral, and seven expressed an unfavorable view of the tenants organization. None was active, nine were definitely in opposition. When the cohesiveness of the residents of each court was measured (by the proportion of their "good friends" who lived in the same court) it was generally true that the greater the cohesion, the fewer the deviates in opinion about the tenant organization ($r = .53$). Tolman Court, which was well unified, produced 62 percent of all sociometric choices of friends from within the court itself; Carson Court, which was more divided in opinion, had only 47 percent of in-court choices. Thus the more clearly the people living near one another composed a cohesive group, the greater the probability that their attitudes would reflect a shared norm.

Group norms may be so strong that new leaders, coming into the group, need to accommodate themselves to the well established customs and traditions. A man who is transferred in to manage a department

Abstract 11

TITLE   Group Leadership and Institutionalization

AUTHOR   Ferenc Merei

PROBLEM   Do incoming leaders have power to revise group norms or must they submit to these norms?

SUBJECTS   Twelve groups of children, age four to 11. Each group consisted of three or four children plus the newly introduced "leader."

PROCEDURE   By observation of free behavior, child leaders were selected; they were a little older; tended to give, rather than follow, orders; to be imitated rather than to imitate; to attack rather than be attacked; and showed strong initiative.

The three or four children who comprised the "group" met in a separate room for 30–40 minutes per day. Younger children played with building blocks; older ones with cardboard, scissors, paint, paste, and picture magazines. After three to six meetings, each group had formed habits, traditions and rules. Then the new "leader" was added. Observers recorded behavior.

SOME FINDINGS   "The group absorbed the leader, forcing its traditions on him. The leader takes over the habits and traditions of children who are younger than himself and who in the day nursery had been his underlings followed his guidance. Now he engages in those activities which the group had developed before he entered it. His own undertakings either remain unsuccessful or gain acceptance only in a modified form suiting the traditions of that group."

In one typical case the ratio of being copied to copying others changed from 9:5 in the nursery to 0:8 in the experimental group; another child leader's ratio changed from 6:2 to 1:6; a third from 6:3 to 5:11.

One girl, a year and a half older, did succeed in imposing her games and her rules on the group; this was the only exception in 26 experiments.

Leadership was still evident, but the new leader soon ordered the children to do what he had observed them to be doing. His directions were adapted to their traditions. Modification of group procedures was slowly achieved by a few more diplomatic personalities who had first suffered several defeats in efforts to introduce change.

SOURCE: *Human relations*, 1949, II:23–39.

will become very unpopular and may fail if he tries to institute procedures which violate the group norms. Abstract 11 shows that even among kindergarten children a new leader—despite evidence of previous successful domination—usually cannot override the group norms.

Norms have been put to effective use in Alcoholics Anonymous. Thousands of men and women who were apparently unable to overcome self-destructive drinking have found it possible to change their individual conduct with the support of this organization. Regular attendance at testimonial meetings helps to re-emphasize adherence to the new code. The member recognizes that his fellows have been through experiences like his own, and they speak his language. He is loyal to them and can count on their support. This program, while sometimes successful, has not appealed to many others who could not identify with its norms.

We must guard against letting the concept of norm lead us to expect too much agreement. While the norms of our society include respect for law and private property, we live among thieves who do not conform to this expectation. Some sociologists regard delinquent behavior as expression of the norm of a subgroup such as a gang or what Sutherland (1937) calls a "profession" of thieves. Merton (1949) proposed that when a society in its norms sets up goals and aspirations, but fails to provide the legitimate means for its members to realize these aims, some will turn to illegitimate channels. Cohen (1955) has carried this argument forward. When lower-class boys find themselves sharing the same plight, with no realistic hope of achieving by respectable means high status and wealth to buy material goods so widely advertised, they set up, not a subculture but a "counter-culture" with norms which give substitute status and sanction a kind of revenge upon middle-class respectability (Cohen, 1960; Cloward, Oberlin, 1960).

There is a repudiation of norms also at the other end of the economic scale. In his studies of suicide, Durkheim (1897) referred to those occasioned by economic crises and depressions as "anomic." The term *anomy* (sometimes "anomie" or "anomia") means being without norms; having no law and order or accepted standards. In economic life, according to Durkheim's thesis, anomy is chronic, since religion has lost its influence, government is more controlled by wealth than controlling, and the profit-making of industry has become a law unto itself. Restraint on private enterprise seems a sacrilege. Hence, the suicide rate, he found to be higher in industrial and commercial occupations than in any other vocation, and highest among those with independent means. These were people who try to live with the illusion that they have transcended the norms which control lesser mortals.

Delinquents and anomics are not the only ones who reject social norms. Most people feel moved once in a while to stand up for a principle that is not popular in their milieu. A study (Brodbeck, *et al.*, 1956) of how parents discipline young children indicated that most of them followed their own ideals rather than what they believed the neighbors generally approved.

Group decision

The operation of norms is responsible for one interesting finding of social psychology which might, at first, seem paradoxical. It is easier to change the attitudes of a whole cohesive group than to bring about a similar change in a single member of that group. Group workers have discovered, as we noted when discussing street gangs, that efforts to "reform" one boy member will probably be frustrated by his loyalty to the gang and their norms and folkways. The more promising approach is to get the whole group to change over to new activities.

The classic experiments in this field were conducted during World War II by Kurt Lewin and his associates (1952). The practical problem was to use easily available foods to improve the nutrition and health of the American people. A procedure in which groups discussed the pro's and con's of the change and joined in a vote (by show of hands), resulted in more change than came about from lectures by experts, talk by a prestige-member of the group, or individual instruction.

A follow-up experiment (Bennett, 1955) endeavored to separate out the factor of mode of presentation (lecture vs. discussion) from the factor of group decision. This study took place during a campaign to get students to volunteer for certain research and service projects. No difference was found between presentation of the case by lecture and by discussion. The two methods were equally effective. What really made the difference was the vote at the end. If the decision were left to each member individually (as after all the lectures in the Lewin experiments), then change was slight. If a decision were required at the time of the meeting, if the prevailing norm were for the change, and if the individual had to register his decision in full view of his fellows, he was very much more likely to commit himself to the proposed change. Fund raisers have often made use of a similar technique: Gifts are called for at a meeting, some members have been prepared to start the ball rolling; everyone who pledges gets immediate recognition, and, eventually, any members who do not give or who give too little (below the group norm) feel very uncomfortable. To give the impression of a high norm, the large gifts are announced first. Most people have experienced the coercive force of group norms. When asked for a subscription for a cooperative gift they commonly ask: "What are other people giving?" and scale their own contribution accordingly. We try constantly to live up to what we think is expected of us, perhaps as a fraternity brother, or a church member, or a trade union member, or a scientist, or as a citizen of our nation.

A critical comparison of Bennett's experiment with the Lewin studies reveals other important differences. The Lewin work was done in the atmosphere of wartime patriotism and involved motives much stronger than readiness to volunteer for a research project. It seems likely also that opportunity to make a group decision was more of a novelty for the Lewin housewives than it would be for psychology students in a university.

In one of the experiments directed by Lewin (Willerman, 1943) it was found that when decision was left to individuals, the readiness to eat whole wheat bread instead of white bread was correlated with individual taste preference. Those who greatly preferred white bread were reluctant to change. But under the conditions of group decision, personal preferences were overriden by other motives. Conformity to the group choice was unrelated to taste for white or whole wheat bread.

Several applications of the group decision technique have been made in industry. Bavelas (1947) found that while the average production in a factory remained at about 60 units, a selected team, encouraged to set for themselves the goal of breaking previous records, made a group decision which made their production soar to 85-90 and enabled them to maintain this pace for at least nine months.

In another factory (Levine, Butler, 1954) group decision was used to combat a tendency by superiors to let their ratings of workers be distorted by a "halo effect." The problem was that workers in low-paid job categories generally received low efficiency ratings even though they performed well, and those workers in highly skilled jobs received favorable ratings which did not always correspond to their actual productivity. A control group of supervisors had no special attention; a lecture group received an explanation of the problem and instructions for improving their ratings; the group discussion led to decision to try to rate the men fairly regardless of the level of the job. Only this last group of supervisors—those who had discussed and decided together—showed significant improvement in their ratings. Other studies have shown that group decision can diminish expressions of prejudice, reduce hostile attitudes, conduce to community action, and aid emotionally disturbed children (Lichtenberg, 1954). A major gain from group decision is *commitment* of participants to carrying out the agreement. Several investigations (Blake, Mouton, 1962; Ferguson, Kelley, 1964) have shown strong preference by group members for the product of their own work over objectively superior products achieved by other groups.

Reference groups

In a simple pre-industrial society, individuals are strongly enmeshed in a given kinship group or tribe. They need not choose; birth places each person. In our complex civilization individuals do choose among many possible group affiliations. The groups in which a person feels that he belongs, or to which he aspires to belong, become his "reference groups." Merton's study, summarized in Abstract 12, illustrates

Abstract 12

TITLE   Contributions to the Theory of Reference Group Behavior

AUTHOR   R. K. Merton

PROBLEM   How the concept of "reference group" can help to interpret various puzzling findings obtained in the study of attitudes of soldiers.

SUBJECTS   Many thousands of enlisted men and officers were tested during World War II under the auspices of the Research Branch, Information and Education Division of the War Department.

PROCEDURES   Merton picks out, from the large mass of data, four pertinent observations which need interpretation.

1. In the Air Force, where promotions were frequent, more men indicated dissatisfaction with the opportunity that "a soldier with ability" has for promotion than in the Military Police, where promotions were very infrequent. Fewer M.P.'s indicated dissatisfaction with chances for promotion. In general, the *less* the opportunity a branch of the service had for promotion, the more favorable its members were toward promotion opportunity.

2. Although most men overseas in wartime felt that those stationed in the United States "had it better," opinion polls did not indicate much lower morale abroad. Thus 32 percent of men overseas reported that they were "usually in good spirits;" the comparable figure for troops stationed in the United States was 41 percent.

3. Married men over 20 years of age were much more likely (41 percent) to say they should have been deferred, single men under 20 were less apt (10 percent) to feel that their induction was unfair.

4. An attitude of "ready to get into an actual battle-zone" was found among 45 percent of new troops abroad; 28 percent of equally inexperienced men who had been shifted as replacements into outfits which had been in combat; and only 15 percent of veterans who had been in combat.

SOME FINDINGS   Each of the above observations can be explained with the aid of the concept of reference groups.

1. Air Force men, comparing their fate with comrades who had moved up rapidly, were more dissatisfied on promotion policies. Their reference group was their own, not another branch of the service.

2. Men overseas compared their fate with others, also overseas; the troops back home were not their reference group.

3. The married men were more dissatisfied because many of them knew of exceptions which draft boards had made; others "in their shoes" got a better break than they did.

Abstract 12—*Continued*

4. Replacements identified with the veterans in the experienced combat units to which they were assigned; their attitudes shifted from what raw troops usually felt, to come closer to the prevailing view in the group in which they wanted to be accepted.

SOURCE: R. K. Merton, and P. F. Lazarsfeld (ed.), *Continuities in Social Research: Studies in the Scope and Method of the American Soldier.* Glencoe, Ill.: The Free Press, 1950, pp. 40–105.

---

the application of a theory of reference groups to interpreting attitudes in the Army.

Whether you consider yourself rich or poor depends upon your reference group. Compared with certain wealthy cliques, most of us would be "poor relations." Compared with villagers in India who are paid only a few cents for a day's work, we are grandly prosperous. To answer other questions about ourselves—are we intelligent? good looking? well adjusted? hard working? happy? right-thinking?—we need to define our reference group. In some circles we would rank at the top, in others, quite low.

Circumstances at any moment may determine which reference group is uppermost in an individual's mind. In one experiment (Charters, Newcomb, 1952) some psychology students were asked to answer a written attitude questionnaire in a classroom group where no reference had been made to their religious affiliation; other students were brought together in homogeneous groups of Catholics, Jews or Protestants, with their common faith emphasized, and given the same questionnaire. The Catholic students especially showed more deviation from Catholic norms when they thought of themselves as psychology students than they did when they came together as Catholics.

Conflict between reference groups

One of the most famous studies in the still young science of social psychology is Newcomb's exploration of political attitudes of Bennington College students during the depression years. The study is summarized in Abstract 13. Those girls whose reference groups, either by actual membership or by aspiration, were composed of campus leaders became more and more "progressive," in accordance with the college atmosphere prevailing at that time. Those girls who felt a little out of their element on the college campus, but who felt at ease in, or wanted particularly to be accepted by, the back-home circles remained conservative. In some cases the conflict between the expectations of the two kinds of reference groups became acute.

The mobility in contemporary American life confronts the individual

Abstract 13

TITLE   Personality and Social Change

AUTHOR   Theodore Newcomb

PROBLEM   How do student attitudes change as they go through a residential college with well established norms of attitude?

SUBJECTS   Students (women) at Bennington College, 1935–1939.

PROCEDURES   Tests of political-economic progressivism (PEP) were given to faculty and student body each year. A "Guess Who" technique secured nominations of girls regarded as outstanding in one or another aspect of personality or campus activity.

SOME FINDINGS   Scores decreased (i.e., became less conservative and more progressive) from an average of 44 for the freshmen, to 41 for the sophomores, 39 for juniors, 38 for seniors and the faculty scored still lower. In 1936, about 66 percent of the parents of students favored Landon for President; he was supported by 62 percent of the freshmen, 43 percent of sophomores and only 15 percent of juniors and seniors.

Freshmen estimated the average attitudes in the college as more conservative than they really were; seniors were more accurate and were keenly aware of the big difference between freshmen and themselves.

A sociometric test, based on nomination by each student of five girls "most worthy to represent Bennington College in a national convention," led to the finding that the students never named averaged 72 in their P.E.P. scores; those most often named averaged 54.

Students identified as "most absorbed in social life and weekends" included none from the lowest sixth (most progressive) on P.E.P. scores and more than half (59 percent) of those from the highest sixth. Students identified as "most absorbed in college community affairs" came often (36 percent) from the lowest sixth; none came from the top sixth. Students whose reference group was the campus leaders were progressive as freshmen and became more so; those whose reference group was their family and social life off-campus were more conservative. "Those individuals who become most fully assimilated into a community most completely adopt the behavior approved by it." Some, anxious for status but lacking certain essential abilities, adopted the prevailing attitudes as a way of identifying with the leaders. Those who participated least in the campus community were unaware of their exceptional conservatism.

SOURCE: New York: Dryden Press, 1943.

with many conflicts. Group norms of the home give way to other norms as the child moves out to his play group, to high school, to college, to the Army, to work, to a home of his own, to a higher job in another community, and so on to retirement. Reference groups are shifted and sometimes their demands seem incompatible. The carefully brought up adolescent finds himself in a peer group where necking is *de rigeur*. The student proctor has been cited in one article (Stouffer, 1949) as a paradigm of conflict; his loyalty to friends pulls him one way; his responsibilities as a representative of the college administration draws him in an opposite direction. Many juvenile delinquents experience some conflict between what important reference groups seem to be demanding of them.

In one study of Jewish adolescents, Rosen (1955) found that if parents and peer group both observed dietary laws, 83 percent of the subjects also observed them and planned to comply with the laws in their own homes after marriage. If both were non-observant, 88 percent of the youth followed this pattern. When attitudes of these two major reference groups were in conflict, 74 percent went with the peer group; only 26 percent with the parents. But for those cases which reported closer ties and more time spent with parents than with peers, 81 percent followed the parental norms.

Another type of conflict may be found in some chaplains with the armed forces; Jesus and the saints say "Love your enemy;" the Army does not. Conflicts which appear to exist within the individual personality can often be better understood as resulting from incompatible norms of reference groups.

Individuality

The attraction of group-belonging is only one side of a dynamic equilibrium; individuals also resist becoming involved in groups. Their resistance takes many forms. The obvious one is withdrawal. Every organization has its turnover and its absentee problems. Some people take pride in not being joiners—they like to accentuate their distinctiveness. A few become hermits. But resistance may also continue although the individual remains on the membership rolls and attends meetings. A member, seeking unconsciously or consciously to keep his individuality intact, avoiding concessions to fellow members, may sit quietly through the meeting, concealing his aloofness through apparent acquiesence. Or he may attempt to dominate the group; in this case he seems to be saying: "If the group becomes completely subordinate to my will, than I can be a member with no threat to my distinctive individuality." In other cases a pair or a clique may unite to oppose the generally accepted pattern of group purpose and action. The individual thus finds it possible to sustain both a feeling of belonging and at the same time his sense of separation.

The inner forces which oppose submergence in the group are like those which make it difficult for some people to make friends or to let themselves fall in love. They seem to be compounded of distrust of, or hostility to, the other, and a narcissistic love for the self with a need to affirm it. Distrust of others probably begins for everyone in the mother-infant dyad. No mother can always and in every way fulfill the demands of a baby. Inevitably, every parent in one way or another disappoints and frustrates the child. If such experiences are the exception, the need to defend oneself against groups is likely to be considerably weaker than the need to belong. Early experiences are, of course, intensified or modified by later social interactions which prove satisfying and dependable or which leave the individual feeling let down; his confidence betrayed.

A feeling about the self develops also from infancy. Some persons grow up with a need to preserve an exaggerated evaluation of their own perfection—their beauty, brains, personality, or saintliness. In moderation, self-approval is healthy. Most neurotics suffer from an inability to feel worth and value in themselves. Even the exaggerated, narcissistic self-love which makes egotists such unpleasant companions may originate as compensation for a lack of genuine self-acceptance.

It is not always easy to disentangle the mixed motives of conformity and self-assertion. Independent critical judgment may, in some cases, lead to the decision to go along with the prevailing view. A thoughtless counter-dependence may lead to negative conformity in which the decision to be different leaves the person still at the mercy of the crowd —he cannot conform even when that would be the right and best course. At present, numerous critics in America are attacking conformity and stressing the distinctive individual. A writer in a popular magazine comments: "Individuality is all the rage now." This kind of expression seems another evidence of acceptance of a prevailing norm.

Primitive societies are commonly believed to be more conforming because they are quite homogeneous. Yet Margaret Mead found among the Manus, three personality types (Mead, 1937). She could identify leaders, dependents, and independents. The leaders were aggressive in initiating lines of action; the dependents followed. The independents went off on their own; one with a tool in his hand; another talking geneology. They paid little attention to others and ignored cooperative plans. Similar types can no doubt be found on any college campus.

There are important values for the individual in group participation, but there are also important values in retaining proudly a distinctive self. Suspicion of certain others is sometimes a life-saver. It would be perilously naïve to assume that everyone we meet has our own best interest at heart, just as it is perilously cynical to assume that no one cares anything for anyone but himself. The person who asserts himself and resists group seduction, or pressure to conform, may be the one to whom future ages erect their monuments. History's innovators, heroes, saints, and martyrs have usually had to be nonconformists.

Some groups have norms which sanction individuality. They approve critical thinking, dissent, and resistance to conformity. They give what Hollander has called "idiosyncratic credit" (1958). They may do this only for high-status members who are admired for their unique behavior, or the privilege may extend to all members. In the following chapter we shall consider some differences in productivity between groups which follow their leader and those which encourage diversity.

Another kind of solution for the dilemma of conformity or deviation is for the individual to discover or to imagine a reference group which would support his views and in which he would not be a deviate. In a heterogeneous society like a large city today, one can find supporters and co-workers for almost any viewpoint. Newcomb (1963) advocates selection of the like-minded as "an adaptation to a world that includes both persons and issues." Then, one need not sacrifice either "belonging" or "principle"—they can be united.

Indeed, one may appeal, not to any living group of supporters, but to the verdict of history or the communion of the saints. William James (1890) said that one might gather strength to brave the condemnation of one's present associates "by the thought of other and better *possible* social judges than those whose verdict goes against me now" (p. 315).

CHAPTER FOUR

Group productivity

Importance of work by groups

An increasingly important part of the world's work is carried on by groups. Corporations today are seldom run by a "strong man;" more reliance is placed on boards, conferences, and committees. An executive in government, business, education or social welfare may spend as much as 90 percent of his working day in cooperative planning with small groups of staff or public. Our laws are written by legislative committees, enforced by operating commissions, and violations judged by groups ranging from local juries to the Supreme Court. Education, which at one time was often dyadic—a tutor and one pupil—now proceeds largely in classes, large or small. Psychotherapy, once limited to a doctor-patient dyad, may be carried on in groups. Research, once the province of the single investigator, is increasingly done by teams. The Manhattan Project of World War II, leading to the first atomic bombs, involved hundreds of distinguished scientists and thousands of assistants.

Group operations have two kinds of potential advantage over action by a single individual. One is in the caliber of thinking, the range of resources, and the critical scrutiny which enter into the problem solving. The other is in the willingness with which people carry out decisions which they have helped to make.

Yet, group sessions often prove quite ineffective. They turn out to be time-consuming, dull, and frustrating. Personalities clash; a few feel driven to dominate in order "to get something done;" others may then resign themselves to accepting whatever the leader wants. Although some students find stimulation in discussion groups, others shun them. "We never get anywhere!" is a common complaint.

Another common objection to work in groups is the fear that individuality may be submerged. In the preceding chapter we commented on the way in which persons may be carried along in the mass emotion of crowds and mobs. Feelings in committees and discussion groups are seldom so extreme, but individuals still may be swayed toward conformity. One of the conditions for good group work is expression of different opinions; this is often difficult because of pressure to get a working agreement.

Actually, as we shall see, groups may sometimes be more sane, moderate, well balanced and wise than their average member. There are some groups in which passions are inflamed and individuals do, as Freud and Le Bon observed, surrender their individual minds and morals, submerging their own selves in a kind of social torrent. There are other groups, however, in which each individual is helped to be more fully himself. A thoughtful group may make its members more rational, more self-critical, and more ready to revise personal prejudices in the light of objective evidence, than these members would be if they were studying alone.

Man has mastered control of steampower, internal combustion engines, electric motors and is beginning to use power from atomic fission and fusion. Our skill in exploiting the immense potentialities of the power of human cooperation has advanced very little from prehistoric times until rather recently. Now, scientific study of group dynamics is opening the way to better utilization of the creative energy of human personalities. We shall review first the evidence on how well groups can solve problems; then we shall go on to study factors which may increase the intellectual productivity of working groups.

Productivity of individuals and groups

Group vs. individual

Between 1920 and 1940, a dozen different studies attempted to determine whether people were more productive if working alone or in groups.

The writer, for example, asked half of the members of a large class of graduate students to work alone, making up as many new words as each could using only the letters contained in a given word (such as "secondary" or "neurotics"). Simultaneously, the other section of the class, in another room, worked at the same anagrams task in small groups of five, with one member writing down the words proposed by all the other members. Then the two sections reversed procedures, and those who had worked alone tried working in groups; those who had begun in groups changed to work by themselves.

Working alone, the average student in ten minutes wrote down 31 words; then in a group of five, using a word of equivalent difficulty, he helped build a group score of 78 words in ten minutes. Those in the other section who began in groups achieved an average of 71 words; later working by themselves, they could find only 34. The range of individual performance was from a low of 18 words to a high of 49. Thus the average group performance with 75 words, excelled not only the average individual working alone, but also the best individual performances. Yet, if all the words found by five group members, when each was working alone, were pooled (eliminating duplicates) they reached an average of 87 words. On this task, group performance was superior to the average individual members; superior to the best individual member; but below the potential which might have been achieved if all individual contributions had been pooled in a "concocted" group.

Another experiment, with varied tasks, is reported in Abstract 14. Group work proved relatively more successful than individual performance especially for those questions in which the right answer, once hit upon, could be quickly recognized.

Following upon this interpretation, R. L. Thorndike (1938) compared group and individual performance when the range of responses was definitely limited (as in multiple-choice tests) and much less limited (as in open-end completion tasks). Groups consistently surpassed the average individual performance in both types of task, but the superiority was a little greater in the free-completion situation, where a larger range of responses could be used.

Solving crossword puzzles has the "Aha!" quality. The right answer, once arrived at, can usually be quickly confirmed by the words which intersect it. In a class experiment by the author with 11 groups, solving crossword puzzles, the average individual achieved a score of 118 correct words; the best individual reached 162 words; the average group performance was 179 words.

In the study by R. L. Thorndike, already cited, the achievement of groups in solving crossword puzzles was compared with their ability to construct a good puzzle. The groups were relatively better at solving a set problem. When it came to constructing a new puzzle, the varied

Abstract 14

TITLE   Do Groups Think More Effectively Than Individuals?

AUTHOR   Goodwin Watson

PROBLEM   Will students working in small groups solve intelligence tests better than they would if working alone?

SUBJECTS   68 graduate students

PROCEDURES   Three equivalent forms of an intelligence test were devised, each consisting of nine tasks suited to bright adults.

Each student took one test alone; then he joined with other students in a group of four or five members to solve the second test cooperatively. The third form was again taken by each individual alone. The two individual performances were averaged to offset practice improvement and show about how well each individual would have done at the time he joined the group performance. Groups had had no previous practice in working together and were allowed only ten minutes per task.

SOME FINDINGS   In total score, 11 of the 15 groups excelled their *average* member; 6 of the 15 excelled their *best* individual performer. Tasks were found to vary in suitability for individual or group solution. In decoding a cipher or in drawing the rigidly correct logical conclusion from certain given facts, or in hitting upon the right word to meet certain specifications, 90% of groups reached a conclusion superior to their average member and 50% excelled their best member. A difficult reading-comprehension test, on the other hand, was better suited to individual performance; only 53% of the group surpassed their average member and 30% their best member. On a creative task—composing the wittiest possible limerick with a prescribed first line—80% of groups did better than their average individual performance, and 30% excelled the best individual creation. A rough overall estimate would lead to the expectation that a typical group, under conditions of limited time and no previous practice, might be expected to attain a level of effective intellectual performance of about the 70th percentile of its members.

SOURCE: G. Murphy, and L. B. Murphy, *Experimental Social Psychology*. New York: Harper and Brothers, 1931, pp. 539–543.

suggestions of individuals altered the pattern on which others were working in a complex and kaleidoscopic way. It proved possible for groups to accomplish more, in a limited time, than the average individual could achieve, but group superiority was not as marked in the process of making up a puzzle as in finding a solution to one already set up.

A study by Shaw (1932) used puzzle problems. One was how to ferry three "missionaries" and three "cannibals" across a river, with a boat which could carry only two at a time, with one cannibal and all missionaries able to row, and the condition imposed that cannibals must never outnumber missionaries on either side of the river. Twenty-one students, working alone, spent from $2\frac{1}{2}$ to 29 minutes on this problem; none of them solved it correctly. Of five groups (4 students in each), three reached correct solutions in times varying from 12 to 34 minutes. Shaw found that groups averaged better than individuals on four of her six problems; on two there were no clear differences.

Another psychologist ingeniously adapted mazes and true-false tests to group performance (Gurnee, two studies in 1937). In the stylus maze, when used as a group task, the group voted on which direction to move at each choice point. This was a somewhat clumsy procedure which took longer than did the average individual performance, but resulted in fewer errors. On a true-false test, covering various matters of fact, the group procedure was simply to vote on each answer, the group answer being that of the majority. No discussion was permitted. Some questions were from a text the class had recently been studying, others were from non-technical chemistry, and still others were based on a film the class had been shown. On the textbook material, the average individual had 72 percent of his answers correct; the average by group vote was a resounding 98 percent correct. On chemistry questions, outside the field of class study, the average score for an individual was 38 percent; by group vote it rose to 47 percent. On the film, the average student had 52 percent correct; group vote gave 64 percent correct. Group vote came out, as a rule, at about the level of the highest individual scores.

Lorge and Fox (Fox, 1955), who compared solutions to a practical military problem (getting a group of men across a mined road with certain available ropes, sticks, trees, etc.), found the quality of solution by 70 groups of five officers each, averaging distinctly higher than the average of proposals by 70 officers working as individuals.

On another practical problem (maintaining morale in an isolated polar weather station) Lorge found, as we did with the little anagrams game of making up words from given letters, that a pooling of all the good ideas gave a better composite than was achieved by any individual or any cooperating group.

In another test of group performance, the author asked subjects to associate a given two-syllable noun with an arbitrary two-digit number. Thus a series "pencil–35, engine–71, etc." was read aloud. Recall was attempted by one section writing individually; by others in groups of four. The average individual scored 20 correct; the average group decision yielded 45 correct.

In a comparison of the ability of individuals and groups to draw logical conclusions, the results after group discussion were found better than those achieved by majority vote or by the average group member. An individual averaged 17.5 correct; the best individual scored 18.8; majority vote without discussion achieved 18.1 (between average and best); but group decision after discussion gave 21.9 correct (Barnlund, 1959).

These several investigations usually show group performance superior to the average individual and sometimes superior to the best individual. In our next section we will try to analyze the main psychological factors which give an advantage to group effort.

Psychological factors in group superiority

What factors generally contribute to making group performance superior and which hamper group problem solving?

The main facilitating factors are: (1) stimulation from the presence of others; (2) pooling of resources; (3) probability of being able to use the insight of an unusually able individual; (4) canceling of chance errors; (5) correcting individual blind spots; (6) cumulative interaction; and (7) security in risk taking. Each in turn will be discussed.

Presence of others

One of the first facts to impress investigators in social psychology is that the individual working in the presence of others performs somewhat differently than he would if working at the same task in isolation. Floyd Allport (1920) published many years ago some data showing that students writing a chain of free word-associations in the presence of several others also doing the same task (they were told not to compete) scored slightly more replies than they did when working at the same task alone. When the task was to write down arguments for or against an idea more arguments occurred to students writing in the presence of others, but the quality was not so good. In a series of routine clerical tasks (crossing out vowels, simple multiplication tasks) six subjects did better working in isolation; 13 did better working alongside others. An experiment on routine tasks with British school children (age 11-13) showed more than 80 percent making higher scores when working alone (Mukerji, 1940). A similar experiment with a group of 40 Ukrainian children trying to recall a series of seven words and seven associated numbers, showed a slightly better performance in the presence of the group (Elkin, 1926). Another psychologist (Travis, 1925) tested the eye-hand coordination of college men alone and later in the presence of an audience of four to eight older students who were strangers to the one being tested. Scores with observers present were a little higher.

The best known research on this problem was done by Dashiell (1930) who varied the experiment, comparing subjects: (a) working entirely alone; (b) working alongside others around two large tables but told not to compete, that their performance would not be compared with others; (c) same situation as (b) but instructed to compete; and (d) working under the close scrutiny of two fellow students who served as "observers." Speed of work at three different tasks was consistently highest under "observation" (d), but accuracy under scrutiny was lowest. Competitive motivation increased speed but not accuracy. Work done in the presence of others also working (non-competitively) was neither as rapid nor as accurate as work when subjects were in a room alone. Putting all the evidence together we can conclude that group members will usually be stimulated by the presence of others to put forth more effort, but that attention to the others is somewhat disconcerting and likely to reduce accuracy.

Pooled resources

In Chapter 1 we reported (Moede's, 1920) measures of increased strength of pull on a rope when additional team members were added. Each new member increased the total pull, but by an amount less than he was able to pull when tested alone. This investigation fits in with the data just reported from experiments on group word-construction and making suggestions for maintaining morale. The performance of five persons is better than that of any one, but each of the five does not contribute as much in the group as he might if he had been working alone. If the task permits each contribution to be made individually and the contributions to be simply added together, the total achievement will be higher than the group achievement. In most group work, the full potential of each member is not utilized.

The real point of working in a group is that members have *different* contributions to make. Suppose, in an experiment, the information needed to solve a problem is distributed among the several members so that each has only a portion of the necessary facts. In these conditions, no single member however brilliant he may be, can achieve precisely the right answer. Only by pooling their resources can the group see all the pertinent resources and difficulties. This kind of laboratory experiment is a small model of many life situations in which the various members of a committee each bring to the group discussion *part* of the necessary knowledge. One reason for making boards broadly representative of various sections of an organization or community is that each will be aware of some relevant facts not known to the others.

Probability of the appearance of an able individual

Another kind of superiority for group thinking arises from the simple statistical probability that since people vary in ability, there are likely to be in each group some members well above the average group level. Assume that we design a problem so difficult that 80 percent of the students in a class are unable to solve it. Suppose, then, we divide the students into groups of five to work on this problem. If one of that top 20 percent is in each group, every group may come out with a correct solution, even though most of the group members were unable to figure out the solution by themselves. A considerable superiority of group performance over the average individual member could result simply by using as the group score the performance of the best individual members.

The several members of a group differ not only in intelligence but also in motivation. Some are more willing than others to do hard work. On practical problems, there is often need for someone to do a time-consuming, painstaking chore. If the problem is left to a single person, he may or may not be ready to put forth the necessary effort. If the problem is the joint responsibility of half-a-dozen committee members, the chance of having at least one of them who will take on the difficult chore is increased. Indeed, a common complaint from class committees developing a group project is that some members shirk and leave most of the necessary work to one or two "eager beavers." This may not be good education—we shall discuss classroom groups later—but organizations are often more concerned about being sure that a certain job does get done. If a task is necessary and important, and if we cannot know whether any given individual will put forth the required effort, assignment to a group is likely to mean that at least one conscientious member does see that the work is properly accomplished.

Chance errors cancel out

Some errors are due to chance or random influences which operate differently on the various members of a group. Suppose some members happen to overestimate while others underestimate. If these are averaged, the result will be more accurate than the typical individual.

In one experiment of this kind (Gordon, 1924), 200 university students estimated the weight of ten similar looking cubes and tried to arrange them correctly from lightest to heaviest. The average individual success was indicated by a correlation of .41. If the answers of five students were averaged, the correlation of this average with the true order rose to .68. If ten individual judgments were combined, the accuracy rose to a correlation of .79; averaging in lots of 20 each gave a correlation of .86 and combining 50 estimates gave a correlation of

.94. This takes place without any discussion or interaction, simply because chance errors tend to cancel out other chance errors.

Some decades ago a German psychologist made a composite photograph of the faces of school children, taking pictures of identical size so that the negatives could be superimposed to give a single print. The composite face of a number of boys turned out to be more regular, and hence more handsome, than any one of the individuals. The composite girl was prettier, but less distinctive, than any of the separate pictures. Even an artificial combination like this minimizes deviations from the norm.

In a roomful of students, where the actual temperature was 72°, each was asked to estimate the room temperature (Knight, 1921). The range was from 60° to 89°, with an average at 72.4°, very close to the truth. In the same study fifteen advertisements, the returns from which were known, were rated by forty judges. Correlations of ratings with the actual pulling power of the ad ranged from —.71 to +.87 with an average at .18. Combining individual ranks into a single group ranking produced a correlation of .63. Ten of the forty judges surpassed the combined estimate.

A study of judgments of the number of dots on a card (there were 3,159) made by individual Air Force officers showed an average error of 3,330; in dyads the error fell to 1,081; in triads to 850 and for a group of six members to 773 (Ziller, 1957). On a judgment task (which facts were relevant to a given problem) scores rose steadily from 3.2 for individuals and 4.2 for dyads to 5.8 for groups of six.

If the individual judgments are all worthless or are consistently wrong, then nothing is gained by combining them. The guess of ten judges on where a roulette wheel will stop has no validity because none of the judges can do better than a zero correlation. When students were asked, for example in Knight's study, to estimate intelligence from photographs, and the average individual was more wrong than right (correlation of —.21) the group judgment was no better (correlation of —.18).

There is no wisdom gained from pooling ignorance, and if each member is wrong, the group does not set things right. Composite judgments are better than those of single individuals only when most individuals are partly right.

Blind spots corrected

It is easier for us to see other people's mistakes than it is to perceive our own. Some people prefer to work alone rather than in groups because, working alone, they are unchecked. In a group, however, someone may say "Wait a minute! Aren't you overlooking this point?" This can be annoying, but correction is useful. In a series of experiments in the Soviet Union, Bekhterev (1924) and his associates demonstrated the utility of social criticism. Pictures were shown for a brief period to groups; each individual then wrote down all the details he could remember. A discussion period followed in which the group tried to reach consensus about each item. The group decision corrected many of the mistaken ideas of deviate individuals.

In laboratory experiments, psychologists have usually used some kind of problem with a single identifiable "correct" solution. Such questions make for easy, valid scoring. There are important differences, however, between questions with one known right answer and the usual tasks of work groups in our society. We do not often assemble committees to solve puzzles all parts of which fall neatly into place after the correct idea is proposed. Their task is usually to forge some kind of workable compromise among conflicting interests, values, and considerations. With real problems it is not so easy to be sure which proposals are "wrong." Yet even in group work on creative tasks, members often contribute by rejecting leads on which time would only be wasted.

In Lorge's studies, reported earlier, of the ability of individuals and groups to devise solutions for typical military problems (getting a patrol group across a mined road; raising morale at an isolated Arctic air base), group discussion frequently disposed of inadequate ideas which individuals, working alone, would have been content to recommend. While most of the best ideas could be traced to ingenious, creative individuals, the group rejected numerous plausible fallacies. Fewer "zany" and unworkable notions were able to get past the screen of group criticism.

If group thinking did nothing more than to correct or eliminate the answers which are much worse than average, that would be an important service to the world. Perhaps we suffer as much from crassly stupid and inept individual acts, which group consideration would surely have rejected, as we do from inability to reach the highest and most creative levels of thought.

Stimulation from cumulative interaction

Participation in group discussion can do more than filter out silly or harmful notions; it may also stimulate ideas which would not have occurred to individuals working alone. A model may be the musical "jam session" which is continuously creative. Each member responds to all the others.

Evidence that discussion adds something to the compilation of individual answers appears in the study by Barnlund (1959), reported earlier. After group discussion, decisions surpassed both the average vote and the best individual answers.

In another experiment (Timmons, 1939) subjects working alone and in groups rated five proposals for changing Ohio's system of paroling convicts. Results after group discussion were found better (closer to what experts believed) than the results achieved by any kind of pooling of individual ratings in statisticized groups, whether based on averages or majority opinion.

The stimulating power of discussion appears particularly in those meetings which succeed in devising a better solution than any single member had in mind when he came. Usually it has been found productive to encourage considerable "free wheeling" in a creative discussion. Fantastic ideas are tossed about for a while because they may help the thinking to take a new and productive turn.

A test of brain-storming techniques in one division of General Motors brought out over 100 ways in which a rough casting might be burred. Not all were really practical, but the objective in a brain-storming session is to prevent premature discard of an idea merely because it would be difficult, costly, disapproved by certain influential persons, or resisted because it upsets traditional concepts or ways of working.

It is not easy, in a practical situation, to adhere to the rule of listing even those suggestions which appear, at first glance, ridiculous. In one instance, reported to the writer, a comptroller refused a department head's request for added personnel to cope with a temporary emergency. He proposed, instead, that all concerned should brain-storm on ways of doing the work with the existing company personnel. One proposal, which the comptroller wanted to reject out of hand was that certain people in his office might be used. The rules previously agreed on forced him to listen, and this solution was later approved by all as the best.

A widely noted study by Taylor, *et al.* (1958), compared the production by college men brain-storming alone with the output from groups of four. The production by individuals working alone were artificially collated in aggregates of four and these "statisticized groups" (Lorge's term) produced more ideas and better ideas than were recorded in the actual groups.

Meadow, *et al.* (1959), found, in contrast to Taylor, that when students had been trained—rather than merely instructed—in the use of brain-storming methods, they produced more, and more creative, solutions.

A project in which groups tried to bring out in discussion all the similarities they could find in two pictures, showed "waves" of stimulation. Proposals would occur along one line until that vein was nearly exhausted. Someone would then suggest another type of similarity. This set off a round of other contributions following the new line. When this flagged, another approach was offered, stimulating a further flow of ideas using a different concept. Shaw (1961) calls the process by which one member of a group takes off from the ideas of a previous speaker "hitch-hiking."

We may now summarize the factors which often contribute to a high level of group performances: social stimulation; range of resources; probability of including some person(s) of high ability or strong motivation or both; canceling out of chance errors; correction of individual blind spots; and cumulative interaction.

Risk-taking

Before turning to the other side of the ledger—disadvantages from which groups suffer—we may note a characteristic which may prove either an asset or a liability.

In Chapter 3 we mentioned that people in groups may be willing to venture further than they would on their own. A series of experiments (Stoner, 1961; Wallach, *et al.*, 1962 and 1964; Marquis, 1962) has confirmed this finding. The problems studied included a change to a job with less security but more chance of financial success; a high return but risky investment; a college where one could be fairly sure of being graduated as against one with more prestige but less certainty of success, and other problems. One study used actual winnings on quiz questions rather than hypothetical situations. The results fairly consistently support the probability of greater risk taking by a group than by the average individual judgments of the group members. One of Marquis' experiments focused on how a group would modify a decision made by its designated leader. Leaders reached their decisions after conducting a group discussion, but on a basis of personal responsibility. Then they had an opportunity for further free discussions with group members. Of 48 possible shifts in the leader's own decision after the second group session, 22 showed no change; two became more cautious; and 24 moved in the direction of taking greater risk. The leader designated was one whose own initial reaction was at the median for his group; hence group members were in equal numbers more cautious and more adventurous than he. Still both group decisions and leader decision involved more risk taking than either the members or the leader would have ventured on their own responsibility. In an experiment summarized in Chapter 5, Ziller (1957) reported that air crews after group discussion chose more risky decisions than their officers would have made.

This area of group production has not yet been studied fully enough to answer all important questions. Experience suggests that frequently boards and committees put a damper on individual initiative. Yet, apparently, at other times and perhaps more often they give support to someone whose ideas are a little more creative and more advanced than those of the average member of the group.

Factors hampering group performance

What, now, are are some of the ways in which groups are less efficient than their members would be if working alone? Six factors can be identified: (1) leaving one's share of the work to others; (2) conflicting goals; (3) failure to communicate; (4) interference of suggestions from various viewpoints; (5) frustration from interference and criticism; and (6) lack of the unity which characterizes the best aesthetic creativity. Most of these are readily apparent and require little explanation.

Leaving work to others

The "let George do it" attitude illustrates the tendency in groups to assume that someone else will take the necessary responsibility. Experience in panel presentations is that some members, if they do not have a specified responsibility, may skimp on preparation and rely on the inspiration of the moment. We have cited several studies supporting the conclusion that added members do not contribute to the group as much as they are capable of doing alone.

Conflicting goals

Members bring into a group project a variety of motives. Some may even want, consciously or unconsciously, to sabotage the group effort. Others have self-oriented needs (Fouriezos, et al., 1950) e.g.: to get the better of certain rivals, to win affection from a pair member, to obtain emotional release for some feelings, to show off, to be a clown, or to withdraw. These all interfere with attention to the group enterprise. Self-oriented needs may interfere with production when working alone, also, but they are likely to be more vivid and demanding in the actual face-to-face relations with others.

Even when members are genuinely work-oriented and anxious to achieve results, they may have different ideas about how to proceed. Each proposes steps toward the goal he has in mind; yet to others, these proposals may seem irrelevant or tangential or ill-timed. The "hidden agenda" is a concept which has proved useful in analyzing the work of a group. All groups proceed on two levels. One is the explicit, avowed rational purpose. The other level is often ignored as if members could really lay aside their private, covert purposes and feelings. Personal ties and resentments "should not" influence certain personnel decisions and may be covered over with calm, objective statistical approaches, but the discerning observer may note that the figures have been marshaled to boost one man and to defeat another.

Failure to communicate

Communication is essential for group thinking, but it may be restricted for many reasons. Some members may feel shy and reluctant to talk. Status differences may inhibit subordinates from appearing to criticize those of higher rank. Some people are apprehensive and defensive and they take an excessive amount of talk and time to get around to any expression of their ideas. Sometimes it is hard to explain to others a distinction one sees quite clearly oneself. Many discussions founder for semantic reasons; words are being used with quite different connotations.

As a rule, the most talkative members are rated as contributing the best ideas in the group (Slater, 1955). However, the deviate and silent member is sometimes the one who, if he had spoken out, would have had a better idea than any the group has heard (Maier, Solem, 1952).

Full, free communication in group decision-making is desirable both for quality of the conclusion and also for its implementation. Sometimes the silent, inarticulate, or vaguely expressive member is concealing his reluctance to support the group decision.

Interference

In the experiment on making up words out of a set of letters, we earlier observed that if it had been possible to add together all the different words thought of by individual members (in a ten-minute period) the total would have been larger than that achieved by any group. Trying to funnel words in quickly through one secretary slowed down the rate of production. Occasionally, too, a word was driven out of the mind by conflicting suggestions from others. Often the contribution of a fellow member is distracting.

Because only one person can talk (and be heard by all others) at any one time, members in a discussion often have to wait to make their point. Sometimes the delay is so long that the whole course of the discussion has changed before the would-be speaker gets his chance to be heard. He may then drop the idea entirely, which deprives the group, or he may bring up his idea belatedly, but this causes the others to backtrack when they have already moved on to other issues.

A good illustration of the interference among proposals was seen in the confused group effort to construct a crossword puzzle (Thorndike, 1938).

Frustration

All the difficulties listed above—the laziness of some members, the self-oriented behavior of others, the confusion of goals, the rambling talk of some speakers, the interference of lines of thought which do not run parallel—produce irritation and annoyance. Members who started out with good intent may give up in disgust, or may explode emotionally, ostensibly over some minor point. The course of group thinking never runs as smoothly as a computing machine.

One of the virtues of group consideration is also an irritant. We noted that group members often catch one another up on errors. This is wholesome for the end product, but a little hard on feelings. It is pleasanter for the individual to write along, developing his own ideas, than it is to offer them for group criticism and have them challenged (rightly or wrongly) at several points.

Insufficient unity for aesthetic creation

Group difficulty in designing a crossword puzzle is an evident case of the problem of endeavor to produce an artistic product by group effort. A work of art must have unity and coherence. A group of musicians can have fun improvising in a jam session but this is unlikely to produce a unified symphonic work. A school of painters can collaborate on a Rubens canvas, but only under the eventual direction of one mind. There have been instances of profitable collaboration—one thinks of Gilbert and Sullivan or Rodgers and Hammerstein—but no great dramas, poems or operas have been group products.

Process in working groups

Three different kinds of analysis mark three different historic periods in the study of group thinking.

"Group thinking" in the 1920's

Pioneer work in the 1920's followed John Dewey's famous analysis (1910) of the steps of individual problem solving. We engage in an on-going activity; an obstacle impedes our progress; we examine it for clues to the situation; we propose to ourselves some hypothesis; we test these, choose the one which best fits the facts, and resume the activity. Manuals for leaders of group thinking such as Harrison Elliott's *The Progress of Group Thinking* (1928) suggest that the place to begin work in a group is with an exploration of the situation in which some difficulty has been felt. Members are urged to tell how the issue has come up in their own experience. People start talking more readily about incidents from their experience than about theories and abstractions. The reports serve an emotional as well as an intellectual purpose. They increase involvement while developing better awareness of the difficulty.

The second step is definition of the problem. Later investigations (Maier, Solem, 1962; Maier, 1963) have supported the observation that groups that are too "solution-minded" attempt prematurely to offer remedies. Then it is found that these solutions have missed the real point of the difficulty and the process must start over.

One of the differences between the novice and the expert in any field is the questions each asks. Getting the right question may be more than half of the process of effective problem solving. A common error (Maier, 1963) is the attribution of causes to personality rather than to situational factors. Another is to perceive some similarity to previous problems, and too quickly to assume that the formerly successful solutions will fit the present situation.

At the third stage, solutions are proposed and examined. Dewey described this process in the individual as dramatic imagination. The thinker constructs a scene showing how the contemplated action would probably develop and work out. At its best, this stage of group thinking represents search and examination rather than attack and defense. Personal feelings are a legitimate factor in solutions to most social problems, but are out of place in testing purely intellectual or scientific or technical answers.

Maier (1963) proposes as screening principles: (1) that solutions taken over from previous problem situations should be regarded skeptically and (2) that when members agree on a solution although disagreeing on their diagnosis of the problem, these answers are also likely to prove unsatisfactory. When generally acceptable proposals have been formulated, it is still important (if often uncongenial in impatient groups) to examine the exceptions.

As the original proposals are examined, amendments and qualifications arise. One advantage of the process of freely moving group thinking over traditional parliamentary procedure is that the best answer is not presumed to be available at the start. Parliamentary procedure starts, officially, with a motion which is seconded. The motion represents a crystallized statement of conclusion before the discussion takes place. Almost inevitably, it discourages revision and re-formulation. If discussion brings out needed changes there may be amendments, amendments to the amendment, and substitute motions. The complications are due to the basic error of trying to formulate the answer, in the original motion, before the problem has been examined or the various alternatives scrutinized and modified. Good group procedure requires that the making of motions be deferred until the period of discussion is concluded; then the motion is likely to be merely a formal statement of the consensus which has been achieved.

Examination and comparison of the various alternative proposals usually reveals a need for additional facts. Apparent disagreement on the value of a line of action may rest upon quite different expectations of what outcomes would follow. At this point the group needs to consult experts, to search the relevant literature, or to design experiments. The importance of the issue under discussion governs the time and resources which can be invested in fact finding.

Eventually the group rejects alternatives which seem less desirable and concentrates on the best available solution. Ideally, the outcome of group thinking is an integration of the ideas, viewpoints, facts, and values contributed by every member. An integrative solution differs from a dominated or a compromise outcome. In power struggles one party—perhaps a single individual or a minority clique or a majority—imposes its view upon the others. Even if the majority triumphs in a perfectly fair vote, the decision is still not an integration. One side dominates and the other has to submit. A compromise is one step better. Each side gives up part of what it wants and gets something in return. The outcome is not wholly satisfactory to anyone. When a genuine integration is achieved, everyone is satisfied. Everyone's wants have been fully taken into account. The aim of group thinking is integration. Often this seems an ideal impossible of achievement. The Society of Friends has long relied upon a persistent quest for consensus in official decisions. A story is told of one congregation which had long been divided over whether to build a new meeting house. A visitor said to the clerk of the meeting after one prolonged session which adjourned with the question still unsettled: "How long do you think it will take to work this out?" "I don't know," replied the Quaker, "but when it is settled it will be right" (Chase, 1951).

The time required to achieve integration is not always wasted. A quick decision may not really be economical if it leaves tensions and the seeds of future conflicts. If people are to continue to work together or to live together as neighbors, a hasty decision which leaves some persons feeling resentful may be costly in the long run.

The final step in the process is putting the decision into action so that the movement of affairs which was interrupted by the initial difficulty can be resumed. If the agreed-upon solution does not "work," i.e., if the process does not move ahead smoothly, thought again tackles the problem of identifying the obstacle and examining new proposals. Living is continuous overcoming.

Interaction process analysis

Two decades later, another form of analysis of group procedure emerged. Bales (1950) in the Laboratory of Social Relations at Harvard, developed a set of categories designed to give a systematic classification of each act of participation in a group. As shown in Table 1, the categories represent polarized dimensions; 1 is the opposite of 12; 2 of 11, etc. The first three are positive emotions; the last three express negative feelings. Categories 7, 8, and 9 request aid; 4, 5, and 6 offer it.

Positive emotional expressions (items 1, 2, 3) are usually more than twice as frequent as negative emotional expressions (items 10, 11, 12). Opinions and information are much more often volunteered (46%) than requested (7%).

Bales (1952) was able to analyze the steps through which a working committee usually moves. A study of 22 committee work sessions, each

TABLE 1—TYPES OF INTERACTION AND THEIR RELATIVE FREQUENCY
(in 96 sessions of 24 different groups) (Bales, 1955)

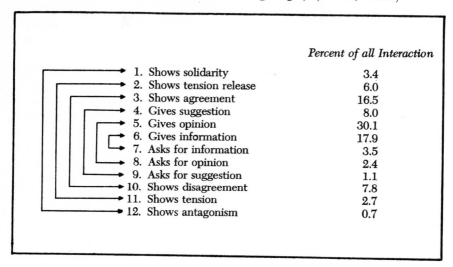

	Percent of all Interaction
1. Shows solidarity	3.4
2. Shows tension release	6.0
3. Shows agreement	16.5
4. Gives suggestion	8.0
5. Gives opinion	30.1
6. Gives information	17.9
7. Asks for information	3.5
8. Asks for opinion	2.4
9. Asks for suggestion	1.1
10. Shows disagreement	7.8
11. Shows tension	2.7
12. Shows antagonism	0.7

divided into a first, second, and third phase, showed that the normal process began with *orientation* ("What is it?"); moved to relatively more concern with *evaluation* ("How do we feel about it?") and in the closing phase gave more attention to *control* ("What shall we do about it?"). As the discussion moved from the intellectual examination of the difficulty in the first phase, to evaluation and decision (control) the frequency of emotional expression increased.

A study (Borgatta, Bales, 1953) of the consistency with which an individual behaves as a group member was made for 126 subjects. The results are given in Table 2. Re-scoring by the same judge gave satisfactory reliabilities (.65–.98). When the same fellow members were working at the same task, behavior categories "show tension release," "shows agreement," and "gives opinion" remained fairly stable characteristics of the individual. When members worked with other associates, no categories showed a consistency as high as $r = .70$. This means that the observed behavior is really interaction and dependent on the relationships with particular others.

The effect of the "others" was particularly studied by Stephan and Mishler (1952). They found that a member placed with others who are highly active in talking and initiating procedure will have a low rate; the same member, associated with quiet members who are slow to take part, will have a relatively high rate of initiation. The behavior of a member is an inverse function of the average interaction rate of his co-participants.

As a rule, the member in the group who is most active in initiating

TABLE 2—SUMMARY OF SOME FINDINGS ON RELIABILITY OF THE BALES
CATEGORIES

	Reliability of Re-scoring by Same Judge One Month Later	Consistency with Same (2-4) Associates (Range for 5 Sets of Data)	Minimum for 126 Subjects in 56 Group Planning Periods with Same Tasks	
			Same Associates	Different Associates
1. Shows solidarity	.98	−.14 to .58	.34	.28
2. Shows tension release	.93	−.62 to .94	.70	.29
3. Shows agreement	.96	.70 to .95	.78	.64
4. Gives suggestion	.81	−.13 to .84	.61	.54
5. Gives opinion	.92	.58 to .94	.74	.53
6. Gives information	.96	−.01 to .98	.69	.61
7. Asks for information	.89	.01 to .97	.51	.41
8. Asks for opinion	.65	−.19 to .99	.43	.38
9. Asks for suggestion	.83	−.03 to .97	.32	.07
10. Shows disagreement	.70	−.53 to .97	.49	.38
11. Shows tension	.92	.02 to .89	.64	.39
12. Shows antagonism	.88	−.25 to 1.00	.62	.07

verbal or other acts is also the one who receives most contributions directed toward him by others (Bales, *et al.*, 1951). The rank order is consistent from the highest initiation to the most passive. The member who seldom contributes is seldom addressed by others.

In another study (Bales, Borgatta, 1955) changes in categories of participation were studied as groups increased in size from two to seven members. All groups were composed of male college students discussing a human relations case study. Four groups of each size were used, and ratings on the twelve Bales categories averaged. The biggest difference related to group size was in category 11, "shows tension." Tension was greatest in groups of two and decreased quite consistently being only half as frequent in groups of six or seven members as in dyads. Correspondingly, joking, laughing, and other indications of a more relaxed attitude appeared more often in the larger group. Perhaps because of the greater interpersonal intimacy, the smaller groups seemed more threatening. Expressions of agreement, understanding and compliance were more frequent in the smaller groups, a finding consistent with the concept of greater tension. Suggestions and direction for others were more commonly offered in the larger group; this too fits with a feeling of less anxiety. Asking for information and for the opinion or feeling of others—a deferential behavior—was observed most often in dyads and triads. Disagreement and rejection of the ideas of others took place more freely in the larger groups.

The Bales categories do not represent the only ways of characterizing observed participation in groups. Heyns (1948), for example, designated some members as "idea men" and others as "reality testers." The "expert" is different from the highly goal-oriented member. Some, in their interpersonal relationships, tend to be supportive, others critical and rejecting. Some smooth over differences ("social harmonizer"); others try to explore and define the contrasting views.

Contemporary group dynamics

We have seen how, in the 1920's, Dewey's analysis of the act of thought was used as a guide to good group discussion. A later stage involved the use of categories for objective observation of ways in which members contribute. More recently, attention has been given to the dynamic factors underlying what goes on in the group. Laboratory studies of groups differing in size, composition, training, in mutual trust, and in cohesion, have led to a new profession of training persons to work more effectively within organizations.

Selection of members. In Chapter 3 we noted that as groups increase in size beyond eight or nine participants, a few members are likely to dominate and others to remain passive. Whether a group will be optimally productive depends also on how fully the necessary information, skills, and viewpoints are represented. The more homogeneous the participants, the less each member adds to the resources present in the others.

Gerard (1953) found that heterogeneous groups reached decisions which were not the average of individual choices, but were closer to the judgment of experts on the ideal problem-solution. Even diversity of temperament may be an asset. One comparison (Hoffman, 1959) of solutions to the problem of getting a squad across a mined road, devised by groups homogeneous in ten traits (measured by the Guilford Zimmerman Temperament Survey) with those devised by more heterogeneous groups showed more originality and constructive quality in the products of groups diverse in personality.

Freedom of communication. Observation of strangers as they begin to interact under laboratory conditions, with no predetermined leader or assigned task, has led one author (Bennis, 1964) to designate the phases of group development as follows:

I. Dependence
   a. Dependence flight
   b. Counter-dependence; fight
   c. Resolution
II. Interdependence
   a. Enchantment flight
   b. Disenchantment fight
   c. Consensual validation

In the first phase members are concerned mainly with the authority problem, supporting or resisting various claims to leadership. In the second they are concerned with the problem of intimacy and mutual trust. In the second phase, they create a false atmosphere of pseudo-harmony; disenchanted, they reject or attack one another. All this precedes the achievement of an atmosphere in which members freely express their views, receive genuine reactions, and are able to be highly productive.

A major obstacle to communication and trust arises from status differences. Those in higher positions can talk freely and be listened to, but often this is a one-way affair. One laboratory experiment (Heise, Miller, 1951) connected three-man groups by earphones in which noise might interfere. When communication was limited to one-way (A could talk only to B; B only to C; C only to A) a task took twice as long as with free back-and-forth talk. Introduction of noise on the line reduced efficiency to less than 20 percent of normal.

Many groups have an explicit or hidden power structure which impedes free communication. A study (Torrance, 1954) of problem solving by three-man B-26 combat crews (pilot, navigator, gunner) in which the pilot is in command, the navigator is a commissioned officer, and the gunner an enlisted man inferior in status to the two officers, showed that when one of the men had the right answer and the other two were mistaken, the pilots were almost always successful in persuading the other two to accept their view (94%). Under similar circumstances the navigators were not quite so successful (80%) and the gunners much less persuasive (63%) even when the low man on that totem pole had the answer the whole group needed.

Adequate time. The superiority of group achievement over individual work is dependent in part on having enough time. A short work period favors the individual response; it takes time for group members to become adjusted to one another, to express ideas, to assimilate one another's contributions, to interact, to criticize, and to integrate proposals. The larger the group the larger the time required.

One study (South, 1927) compared groups of three members and groups of six working at four different tasks: solving a bridge problem, solving a mechanical puzzle, matching emotions to photographs, and giving qualitative grades to English compositions. In the latter two tasks, in which it was difficult for the group to check which rating was most nearly correct, the larger groups took longer. On the first two tasks, which have an "Aha!" quality so that once the right answer is found it can be immediately recognized, the larger group with its greater resources of talent to draw upon, usually found the correct solution more quickly.

In another study (Hare, 1952) groups of Boy Scouts were given 20 minutes to discuss the relative importance of 10 pieces of camping equipment for a certain trip. Some groups contained five boys; others 12 boys each. In the smaller group, only 3 percent complained of too little time; but 22 percent made that criticism in the larger groups. Given the limited time, the small groups achieved more consensus than did the boys in the 12-member groups.

Fox and Lorge (1962) reported that in a 50-minute period individual written proposals were generally better than group products; with more time and training, group products surpassed individual solutions.

Anderson (1961) repeated our earlier study of group performance in making up words out of certain letters. Whereas we found, in a 10-minute period, that groups did not record as many different words as the total of individual papers would have provided, Anderson's groups, given 20 minutes, did achieve as many as the total of all individual responses. He also showed three-person-groups scoring about 17 percent more than did dyads.

Cohesion. Is a close, warm friendly group more or less efficient than one in which a more impersonal, matter-of-fact, businesslike attitude prevails?

Friendliness among the group members may work either way. On the one hand, when members are friendly they may waste a lot of time talking and joking about matters not closely related to the task. On the other, general good feeling in a group usually makes it easier for members to express themselves and to exchange views. A study of performance of military squads (Abstract 15), showed that groups in which members liked one another were actually more efficient in solving combat problems. Of course the correlation might equally well mean that more efficient groups develop more affection among members.

It is characteristic of the cohesive group that members cooperate readily with each other. One study (Haythorn, 1953) showed that groups which rated high in cohesion also rated high in productivity. In contrast, groups in which members made themselves disliked by dominating, eccentric or suspicious behavior were less productive. Again, the correlations could be interpreted either way.

Abstract 15

TITLE   The Use of a Sociometric Test as a Predictor of Combat Unit Effectiveness

AUTHOR   Daniel M. Goodacre, III

PROBLEM   Can a sociometric scale measuring group cohesion effectively predict group performance?

SUBJECTS   72 men in 12 reconnaissance platoon squads.

PROCEDURE   Each man was asked to indicate the men in his squad whom he would *want* and those he would *not want* to be with in a variety of situations, i.e., at a dance, during an attack, etc. The total number of men who were listed as wanted by the members of the group, minus the number of men who would not be wanted in any of these situations, was considered as the measure of group cohesion.

A field problem for scout squads from reconnaissance platoons was developed as a criterion of the effectiveness of the squads' performance. Twelve tactical situations, such as air attacks, outposting of road junctions, etc., were simulated.

SOME FINDINGS   The score that each squad obtained on the sociometric scale was correlated with the ease with which they solved the field problems. This correlation was .77. The probability of this relationship's being a chance one is less than one in one hundred.

SOURCE: *Sociometry*, 1951, XIV:148–152.

A group which has been organized for some time and is accustomed to working as a team can withstand considerable internal conflict. French (1941) gave groups tasks which apparently could be done but were actually much more difficult than they seemed. *Ad hoc* groups—arbitrarily set up at the time of the experiment were soon disrupted by the frustration. "Traditioned" groups—basketball or football teams which had played together—expressed more interpersonal aggression but still did not break down or give up. There was more sense of freedom, more we-feeling and more equality of participation in the traditioned groups. If the tasks assigned were of a kind which a highly motivated and persistent group might be able to solve, indications were that more of the cohesive, traditioned groups would have succeeded.

Not all studies find that cohesion increases efficiency. A strong sense of belonging makes the individual want to conform to the group norm but the group norm may favor either better work or less careful work.

In one experiment (Schachter, Ellertson, *et al.*, 1951) twelve groups of three girls each were led to feel very congenial; twelve more groups were led to feel disappointed in their associates. Some groups of each type received suggestions (believed to come from fellow group members) to speed up; other groups received notes which read something like: "Let's take it easy; I'm tired." Members in more cohesive groups were more inclined to follow the suggestion, whether for increased or for decreased production. Experience in industry has shown similar influences; organized workers may decide to speed up or to slow down production; if group loyalty is strong, these shared understandings are very potent.

A group climate which values only harmony and cordiality leads to repression of differences and criticisms, thus facilitating acceptance of defective or inferior products.

Training and experience

Most laboratory experiments on group thinking have been carried out with *ad hoc* groups, usually made up of students arbitrarily assigned to do certain tasks together. The real work of the world is seldom done this way. Committees work together for some time; boards may operate with much the same membership over years. These become traditioned groups; they are accustomed to certain ways of working together.

When individuals are first brought together to work as a group, they go through a necessary period of adjustment to one another. They need to test and evaluate each other and are likewise concerned about making a favorable impression on their fellow members. All of this interferes a little with efforts to concentrate on the task before them. They have to resolve any conflicts of power and mutual acceptance before the atmosphere for work is established. Traditioned groups can usually coordinate their contributions more easily. Sometimes, however, previous work together has led to rivalry, antagonisms, and other negative attitudes which impede communication.

Training in how to work as an effective group member is usually helpful. Fox (1955) in one set of experiments found no difference in the quality of solutions to the problem between the average individual and an average group brought together for the first time in an arbitrarily assembled group. Later, after men had had six months of training, group performance was substantially better than achievement by the average member working alone. Lorge (1953) also found that groups could improve their skill in cooperative planning.

Education has been slow to recognize its obligation—even the possibility—for training people to work effectively in groups. The tradition of the school room has been that each pupil does his own work and is graded on individual performance. Cooperation with the teacher is looked upon as an admirable character trait, but cooperation with fellow pupils without permission is still often regarded as cheating.

Since so much of the work of modern society is assigned to committees, commissions, boards, and other organized groups, and since the high ability of an individual working by himself does not guarantee a high contribution from him as a group member, an education that is only individualistic proves inadequate. Skill in working as a group member can be taught, just as skill in reading, mathematics, typing or swimming can be taught. The following list of objectives can be used as a check list for observing behavior of group members before and after training.

Some goals in training for group participation

The following qualities characterize an effective group member:

1. Aspires to become more effective; realizes he has much to learn.
2. Discounts his first impressions of others; keeps open and receptive.
3. Observes and listens carefully.
4. Expresses himself as frankly and openly as possible.
5. Confronts disagreements; examines differences rather than evades or smooths over.
6. Is not defensive; accepts his limitations; recognizes that it is easier for others to accept his human failings than his claim to superiority.
7. Re-examines problems before proposing remedies. Is problem-minded rather than solution-minded at the beginning. (Maier, Solem, 1962).
8. Checks his perceptions and understandings, seeking consensual validation. (Do others agree?)
9. Builds on the contributions of others; uses their resources where they supplement his own.
10. Defends the opportunity of minorities and deviates to be heard and understood.
11. Avoids lengthy statements or dialogues which interest only the two members involved.
12. Is comfortable with periods of thoughtful silence.
13. Keeps alert to the need for better evidence and proposes ways to obtain it.
14. Shares in watching the continuing processes in the group, summarizing at appropriate turning points.
15. Tests proposed decisions to discover how extensively and genuinely these are supported.
16. Recognizes the value, in a continuing group, of maintaining morale; does not neglect the emotional aspects which make it satisfying for members to work together.

Practice: role-playing

Reading and approving a description of the good group member does not enable a person to act the part. The skills of group participation, like other skills, require practice and can be improved by coaching. The coach in this activity is usually an observer who records behavior of members during a group session and reports on what he has seen. Self-perception is often at variance with the facts. Highly active members may be more aware of the times they held themselves in check and waited for others to speak than of the fact that they talked more than any others in the group. Members may play one role monotonously in the group—may speak, for example, only to challenge some remark made by another member—without being aware of the stereotyped quality of their participation. They may show themselves as very defensive and yet be quite unaware of the impression they give. In accord with the consonance hypothesis they may interpret anything said by members whom they like as agreement and anything said by disliked associates as disagreement, although an objective observer would find both judgments erroneous or exaggerated.

One device used in training is role-playing which means spontaneous, unrehearsed acting out of a group situation. The training may begin with expression by some member that he has difficulty in preventing others from dominating the discussion or that he wishes he could more easily "show solidarity." After a bit of discussion to arouse interest, a typical situation is devised. The member may wish first to watch someone else play the part he finds difficult; eventually he tries it out. Now it is no longer a matter of theory; he has to perform. In the examples chosen, he would have to restrain the aggressive talker or express solidarity in an acceptable way. Role-playing scenes are best quickly cut after the main act has been finished. They can be repeated with other actors or with agreed on variations to make the task easier or harder. Frequently, audience discussion follows each role-playing, bringing out suggestions for improving future performances.

Training in a T-group

Application of what is known about emotional factors in productive groups to the improvement of the skills of participants has led to the emergence of a social invention called a "T-" (for Training) group (Bradford, Gibb, Benne, 1964). The training takes place in self-directing, self-observing groups usually containing eight to twelve members. The "laboratory method" implies that participants learn mainly from their own observation and experience rather than from lectures or reading. The skilled professional trainer does not serve as a group leader but rather helps the group members to discover and to operate their own leadership resources. The T-Group is sometimes called "sensitivity training" because participants become more aware of their own feelings, the feelings of other persons, and of the way their own behavior affects others. (The writer prefers "sensibility" training.) Further, the group strives for frank, free, open communication on a basis of mutual trust. This climate, when achieved, permits the group to use more fully the potential resources of all members, to reach decisions based upon true consensus, and to engage creatively, flexibly, and adaptively in cooperative action toward shared goals.

T-Group training dates from some experimental innovations introduced at Bethel, Maine, in 1947, by Kurt Lewin, Leland Bradford, Ronald Lippitt and their associates. Each year since then, in increasing numbers, business executives, chiefs of government units, community leaders, and other persons who exercise influence have sought improvement in interpersonal and organizational effectiveness through some such laboratory training. Because so many of the professional trainers have come from the discipline of social psychology, there has been continuing research to test the effectiveness of procedures (Durham, Bigg, 1961; Weschler, Schein, 1962).

The effects of feedback to members on their performance in a group have been studied in a series of well designed experiments by Gibb at the University of Colorado (1955). Students who were given nine weeks of training in such activities as observing group process, using interaction categories to classify behavior in a group, and role playing in typical group situations, gained (on before and after tests as compared with a control group) in ability to see themselves objectively. They were better able to rate themselves as others would rate them. Another experimental group which had similar training, but the added factor of learning how they had been rated by their fellow group members on several occasions, showed an even greater gain in accuracy of estimating how their personalities would be rated by a new and different group of associates.

Other studies at the Human Relations Laboratory in Colorado have shown that the productive efficiency of problem-solving groups is increased by feedback from process observers. Emphasis in the feedback upon how group members seem to be feeling proved more helpful than emphasis upon their understanding of the task and their methods of intellectual work. Feedback oriented toward feeling did more than task-oriented feedback to raise the level of satisfaction in the group and to encourage more nearly equal participation by all members. When the feeling feedback was positive—indicating praise and approval—the effects were more beneficial than when the feedback dealt with negative feelings. The observer who communicated the report on member behavior was received by the group in accord with the consonance hypothesis. If he emphasized positive feelings, the group saw him as a pleasant, congenial, warm person. If the same individual, in reporting to another group, referred mainly to negative feelings, he himself was perceived as cold, critical, interfering and not helpful to the group.

Clark (1963) reported that noticeable improvement in skill of communication was observed in four of ten participants; one grew less free and open. A major factor differentiating those who improved most was their sense of warm support from others in the group.

A study (Massarik, Carlson) using the California Psychological Inventory, showed that sensitivity training enables the average participant to feel freer and more spontaneous. Miles (1960) demonstrated that school principals who went through a two-week T-Group training improved communication with their co-workers and were able to achieve a larger number of genuinely shared decisions. Change after eight months was reported by associates in 73 percent of participants and in 29 percent of controls.

A careful study with controls was made by Boyd and Ellis (reported by Buchanan, 1965). Ten men who had been in laboratory training were compared with a matched number who had attended a seminar built around case discussions and lectures. A third comparable group served as controls. Data were collected from supervisors, peers, and subordinates six weeks after training and again six months later. The question was: "Have you noticed any change in X's behavior?" Desirable, positive changes were reported for 64 percent of those who had been in T-groups, but by only 23 percent of the seminar group and the control group. The changes appearing notably in the laboratory training were: better listening; better participation in meetings; and increase in flexibility.

A particularly interesting finding was that, in analyzing what is needed to improve a problem situation, 58 percent (of 42 laboratory participants) showed an increased tendency to think of their own behavior as a factor needing some change.

Abstract 16 of a larger study shows that T-Group training brought substantial and significant increases in sensitivity, openness, awareness, and other factors clearly related to better conduct of human relations.

Another study (Gibb, Allen pending) emphasizes a different kind of gain from sensibility training. "The T-group trained . . . were more vigorous in challenging the ideas of other group members, more 'hard-nosed' in their comments, more open in their criticism of persons, ideas, etc. This runs counter to a common stereotype about Bethel training." A related finding in this same research was that after training (as compared with a before-training test), members participating in a series of group-decision tasks had fewer private unexpressed reservations about the jointly made decisions. Later (Chapter 13) we shall note the use of T-Group training to improve executive action in business and industry.

Abstract 16

TITLE · · · The Effect of Laboratory Education upon Individual Behavior

AUTHOR · · · Douglas R. Bunker

PROBLEM · · · How do adults change as a result of T-group and laboratory experiences?

SUBJECTS · · · 346 persons who had attended three-week (in 1960) or two-week (in 1961) training laboratories; compared with an equal number of matched controls.

PROCEDURE · · · Each participant rated himself eight to ten months after he had returned to his job. In addition, each was rated by from five to seven work associates: supervisors, peers, and subordinates. The questionnaire asked an open-ended question about changes in behavior in working with people.

Responses were coded by a procedure giving better than 90 percent agreement among coders and also more than 90 percent on a recoded sample.

SOME FINDINGS · · · 1. Ratings placed three times as many men who had experienced laboratory training, as compared with controls, in the top third in amount of change observed.

2. Five times as many of the laboratory-trained group reported one or more changes verified independently by an associate.

3. The areas in which change among the laboratory-trained most exceeded change among controls were:

   a. increased sensitivity to others (35 percent *vs.* 10 percent)
   b. greater acceptance of others (49 percent *vs.* 29 percent)
   c. more openness to new information (42 percent *vs.* 23 percent)
   d. more receptive listening (34 percent *vs.* 16 percent)
   e. greater awareness of behavior (34 percent *vs.* 16 percent)
   f. heightened sensitivity to group processes (24 percent *vs.* 9 percent)
   g. better ability to relate to others (36 percent *vs.* 21 percent)
   h. more comfortable and at ease in social interaction (36 percent *vs.* 23 percent)
   i. more insight into self and role (36 percent *vs.* 24 percent)
   j. increased interdependent cooperation (38 percent *vs.* 27 percent)

SOURCE: *J. appl. behav. sci.*, 1965, I: No. 2.

Group work in the classroom

Groups facilitate learning

It has sometimes been assumed that the ideal educational procedure is tutorial, one teacher working with a single student. From this point of view, school classes are a necessary compromise in the interests of the economics of mass education. Actually there are some indications that individual learning may be facilitated by working in a group or class with others.

After discovering that a typical student group, deciding by vote at each point, could learn a maze faster than could 98 per cent of the individual members, working alone (Gurnee, 1937), a psychologist decided to explore the learning of each individual whether working alone or in the group. He used both a maze test and a series of arbitrary choices between two numbers presented on cards. Those who had worked for six trials as members of a group made fewer errors, in an individual test, than did those who had had six trials alone (Gurnee, 1939). The superiority of learning in the group situation may lie in the fact that the group choice was more often correct; hence budding errors were checked almost at their inception and with some sense of deviation from the group. Correspondingly, right responses were reinforced and a sense of group approval was added to the strengthening effect accompanying individual success.

In an extensive series of experiments (1,200 students) Robert Thorndike (1938) tested the ability of individual students to select the right answer for questions concerning geography, economics, and current events, and also to choose the better of two poems. Students were then given ten minutes to discuss these questions in small groups and were re-tested. Apparently the discussion helped. Mean scores increased.

The McAdory Art Test consisting of 72 plates, each presenting four variations of a picture, was given to 168 college girls. Five days later, they met in groups of four to discuss half the items in the test. After five more days the original test was given again. On the items discussed, the average student gained nine points; on the remaining items five points. A control group, given the before-and-after test with no intervening study or discussion, gained only one-half point (Simpson, 1938).

If the discussion time had been spent in individual reflection and re-study of the task, would there have been a similar gain? This was tried by Timmons (1939). Students read material on improving the Ohio system for paroling convicts. They ranked five proposed solutions which had been ranked by experts on the matter. Some students then took part in group discussions; others re-studied the given factual material. A re-test showed substantially more gain in retention from the group discussion.

An experiment in learning nonsense syllables was tried with students at the Sorbonne in France (Perlmutter, de Montmollin, 1952). Half the class worked first as a member of a three-man group; the other half worked individually. Those who had begun in a group had a significantly better total score. Apparently working first in the group not only gave a higher initial score (groups always did better than individuals) but also laid a basis for better individual work later on.

As long ago as 1926, an experiment was reported which used an actual classroom situation (Barton). High school pupils in first-year algebra were divided into two sections, alike in I.Q., in preliminary training, and in performance on an algebra test covering work up to that point. For four periods, members of one section then did individual assignments while the members of the other section worked by discussion in small groups. Retests showed more gain from the group discussion.

A more recent project (Hurst, 1960) compared lecture, group discussion, and group decision procedures (the last required students to agree on recommendations for handling proposed cases) as a way of teaching a unit in educational psychology. Tests of factual knowledge, attitude, and ability to apply the facts were used. No significant difference in factual knowledge was found, but the students who had been required to reach group decisions did best on tests of ability to apply what had been taught.

As we saw in the preceding chapter, group participation draws most individuals toward acceptance of the group norm. In one experiment (Pennington, et al., 1958) both group discussion and group decision were found to contribute about equally to convergence of individual estimates toward the group mean or the consensus.

The decision whether students should work mainly alone or in groups will depend upon the educational objectives. Creation of a painting or a poem expressing one's unique experience is clearly a task for the individual left to himself. If the objective is to stimulate the student's awareness of differing viewpoints and to get them to criticize his former assumptions—as in many courses in philosophy, law, ethics, business problems or in the interpretation of current events—then group procedures are clearly desirable. They serve also to increase self-awareness and should be part of any good training in psychology or mental hygiene. If skill in working with others is essential, as it is for business leaders, industrial managers, public officials, teachers, clergymen, social workers, and theatrical directors, then experience in small groups offers excellent laboratory opportunities.

A study (Watson, 1953) in which graduate students of education rated their small-group activity (within a large class) shows many problems still unsolved. About two-thirds of the students found their leaderless small group discussions very satisfying and more rewarding than most graduate courses. For 15–20 percent the experience was rated as "marvelous" and "as educative as any experience I ever had." But for another 15–20 percent the group proved frustrating, unsatisfactory, and a waste of time. While some groups averaged better than others, there were often both "high" and "low" ratings in the same group. No group was rated consistently high or low by all its members. A typical group proved very valuable to some members, good to others, and a waste of time for still others. Size of group (varying from five members to 15) was not a major factor in success. Whether the group worked cumulatively at one long project or discussed a different topic each week made no noticeable difference in member satisfaction. There was no consistent relationship between the academic grades of students and their appraisal of the value of their group experience. It was rather surprising that students who entered the group acknowledging some prejudice against that kind of education emerged just as well satisfied as those who had previously found group discussion very rewarding. We conclude that working together in small groups is likely to be a highly educative and satisfying experience for *some* students. We do not yet know how to define the factors which make the group work so productive for some and so unprofitable for others.

Group psychotherapy

A paraphrase of the UNESCO charter might run: "Since neuroses begin in interpersonal relations, it is in interpersonal relations that the defenses of mental health must be built." All psychotherapy (except, perhaps, auto-suggestion) is interpersonal, but in group psychotherapy special attention is paid to the feelings which members create in one another. The psychotherapeutic group is no less a working group than is a classroom group, a community committee, or a board of directors. Its goal is more like that of the classroom group, however, because the aim of each member is to gain as much help as possible for himself. Most committees have one common problem toward which each member contributes; in the psychotherapeutic group there are different sets of problems in each member. It would be no advantage—it may even be a disadvantage—to assemble a group all of whose problems are very similar. In a group so homogeneously ill, members might well sustain illusions, distortions of reality, and rationalizations of their fellow members. Differences of age, sex, occupation, and emotional history can all be useful in the psychotherapy group.

The therapeutic power of the group results from a combination of factors. First and foremost is the therapist. A group of disturbed personalities, meeting without a competent therapist, might well hurt more than help each other. More will be said about the therapist in the next chapter. His capacity to be aware, at every moment, of what is going on within each member and between or among members, spoken or unsaid, and his ability to use either words or silence to facilitate constructive emotional growth is the central healing factor.

Catharsis—pouring out one's troubles to others—is a well-recognized aid in emotional adjustment. Troubles too long nursed in private grow unbearable. Most people have experienced the relief of getting certain problems "off their chest." The fellow group members who merely listen render a real service.

Many people are further helped by awareness that others have similar problems. Too often members have assumed, sometimes for many years, that their problems were unique. They are surprised and relieved to find that other people also have strange fears, trouble with parents, resentment toward siblings, worry over trivialities, thoughts that are usually considered improper, and even, at times, homicidal or suicidal impulses. Part of the effectiveness of Alcoholics Anonymous has been awareness by participants that alcoholism is a shared rather than a uniquely individual problem.

In an earlier chapter we referred to the multiple transference or parataxis which is so vividly seen in group psychotherapy. Each member is reacting not only to the actual persons in the room, but also to what those persons symbolize for him. One member may hate his neighbor because that neighbor reminds him (maybe unconsciously) of a brother who seemed to him to be favored at home and in the community; he may expect a rebuke from an elderly lady whose appearance and manner suggest to him his nagging grandmother; he may feel quickly attracted to someone who in some way resembles an earlier love. Part of the process of group psychotherapy consists in analyzing and untangling these hidden expectations. The neighbor is not really a rival sibling; the elderly lady may be much more tolerant than Grandmother was; the object of infatuation at first sight may prove very uncongenial on further acquaintance. In group psychotherapy members learn to recognize the distortions which have previously corrupted their interpersonal adjustments and to make suitable corrections.

Group members are often able to give each other helpful insights, and this ability increases as their own adjustment to life improves. When a group works together for some time, each member gets to know something of the early life of every other, his joys and sorrows, his hopes and frustrations, his day dreams and night dreams. Frequently one member will recall to another some incident which illuminates a present problem. The group thus provides an enlarged memory for each individual. Every disturbed person has emotional "blind spots" which keep him from discovering easily in himself relationships which other group members can see quite easily. When the member has come to feel comfortable enough in the group to be able to accept such interpretations of his own behavior, his fellow members have a great deal to offer.

Despite their personal problems, which are very absorbing, members of psychotherapy groups come to feel strong linkages with their fellow members. When one member, previously too fearful to come unaccompanied to group meeting, finally made the trip on his own, there was real jubilation in the group. And the awareness that his fellow members would all be celebrating with him played a significant part in his own determination to meet the challenge.

Negative, hostile, aggressive, and rejecting feelings toward others are also expressed in group psychotherapy. Frequently one member threatens to withdraw because he "can't stand" some other. Such feelings are freely expressed and accepted by the experienced group. Often the member who feels upset can be led to see this as a re-enactment of feelings he has had many times before. His proposed solution—running away—can be examined to see how well it has worked on previous occasions. Other members tell how they have learned to deal with some of their own, similar negative feelings. Eventually the disturbed member may be able to experience his feeling of antagonism on a new level. Always before it has been "out there"—caused by the bad other. One must run from the bad or be destroyed. Here in the group, the feeling gradually changes. The member faces his hostility as something produced by himself and with a variety of action possibilities he has never tried before. Negative feelings are among the most constructive opportunities for the therapeutic work group. No group in which everyone is always polite and considerate to everyone else is likely to be very therapeutic. On the other hand, free vent to interpersonal hostility is no panacea. A bout of mutual vituperation if not constructively analyzed, can do far more harm than good.

Bach (1954) has described sequential stages in the life of a therapy group as follows:

1. Initial situation testing accompanied by stereotyped attempts at rational problem solving.
2. Leader dependence. Didactic, directive processes.
3. Familiar dependence. Cathartic verbalization.
4. Associative compeering. Testing of interpersonal affects.
5. Fantasy play. Contextual associations.
6. In-group consciousness. Improved self-perception.
7. Work group ready for genuine problem solving.

Some evidence of the effectiveness of group psychotherapy is beginning to appear. Drs. Powdermaker and Frank (1953) evaluated changes taking place in 124 Veterans Administration patients under treatment. Some received only group psychotherapy; others received a combination of group and individual treatment. Among 18 patients who had been in group psychotherapy for from one to two years, all had shown some improvement and 15 of the 18 were rated as considerably or greatly improved.

Another study (Gorlow, Hoch, Telschow, 1952), based on analysis of verbatim records of three groups over about 20 sessions each, showed that there was a steady increase in such positive kinds of behavior as self-acceptance, acceptance of others, insight and understanding, and plans for positive action. Negative behavior (expressions of resentment toward self or others) was low at first, increased to a peak in the middle of this period of treatment and then decreased. Presumably patients had to feel some sense of security in the group before they could express such feelings.

Verbal expressions by patients during group sessions conducted by the author show: (1) appreciation of a sense of belonging in the group; (2) increasing spontaneity and ability to express real feelings; (3) reassurance that their problem is not unique but is shared by others; (4) relief at getting said some things they have never talked about before; (5) increasing sensitivity in perceiving the feelings of others; (6) recognition of recurring patterns in others and (later) in themselves; (7) gradual disappearance of symptoms which force patients to seek help in group psychotherapy; (It is interesting that patients often do not see any specific event or insight which freed them; they know only that they improved and that the group experience had something to do with it.); (8) increasing ability to be helpful to one another (not by being merely polite but by well directed, penetrating, yet well received, comments) in the therapeutic group; and (9) increasing competence in social relations outside the group.

Large meetings

Thousands of large meetings take place in this country every week: convention sessions, college lectures, parent-teacher associations, sales organizations, community service agencies, church groups, luncheon clubs, and many more. Some—like a pep rally, a political convention or a religious festival—are designed more for emotional impact than for intellectual work. Careful planning, in the light of well established principles of social psychology can do much to make meetings more productive.

The writer, lecturing to a large class in which students had been assigned their seats arbitrarily, noted that resulting grades on objective tests rose in a fairly steady gradient from the back of the hall to the front row and from the wings in toward the center. Sheer distance from the teacher seemed to affect what was learned. Griffith's (1923) observation's agreed, except that he found the very front row also peripheral. Other observations (Nagoon, 1932; Farnsworth, 1933) suggest that student achievement is highest in that part of the room to which the lecturer pays most attention. If a lecturer cannot see his audience and thus gets no visual cues to which he can respond, learning is seriously hampered (Leavitt, Mueller, 1951).

Lectures, at best, are not well recalled. A series of studies (Jones, 1923) using systematic quizzes after each of 42 lectures in psychology to college students, showed 62 percent of main lecture points remembered at the close of the talk, 37 percent a week later, and 23 percent after two months.

A major reason for the ineffectiveness of the large session is the passivity of most of the listeners. Various devices have been tried to stimulate participation and learning. Knowledge that a quiz will come at the end of the hour increases retention.

We have seen earlier that in groups larger than seven, one person often dominates while several members remain silent. A natural proposal is to break up the larger meeting into small groups. These have been called "buzz groups." Sometimes they are used at the beginning of a meeting to permit many members of the audience to describe experiences relevant to the evening's problem. Sometimes the issues are presented by one or more speakers, and buzz groups then thrash out reasons for taking one side or another. Or buzz groups may be used deductively at the end of a presentation to suggest possible applications of the proposed thesis.

Another device, especially useful when the audience is watching films or role playing, is to divide the large group into several sections, assigning those seated together in one area to identify with one character, those in a second area to try to feel themselves in the place of another character; a third section to project backward in time to what probably happened before the scene was presented, while the fourth section projects forward to imagine what will happen later. Any such assignments make members of the audience more alert and involved.

A panel has advantages over a single speaker, especially when members represent contrasting views on a controversial issue. Some panels degenerate into a set of speeches; good panels are conversational with give-and-take as lively as tennis volleys.

A forum, in which the audience asks questions (in writing or orally) of the speaker often transforms silent passivity into animated response.

Some congresses have papers sent out in advance to be read by participants before they come to the meeting. Then the actual session can be spent in back-and-forth questions and replies.

Large bodies which regularly convene, like a legislature or parliament, expect most of the creative work to be done by committees. Projects have to be developed into well formulated "bills" before the large body can act; if revisions are needed the usual procedure is to return the bill to a small working committee.

Any large meeting which is to accomplish something needs to be planned in a context; it is not an event by itself. There will normally be considerable advance preparation by small groups to define the purpose of the big meeting, to collect pertinent data, to arouse interest and to coach the chairman and speakers. Assuming that the large meeting is successful in contributing its part to the continuing process, smaller groups will need to follow up on the information, attitudes, and decisions which have emerged from the big session.

In our discussion of groups, small and large, we have drawn upon illustrations from classrooms, committees, and therapeutic groups. The effectiveness of any task-centered group is dependent in considerable measure upon the skill of its leader. In the ensuing chapter we shall examine similarities and differences in the roles of several kinds of leader.

CHAPTER FIVE

Leaders, teachers, therapists

Definition

The word "leader" has many connotations: pioneer, boss, superman, expert, demagogue, seducer, conductor, instructor, chairman, dictator, ideal example, helmsman, titled official, manipulator, or wise man. The leaders of history have been of many types.

Definitions of leadership commonly emphasize one or another of its many characteristics. Some start from the relatively high *status* or position occupied—leadership is seen as a structural feature of a social system. Other definitions emphasize popularity or *esteem*—the way the followers perceive the eminent member. Most small-group studies define leadership as power or *influence*. Thus if L's presence or activity induces change in F's experience, and particularly if L can get F to move toward or away from some goal, then L exercises leadership and F follows. Cartwright (1959) suggests that L usually sets up ambivalence in F; to some extent F wants to move in the direction urged by L, but L's efforts also arouse some resistance in F. Hence L's power to influence is the remainder after F's resistance tendency is subtracted from his tendency to accede to L. A variant of this definition is to emphasize the belief of followers about L's ability to aid or block them in their efforts to reach their goals.

Still other definitions enumerate the *functions* a leader performs. He is the central figure about whom the group clusters. He initiates structure and proposals for group activity. He makes more attempts than others to influence people and is usually successful. He is a communication center to whom and from whom most messages flow. He is also a symbol, a representative, and spokesman of the group in outside relationships. The leader may also be defined as the one whose presence and activity makes most difference in the way in which a group behaves.

Later in this chapter we shall be concerned with two particular kinds of leader—the teacher in his class and the therapist conducting a group. Their leadership is evident partly in their status, partly in their ability to influence the pupils or patients (not without some resistance!), and can be seen also in their actual behavior as they initiate structure, direct the flow of communication, and, by their presence and activity, exert a major effect upon what their groups do.

Identifying leaders

It is not always easy to determine who leads. In social interaction each person has some effect or influence upon the others. In marriage or friendship one partner may temporarily be the active leader, then the roles may be reversed.

Performance

Performance and status may serve to identify the generals who win battles, the rulers who promote the welfare of their nation, the corporation presidents whose companies achieve success, and the community leaders who get things done. The effectiveness of supervisory leadership in business was evident in one study (Feldman, 1937) of the efficiency of several sections of clerks in an insurance company. When supervisors were shifted about, the relative performance of sections changed. Some supervisors seemed able to raise the efficiency of any section to which they were assigned. This is a clear demonstration of one kind of leadership.

Another study in which members of groups communicated in writing while solving problems found that when groups chose leaders, the members chosen for leadership had ranked high in number of messages sent and in number of items of information and thought offered (Shaw, Gilchrist, 1956).

Reputation

Many studies rely on reputation as an adequate indication of leadership. Those persons who are generally regarded as leaders in any organization usually have earned this distinction. An inquiry conducted in a boys' camp (Lippitt, Polansky, *et al.*, 1952) posed the question: "Who is best at getting others to do what he wants them to do?" Reputation for being influential showed a high correlation with the actual frequency with which boys tried to influence others, were successful in getting others to change, and were modeled or imitated by the other boys. Hunter's (1953) exploration of the persons frequently nominated as centers of power in a medium-sized city enabled him to identify some 40 persons who made the most important decisions. They were what Kurt Lewin (1951) has called "gate-keepers." They allowed or blocked the passage of others. In the city under study, incidentally, although one-third of the population was Negro, not one of the 40 was of that race.

A study (Bigg, 1950) of choices made by young men who had worked together in groups of ten for three three-hour sessions, showed a large overlap between the group choice of a leader for the next session and member choice of personal friends. It seems probable that causation here works both ways. Popular persons are nominated for leadership and prominent persons are sought after as friends.

One difficulty has emerged in attempts to identify leaders by asking others—e.g., in the armed forces—which persons they would most like to have lead their group in an activity. The same persons who are nominated for leadership are likely also to be nominated as chosen "followers" (Hackman, Moon, 1950). Both nominations reflect liking for and trust in the other person; the distinction between leading and following is submerged in the general desirability of the companion.

Actions

Activities of the individual during social interaction may be used to determine his leadership. The number of attempts that he makes to initiate influence, the degree of assertiveness in his attempts, the absence of evident resistance to his attempts, and the actual number of attempts which succeed, all correlate about .60 (Levinger, 1959).

The leaderless group discussion (LGD) has emerged as a particularly good setting in which to identify leadership characteristics. It was used extensively by the Office of Strategic Services during World War II. Bass (1960, p. 189) summarized 17 different studies which have tested the correlation between the performance of men in LGD and their demonstrated leadership in fraternities, in Reserve Officers Training Corps, in bomber crews, as foremen in shipyards, or as Civil Service administrators. The correlations average about .40—high enough to be respected but not high enough for reliable individual selection. The correlation is higher when the leadership role is in the same kind of situation. Leadership behavior in one LGD correlates as high as .90 with leadership behavior in the same group a week later. If the second situation is also an LGD but with a different set of persons, the correlation drops to about .70. An LGD rating can predict leadership in a debate with a correlation of about .60, but can predict leadership on a physical construction task with a correlation of only .30. As the difference in task and situation increases, the usefulness of LGD behavior as a predictor diminishes.

One exception to this rule may be seen when the members come into the LGD with important status distinctions. Thus if the president of a corporation participates in a nominally "leaderless" discussion with a group of employees of much lower status, they will defer to him and he will show most of the behavior patterns, characteristic of the leader, regardless of what may be the subject of discussion. He will be the one who talks most (despite, perhaps, his good intention to draw out the others), the one to whom most communication is addressed, the one who gives pertinent information, the one whose objection leads immediately to dropping a proposal, the one whose expression of favorable support quickly brings acquiescence from the other members (Bass, Wurster, 1953).

It is a little surprising that the single factor of time spent talking in an LGD should prove to be so highly correlated with other indices of leadership. Everyone can, of course, recall groups in which someone made himself quickly unpopular by attempting to monopolize the discussion. Over the short range, amount of time spent talking in such a case would correlate negatively with leadership. But the nuisance is usually squelched or excluded as the group continues its work. Studies (e.g., Slater, 1955) have shown that generally the ones who speak most are nominated as having contributed the best ideas. Bass (1951) found that time spent talking in an LGD correlated .65 with success in leading management training. French (1950) found leadership in a college group correlated over .90 with verbal output in an LGD. In a study (Shaw, Gilchrist, 1956) which limited communication to written messages back and forth among members, those who sent most notes were the ones rated highest for "leadership."

Homans (1950) examined five different social systems and found similar leader behaviors in all of them. Leaders consistently initiated interaction; lived up to group norms; neither blamed nor praised members in the presence of others, and avoided giving orders that might not be obeyed.

Personality traits

While different groups and different activities require different characteristics in leaders, some individuals seem to rise to leadership in a range of settings. Before Benjamin Franklin reached 30 years of age, he had been chosen Public Printer for the colony of Pennsylvania, had founded the famous and influential Junto club, had brought out the most widely read publication in America (*Poor Richard's Almanac*), had founded the first circulating library, and been elected Grand Master of the Freemasons Lodge of Pennsylvania. The next year he inaugurated the first fire-fighting company in Philadelphia and was chosen clerk of the Pennsylvania Assembly. He was one of the most successful business men in the colonies, but had enough interest in scholarship and research to be the founder (he was then 37 years of age) of the American Philosophical Society. From then on until, when, over 80 years of age he led in the group enterprise of devising the Constitution, he served in a variety of leadership posts in politics, the Army, science, diplomacy, and education, founding the Academy which became the University of Pennsylvania. A biographer (Fäy, 1929) writes, "Nobody could approach him without being charmed by his conversation, his humor, wisdom and kindness."

Intelligence

Intelligence is certainly a prerequisite for Franklin's kind of leadership but it may be doubted whether Franklin or John Adams or George Washington possessed the highest I.Q.'s of their period (Cox, 1926). A follow-up of the careers of 1,000 highly intelligent children from California showed that relatively few of them had reached the roster of famous leaders (Terman, 1947). Twenty-five years after their childhood selection, none had attained high political office, or the presidencies of corporations or colleges. Only 5 percent were in *Who's Who* and 13 percent in *American Men of Science*. There is evidence (Hollingworth, 1924) that when individuals have remarkably high intelligence they are too far beyond the rank-and-file to communicate readily and to arouse trust and confidence. The very highly intelligent may lead in scholarship, but are unlikely to win out in the competitive struggles of business, army careers, politics or statesmanship. Leaders undoubtedly average above the median intellectual level of their followers, but mental ability by itself is no guarantee of influence, prominence or power. Bass (1960) estimates an average correlation (based on 24 studies) of about .30 between verbal intelligence and leadership behavior.

Physical superiority

Franklin was taller, heavier, and better looking than most of his peers. Physical superiority is an essential element of leadership in gangs. Doc had to fight and defeat every other member of his street-corner group (Whyte, 1943). In one of the early studies, Gowin (1915) found from insurance company records, that bishops were taller, on the average, than clergymen; that railway presidents were taller than station agents;

that sales managers were taller than salesmen; that university presidents were taller than the average professor.

A study (Partridge, 1934) in a Boy Scout camp showed that the boys chosen as leaders and actually most influential were a little older, taller, heavier, stronger, and faster, as well as more intelligent. The limitations of this kind of generalization are apparent, however, when we think of some leaders of small physique, like Napoleon or Gandhi, who have won tremendous loyalty from their followers.

Personality adjustment

The value of emotional adjustment for leadership is controversial. Some leaders, like Adolf Hitler, have shown signs of emotional maladjustment. Data on more modest scales of leadership—for example among boys in a camp—show that the leaders tend to be a little above average in their emotional health as in their physical prowess. Rosen (1959) reports a correlation of .48 between success in influencing other campers and score on an adjustment index. Among naval cadets (Izard, 1959), those who had gone to the infirmary for what were diagnosed as psychosomatic complaints, were distinctly less likely to be nominated by their fellows as showing a potential for leadership.

Drive

Most leaders seem superior to their followers in energy, drive, determination to succeed, and in self-confidence. They lead because they want to; they work at it; they do not easily give up. Leadership usually implies success in some kind of struggle. Apathy and opposition must be overcome. This requires stamina. Several studies show that successful executives are high in need to achieve and desire for excellence in their performance (Cox, 1926; Gardner, 1948; American Management Association, 1948; McClelland, Atkinson, et al., 1953). Observation of girls most apt to be chosen by their fellow pupils in an institution for delinquents, showed the leaders to be far more enterprising, active, and involved in acts of initiative (Jennings, 1943). A study of 50 school executives showed that those who most highly valued moving up on the scale of promotion and advancement had actually been most mobile in advancement in their careers ($r = .39$. Seeman, 1958).

A "virtuous circle" operates in leadership. Those with more than average self-confidence are more likely to try to influence a group; successful results then add still more to their confidence. (Bass, 1960, pp. 298, 299).

Embodiment of group norms

Another general characteristic of leaders is that they exemplify the norms and ideals of their group. Pigors (1955) has said: "Followers subordinate themselves, not because the leader is utterly different, but because he is the same, only more so. They follow because they can understand and appreciate what their allegiance involves." Merei (Abstract 11) showed successful leaders adopting the norms of their followers.

In Doc's street-corner gang (Whyte, 1943) the leader was expected to be an outstanding bowler, also to help members who needed money or were otherwise in distress, to be fair, and to keep all promises. Scientists choose as their leaders men whose work has set high scientific standards. Members within the same group but with different needs choose different leaders who meet their requirements. Thus Jennings (1943) found that those who chose Jean responded to her enthusiasm and enjoyed her showoff tendencies. Quite a different set of girls in the same institution chose Jacqueline, who was quieter, more sensitive, and seemed better able to understand the moods and needs of others.

Change in situation

A change in the situation may bring about the rejection of old leaders and the emergence of new ones. In J. M. Barrie's play, *The Admirable Crichton,* a shift from a well organized city house to a desert island transforms the servant to master. The type of American financial leader normally prominent lost much of his influence from 1932 to 1934. Chapter 6 will show how often changed situations alter behavior and attitudes.

Cumulative success

A virtuous circle can operate also in the interaction of reputation and leadership. A pupil is elected or appointed to some minor post. This calls attention to him and gives him a little prestige. If he is a congenial person and does his job reasonably well—no better, perhaps, than many others might—he is in line for the next higher position. Gratified, he exerts himself to serve, to please, and to succeed. So he moves ahead again. Emergence at a high level of leadership is commonly the result of numerous earlier successes, each of which led to the next opportunity.

New responsibilities tend to flow to those who already have some reputation. "Forms of power and influence are agglutinative; those with some forms tend to acquire other forms also" (Lasswell, Kaplan, 1950). Even in families, those husbands who have done best in prestige and income outside the home are more apt to be granted rights of dominance on decisions within the home (Wolfe, 1959).

A vicious circle operates also in leadership. Disappointed over not being chosen, an individual often behaves in such a way that he is even less likely to be given leadership responsibility another time. Once a pupil—or an adult—has acquired a reputation for being unreliable (even if undeserved) he is finished. The reputations of some cumulate toward high prestige, but a man given a bad name can be undeservedly rejected.

Inconsistencies

Evidence that leadership is not a single consistent trait can be found in the many instances in which a man with a record of past success fails at some new undertaking. Distinguished generals have often become heads of states, but not always with continuing acclaim. Ulysses S. Grant was not a great President and later, as head of a banking house, his failure was calamitous. Woodrow Wilson headed a university with distinction and led the United States triumphantly through World War I but his ability and enormous prestige did not assure his success as a builder of a world organization to keep the peace.

Conclusion

The effort to find some key trait that is common to the personality of all leaders and will always result in successful leadership has been unrewarding. We prefer to think of leadership not as inherent in some individual, but as describing a form of social interaction. Leadership is as much dependent on the traits and needs of the followers as it is of those who provide the initiative and direction. The interrelationship between leaders and the led is clearly evident in the case of authoritarian leaders. It takes at least two persons with complementary needs to make possible any dictatorship.

Authoritarian leaders

Most leaders throughout history have been authoritarian. Whether they led by virtue of an inherited title, their ability to persuade, or their power to coerce, they stood *above* their followers. They made the decisions and their followers, with more or less good will, accepted them.

Authoritarian leadership implies interaction. If we see strong leader dominance in groups from nursery school (Parten, 1932) to the modern corporation (Argyris, 1957) there must be corresponding readiness to accede to such control. Bass (1960, p. 226) quotes a National Research Council book: "No amount of legal authority over the grizzly bears of British Columbia would enable you to get yourself obeyed by them out in the woods." Authority becomes power only when subordinates accept it.

All human beings begin life in total physical dependence. As babies we were once wholly dependent on parents who were bigger, wiser, more competent and powerful. Most human beings go through life with some tendency—the transference, as discussed in Chapter 2—to respond to father-substitutes who seem bigger, wiser, more competent and powerful. We bring out of childhood a built-in readiness to follow authority figures. We invent supermen to fit the pattern of our needs. The real problem for social psychology is not the authoritarian leader but the emergence in some situations of other forms of leadership. From the earliest days of prehistoric and even pre-human existence, the herd has had its strong and dominant leader. When any situation becomes extremely frustrating, even competent and normally self-reliant adults search for someone on whom they can depend to set things right in what Erich Fromm has called "escape from freedom."

In discussing, in the preceding chapter, how groups proceed to work together, we noted that they usually have to deal first with the power question. They want to know who is going to lead. If the official status leader abdicates, as in some T-groups and therapy groups (Bradford *et al.*, 1964; Bion, 1949–1951), members struggle to replace him. They feel frustrated by the lack of direction. Discouragement turns to apathy and a desire to withdraw. A "strong leader" seems to be the way out. A general sense of frustration and despair in Italy and Germany preceded the rise of Mussolini and Hitler. After study of 35 dictatorships, Hertzler concluded that usually disillusion, resulting from problems too great for the old regime, led to the demand for a strong leader (1940). Hook (1943) has reported that, historically, the more acute the social crisis, the greater the demand for a hero-savior.

In very large groups, members commonly expect the good leader to make decisions for them without consulting them (Hemphill, 1950). They accept direction as a matter of course or of preference. The average member invests relatively less of himself in his large group affiliations. To surrender decision making for this little segment of his life, is no great sacrifice of autonomy. Indeed, to try to participate effectively in the affairs of a large college, church, trade union, or political party would be very time-consuming. It is simpler to let the responsible officials run the organization.

Sometimes the authoritarian leader, with the wholehearted support of his numerous followers inaugurates important social changes. William James (1880) was one of the many (Jennings, 1960) who espoused the "great man" theory of history. Carlyle's *Heroes and Hero Worship* minimizes the contribution of other social forces and exalts the divine revelation which comes into the world through prophets like Mahomet, poets like Shakespeare and Dante, priests like Luther and Knox, and rulers like Cromwell or Frederick the Great.

Arnold Toynbee in his extensive *Study of History* (1934) distinguishes between the creative leaders, who arouse *mimesis*, or spontaneous loyalty, and those leaders who dominate by coercion. In its most vital period of development, a civilization generates creative leaders. Later, when the social aim diminishes to consolidating the prestige and position the state has already won, the leadership becomes merely dominant. A related distinction has been made by Pareto, an Italian political theorist (1916). He has introduced the conception of a "circulation of the elite"; the "lions" do the pioneering; then the "foxes" follow and shrewdly gather in benefits for themselves. Eventually new lions arise to challenge the corruption and drive out the foxes.

The craving to be dependent contends with another strong human drive for autonomy and independence. Authoritarian leaders usually combat this unwelcome resistance by reliance upon tradition, threat or personal gifts. They lead by custom, by coercion, and by charisma. We shall explore each type briefly, but it should be recognized that in life most leaders use a combination of assets. The commanding general on a post leads partly by virtue of his abilities, partly by virtue of the respect given his position, and partly by his power to punish any who disobey. The professor in a class also combines in his leadership some admiration for his talent, some deference due his position, and some conformity because otherwise the student might suffer.

Charismatic leaders

Charismatic leaders are fascinating. Biographers try in vain to account for the magnetic attraction which centers in certain outstanding personalities. The term "charisma" implies some sort of divine grace, miraculously bestowed. Garibaldi won the loyalty of his Roman soldiers with an unusual appeal: "What I have to offer you is fatigue, danger, struggle and death; the chill of the cold night in the fall air, and heat under the burning sun; no lodgings, no provisions, but forced marches, dangerous watchposts, and the continual struggle with the bayonet against batteries—those who love freedom and their country may follow me!" Winston Churchill offered "blood, sweat and tears" but sustained the faith and courage of millions. One thinks of Alexander, Julius Caesar, Washington, Robespierre, Bolívar, Lenin, Sun Yat Sen, and Gandhi—so widely different in personality and yet all able to inspire confidence and to demand sacrifice of even life itself from their followers. The attempt of most biographers and historians has been to discover the secret somehow in the character, personality, mind, or invisible aura of the charismatic leader himself. While most famous leaders do have considerable ability and strength, the differences between them and other human beings of their time is not of the same order as the differences in reputation.

Our social psychological definition of leadership has turned attention from the traits of the leaders, to the process of mutual interaction. Men want their rulers to be great; this enhances their own dignity. Yet the repressed need for self-direction and autonomy may break out in a rejection of the idol which is as unwarranted as the earlier adoration. Charisma has its inverse side. The masses need supermen but they also need scapegoats and villains as targets for projected resentment and hatred. Mussolini and Hitler at the peak of their influence were regarded by their followers as supermen; after defeat, the mobs despised them. Popular adoration is notoriously fickle. Shakespeare has immortalized the shifting loyalty of Roman crowds from Caesar to Brutus to Mark Antony.

A long line of faith healers from primitive medicine men to the evangelist Aimee Semple McPherson and contemporary miracle workers, testifies to the powerful effect which one man's faith in another may exert, even upon bodily processes. Franz Mesmer started his career in Vienna in 1777 with his apparent cure of a case of blindness by the use of magnets. Soon he discovered that stroking by his hands alone could produce similar therapeutic effects upon patients. Crowds besieged him in Paris despite reports by distinguished scholars accusing him of being a charlatan. It is not necessary to assume that Mesmer was dishonest. The results he achieved no doubt led him to conclude that he did possess mysterious powers. But 50 years later hypnosis was identified and provided the explanation for Mesmer's accomplishments.

In charismatic leadership we see the effects of something like hypnotic suggestion reinforced and magnified by social support. Often the leader's reputation for greatness reaches the followers in advance of their actual contact with him. They come to hear him, prepared to be awed. Stories of his achievements may run far beyond the facts—including such tributes as belief in his miraculous birth and precocious childhood. Even those who have come prepared to scoff find themselves powerfully influenced by the enthusiastic responses of their neighbors in the audience. It is told of one man that when Wendell Phillips had finished a stirring oration against slavery, and the audience arose with wild applause, one skeptic was seen struggling against the counter currents of the crowd. He was observed stamping his feet and beating his hands together as enthusiastically as anyone in the hall, but shouting as he applauded: "The confounded liar! The confounded liar!"

Special readiness to follow and the social pressure from other submissive followers make for a response which may become magnified in recollection and in the re-telling. Those who once saw or shook hands with a folk hero are unlikely to diminish their own prestige by allowing his to wane.

The great charismatic religious leaders provide impressive evidence of the cumulative growth of a following. Moses, Buddha, Confucius, Jesus, and Mohammed each came in actual contact with only a few followers and were seldom widely acclaimed. Yet each in time became a figure who seemed to meet the spiritual needs of millions of adherents. It is no disparagement of the historic leaders themselves to recognize that their followers have created around the actual personality a somewhat different symbolic pattern which remains at the heart of the continuing religious movement.

Charismatic leaders are sometimes invented. Most peoples have tales of gigantic heroic figures. It is hard to disentangle the historic acts of a Perseus or Theseus or Sampson or Sir Lancelot from the accumulated legends. Was there ever a Paul Bunyan? It does not really matter. Surely the need that is met today by a figure like Santa Claus or Superman is independent of any historic figure. Each culture forms the heroes it unconsciously needs.

Leaders by custom

Leaders by custom occupy those positions or roles in the social system toward which followers are supposed to be deferential. The deference need have no relationship to the actual abilities of the person occupying the dominant position. In monarchical societies, the king may be feeble-minded or corrupt or insane, but he remains the King. A tribal chief or the owner of a business may likewise have inherited a position which has no relation to his own merits. The right to direct and control is associated with the position, not with its incumbent at some particular time. The obligation to obey the authority figure is felt to be bound to the position rather than to the occupant. This important social fact may be symbolized by the king's crown, the mace in Parliament, the judge's robe, the policeman's badge, the priestly vestments, or the deed to the land. We shall be exploring further in Chapter 6 the extent to which positions and roles control social behavior. Here we note that customary leadership provides an excellent illustration of our thesis that authority figures need not necessarily have any kind of superiority apart from their titles and official symbols.

A confirmed bureaucrat is another type of the leader by custom and position. His personality is wholly submerged in his role. When he leads, it is only in accord with the prescribed rules and expectations which he is careful never to exceed. He is acutely aware of his obligations to those above him in the hierarchy and expects the same unqualified acquiescence from his subordinate functionaries.

Coercive leaders

The warden of an old-fashioned prison or the head of a concentration camp may control by coercion alone. It is not necessary that the followers he dominates feel the slightest loyalty to the man or to his position. He controls their lives simply by his power to beat them, torture them, or kill them.

Not all coercion is so unlimited. An army officer giving an order to an enlisted man, an employer directing an employee, a teacher telling a child what he must do, or a traffic policeman stopping a motorist is only under specified conditions entitled to say, "Do this or else!" From time to time we all feel pushed around by authority figures toward whom we feel no devotion or even respect. We obey out of fear of the consequences of disobeying.

The ruler by coercion is in an unstable situation. Outward conformity may be accompanied by inner rebellion. The need for autonomy may be suppressed but its emotional drive is not eliminated.

The coercive leader is surrounded by advisers who fear him. No one dares to bring him unwelcome news. Hence he is likely to be ill-informed about anything which does not exalt his own self-esteem. Since his subordinates are afraid to venture on their own initiatives, they appear to be without ideas or courage. The "self-fulfilling prophecy" operates: the leader assumes his subordinates to be stupid, incompetent, and dependent; their action confirms this expectation. They dare not show the tyrant their orginality, initiative, and capacity for self-direction. Coercive leaders seldom develop competent successors.

Every coercive dictatorship contains within it the seeds of its own destruction. Resentment smolders in followers and may flare up against the dictator unless it be deflected against weaker scapegoats. "Uneasy lies the head that wears a crown." Every dictator finds himself surrounded by those who would like to be dictators. Whyte (1943) found that the chief threat to a gang leader is one of his own lieutenants. Many a dictator has been deposed by a cabal in which persons he himself raised to important military or cabinet posts played a major part. Hitler and Stalin purged as their most threatening rivals some of those who had been closest to them during their rise to power. Ruthless repression may sustain the tyrant in power for a time, but, as another saying has it, "One thing you cannot do with bayonets is to sit on them."

Technological changes in weapons of destruction may modify the processes of social control. When everyone fights with his fists, a stick or a stone, the followers can readily combine successfully against a single leader. When every man had a gun, rebels could outnumber and outshoot the king's men. Atomic weapons are another story. Immense destructive power can now be concentrated in the hands of a very few—conceivably in the hands of a single ruthless maniac. The people of the world could one day find themselves coerced by a leader and his gang with no scruples about the destruction and maiming of millions. A whisper of a suspicion of revolt would provoke retaliatory destruction of vast populations and areas. Eventually such a dictatorship, too, would collapse but "eventually" could prove to be an intolerably long time.

Experts

The type of authoritarian leader most acceptable in the modern world is the expert. As knowledge has increased so rapidly, the public finds itself unable to rely on tradition, childhood schooling, or firsthand exploration. To learn the latest about outer space, world affairs, national economics, state laws, electronic data processing, Parisian styles, television sets, child care, or diet, we rely on experts. We must.

Experts differ in their readiness to share their special knowledge. Some physicians and dentists make an effort to explain as much as the patient is interested in learning. One mark of the quack is his desire to mystify. He tries by hocus-pocus to give the impression of esoteric knowledge, far beyond what any ordinary man could hope to grasp. The problem of experts in some fields—nuclear energy, for example— is that despite their desire to enlighten, they cannot explain their work to people who are unfamiliar with the basic concepts of modern physical science and mathematics.

The public is therefore forced to turn to other experts to validate the testimony of the first group. To the uninitiated, a conflict in viewpoint seems to be a problem of deciding which experts have the most prestige. But sometimes the established authorities are wrong.

Most leaders are, to some extent, experts. The leader of a combat air crew is usually an expert flyer (Jenkins, 1947). The leader of a construction firm must know his business. A judge should know the law. An orchestral conductor must be superior to most of his players in his understanding of the total musical score.

In experimental situations, the person in command of the pertinent facts usually becomes, at least temporarily, the leader. (Hemphill, *et al.*, 1954; Wolman, 1956). It has been reported that the late Senator Robert M. LaFollette, Jr., achieved his eminence partly by studying the technical reports on pending legislation to the point where he was better informed than his opponents. As problems of management and administration have mounted in complexity, outstanding executives rely less upon personal drive and magnetism and more upon their ability to marshal, organize, and interpret the relevant facts.

Other central figures

Since leadership depends so largely on the feelings of the followers, there can be as many types of leader as there are shared needs among people. The charismatic leader is admired and almost worshiped; the coercive leader is feared. But a process of interaction between a central figure and those who are responding to him may involve many motives other than admiration or fear. Among the ten types of leadership-followship identified by Fritz Redl (1942) the first and second involve admiration; the third, fear; but other emotions predominate in the remaining patterns. Redl's ten types are as follows:

1. The patriarchal sovereign.
   Followers look up to him, seek his approval, fear his disapproval.

He incorporates their "superego" or conscience.
2. The leader.
   The followers wish to be like him; he is their "ego ideal."
3. The tyrant.
   The followers fear him.
4. The love object.
   The followers all choose the central person as object of their affections.
5. The hate target.
   The followers are united by their shared hostility to this central person.
6. The organizer.
   The central person enables the group to do something they could not do without him; he is the necessary facilitator.
7. The seducer.
   The followers who have been in inner conflict respond to the central person's action; since he started it, the barrier is broken down and others may sin with less anxiety and guilt.
8. The hero.
   The followers who have been in inner conflict, respond to the central person's action; his bravery helps each follower to overcome his own cowardice.
9. The bad influence.
   Since the central person feels no conflict about his "bad" behavior, the followers can act with less guilt and anxiety.
10. The good example.
    Since the central person feels no conflict about his "good" behavior, the followers feel confidence in similar behavior. Both 9 and 10 are neatly explained by Redl as "infectiousness of the unconflicted personality constellation upon the conflicted one."

The authoritarian personality

Some people like to dominate or be dominated. They see the world as a continuous struggle in which the stronger come out ahead and the weak submit. This personality pattern, called the "authoritarian" or "antidemocratic" has been extensively investigated by social psychologists. It is measured by an instrument called the "F- (for fascist) scale." Interest has been stimulated especially by the fact that this concept links the dynamics of individual personality with positions on vital social issues.

The history of the research illustrates its connection with political viewpoints. Before Hitler came to power in Germany a group of German social scientists was already apprehensive. They asked themselves what force might possibly hold back the rising Nazi tide. They could not

Abstract 17

TITLE The Authoritarian Personality

AUTHORS T. W. Adorno, Else Frenkel-Brunswik, D. J. Levinson, and R. N. Sanford.

PROBLEM Is there a type of personality which is particularly susceptible to antidemocratic propaganda and hence potentially fascistic?

SUBJECTS Some 1,500 men and women in colleges, professional groups, labor groups, service clubs, middle-class groups, church groups, psychiatric clinic, state prison.

PROCEDURES Tests were developed for Anti-Semitism (AS-scale), Ethnocentrism (E-scale), Political-Economic-Conservatism (PEC-scale) and Implicit Anti-democratic Attitudes. The last named has become widely known as the F-scale, because it is concerned with susceptibility to fascism. Many subjects were also interviewed, given TAT and other projective tests.

SOME FINDINGS Intercorrelations of the several scales suggest a common factor:

	F-Scale	A-Scale	E-Scale
AS	.53	—	—
E	.73	.68	—
PEC	.52	.43	.57

The type of personality associated with the term "authoritarian" has components of: (1) conventional values; (2) authoritarian submission, as shown for example in not questioning family or religious standards; (3) authoritarian aggression; (4) anti-intraception, which is expressed in opposing introspection, paying attention only to the objective and external rather than to inner thoughts and feelings; (5) superstition-stereotypy; (6) pseudo-toughness; (7) concern with power; (8) cynicism about human nature; (9) projectivity, meaning a tendency to imagine strange, evil, destructive forces at work in much of life; and (10) preoccupation with sex as dangerous and immoral. TAT pictures are often interpreted by those with high F scores as involving an act of impulsive aggression (manslaughter, rape, murder) which is condemned and for which the offender must suffer severe punishments. Parents are seen as dominating and children as submissive. Men are domineering toward women. Sex is seen as an instrument of power for achieving conquest and status.

Subjects scoring low on the F-scale show more self-acceptance, more matter-of-fact attitudes toward parents and other relatives. For low scorers sex is more apt to imply warmth, companionship, and mutual affection. Low-scoring persons are more tolerant and understanding; high scorers are more repressed, rigid, and inclined to project disturbing feelings onto suspected threats from outside themselves.

SOURCE: Published by Harper and Brothers, 1950. See also summary in Swanson, Newcomb and Hartley, *Readings in Social Psychology.* New York: Henry Holt (revised), 1952, pp. 612–622.

trust the Prussian army or the aristocracy which were closely allied. They saw little strength in the wavering middle classes who never fought for anything or in the unorganized peasants. Only the working class might have the necessary power, but research indicated that children of workers were as firmly bound by autocratic paternal authority as any others. Democracy had no real strength in German family life; hence, the social scientists concluded, it could have no solid foundation in the political affairs of the nation. These social scientists decided to leave Germany even before the Nazis came to power.

After emigrating to the United States, this group asked themselves, "Might fascist movements succeed also in the United States? Can it happen here?" Their hypothesis was that a certain type of personality is especially susceptible to the appeal of authoritarianism. They argued that, in a democracy, the bent toward being a dictator or submitting to a dictator is a constant peril. By tests, interviews and case histories they tried to discover what sort of person seeks to dominate others or to be dominated by others. The general outline of their study is in Abstract 17, and this is followed by a case study of a high scorer.

Case 2: Mack—A Student High in Authoritarian Ideology

Mack, a 24-year-old undergraduate, plans to study law. He is of Irish extraction. Mack's mother died when he was six and his sister ten. Their father worked in a lumber mill. Mack finished high school, had a year in business college, then a wartime Civil Service job as a clerk in Washington for a while, and was in the Army but given a medical discharge because of "stomach trouble." His upbringing was strict. His mother and the aunt who took over after the mother's death insisted on regular church attendance, but since high school Mack has been busy with other things. He was a sickly child. His father was stern, shy, disliked meeting people, and had a quick temper.

On the test of "Anti-democratic Trends" (the F-scale) Mack scored higher than the mean of any group tested except the men in the San Quentin prison. Among the items which contributed to his relatively high score were the following, to which he agreed:

	Mack's response
(Conventionalism) "What a man does is not so important so long as he does it well."	+2
(Authoritarian submission) "It is essential for learning or effective work that our teachers or bosses outline in detail what is to be done and exactly how to go about it."	+3
(Authoritarian aggression) "Homosexuality is a particularly rotten form of delinquency and ought to be severely punished."	+2
(Anti-intraception) "Novels or stories which contain mainly action, romance and adventure are more interesting than those that tell about what people think and feel."	+2

(Power and toughness) "To a greater extent than most people realize our lives are governed by plots hatched in secret by politicians."

+3

(Destructiveness and cynicism) "When you come right down to it, it's human nature never to do anything without an eye to one's own profit."

+3

(Projectivity) "The sexual orgies of the old Greeks and Romans are nursery school stuff compared to some of the goings-on in this country today, even in circles where people might least expect it."

+1

(Sex) "Sex crimes, such as rape and attacks on children, deserve more than mere imprisonment; such criminals ought to be publicly whipped."

+2

Following are some direct quotations from the interview with Mack. *Politics:*

I worked there in Washington and saw things I would put a stop to. There is a concentration of power in the bureaus . . . I was the right-hand man of the General there when the OWI was introduced . . . It was fun knowing about the background, knowing about the secret committees . . . Eventually the President will have to appoint a strong Cabinet to run things for him. There is no doubt that the system is becoming more centralized . . . Dewey's honesty and straightforwardness appeal to me greatly but a man has to use some underhandedness to get across the highest ideals.

Minorities: Mack agreed with the statement: "Negroes have their rights, but it is best to keep them in their own school districts and schools and to prevent too much contact with whites." He asserts: "It would be a mistake to have Negroes for foremen and leaders over whites." He also would agree that: "Citizens or not, no Jap should be allowed to return to California."

Crime: Interpreting a TAT picture of an older and younger man together Mack said: "The young fellow indicates the type of person who might do violence if pushed too far . . . I think he could easily murder somebody on being oppressed."

Searching for some questions which would predict anti-Semitism without specifically referring to Jews, the Anti-Defamation League found that agreement with the following five propositions correlated highly with the score on both the F-scale and the scale of Anti-Semitism.

1. The most important thing to teach children is absolute obedience to their parents.
2. Any good leader should be strict with people under him in order to gain their respect.

3. Prison is too good for sex criminals. They should be publicly whipped or worse.
4. There are two kinds of people in the world: the weak and the strong.
5. No decent man can respect a woman who has had sex relations before marriage.

Among the many correlations with the F-scale, the following are typical. High authoritarians have been found to be significantly:

1. more prejudiced against unpopular minorities (Campbell, McCandless, 1951).
2. committed to traditional views of the proper roles for husbands and wives (Levinson, Huffman, 1955; Nadler, Morrow, 1959).
3. more conservative or reactionary in political attitudes (Gump, 1953).
4. less able to participate effectively in democratic or leaderless groups (Bass *et al.*, 1953).
5. unable to make accurate estimates of attitudes of others (Christie, Cook, 1958).
6. more frequently Catholic; less frequently Unitarian, Congregationalist, Jewish or non-religious (Levinson, Schermerhorn, 1951).
7. more frequently studying engineering than psychology or other social sciences (Davidson, Kruglov, 1953).
8. more suspicious and exploitive in human relations (Deutsch, 1960).
9. more apt to come from culturally underprivileged backgrounds and to be low on education. The correlation of F-scale with intelligence or with years of education in samples of adults runs $-.50$ to $-.60$ (Christie, Cook, 1958).

In the course of the research on the F-scale, several improvements have been made on the original technique. For example, the items were all stated in such a form that acquiescence gave high F scores. Christie *et al.*, (1958) worked out a balanced version which made it possible to correct for response-set and to measure authoritarianism and acquiescence as separate variables. A second criticism has called attention to the bias of the F-scale toward identifying right-wing authoritarianism of the pro-fascist variety. Hence Communists usually score very low. But there is obviously a left-wing or pro-Communist kind of dogmatism, intolerance, tendency to domineer, and to exploit others. Rokeach (1956) has developed a Dogmatism Scale which focuses on rigid, stereotyped thinking, whether tending left or right politically. This updates a scale measuring "Fair Mindedness" developed by the author (1925).

Authoritarian dictatorships are not simply strange, subversive foreign systems of government. There are numerous parents, teachers, supervisors, employers, and officials in every community whose bent is toward command and whose interest is power. The struggle for democracy is not primarily a matter of foreign relations. Discomfort in egalitarian situations and distrust for democratic procedures are deeply rooted in almost every institution of American society.

Benevolent despot

Some political scientists have argued—in line with theologians—that the ideal government would be that of an absolute dictatorship by an all-wise and benevolent despot. The trouble in practice seems to be the discovery and certain identification of any such human being. Democracy is resigned to making the best of what we have—fallible individuals who are able to pool their resources in making decisions more often right than wrong. We turn now to a study of democratic leadership.

Democratic leaders

Chapter 4 introduced a distinction between mobs and democratic groups which corresponds in many ways to the distinction between authoritarian and democratic leadership. Under an authoritarian ruler, the individual member merely submits. His own insight, knowledge, feelings, and will are subordinated to the orders given him by the leader. He is a puppet, not a responsible person. Democratic leadership is quite different; it calls forth the maximum contribution from each member; it respects his ideas, his values, and his capabilities. Democratic leadership helps each member to be more fully and completely himself than he would be if the group had no leadership.

Not laissez faire

Democratic leadership challenges a common assumption that a group must either have a dominant leader or dissolve in anarchy. A democratic leader is not one who passively permits each person to do as he chooses. The democratically led group is a real working group, with common goals and effort efficiently directed toward those ends. The goals in a democratic group are worked out by the members and the leader planning together. So are the methods to be followed. Duties are assigned by the group to its members. The group evaluates its own progress or lack of progress. Each of these steps—setting goals, planning, working, evaluating—requires good leadership.

Not merely permissive

Some pseudo-democratic groups are actually under temporarily suspended authoritarian domination. The term "permissive" suggests that someone has the power to deny or to permit. The power figure may withdraw into the background, but his influence is felt, although it is not overt and explicit; group members are left to guess how much the real ruler will tolerate.

A student council in a college may be genuinely democratic if the limits of its power are laid down in rules and members are free within those bounds to set goals, to plan, to carry out and to evaluate without interference from higher authorities. Frequently, however, the allegedly democratic student group is told that it is free, only to find that the faculty, deans or other administrative officers impose their well-meant but unwelcome control.

Very similar problems arise within large corporations. In a phase of decentralization, powers are delegated to local managers or to standing or special committees. When these new responsibilities are undertaken, however, it may turn out that work has to be done to suit some higher official. The frustration of discovering arbitrary control behind a democratic facade is conducive to cynicism.

Participatory

It is ironical that democratic leaders, despite their respect for the viewpoints of members, often exert more influence than those who try hard to dominate or persuade.

Two kinds of discussion leadership, called "participatory" and "supervisory," were compared in their influence on the attitudes of college students toward twelve possible candidates for President of the United States (Preston, Heintz, 1949). The participatory leaders were trained in techniques of leading democratic group discussions. The supervisory leaders were not trained, but were asked only to get the group to reach a decision within half an hour without any expression of the leader's opinion. Before-and-after ranking by the students showed that discussions led by participatory leaders more significantly changed the opinions of the individual members.

A similar study (Hare, 1953) was carried on with Boy Scout groups who discussed the value of each of ten items of equipment for a proposed camping trip. The discussions were led by patrol leaders slightly older than the boys. Participatory leaders achieved more consensus among their members and, as in the college discussions, more individuals changed their earlier opinions after a democratically conducted session.

A wise leader, recognizing the danger of undue influence and of too ready an acceptance of his ideas, may wait quietly to see whether others develop the point he has in mind. If the point is not brought out, and it seems important, the leader will then feel free to make his contribution. He will do so, however, in a way which invites others to disagree or to criticize. His aim is to enable the group to find a wiser answer than his own or that of any single member.

Supporting the minority

An important function of the democratic leader is to prevent majorities from silencing minority viewpoints. A film, *Twelve Angry Men*, tells the story of a jury in which all but one member are ready to vote "Guilty." As discussion proceeds, enforced in this case by the unanimity rule rather than by a leader, more and more evidence comes to light, leading members to question their initial position. At the film's end, all are persuaded that the 11 were wrong and the one was right. One experiment (Maier and Solem, 1950) in groups with and without leaders showed that the greater success of the groups with a trained leader came largely as a result of his effectiveness in preventing a stampede and of his insistence on exploring the ideas of those who took a deviate position.

Task and maintenance

Chester Barnard (1938) in a famous analysis of the work of the business executive concluded that in every successful group two problems must be solved: (1) performing the required task, which Barnard calls "achievement," and (2) keeping members well satisfied, which Barnard refers to as "efficiency." Sometimes a closely similar distinction is made between the *external* demands set up by a group, e.g., a task, and the *internal* demand, which is to bring satisfaction to group members.

The leader's functions related to group maintenance include: keeping interpersonal relations friendly, encouraging participation, providing for self-direction, setting conditions for emotional expression, easing communication, responding sensitively to emotional needs of members, offering warmth in personal relations, listening attentively to members, showing liveliness and good humor, respecting dignity, expressing solidarity, and helping members to feel pride in belonging.

The leader's functions related to achievement or task-mastery include: helping to set and clarify goals, drawing out resources within the group, making other resources available, testing proposals, exercising judgment, preventing discouragement and strengthening persistence, keeping personalities from distorting discussion, pacing activity in relation to available time, establishing standard operating procedures, offering good ideas, and enabling the group to measure its progress.

These two broad categories of function—group maintenance and task-achievement—need to be kept in balance. If a group becomes over-concerned with one, the other may suffer. A group which becomes highly task-centered but neglects the feelings of members cannot count on their continued help. (A group which becomes too conversational may be abandoned by its members because it accomplishes little.) Blake (1964) in his *Managerial Grid* suggests that it is possible to attain a maximum simultaneously on both dimensions, concern for production and concern for people. He rejects the compromise position which would sacrifice something of each. The manager's problem will be discussed further in Chapter 13.

Sometimes two different types of leader, representing these two functions, can be found in the same group. Twenty small groups of male undergraduates, after meeting and working together four times, voted for the most popular member, the one who contributed the best ideas, the one who did most to guide the discussion, and the one who stood out most definitely as a leader. The man chosen as leader was also the discussion guider in 80 percent of the cases, the idea man in 59 percent of the cases, and the most popular in only 25 percent of the cases. A record of time spent speaking showed that the most talkative was regarded as the leader (or vice versa) in 55 percent of the cases; the person to whom most remarks were made was the leader in 65 percent of the cases (Bales, 1953).

Another study (Slater, 1955) of 44 groups in which the idea man (who is rated by other members as having contributed the best ideas for solving problems) is different from the most popular man in the group, used the Bales categories to define characteristic behavior differences for these two roles. The most popular men introduced more statements of positive feeling (shows solidarity, tension release, agreement). Idea men contributed more suggestions, opinions, and orientation. The most popular also asked more questions than did the idea men.

The relative concern for task and maintenance may well determine what type of member or leader the group will want. Wolman (1956) planted two members in student groups. One demonstrated the behavior characteristic of a good group member, as outlined in the preceding chapter, but he did not know the facts the group needed. The other behaved rudely and sarcastically, but he knew the answers to the kind of questions the group had to answer. Members were preparing to take a test on biographical details of famous psychologists. With this sort of task, the group preferred the knowledgeable expert, however unpleasant his manner, to the agreeable, but uninformed, man.

Understanding other members

It is important, for both achievement and efficiency, that a democratic leader be aware of the interests, knowledge, capacities, and feelings of group members. A leader who has had long experience with a given group has a great advantage in this respect over a newcomer. A study (Chowdry, Newcomb, 1952) in which leaders chosen by various groups were asked, along with other members, to estimate group opinion on various issues showed that—especially on issues related to the work of the group—the persons chosen as leaders made the best estimates of group opinion. Non-leaders who were reasonably well accepted in the group were second-best. Most erroneous estimates were made by isolates who were not sociometrically chosen by other group members. On issues not especially pertinent to the group (religious issues in a medical fraternity) leaders were not noticeably above average. What they demonstrated was not general all-around empathic ability, but familiarity with the affairs and norms of their particular social unit.

Another report (Kates, Mahone, 1958) deals with leadership rating and value profiles for students in a girls' dormitory and for members in a young people's religious organization. The value profile was based on a questionnaire concerned with interests, ethics, and philosophy. The students who most nearly approximate the norm of their group were rated higher on leadership.

Many leaders find it easy to understand members of their group because they are themselves so near the group mean. When they project their own values onto other members they are not far wrong. Those whose interests and values are quite different from the standards of the group will probably not become leaders; if they do, it will be because they have learned to understand feelings rather different from their own.

Concern for other members

The democratic leader, as a rule, not only knows his fellow members; he also cares about them. He is not remote and detached; he is involved. A study (Jennings, 1943) of the girls chosen to represent their cottage on the student council of an institution for delinquent girls showed that one of the most marked, differentiating characteristics of these leaders was their readiness to go to the administration on behalf of other girls. They made the welfare of their cottage mates their business. This technique resembles one practice of the political bosses. Precinct and ward leaders of a political machine make it their business to know the needs of voters in their area and to try to help where they can. The democratic leader differs from the political boss in that the politician's concern may be only a device for winning support. The democratic leader's concern is genuine and persistent.

Leaders in groups with democratic norms are best liked when they are regarded as *considerate* of their fellow members. In scores of studies of attributes of chosen leaders, most successful supervisors, best bosses, and skillful politicians, the following traits appear repeatedly:

"Friendly"
"Appreciates achievement"
"Gives praise when due"
"Stands by us"
"Gives support"
"Is warm"
"Easily approachable"

"Doesn't put on airs"

"Asks our opinion"

"Shows respect for us"

The armed forces have a tradition more authoritarian than democratic, but the best officers rely more on good human relations than on the authority to give orders and penalties. A study of the way 300 combat crew members rated successful commanders showed that the profile most prominent in the minds of the men was composed of elements like "friendly and approachable," "finds time to listen," "looks out for the personal welfare of crew members," and "does personal favors for crew members" (Halpin, Winer, 1957).

When children in an elementary school were asked to tell about two classmates, one who had previously rated high in ability to get others to do things for him and one who rated low in this measure of influence, the outstanding difference in the boy with the higher rating was his friendliness: "acts friendly," "a good person to do things with," "asks you to do things in a nice way," "doesn't start fights," "knows how to act so people will like him." Other qualities sometimes associated with leadership—expertness, brightness, physical prowess, similarity of interests, good appearance, and generosity—were all less differentiating than was the friendly manner (Gold, 1958).

Too close a relationship between the leader and his group members seems sometimes to be a liability. If the chief subordinates his own interests and values to pleasing the group, he loses strength. If he is too solicitous, he may seem artificial. If he likes everyone equally, he may not be objective enough to use wisely the human resources of his team. Thus Fiedler (1955, 1957) has found in basketball teams, work groups and combat crews, that the more effective leaders perceived a wider gap between their "best member" and "poorest member." The efficient leader keeps enough social distance between himself and his subordinates to be able to see them objectively.

This finding does not really contradict the thesis that the leader feels a genuine concern for his team members and treats them with courtesy and consideration. It warns against the leader's submerging his personality and insight in close friendships with all the members of his group.

Competence

Successful leaders usually possess more ability than the average group member at some tasks which the group values highly. A leader for a combat air crew must be an outstanding flyer (Wickert, 1948). In the Norton Street Gang (W. F. Whyte, 1943) bowling was the most significant activity, and status in the gang was closely related to bowling scores. The leader, Doc, ranked high, although one or two members sometimes surpassed him. Whyte states: "The leader need not be the best baseball player, bowler, or fighter but he must have some skill in whatever pursuits are of particular interest to the group."

Studies in the Air Force (Ruch, 1953) showed that good leaders originated new procedures and plans. A similar study of administrators and executives in civilian life (Rupe, 1951) again emphasized the competence of the leader at understanding the group's situation and developing good plans.

Whether leaders were officially designated or left to emerge from an unstructured discussion (Carter, *et al.*, 1951), the leader was observed to differ significantly from the average group member in two functions: "Diagnoses situation," and "Gives information on how to carry out action." The leaders of groups trying to solve problems of logical reasoning, mechanical assembly, and controversial discussion attempted to supply information about four times as often as did the average member. This proved equally characteristic of both the appointed and emergent leaders.

The competence of a member in the first of a series of tasks may set his leadership status for subsequent group endeavors. One study (Hemphill *et al.*, 1956) in which groups tackled four problems (mechanical assembly, strategy, construction, and discussion of ideas) found that whenever a member had been supplied with special information which enabled him to direct the group on the first task of the series, he tended to continue attempts to lead even though on subsequent tasks he had no special information and another member had been given the pertinent facts. Particularly in a crisis, when familiar ways of operating break down, the suggestions of a competent leader are sought. Hamblin (1958) devised a game in which play by the old rules suddenly was scored as "error." In these experimental groups, the emerging leader had more (three times as many) of his suggestions accepted by the other two members of the triad than did the average member. No such reliance on a single member's ideas was found in a control group where the rules of the game remained unchanged.

Ego strength

A democratic leader needs a rather different kind of self-confidence from that of the dominant authoritarian. The democratic leader must be sure of himself, not as a controller but as a contributor and coordinator. Sharing responsibility with his group, he must be able to admit that he does not have all the answers and that each of the other participants is superior to the leader in some respects. It takes more genuine self-acceptance to cooperate effectively than to pretend infallibility. One must be able to admit limitations honestly without minimizing real strength. If members are to be frank in expressing criticism, they must perceive the leader as strong enough to take it. A study of people who were described as leaders because of their popularity and influence in 23 therapeutic groups showed that these persons were the most candid in revealing their own feelings (Taylor, 1957). Experience in therapy and other kinds of training groups indicates that ego-strength, which permits the individual to express his own feelings frankly and to accept the feelings—both positive and negative—of others, can be increased.

Training democratic leaders

Most of the characteristics required for good democratic leadership can be improved by appropriate training. Knowledge can be acquired; attention can be directed toward the maintenance as well as the achievement needs of the group; the leader's own defensiveness can be reduced, and his perception of himself and others sharpened; skill in speaking to and influencing others can be learned.

Several studies support the conclusion that trained leaders perform better than those with equally good intentions but without training. Maier (1950) compared efforts to solve an industrial problem by 17 groups having trained leaders with 29 groups in which the leader had no special training for democratic discussion. The best solution was attained by about 70 percent of the groups with trained leaders, but by very few of the other groups. Leaders who had had some training were found, in experiments, already cited, to be more effective at getting agreement in a discussion group of college students (Preston, Heintz, 1949) and in a group of Boy Scouts (Hare, 1953).

Good training focuses on behavior as well as on theory. Studies of leadership ideology of school administrators and of aircraft commanders showed little relationship to their actual behavior (Halpin, 1955). Industrial studies indicate that men who think they are are quite democratic in relations with subordinates may be perceived quite differently by those whom they supervise. It is not enough to give courses on principles of good human relations. Men too easily learn the approved phrases without corresponding modification of their controlling habits. Hence role-playing has become increasingly important in leadership training.

Role-playing

Role-playing serves many purposes but is especially helpful in increasing empathy. Conflicts such as commonly arise between a mother and daughter, a supervisor and a worker, a husband and wife, or two leaders of competing organizations are often illuminated if each can be induced to act out the role of the other. Putting oneself in another person's role and trying to talk spontaneously with his interests in mind brings important changes in understanding and attitude. Or, seeing how someone else acts out a role which is difficult for you—expressing criticism of a fellow group member, for example, so that it will be accepted rather than resented—may improve your own performance in the actual situation next time.

The scene for role-playing is structured with a beginning; conversation is as natural and spontaneous as possible; the leader says "Cut" as soon as the main point has emerged. There may be criticism by the group of the way some of the roles were played. Usually a second set of persons will re-enact the same scene, showing how a different approach works out. Role-reversal is another variation. The person who played the aggressor in the actual occurrence may exchange roles with his victim. Another variation in technique is to make explicit the feelings which are hidden beneath what is being openly said. Sometimes this is done by the role-player himself raising his hand to stop the action while he makes an explanatory aside about his own feelings in the role. Then action is resumed as if nothing had interrupted it. Or an alter ego may be played by another person who stands behind the role player and accompanies the overt expressions with an attempted interpretation of what the actor is thinking but not openly expressing.

Role-playing, properly used, serves to enlarge and correct perception of the feelings of others, and to try out new ways of responding and interacting. Since the action takes place in a setting of play-acting and is not irrevocable as in the real life situation, there can be freer experimentation with one's own behavior. Those who watch and comment on the role-playing, although not so actively involved, often find themselves identifying with some of the actors and modifying their own ways of meeting such situations.

French (1944) reports a successful experience with an authoritarian Scoutmaster of the old school who was re-trained by role-playing to use a more democratic approach. The evidence indicates that even those leaders who have spent many years in traditional activities can learn a different method of work.

Another Bavelas experiment is summarized in Abstract 18. Schools of education give students courses in teaching for periods of two years and more, but seldom are they able to show changes in teaching behavior comparable to those which Bavelas achieved in three weeks. Probably the discouraged state of his students at the beginning of training was one factor in making them ready to change. Group leaders who are quite complacent about their habitual procedures would be more reluctant to try new methods. Other elements were the direct attention to behavior and small-group support for each learner.

Who improves most, given opportunity for leadership training? The Bavelas studies suggest that persons who felt they had been failures responded well to training in a quite different method. In contrast,

Abstract 18

TITLE   Morale and Leadership Training

AUTHOR   A. Bavelas

PROBLEM   Can poor leaders be quickly transformed into good leaders?

SUBJECTS   Six Works Progress Administration recreation leaders in a community center; three were retrained, the other three served as controls. Ages varied from 35–45; experience in recreational leadership averaged three years. All had been rated as poor or unsatisfactory group leaders.

PROCEDURES   All six leaders were observed on the job and their behavior with children was recorded in frequency of each category. Training consisted of a kind of "clinic on the job." Leaders observed one another at work. They observed the trainer working with their group. They role-played possible ways of handling incidents. They studied and criticized motion picture films of the way in which they had actually responded to situation on the job. They noted improvements from session to session in the records of their work. Theory was given incidentally in relation to actual behavior. Training occupied two hours a day, four days a week for three weeks. Then all six leaders were again observed and their behavior with children recorded.

SOME FINDINGS   Trained leaders gave fewer directions after training and vested more responsibility in the children. Untrained controls did not change. The success of the trained leaders was further evident in the fact that the number of children voluntarily attending their group doubled, pupil enthusiasm rose and remained high; the quality of the work produced improved.

SOURCE: G. Watson (ed.), *Civilization Morale*. Boston: Houghton Mifflin, 1942. pp. 143–65.

Klubeck and Bass (1954) found that training was relatively more effective with college girls who already ranked high in leadership status. Perhaps the explanation of the difference may lie in the degree of change promoted by the training. The high-level leaders could readily learn some improved techniques which fitted their general style. Bavelas was trying—and succeeding at—the more difficult task of bringing fundamental change from autocratic to democratic methods. Further experiments are needed to test this and other pertinent hypotheses.

Comparisons of types of leadership

The most famous study on the effect of various types of leadership is that which Ronald Lippitt conducted in association with Kurt Lewin and Ralph White (1939; 1960). Clubs of 11-year-old children were run by leaders who adopted for a period autocratic (themselves planning for and directing the youngsters), democratic (joint planning with group decisions), or laissez-faire (no leader intervention) methods. During the period under autocratic leadership pupils were more dependent and more egocentric (*I* vs. *We*). When rotated to a democratic leader, the same children evidenced more initiative, friendliness, and responsibility. These children continued to work even when the leader was out of the room. Their interest in the work and in quality of product was higher. Aggressive acts were frequent under authoritarian or laissez-faire leaders.

The findings portray typical reactions of members to a dominating leader. Most members submit, conform, and remain uninterested. A few grow resentful, but unable to attack the powerful figure of the leader, they make a scapegoat of someone more vulnerable. Only rarely does a member have the courage to rebel openly against the autocratic leader. An analysis of stenographic records showed that in groups in which there had been more open expression of hostility toward an autocratic leader there was increasing feeling of warmth and solidarity among the members themselves. In the comparison of participatory (democratic) and supervisory (autocratic) leaders of college student discussion groups, mentioned earlier in this chapter (Preston, Heintz, 1949), there were similar responses to the democratic leadership: more satisfaction with production, with the group, and the leader.

Another comparison of group discussions led by democratic and autocratic leaders (Fox, 1957) again showed that the democratically organized group was able to achieve more consensus and a higher level of satisfaction with the group decisions.

One way of characterizing the difference between these two forms of leadership is to note that the attention of an autocrat is directed toward winning or forcing compliance. The democrat has no problem in gaining assent; his concern is to upgrade the process by which the decision is reached (Maier, 1963). Maier does not try to prescribe a particular process; he recognizes that a good leader's methods will vary with the nature of the issue, the participants, and the feelings involved.

In the study reported in Abstract 19, decisions made by the leader without consultation were less well accepted than those made in some kind of discussion. Also impressive was the fact that men given the opportunity to decide for themselves were more likely to make the more dangerous choice; a characteristic of group decisions discussed in the preceding chapter.

The greater the ease of communication among group members the

Abstract 19

TITLE   Four Techniques of Group Decision Making under Uncertainty

AUTHOR   Robert C. Ziller

PROBLEM   How will groups react to decisions made with varying degrees of leadership authority and group participation in making the decision?

SUBJECTS   44 air crews (approximately 500 men) ranging in size from 8 to 13.

PROCEDURES   Each crew, with leader (crew commander) present, was read a problem (survival and escape in enemy territory, involving a decision whether to cross dangerous ice or make a lengthy detour around it). Four methods, assigned at random, were used: (a) *Authoritarian:* all think silently; leader presents his decision to crew and reports it to experimenter. (b) *Leader Suggestion:* silent thought; leader presents suggestion for decision to crew, asks their comments; after ten minutes leader reports essentially his own decision. (c) *Consensus:* leader begins group discussion in which he participates. After 15 minutes leader reports group consensus. (d) *Chairman:* leader serves only as chairman, offering no suggestions, remaining neutral. After 15 minutes leader reports decision of group. Following the report of the decision, all group members filled out a nine-item questionnaire reporting their reactions to the decision and the method of reaching it.

SOME FINDINGS   Members were least well satisfied with decisions made by (a) the leader as solely responsible. They were more willing to accept (b) decisions they had had an opportunity to discuss; best were the decisions (c) and (d), resting on group consensus.

When type of leadership was compared with actual decision made, it was found that leader-focused decisions (a, b) were almost equally divided (11 decisions to go around the ice; 13 decisions to cross); when the decision was group-focused (c, d) more decisions were made involving greater personal risk to members (3 to go around; 17 to cross the ice).

When decisions were made by the leaders, the crew members considered the problems less difficult than those which the members solved through participation.

SOURCE: *J. appl. Psychol.,* 1957, XLI:384–88.

higher the probability that democratic leadership will be successful. Shaw (1955) found that errors of decision in a "wheel" with one central position and three peripheral positions, each communicating only with the center, were greater with a democratic leader at the center (3.8) than with an authoritarian (1.3). But in the "common" net, where each of the four members could communicate freely with every other, there was no difference between the two leadership styles.

Hierarchical organization, with emphasis on status differences, typically restricts free communication and leads to preference for autocracy. Bass (1960, p. 407) cites a study of 100 groups supporting the conclusion that the greater the status differentiation, the stronger the tendency toward coercive leadership.

The clear differences in prestige level in industry make it difficult to use the techniques of democratic leadership. This point will be discussed further in Chapter 13. Factory workers are accustomed to a large measure of direction and to little participation. One study (Fleishman, 1954) showed that industrial workers preferred the leadership of foremen who were benevolent autocrats. The men did not ask to be consulted; they preferred to be told clearly the rules and their responsibilities. They did want a foreman to show some personal consideration, to pay attention to them as individuals, to be fair and also encouraging. But studies in the United States have shown that rank-and-file workers usually have little interest in participating in the responsibilities of their own unions and still less in sharing the tasks of management.

There is some evidence that this attitude reflects the autocratic pattern of top management. If foremen and other supervisors are encouraged to participate in democratic decision making with their superiors, this pattern of preference for democratic leadership carries down to the men they supervise (Pelz, 1951).

A study of decision-making conferences suggests that the amount of participation by members was unrelated to their degree of satisfaction, but that their answer to the question: "Did you feel free to participate as much as you wanted to?" was positive in the more satisfying meetings. In other words it is not so important that everyone share in leadership as it is that everyone feel that he could exercise influence if he wanted to (Marquis et al., 1951). Experience with faculties in colleges generally confirms this observation. The typical faculty member does not want to participate in all the administrative affairs. His view of the democratic institution is that someone else can run it as long as things go to his satisfaction; when they do not, he wants effective channels of influence.

We have seen that the preference for democratic leadership varies with the group, the task, and the situation. In times of crises there is a popular tendency to regress to dependence upon an authoritarian leader, preferably a charismatic figure symbolizing strength (Hamblin, 1955). Democracy is still a new social experiment. Not many families, schools, factories, businesses, clubs, communities, hospitals, military units, or churches operate with skilled democratic leadership. We Americans profess strong allegiance to Democracy, but our actual skills in democratic operation are few and fragile.

Distributed leadership

A democratic leader usually gets better results than does an autocrat. But if the members of a small group were all well trained and able to carry out the functions of a good group member as listed in the preceding chapter, would any one person need to be the leader?

Every group requires leadership, but that leadership need not be vested continuously in a single individual and exercised only by him. One person may be the leader when it comes to calling the group to order, another in describing the troublesome situation; a third may be an expert leader with more facts to contribute than any other member in the group; a fourth may be a leader because his judgment and character are so highly respected; a fifth may be the leader in that he possesses the most power, or is closest to the centers of power.

In some groups only the official leader defines the problem, calls on members to speak, keeps the discussion on the issues, summarizes, protects minorities, tests consensus, and announces conclusions. Members leave these jobs to the leader. If he fails, the group fails.

Advantages of distribution

There are several advantages in regarding leadership functions as proper for every member. First, if all group members are aware of responsibility for a given act of leadership, it is almost certain to get done. If one fails, another will try. Second, a sense of responsibility for the process keeps every member alert, involved, and responsive. It avoids the situation, too common, in which a leader works hard while the group remains apathetic. Third, group consensus is more likely to be correct than the judgment of any one member—even the best in the group. When it comes to deciding whether a group has said essentially all that it wants to say on a given point, no one person can know the facts as well as the composite group knows them. Finally, members feel more closely identified with the achievements of a group in which they have themselves been active leaders than they would feel in a group that was under the direction of someone else.

A study of leadership in Army squads that were especially effective in combat on the front line in Korea is summarized in Abstract 20. The evidence indicates that even in the military hierarchy, leadership functions are somewhat distributed. It is interesting, too, that among all the kinds of service leaders might render, the one most important for

Abstract 20

TITLE   Leadership in Rifle Squads on the Korean Front Line.

AUTHOR   Rodney A. Clark, *et al.*

PROBLEM   What kinds of leadership are evident in squads especially effective in combat?

SUBJECTS   81 rifle squads on the Korean front lines in the winter of 1952–53.

PROCEDURES   Questionnaires and interviews on civilian and military background of each man, his weapon information, attitudes toward his group and fellow members; criterion information about combat performance of 69 of the squads.

SOME FINDINGS   Official squad leaders did not do all the leading (managing, defining rules and procedures, performing as model, teaching, and sustaining with emotional support).
In 69 squads, 66 of the designated leaders, 49 of the designated assistant leaders, and 35 other men were observed in performance of leadership functions. The type of leadership activity most commonly seen was "managing," but combat efficiency was more highly correlated with the frequency of sustaining (r = .57), teaching (r = .46), and modeling (r = .43). Feeling of group loyalty correlated .30 with reported effectiveness in combat.

SOURCE: *Hum RRO Technical Report 21*, September, 1955. Reproduced by Document Service Center, Knott Building, Dayton 2, Ohio.

raising group effectiveness in the stress of combat was sustaining morale by emotional support. This is a type of service to the group which any member can give about as well as can the designated official leader.

In a study of problem solving by aircraft crews (Torrance, 1953) it developed that the important factor was not the presence of the leader or his democratic methods, but the presence or absence of diagnostic scales for directing the attention of members to significant factors in group performance. If the scales were used, either by a leader or without any designated leader, the group performance improved markedly. If no scales were used, having a discussion leader was of no help. The scales made it possible for each member to participate in a major leadership function—the diagnosis of procedure and suggested improvements.

The preference of groups for centralized or distributed leadership varies with the nature of their task, its urgency, and also with each member's skill in group participation. A study (Berkowitz, 1953) of 72 conferences of industrial, business or government committees showed very little relationship between "functional differentiation of the leader" (i.e., the leader behaving in ways different from members) and the ratings assigned the session on cohesiveness (r = .15), satisfaction of members (r = .33) or productivity, defined as covering every item on the agenda (r = −.04). Most businessmen have been accustomed to authority exercised by a responsible leader and might be expected to be a little more comfortable when that procedure is followed.

Member growth

People grow largely as a result of what they do for themselves rather than because of what is done for them. The leader who makes decisions for others may get quicker results, but he fails to equip his followers for making decisions wisely for themselves. The best leader makes himself dispensable; he develops capability and responsibility in the group.

Teachers

Teachers usually lead groups; individual tutoring is the exception. While education in classes may have been introduced primarily for economic reasons, the group setting often facilitates learning. In the preceding chapter we reviewed comparisons which showed that groups think better than their average member—sometimes better than their best member. Working at certain kinds of tasks in groups, pupils may learn more than they would learn if they worked alone. It does not follow that all learning should take place in groups. Some kinds of concentrated study and creative art may require solitude. Other important kinds of learning—skills of behavior in social relationships, for example—can take place only in groups.

Roles

Earlier in this chapter we listed ten roles which "central figures" play in groups (Redl, 1942). Four of them are especially appropriate to the relationship between pupils and teachers. One is the love object. A teacher may be leader of the class because the pupils are drawn by affection. The parent's natural question to a child returning from his first day at school is "How do you like your teacher?" This is a vitally important question which may affect the pupil's ability to benefit from the teacher's knowledge or instruction.

One college teacher of a large lecture course arranged to have 15 minutes of personal interview with each of a fair sample of the students in his course. During the interview they talked of the student's home, his family, his extracurricular interests, anything except the course work. All students heard the same lectures and took the same objective tests, but those who had been interviewed and given even that brief testimony of personal interest by the instructor did noticeably better on the tests. Achievement is clearly influenced by the rapport between teacher and learner.

Another type of central figure is the patriarchal (or matriarchal) sovereign whose approval is sought because he represents what is right. A traditional school attitude is respect for the teacher as a symbol of what the learner ought to want, of all that is regarded as fitting, right, and proper. Psychoanalysts recognize that each person has a part of himself, the superego, which threatens the ego with punishment for any deviation from the approved, undeviating path. The extent to which a pupil prefers a strict, severe teacher depends upon the pupil's own superego development. Unfortunately, those young people who need further restriction least are the ones who most welcome it and can best relate to a very demanding teacher.

An especially constructive pattern for the teacher-learner relationship is the ego-aid. The pupil sees the teacher as a useful aid in the accomplishment of the pupil's own objectives. While some coaches may be love objects for the students they train, and others may be like the superego figure of the arbitrary old tyrant who must be obeyed at whatever cost, most coaches are seen as aids to skill. What most learners ask of a coach is not that he love them, or approve their character, but that he develop the ability to run faster, kick farther, pitch more strike-outs, throw more baskets or swim better. The teacher in this concept is seen as an ego-facilitator, helping the learner do better what he already wants to do. An example is the experiment (Jack, 1934) cited in Chapter 2, in which pupils gained self-confidence because they had learned a new skill.

Still another role of the teacher is that of ego-ideal. The ego-ideal is the model the pupil tries to emulate. A tendency to seek out admirable people as models for imitation is strongest during childhood and adolescence but continues well into adult life. Many adults at one stage of their psychoanalysis wonder whether they should not change their vocation and become analysts. Many young men study biographies of business leaders and try to walk in the footsteps of the successful. In almost any university one may find an instructor who has copied some of the trivial idiosyncrasies of the famous head of his department.

These several types of teacher are theoretically distinct but in practice are likely to be combined. A successful teacher may represent some degree of affection, some embodiment of conscience, some assistance toward pupils' goals, and in some measure an ideal whom pupils would like to resemble. Every successful teacher offers a unique combination of these factors. A teacher who is not admired, respected or liked and whose efforts are not seen by learners as helpful in their purposes, has little likelihood of teaching anything. The failure, however, is not *in* the teacher; it is in the relationship. The same person could possibly be helpful, well liked, respected, and admired when working with a different group of learners.

The best teaching technique depends upon the emotional state of the particular learner. Pupils who have lost confidence in themselves respond better to incontrovertible success experiences than to challenges, criticism or praise. Pupils long accustomed to easy achievement are likely to be challenged by unusually difficult projects assigned by a teacher who remains dissatisfied with mediocre results. Individual learners differ from one another in the type of teacher from whom they learn best. The same learners may differ also from day to day. Even brief experiences during the day may affect the readiness of the pupil to respond.

Several studies (Walters, Karal, 1960; Walters, Ray, 1960; Erickson, 1962; Lewis *et al.*, 1963) have demonstrated that pupils who have been left in social isolation for several minutes just before a learning task were more quickly conditioned to give the responses personally approved by the experimenter ("Good!" "That's right!" "Fine."). One explanation offered has been that social hunger is increased by the lonely period. An alternative is that a mild anxiety is created which makes a word of commendation especially effective. This latter theory is supported by a finding (Lewis, Richman, 1964) that pupils treated in a brusque and unfriendly manner on the way from their classrooms to the experimental room were more quickly conditioned by approving comments than were pupils with whom the experimenter had tried to establish a warm and friendly relationship. That social isolation was more effective than the inconsiderate treatment may be explained by supposing that a child left alone in a strange setting may feel more anxiety than one who encounters the familiar experience of a cold, cross teacher-figure. The pupil's reaction may well have been hostility and rejection rather than anxiety.

Autocratic—democratic

Teachers, like other group leaders, may be generally authoritarian, laissez faire, or democratic. The evidence from the Lippitt-Lewin study, although collected on groups of only five members in a club, probably applies also to a classroom with 30 or 40 children. The autocratic teacher creates a climate in which children usually submit with outward docility but in which they accumulate inner resentment. The repressed hostility may lead to dislike of school, ineffective study, and occasional attacks on other pupils who become sanctioned targets because the teacher also regards these pupils as stupid or a nuisance. A laissez-faire teacher, who would permit any sort of disorganized and random activity without interference would produce in the classroom the same kind of dissatisfaction which appeared in the clubs. Eventually, perhaps, the pupils themselves would set up a structure of school work. Indeed, this is what did happen in several very free schools that the author visited in Europe. For several days—sometimes weeks—pupils who were left free to do as they pleased simply dallied. But they became visibly bored and eventually went to the teachers and proposed organized activities and even lessons (Neil, 1960). The Lippitt-Lewin experiment, covering only one free hour in a highly organized day, provided no opportunity for this self-direction to emerge. In a democratically organized classroom, we would expect to find, as in the clubs, more cooperation, more friendliness, more work-minded attitudes, and better learning.

Experimental results

A few experiments have been reported and they consistently confirm our expectations. Two groups of students in one study (Bovard, 1952) saw the film "The Feeling of Rejection." For one group the teacher was more of a directive influence; in the other, the group conducted its own discussion. Analysis of the tape recordings indicated freer expression of student feeling, more personal identification with the heroine, and more evidence of understanding in the group in which the teacher was less directive. In another investigation two teachers each taught two groups, one leader-centered and one group-centered. These correspond approximately to Lippitt's autocratic and democratic leadership. Each student, near the end of the (psychology) course expressed his feeling about every other member on an anonymous 11-point scale. Stronger feelings were expressed in the classes which had experienced the more democratic atmosphere, and these were usually positive. More interaction with fellow students brought greater liking for them.

Anderson and Brewer (1945–46) studied responses of second and third grade pupils to dominating, autocratic teachers and to integrative, democratic teachers. Under the democratic teachers, pupils were more interested, and showed more initiative. The authoritarian teachers produced conformity or resistance, with more misunderstanding and conflict.

Another study, typical of many, tried lecture methods with some sections of college students and group discussion of cases with others (Hurst, 1960). All students were tested for: knowledge of facts and principles; ability to apply the relevant principles in selecting appropriate behavior for 20 new short case incidents; and general attitudes on teacher-pupil relations. Statistical analysis indicated that the group decision sections, where students took more responsibility, had a clear advantage on the tests of attitude and ability to make applications. There was no significant difference between sections on the test of knowledge of facts and principles.

In a different kind of experiment, the value of student participation was tested in relationship to the single variable of feedback (Leavitt,

Mueller, 1951). Zero in feedback was represented by a section to which the instructor talked without ever seeing the class or hearing anything from them, conditions resembling a television talk. Under these conditions there was least learning. Number of correct scores increased with visibility of the class (the usual lecture situation). When brief student responses, such as "Yes" or "No," were permitted, learning was still better. Free responses from the class were most conducive to correct learning.

Democratic leading is concerned with the relationships within the class as well as the teacher-student interaction. An experiment reported by Deutsch (1949) compares groups in which each student competes with every other, with a plan by which students cooperate within their group but compete as a group with other groups. The emotional reactions of the cooperative groups resemble in many ways what Lewin and Lippitt found with democratic leaders; the ego-assertion and hostility in the competitive groups resembled more the climate created by autocracy.

Difficulties in democratic teaching

It is not easy for most teachers to sustain the role of democratic leader. Many factors combine to push them toward authoritarian control. One is that they are usually bigger and stronger than the pupils they teach. Another is that they are more expert; they know more of the right answers. A third factor lies in their own experience in school; most teachers during their school years had only autocratic teachers. Teachers tend to teach as they were taught. An extremely potent factor is the expectation of the principal, the supervisors, fellow teachers, and the community. In most communities the teacher is expected to rule his little kingdom with a firm hand. The children must not get out of hand. Steps toward democratic freedom are viewed with alarm as likely to lead to anarchy. Even the children have come to think that a strict teacher is a good teacher. Should an adventurous teacher try to pioneer by introducing a freer atmosphere in his classroom he is likely, at first, to meet the kind of experience which characterized the transition in the Iowa experiment from autocratic to democratic leadership. Children who had been over-directed had built up a considerable head of steam which they released by wild behavior during the first days of freedom. Eventually they settled down to cooperative work, but the experience of the first day or two could easily discourage a teacher attempting this form of leadership for the first time. Threatened by the hyperactivity of children escaping from repression, by critical attitudes among colleagues and supervisors, by his own uncertainty and inexperience with democratic procedures, it is quite understandable if the teacher retreats to a policy of domination.

A study (Jenkins, Lippitt, 1951) of the views which parents and pupils hold of teachers showed a strong emphasis by students on the need for teachers to be "fair." This implies power in the teacher to impose unfair demands—surely an authoritarian role. Again, 73 percent of the teachers approve pupils who are "respectful" and "obedient." Dominance by the teacher and submission by students seems to be the pattern generally approved. Incidentally, the relationship of teachers to parents turned out to be a rather one-sided need by school personnel to be accepted as friends by the other adults of the community.

In large classes the pressure toward teacher direction is increased. An instructor usually decides on the topics, class procedures, tests, and grades with little or no student participation. One consequence is that students whose grades are unsatisfactory usually place most of the blame onto the instructor, his tests, his procedures, and his idea of what is important (Hartley, 1952, p. 590).

Rogers (1951) has reported some success in teaching psychology and counseling by non-directive methods. The student-centered teacher, as described by Rogers, is more permissive than the democratic leaders in the Lippitt experiment. He comes closer to laissez faire, except that he does undertake to observe closely what is going on and to reflect back to the group their apparent feelings about what they are doing. The student-centered teacher is especially concerned with helping the students discover their real situation, while the demoncratic teacher participates more in the processes of planning and acting together.

One point of common misunderstanding needs to be clarified. However democratic or student-centered or permissive a teacher may be, there are always limits. A clear recognition of these limits is often reassuring to the pupils as well as to adult critics. Freedom in the classroom does not imply tolerance for every kind of acting-out of impulses, for irrelevant or disturbing behavior. There are positive goals for the class and for the school; any method must be appraised by the extent to which it advances or retards progress toward the accepted ends of education.

The teacher and group norms

It is commonly assumed that the teacher establishes the climate of his class—by his personality, his standards of scholarship, his methods, and his requirements. He functions, however, within groups which may have generated norms conflicting with his, especially when teaching students in secondary school and college. In different communities, youth vary widely in their valuation of school work (Coleman, 1961; Tannenbaum, 1962). Even at Harvard University, two sections of graduate students in the School of Business were found to develop different norms (Orth, 1963). Section A valued, and produced, popular social mixers. Section E valued, and produced, critical individualistic intellectuals. Neither section developed the active, cooperative self-direction of learning which the faculty valued and sought to create. The little experiment by Merei (Abstract 11) indicates that even a strong leader may not succeed in altering established group norms.

Therapists

The leader of a psychotherapeutic group has a role similar to that of the democratic leader of a youth group or the student-centered teacher in a classroom. All three confront individual differences and abilities and are responsible for developing a group climate that will lead members to engage in productive work.

A therapist usually deals with more disturbed personalities than are found in clubs of the community center or classes in the high school. There are exceptions, of course. It is easy for the layman to exaggerate the differences between the average personality and the neurotic. Almost everyone at some time during his life could benefit from psychotherapy. But because the psychotherapist's patients are generally more deeply disturbed, he has to discipline himself more carefully. Most effective leaders for therapy groups have experienced the self-revealing processes of some kind of psychoanalysis and have been trained by supervisors with insight. Unlike most teachers and group workers, the psychotherapist is equipped to recognize the pathological patterns that appear and reappear in disturbed persons. Some believe that medical training provides the best foundation for work with these cases. The psychotherapist who has had medical training is called a psychiatrist. Others advocate basic training in psychology, clinical psychology, and social psychology for the psychotherapist. Increasingly, social workers are also entering the field, treating groups of parents, groups of adolescents, or groups of other clients formerly seen individually.

Therapists working with alcoholics compared the effectiveness of procedures based on: (a) learning theory; (b) psychoanalytic theory; and (c) client-centered theory. The greatest gains were made under the last style of leadership in which the therapist reflected back to them the feelings of members (Ends, Page, 1957). The least gain came from the most directive and manipulative approach, controlled by learning theory. Follow-up after 18 months showed that the client-centered approach maintained its significant lead.

Another report (Halkides, 1964) compares ten highly successful cases with ten least successful cases. For each case, nine counselor-client interactions units were selected at random from recorded interview early in the treatment and nine from another record of a session near the end of treatment. These 360 excerpts were scrambled in a random order and rated for several characteristics. The items from "successful" cases were found to differ from the "least successful" (.001 level of statistical significance) in higher ratings for: "degree of empathic understanding manifested by the counselor;" "degree of unconditioned positive regard for client, manifested by the counselor" and "genuineness or authenticity of counselor's expression of his own feelings."

Analysis of their procedures shows that good psychotherapists share certain similarities, regardless of the discipline under which they were trained. One study (Fiedler, 1950) of individual psychotherapists adhering to several different schools (Freud, Adler, Rogers) showed that the successful and experienced practitioners resembled one another more than they resembled the novices in their own school. The practitioners agreed that the ideal therapeutic relationship is one in which the therapist stays close to the patient's problems, helps the patient feel free to say what he likes, keeps the patient active, accepts all the patient's feelings as understandable, and gives the patient the freedom to make his own decisions. The therapist, according to this consensus among therapeutic schools "is able to participate completely in the patient's communication," and he "sees the patient as a co-worker on a common problem." The distinguishing feature of the successful therapist was that he seemed to be fully aware of what the patient was communicating. This awareness is as true of a leader in group psychotherapy as of therapy with a single patient. The therapist in charge of a group must keep constantly in rapport with the feelings of those who are not speaking as well as of the one who, at any moment, holds the floor.

The categories devised by Bales (Chapter 4) to record participation in a group have been used also to report what a therapist does (Fiedler, 1950). The following table summarizes the type of response made to 27 typical statements of supposed patients, by 25 psychiatrists, 7 psychologists, and 9 social workers. Some had been trained as psychoanalysts, others had worked with Rogers on client-centered therapy. Bales' categories 2 (Shows tension release), 9 (Asks for suggestions), and 11 (Shows tension) appeared so rarely that these have been omitted from the table. Differences among the three professions (medicine, psychology, and social work) proved negligible. Leaders with a psychoanalytic approach did more exploration of feelings and more interpretation. Those trained in client-centered counseling were more apt to re-state, clarify, and reflect feelings. These differences were especially marked among the less experienced therapists. With greater experience, the therapeutic leaders became less doctrinaire and were able to utilize more of the procedures which the other school found helpful.

A study (Lennard, Bernstein, 1960) of 64 sessions for each of eight patients, conducted by four therapists who varied considerably along the activity-passivity dimension showed many similarities growing out

TABLE 3—FREQUENCY OF EACH TYPE OF RESPONSE BY THERAPIST

	Categories		*Responses*			
No. Bales		*Psychotherapeutic Form*	*Psychoanalytic*		*Rogerian*	
			Less Experienced	*More Experienced*	*Less Experienced*	*More Experienced*
1.	Shows solidarity	Reassures	5%	6%	2%	4%
2.	Agrees	Permissive acceptance	16%	16%	4%	6%
3.	Gives suggestion	Defines, proposes	4%	8%	1%	3%
4.	Gives opinion	Interprets	12%	8%	2%	6%
5.	Gives orientation	Restates, reflects	11%	17%	90%	59%
6.	Asks orientation	Asks factual questions	8%	6%	0	0
7.	Asks opinion	Explores feelings	38%	33%	1%	18%
8.	Disagrees	Ignores requests, complaints; thwarts	6%	4%	0	2%
9.	Shows antagonism	Aggressive remark	1%	1%	1%	2%
		Totals	100%	100%	100%	100%

of the nature of the interaction. The authors refer to a "latent system process" which operates in the dyad much as unconscious motivation may operate in an individual. At first, considerable attention must be given to orientation by both the therapist and the patient. Later affective statements by the patient are commented on by the therapist.

The investigators found that over a period of time, the propositions of patients and therapists became more and more similar in theme. The pairs developed harmonious roles. The amount of reference by patient and by therapist to the immediate, current relationship of the two persons concerned correlated .72 in the first two sessions, but rose to .88 during the third and fourth month. Frequency of reference to feeling and emotion (again between patient and therapist) correlated only .23 for the early sessions, but .70 during later months. Regardless of theory, the evolving realities in the dyad led to congruent therapist behavior. When patients were pouring forth their stories, all therapists listened. When patients were blocked, hesitant, and confused, most therapists naturally asked more questions or offered more specific suggestions to get the process going again. There was some evidence in these studies that when therapists were too quiet and noncommittal, patients felt it harder to communicate and were more apt to withdraw from therapy. While good leaders, teachers, and therapists learn to listen and to wait, it is possible to become too unresponsive. All leadership calls for two-way communication. The best leaders are seen as authentic persons (Rogers, 1963). An attempted integration of the findings from scientific study of "group dynamics" and those from clinical experience with group psychotherapy is offered by Durkin (1964). Her interpretation of reactions of the group to its leader may be helpful:

> At the beginning the members . . . tend to perceive the therapist in the image of the good, all-giving, omnipotent mother. They expect final answers and formulae for cure from him and seem willing to accept whatever he says. During that period they are likely to be very much afraid of the group as a whole. As they gradually become disappointed in the therapist's magical power, they become angry that he will not wave his wand in their behalf and begin to cast him in the role of the "bad mother" . . . Eventually . . . they begin to see the therapist much more realistically and become more able to treat him as a peer.

Need for more theory

Some of the concepts needed for the study of small groups and their leadership have been introduced in this and earlier chapters. The reader will have become familiar with the idea of social interaction; concepts of convergence and consonance; terms like "norm," "conformity," "reference group," and "the authoritarian personality." As we prepare to understand, later in this book, the social psychology of public opinion, business, race, and international relations, we shall need some additional theory. This will be the subject of the following chapter.

CHAPTER SIX

Structure – process – attitude

The S–P–A theory

Here we will present a conceptual system within which to integrate many of the experimental findings of social psychology. Specific findings become part of the science as they fit into general theories and larger systems. The concepts which emerge in this chapter will be applied throughout the remainder of the book. Mass media, race relations, business operations, and other phenomena of our culture will be interpreted largely in terms of the approach developed in this chapter. The specific influences which mold attitudes will not be examined at this point. Sources of attitudes and ways of changing attitudes will be explored systematically in the next two chapters. Here we shall be concerned with a basic way of thinking about how attitudes and behaviors relate to the objective pattern, or *Gestalt*, of situations.

Basic concepts

Response to situation

Much of psychology explains why different persons, if placed in much the same situation, behave differently. These differences in response among individuals may be attributed to heredity, to native intelligence, to age or stage of development, to previous learning, to conditioning, or to the persisting influence of powerful emotional experiences. Differential psychology, genetic (or developmental) psychology, psychometrics, psychology of personality, abnormal psychology, and clinical psychology are concerned mainly with accounting for *differences* in the response of different persons to situations essentially similar in structure.

Social psychology, like anthropology, is concerned also with the other half of the human picture—with *similarities* of response among various personalities. Despite all differences of personality, most people in a given culture show generally similar patterns as they satisfy needs for food, clothing, shelter, companionship, sex, and security. In our own society, most of us are accustomed to sleeping at night, rising in the morning, and having an American-type breakfast, going off to school or to work, eating again at around noon, and perhaps relaxing during evenings and holidays. We have common understandings about birthdays, weddings, child care, schools, jobs, money, newspapers, automobiles, elections, laws, government, life insurance, and funerals. Later we shall explore some of the differences between one culture or subculture and another. In this chapter the emphasis is upon consistent meaning, feelings, and behavior among different individuals in response to a common and recurring situation.

Whatever brings about the typical response to a certain situation continues to operate so long as the situation remains constant. When the situation changes, behavior and feelings change correspondingly. When storm clouds suddenly appear on a hot summer afternoon, thousands of persons on a crowded beach simultaneously begin hastily to gather up their robes, blankets, umbrellas, radios, and lunch baskets and to move in a continuous procession toward shelter and transportation home. Another illustration is graduation from school. Student life, for college seniors, has its well established characteristic schedule, responsibilities, and privileges. After Commencement, with college days over, typical changes occur in schedule, responsibilities, and privileges. The diploma marks a transition to a different set of behaviors and feelings.

Field theory

The view to be presented in this chapter derives from what is sometimes called the "Field Theory" (Deutsch, 1954). The essential idea is that objects in a field take on their dynamic character as a result of their position in the field. The movement of a bit of iron toward a magnetic pole is not due simply to innate traits of the moving part, but to the pull exerted by the field at the point where the particle is placed.

The course of a stream is not inherent in the water, but follows the topography of the bed and banks. Likewise, most human behavior is responsive to its setting. In one group we lead; in another we participate equally with others; in a third, we are silent and apprehensive.

To account for these differences in behavior we must look to the situation or field in which the action takes place. Except during conflicts, we seldom focus on *ourselves* as we respond. Like an experienced cyclist, we follow the course of the road, avoid stones and puddles, quite automatically as we move toward our goal.

Social system—position—role

Social scientists have developed a set of concepts for describing and understanding similarities of behavior in a culture. Every society includes a number of subunits of organized interaction which may be called *social systems* (Linton, 1936). A family, a college, a business, a baseball team, or a hospital is a social system. The social system may be as small as a newly-wed couple or as large as an army, the Roman Catholic Church, or the United Nations.

Each social system is composed of inter-related *positions*. Some sociologists, anthropologists, and social psychologists prefer the term "status" rather than "position." Since, in popular usage, status often implies a differential of prestige in a hierarchy, we prefer the more neutral term, "position." People may occupy different positions in a social system— on a baseball team, for example—and yet be equal in prestige status. In a family, the positions are indicated by the words father, mother, son, daughter, grandmother, aunt, and so forth. In a college there are positions such as those of freshman, senior, faculty, janitor, librarian, dean, or president.

For every position there are expected behaviors which may be called *roles*. In baseball, the role of the pitcher differs from that of the catcher, batter, short stop or left fielder. Each position calls for appropriate role behavior. The several positions in the social system of the family imply distinctive roles with certain obligations and privileges for a father, mother, oldest son or daughter or baby. Each position in the social system of the Army has well defined roles associated with it. The role behavior appropriate to any position in a social system is largely independent of the unique personality characteristics of the particular individual who may occupy it at a given time. However different in personality make-up the teachers in a school, the priests in a church, or the clerks in a store may be, there are fairly well understood ways which any teacher as teacher, any priest as priest, or any clerk as clerk is supposed to behave. Some things are required by the job. Whoever may become the new mayor of the town is expected to perform the official duties associated with that position. Individuals, with all their special traits and private lives, may come and go but positions continue to make fairly stable demands. In a hospital, an administrator, a doctor, an X-ray technician or a nurse may leave and be replaced by a very different individual but the role behaviors appropriate to these positions remain fairly fixed. There are certain things that a doctor, nurse, technician or administrator must do, willingly or unwillingly, and other things he may not do, whatever his inclinations.

Norms

Since there needs to be, and usually is, a fair degree of agreement within the social system on the role-behavior which is thought appropriate for a given position, this consensus may be called a *norm*. The term norm was introduced in Chapter 3 to describe the understanding, attitudes, codes of behavior and frames of reference which are shared by members of a group. Among the most vital norms for any group are those which define role expectations for the main positions. In a family, for example, the expectations of behavior appropriate to father, to mother, to son, to daughter, and to other relatives, are of very great importance. Where the role-expectations and role-behavior agree and the norm is firmly established, the members take it all for granted. Discussion and controversy arise when behavior does not accord with expectations or when expectations differ.

Varying conceptions of a role

Although role, as the dynamic aspect of any position, seems to be a simple concept, we have already begun to notice a distinction between the expected role and the enacted role. We also note possible differences in the role various persons associate with a given position. One of the problems of a modern teacher is that some supervisors, colleagues, pupils, and parents think a teacher should properly behave in one way while others have a different picture in mind. The result is role-conflict. Role-conflict may be related to differences among the following:

(a) self-definition of the role
(b) role-expectations by others
(c) actual role-behavior
(d) role-behavior as perceived by self
(e) role-behavior as perceived by others

As an example we may note a wholly imaginary college professor bicycling from the campus into town, wearing a beret. The corresponding views might be

(a) I am continuing an activity I found enjoyable as a student in Europe (self-definition).
(b) A professor should dress conservatively and behave with gravity (definition by others).

(c) Riding the bicycle, wearing the beret, nodding at acquaintances (actual role).

(d) I guess I look gay, relaxed, calm, youthful, attractive—not as stodgy and conventional as those others (self-perception).

(e) How nutty some professors are (perception by some others).

Role and feeling

How we feel varies with what we do. The same person will experience different feelings in the various roles of roommate, unsatisfactory student of French, top student in chemistry laboratory, ordinary second trumpet in the band, good tennis player, reader of a letter from lonely parents, borrower of money from a friend, and escort for a girlfriend on a date, although all of these and other roles may have arisen during one day.

Princes and princesses who are to inherit a throne are trained from infancy to the behaviors appropriate to their role. Their feelings are also adapted to the requirements. At levels of less prestige, there are similar prescriptions. In French Canada (Miner, 1939) the eldest son, to whom the farm property passes has a different set of experiences from those of his brothers who may expect to be priests or go into teaching or business. The eldest comes to think of himself as the farm proprietor long before he officially assumes the role; during boyhood he sees changes in agriculture, markets or taxes as they will one day affect him.

From structure to attitude

In our culture tradition has emphasized the dependence of behavior on attitudes. Evangelical Christians have been brought up to believe that "out of the heart are the issues of life." Proposals for social improvement have typically taken the form of first changing people's feelings and then finding appropriate expression in changed laws and institutions. The central figure in reform movements has been the missionary, reformer, orator, or pleader who could move men's hearts. Once the inner changes had been brought about, it was rather taken for granted that the objective arrangements would be correspondingly altered. The movement toward American independence has been seen as beginning with impassioned speeches like those of Patrick Henry; opposition to slavery with the appeal of *Uncle Tom's Cabin,* William Lloyd Garrison's *Liberator,* and the superb oratory of Wendell Phillips. In the next chapter, these processes of influence will be examined. In the behavioral sciences today the flow of causation is more often viewed in the reverse direction. A social system having a certain pattern or structure establishes positions with prescribed roles. In the process of carrying out these roles, individuals develop corresponding outlooks, attitudes, and

Abstract 21

TITLE   The Chinese Indoctrination Program for Prisoners of War: A Study of Attempted Brainwashing

AUTHOR   Edgar H. Schein

PROBLEM   How did the Chinese (and North Korean) Communists succeed in influencing so many American prisoners to collaborate to some extent?

SUBJECTS   Twenty repatriated Americans who had been prisoners of war in North Korea.

PROCEDURE   Interviews (2 to 4 hours) with each man at Inchon, Korea, and on a transport returning to the United States.

SOME FINDINGS   1. Social relationships were manipulated to break down reliance on customary patterns. Both commissioned and noncommissioned officers were separated from the other men. If any effective organization emerged among the prisoners, the key figures were removed. Sometimes young, inept or malcontent men were appointed to squad command, a procedure that was often gratifying to the nominated leader but actually disorganizing in its effects on the group. Religious services were forbidden. Mail from home was held up to create an impression of domestic unconcern and neglect. Spies and rumors of informers led to suspicion among the men, who became afraid to trust anyone. Continuous reports of collaboration by other prisoners suggested a new acceptable norm.

2. Rewards were distributed in accordance with sound learning theory. Men who signed Communist petitions served on peace committees, talked on the radio, etc., were given better food or living conditions or more status and freedom of movement.

3. Direct propaganda was used in daily lectures, discussions off and on through the day, news broadcasts and reading material. Repetition was characteristic. The Americans were usually confused about just why they were fighting and hence more open to Communist logic. Their understanding of Communism was often small and clouded.

4. Personal persuasion was also employed. Each individual case history was studied; the class status of the man's family was interpreted to him as guilty exploitation of the workers or as justifying his siding with the working class. Injustices were emphasized, and the atmosphere was one of friendliness, fairness, and warmth.

5. Minor infractions of the many camp regulations were used to threaten men with severe punishment unless they publicly confessed their wrong-doing. Then the error was analyzed to bring home to the offender his mistaken perception or motivation. The effect on self-confidence was humiliating. Promises to try to improve were elicited. Many men found subtle ways of complying with the letter of the demands while evading the intent.

Abstract 21—*Continued*

6. No mysterious drugs or hypnotic techniques were employed in brain-washing. The psychological pattern of physical deprivation, weakened social support, reduced self-assurance, accompanied by logical arguments and rewards for cooperation, represents only the rational application of psychological principles familiar to the West.

SOURCE: *Psychiatry,* 1956, XIX:149–172.

feelings. A change in the system brings changes in positions and roles, and the changed interaction alters the way participants are feeling. The general formula runs S→P→A: from Structure to Processes to Attitudes.

There are social interactions which proceed from the attitudes of individuals to affect the procedures and the structure of social systems, but these are fewer and less influential than those which flow in the S→P→A direction.

In practice, both religious and secular institutions have often followed the S→P→A sequence. Retreats, monasteries, and nunneries set up situations designed to restrict interaction and so to intensify the desired attitudes. In military training, camp life is an essential factor in separating the recruit from the habits, comforts, and attitudes of his home. An impressive example of the manipulation of a situation to affect attitudes is found in reports of so-called brainwashing of captured Americans in North Korea. Abstract 21 indicates that while efforts to influence attitudes directly by argument and persuasion were employed, the unusual effectiveness of these techniques was probably due to the structure of a situation which cut men off from earlier ties and rewarded them for new kinds of interaction.

Another social scientist (Biderman, 1963) has challenged a popular view that American POW's behaved weakly or shamefully under the stresses described in the Schein report. Despite the pressures, few gave in.

Dimensions

What variables in the structure of the situation, S, are particularly potent in affecting behavior processes and psychological characteristics? The earliest and most influential are the relationships determined by the structure of the primary group—the family. As the child matures, he associates with neighborhood groups; their make-up modifies his way of looking at life.

In larger social systems, we shall examine they way in which such factors as (a) size; (b) spatial arrangements; (c) the structure of productive work; (d) the prestige hierarchy; (e) sanctions; (f) power, and (g) conflict operate to shape the processes of interaction which, in turn, form the mentality of individuals. Each of these parameters of the social system will be examined in the sequence just named.

Primary group structures

It is not just the particular personalities in the family, but their roles and relationships which establish the matrix for the psychological development of the individual. A sociologist, Talcott Parsons, has expressed the idea cogently. "The *goals* of the human individual, in the human personality sense, are not primarily given in his biological constitution, but must be learned in the process of socialization. . . . Not only are other human beings, as discrete objects, individually and severally the most important objects in the child's, and indeed any human being's, situation of action, but the *system of relationships* in which these objects stand to each other, and which includes the child himself, constitutes the most fundamental *structure* of the situation or environment in which his action takes place. A child, throughout his life cycle, is never exposed to just one person or 'social object' but always to structured *systems* of social objects."

The only child, at an early stage, learns relationships mainly to adults who are deeply interested in him. The only child's expectations do not fit his first encounters with other children or with indifferent or hostile adults. Children born into large families may become skillful mainly in relating to slightly older or slightly younger peers. An informed report (Beaglehole, Ritchie, 1961) on Maoris living in Rakau, New Zealand, attributed the warmth and social spontaneity of adults to a sequence of experiences in the family: (a) absorbed attention of parents during the first year of life; (b) displacement then by the next child; and (c) diversion of the affiliation needs from the parents to a peer group.

The size of a family or kinship unit housed together varies in different cultures, and these variations in size have been found to be related to ensuing attitudes. Children in the larger units are less involved in intense emotional relationship with their particular father or mother. Uncles and aunts (or equivalents) are at hand to serve some of the children's needs. When grandparents live in the same house, they are in a position to supervise their married children. This tends to perpetuate some family traditions ("for the sake of the old folks") and to prolong some resentment in the parents who would like to outgrow the pattern of childhood dependence. Whiting and Child (1953) note that sororal polygony (one husband marrying two or more sisters) has the advantage that the several wives have been interacting since babyhood and are quite accustomed to living together. Their personalities are much less changed by marriage than if each had gone off with her husband to a new and distant home. There are other personality differences related to size of family. A humorist commented that one of the important things learned in a large family is that it is futile to expect justice.

When the large family—the tribe or clan—lives together, a child feels related to many aunts, uncles, and cousins as well as to his own parents and siblings. His security and status are less precarious; they cannot be altered because he happens at some moment to displease his particular father or mother. He belongs in a larger system. The wife may feel the continuing support of her brother and her clan in a way which guarantees that they will take responsibility for her if her husband does not prove compatible.

In modern American marriage, the couple usually leave their family of origin. The bride is uprooted from the home she has known and becomes almost wholly dependent on her husband. "Going home to mother" is seldom practicable. Children usually have only a weak relationship to relatives outside the immediate family. The new family is more autonomous and independent, but the members are very dependent on one another.

The order in which children are born gives each a differentiated role within the social structure. Oldest children, for example, are inevitably displaced as others come along. They are expected to help more in the home and to set a model for younger siblings. They are likely to develop a greater sense of responsibility and more hostility, guilt, and anxiety. Schachter (1959) found the older children more in need of reassurance from companions, more conformist, more likely to become alcoholics, more prone to seek psychotherapy, and more likely to join organizations.

Most family systems assign to girls a different status from that of the boys. Some of the effects of sex-stereotypes will be discussed later, in Chapter 12.

A particularly interesting deviation from our system of family life is found in the child-rearing institutions on communal farms (*kibbutzim*) in Israel. Children grow up with their age group and are cared for by professionally trained persons. They may be with their own parents only for play periods after work and on holidays. Available studies seem to indicate no serious emotional deprivation. The two most frequent noted characteristics of *kibbutz* children are: (1) easy, warm, friendly, trusting relationships to adults, extending even to visiting strangers, and (2) lack of drive to mate sexually with young people of the opposite sex with whom they have grown up. Some explain this second attitude as a consequence of the relaxed, family-like, intimacy of children who have bathed and slept together since infancy; others suppose that at adolescence such intimacy arouses unusually powerful repressive forces (incest taboo), leaving the individual free to respond emotionally only to strange lovers.

An interesting observation by anthropologists (Whiting *et al.*, 1956) is that those societies in which family patterns encourage exclusive and intense emotional relations of a boy to his mother are likely to develop initiation rites for adolescent boys, involving painful hazing, periods of isolation, trials of endurance, and sometimes genital mutilation. After passing these trials, the boy is presumed to have outgrown the emotional ties of childhood and is permitted into the secrets, lodges, and councils of the adult males.

It is sometimes argued (Maslow, Diaz-Guerrero, 1960) that the problem of delinquency in contemporary American life is caused largely by the weak role assigned to fathers. The authors point out that in Mexico, although "broken homes" are frequent and fathers may spend very little time at home with their children, the delinquency rate is low. This is attributed to the strong position of the father in the traditional Mexican communities. Although physically the father may be absent, he is psychologically very much in the picture. The father in the United States, these writers maintain, has no such assured status. Even if he is physically present he may be psychologically a nonentity. The hypothesis is interesting because it postulates another connection between structure of the primary group and the ensuing attitudes. The evidence, however, for the proposed connection between ineffective fathers and delinquent children is not yet persuasive. There are such cases, but there are also numerous cases of delinquents whose fathers brutally dominate the home.

The term "primary group" applies to all very influential face-to-face relations and so extends beyond the family. The gangs described in Chapter 3 define patterns of interaction among boys in many city neighborhoods. Social cliques may be exclusive and define certain other ethnic or national or religious or occupational groups as unacceptable.

On the point of social acceptance, certain animal studies, while having only qualified relevance to human social behavior, offer interesting hypotheses about connections between S and P and A. An alley cat has traits that are different from the cat raised on cushions and cream. Rats that are given too easy a life turn out to be less effective at problem-solving (Hebb, 1949). Puppies reared in cages may be quite healthy and noticeably less timid than those which run about normally (Thompson and Heron, 1954). The ducklings (described in Chapter 2) which were placed in an unusual situation of dependence for maternal care on a Greylag goose interacted and formed a sexual preference different from that which might have been regarded as instinctively normal for the species (Lorenz, 1952). Kittens brought up with puppies or with mice show friendly rather than hostile attitudes (Haldane, 1947). Bass which grew up alone in secluded spots, sheltered by vegetation, ate any little fish which strayed into their territory. When the ponds were cleared before they were stocked, all the fish grew up together, visually aware of one another. They shared food and "nobody tried to eat anybody" (Montague, 1950). Such attitude studies in animals do not prove that racially integrated neighborhoods, schools, work groups or playgrounds will reduce prejudice in children. We shall examine the evidence on this point in Chapter 11. What is demonstrated here is that organization of the social environment can even modify behavior usually regarded as instinctive in animals. We noted earlier (Chapters 2 and 3), the general rule that increased interaction fosters friendlier feeling. Thus we would expect that changes in a school, business, or community which remove some people from one social setting and place them in another, will cause some previous friendships to fade out while new ones develop. Children are sent off to camps and to boarding schools to permit a break from home-bound attitudes and to encourage the acquisition of a different outlook.

We shall look next at several characteristics of larger social systems which affect interaction patterns and intrapsychic preferences. The first of these parameters is size.

Size of social system

We have noted that size of family has an effect on members; the same is true of other groups. When a group is too large (as reported in Chapter 3), several do not speak, and, as their interaction decreases, they care less for the group and the group cares less for them. When the leadership activity of each individual is measured, recording his initiative and his ability to influence others in a leaderless group discussion, the scores vary inversely with the size of the group. In one study, when only two members participated each was found to rate a leadership score of 23; when there were six members each averaged 17; with 12 members the rating went down to 12 (Bass, 1959).

The size of an audience affects both the speaker and the members. It is inspiring to speak to thousands; dismaying to address a scattering of listeners in a large auditorium. In a small room, the field would not seem so empty.

Size has been found to be an important factor affecting processes of supervision. If a supervisor has only a small number of subordinates, he can keep very close watch over their work. Although this might seem desirable, studies by the Institute of Human Relations at the University of Michigan have led to the opposite conclusion (Chapter 13). People do not like to work with a supervisor hovering over them. Their morale is better when they feel that they are trusted with freedom to do their work in their own way. Hence, some companies have changed their pattern of organization toward giving a supervisor much larger numbers of workers to control. With a large group of subordinates it becomes impossible to oversee every move of every individual. Obviously, more independence and autonomy must be granted. A change in the size of the supervised unit (S) thus leads to a change in the closeness of supervision (P) and affects morale (A).

The size of units in which racial integration is practiced has been shown to be an important variable. The study in Abstract 22 indicates that white soldiers whose immediate associates were white were less favorable to the Negro companies or battalions than were white troops who interacted with Negroes in their same companies. The larger the unit which was racially homogeneous, the less interracial interaction took place and the less favorable were attitudes of each race toward the other. When Negroes and whites in the same company shared the daily routines of the barracks, mess hall, drill, and other duties, the effect on attitudes was to create the highest level of mutual acceptance.

The size of a community affects the processes of interaction and the consequent attitudes of its citizens. A sparsely settled area fosters individual self-sufficiency. In a village, everyone knows his neighbors and knows that they keep an eye on him. In the great city, the individual feels the freedom of anonymity. In the small town, one must adapt, without choice, to old and young, rich and poor, bright and dull, moral and immoral (Hicks, 1947). In a large city, one can more freely choose one's associates from a wide assortment of types and interests. In cities, primary group attachments are weakened and traditions are forgotten. Radical movements, in politics, art, fashions, and morals, usually start in cities (Chapter 15).

Changes in American character have come with the transition from the small settlements of pioneer days to the modern metropolis. Where human contacts are superficial and transient, surface effects are sought more than depth and lasting qualities. The role of the anonymous "they" who own the city houses, provide urban transportation and water, bring goods to the supermarket, and schedule the movies and television leaves the individual free from many responsibilities which he would normally assume if living in the country. *Stadtluft macht frei* (City air makes one free) says an old German proverb quoted by the urban sociologist Park (1916). Free, and irresponsible, "wheeling and dealing," "speed it up," "here today and gone tomorrow"—these are common attitudes of the highly mobile city life. The loose social organization of the city permits development of a wide variety of occupations, personality types, attitudes, and interests. These observations on size of community involve spatial proximity as well as numbers, and we proceed next to a review of spatial structures.

Abstract 22

TITLE　Opinions about Negro Infantry Platoons in White Companies.

AUTHORS　Information and Education Division, U.S. War Department

PROBLEM　What did white soldiers think (in 1945) of integration with Negro troops? Were those who had had such experience more or less favorable?

SUBJECTS　250 officers and 1,710 white enlisted men in European Theatre of Operations field forces.

PROCEDURE　Survey by trained interviewers.

SOME FINDINGS　Question: Has your feeling changed since serving in the same unit with colored soldiers?

ANSWER:　77 percent of officers with such experience reported more respect and more favorable opinions; 19 percent no change; 4 percent no answer. None reported less favorable attitudes.

QUESTION:　Some Army divisions have companies which include Negro and white platoons. How would you feel about it if your outfit was set up something like that?

Answer:	Would dislike it
1,450 men with no experience with Negro troops	62%
180 men in same regiment or division but not in a company which includes Negro platoons	22%
80 men in company with Negro platoons	7%

SOURCE: *Report No. B-157*, Information and Education Division, Army Service Forces, Washington, D.C., U.S. War Department, 1945.

The seating arrangement in a room modifies the interaction patterns and the consequent attitudes. A lecture hall is laid out to suggest focus on the speaker. Members of the audience are most likely to converse, if at all, only with their near neighbors. The same determining forces lead passengers on a train, bus, or plane to limit their remarks, as a rule, to their seatmates. On an ocean voyage those in neighboring deck chairs are apt to strike up an acquaintance. If a room is designed to facilitate discussion, the seats are arranged in a circle so that each participant can see every other. Sometimes they sit around a table. Steinzor (1950) observed that when groups were seated in a circle, members interacted most with those who sat opposite them; least with their neighbors on either side who were out of the direct line of vision.

Another observer, Sommer (1961), recorded the spontaneous geographic arrangement of visitors (to a mental hospital) who were asked to sit down around a table for a few moments of discussion. One was arbitrarily appointed to lead the discussion. The designated "leader" almost always chose the seat at one end of the table and the other members chose the seats at the "foot" of the table opposite the leader. When the visitors were sent by two's to wait in a room with two parallel couches, their choice of seats depended on the distance between the couches. If the couches were 2 feet to 3 feet apart, dyads usually sat facing one another (ratio 3:1). With 4 feet or more between couches, members almost always sat alongside each other (ratio 9:1).

Spatial arrangements at work are even more potent because they operate for something like 40 hours a week. A sociometric study of 494 factory workers (James, 1951) showed that those who worked near one another or who worked on a joint project were especially well acquainted and likely to be friends. In the Western Electric plant at Hawthorn the inspection group who worked together at the front of the room formed one clique and the soldering group located at the back of the room, another (Roethlisberger, Dickson, 1939). A study of 70 bomber crews (Kipnis, 1957) showed that choice of a partner for a work task or a social companion was strongly influenced by physical arrangements facilitating interaction.

One corporation found its efficiency reduced by poor communication among departments. Sometimes two or more departments duplicated work; both collected the same statistics; jurisdictional disputes arose over who should be doing what. Departmental empire building and rivalry intensified tendencies to claim credit and put blame elsewhere. The solution was to move the vice presidential offices. Formerly each vice-president had been close to the department he directed; some occupied whole floors; others were in separate buildings. The change brought all these department heads onto one floor where they would see one another several times each day. Interaction brought better communication and improved cooperative attitudes. The good of the corporation as a whole took precedence over the concern for only the VP's own distinct area. Psychological change proceeded from spatial change.

Historians recognize that the exploration of a new country follows routes laid out by Nature. Rivers become highways to the interior; high mountain ranges are barriers. Colonies form first along the coast and develop their own traditions and norms. Out on the frontier the isolation fosters different styles of life and different attitudes.

An ecological study of attitudes as shown by the vote in South Carolina for "Dixiecrat" Thurmond in the 1948 presidential election showed that districts with a larger percentage of Negro population cast more votes for this segregationist candidate ($r = .39$) and that districts most largely rural also cast more such votes ($r = .41$). These are partial correlations, with other factors statistically held constant (Heer, 1959).

People who live near one another interact more often and are more likely, consequently, to develop similar attitudes. One study (Caplow, Forman, 1958) reported a correlation of .48 between frequency of interaction and geographic nearness for families living along a single lane. The correlation may reflect the decision of families that see each other frequently to live near one another. But in other instances strangers brought into proximity become good neighbors.

Studies of the shopping habits of farm dwellers who lived between two towns showed that the proportion of the shopping done by a family in one town rather than the other varied with the size of the town and inversely with the square of the distance between the farm home and the town (Reilly, 1929). Frequency of telephone calls between cities likewise varies with the size of the city and inversely with the distance between them (Sipf, 1947). Dodd (1953) found that the spread of a slogan among housewives in a community depended largely (72 percent) on the interactions between women whose homes were not more than 100 yards apart. Only 37 percent heard about the slogan from an informant living more than a block away. These studies—largely sociological—are significant for social psychology because psychological variables in perception, feelings, and behavior seem to be predictable from parameters of the social field.

A study in Arkansas (Loomis, Davidson, 1939) found that geographic location within a community was a major factor in determining which families associated with which others. Families that associated with one another also belonged to or made use of many of the same organizations. The relationship here is probably circular: Proximity, friendship, and participation in community agencies all affect one another. Further evidence of similarity in attitudes among associated families appeared when those who migrated out of the community tended to visit mainly with other families who had also left town; those who remained associated mainly with others who remained.

A study of attitudes of residents toward a tenant council (Festinger, *et al.*, 1950) showed that those living around the same court, and hence interacting more often, tended to be in general agreement. Some court groups favored the council; others were opposed. Those who deviated within groups were typically less than 30 percent. The more cohesive the court (measured by sociometric choice), the fewer the deviates. Even so minor a spatial factor as having apartment doors opening onto the same inner court increased both cohesion and similarity of attitude.

Experience in interracial housing projects adds evidence for our hypothesis. When certain buildings were reserved exclusively for Negro or for white families, cohesion developed among residents within each of those buildings, but families in a separate building or of a different race were regarded with suspicion (Deutsch, Collins, 1951). When race was disregarded and families located in order of application—the so-called pepper and salt mixture—many families found their immediate neighbors to be of a different race. Through the normal processes of interaction, acquaintance and friendship soon developed across the barriers of race. Another study (Wilner, Walkley, Cook, 1951) indicates that eventual feeling about fellow tenants of the other race could be predicted more accurately from proximity in the building than from the attitude (favorable or prejudiced) which the tenants had when they moved in.

Interesting evidence of homogeneity of attitudes among those who live in close proximity appears in surveys of different types of city neighborhood. Studies of delinquency (Shaw, 1942) reveal that certain areas within cities have especially high rates of crime among youth; other are relatively low. In Chicago, a region just outside the business district of the "Loop" had for decades been high in delinquency rate. The actual population of the area had changed: Irish, Italian, Polish, and Negro people had each predominated for a time. But, regardless of race, nationality, or religious affiliation, the youth in this area were a problem for the police. Deteriorated housing, lack of community facilities, and other structural factors in the region kept young people on the streets and in gangs. Gangs in a given area developed delinquent norms which lived on in the group while particular individuals came and went. In several run-down areas of New York City the only measure which broke up the antisocial traditions and action patterns was physical relocation. When the old Hell's Kitchen tenement houses were torn down and the residents were forced to live in other sections, the new apartment houses which replaced the slums brought new standards of conduct into the neighborhood.

Structure of productive work

People who do different work develop different attitudes. The farmer in all lands is bound to manual labor, rooted in the soil, and moves with the cycle of seasons. A changed agricultural technology produced a new type of modern American farmer who works with machines and the applied sciences, who uses the commercial and cultural resources of cities, who may participate in county, state or national politics, and whose outlook is no longer narrow and provincial. Yet, all farmers have some concerns in common which differentiate them from factory workers, magazine writers or movie stars. Professor Robert E. Park, one of the earliest students of the sociology of city life, observed: "The effects of the division of labor as a discipline, i.e., as a means of molding character, may (therefore) be best studied in the vocational types it has produced. Among the types which it would be interesting to study are: the shopgirl, the policeman, the peddler, the cabman, the nightwatchman, the clairvoyant, the vaudeville performer, the quack doctor, the bartender, the ward boss, the strikebreaker, the labor agitator, the school teacher, the reporter, the stockbroker, the pawnbroker; all of these are characteristic products of the conditions of city life; each, with its special experience, insight, and point of view determines for each vocational group and for the city as a whole its individuality" (1916).

Adam Smith in one of the classics of economics noted that "The difference of natural talents in different men is in reality much less than we are aware of; and the different genius which appears to distinguish men of different professions when grown up to maturity, is not upon many occasions so much the cause as the effect of the division of labour" (1776). Here he supports the sequence of our thesis: form of work (S–P) leads to distinct psychological attributes (A).

Millar (1793) writing at about the same period, related regional and national characteristics to the prevalent occupations: "In searching for the causes of those peculiar systems of law and government which have appeared in the world, we must undoubtedly resort, first of all, to the differences of situation, which have suggested different views and motives of action to the inhabitants of particular countries. Of this kind are the fertility or barrenness of the soil, the nature of its productions, the species of labor requisite for procuring subsistence, the number of individuals collected together in one community. . . . The variety that frequently occurs in these and such other particulars must have a prodigious influence upon the great body of the people; as, by giving a peculiar direction to their inclinations and pursuits, it must be productive of corresponding habits, dispositions and ways of thinking."

A study (Stogdill *et al.*, 1956) of naval officers who had moved from one assignment to another indicated that more than half of the variance in what men did was determined by the job rather than by the personality of the man. While there were noticeable traits of behavior carried by the particular individual as he moved from one job to another, there were even more characteristics necessarily required by the position and evidenced by one man after another as he assumed the particular role.

Organizational structure has been studied in the laboratory by varying channels of communication. Leavitt's (1951) findings, presented in Chapter 3, show satisfaction varying with centrality in the structure. Key men are high in interaction and obtain the most psychic reward. Replications (Guetzkow, 1954; Shaw, *et al.*, 1957) also found that the all-channel network, in which each is free to communicate with every other, leads to greater satisfaction among participants, partly because they experience less sense of restraint.

A study (Kornhauser, 1962) of the mental health of factory workers led to the conclusion that the kind of the work men were doing affected their emotional adjustment. Each worker was rated for tension, anxiety, hostility, social withdrawal, alienation, and dissatisfaction with himself and with life. Kornhauser classified 57 percent of skilled workers as having good mental health; 37 percent of semi-skilled workers as good; but only 12 percent of those doing repetitive work as having good mental health. He investigated the possible effect of differences in education, but found that this was not a significant factor. The emotional state of the men was most closely and clearly correlated with what they had to do to earn their wages and with "associated life conditions."

In another Detroit study, several ministers took jobs on assembly lines in factories and kept diaries of their experiences. One of their observations was that, to their surprise, they found themselves adopting many practices they had condemned from the pulpit. They swore, cheated, lied, hated, loafed on the job, and behaved in ways closely resembling the actions of other workers in similar situations.

An unusually clear demonstration of the effect of a changed situation on attitudes is found in Lieberman's report (1956) on workers who became foremen or shop stewards. An attitude inventory was given to 2,500 workers. During the ensuing year, 23 of these men became foremen and 35 became shop stewards. In the new job, foremen were more pro-management and shop stewards were pro-union. Inspection of their earlier responses showed no significant differences between the attitudes of the men who later became company officials and those who later became union officials. After they stepped into the new role, they each took on the attitudes of the related reference-group. Foremen became more like other managers; shop stewards became more like other trade union leaders.

Most people are capable of both competitive and cooperative behavior; which pattern they adopt may depend on the work situation. Mintz (1951) showed that when subjects were stimulated to compete at drawing cones up through a narrow-necked bottle, frustrating jams ensued. When they were instructed to cooperate, the subjects perceived their tasks differently, were successful in permitting every member to draw out his cone within the time limit, and felt pride in their achievement. Some games, like tennis, stress courtesy and minimize taking any unfair advantage of an opponent. The same player may behave differently on the tennis court than he would in a football contest. Workers also respond to the overall climate of their enterprise. We described earlier the change in children when bricklaying was undertaken as a team enterprise rather than in individual competition (Tseng, 1952). Parallel changes have been observed in engineering students, working cooperatively or competitively at problem solving (Deutsch, 1949). The conforming traits of the "organization man" (Whyte, 1956) may well have arisen as a consequence of the change from small competitive enterprises to immense corporations which now encourage a high degree of cooperation within the company and agreements to prevent price wars among the leading companies.

Technological changes, such as the introduction of automation in industry, alter the work structures, the positions and roles, and the attitudes of workers. One pertinent study (Mann, Hoffman, 1956) compares a new electric power plant with the older plant which continued to operate nearby. Many jobs, such as the regulation of supply of coal and air and water to the boiler, which are manually operated by a fireman watching gauges in the old plant, are controlled by automatic devices in the new plant. Fewer employees are needed in the new plant and jobs have been redefined. Operators in the new plant have had to master parts of the production process which were quite outside their former specialized function. As a consequence they have been rotated through several working situations and report a higher level of job-satisfaction with their expanded knowledge and responsibilities. Maintenance workers who were formerly skilled in a single craft—mechanics, electricians, welders, pipe-fitters, and others—have been replaced by multiple-skill members of a team. The latter are less identified with a particular trade. The large capital investment in the plant has led to continuous operation which has created dissatisfied workers who do not like rotating shifts. Changes in equipment have thus brought a variety of changes in operating procedures and have caused corresponding changes in the attitudes of the employees.

Prestige hierarchy

In most social systems some positions are regarded as "higher" and as bringing more prestige to the occupants. Persons who move up in the hierarchy obtain ego-satisfaction and show increased self-regard. Those who move "down" in such a structure are likely to become frustrated, disappointed, hostile, alienated or self-rejecting.

Security of status has an important influence on attitudes. In older societies where differences of caste or class have been thought of as Divinely prearranged and sanctioned, each level takes its rights, privileges, and duties for granted. The secure upper class members are relatively free from pressure to conform. They may do about as they please. Secure lower-class members experience little craving to rise. American society does not ordain fixed status for most of its members. The business executives who head departments in dynamic companies would like to be promoted to vice-president; they fear replacement or demotion. They are under constant strain which sometimes produces ulcers. Those lower in the scale, having been taught that everyone has a fair chance to rise and being under constant appeal from advertising to aspire to higher standards of living, struggle to get a foothold on the next rung of the ladder. Some eventually resign themselves to permanent ceilings and find ways to take life as easy as possible without losing their jobs.

Some insight into the attitudes generated by status levels can be obtained from simple laboratory exercises. A study (Kelley, 1951) of college students assigned to high status ("the best and most important job in the group") or low status ("menial and routine, a poorer job") jobs in an experimental task brought out a connection between lower status and the introduction of more communication irrelevant to the task. Low-status members more often failed to understand directions.

Another difference in communication was that the high-status students more freely criticized their subordinates but said little about any problems they themselves found in their work. They seldom criticized any other high-status persons. They apparently fell into an upper-class defensive pattern of admitting no defects in themselves or their own jobs, while directing their accusations at the lower status workers. A control group, doing the same work without any definition of high- or low-status jobs, expressed significantly more criticism toward fellow workers, whatever their job. The experimenter concluded that the introduction of a sense of hierarchy operates as a general restraint on the free expression of criticism. An interesting angle is the difference in expression of criticism between low-status workers who were frozen in their type of job, and those who were told they might win promotion to a higher level task. Those who viewed themselves as potentially mobile were less free in their criticism of the higher-up's.

Factors which impede interaction within a work group also influence the resulting attitudes. In Chapter 2, Bavelas' experiment was described. When the situation (S) permitted free two-way communication (P) the outcome was a friendly attitude (A). When telephone communication from one party was arbitrarily restricted to "yes" or "no," as it often is in the reaction of a boss to a request, the ensuing attitudes became hostile.

In Chapter 10, we shall see that members of socio-economic classes who have little direct communication with other classes develop distorted stereotypes. In "Middletown" (Lynd, 1929) two generations ago the boss and workers called one another by first names; they sat beside each other in church and sent their children to the one public school. In a large modern corporation, size, structure, and geographic separation of the absentee directorate mean that workers usually have little if any contact with top management and none at all with the board of directors. This social structure perpetuates stereotypes of the boss as a bloated "Moneybags" and of the "lower class" as irresponsible, ungrateful, and lacking in sensible thrift. Each class can readily become a scapegoat onto which the other projects its distress.

A study of changes in attitude related to high-prestige Greek-letter residences on a college campus (Siegel, 1957) showed that those freshmen who wished to join such groups scored higher on the antidemocratic (F-scale) test; those who had a year of residence there remained high in F-scale scores; but those who had lived a year in lower-prestige residences became more democratic in their attitudes.

A study of race prejudice among white college students found that an important factor was "equal status contacts" (Allport, 1954). If contacts were limited to a situation in which one race had prestige and dominance, while the other was subservient, communication processes were impeded. Each said to the other only certain "appropriate" things. Prejudice could easily remain undiminished. Contacts based on equality, between co-workers or fellow students, led to freer communication and more genuine mutual appreciation of one another as fellow human beings. A study (MacKenzie, 1948) was made of attitudes among Civil Service employees. The study indicated that employees who had known Negroes only in subordinate positions, such as cleaning women or porters, had more illusions about white superiority than those who had known Negroes as co-equal fellow workers or as supervisors.

This principle of equal-status interaction as an antidote for prejudice will be very useful in Chapter 11, when relations among ethnic groups will be more fully considered. Without noting differences in the prestige structure it would be difficult to account for the fact that resistance to desegregation is strongest in those areas in which Negrowhite ratio is 50 percent or more (Tumin, 1957). Obviously there are numerous inter-racial contacts in such a situation, but they operate within a pattern of white supremacy and Negro subordination. Under these conditions, interactions reinforce the existing norms. The basic issue in the Supreme Court decision of 1954 on public school desegregation was whether schools could be racially separate and yet equal. In a society of equal status, separation would not necessarily be derogatory for either race. Given the prestige structure of most American communities, North or South, residential and school segregation implies separation because of inequality. It reinforces attitudes of prejudice.

Sanction structure

The S-P-A formulation applies to all attempts to influence behavior and attitudes by manipulating the sanctions, i.e., the rewards and punishments. A prime example is legislation. When the laws provide premiums for certain kinds of behavior and penalties for not conforming, most people follow the legally prescribed path. Moreover, they come to feel that this is quite right and proper; they internalize the traffic lights (laws).

Psychologically, the sanctions operate mainly through reenforcement or positive rewards of satisfaction when certain acts are performed. The restraining influence of fear of punishment leads to avoidance of the situation, the agent of control, the punishment, or perhaps to avoidance of the prescribed act. In any case, actual effects are more potent than promises.

Every successful parent and teacher has learned that children respond to what one does rather than to what one preaches. Empty threats and enticements do not have a lasting effect. A parent may say, and believe, that he wants his child to be helpful in the home. If, however, the child finds that nothing happens when he fails to fulfill a request for some work, and that when he does do so, no one expresses any special appreciation, such actions build tendencies to evade home tasks. A teacher may claim that he is interested in stimulating an attitude of inquiry in his students. If, however, he brushes aside student questions and grants high semester grades on the basis of correct answers to his factual questions, his students will tend to stress mastery of facts over thoughtful exploration of the unknown. A manager may say that he values initiative and enterprise in his subordinates; if, however, he rejects their proposals and rewards the yes-man, his organization will breed conformists. Colonial powers, asserting that they want to develop the capacity of the natives for self-government, have often suppressed every emerging leader who exercised initiative and won a following.

In Mintz's experiment it would not have been very effective to urge subjects to be "cooperative" as long as the rewards and punishments were based wholly on individual achievement. In Deutsch's experiment some groups worked cooperatively because they shared a common fate. They all had to survive or perish together. The control groups allowed one individual to win his reward at the expense of others.

In a similar experiment (Katz et al., 1958) subjects were asked to build designs with erector units, to solve puzzles, to discuss human relations problems, and to roll a ball along a large spiral, a task which required manual skill. Some subjects knew they were being rated and given bonuses for individual performance; others were given bonuses only for the performance of their whole group. Group rewards inspired more helping of others, more giving of suggestions, and less rejection of others' ideas.

Power structure

In earlier chapters we have seen that groups under autocratic leaders develop behavior and outlook different from the patterns fostered by democratic leadership. In the famous Lewin, Lippitt (1940) experiments, one variant was to exchange a single member. Bob had been in a group with an autocratic leader and had shown the behavior characteristic of his fellow members—outwardly docile with repressed hostility. Bill had been in a democratic group characterized by friendly talk, cooperative planning, and interest in the work. When the two changed places, each took over the patterns which had previously marked the other. Apparently neither heredity nor early childhood experiences made the boys egocentric or cooperative, social or hostile. When they moved into a new S, the processes of interaction, P, changed, producing distinctly different attitudes, A.

Another report (McCandless, 1942) describes what happened in a state training school when one of two comparable cottages shifted from the autocratic leadership which had been traditional in both to a more democratic style of control. In both cottages, before the change, the more dominant and aggressive boys had been most popular. After the change, this relationship fell to zero in the cottage that became democratic; the other did not change.

The conflict pattern

The same persons, in the same physical settings, under the same leadership will behave differently when their group becomes involved in a contest or conflict. The whole psychological field is altered. A club or church or political party or union in which one may have been only mildly interested may become a vital reference group when it gets into a bitter struggle. A fight over a school bond issue may alienate close neighbors and long-time friends. In time of threatened war, national loyalties are emphasized and domestic controversies may be laid aside "for the duration."

A fascinating new line of research observes how human behavior changes under threat. Several experimenters have used a game called "prisoner's dilemma" (Deutsch, 1960). The rules are designed to make it possible for both parties to win modest rewards if both cooperate. However, if one party deceives the other and takes full advantage of him, he can win heavily at the expense of the victim. Under such rules, will subjects trust one another? One in this series of experiments showed that when one or both parties in a bargaining situation possess a weapon with which to threaten the other, the power struggle destroys cooperation and brings losses to both.

Total milieu

In this chapter we have looked at one dimension of the structural situation after another: positions, roles, size, spatial arrangements, organization of production, prestige, hierarchy, sanctions, power patterns,

Abstract 23

TITLE   Individual and Mass Behavior in Extreme Situations.

AUTHOR   Bruno Bettelheim

PROBLEM   What happens to human beings in such an atmosphere of terror and torment as a Nazi concentration camp?

PROCEDURE   The author was confined in Dachau and Buchenwald during 1938–39. He observed his fellow prisoners who, despite their malnutrition, had to perform hard labor and were tortured. Differences in reaction between new prisoners (less than one year in the camp) and old prisoners (three years or more) were noted.

SOME FINDINGS   1. New prisoners thought of return to the outer world; old prisoners of how to adjust to camp conditions.

2. The group, in the interests of its own security, imposed on all members regression to infantile behavior, living in childlike dependence on the guards, unable to plan beyond the present moment, indulging in fantasies and groundless boasts.

3. Old prisoners eventually accepted the values of the Gestapo guards. They took over verbal expressions and copied acts of physical aggression toward newcomers and the weak. Torture of suspects by the prisoners themselves imitated Nazi models. With bits of material old prisoners tried to make their costumes resemble uniforms of Nazi guards. They prided themselves on exhibitions of toughness. A game of seeing who could take the most blows without complaining was played by guards and copied by prisoners. Nazi racial discrimination was also adopted by some of the old timers.

SOURCE: *J. abnorm. soc. Psychol.*, 1943, XXXVIII:417–452.

and so on. Changes along any of these dimensions of S require corresponding changes in P and in A. Our final proposition is that situations are integral, and the total milieu has a combined influence.

At the worst extreme of the scale is a horrible milieu like a Nazi concentration camp. In Abstract 23, Bruno Bettelheim's observations are summarized. Long-term prisoners in a concentration camp became as free of conscience and as brutal as their depraved guards. It is a moving and frightening demonstration of the power of the S-P-A line of control. It is also significant that the rehabilitation of men who had been war prisoners in camps less cruel than Buchenwald also seemed to require special therapeutic treatment. The British developed for this purpose "Civilian Resettlement Units," which were transitional settings, part way between camp conditions and civilian life. At the positive end of the scale are utopias, designed to bring about behavior and attitudes which bring most satisfaction. In *Walden Two* a psychologist, B. F. Skinner (1955), describes a total milieu which he believes would foster the best human relations.

In this chapter we have seen how changes in the structure of a situation lead to adaptations in social interaction and bring consequent changes in attitude. Within this broad framework, we will examine more closely, in Chapter 7, the psychological processes by which attitudes arise and are modified.

CHAPTER SEVEN

Attitudes

Development

Definition

In the preceding chapter the term *attitude* was used without full definition or exploration. We have observed that the structure of situations affects processes of interaction and out of these grow attitudes. What, more precisely, does the word mean?

Attitude is a *construct* inferred from the direction that behavior takes. Attitudes predispose organisms toward some objects and away from others. The construct refers to a presumed state of the organism which eventuates in the observed action. Attitude and changes in attitude may be expressed in words or may be deduced from other behavior. The look that passes between two lovers reveals attitude and response to attitude. So does the look that passes over the face of the person who is offended, frightened, amused or scornful. A clenched fist may betray an attitude, even while behavior is being carefully regulated to appear calm and pleasant.

An attitude may be further defined as a disposition or readiness to act or to react in a certain way toward a given stimulus or class of stimuli. An attitude exists in the relationship between a person and some kind of object. The object of an attitude may be inanimate things (airplanes), living things (roses, mice, persons, groups, institutions, communities, nations), or experiences (hearing jazz, climbing mountains, going to college, dying) or ideas (mathematics, Christian doctrine, monogamy).

An attitude is a construct. It is a concept which is assumed to mediate between objectively observable stimuli and the subsequent response. The direction of attention, the nature of perception, the significance attributed to what is observed, and the readiness to accept or reject this meaning are all consequences of the presumed attitude. The most prominent dimension of attitude is like-dislike; a tendency to accept or to reject; to go toward or away from; to seek or to avoid. Attitudes involve feelings, not pure intellectual classification. The attitude may be made to appear rational and logical, but beneath the surface syllogisms lie emotional concerns. Attitudes express values.

Other dimensions of attitude are salience, duration, stability, and range. *Salience* refers to the importance and urgency attached to the attitude, its significance in the life of the person holding that attitude. Attitudes toward the self or toward loved ones are usually more salient than attitude toward historic figures, but there are exceptions. Circumstances may make an attitude suddenly more salient. For example, during controversies, such as elections, we may be aroused over individuals who usually mean very little to us. Attitudes may also be of long standing or recently acquired. Short-lived attitudes may be called whims or crotchets. Attitudes may be stable and resistant to change or very tentative and fragile. They may be sharply differentiated, covering a very limited range, like the attitude toward a painting, or be as broad as an attitude toward one's fellow man or toward friendliness, indifference or the cruelty of the universe. Highly specific reactions may be regarded as opinions which focus a more general underlying attitude on a particular person, object or idea. Thus, a man's *opinion* about a particular statement issued by a certain labor leader may be determined largely by a general pro-labor or anti-labor *attitude*. The broad attitude induces many specific opinion reactions.

Perception and attitude

In the preceding chapter, it was asserted that attitudes flow from the structure of situations as perceived and reacted to by persons. The perception itself, however, is influenced by attitudes which were formed from earlier experiences. What one sees, hears, or feels in the world about him depends in large measure upon what he is prepared to expect. It is common for two persons to look at the same stranger, the same work of art, or the same collection of objects in a store window and "see" quite different images. Each makes of the sensory stimulation a meaningful perception which grows out of his own background and expectations. A modern painting may be experienced as a confused mass, a riot of color, a display of technical virtuosity, or a meaningful expression of the artist's insight. A man seeking a suitable gift for a girlfriend will "see" in a department store a quite different set of objects from those he would notice if in quest of a tool for his shop.

Attitudes—defined as readiness to respond—are involved in all perception. We do not first see and then recognize and evaluate our perceptions. The attitudes are built into the very process of perception.

An excellent demonstration of the effect of mood in perception was carried out by hypnotizing subjects, suggesting feeling to them, and noting how this influenced their interpretation of pictures. If they were told to be relaxed, happy, and contented, they saw the people in several pictures as "mellow" or "having fun," "really living." If the induced mood were critical and antagonistic, they saw the same people in the same pictures as exploited, filthy, disgusted, "looking daggers." In the mood of anxiety, they saw the same people as worried and likely to get cut or drowned (Leuba, Lucas, 1945).

Source of attitude

Attitudes are an important part of social psychology, partly because they affect responses to other people, to groups, and to social policies, but also because most attitudes arise in a social context. In Chapter 2 we noted that chronic attitudes of trust and optimism or of distrust and resentment may carry over from that first encounter of the impressionable infant with the nursing mother. More than a century ago, Alexis de Tocqueville (1835–40) cautioned his readers not to suppose that a man's vices and virtues begin when he steps into an adult role.

> This, if I am not mistaken, is a great error. We must begin higher up: we must watch the infant in his mother's arms; we must see the first images which the external world casts upon the dark mirror of his mind, the first occurrences which he witnesses; we must hear the first words which awaken the sleeping powers of thought, and stand by his earliest efforts, if we would understand the prejudices, the habits, and the passions which will rule his life. The entire man is, so to speak, to be seen in the cradle of the child.

An adult's attitude toward Catholics, Republicans, or Negroes, for example, is likely to have been conditioned by the religious, political, and racial attitudes of his parents. One study (Newcomb, Svehla, 1937) of 500 students and their families showed that children usually agreed with their parents ($r = .63$) and their brothers and sisters ($r = .60$)

on attitudes toward the church. On other attitudes (toward Communism and toward war) the correlations ranged from .37 to .56. A later study (Helfant, 1952) showed that the attitude of high school students on current international issues agreed with parental attitudes to the extent of a low positive correlation of about .20.

In Chapter 3, we introduced the idea of "reference groups." Individual attitudes usually derive from group norms. If not the family, then the peer group, the campus fraternity, business associates, or neighbors contribute the standard expectations which the learning individual acquires. Newcomb's Bennington College study (Abstract 13) showed a conflict between conservative attitudes inculcated at home and the more liberal atmosphere of that college in the depression years. Sometimes it became quite explicit. Newcomb quotes one student who said: "Family against faculty has been my struggle here. As soon as I felt really secure here I decided not to let the college atmosphere affect me too much. Every time I've tried to rebel against my family I've found out how terribly wrong I am, and so I've naturally kept to my parents' attitudes." More typical was the girl who said: "I came to college to get away from my family, who never had any respect for my mind. Becoming 'radical' meant thinking for myself and, figuratively, thumbing my nose at my family. It also meant intellectual identification with the faculty and the students I most wanted to be like" (Newcomb, 1943). A follow-up of girls one, two or three years after leaving Bennington showed that those who had spent three or four years on the campus changed their attitudes during college and afterward held to the college norm. As freshmen they had an average conservatism score of 74; this dropped gradually to 62.6 at graduation time. The follow-up average was 61.9. Twenty-five years later, these women voted for John F. Kennedy (60%) rather than Richard M. Nixon (40%) and in the most liberal half of the student population, as measured in 1935, the proportion preferring Kennedy in 1960 was 83 percent. Despite relatively high incomes (three out of four were judged to be over $20,000 a year) these Bennington alumnae were not conservative; 76 percent approved a controversial expansion of social security to give inexpensive medical care to the aged ("Medicare") and 61 percent supported the admission of Communist China into the United Nations (Newcomb, 1963). Newcomb explains the persistence of the *Weltanschauung* acquired in college years, by the fact that the alumnae have continued to associate with friends and groups selected partly because of congruent attitudes. Reference groups form and sustain the attitude, while attitude influences choice of associates. The relationship is circular.

A study of voter attitudes toward the presidential candidates in 1940 will be summarized in the following chapter (Lazarsfeld, Berelson, Gaudet, 1944). Two of the findings are relevant to the source of attitudes. Among 413 voters, only 4 percent voted for a candidate different from the one supported by some other member of their family. If a voter changed his mind, it was usually because his family or companions at work or friends differed from him in his original choice. Face-to-face contacts were the major influences.

It is sometimes supposed that race prejudice originates with unpleasant experiences with members of the rejected race. This does occasionally happen and examples will be cited in Chapter 11. More frequently, however, race prejudice is acquired by a kind of psychological contagion from one's own reference group. A small white boy in a rural Southern area sat in the back of a slowly moving pick-up truck, holding his toy gun and shooting "Bang! bang!" at whatever took his fancy as a target. "Hold yer fiah sonny," said his father, who was driving, "until ya see a niggah!" Accumulation of such little incidents will mold that boy's attitude toward the other race.

Attitudes toward other people are often strengthened by what is called the "self-fulfilling prophecy." What one expects others to be like may determine what they do. A student who comes to college expecting that his new acquaintances will dislike and reject him does not meet other people half way. His guard is up; he is looking for signs of a slight. Others quite naturally turn away from him to more friendly companions. "See," he might say, "I was right. I knew they'd reject me." Another student who comes to the campus expecting that almost everyone will be congenial, frank, friendly, good-natured, and warm finds a correspondingly pleasant confirmation of his expectations. The self-fulfilling prophecy operates also on a larger scale. If representatives of a colonial power believe that the natives are child-like, stupid, and dependent, they will treat them this way. Educational opportunities will not be provided. Decisions will be made for and not by the local people. Their anticipated dependence and ignorance will become only too obvious. Not until the natives achieve independence is it possible to demonstrate that the attitude of the governing minority created the characteristics attributed to the governed.

The experiment by the German psychologist, Zillig (1928), described on page 85, demonstrated that perception may be distorted to make it confirm our expectations. These findings support the principle of consonance presented in Chapter 3. Bad people are popularly supposed to do bad things.

Another illustration comes from a cartoon showing some people in a bus or street car. One man is a Negro, the other white. One white man is arguing with the Negro. One man has a razor. Actually it is the white man who has the razor, but the experimenters found (Allport, Postman, 1945) that white college students who had glanced at the cartoon tended to recall the razor in the hand of the Negro. The stereotype prevailed over the reality.

Sequence in attitude formation

Most psychological processes move through a normal sequence from a rather vague, undifferentiated state, to more and more sharply defined reactions in some specific form, and finally to an integrated pattern. Attitudes develop in a similar sequence. The term "Moslem" may have no meaning for a child, or a rather dim reference to some sort of different being. Later, he may learn something he likes or dislikes about the creed or history of Islam or may associate the word with a picture of a man wearing a fez. Eventually, in the integrated stage, his attitude toward Moslems is likely to be part of a larger complex of attitudes toward organized religions or toward the Middle East. Attitudes, like perceptions and skills, grow from the undifferentiated, to the differentiated, and finally to the integrated.

Our own attitudes seem best

A characteristic of most attitudes is that they seem wholly right and proper to the one who holds them. This is not surprising. Most attitudes were formed because they were associated with admired persons or were group norms. It is easy to conclude that anyone who does not share our attitudes must be rather stupid or bad. In a static society, with little change or mobility, where most persons spend all their lives in the same social context that first formed their attitudes, the conviction that one's own way of life is right and best causes very little trouble. It leads, of course, to ethnocentrism and to hostility toward strangers or foreigners with a different set of attitudes. In our present complex and changing world, however, we eventually find ourselves interacting with other persons who have different moral standards, opposing political views, and other national loyalties. Ethnocentrism is a liability in our shrinking world.

Stability

Basic attitudes remain stable

Attitudes sometimes seem too fleeting for study. They are related to feelings which seem to shift kaleidoscopically from hour to hour. Actually, however, most persons have a fixed core of basic attitudes which change very little. The attitude of many Republicans toward their G.O.P., of many Roman Catholics toward their church, of white South Africans toward blacks, of music lovers toward Beethoven, of a baseball fan toward the national game remains constant over many years. Equally stable are the basic attitudes of parents toward their children, of national patriots, and the dislike some pupils have for mathematics. Unconscious attitudes of hostility toward the opposite sex or toward younger siblings or unconscious guilt feelings may dominate one's social outlook from early childhood to death. The effort of psychotherapy to correct some harmful attitudes contends with powerful resistance against any change.

The human organism has many built-in stabilizers. The physiologist, W. F. Cannon (1932), has described under the term *homeostasis* the tendency to return to normal equilibrium after some disturbance of metabolism, blood sugar content, temperature, heart beat, or other bodily processes. A parallel tendency can be seen in attitudes. Psychologically, persons defend their basic patterns of attitude. As Lord Grey once put it: "Mental digestion ceases to be able to assimilate anything except what nourishes convictions already formed."

One method of defense is selective attention. We tend not to see truths which would challenge our prejudices. The writer has led study tours in many foreign countries and has had abundant opportunity to observe how, in the Soviet Union, for example, Americans predisposed to finding misery can see little else, while those expecting to find admirable features can overlook what does not fit their expectations. People usually subscribe to newspapers and listen to news commentators who share their opinions; they cancel subscriptions, turn off the television, or toss the pamphlet in the wastebasket if the ideas advanced are not in accord with pre-established attitudes. Most worshippers, attending churches of their own persuasion, try to avoid reading books or listening to talks which might lead them to question their faith. Study of reader responses to an article connecting lung cancer with cigarette smoking showed that the article was twice as likely to be read by a non-smoker (Cannell, MacDonald, 1956). A persistent problem for propagandists, discussed again in the following chapter, is that non-captive audiences go to hear only those speakers with whom they already agree.

If, despite the normal selective process of like-seeking-like, a person does encounter evidence which challenges his present outlook, there are second-line defenses. He may, for example, explain away the apparent contradiction. Seeing something good in a country he dislikes, the traveler may argue that it is a sham, set up just to mislead visitors. Seeing something bad in a country he admires, he may argue that the country has nevertheless made great improvements.

One early study of attitudes (W. S. Watson, Hartman, 1939) showed that theists and atheists, after evaluating 20 arguments related to the existence of God, were a little more likely to recall the ones which favored their own position. Abstract 24 shows how attitude toward communism affected recall of biased content.

A similar study of attitudes, in 1940, toward the New Deal, showed that in response to a neutral speech (equal number of statements favoring and opposing) students who were pro-New Deal recalled 58% more of the points they agreed with than of those they opposed; students

Abstract 24

TITLE   The Learning and Forgetting of Controversial Material.

AUTHORS   J. M. Levine and G. Murphy

PROBLEM   Is material which is congruent with the learner's attitudes more easily learned and better remembered than would be material which conflicts with the learner's attitudes?

SUBJECTS   Five pro-communist undergraduates; and five anti-communists.

PROCEDURE   Two prose passages were used, one moderately pro-communist, the other excitedly anti-communist.

Members of each group were asked to read each passage twice at normal reading rate. After 15 minutes subjects were asked to reproduce the material.

The learning exercise was repeated once a week for four weeks.

During the forgetting period (five weeks) memory for each passage was tested without re-reading.

SOME FINDINGS   (a) Learning period

Pro-communist material better learned (+17%) by pro-than by anti-communists.

Anti-communist material better learned (+36%) by anti- than by pro-communists.

(b) Forgetting period

Pro-communist material better recalled (+73%) after five weeks by pro- than by anti-communists.

Anti-communist material better recalled (+217%) after five weeks by anti- than by pro-communists.

SOURCE: *J. abnorm. soc. Psychol.*, 1943, XXXVIII:507–517.

anti-New Deal recalled 20% more of the anti-New Deal statements than of the pro (Edwards, 1941).

Because of what is noticed and recalled, the usual effect of a balanced, two-sided presentation is to strengthen existing biases. In the days when Prohibition was a controversial national issue, some students read logical passages and emotionally persuasive passages on both sides of the issue. More were strengthened in their initial convictions than converted to an opposing view. When they read (or heard) only material opposing their initial outlook, there was some shift beyond what was evident in the control group. Neither the logical nor the emotional appeal was significantly more influential than the other (Knower, 1936).

Still another line of defense against change is to discredit the source.

A speaker who expresses views which run counter to dominant attitudes in an American community today may be disregarded if he can be labeled an outside agitator or a communist. One of the difficulties of propaganda abroad, whether it be the Voice of America transmitted to other lands or foreign broadcasts to us, is that if listeners hear what contradicts their former views, they can easily dismiss the whole statement as untrustworthy. Some Americans, in 1958–61, dismissed the reports of the first Sputnik and the first manned travel in space as "Russian lies." Most advertising has to contend with the general expectation that companies will make exaggerated claims for their products.

If one finds it impossible to ignore or discount dissonant communications, he may distort them. A series of cartoons, intended to ridicule prejudice, portrayed a "Mr. Biggott" as biased and disagreeable. Particularly prejudiced subjects failed to get the message; they distorted the comic strips to accord with their own views (Cooper, Jahoda, 1947; Kendall, Wolf, 1949).

Changing attitudes

Attitudes do change

Despite all homeostatic tendencies, rationalizations, and such defensive devices as selective attention, selective memory, discrediting the source, and distortion of meaning, attitudes do change. More superficial attitudes, such as our impression of someone we have just met casually for the first time, may change markedly within a few minutes. As we grow older we become aware, too, that deeper attitudes have changed. We no longer feel and believe as we did when we were children. Sometimes the change proceeds from alteration in the external situation (S-P-A); sometimes from developments within ourselves.

One way in which attitudes are changed is learning from one's own experience. A boy enjoys a certain Western drama on television; he watches it intensely for weeks, even months. But gradually he loses interest. The anticipated excitement does not come. He finds himself bored with the repetitious, stereotyped plot. He has outgrown this favorite program. Another illustration is the change in attitude toward newcomers in a community. Some, as we say, "wear well;" others disappoint us. A naïve traveler may begin with suspicion of the "foreigners" around him who speak a strange language and live by different customs. Yet repeated experiences of friendliness, helpfulness, and trustworthiness may form a quite different attitude. Then a single experience of dishonesty or unkindness may obliterate all the good impressions. So the attitude fluctuates with new experience. Over a long period it may stabilize at some balanced level. Adolescent impressions of the opposite sex have something of the same changeable quality. A few experiences (or reports from others) lead to unwarranted generalizations which are corrected by further experience. Changes in situations lead, as we said in the preceding chapter, to changes in behavior and attitudes. It is often observed that a man who grew up in poverty and shared the attitudes of his associates may become economically more conservative as his income rises; if he loses his investments and salary, he may become more radical.

We shall study changes produced by (a) conditioning and learning; (b) the influence of important other persons; (c) new information; (d) logical arguments; and (e) changed reference groups.

Conditioning and learning

One of the earliest laboratory experiments in attitude change was the case of Albert, reported by John B. Watson in 1921. When Albert was 11 months old, he was apparently afraid of nothing except a sudden loud noise. When the banging of a steel bar occurred every time Albert touched a white rat, the fear response was conditioned to the white rat and generalized to a white rabbit, cotton, wool, and a fur coat. The case of Peter was studied (Jones, 1924) to see whether the conditioning technique could remove a fear. Peter, who was just under three years of age, would scream in hysterical fright at sight of a white rat, white rabbit, or a white piece of fur. Reconditioning was attempted first by introducing the white rabbit in a social play situation. Three other children who were not afraid of the rabbit were selected to play with Peter. When they were playing happily, the rabbit was introduced. The other children petted it and Peter was reassured. After seven sessions he would give it a little pat. Unfortunately, Peter then came down with scarlet fever and was away for two months. On his return, he and his nurse were badly frightened by a big dog. In the laboratory, he regressed to his original fear response to the white rabbit. Then re-conditioning started with food as the unconditioned stimulus. When Peter was happily eating, the rabbit was brought out in a wire cage, and set as close as it could be without upsetting Peter's eating. Slow progress was evident. The importance of social factors is underlined by the fact that the next big rise in Peter's tolerance for the rabbit came on the day when another child was with him and this boy showed acceptance of and interest in the rabbit. Another big improvement came on the day when another child held the rabbit as Peter was eating. After about 40 sessions, Peter freely fondled the rabbit.

An experimental effort to influence the freedom with which persons expressed opinions was based on the conditioning theory (Verplanck, 1955). The experimenters (there were 17 students taking this role) conducted a conversation according to a prearranged schedule, unknown to the other participants. For the first ten minutes, the number of opinions expressed by the second party was simply tallied. During the second ten minutes, every opinion expressed was "reinforced" by a friendly accepting response. The relative frequency of opinion statements by this partner nearly doubled during this period. There followed a third period of "experimental extinction" in which statements of opinion by the partner were ignored or disagreed with. Either procedure reduced the frequency of opinion statements to the original level, arousing also some hostile reactions to the strange and unpleasant behavior of the experimenter.

A subsequent study (Binder *et al.*, 1957) gave results suggesting that responses from an attractive girl student produced more change in the content of sentences made up by male students than did responses from a tall, heavy, dominant, mature man using the same conditioning technique.

A demonstration of the formation of attitudes by a classical conditioning technique was carried out with names flashed on a screen while an experimenter pronounced a word which subjects were asked to repeat silently to themselves. Most names were accompanied by neutral terms but "Tom" was always followed by an unpleasant word (e.g., ugly, failure) and "Bill" by a favorable term (e.g., happy, gift). As a result, the rating on a +3 (like) to —3 (dislike) differential scale came out +0.6 for Tom and +2.2 for Bill. In another group where the associations were reversed, Tom rated + 1.3 and Bill —0.1. In a variant of the experiment, nationality names were used. If "Swedish" were followed by unpleasant words, the Swedes rated +0.6; if by pleasant words, they rose in favor to +2.2 (Staats, Staats, 1958). This is the technique of the advertiser who repeatedly associates his product with the most attractive words and images.

Another version of the attitude-conditioning experiment associated nonsense syllables with "good" names like George Washington and Helen Keller, or with "bad" names like Stalin and Hitler. Subjects were ostensibly supposed to memorize the nonsense syllables. Later they were asked to react to each nonsense item on eight scales ranging from "like" to "dislike," from "beautiful" to "ugly," etc. On scales, again ranging from +3 to —3, the previously meaningless syllables seen during the pronunciation of names of bad characters, rated, on the average, at —0.9; those seen while hearing the name of an admired person, averaged +1.9, a difference significant at the .001 level (Blandford, Sampson, 1964).

Other educational and therapeutic experiences have been devised to affect attitudes. One experiment successfully modified attitudes of young children toward a task by constructing situations in which the structure (S) leads to processes of successful operation (P) and gradually builds the attitude of self-confidence (A). Twelve pre-school children who had reacted to a difficult task by crying, begging for help, or becoming angry and destructive, were trained for similar tasks which were extremely easy but which grew gradually harder. Their interest in the task increased; they cried less, and they no longer showed angry or destructive behavior. A control group showed no significant change (Keister, Updegraff, 1937).

Influence by important other persons

A norm is usually thought of as the majority view and as supported by the prestige figures of the group. Hence, evidence of disagreement with the majority or with the leader provokes a sense of dissonance, alienation, and need to revise attitudes.

One of the first studies on this problem (Moore, 1921) explored attitudes toward the offensiveness of common acts of minor misbehavior and toward dissonant musical chords. One experimental group was told the choice of the majority; a second was told the decision of an expert in the field; a third served as control. Controls when retested changed 16 percent of their responses; those who received expert opinion changed 47 percent; and those who received majority opinion, 53 percent. Both of the latter groups moved toward agreement with the alleged norm.

In another early experiment (Wheeler, Jordan, 1929) students were given 50 controversial questions on campus and public affairs. These were repeated a week later with no effort to influence responses. Changes appeared in 30 percent of the individual answers: 22 percent of these went toward the majority viewpoint; 8 percent went against it. Apparently, individuals sharing ideas with others had produced some movement toward the group norm although this had never been explicitly reported. After another week, those items on which at least two-thirds of the class agreed were given a third time, with information on the answers preferred by the majority. In this case, 64 percent of the responses were changed: 60 percent in agreement with the majority, 4 percent against it.

In another experiment (Marple, 1933) subjects expressed their opinions on 75 controversial issues of the day. A month later, the questionnaire was repeated, but with this difference. One-third of the subjects found one response to each question already checked. They were told that this was how a majority of their group had responded the month before. In this subgroup about half of the subjects who were not in agreement with the apparent norm, changed their answer to make it reflect what "most people" believed. Another third, in the Marple experiments, also found a response checked, but were told that this represented the best answer in the opinion of 20 "experts." Here again, nearly half of the deviate answers were changed to bring them closer into line with authority. The last third served as controls; they showed high consistency between answers on the first and second inquiry.

The finding that people often change their views to accord with their associates reminds one of the Asch conformity experiments reported in Chapter 3. Another study by Asch (with Block and Hertzman, 1940) asked students to rank ten professions (business, dentistry, engineering, law, politics, etc.) for intelligence required, social usefulness, and other desirable characteristics. One subgroup had been told that a study of rankings by 500 college students rated politics highest. This subgroup rated politics as fourth among the ten. Another experimental subgroup was told that politics had come out lowest in the ratings previously assigned by 500 college students. In this subgroup, politics dropped to ninth place. In a control group, with no statement about how others felt, politics ranked eighth. Asch interprets the change as based on a re-definition of "politics;" the high ratings give the connotation of statesmanship; low ratings suggest ward heelers. Later in this chapter we shall report Lewis' (1941) work, done with Asch, on rationalization of changed reactions to various political slogans.

These experiments have shown how individuals modify their responses to conform with a known reference group. Dissonance may also be reduced by imagining that the group feels as the individual does. One study (Wallen, 1943) asked 237 college women to estimate what proportion of students on the campus of this small college for women expected the United States to go to war with Germany, favored the Selective Service Act, and supported the St. Lawrence Seaway. Each student reported also her own view on the same three questions. Correlations between own opinion and the size of estimated support on campus ran .56, .39, and .45. Without firm knowledge of campus opinion, each girl expected that most others would agree with her. Those who themselves answered "Yes" estimated that 56 percent agreed with them; those who themselves answered "No" expected 65 percent of the student body to be on their side. The same phenomenon is seen in elections in which both sides seem certain of victory before the ballots are counted.

In 1940, when public opinion in the United States was divided on staying out of the European war, a public opinion poll asked whether, if Germany won, the United States should try to have friendly relations and trade with that country. The question was presented to people in two forms. One form was, "Lindbergh says . . . (. . . .)." The other named no one and began, "It has been suggested that . . . (. . . .)." Lindbergh, of course, was a national hero at that time. Use of his name in stating the proposition increased agreement from 46 percent to 57 percent in comparable populations (Cantril, 1944).

In a typical study of the impact of prestige, large (150–160 each) and comparable groups of students rated their acceptance of 30 statements when these were (a) attributed to admired persons; (b) attributed to disliked persons; (c) presented with no source. For example, a statement that there is nothing sacred or unalterable about the American Constitution was rated +1.1 on a scale from +2.0 (complete agreement) to —2.0 (complete rejection). A group who were given the same statement as a quotation from Woodrow Wilson rated it +1.7, a higher degree of acceptance. Those who saw it attributed to Al Capone, a gangster, rated the same proposition +0.5, a difference statistically significant (more than 5 times its standard error) (Saade, Farnsworth, 1934).

A statement about revolution attributed to Thomas Jefferson was more readily accepted than was the same proposition attributed to Lenin (Lorge, 1936). Lorge interpreted the influence of prestige suggestion as a case of the power of *settled* attitudes (toward the authors) over *tentative* attitudes (toward the specific utterances).

Stereotyped labels may also influence acceptance or rejection of a proposition. Political statements attributed to "radicals," "fascists," or "Communists" were less likely (about 30 percent less) to be accepted than were the same propositions when presented without such a label (Menefee, 1936). Quite possibly, the meaning of the propositions changed when the labels were attached.

An accepted teacher represents an influential norm. Usually—but not invariably—students tested before and after a course move toward the position presented by the instructor. One illustration is a study (Stagner, 1942) of 140 summer session students attending a course on nationalism (in 1938) at Western Reserve University. Most of the nine lecturers supported an internationalist viewpoint. On tests given before and again after the lectures students showed an increase (57 to 69 percent) in support of a League of Nations with strong armed forces of its own and a decrease (76 to 65 percent) in advocacy of educating American children to believe that the United States has always stood for peace and justice. It is important to note that the impact was not overpowering; in neither case did a majority become a minority. On other pertinent questions changes were less than on these two. A course on Immigration and Race Problems (Smith, Mapheus, 1939) brought about more favorable attitudes than were produced in a control group which gave little attention to race. Explanations for such changes must take account of several factors: the prestige of the instructor as an expert and as a symbol of what is right; the cogency of the arguments offered; the desire of pupils to emulate or to please the teacher; the influence of fellow students who for one reason or another agree with the instructor.

A study (Kroll, 1934) of liberal-conservative attitudes of 183 high school students showed that three teachers who were only slightly more liberal than the pupils had little influence on these attitudes, but that three teachers who were strongly liberal produced a marked change (13 times its S.E.) in their pupils. Experiments with before-and-after tests of student attitudes toward Negroes, soil conservation, capital punishment, social insurance, and trade unions showed that 15-minute high school teaching units were usually effective in changing attitudes. Follow-up tests after two months and four months revealed some regression toward initial attitudes (Remmers, 1938) but even after a year some effects persisted. A typical result is the finding that attitudes toward Negroes averaged (300 cases) 5.26 before the unit was taught, rose to 6.59 after the unit, two months later dropped to 6.09, and six months after the instruction had returned to 5.97 but still remained substantially above the initial level (Hall, 1938).

One investigator (Longstreet, 1935) tried to teach history in high school so that pupils would become less militaristic in outlook. He produced a significant decrease in favorable attitudes toward war, although in three control schools during the same period, the usual history course produced no change.

Teachers, of course, do not always succeed in attempts at influence. One teacher (Campbell, 1934) tried in vain, during a one-semester course in economic geography, to make high school students more "world-minded." Students taking some courses in race relations likewise failed to show a statistically significant improvement in attitude (Droba, 1932; Young, 1932). These studies were made early in the history of research on this problem and do not provide data with which to answer the obvious question of why some teachers influence attitudes more than others. One possible factor is the initial attitude of students. As we shall emphasize later in this chapter, people who hear a point of view for the first time are more easily influenced than those who have previously heard and rejected the ideas being presented. Another factor is certainly the appeal of the teacher himself as a symbol of prestige and of the students' ideals. Attitudes of pupils toward schoolbooks and tests may also play a part.

People tend to be more influenced by leaders in their own field. Teachers, for example (Kulp, 1934), changed more of their responses to agree with norms attributed to "leading educators" than they did when the same answers were attributed to some experts in the social sciences.

In Chapter 3 we noted that conforming behavior may be psychologically motivated by a desire for guidance in a puzzling situation (informational), or by a desire to please others (ingratiating) or by pressure to join in group solidarity (normative). Shifts of attitude toward agreement with the majority or with distinguished persons are commonly of the first type. The individual is uncertain and relies on what he thinks may be superior wisdom.

Information and attitude

A persistent problem in the study of attitudes concerns the extent to which they are influenced by cold facts. Certainly an irate mob is un-

Abstract 25

TITLE   Interrelationships of Attitude and Information.

AUTHOR   Meredith W. Green

PROBLEM   Does information about Negro achievements affect attitudes of white adolescents?

SUBJECTS   224 white pupils in 9th and 10th grades of a Virginia high school.

PROCEDURE   Subjects were tested for knowledge about Negroes and for attitudes toward Negroes. They then read for 40 minutes material which presented facts about Negroes and their achievements.

SOME FINDINGS   Intelligence of pupils was related to initial information about the Negro ($r = .43$) and to a more favorable attitude toward increasing opportunities for Negroes ($r = .36$). Initial information score and attitude score were also correlated ($r = .48$); pupils with more favorable attitudes were also better informed. As a result of reading the assigned material, information scores rose substantially from an average of 139 to 202 (a gain 23 times its S.E.). Attitude scores after reading the assigned material became more favorable to increasing Negro opportunities, from an average score of 175 to one of 195 (a gain 10 times its S.E.).

Those pupils who learned most on the information tests also made significantly larger changes in attitude.

SOURCE: Unpublished doctoral dissertation manuscript. Teachers College, Columbia University, 1952.

likely to be swayed by statistics and logic. But many attitudes are connected with systems of interrelated intellectual concepts and can be modified when these concepts change. Information that an acquaintance has said pleasant or unpleasant things about us can change correspondingly our attitude toward him. Abstract 25 presents evidence that giving white pupils in a Southern school information about Negro achievements affected their readiness to extend opportunities for Negroes. The same interpretation can be made of teacher influence. Certainly the information presented by the instructor is one of the strong factors in subsequent attitude changes.

In Chapter 14 is a table listing the remarkable changes in the United States' friends and enemies over the years. The development of public opinion polls has made it possible to study the movement of attitudes in response to events in the news. One early example was the polling of 222 adults in September, 1938, before Munich and again in October and November. On the proposition that the United States should build up its military strength, support rose from 32 percent in September to 43 percent in October and 54 percent in November (Riess, 1939). Cantril (1940) has graphed the course of public opinion as America moved toward participation in World War II. Each time the people learned of Hitler's attack on another country, the pro-war attitudes in America mounted. When the public was informed of the first Sputnik launched into space, American attitudes toward Russian science and toward our own programs of education in science were affected.

Being generally well informed has been found associated with emerging rather than outworn attitudes. A test of "liberalism" on issues of race, politics, and international relations showed that among 400 high school students those who were most liberal were also higher in factual knowledge of history [r = .58] and in amount of reading of journals of opinion [r = .37] (Wrightstone, 1934). In the Purdue poll of high school students, knowledge of social science accompanied attitudes supporting the Bill of Rights and opposing Marxist, Fascist or super-patriot creeds, despite the fact that correlations were low, only .10 to .20 (Remmers, 1963). Lentz (1939) found that more liberals than conservatives were in the upper third of their high school graduating class. Dexter (1939) found that radicals were better informed than conservatives. Harper (1927) found that more years of education meant more liberal scores (r = .52). Students given the Harper test of liberal-conservative attitudes at the beginning and end of a sociology course showed an increase of liberalism (5 times its S.E.). The correlation between objective tests of factual information and increased liberalism was high—r = .73 (Salner, Remmers, 1933). Knowledge of current events, based on a *Time* magazine quiz, correlated only .20 with preference for liberal policies on specific issues, but this was enough to give the most liberal quartile an average score of 71, significantly higher than the 61 average attained by the most conservative quartile (Pace, 1939). A study in Kansas during depression years showed (as did Newcomb's Bennington College study) a steady increase in liberalism of student opinion from freshmen through seniors and the highest levels among graduate students. Neither study clearly separated the impact of new facts from that of the prevailing social norms. The students majoring in social science were significantly more liberal than were those majoring in the humanities or in the physical sciences. The more social science courses a student had studied, the higher his liberalism score (Boldt, Stroud, 1934). Another study of college students (Murphy, Likert, 1938) showed correlations of .40 or .50 between academic grades as a measure of scholarship and liberal attitudes on race and international relations.

On the specific issue of international relations, a liberal attitude (international in outlook) has been found to be positively correlated with more intelligence and more study of social science (Harris *et al.*, 1932; Kolstad, 1933). On race relations, more liberal acceptance of Negroes by whites was strongly correlated with high scores on 40 information items (Reckless, Bringen, 1933).

These factual findings can be interpreted in several ways. Does the information bring about the favorable attitude, or does the attitude open the mind and arouse interest in acquiring more knowledge? Which is cause and which is effect? Or are both due to higher intelligence or more cultured homes? Green's experiment (Abstract 25) indicates that new information can modify attitudes in a liberal direction. But concern over a situation may well lead to acquisition of new information.

The role of attitude in affecting the acquisition and use of new information is evident in a study of immigrants to Israel (Shuval, 1959). Those who came with a Zionist orientation and enthusiasm were generally better informed than non-Zionists when they arrived, and their superiority in knowledge over the non-Zionists *increased* after both groups had spent six months in the country.

According to Festinger's (1957) theory of cognitive dissonance, people whose attitudes lead them to take certain actions, such as moving to Israel, transfering to another college, or buying an expensive article, seek to reduce any lingering doubts or dissonance by finding facts to justify their actions. A study (Ehrlich *et al.*, 1957) of persons who had recently bought a new car showed that they were more apt to read car advertisements particularly for the make of car they had just bought than were owners of older cars. Apparently they sought confirmation of their good judgment in making this important choice.

The source of information affects its credibility and influence. The relative influence of different sources and media will be considered more fully in the following chapter. Usually an attractive communicator enhances the probability of acceptance of the message. If subjects are clearly forwarned that a persuasive communication comes from a biased, incompetent, untrustworthy source, they show very little attitude change. A similar warning placed at the end of a piece of propaganda was found to come too late to reduce the susceptibility (Kiesler, Kiesler, 1964).

It is not necessary, apparently, for a communicator to be lovable in order to be influential. Smith (1961) reported that Army men, given reasons for eating fried grasshoppers and left free to make their own decisions, were not more likely to adopt the recommendation of the man whose manner was friendly rather than forbidding. Perhaps, in Army life, friendliness does not signify trustworthiness. Zimbardo (1964) has duplicated the experiment with college students. He found the more disagreeable communicator more likely to persuade subjects to undertake the disagreeable experiment.

When information has brought about a change in attitude, will the

Abstract 26

TITLE   Persistence of Induced Opinion Change and Retention of the Inducing Message Contents.

AUTHORS   William A. Watts and William J. McGuire

PROBLEM   Is persistence or decay of an opinion change closely related to memory for, or forgetting of, the cognitive material which accompanied the change? Does apparent trustworthiness of the source make a difference?

SUBJECTS   191 students in an introductory course in education.

PROCEDURE   As a result of pre-testing, four issues were selected because students were generally opposed to the propositions:

(a) Puerto Rico should be admitted to the Union as the 51st State.

(b) Courts should deal more leniently with juvenile delinquents.

(c) The Secretary of State should be elected by the people, not appointed by the President.

(d) The state sales tax should be abolished.

Each statement was rated on a 15-step scale from 1 "Definitely disagree" to, 15, "Definitely agree."

Students rated their opinion on an issue; then read a persuasive 600-word message including facts and figures, favoring the proposition, and attributed either to a competent or apparently untrustworthy source.

Other tests asked for recall of issues; of the point of view favored by the message; and of specific arguments advanced in it.

Recall was measured immediately, after one week, two weeks, and six weeks.

SOME FINDINGS   Opinion change based on an allegedly competent, official source was 3.0 scale steps; the change after reading the same message attributed to an apparently untrustworthy source was only 1.9 scale steps.

After six weeks, however, the influence of the competent source had declined steadily to 0.7 scale steps; that of the untrustworthy source declined only to 1.1 scale steps. Only 34 percent were able to identify the source after six weeks.

Immediately after presentation 72 percent were able to recall three relevant arguments; after six weeks only 11 percent could do so.

The opinion change remaining after six weeks was 31 percent of the immediate change; argument recall after six weeks averaged only 11 percent of the original recall.

SOURCE: *J. abnorm. soc. Psychol.*, 1964, LXVIII:233–241.

change persist after the facts have been forgotten? Abstract 26 indicates that it may.

Logic and feeling

Attitudes support, and are supported by, a cognitive structure. For example, because we believe that a college education will create a broader understanding of life and greater chances for success, and because we value these ends, we have a positive attitude toward college education. Two factors are interrelated in the logical conclusion. One is the probability that certain consequences will occur. The other is the value (positive or negative) attached to each consequence. Theory suggests that the two factors be multiplied, since if either the probability or the value rating is zero, the factor will have no influence.

The formula may be written $A = (p_1v_2 + p_1v_2 \cdots \text{(to } n)\ p_nv_n)$ where p is probability and v is value, for consequences to n.

Rosenberg (1956) tested the attitude of 117 students toward allowing Communists to address the public. He also obtained from the students the value they placed on 35 items—e.g., "being strongly patriotic" or "all human beings having equal rights"—and their judgments about the probable connection between Communist speakers and the attainment of each value. In another project the issue was "allowing Negroes to move into white neighborhoods." In each case the sum of the products of value and instrumentality correlated highly with the independent measure of attitude.

In more recent studies Rosenberg (1965) has explored the question: If an attitude is reversed (e.g., by hypnosis) will the cognitive associations be revised to become consistent? Tests revealed marked changes in both the estimates of value and those of instrumentality for items related to the central issue on which the attitude was temporarily altered. No such changes occurred in control subjects. For example, it was suggested to a medical student who was strongly opposed to federal medical insurance that on awakening from hypnosis he would be strongly in favor. The suggestion was effective. On the scale, he rated himself strongly favorable. Before hypnosis, he had been in favor of "change, variety and new experience" but saw no connection between this and the federal insurance. After the change in attitude toward medical insurance he argued that physicians in such a program would gain a wider variey of experience. Another of his values was "the right to participate in making decisions which affect one." He saw this value threatened by federal health insurance. After hypnosis, he could no longer see any connection between this value and the proposal. In the above instances the probability of a connection was altered. In others, the value changed. Thus, before and after the hypnotic suggestion this student saw a strong connection between "a good standard of living assured to everyone" and federal health insurance. But his original value rating put the "good standard of living for everyone" at —3; i.e., undesirable. After hypnosis it changed to +5; very desirable. The p v in the formula was not completely consistent with A for every item, but deviations were regarded by the subject as unimportant.

After removal of amnesia, subjects were told they would return to "normal." Their attitudes became like those originally expressed. But as late as ten days after the experiment, some subjects still retained some cognitive assumptions more consistent with the experimentally altered position. Also, some propositions originally asserted with confidence had become questionable. Presumably the enforced exposure to considerations that they would never previously have entertained had left its mark. But in general the cognitive system shifted with the attitude change.

These findings illustrate both rationality and rationalization. People usually want their beliefs and attitudes to be consistent. A strong attitude is supported by what seem to be "good reasons," even if sometimes the reasons are rationalizations developed to keep consonance in the psychic system.

In another ingenious experiment which has become famous in social psychology, Lewis (1941) asked adults to rank ten political slogans. Having previously determined the political views of these respondents, she reported to them some unexpected and challenging new data. She told them that one of their leaders and heroes had made a very different ranking. Staunch conservatives were told, for example, that Herbert Hoover had given a fairly high rating to "Workers of the world, unite" and a low rating to "Balance the budget!" Communists and pro-Communists were told that the head of the Communist Party (Earl Browder, at that time) had given a high rating to "America First" (a slogan being used by extreme isolationists) and only average rating to "Workers of the world unite!" The little experiment did not basically alter the adults' attitudes, but the surprising information was assimilated by rationalization. Thus, if Hoover were admired and said to believe that workers should unite, he must have meant that they should unite with their employers and fellow workers in loyalty to the company and to their country. A Communist who accepted the alleged high rating of "America First" by the head of his party, explained that Browder undoubtedly meant that Communists in America should try first of all to win over America for the Communist cause. Thus the cognitive interpretations were made to reconcile the apparently contradictory data with no change in basic attitudes.

Another method by which logical consistency may be preserved in this type of experience is to attribute devious motives to the supposed author of the statement. Students who held the author of an acceptable proposal in low esteem usually rated his motives as "condemnable" (Horowitz, Pastore, 1955).

When an attitude is challenged by contradictory evidence, intellectual consistency requires that the evidence be rejected, discounted, or re-interpreted in order to sustain the pre-existing attitude. Strong attitudes seldom give way before a few incompatible facts or arguments.

Changed reference groups

The most effective technique for altering attitudes is to change refer-ence groups. This accords with our S-P-A formula. In the preceding chapter we reported that workers who became foremen began to think of themselves as company officials and identified with the corporation. Those who became shop stewards gradually became convinced of the soundness of the union viewpoint (Lieberman, 1956). Other studies, to be presented in Chapter 11, show that Northern students who attend a Southern college (Sims, Patrick, 1936) or Southerners attending a North-ern college change their attitudes on race relations (Eddy, 1961). An investigation of adults who had undergone a marked change in prejudice showed that most of them connected the shift in attitudes with having moved from one region to another (Watson, 1950). The change in atti-tudes of students at Bennington during depression years is, as mentioned earlier in this chapter, a notable example of the effect of a new reference group, although as we have observed, new knowledge was also influential.

Many students who attend summer conferences organized by re-ligious groups have experienced the "pull" of the special atmosphere toward taking seriously many ideals not so vigorously championed by their hometown reference groups. These students may also have felt a letdown when they returned to their normal social setting.

An organization like Alcoholics Anonymous, which has been unusu-ally successful in maintaining changed attitudes toward drinking, relies heavily on group influence. The new member is assigned to friends who look out for him and on whom he can call whenever he needs them. He is urged to come to meetings in which other members testify to their loyalty to A.A. In much the same way, the Salvation Army pro-vides the convert with a group of associates who will help sustain his new way of life.

What attitudes change?

We have reported changes in attitudes as a consequence of condition-ing, learning, majority influence, prestige models, new information, logic, or changed reference groups. But not all attitudes are equally suscep-tible to such influences. What makes an attitude easy or difficult to change?

At his first encounter with a strange object, the individual has no clearly defined attitude. He tries to place the new object into some familiar category so that he will know how to respond. Imagine a student hearing for the first time about Zen Buddhism. His attitude might be based on the presumption that "Zen" is foreign, or religious, or fashionable, or mysterious. The hypothetical student might have strong attitudes toward things mysterious, fashionable, religious or foreign. Much might depend on his feeling about the person who uses the word or the magazine in which he reads it. In any case, his initial attitude will not be strongly anchored. It should be easy to influence. Thus, a campus newspaper once experimented with a planted story about a little known public figure—a Prime Minister of Australia. One story was favorable, another very critical. Tests showed that students' opinions were strongly influenced by which story they read (Annis, Meier, 1934). Similar reports about a President of the United States would have little chance to influence the more firmly set attitudes of readers. An argument on architecture or dieting might influence laymen, although it would be quickly discounted by experienced architects or nutritionists. The first hypothesis, then, is that the more sophisticated the audience on a given issue, the harder it will be to alter their attitudes. The more naïve they are on the particular issue, the more easily they will be influenced.

Another dimension of attitude which affects its mutability is its salience for the holder. It is relatively easy to change opinions about matters which seem peripheral, remote, and trivial to our lives. It is another matter to move us in a direction which is central to our lives and involves our sense of worth and meaning. This is related to the finding (Rokeach, 1960) that it is usually easier to change the opinions of persons who are near the middle-of-the-road than of those who are more intense and fanatical, who choose the extremes.

Among attitudes that are easily changed are those reluctantly held. A change in the direction of wishes, on the other hand, is usually welcome. Cantril (1938) has shown a substantial correlation between what people would like to have happen in the future and what they believe is likely to happen. There seems to be a general tendency toward optimism, at least in the United States. (More on this in Chapter 9.) Quite possibly studies within cultures which have suffered more tragically would yield different expectations.

Attitudes that are firmly grounded in cognitive structures are particularly resistant to change (Rosenberg, 1956). This proposition relates to several earlier observations. Objects relatively new to us, and not especially salient or pleasant, are likely to have only insubstantial rational support. On matters, however, with which we have long been vitally concerned, we are likely to have collected an abundance of hard facts as well as plausible arguments.

Persuasible moments

An individual varies from time to time in the ease with which he can be influenced. In the Mausner experiment (reported in Chapter 2) students who had recently experienced a series of failures were especially prone to concur with their partner's view. In the Bavelas study (reported in Chapter 5) recreational leaders who knew they had not succeeded with autocratic methods were particularly good at learning a new democratic approach.

There are times in the life history of every person when there is a special readiness for many changes in attitudes. The beginning of a new stage of life is likely to arouse a special degree of receptivity to new ways. The child is ready to discard some old ways when he first goes to school, when he moves from grade school to high school, when he goes away to college, when he takes his first job, when he marries, and when his first child is born. Kurt Lewin (1947) spoke of the need to "unfreeze" old attitudes, to re-orient the individual, and then to "freeze" or make stable the new attitudes. When individuals sever their old moorings by moving from country to city or from the parental home to one of their own, old patterns are broken.

A crisis or traumatic experience is likely to force open new paths of thought. John Dewey (1910) said that thinking begins after complacency is disturbed. A problem for creative thought arises when customary behavior does not bring expected results.

Davis (1930) found that a number of Russian Communist leaders had been brought up in conservative environments but had been suddenly converted as a result of unusual, shocking, or painful experiences. Not infrequently, community action to correct hazards cannot get started until some tragic incident jars public opinion. It is traditional that reform must come at the opportune time. But the precipitating incident, although it may unfreeze the old syndrome, does not immediately create the new pattern of feelings.

When a long-standing and cognitively supported attitude is upset, it takes time to assimilate the change. This may account, at least in part, for the "sleeper effect": A message may seem to have less effect immediately after presentation than is apparent weeks later. The seed of a new attitude has been planted, but it needs time to grow. In the next chapter we will show that a communication from a source of low credibility may have a stronger effect with the passage of time, when the source has been forgotten.

A summary of the processes by which behaviors are changed has been offered by Kelman (1958). He suggests three types of change: compliance, identification, and internalization. Glidewell in an address (N.T.L., 1962) renamed these alliteratively "bargaining, belonging, and belief." The first type is forced on the person, and he conforms only so long as he is rewarded and under surveillance. The second depends on the subject's desire to please the influencer; he conforms so long as he cares about the person's approval. Only the third represents a change in genuine personal conviction.

Persuasible personalities

Are some people generally more open to persuasion, whatever the issue and whatever the direction of influence? Are others more resistant?

Some 185 eleventh graders were given an attitude test covering 15 current issues (Janis, Field, 1959). They then read booklets of argument on one side of these questions. They were tested after one week to see how much their opinions had changed. Later they read arguments of opposing points of view and were again retested. Those who changed most on the first arguments also changed most on the counter-arguments (r = .30). Self-rating on personality did not correlate significantly with actual change. This research indicates that it is possible to identify some individuals who can more easily be persuaded by reading arguments. The study is not broad enough to reveal whether these same people would also be more gullible in response to advertising or more sensitive to cues in a social situation.

A series of studies (Hovland, Janis, 1959) indicates that many of the popular notions about general gullibility have not been confirmed in careful tests. Intelligent people are not always critical and hard to influence; they sometimes accept new evidence more quickly than do the less intelligent. Highly imaginative adolescents are not necessarily more easily influenced than their more practical and prosaic peers. Tough, aggressive, argumentative persons are not noticeably more resistant to persuasion than those of quiet and mild manners who preserve a rigidly closed mind.

One personality trait that does seem to be related to persuasability is low self-esteem. In Chapter 2 we showed that subjects who thought they had done very poorly in a series of laboratory exercises were more likely to conform to what their partner thought was a correct estimate (Mausner, 1953). A study of college men who were tested before and after reading arguments concerning the probability of three different events showed that those who changed their opinions most readily were also likely to be those who reported feelings of social inadequacy (Janis, 1954). In a second study of this kind, it was found that the more persuasable college men reported more fear of failure on tests and more avid need for social approval (Janis, 1955). Students who, on a scale of other-directed vs. inner-directed tendencies, registered a high need for security, social approval, and conformity were more likely to change their opinions (significant at .01 level of probability) (Linton,

Graham, 1959). When two subjects, one high in self-esteem and one low in self-esteem, cooperated in interpreting a psychological case history, the partner higher in self-regard was much more persuasive (Cohen, 1956). Depressed psychotic patients have been found especially easy to persuade (Janis, Rife, 1959). Persons low in self-esteem are reported to identify more readily with other individuals (Stotland, Hillmer, 1962).

The authoritarian personality might seem to define one kind of person who would be dogmatic and hard to influence. One study (Canning, Baker, 1959) found that students who had scored high on the F-scale, when tested in Sherif's autokinetic exercise, did converge less toward their partner than did the low-authoritarians. However, one dimension of the F-scale is "submission to authority," and on this particular cluster of characteristics another study (Cohen, 1956) found no difference between persons who changed their opinions and non-changers. What did appear was that the eight (of 47) students who resisted so hard that they changed opinions in a direction counter to the attempted persuasion were very low in "submission to authority" and very high in "cynicism." Another cluster difference relates to the dimension called "anti-intraception." Non-changers were impatient with self-scrutiny and prone to action; changers of opinion were more introspective. The relationship of total F-scale score to persuasability is not simple; the various parts of the scale seem to operate in contrasting directions. A study by McClintock (1958) agrees with Cohen that greater self-insight accompanies openness to change and freedom from ethnocentric prejudices. In the same direction is the conclusion of another study (Katz *et al.*, 1956) that persons who are highly defensive are resistant to influence. If they are less defensive and more ready to listen to others, they are less likely to cherish prejudices.

Immunization against persuasion

The individual who has always supposed that everyone agreed with his own attitude is in for a rude shock when he finds people he admires holding opposing views. He may be more vulnerable than another person who has been forewarned that some people think differently. One reason why some American soldiers yielded to the "brainwashing" of Communists during the war in Korea, was that they had not been prepared to refute the Communist line of persuasion. The person who has already heard the arguments against his position, has evaluated them and found their weaknesses, is far better armed than the one who has been given only a positive indoctrination.

Abstract 27 shows that students who were prepared to refute counter-arguments were still influenced by them, but much less than were students without such immunization.

Abstract 27

TITLE   The Relative Efficacy of Various Types of Prior Belief-Defense in Producing Immunity against Persuasion.

AUTHORS   William J. McGuire and D. Papageorgis

PROBLEM   Will exposure to possible counter-arguments (with refutation or support for present beliefs) strengthen the ability to defend present beliefs? Which is more effective—mobilizing arguments to bolster present beliefs or refuting possible counter-arguments?

SUBJECTS   130 freshmen at a university.

PROCEDURE   Subjects indicated strength of their agreement (on a 15-interval scale from definitely false to definitely true) with each of four propositions concerning health:
a. Chest X-rays should be taken once a year.
b. Penicillin benefits mankind.
c. Mental illness is not contagious.
d. Teeth should be brushed after every meal.
The first immunizing session required writing a 20-minute essay defending a belief. Half of the subjects wrote supporting arguments; the other half developed refutations for possible counter-arguments.
A second immunizing session presented supporting arguments or refutations of counter-arguments.
There followed exposure to strong arguments against (a) beliefs which had been treated in the immunizing sessions and (b) beliefs which had not been so treated.

SOME FINDINGS   Untreated beliefs, subjected to strong counter-arguments, dropped from 12.6 to 6.6 on a 15-point scale.
Immunized beliefs rose during the immunizing sessions from 13.3 to 14.1; the counter-arguments reduced this acceptance to 8.0; the final level remained significantly higher than for non-immunized. Refuting imagined counter-arguments was significantly more effective than cumulating supportive arguments (p = .001).

SOURCE: *J. abnorm. soc. Psychol.*, 1961, 62:338–345.

Measuring attitudes

At the beginning of this chapter it was reported that our everyday estimates of the attitudes of others are based on their facial expressions, gestures, and behavior as well as on what they say. Scientific study of attitudes, however, demands more careful control of our indices. Questions and observation techniques should be carefully devised, tried out, and revised. To measure an attitude in one person may require both range and depth of inquiry. To measure opinion in a section of the public may require a large and carefully selected sample of respondents. We shall study public opinion polls first, because responses are typically gathered by a very simple procedure: asking a single question or a few interrelated questions. The issues are presumably those on which direct answers can be trusted to correspond to real attitudes.

Polls

Public opinion polls originated with straw votes collected by political leaders, newspapers, and magazines to determine how various sections of the population would vote. Beginning in 1916, a famous series was conducted by the *Literary Digest* magazine. The elections of Herbert Hoover in 1928 and of Franklin D. Roosevelt in 1932 were predicted correctly. Then, in 1936, despite millions of ballots, the *Literary Digest* poll went sadly astray. It predicted 32 states for Alfred Landon, who carried only two—Maine and Vermont. This fiasco precipitated modern scientific polling. The key to accuracy is not the form of the question or the size of the sample—current polls are never as large as the *Digest* polls—but how *representative* is the sample. The *Digest* mailed ballots to automobile owners and names listed in telephone directories. This biased the sample in favor of prosperous voters, who were more likely to be Republicans. The poorer voters were less likely to receive ballots, but they did vote for Roosevelt at the polls.

Since 1936, the technique of polling has been improved in many ways. Samples are made up carefully to ensure that every region, every economic class, both sexes, each age group, each religion, every level of education, etc., are proportionately the same in the sample as in the total population. Special care has been taken, when forecasting elections, to distinguish between those who will and those who will not take the trouble to vote on election day. Interviewers have been trained to ask questions without disclosing their own points of view. Questions have been pre-tested to avoid possible misunderstandings. As a result of these and other technical advances, public opinion polls now provide remarkably reliable data on a wide variety of issues. Polls on such controversial issues as federal aid to education, value of trade unions, approval of the President, foreign policy, health care programs, farm policy, criticism of television, treatment of delinquents, changing moral standards, and status of the sexes are usually easier to interpret than are election forecasts. Opinon is usually more unevenly divided and when the results show 75 percent for and 25 percent against, a possible slight error of 2 or 3 percent makes little difference. In close elections, however, when opinion is 49 percent one way and 51 percent the other, and when forecasts must be made state by state, the difficulty of interpretation is much greater.

242

A summary (American Institute of Public Opinion, Feb. 9, 1964) of poll results compared with election returns in 14 campaigns from 1936 to 1962 showed all but one (Truman vs. Dewey, 1948) correctly predicted. The discrepancy between forecast and outcome in percentage of popular vote accorded the winning party averaged 2.9 percentage points. For the most recent seven elections, the deviation averaged only 1.8 percentage points. Better techniques of sampling and of allowance for non-voting contributed to the improvement.

Public vs. private

When an interviewer comes to a citizen and asks for an opinion, the response given may or may not correspond to the real, inner attitude of the citizen. It may be more important to him to make a good impression on the interviewer than to voice his true opinion on the issue. Some studies (Cantril, 1944; Stember, Hyman, 1949) have shown that interviewers, despite efforts to be objective, are likely to get the opinions they approve or expect. White interviewers do not get quite the same frankness from some Negroes that Negro interviewers might get: Whites may be told what respondents think they want to hear.

A study in New York showed that interviewers who looked Jewish or introduced themselves with names considered Jewish found less anti-Semitism in the samples they polled (Robinson, Rhode, 1946). Most public opinion polling organizations use college-educated, middle-class women as interviewers, and there is evidence that many working men do not express themselves freely to such a stranger.

In an intensive study of a community called "Elm Hollow" (New York State) 90 percent of the Methodists in 1930 publicly opposed card games. When the participant observer had lived longer in the community and had become accepted and trusted as a friend, he found that in private only 20 percent of these Methodists expressed opposition to card games (Schanck, 1932).

Form of question

It is not as easy as it seems to ask a really effective attitude question. An effective question is one which is understood in the same way by the interviewer and the respondent. The question seeks information which the respondent has available and is willing to give to the interrogator at the time he is asked. It is phrased unambiguously. It focuses on a single issue (unidimensional) and does not create confusion by raising several attitude issues in one query.

Some polls begin with a screening question to eliminate respondents who might not know what was being asked, but would nevertheless offer an opinion. For example, a question on approval or disapproval of high school fraternities might be preceded by a screening question designed to find out whether the person interviewed understands what a fraternity is. Sometimes the screening question begins: Have you heard or read anything about the XYZ bill now in the legislature?

Several forms of opinion questionnaire are commonly used. The "fixed alternative" question limits response (as in true-false or multiple-choice tests) to certain specified answers. This has the advantage of objectivity, but leaves us ignorant of what the respondent might have said if he had been free to define his own position. The "open end" question provides this freedom, but presents difficulties in interpretation. Different interviewers and coders may record and code responses differently (Hyman, 1954). Some interview procedures involve also "probing" questions, designed to get at something which lies behind the overt conclusion expressed by the respondent. A probing question may ask "Why?" or for examples, or simply "Can you tell me more about your feeling?" Thus it verges on a clinical interview.

Questions must not be leading or biased, tending to predetermine the answer. Phrases in a question may encourage acceptance or rejection. The proportion of the public favoring birth control was substantially increased when the question was prefaced by: "To enable parents to plan their families more wisely." The statement, "Because every man is entitled to safe and healthy working conditions, labor (in defense industries) should be allowed to strike for them" received 45 percent approval, with 45 percent denying the right to strike in a defense industry. Different phrasing of the question brought a quite different response: "Because working conditions in this country are the best in the world, labor (in defense industries) should not be allowed to strike about them." With this preface, 74 percent were for denying the right to strike, and only 17 percent supported it.

Kornhauser (1946) has raised the general question about whether polls are unfair to organized labor. Most polling organizations depend on the sale of their product to newspapers or other large corporations. Among the examples of loaded questions cited by Kornhauser are the two following:

"Westbrook Pegler, the newspaper writer, claims that many labor union leaders are racketeers. Do you agree or disagree with him?"

"Do you think that the soldiers when they come home should have to join a union in order to get or hold a job?"

During any public controversy, certain facts, incidents or arguments are stressed by one side; other facts, incidents, or arguments are presented by the other side. A poll may be biased in the content it emphasizes, even though the specific questions are fairly phrased.

Tests and scales

A public opinion poll usually presents one question on a given issue. Attitude tests measure responses to a battery of questions related to a particular issue, e.g., racial integration, church attendance, capital punishment, monogamy, the United Nations. The form may be true-false or may range from "strongly agree" through a five-step or seven-step scale to "strongly disagree." Answers to 20 or perhaps 50 questions, all concerned with attitude toward one object, give a more complete and reliable measure than could be obtained from any single item.

The three technical questions commonly asked regarding a test concern its *objectivity, reliability,* and *validity.* If a test is objective, then its scores are independent of the person giving and scoring it. Any two competent persons would come out with the same score. If a test is reliable, it will give much the same result for the same subjects on two similar occasions. A reliable measure is consistent and dependable. It does not fluctuate haphazardly. One way of determining reliability is to give the test twice to the same group; if it is reliable, the high scorers should again come out high; the low scorers should remain consistently low. A more common technique in attitude tests is to correlate scores on half the items (all odd-numbered questions, for example) with scores on the other half (the even-numbered items) and then make a statistical correction for the abbreviation.

A valid test is one which really measures what its name and interpretation imply. If it is supposed to be a test of attitude toward Communism it should reveal what the persons tested truly believe. Obviously the questionnaire itself cannot guarantee validity. How frankly people will express themselves depends on the whole situation, especially their degree of trust in the person giving the test. For an attitude test to be valid, the respondents must be both able and willing to reveal how they feel. A test may be valid when the respondents want to cooperate, but invalid when they want to conceal their views.

Say or do

Attitude tests are not intended to measure conduct. They focus on certain tendencies to act or on opinions about action, but they may not be valid measures of other forms of behavior. In their classical investigation of character, Hartshorne, May, and Shuttleworth (1930) found that moral knowledge correlated .46 with measures of honest behavior, .30 with actual cooperation, and .34 with persistence in conduct. The test of attitudes of good citizenship had a reliability (self-correlation) of .84; it was a dependable measure of what children would say in response to a paper-and-pencil test; it had less value as a predictor of conduct. Borgatta (1951) compared what subjects said they would do in defined situations (Rosenzweig Picture Frustration Test); what they did in role-playing their behavior; and what actually happened when they were observed without their knowledge. The three modes of response were not significantly correlated. In a second study, Borgatta (1955) found again that paper-and-pencil reports did not predict how an individual would operate in a group, but that role-playing and actual behavior did correspond. Halpin (1957) found that school superintendents and aircraft commanders described their behavior in terms significantly different from what subordinates said these leaders did.

Many opinions are important in themselves and do not require further implementation. A vote is an expression of preference; it is intrinsically meaningful. A referendum is a form of social action geared to attitude questions. Most citizens have little opportunity to "act" on their beliefs about government foreign policy except as they express their approval or disapproval orally or in writing. Their pertinent "conduct" is only verbal.

Attitude scales do not always have to be validated against other indices of conduct. In one famous study, La Piere (1934) found that only one of 184 restaurants refused to serve him when he traveled across country with a Chinese couple; yet when he asked the same establishments later, in a questionnaire, whether they would serve Chinese guests, 91 percent of the 128 replying said they would *not*.

Disguised tests

It is apparent that when subjects believe that their responses will influence their acceptability for a position, their self-description on an inventory is likely to be distorted to create the impression they would like to make. Edwards (1948) has tried to construct scales in which "social desirability" is equal for all the alternative answers. Another technique is to conceal the purpose of the instrument. Tests of prejudice and dogmatism may be called simply "Opinion Inventories" (Watson, 1925; Rokeach, 1960). In the preceding chapter we noted that anti-Semitism could be fairly well measured by a scale which did not mention Jews.

Scaling

The concept of measurement implies some kind of scale. When one person answers 17 of 30 questions about war in a pacifist direction, a second person answers only 12 of the questions in a pro-pacifist way, and a third gives only three such responses out of the 30 items, it is assumed that these scores: 17, 12, and 3 are approximate measures of the strength of pacifist attitudes. Yet it might be conceivable that the three accepted items could represent a deeper pacifist conviction than the 17, if the latter happened to be rather superficial and to involve far less commitment.

One of the first efforts to devise a social psychology scale made up of sequential steps was Bogardus' *Social Distance Scale* (1925). He defined seven steps for acceptance of foreigners. Least intimate was admission to this country. People unwilling to admit a certain group

(Chinese, Jews, etc.) even as visitors to this country, would not accept them as citizens, fellow workers, neighbors, friends or new members of the family. "Social distance" declined as intimacy increased. The least social distance and greatest acceptance was indicated by willingness to admit some of the ethnic group to "close kinship by marriage." It was found that this answer included willingness to accept also less close relationships. In a study of attitudes toward immigrants, Bogardus found that most native Americans felt least social distance toward Canadians and most toward Turks. The Bogardus scale has been shown to have a high reliability of .90 or better and to give fairly consistent results over a period as great as twenty years (Bogardus, 1947). A similar scale used in the Middle East (Dodd, 1935) ranged from a score of 0 for "I would marry one of them" to 100 for the very extreme position: "I wish someone would kill them all."

Another kind of scale carries over into the field of attitudes a psychological principle firmly established in studies of perception: "the method of equal appearing intervals." The gist of the rule is that when judges are asked to estimate which of two lines is longer or which of two weights is heavier, the proportion of correct judgments increases as the actual difference between the two increases. Thurstone (1929) proposed that by finding the proportion of judges who, regardless of their own views, believed Statement A more favorable to the scale object (Church, War, Negro, etc.) than Statement B, the real distance between A and B could be measured. He and his co-workers developed a number of highly reliable attitude scales in which each item carries a numerical value derived from estimates, made by a large number of judges, about its position along a single dimension in comparison with other statements of the scale. While the Thurstone method is mathematically gratifying, the reliabilities are not higher than those obtained by simpler procedures (Edwards, Kenney, 1946). Other scaling techniques (Guttman, 1944; Edwards, 1948) also utilize the expectation that everyone who accepts a position with scale value 4, for example, should logically accept all items scaled as 1, 2, or 3. If he is unwilling to accept an item scaled as 5, he should also reject items higher in the scale. Items are selected and statistically scaled to meet these requirements.

Other dimensions of attitude

An attitude is not fully measured when its position along a scale from pro to con has been established.

One important quality is *intensity* or salience. Two people may agree in opposing higher taxes, but one may feel lukewarm and the other very bitter. Usually the people in the middle of the scale feel less intensity than those near the positive and negative extremes (Cantril, 1946).

In opinion polls, citizens may be asked: "What are the main problems that concern you?" Someone may not think of mentioning automation, but if asked specifically, might say that automation is a serious problem for this country today. If it were very salient for him, he would have mentioned it in response to the general inquiry. He is aware that it is serious, but he is not personally concerned. Two citizens may agree that something ought to be done to improve public schools, but for one the issue is so salient and his feelings so intense that he attends open school board meetings; the other may say that he realizes its importance, but his lack of activity indicates that the issue is not really salient for him.

A third dimension is *confidence*. Some attitudes are held with strong conviction of correctness, even though the issue is not salient and the feelings are not intense. Degree of certainty, like intensity, however, is likely to be higher at the extremes of a scale. People who are not very clear about their views are more inclined to choose a safe, middle-of-the-road position. On the other hand, confidence is highest toward statements on which there is the largest amount of group agreement (Johnson, 1946). Cognitive support is also an important factor in confidence.

A fourth aspect of attitude is *specificity vs. generality*. Two persons may score at about the same level in acceptance of welfare legislation by the Federal Government; yet they may differ markedly in that one person knows the pending legislation and what provisions of each bill he approves or rejects; the other may have a general, diffuse concept that government ought to do more—but not too much—for the poor.

In all the abundant literature on attitude measurement there are few, if any, examples which include data on all of the variables: scale position (from agree to disagree), intensity, confidence, cognitive support, and differentiation or specificity.

Perception of attitudes of others

The individual's own attitude affects the way he looks at the views of others. As shown in the study summarized in Abstract 28, persons near the extreme of an attitude continuum are relatively intolerant, even of positions which others might see as close to theirs. Latitude of acceptance is greatest for those who are themselves near the middle of the scale.

Attitude syndromes

An American citizen today who has a highly favorable opinion of the National Association of Manufacturers does not usually hold that attitude as a distinct opinion unrelated to his other social, political, and economic views. Although there are individual exceptions, we might

Abstract 28

TITLE   Some Needed Concepts in the Study of Social Attitudes.

AUTHOR   Muzafer Sherif

PROBLEM   How do individuals with different attitude positions and different degrees of intensity view the range of attitudes along a scale?

SUBJECTS   406 college students.

PROCEDURE   Each subject checked a scale of nine statements related to the election of a Republican or Democratic President (in 1956). He selected the "most acceptable" and "other acceptable" statements, also the "most objectionable" and "other objectionable" statements. Statements neither acceptable nor objectionable were designated as noncommittal.

SOME FINDINGS   Those subscribing to extreme pro-Republican or pro-Democratic positions showed a narrow "latitude of acceptance," extending only two steps away from their own. They showed a correspondingly large latitude of rejection covering five or six steps of the nine-point scale.

Those whose "most acceptable" position fell near the middle of the scale rejected only the two most extreme positions.

SOURCE: J. G. Peatman, and E. L. Hartley (eds), *Festschrift for Gardner Murphy*. New York: Harper and Brothers, 1960, pp. 194–213.

expect the N.A.M. adherent to oppose higher income taxes, to oppose federal power projects, to favor restrictions on trade unions, and to resist any extension of public health services. A study in the 1930's (Murphy, Likert, 1938) showed that those who did not regularly vote Democratic or Republican but who called themselves Independents or Socialists, were more inclined to favor racial desegregation and international cooperation. These broad groups of attitudes are commonly called "conservative" or "liberal."

A study of various areas of possible conservatism (education, religion, sex attitudes, government, etc.) showed that conservatism in one area was usually, but not always ($r = .45$), accompanied by conservatism in the other areas (Lentz, 1938). More conservatives than liberals have admired Gen. U. S. Grant, Kate Smith, Huey Long, Babe Ruth, Bing Crosby, and Edgar Guest. More liberals than conservatives have admired Norman Thomas, Immanuel Kant, H. G. Wells, Joseph Lister, and Charles Swinburne (Lentz, 1939). More conservatives attend church regularly; more liberals read progressive periodicals. A study using the

Bogardus Social Distance scale, showed that acceptance of various ethnic groups was positively related to economic liberalism ($r = .45$) and to an international rather than a nationalistic attitude ($r = .54$) (Murphy, Likert, 1938). When an issue becomes salient for a large part of the public—as did civil rights for Negroes in 1965—supporters are likely to include many who remain conservative on other policies of an economic, social, political, and international nature.

A factor analysis of scores made by the same persons on ten different Thurstone scales pointed to two general factors: one which might be called humanitarianism, apparent in opposition to capital punishment and war, and another, religious modernism, manifest in belief in evolution and favoring of birth control (Ferguson, 1939).

Progressives and conservatives

I often think it's comical
How Nature always does contrive
That ev'ry boy and ev'ry gal
That's born into the world alive,
Is either a little Liberal,
Or else a little Conservative.

(W. S. Gilbert in *Iolanthe*)

How does Nature "contrive" the development of the basic attitudes which distinguish those who welcome change and those who resist it?

We need not expect that everyone who is progressive in politics is necessarily so in his ideas on religion, morals, education, art, and fashion, but all studies show some correlation among these different kinds of progressivism. Those who are suspicious of new ideas and like the old ways best may make certain exceptions, but the syndrome is consistent enough for study.

There is, as yet, no persuasive evidence that these attitude differences are innate. Studies of identical twins raised in different environments, (Newman, *et al.*, 1937), show that one may be spontaneous and the other restrained; one less conventional than the other in moral outlook; one excitable and the other phlegmatic; and one more independent than the other. These traits are not identical with the progressive vs. conservative dichotomy, but they come close enough to support a presumption that contrasting attitudes toward change have been learned.

Parents, friends, and teachers play a major role in the formation of all fundamental attitudes. One comparison of 47 political "radicals" and 47 "conservatives" showed that 40 percent of the radicals had heard radical theories discussed at home; none of the conservatives recalled such experiences. While 21 percent of the radicals had radical friends, only 3 percent of the conservatives had such associates. The experience of radicals included belonging to a trade union in 47 percent of the cases; only 9 percent of conservatives had been a member of a labor union. Radicals had been more often exposed in early life to left-wing books and newspapers. All the 47 cases of conservative adults showed that conservative influences predominated over radical influences at at every stage of their development. Even among the radicals, however, conservative influences were strongly present. Only a third of the 43 radicals grew up with more radical than conservative associates. Most radicals had heard conservative ideas expressed at home; most of them had conservative friends and read some conservative papers. The distinction was that the persons who had become radicals had had some childhood exposure to progressive ideas, the conservatives had had almost none (Breslaw, 1938).

What makes some people ready for, and easily influenced by, ideas of innovation? A comparison (by the writer) of 50 graduate students who describe themselves as radical in their economic, educational and religious ideas with an equal number who oppose radicalism brought out a few interesting differences.

1. More radicals (28 percent vs. 12 percent) grew up in a city of more than 500,000 people.

2. More radicals (50 percent vs. 36 percent) were only or oldest children. This finding replicates Vetter's (1930) observation that 51 percent of the radicals in his study were only or oldest children, as compared with only 32 percent of the conservatives.

3. More radicals believed their families below the average income of the community (44 percent to 22 percent).

4. More conservatives reported demand for strict obedience at home 70 percent vs. 44 percent).

5. Studying and poetry were rated as more important by radicals than by conservatives.

6. More radicals (26 percent vs. 10 percent) felt that they did not receive at least average attention from the opposite sex during adolescence.

7. More conservatives complain of shyness and timidity (30 percent vs. 18 percent).

8. More radicals complain that they tire very easily (42 percent vs. 18 percent).

9. More radicals report that they were regarded as unusually studious and sometimes as a "teacher's pet" (44 percent vs. 32 percent). (Both groups are high because all subjects are graduate students of education.)

10. More radicals would prefer a life of change and adventure to one of peace and serenity. (78 percent vs. 58 percent).

There were no differences between radicals and the others in age, marital status, size of family, or self-estimates of childhood happiness or present happiness.

Watson carried out during the Depression another study of radicalism (Abstract 29). In 1934, millions of Americans had been unemployed for many months. A drastic drop in stock prices, foreclosures of farm mortgages, and bank failures added to the climate of uncertainty. Numerous programs for economic reform and revolution were being proposed. Even under these conditions only about one in five of the unemployed men in and around New York had adopted a radical attitude. The study shows further that high mental ability, as evidenced by intelligence test scores and by level of education, increased the probability of radicalism. Among personality traits, a considerable degree of independence characterized the radicals. Personality problems seemed more frequent among the non-radicals.

Other studies have usually concurred in finding liberals, progressives, and radicals above the mean in intelligence, education, and factual knowledge. The correlation between "radicalism" and intelligence in a group of 70 women teachers college students in London was .25. Thurstone found a correlation of .44 in a different sample. College students with A grades made 53 percent of possible radical choices while those with a D average made only 4 percent (Moore, Garrison, 1932). Lentz (1939) found 24 percent more radicals than conservatives in the top third of their high school class. Correlations of "liberalism" with intelligence, scholarship, and information about current affairs were reported earlier in this chapter.

A related finding is that the innovators are more apt to come from homes that are culturally privileged. Lentz (1939) found more radicals whose fathers were professional men and more conservatives whose fathers were unskilled laborers. A study of voters for Norman Thomas, Socialist candidate for President of the United States in 1932, showed that among professionals he won 15 percent of the votes, only 9 percent of factory workers, 5 percent of clerical workers, and 4 percent of farmers (Robinson, 1933). Radicals come from homes with more books and have traveled more widely than have conservatives (Lentz, 1939).

On the personality of progressives, studies are not in agreement. In one of the earliest studies Moore (1925) found male undergraduate radicals different from conservatives in that the radicals were less susceptible to majority influence, more adept at learning mirror drawing, inclined to sacrifice accuracy for speed, and deviating more in word associations. Washburn (1930) repeated the experiment with girls at Vassar and failed to get the same results.

Moore's work was confirmed by Lewis (1941) in his finding that radicals were less likely to shift their opinions after they had been informed that a majority of fellow students disagreed with them.

Another early study (Allport, Hartman, 1925) found that freshmen

Abstract 29

TITLE   Some Characteristics of Adjustment Service Clients with Radical Opinions.

AUTHOR   Goodwin Watson

PROBLEM   During a period of severe economic depression, what kind of a person becomes a radical?

SUBJECTS   745 adults who came for free educational or vocational counsel during the spring of 1934 in New York City. Most were unemployed.

PROCEDURE   The index of radicalism was based on the statements:

"Even though the present economic system may have its faults it should not be radically changed." (Disagree)

"Socialism might have its defects but it would be better than the present system." (Agree)

"There is no justification for a strong radical party in this country." (Disagree)

"All basic industries should be governmentally owned and operated." (Agree)

"A revolution might be a very good thing for this country." (Agree)

Reliability of the index was .78.

19 percent were classified as "radical."

Other data were collected by questionnaires, tests, and interviews.

SOME FINDINGS   1. Verbal intelligence and education were high for radicals. Among those who did not go beyond eighth grade only 4 percent became radicals; among those whose schooling stopped during high school, 10 percent became radicals; among high school graduates, 16 percent became radicals; among college graduates 21 percent; with post-graduate education, 45 percent became radicals. With education constant (all high school graduates) those in the top 10 percent in their intelligence test scores, showed 46 percent radical; those below average in intelligence, only 9 percent radicals. Interest in more study was expressed by 64 percent of the radicals and 42 percent of the non-radicals.

2. Radicalism was most common in the age group 20–29 (22 percent radical); least common among those over 40 years of age (8 percent radical). A related fact is that single persons without dependents were more radical than were those married with children.

3. Occupations highest in proportion of radicals were those requiring considerable verbal facility: writers, teachers, advertising writers, actors, scientists. Least radicalism was found among sales persons, factory workers, shipping clerks.

4. Radicals constituted 24 percent of the native-born children of foreign-born parents but only 18 percent of the foreign-born and 15 percent of the native-born of native-born parents.

Abstract 29—*Continued*

5. The non-religious were more apt to be radicals (47 percent) than were Jews (25 percent) Protestants (13 percent) or Catholics (7 percent).
6. Radicals rated themselves (on the Bernreuter test) as more self-sufficient and less dependent.
7. High nervous instability was reported by relatively more non-radicals than radicals.
8. Many commonly hypothesized differences between radicals and conservatives were not confirmed. Radicals showed no more personality problems than the non-radicals. Radicals were as happy as the non-radicals. Excessive demand for obedience in childhood was more characteristic of conservatives. Shyness and timidity in social relations were more characteristic of conservatives. Radicalism was not more common among those unemployed than among those still employed and did not increase significantly among those who had been unemployed for two years or more.

SOURCE: *Common Sense,* 1941, X:7–9, from "What Makes Radicals," together with unpublished data.

who reacted against change rated themselves as more self-reliant and dogmatic, while radicals rated themselves as more introverted, tender-minded and less assertive. For this finding there are corroborative data. Lentz (1939) reported that conservatives have more "dates" than do radicals. Conservatives are more militaristic and athletic. Radicals identify more with the underdog. Rorschach test results suggest that radicals are only slightly (r = .16) more introversive (Sanai, Pickard, 1949). More liberals study psychology and philosophy; more conservatives major in business and engineering (Murphy, Likert, 1938). More liberals are introverts and pessimists (Kerr, 1944).

There is little evidence to support a widely held theory that radicals are emotionally unstable. Vetter (1930) found the Maladjustment score for "radicals" to be 51; for "liberals" it was 54; for "conservatives" it was 53; for "reactionaries" it was 62. Only the last group differs significantly from the others, but the radicals reported the fewest symptoms of disturbance. "Emotionality," based on Rorschach observations, did not correlate with radicalism (Sanai, Pickard, 1949).

An important distinction may be made between the sense of frustration of radicals with and without an appropriate channel of action. A study of some 300 persons between the ages of 18 and 35, during the period of economic depression shows that those intellectuals who became theoretical radicals tended to develop an introverted and escapist attitude. Those who joined a movement and found an action role for themselves were more extroverted, realistic, and effective (Diamond, 1936).

Perhaps radicals identify less closely with their parent of the same sex than do most adults. An early study of 70 male undergraduates showed a correlation of .54 between radicalism and an estimate of antagonism toward their fathers (Klein, 1925). A later study of a more varied sample reported a correlation of .30 between antagonism to the father and rejection of his ideas (Newcomb, Svehla, 1937). Such studies do not disclose whether the emotional relationship is cause or result of a political disagreement. It might be both.

No review of psychological causes of radicalism should minimize the realistic, basic economic factors. Periods of depression breed drastic criticism of the old order. Those who are most rebellious are likely to be those who feel unjustly treated. Thus in Vetter's (1930) study, the average annual income (about 1928) of familes of conservatives and reactionaries was over $9,000; for radicals it was only about $1,000. In Breslaw's (1938) study the average income of conservative homes was $5,000 while the radicals averaged only $3,200.

A comparison of counties in North Dakota and Minnesota which voted for more radical candidates (Non-Partisan League; Socialist) and those which had more conservative voters showed voter radicalism significantly associated with poorer farms, poorer buildings, and relatively higher mortgages (Lundberg, 1927). A later chapter on social change (Chapter 15) will discuss other factors which make for efforts to alter the social system. The correlation of economic data with psychological outlook will be developed further in our study of socio-economic class (Chapter 10). Different economic conditions generate interactions which result in characteristic attitudes (S-P-A).

Other syndromes

William James in a psychological classic (1890) proposed a dichotomy of attitudes which he called "tough-minded" or "tender-minded." A sociologist, Sorokin (1941), has used the distinction between *ideational* and *sensate* values to classify entire civilizations and epochs. For several centuries American life, as Sorokin views it, has been overweighted toward the sensate, with emphasis upon scientific truth, technological development, and material satisfactions. Is there a consistent complex of this kind, or would more careful analysis and attitude testing show sensate values in certain situations and idealistic or ideational in others? This test has not yet been made. Freudian theory leads to a different typology illustrated by "oral" persons, who love food, drink, words, and prefer the role of dependence upon those who will nurture them; "anal retentive," characters who are grasping, miserly, interested in collecting, and rather suspicious of other persons. Jung has given us the concept of the introvert, whose values come largely from the inner self and the extrovert, who seeks to gather for himself the values which predominate in the world around him. No adequate tests or factor-analyses have yet been made to demonstrate whether these theoretical types do correspond to actual responses.

The data on authoritarian vs. democratic personalities remains one of the syndrome contrasts best supported by research. A recent report of antidemocratic attitudes among teen-agers (Remmers, 1963) confirms the association of authoritarianism with ethnocentrism, prejudice, and social discrimination.

"Values" are generally considered to be broader and more basic than attitudes or opinions. Allport and his co-workers (1960) have built a test based on Spranger's typology of values: theoretical; economic; aesthetic; social; political; religious. One difficulty with this approach is that people may be interested in some theories but not in others, e.g., responsive to power (political) in some situations but seeking aesthetic satisfaction in others. Broad general preferences may be established, but the problem of the best taxonomy of attitudes remains unsolved.

In the chapter which follows, the influence of propaganda on attitudes will be examined. Many observed syndromes may be a consequence of reading certain newspapers and watching certain television presentations, but the relationship is circular. People select what will support previously formed attitudes.

CHAPTER EIGHT

Mass communication and propaganda

Importance and development

Social interaction in modern times takes place on a much larger scale than that of primary groups in which individuals may talk face to face with one another. Norms are formed by families and peer groups but also are shared by whole nations or groups of nations. If millions of persons are to be integrated in some kind of common life as consumers, employees, residents of a city, voters in a nation, and citizens of a worldwide community, influence must be exerted by methods which reach far beyond those of conversation. How are shared attitudes created among masses of individuals, most of whom never see or speak to one another?

The media of mass communication (it is not quite precise to call them "mass media") may be defined as media directed toward a relatively large, anonymous audience.

The first source of influence upon a large group was probably oratory. Powerful speakers reached thousands at a time. They told stories, sang songs, conveyed messages, proclaimed laws. The spoken word still remains highly effective. Despite criticism, the lecture method continues to be generally used in higher education. Studies (Chen, 1933; Cantril, Allport, 1935) have shown that the living presence of a speaker is usually more influential than is his voice over a radio.

A greater extension of human communities became possible with the invention of writing, and later, of printing. Communication conquered distance by means of letters, pamphlets, newspapers, books, and magazines. Studies of the relative influence, among good readers, of the same material when printed or spoken are inconclusive, but print has the advantage that it can be widely distributed, re-read from time to time, and studied in detail. Printed media have the disadvantage that even in generally literate societies there are still millions who have difficulty comprehending material which, if explained orally, could be clearly understood.

A very great advance was made, early in the twentieth century, when motion pictures were developed. One no longer needed to translate ideas into letter symbols and words, or verbal descriptions into imagined scenes. The story of an event could be presented as if it were taking place before one's eyes. A well-made silent film often required no words.

Soon came radio to carry the spoken word, simultaneously, to innumerable listeners. Then talking movies. Today the mass-communication field is increasingly dominated by television. Television transmits a motion picture simultaneously to millions of viewers scattered over an entire nation, or even—via the Telstar satellite—across the seas. Television, especially in color, can be similar to first-hand experience. People who have never seen a real mountain, a Japanese house, a Brazilian jungle, a ceremonial dance, or a ship at sea, can get realistic facsimiles on their television screens. Before the days of movies and television only a few Americans ever saw the President or heard him speak. The television program and the talking movie are, technically, great improvements over printed words, which must be reconstructed into images that may distort or fall short of the immediate experiences they describe. If books are still richer in ideas than are film libraries, the reason is not in the media themselves but in what men have thus far done or failed to do with each.

Increasingly Americans are dependent upon what is broadcast for their entertainment and for the knowledge they need to function as intelligent citizens in the modern world. This is largely one-way talk. The listener has little comeback. The eminent broadcaster seems elevated far above the average man. The medium provides him this stature. What happens to democracy when, instead of cracker-barrel discussions in small country stores, citizens, sometimes millions, receive a one-way communication from a single source? A dictator might willingly offer the people all the machinery of free elections if he could control the flow of information which shapes public opinion.

Propaganda may be defined as the effort to influence opinions and attitudes toward conclusions which will be accepted without critical evaluation of the reasons pro and con. Do the media of mass communication tend more toward propaganda than education? Are we in danger of being manipulated into a conformity of standards and pleasures suited to the interests of the few who are able to control the communication channels? Is aesthetic taste being reduced to some lowest common denominator far below what might be attained?

To answer such questions of social and psychological significance we need measures of the effectiveness of a magazine article, a speech, or a television broadcast. Impressionistic reactions are untrustworthy. Lincoln believed his Gettysburg address to be a popular failure. Ministers and teachers are likely to get feedback mainly from those listeners who strongly approve. Dependable evidence requires impartial surveys, before and after the message, and comparison with control groups.

Is public opinion easily manipulated?

Much of the discussion and prevailing opinion on this important issue rest upon a few impressive instances of success or failure in the employment of mass communications. We begin this chapter by citing first several instances of successful propaganda attempts and continue with several examples of failure in similar efforts. Then we shall need to examine social psychological hypotheses which may account for the contrast in outcomes.

During a war, modern nations successfully indoctrinate nearly all of their citizens with a firm belief in the virtue and eventual triumph of their own cause; clearly one side or the other has been duped.

Movies have a strong effect on the attitudes of high school pupils according to an early study. Pupils who were tested on their attitudes toward Negroes before and after seeing the film, *The Birth of a Nation*, changed markedly—26 times the S.E. Diff.—toward dislike and rejection of the Negro. Pupils given similar scales of attitude toward the Chinese, and shown the film *Sons of Gods* changed markedly (18 times the S.E. Diff.) in the direction of admiration. Retests after five months showed 62 percent of the change still remaining and a second retest after 19 months gave a similar result (Peterson, Thurstone, 1933). A wartime movie, *Naples as a Battlefield*, was similarly shown by before-and-after attitude tests to have changed the opinions of 71 percent of an American audience, leading them to want to send more food to Italy (Bureau Applied Social Research, 1944).

Many studies of the effects of advertising have shown occasional dramatic results such as thousands of responses from one brief adver-

tisement in a nationwide network show. Products more often advertised are more often purchased. There are instances of companies which
cut down too far on their advertising and lost their market. A careful
study in a Long Island community of 800 homes equipped with television compared with 800 which were not (in 1949 when the medium was
new) showed that every brand advertised on television was bought by
a larger proportion of families with television than was true for control
families; conversely, competing brands which were not promoted by
television were, in every case, purchased more frequently by the people
whose homes were not yet equipped with TV sets (Coffin, 1950).

The apparent success of the Communists in selling their program,
despite its many unpopular demands, to a substantial proportion of the
Russian, Chinese, and other Communist-dominated people has aroused
concern over the possible impact of subversive propaganda in our own
country.

Equally impressive, however, is some evidence on the other side
of the issue: Presidents F. D. Roosevelt and Harry Truman were elected
despite the fact that a large majority of newspapers opposed them. A
study (Lundberg, 1926) of the attitudes of 940 adult residents of Seattle
on four public issues of the 1920's showed little relation between the
editorial position of a man's favorite newspaper and his own views. The
readers' choice of newspaper was more influenced by its comic strips
than by agreement with its political positions. Mott (1944) reviewed
presidential campaigns from 1792 to 1940 and found that the majority
of newspapers were as likely to support the loser as the winner.

The best known study of changes in voter attitudes during a presidential election was made by Lazarsfeld and his associates in Erie
County, Ohio, in 1940. Despite the flood of campaign pressures between
May and November, only 5 percent of the representative panel of voters
switched from one party to the other. The initially "undecided" usually
voted in accord with the majority of their families and friends (Lazarsfeld *et al.*, 1944).

A similar study in Elmira, New York, during the 1948 presidential
campaign showed only 3 percent of the voters switching from one party
to another between late August and the November elections (Berelson
et al., 1954).

Challenging the first conclusions about the impact of movies is a
finding (Hulett, 1947) that the film *Sister Kenny*, which gives warm
support and approval to her contribution to the treatment of polio-
myelitis, had no clear effect on the opinions of 60 adults who saw the
film as compared with a control group who did not. The groups were
much alike in their opinions of her somewhat controversial method for
treating polio victims and were also alike in their estimate of the National Foundation for Infantile Paralysis, which opposed her procedures.

The omnipotence of advertising is likewise open to question. The failure of the Ford Motor Company to sell Edsels was not due to lack of promotion. No advertising agency can guarantee substantial sales increases as a result of increased expenditures. Yet advertising has many advantages over ideological propaganda. It is very limited in its aims, often trying only to shift the consumer from one brand to another which is really quite similar and equally accessible. The same advertisement may be repeated again and again. No basic change in attitude may be involved and usually the consumer's response is made very easy: "Just pick up the phone and call XY-1000—our operator will be waiting for your call!" This is a far cry from inducing the public to get busy and organize for a cause.

Two experiments with citywide campaigns using all available media to promote certain attitudes have shown little effect. One, in Cincinnati, was intended to increase knowledge of foreign affairs and support for the United Nations. Newspapers, radio, television, and public meetings contributed what they could. Public opinion polls, before and after the campaign, showed little change and little difference from comparable cities which had experienced no such campaign. In the preceding chapter we called attention to the devices of selective attention, selective recall, and reinterpretation which served to resist a change in attitude.

The second campaign (Springfield, Mo.; studied by Columbia University's Bureau of Applied Social Research, 1954) was carried on intensively for one week through several media, endeavoring to create a favorable image of the oil industry and its contribution to America and the world. Polls before and after showed 13 percent of the panel becoming more favorable to the oil industry while 9 percent became less favorable—hence a net gain of only about 4 percent of this sample of the public.

We have presented examples of the effectiveness of propaganda and other instances in which it had little effect

How can the often contradictory findings on the effectiveness of propaganda be reconciled? The answer seems to be that when people have opinions, they usually find reenforcement among the many messages which are available in print or talks or pictures. Seldom are their basic attitudes and values changed. If people have had little previous knowledge or concern, they may be influenced by what they are told or shown, but the new learning must fit into a pre-established personal system of concepts and values. Propaganda is not a simple matter of telling or persuading. People accept only what they find acceptable, and their views are anchored very largely to the views held by their families and friends.

John Crosby, a former television critic for the *New York Herald Tribune,* once proposed: "It might be stated as Crosby's law that the more important a subject is, the less influence the guy with the mike has. In matters of most profound importance to the individual—say, religion—I doubt that the Murrows, or Godfreys, the Winchells or anyone else could sway a single soul a single inch" (Klapper, 1960).

Whether a particular message has influence depends on many factors—its source, its form and content, the medium of transmission, and the audience receiving it. A well known formulation is: "Who says what, to whom, by what means, and with what effects?" We shall begin our analysis with "Who says," i.e., the source.

Who says? The source

The first text in social psychology published in the United States (Ross, 1908) called attention to opinion-influence. "Every editor, politician, banker, capitalist, railroad president, employer, clergyman or judge has a following with whom his opinion has weight. He, in turn, is likely to have his authorities. The anatomy of collective opinion shows it to be organized from centers and subcenters, forming a kind of intellectual feudal system."

Later, public opinion studies (Roper, 1955) suggested a differentiation of six concentric circles.

1. At the center a small circle of Great Thinkers
2. Around them a narrow band of Great Disciples
3. Next ring composed of Great Disseminators
4. Next, Lesser Disseminators, influential locally
5. A very large group of Participating Citizens
6. Farthest out, the Politically Inert.

The sixth group learn from the fifth, the fifth from the fourth, and so on up. He believes that this structure, operative historically in religious and political movements, is also evident today in the media of mass communication. Books, magazines, news commentary, and other serious talks usually pick up ideas originated by Thinkers or Disciples and promote their flow from Great Disseminators to Lesser Disseminators or to Participating Citizens. The Politically Inert probably learn mainly from personal conversations with family, neighbors, and other friends. Rumors circulate from those supposedly better informed to the less informed.

An empirical study (Katz and Lazarsfeld, 1955) in a city of 60,000 people (Decatur, Ill.) was based on interviews with a cross section sample of 800 women who were asked about their behavior in four areas: marketing, fashions, public affairs, and movie going. They were asked also to name "sources" they believed trustworthy in each area and those persons with whom they had talked over certain recent choices or events. Influence on public affairs came mainly from persons with higher socio-economic status (of those with high status, 19 percent were leaders; middle status, 12 percent; low status, only 6 percent leaders). The public affairs leaders were also better informed than the average person in their socio-economic class. More opinion leaders in matters of current affairs were men. More of these influential persons read five or more magazines and one or more books per month.

The power of personal influence as contrasted with media of mass communication is evident in the following data:

On 386 shifts in brand purchased
    28 percent were directly or partly influenced by personal contacts
    22 percent by radio (survey made in 1949)
    10 percent by newspapers
     7 percent by magazines

On 584 choices of movies to attend
    18 percent were directly or partly influenced by personal contacts
    11 percent by newspapers
     7 percent by magazines

On 502 fashion changes (hairdo, clothes)
    38 percent were directly influenced by personal contacts
     8 percent by magazines

The flow of influence was pictured by Katz and Lazarsfeld as a two-step process from print or radio to influential persons and from influential persons to the rank and file. In the total sample, 60 percent were rank and file; 27 percent were leaders of opinion in one area only; 10 percent were leaders in two; and only 3 percent were leaders in marketing, fashion, and public affairs.

Further evidence for the importance of direct personal contact as contrasted with more general propaganda comes from an experiment in practical politics when the city charter revision was to be voted on in Ann Arbor, Michigan. Sixty-three citizens who said they opposed the charter revision or reported themselves undecided were arbitrarily assigned to one of three groups. One group of 20 was visited and given personal persuasion to vote for charter revision. A second group of 22 received four mailings of propaganda, some emotional and some objective and factual, but all in favor of the revision. The remaining 21 cases served as controls. In the election, 19 percent of the control group supported charter revision; 45 percent of the group receiving the printed material voted for the revision; while 75 percent of those who had been personally contacted voted for the revision (Eldersveld, Dodge, 1954). Those who had been talked to reported that they later read more of the newspaper articles on charter revision than did the control group or those on the propaganda mailing list.

Within each medium certain newspapers, magazines, commentators or programs become trusted sources for a section of the public. One study showed, as might have been expected, that listeners who liked Drew Pearson were more influenced in their opinions by hearing a tape of one of his broadcasts than were listeners who had previously indicated no particular liking for him (Freeman, *et al.*, 1955). A report on people who bought war bonds in response to an all-day marathon broadcast by Kate Smith (Merton, 1946) showed that they had an image of her as sincere and unselfish; they admired her, trusted her, loved her. One woman said: "Next to God, she is for me."

Public adoration has always constituted a peril for prominent people. Statesmen, business leaders, movie stars, well-known writers, top athletes, or renowned ministers are in constant danger of accepting the public's image of themselves. Even a college teacher who lectures authoritatively to a few hundred students and grades them may be tempted to overrate himself. Television has magnified the opportunity of certain individuals to become demigods for masses of followers. The writer was surprised to discover that a single appearance on an evening television show suddenly made him a "celebrity" among townspeople who had previously taken no particular note of him.

An influential source need not be a person of high competence or prestige. One study has explored the relationship between the image of a communicator as competent and the self-esteem of his listeners (Dabbs, 1964). The study showed that young men low in self-esteem were more influenced by a message (concerning Army life) coming from someone who had shown little initiative, lacked self-confidence, and felt somewhat depressed than they were by the same message attributed to a man of enterprise, activity, self-confidence, and optimism. Presumably it was easier for these discouraged listeners to identify with, and to trust, someone who, like themselves, had not been highly effective in coping with life's predicaments.

A remarkable finding (Hovland and Weiss, 1951) is that people may remember a message but forget that it did not come from a credible source. The Hovland-Weiss study offered information about health, the steel shortage, atomic submarines, and the future of movie theaters. Some of the audiences studied believed that the messages came from reliable sources; others were told that the information came from the Soviet newspaper *Pravda* or from gossip. Credible sources brought a change in 23 percent toward acceptance of the information; unreliable sources only 7 percent. But one month later, only 12 percent accepted the message from the reliable communication, while 14 percent accepted the message which had had low credibility. The surprising and important discovery in the Hovland and Weiss study is that the ideas set forth may be retained and be influential after the source has been forgotten. This finding is in accord with the common experience of remembering a fact or allegation but having to add: "I've forgotten now where I read (or heard) it."

A similar study (Kelman, Hovland, 1953) presented to high school seniors a radio talk on the value of leniency in treatment of juvenile delinquents. Some pupils thought they were listening to an able judge experienced in a juvenile court, others that the speaker was an unidentified man in the studio audience, and a third group heard an introductory interview which brought out that the speaker had been a delinquent and was now out on bail after arrest for another alleged offense. Agreement with the argument was greatest when it was attributed to the judge and least when the speaker was identified as a delinquent. In another related experiment (Hovland, Mandell, 1952) dealing with opinions about currency devaluation, the fact that the source might have ulterior motives had little influence. The suspect source in the latter experiment was introduced as head of an importing firm, likely to benefit by currency devaluation. The supposedly trustworthy source was a distinguished economist from a leading university. The subjects—college students—expressed more approval for the fairness and objectivity of the university economist, although the content presented was identical. Opinion change turned out to be very much the same for both the trustworthy and the untrustworthy source.

In the Kelman, Hovland study of attitudes on the treatment of delinquents the temporary advantage of the statement coming from the judge was soon obscured by time. In a retest after three weeks, the propaganda for leniency was just as effective when having come from a delinquent as when from an experienced judge. (See also Abstract 26.)

These observations have disturbing implications. In each instance an untrustworthy source did exert considerable residual influence. We are all aware that advertisers, reformers, political candidates, and other propagandists are likely to overstate their case. We probably assume that it is not important because we like to believe that we consider the source and discount biased claims. But it often develops, perhaps a month later, that we may still remember the claims without remembering the reasons for discounting them. Could this tendency account for Dr. Joseph Goebbels' confidence in the effectiveness of the Big Lie when he was Hitler's Minister for Propaganda and National Enlightenment? At first such propaganda will be viewed as a self-serving distortion; later it may be recalled without any such cavil.

A source that is not recognized as an attempt to influence opinion may be particularly potent. When the listener feels under attack, he braces himself to refute and to resist. When a message comes to him without, apparently, being intended for him, he may have his guard down. Thus subjects who were told that the experiment was intended to change their opinions changed less than did more naïve subjects (Kerrick, McMillan, 1961). In another study, those who happened to overhear a persuasive communication were more influenced than were others who knew that the speaker was addressing them (Walster, Festinger, 1962).

Says what? The message

Drawing upon the studies of attitude changes reported in the preceding chapter and supplementing these with some research on the effectiveness of various techniques of persuasion, we can formulate some characteristics of effective mass appeals:

1. *The message identifies the communicator with his audience.*

Listeners or readers want first to know whether one is with them or against them. White Southerners will listen more attentively to a talk on changing race relations by someone who begins by establishing his connections with the Old South and its traditions.

An instructive example may be found in an experiment where two speakers talked to similar audiences about Henry Ford. Both audiences had a generally high opinion of the automobile pioneer. The content of the message was the same for both audiences. With one audience the speaker frankly stated that he intended to try to decrease their admiration for Ford. With the other audience, the speaker began by saying that his objective, despite some inevitable criticism, was to raise their estimate of the man. The positive approach was more acceptable for these audiences. The audience which started with the assumption that the speaker agreed with them changed five times as much in the direction of his critical argument as did the audience which was initially repelled by an expectation of disagreement (Ewing, 1942).

2. *The message is more effective if it is simple, clear, and explicit.*

Alexis de Tocqueville has said: "A proposition must be plain to be adopted by the understanding of the people. A false notion which is clear and precise will always have more power in the world than a true principle which is obscure or involved." Although historians are aware of the complicated factors causing a war or revolution, each side reduces that complexity to simple slogans which move the masses.

A teacher, speaker or writer often prefers to present the evidence and to let the pupil, listener or reader draw his own conclusions. Thus he encourages the growth of the person, who develops the ability to think for himself. This method, however, cannot be depended upon to produce the outcome which the typical propagandist seeks.

A comparison of two tape recordings dealing with devaluation of the currency (Hovland, Mandell, 1952), both of which presented the same facts but one of which added an explicit statement of what the evidence proved, showed a net change in the direction of the propaganda amounting to 19 percent for the facts alone, but to 48 percent for the same facts with the pointed conclusion added. When the facts alone were given, 11 percent of the audience came to a conclusion opposite to the one the speaker intended; when he drew the conclusion, only 3 percent moved counter to his intent.

When high school students were shown a film on civilian defense against atomic weapons, they learned much more if they were tested and then told the correct answers (Michael, 1952). Making explicit what they were supposed to have learned increased substantially those particular learnings.

Experienced advertisers seldom leave the listener to draw his own conclusion. They tell him what to buy and often spell out precisely how he is expected to respond.

The fewer the distractions in the message the more likely it would seem to carry its point. Yet a qualification has been introduced by some recent research. When an oral presentation was directed against a resisting audience (in this case, arguing against fraternities to fraternity members), an accompanying film not related to the content of the talk and presented as an abstraction resulted in greater acceptance of the message (Festinger, Maccoby, 1964). The distraction is hypothesized to have retarded mobilization of the resistance. Perhaps the distraction made it harder to concentrate on resisting the arguments.

3. *Pleasant words (or symbols) are connected with what is to be accepted and unpleasant words (or symbols) with what is to be rejected.*

Successful advertisers associate their product with such emotionally pleasant words as beauty, charm, trust, youth, health, success, moonlight, and roses. Wartime propaganda pictures our side as good, strong, right-minded, peace-loving, admirable, and virtuous. Our opponents are bad, weak, sinister, hostile, despicable, and vicious. Our symbols are truth, light, and the indomitable spirit. Our enemy is portrayed as beastly, treacherous, and fiendish. Hayakawa (1941) tells how the British press during the early stages of the Boer War described the enemy as "sneaking and skulking behind rocks and bushes." Later, after the British were able to master similar tactics, their press commented on how cleverly the British soldiers employed the natural terrain for cover.

Sargent (1939) prepared a table showing how the *Chicago Tribune* at that time used loaded terms for items expressed in a more neutral fashion in *The New York Times*. For example:

New York Times	*Chicago Tribune*
Government regulation	Regimentation
Labor organizer	Labor agitator
Crop control	Farm dictatorship
Foreign	Alien
Progressive (La Follette)	Radical (La Follette)

4. *The message is more effective if it says or implies that most people or the most prominent and influential people agree.*

In Chapter 8, we reported evidence of a tendency to shift attitudes to conform with what is believed to be the prestige or majority opinion. In propaganda this is sometimes called the "band wagon" effect. It is illustrated in the case of one young man, just turned 21, who studied carefully the polls and forecasts before casting his first vote. "I want my first vote to pick the winner!" he said, equating his suffrage with a bet on a horse race.

Most people feel more comfortable with the assurance of support from others. Even when they are in a minority they may imagine that most others agree with them or that there is a last-minute wave of enthusiasm turning people to their side. A study (Gorden, 1952) of 36 members of a student co-op who lived together and knew each other quite well showed that those who tended to be anti-Communist estimated the opinion of the whole co-op as more anti than it really was; the opposite was true of those more lenient toward Communism. Both sides cherished the reassurance of feeling that their view was the more popular one. Similarly Newcomb (1943) found the conservatives at Bennington mistakenly supposing that most girls on campus shared their views.

In promotion of fashions, more emphasis is laid on prestige figures than on majority support. The prospective purchaser is made to feel that this clothing, cosmetic, fur, or jewelry will associate him (or her!) with the best dressed and most glamorous personages.

5. *Messages are more effective when they repeat, reiterate, and say it again.*

One of the principal techniques of advertising is the campaign. A single ad can only rarely be effective. A good campaign uses several media and carries on over several days or weeks. The effects are cumulative. The first appeal may be disregarded, but by the fourth or fifth time, the audience begins to pay attention. The Kate Smith marathon appeal (Merton, 1946) went on in 60 slightly different versions every few minutes all day long. An advertisement for two new products, appearing only four times in local newspapers, produced little effect. Eight insertions brought some response but it soon died down. Sixteen appearances were required to bring substantial increase in purchases. (Stewart, 1963)

A series of three talks—on prohibition or on war—showed a steady increment of influence from the first, to the second, and to the third (Gardiner, 1935).

In the Springfield, Missouri, campaign to promote a favorable image of oil companies, the propositions most frequently asserted during the week turned out to be the best remembered (Bureau Applied Social Research, 1952). Television ads are repeated so often that the viewer may wonder whether they do not lose effectiveness. It is the melancholy truth than an ad may be repeated "ad nauseum" for some but still be increasing its general impact. A feeling that the repetition has become tiresome does not destroy the message, at least for some. Decisions on how long to continue have usually been made after tests, the results

Abstract 30

TITLE   Effects of Fear-Arousing Communications

AUTHORS   I. L. Janis and S. Fishbach

PROBLEM   Will propaganda which contains a threat be more or less effective than a purely factual communication?

SUBJECTS   200 high school freshmen

PROCEDURE   A 15-minute illustrated (film-strip) lecture on dental care was prepared in three different forms:
    A. Strong-fear appeal; painful decay, diseased gums, teeth extracted; gory illustrations
    B. Milder appeal
    C. Purely factual on growth and care of teeth
50 subjects heard each form; 50 served as controls. Tests and questionnaires were given one week before the talks, immediately after, and one week later.

SOME FINDINGS   No significant differences in amount of factual information conveyed by the three talks.

Questions on how students currently brush their teeth, the type of stroke used, the frequency of brushing and the time spent brushing showed no net change for the control group; 36 percent improvement for the factual group (C); 22 percent improvement with the mild appeal (B); but only 8 percent for Group A with the emotional, fear-arousing appeal.

A later counter-appeal ("It does not matter what kind of toothbrush a person uses") supported by "a well known dentist," brought positive agreement (up to 20 percent) from the control group but more disagreement from all three groups who had heard the original illustrated talk. Again the purely factual group showed most resistance (−40) to the counter-appeal and the group which saw the pictures with lurid detail least resistance (−8) The authors conclude that: "When fear is strongly aroused but is not fully relieved by the reassurances contained in a mass communication, the audience will be motivated to ignore or to minimize the importance of the threat."

SOURCE: *J. abnorm. soc. Psychol.*, 1953, XLVIII:78–92.

of which are rarely published, but which warrant some scientific respect for the policies followed.

6. *Messages which use positive rather than negative (threat) appeals are more effective.*

In propaganda, as in learning, the carrot in front is more effective than the stick applied behind. Warning and scoldings produce avoidance responses. The audience ceases to listen or quickly dismisses the unpleasant thoughts.

The experiment summarized in Abstract 30 grew out of the observation that movies on sex hygiene which dramatized the dangers of promiscuity had been rather ineffective with the armed forces.

The same principle appears again in a study of reactions to mailed propaganda on treatment of mental illness (Nunnally, Bobren, 1959). Some messages were designed to create high anxiety, for example, imagining oneself going through electric shock therapy—the electrodes attached, the shock, tension, muscle spasms, and resulting loss of consciousness. Low-anxiety messages made treatments appear simple and welcome, e.g., relaxing in a warm bath. More public interest was aroused by low-anxiety messages. In this experiment, some messages were framed with a happy ending. These, again, stimulated more attention and approval than those which left the reader with a problem.

Another example was reported by a minister of our acquaintance. For some months he preached challenging or reassuring sermons on alternate Sundays. His congregation particularly praised those sermons that served mainly to comfort and to reinforce what they already did and believed. Some were quite explicit about not liking the preaching which left them uncomfortable. The minister did find, however, that he had more requests for private interviews following the challenging sermons.

A further pertinent observation is that studies of the ability of readers to recall various advertisements from specific newspapers or magazines consistently show a low recall for notices by funeral directors and cemeteries.

7. *Messages combine emotional and rational appeals.*

Several psychologists have tried to test which are more effective, emotional or rational appeals. When a social psychologist, George Hartmann, was a Socialist candidate for Governor of Pennsylvania he applied his psychological training to his campaign by using in one ward of Allentown leaflets making an emotional appeal; in another, leaflets making an appeal to facts and logic; while a third ward served as a control. He found the small Socialist vote in all three wards increased over the previous election (this was in the depression years, the mid-thirties), but the increase was greatest in the ward where the emotional appeal had been made. (Hartmann, 1936).

Another test used prohibition of alcoholic beverages as the issue and university students as subjects (Knower, 1936). Of four messages, one made a factual appeal and one an emotional appeal for each side ("wet" and "dry"). Difference in attitude test scores before and after reading the messages showed a slight advantage for the rational appeal favoring prohibition and very nearly equal results from the emotional and rational appeals opposing prohibition.

A particularly effective emotional appeal was the one made by Kate

Smith in her marathon broadcast to sell war bonds during World War II (Merton, 1946). All citizens felt involved in the war and concerned about members of their families in uniform. In this general setting, the Kate Smith broadcast emphasized three themes: (1) the sacrifices of our boys in combat; (2) sacrifices being made by other purchasers of bonds; and (3) Kate Smith's own implied sacrifice as she persisted hour after hour, despite fatigue. Listeners were made to feel guilty and remiss and thus driven to telephone their orders for bonds. Once this was done, many listeners reported a purging sense of release: "I felt that I had done something real on the phone . . . to bring the boys home!" Tension was built up by the appeal and released by the desired action.

No psychologist seems yet to have tested the plausible theory that a combination of appeals would be better than either emotional or rational approaches alone. If some people are more moved by human interest and emotion-arousing tales, and others by reasoned factual presentations, why not offer both? Many advertisements now command attention with some striking picture or phrase but go on to refer to laboratory tests or other rational persuasion.

8. *Events are great educators; news messages arouse more interest and less resistance than does evident propaganda.*

The Minute Men of Concord, in 1775, fired a shot virtually "heard round the world." Fort Sumter, the Alamo, Hitler's invasion of Poland, and the attack on Pearl Harbor changed attitudes far more effectively than any oratory could. The first Soviet Sputnik had more impact on world opinion than thousands of words of Russian propaganda. In the preceding chapter, Cantril (1940) was cited as reviewing evidence of how events influenced American opinion on entering World War II.

Public relations professionals have learned to utilize the news technique. News can be reported or manufactured to taste. An editor receiving a release singing the praises of some actress will probably toss it into the wastebasket. But if the press release tells of the actress adopting a lion cub as a pet, or being robbed of her valuable jewels, being lost in the woods, or being elected "Bedmaker of the Year," this is *news* and may receive big headlines.

Newspapers have traditionally marked columns "Advertisement" and often used different type styles to prevent the insertion of advertisements in the guise of news stories. Despite this, a fair amount of news has been reported or slanted with propaganda intent, and some of what is labeled advertising presents news of improved products or new tests of familiar ones.

9. *If people are likely, sooner or later, to be exposed to counter propaganda, it is most effective to present both sides of the question at once.*

In so far as totalitarian states can succeed in controlling all that their subjects hear and read, they find it effective to present only one side. One study (Thistlewaite, Kaminetsky, 1955) attempting to influence attitudes regarding U.S. participation in the Korean War found that a tape which did not mention any argument on the other side was more effective in arousing immediate agreement than were those which attempted to refute the probable objections. But this leaves people vulnerable to counter-influence if they ever learn that there is something to be said on the other side.

A wartime opinion study (Newcomb, Hartley, 1947, pp. 566–579) shows that propaganda strategy depends on the sophistication of the audience. If listeners are well educated or well aware that there are two sides to the question, they are not favorably impressed by a message giving only one side.

A subsequent study (Lumsdaine, Janis, 1953) attempted to influence American high school students, in the spring of 1949, to believe that Russia would be unable to produce atomic bombs for at least five years. The arguments emphasized the absence of know-how and lack of uranium deposits. One group of students heard only this side of the debate; the other group also heard comments to the opposite effect, such as the ability of Russian scientists and the phenomenal recovery of Russian industry after the war. After a week, half of each group was exposed to a transcribed radio program in which a speaker argued that Russia probably already had an A-bomb and would have the weapon in quantity within two years.

The effect of the initial messages is indicated by 64 percent acceptance of the arguments in the one-sided presentation and 69 percent acceptance of these same arguments by the students who also heard some comments on the other side. The big difference appeared after the exposure to counter-propaganda. The group which had originally heard only one side lost their confidence in the message. Only 2 percent agreement remained. The group forearmed by having had both sets of consideration in advance, retained a 61 percent accord with the intial contention that Russia would be unable to produce the A-bomb within five years.

The two-sided presentation requires a delicate balance between neglect of and overemphasis on the opposite view. In the wartime study, the counter-arguments were presented and demolished. In other studies where both sides were given approximately equal emphasis, the results cancelled out. Persons who read a message favoring the Tennessee Valley Authority (TVA) changed in that direction; those reading a similar passage opposing it accepted that view; those who read both remained virtually unchanged (Sims, 1938). Similar results were obtained with arguments for and against a career in civil service (Schanck, Goodman, 1939).

One who hopes to present his opponent's case and still advocate his own has to achieve what might be called an apparently impartial partiality. He has to appear to be fair or he will alienate those who are initially inclined to the opposing view. It is a real advantage in such a situation to be able to state the other side in words which are acceptable to those who believe it. This accords with our first observation on the value of some identification with the dissenters. The effective debater does not misstate the opponent's position; he demonstrates that he can refute the position even though he has stated it fairly.

10. *Effective contentions are those which remain within the limits of the audience's latitude of acceptance.*

Two dynamic factors must be balanced. Imagine a conservative audience inclined to believe that coexistence with communism is impossible. Suppose a liberal speaker wants to persuade them that coexistence is both possible and highly desirable. He might fail in either of two ways. Wishing to win the confidence of his audience, he might take an extremely mild position, admitting the serious difficulties in coexistence. The audience would then sense considerable agreement and would tend to overlook the little points of difference. Listeners would then see a reinforcement of their previous beliefs. Or the speaker might stress a pacifist view to the point where the audience would lose all confidence in his realism and reject his appeal entirely. The speaker would thus have gone beyond the audience's latitude of acceptance and aroused negative rejection reactions. The point of maximum effectiveness with any listener is as far toward the speaker's end of the scale as the listener is willing to recognize as deserving serious consideration.

It is frequently observed that people who feel strongly about a subject are less likely to be moved by a communication than are those who are less deeply committed. The social psychological concept of latitude of acceptance is useful in interpreting these observations. In an experimental study on this point students were asked to read aloud to six fellow students passages very critical of the role of the church. Students who were themselves alienated from the church or who were neutral in their initial attitudes were much more affected by the experience of communicating this kind of information than were students who initially felt a strong commitment to the church (McGinnies, et al., 1964). Tannenbaum (1956) also found that a speaker who took a position outside an audience's latitude of acceptance was himself rejected and his ideas received no serious consideration.

In the study by Sherif (Abstract 28), attitudes of voters varied from those who believed that a Republican victory was "absolutely essential from all angles" through a neutral mid-point to those who held that a

Democratic victory was "absolutely essential from all angles." The data showed that those who held extreme views had a narrow latitude of acceptance and rejected not only neutrals but even those who tended moderately toward the position held by the extremist.

Provided a message falls within the latitude of acceptance, the further it diverges from the subject's previous attitude, the greater the change it will produce (Cherrington, 1934; Harvey, *et al.*, 1957; Fisher, Lubin, 1958; Cohen, 1959; Zimbardo, 1960; Aronson, *et al.*, 1963). Under conditions of high involvement, the latitude of acceptance for deviant viewpoints is narrow, and discrepant messages may produce no change or even a negative change (Hovland, 1959; Freedman, 1964).

A true report may be rejected if it falls beyond what the listener is prepared to accept as true. During World War II the actual menus of German prisoners held in American prisoner-of-war camps were distributed to persuade German soldiers to surrender. The propaganda failed because the German soldiers regarded the claim that prisoners in American camps were given eggs for breakfast as incredible and ridiculous.

A classic in the history of advertising made effective use of the step-by-step method of attitude change. An advertisement in the early 1920's showing a woman smoking a cigarette would probably have been shocking and would have aroused resentment as well as rejection. In 1926, however, Chesterfield portrayed a young couple at sunset by the seashore. As the man lit his cigarette the woman said, "Blow some my way!" In 1929, Lucky Strike pictured a young woman, her mouth puckered as if she were blowing out smoke, but there was no visible smoke and all the cigarettes were still in the pack. (Pictures reprinted in *Time*, April 11, 1960, p. 105.) As latitude of acceptance broadened, it became possible to portray women smoking cigarettes and considering cigarillos, but cigars and pipes remain for the present male symbols.

11. *Effective messages make personal appeals.*

The public is usually more interested in other people than in ideas or things. Everyone's interest is centered in himself and those he loves. The most effective approach is human. *The New York Times* for years has dramatized the appeal of social agencies with the human interest of its "Hundred Neediest Cases." Orators arouse the keenest interest when they start a personal anecdote. Among the most popular radio serials and television programs are those which relate episodes close to the life of the audience. Advertising impact is greatest when the product is seen as a way of enhancing personal charm, prestige, or satisfaction.

The late Edward R. Murrow in an interview (Murrow, Lyons) commented that one of his most successful television programs was created when, after filming many pictures of the buildings, laboratories, and activities of the Institute for Advanced Study at Princeton, he discarded almost all of it except the long interview with Robert Oppenheimer, Director. Again, he learned the importance of the personal when, after showing pictures of a block of uranium and its equivalent in energy, 2,800 coal cars, the program included a ten-minute interview with Admiral Hyman Rickover. Murrow observes: "No one really saw our coal cars or our little block of simulated uranium. Admiral Rickover, yes, they remembered, for the simple reason that here was a man who (1) knew what he was talking about, (2) had fire in his belly about it, and (3) was able to communicate. I think one thing at least we have learned out of television and that is that there is no substitute for a good picture of a man talking with conviction and with knowledge of his subject."

12. *Messages which stimulate participation carry more impact.*

What is learned depends upon how the learning organism has been active. Learning is not "taking in"—it is discovering the consequences of what one has just done. The more passive the audience, the less it learns.

If some students read a passage silently while others read it aloud to others, the latter, being more active, are more influenced by the content (Janis, King, 1954). When some are asked to improvise a presentation, they are more influenced to agree with it than they would be if they simply read the material aloud (again in King, Janis, 1956).

The study summarized in Abstract 31 shows that those who acted a role favoring racial integration in a housing project changed their real attitude in the same direction. The active role-players changed more than did those who observed the playlet, but the observers changed more than the control group. Not only did the acceptance of interracial housing increase, but the attitudes toward the Negro also grew more favorable. In a review of many studies in which learners made active, overt responses, this mode of studying was found generally superior to mere passive receptivity (Lumsdaine, May, 1965). Most of the evidence comes from gaining knowledge and skills, but the same rule also seems to hold for acquiring changed attitudes.

Debaters often report that after having been arbitrarily assigned to defend one side of an issue, they end up believing in the rightness of that position (Hovland, Janis, Kelley, 1953, p. 218). Churches and other organizations engaged in fund-raising find that the man who tries to persuade others to contribute succeeds at least in convincing himself. High school students who, after hearing propaganda for lowering the draft age, wrote out their own views for publication in the school paper proved more resistant to counter-propaganda against a lowered draft age than did control students who also had heard the original arguments (Hovland, *et al.*, 1957).

Abstract 31

TITLE — Modification of an Emotionally Held Attitude Through Role-Playing

AUTHOR — F. M. Culbertson

PROBLEM — Does participation in role-playing change an emotionally loaded attitude?

SUBJECTS — College students (95 experimental; 20 controls)

PROCEDURE — A pre-test measured attitudes toward Negroes held by the S's. The specific attitude measured was one toward allowing Negroes to move into all-white neighborhoods. General attitude toward Negroes was measured with a Likert scale. Two weeks after the pre-test S's were involved in a psychodrama on integrated housing. Members were assigned randomly to be role players or observers. All roles were pro-integration. A post test was administered ten days later.

SOME FINDINGS — Increase in approval of integrated housing was found in 10 percent of the controls; in 30 percent of those who had observed the scenes; in 40 percent of the participants. More generally favorable attitudes toward Negroes were reported in 5 percent of the controls; 36 percent of observers; and 43 percent of participants.

SOURCE: *J. abnorm. soc. Psychol.*, 1957, LIV:230–233.

Students who saw a film (*The High Wall*) which opposes ethnic prejudice were tested on information and attitudes before and after the presentation. Half of the students took part in a discussion of the film led by a passive, non-directive leader. Those who were present or engaged in this discussion retained, a month later, more of the film's impact than did those who did nothing more than watch the picture. (L. Mitnick, E. McGinnies, 1958). Even so simple a form of participation as answering test questions can add noticeably to the influence of a communication. A pre-test alerts people to watch for certain facts or attitudes in the message.

Once people begin to think about issues, they move toward greater consistency in their views. When students were asked to rate their belief in 48 randomly arranged propositions (which actually could be related in 16 logical syllogisms), the answers revealed numerous inconsistencies. Students rejected some conclusions while accepting both premises; they accepted other conclusions despite rejection of one or another premise on which the conclusion rested. Going through the test, however, and being forced to pay some attention to items which could be brought into logical relationship reduced the inconsistency on re-test a week later (McGuire, 1960.)

To whom? The audience

Communication is a two-way process. Even in the more remote contacts of broadcasting the audience plays a part in determining what is sent out. Through regular ratings and other surveys, broadcasters keep continuous estimates of how many listen to each program. The advertisers, who support most radio and television broadcasts, pay in some rough proportion to size of audience. Even sustaining programs, financed by the broadcasting companies themselves, do not survive if they fail to attract and hold listeners.

The audience depends on the medium. Better educated people generally prefer print—newspapers for news, books and magazines for entertainment and enlightenment. They turn to records and FM radio for music. Children and adults with less education prefer pictures, action, and talk. Each medium selects its own audience and is influenced in turn by the characteristics of those who consistently use that medium. The audience and medium converge as each modifies the other. Devotees of Westerns or daytime serials are as conservative in wanting the standard pattern as are ballet or grand opera audiences.

The radio audience consists of those for whom radio is regularly important. It is not defined by radio set owners; many owners seldom use their radios. Even peak programs rarely enlist half the set owners. Those who listen only to certain specially selected programs are marginal to the real radio audience for whom listening is chronic and consistent. There is likewise a television audience which chooses the medium rather than the particular show. A Neilson rating of a television show showed that only 3 percent of the viewers began their watching with that particular program; 97 percent were holdovers from a preceding show (Bogart, 1956, p. 75). They were generally television-minded, not followers of a certain type of program or a certain star performer. Half of the homes with television account for two-thirds of the viewing (Bogart, 1956, p. 64). The top 20 percent of households in television watching had their sets turned on for an average of *nine hours* a day, as recorded by Nielsen's automatic recording. Clearly, many occupations would not permit this extensive participation. Perhaps because other recreation is less diverting, farm families watch television more than do city dwellers.

Thomas (1962) has observed that the emergence of a new audience, responding to a new medium of communication, arouses the distrust, apprehension, and hostility of the old order. The clergy, the main spokesmen of the European community during the Middle Ages, were fearful of the power of the printed page to mislead their congregations. Educated readers and writers 500 years later pointed with alarm to the lower cultural level of the movies. The newly created audience is a social entity unresponsive to expectations formed around previously recognized groups and organizations. When radio and television created a new audience, they, too, were widely disapproved.

> The public official disliked it (the medium) because it appeared to yield to no existing methods of administrative direction or control . . . ; the educator disliked it because it both resisted and exposed the bias of his traditional methods (based on print); the artists and literate loathed it because it so rapidly invaded their private domain and because, though it has frequently made them richer in pocket, they have consistently believed they were poorer in spirit; the broadcaster came to hate it because it has . . . seemed fickle in its tastes and interests, and because everyone comes to hate a powerful communicant that communicates only by the crudest type of yes-and-no responses; the merchant distrusted it because it seemed to assimilate his blandishments, acting with frivolity in response to his most persuasive appeals and because he could never afford to ignore it; and finally the public despised it because it upset existing channels of communications and control, and has in general maintained a blasé indifference to the most sacred public affairs and events. . . . . . Though each of the interests represented in general by educator, politics, marketing and perhaps religion, approached the population with great expectations that their sway would be automatically extended, they found instead of students, members of the public, consumers, or communicants—the Audience. (Thomas, 1962, pp. 271–273)

Self-selection

One of the dominant and distinguishing characteristics of a free society is that people may choose the media they wish to patronize. Fascist, Communist, and other dictatorships create captive audiences, compelled to read the official line, if they read at all, and to listen, in public gatherings and in private homes, only to those broadcasts which support the regime.

A consequence of the freedom to select, as noted in the preceding chapter, is that the audience usually reinforces its preconceptions. During political campaigns, Democrats listen almost exclusively to Democratic speakers and seldom read any literature put out by Republicans. This is the converse of what Republicans do. Even when both groups (in a captive audience) had to listen to a speech by Democratic President Franklin D. Roosevelt, the change of attitude in Republicans was less than one-third (.40 to 1.35) of the change in those already Democratic (Remmers, Whisler, 1937). Those who have no particular concern about an issue (have a wider latitude of acceptance) are more influenced when the discrepancy between their present position and that of the message is large, but those who have a firm conviction (and a narrow latitude of acceptance) are more easily influenced if the message is not too different from what they already believe (Rosenberg, et al., 1960).

The reciprocal effect of an audience upon those who generate the contents of the message is that anything unpopular is likely to be excluded. Hence the mass media become replete with platitudes and clichés. People want to hear what they already believe; writers, publishers, and broadcasters try to give people what they want. Prevailing stereotypes go unchallenged. The "good guys" must win. One must be very careful to say only the obviously acceptable if one is anxious not to offend and not to alienate any of the huge mass audience.

Edward R. Murrow, who was one of America's foremost television journalists, has said: "I believe this country is in grave and perhaps mortal danger, and that to a large extent during the hours between 8:00 and 11:00 in the evening the television audience is being fed a diet that tends to cause it to be indifferent, that tends to insulate it from the realities of the world in which it lives " (Murrow, Lyons). What Murrow does not say is that the evening programs are entertaining rather than educational because that is what most of the audience wants.

Audience predisposition and effects

The audience not only selects reading or pictures or speakers in accord with its predisposition but, as reported in the preceding chapter, it may distort what is heard and what is recalled, to minimize any need for change in established attitudes. There are numerous telling observations of the way in which readers or listeners modify what is presented so that it will fit their expectations and beliefs.

Kishler (1950) found that the people most affected by a pro-Roman Catholic film (*The Keys of the Kingdom*) were those who were themselves Catholics and who esteemed the priest who was the main character.

When the comic cartoons, entitled *Mr. Biggott*, were created to show a prejudiced man as a most unattractive personality, their obvious message was misunderstood by more than two-thirds of the prejudiced viewers. Many of these viewers protected their bias by seeing the cartoons as devices employed by Jews and aliens to stir up trouble in America. In another example, when Mr. Biggott needed a blood transfusion and would accept only "sixth-generation American blood," one segment of the audience approved his patriotism, others, who were tenth-generation Americans, saw him as a comparative newcomer.

When the film *Crossfire* connected anti-Semitism with murderous impulses, in an attempt to make it abhorrent, some prejudiced viewers merely concluded that their feelings, which were not so aggressively destructive as those portrayed in the film were not really anti-Semitic at all (Raths, Trager, 1948). The British film *Naples Is a Battlefield* clearly attributed the destruction to the Allied invaders, but was interpreted by many Americans as showing how destructive the Nazis had been (Klapper, 1961).

An impressive instance of how far an audience can go in finding evidence to confirm its expectations comes from the Forest Park experiment on introducing a bit of fluorine into the city water. The object was to prevent dental cavities, especially in children. The papers announced that on a certain date—a Tuesday—the experiment would begin (although actually it was delayed until Friday). Promptly on Wednesday complaints flowed in from the public. The water tasted bad. Tea and/or coffee was spoiled. Several people became ill from the change. All this before the day when the fluorine was actually introduced.

What the audience wants or finds may be influenced by the mood of the moment. One experimenter gave spelling tests to two comparable groups of children and then showed a film containing highly aggressive acts. One group had had an easy spelling test and had done very well. They remembered more of the neutral, informational content of the movie than the other group. The other group had received very difficult spelling words, done poorly, and recalled chiefly the scenes of aggression (Bogart, 1956). The generalization might be that the needs and frustrations of the audience are likely to influence what they select from the media presentations. Any one television show may feed a variety of human passions, depending on the emotional state of the audience.

The duration and spread of rumors, whether through word of mouth or repeated in print or broadcasts, depends greatly on the emotional condition of the audience. Allport and Postman (1945) found wartime rumors serving to justify and rationalize the anxiety the public felt. Over 90 percent of 1,000 rumors they were able to trace expressed hostility or fear. Few expressed wish-fulfillment. As rumors were experimentally repeated they grew shorter (lost about 70 percent of their idea content during four repetitions); they "sharpened," adding emphasis to the more odd, striking, or emotion-charged points; and became "assimilated," i.e., tailored to fit the preconceptions, expectations, and acceptable interpretations of the people, who heard the rumor and passed along what they understood it to mean. The impact of any message from the mass media may be altered as it is passed by word of mouth to those who did not receive the initial communication.

The unreachables

The well informed are most likely to be attentive to new published or broadcast information. A public opinion study (Hyman, Sheatsley,

1947) showed that the more people already know about foreign affairs, the more interest they have in current issues. The authors of that study conclude: "There is something about the uninformed which makes them harder to reach, no matter what the level or nature of the information." The unreachables are likely to be low in level of education, more likely to be rural than urban, and more commonly women than men. Organizations which endeavor to enlighten citizens about issues of health, education, welfare, or governmental policy are constantly frustrated because, whatever the medium of propaganda, they reach easily the people who least need the enlightenment and cannot reach those most in need of education.

The uninformed (sometimes called the "know-nothings") are more numerous than we, in an enlightened democracy with universal public education, like to think. About one-third of adult citizens seem never to have heard of the Bill of Rights; others have very vague or mistaken ideas; only about 20 percent can correctly identify it (Hyman, in Katz *et al.*, 1954, p. 41).

In a public opinion poll, taken in May, 1946, citizens were asked how much interest they had in each of eight current issues; among them our relations with Russia, the newly developed atomic bomb, our policy toward Germany, and the United Nations. Eleven percent had little or no interest in any of the eight questions; about 25 percent were apathetic toward six or more of the eight live issues. Those who were more interested, as might have been expected, were also better informed (Hyman, Sheatsley, 1947). In a 1945 poll, only 41 percent could identify the Tennessee Valley Authority (TVA) (Cartwright, in Katz *et al.*, 1954, p. 228). At the peak of the presidential campaign between Thomas E. Dewey and Harry Truman in 1948, 10 percent of the potential voters did not know whether Dewey was a Democrat or a Republican. It is not uncommon to find that persons who are quite uninformed still hold strong prejudices on current issues. A survey for the Council on Foreign Relations (1964) showed that more than one-fourth of the public were not aware that mainland China was ruled by Communists.

David Riesman (1950) has distinguished between the new and the old type of unreachable. The old type is represented by a Negro cleaning woman of middle age. She says she is not interested in politics—leaves that to her husband. She believes the best man wins, but Democrats or Republicans are all the same. "The Bible says there will always be war." "Ours is the best country."

The new type of unreachable is the indifferent youth—socialized but passive. He is ready to take whatever comes—be it bonus or atomic fallout. He is apathetic because he feels alienated. Nothing he thinks or says would make any difference. So why try to understand?

People who do not read newspapers, books or magazines and do not listen to radio or watch television are not necessarily uninformed and out of touch. Most people learn more from other persons than from publications or broadcasts. Roper's chart, presented earlier, showed the "politically inert" learning from more active citizens. This is supported by the evidence on how women learn about fashions and movies (Katz, Lazarsfeld, 1955).

By what means? The media

Messages come to persons by direct speech; newspapers, magazines, and books; by radio, movies, and television. In the United States eight out of ten persons listen more or less regularly to some radio programs; nine out of ten read one or more newspapers with some regularity; and nine out of ten are television watchers (Survey Research Center, 1958). Each medium creates its own audience. It also accentuates the importance of the kind of material which it transmits. Thus print led to reading and professional writing. Radio made music more available and more important in our culture. Television has played up sports and other spectacular occasions. A social psychological analysis of the media must be concerned with interaction: the way the audience is affected and the influence the audience can exert.

Speaker to assembled audience

Before the advent of printing the orator was the main source of public influence. People listened to news disseminated by a crier, to sermons by the clergy, speeches by politicians, and tales by story tellers. The emergence of new media has not eliminated the word spoken in the direct presence of an audience. Millions listen to sermons every Sunday. Political rallies are still addressed by candidates. Speakers entertain, enlighten, persuade or bore listeners at club meetings, after dinners, and at conventions of many kinds. Lectures abound on every college campus.

Abundant data support the conclusion that people are influenced by such talks. Shakespeare dramatized in Julius Caesar how Brutus swayed a crowd to his support, only to have them persuaded to an opposite view by Mark Antony.

An early dissertation (Chen, 1933) attempted to modify, by speeches, attitudes of American students toward Japan and China during the 1931 conflict over Japanese occupation of Manchuria. Some 500 students in six different groups were given 15-minute talks that were pro-Chinese or pro-Japanese, and in each instance tests administered before and after the talk showed marked change in the advocated direction. A follow-up about six months later, however, revealed that attitudes had drifted back to something like their original levels (Chen, 1936).

An impressive fact that has emerged from numerous studies is that audiences promptly forget most of what they have been told. An early study (Jones, 1923) concluded that what college students remember from a lecture averages 62 percent at the close of the talk, 50 percent after three or four days, 37 percent after one week, 30 percent after two weeks, 23 percent after eight weeks.

In a study of debates before 118 audiences, Woodward (1928) found that listeners who had definite opinions before the debate usually reported their opinions strengthened by what they heard. Only 17 percent admitted that the evidence presented had caused them to question their prior convictions. On the other hand, 84 percent of the originally "neutral" were moved by the debate to favor a pro or a con.

In the preceding chapter we noted that lecturers presenting an internationalist viewpoint also brought about corresponding shifts in student attitude (Stagner, 1942). Abstract 32 shows that lecturers who addressed naïve subjects had far more impact than those who talked to audiences which had studied and held firmly set attitudes.

A speech before an audience has one psychological advantage over other media. Each listener is aware—as he is not when he reads, listens to radio, or watches television—of the responses of others around him. Their facial expressions, gestures, and other bodily attitudes affect him; A kind of rapport develops, encouraging a concerted response (Hollingworth, 1935, p. 16). Members of an audience are more likely to be carried away with enthusiasm or anger than the same persons would be if hearing the same talk in isolation. Listeners in the front and center of the room are likely to be more influenced than those at the back or on the outskirts (Griffith, 1928).

Many studies have analyzed techniques of effective speech making. Lengthy sentences induce boredom (Hollingworth, 1935, p. 58). Attention is livelier at the beginning than toward the end of a long talk. A comparison of the effect of the same material read from manuscript or freely delivered showed the latter to be substantially more effective (H. T. Moore, 1919). Exploring how best to give special emphasis to certain points in a speech, Jersild (1928) found in order of importance: three to five repetitions most effective; verbal emphasis—"Now get this!" —next; and of less influence: primacy (place at beginning of the talk), a significant pause preceding the statement, recency (final statement), loudness. Banging fist on table at close of statement added least in emphasis. Woolbert (1920) observed that audiences are particularly impressed by statements made with extreme change of voice—pitch, intensity, rate of speech, and quality. Monotony—no change—was least effective.

The effectiveness of speeches as propaganda is limited by the audience which selects its speakers. Does the medium of a speaker facing an audience provide opportunity for all sides of important questions to be pre-

Abstract 32

TITLE   Methods of Education in International Attitudes.

AUTHOR   B. M. Cherrington

PROBLEM   What procedures most effectively change nationalistic attitudes?

SUBJECTS   Eleven projects, ranging in size from 15 to 116 adults or college students.

PROCEDURES   Tests (Harper's Opinions on International Attitudes; Thurstone's Attitudes Scale toward War; an Attitude Scale toward Disarmament) were given before and after various types of project—some lectures, discussions, and study tours.

SOME FINDINGS   1. A 10-day summer conference for students decreased nationalism (11 to 9) and increased international attitudes (63 to 72).

2. A 12-week college course increased internationalism scores (55 to 69). A summer course on international affairs raised scores of graduate students (71 to 85).

3. A selected group of American students studying international affairs at Geneva, Switzerland (1930), changed very little (76 to 78).

4. A speech by a pacifist to 85 college freshmen and sophomores brought a less favorable attitude toward war. (From 4.06 to 2.99 on the Thurstone scale.) After six months, about half the change remained (3.60). A parallel group reading a pamphlet written by this pacifist speaker (but not exposed to his speech) made a similar change (immediate, from 4.14 to 2.89; after six months, 3.35).

5. A study group of well-educated, widely-traveled, middle-aged club women, meeting once a week for two years, showed very little change (insignificant drop of internationalism score from 55 to 52). A study group of younger business and professional men, meeting once a week for one year, showed moderate increase in internationalism (68 to 75).

SOURCE: New York: Bureau of Publications, Teachers College, Columbia University, 1934.

sented? Freedom of speech is guaranteed in the Bill of Rights and is one of the cherished characteristics of American democracy. The medium of speech from a soapbox on a city street or in a hired hall is the means of communicating to the public which is most readily available for nonconformists. There is, however, a substantial part of the public which would not allow speakers to present disapproved views. Thus Stouffer (1955) reports that 31 percent of a national cross section would not, if it could be prevented, allow a person to make a speech in their community favoring government ownership of big industries. Another 11 percent were undecided, leaving only a small majority (58 percent) supporting this basic civil right. On the issue of allowing an atheist to speak his mind, 60 percent were against it, and only a minority (37 percent) would stand up for free speech. If the speaker were an admitted Communist, 68 percent would not allow him to address an audience.

A poll of high school students (Remmers, Radler, 1951) showed that 34 percent agreed with the proposition, "The government should prohibit some people from making public speeches," 13 percent were undecided, leaving a quite meager majority (53 percent) to defend the Constitutional position that government must not abridge freedom of speech.

The printed word—newspapers

Newspapers, magazines, books, pamphlets, advertising circulars, and posters carry innumerable messages to literate readers. Again, there is impressive evidence that people are influenced in their understanding and outlook by what they read (D. Waples, *et al.*, 1940). Most of the studies in attitude change, reviewed in the preceding chapter, have depended upon printed material.

How much we rely on newspapers is shown in a study (Berelson, 1949) based on interviews with a sample of New Yorkers while the deliverymen for eight major New York newspapers were on strike in 1945. Almost all respondents felt vaguely uncomfortable, deprived, and out of touch, although only about one in three could identify any serious news event which he wanted to follow up. Others missed the announcements of radio and motion picture shows, recipes, and fashion news. Those who had developed a continuing interest in certain comic strips or an appetite for the zestful crime and love-nest stories of the tabloid missed these stimulants. For many, the disturbing element was not the absence of certain information but a disruption of their customary routines. "It's a habit," said one man, "when you're used to something you miss it."

Newspapers, because they are influential, are commonly criticized for slanting the news or for sensationalism. More than a century ago de Tocqueville accused the American press in these words: "The characteristics of the American journalist consist in an open and coarse appeal to the passions of his readers; he abandons principles to assail the characters of individuals, to track them in private life, and disclose all their weaknesses and vices" (1830–40, p. 237–238). In 1941, a Commission on Freedom of the Press, headed by Robert M. Hutchins, presented the results of a three-year study. The commission defined the approved role of the press as follows: "Today our society needs, first, a truthful, comprehensive and intelligent account of the day's events in a context which gives them meaning; second, a forum for the exchange of comment and criticism; third, a means of projecting the opinions and attitudes of the groups in the society to one another; fourth, a method of presenting and clarifying the goals and values of the society; and, fifth, a way of reaching every member of the society by the currents of information, thought, and feeling which the press supplies."

Many American citizens are not satisfied that their newspaper gives a wholly truthful and comprehensive account of the day's events. Even less often are news reports placed in a context sufficient to bring out the full meaning. Most readers are aware that there are other viewpoints not fairly presented by their particular newspaper.

The Hutchins commission raised the charge of sensationalism as follows: "To attract the maximum audience, the press emphasizes the exceptional rather than the representative, the sensational rather than the significant . . . In most news media such matters (trends of great social consequence), are crowded out by stories of night club murders, race riots, strike violence, and quarrels among public officials." The commission subsequently cited as an example the day-by-day reporting of the working out of the Charter of the United Nations at San Francisco, in which "a series of personal items modeled after the Hollywood fan magazine" gave a distorted impression of the serious work being undertaken and the worldwide importance of the achievement. In a later chapter, concerned with the social psychology of international relations, we shall refer again to the tendency of the mass media to dramatize conflicts.

The charge of sensationalism does not apply to all newspapers. Some publications, like the *Times* of London or *The New York Times,* maintain both dignity and responsibility. Other newspapers, including a number of tabloids with more space for pictures than for words, play up crime, sex, and tragedy. The story of mass hysteria, fostered by one newspaper, was told earlier in Chapter 3.

The charge of conservative bias in the press arises from the ownership and control of these channels of communciation. A daily newspaper in a large city represents property worth millions of dollars. Virginius Dabney, editor of the *Richmond Times-Dispatch* is quoted by the commission as follows: "Today newspapers are Big Business and they are run in that tradition. The publisher, who often knows little about the editorial side of the operation, usually is one of the leading businessmen in his community, and his editorial page, under normal circumstances, strongly reflects that point of view. Sometimes he gives the editor a free hand but far oftener he does not. He looks upon the paper primarily as a 'property' rather than as an instrument for public service."

In the early years of American history, many small newspapers competed for attention. About 1909, the number of dailies reached its highest

TABLE 4—CONTENT ANALYSIS OF *Reader's Digest* (JANUARY 1963)

Theme	Columns
1. Combating Communism	94
2. Economic progress: planning, private enterprise, and government	42
3. Adventure: travel, escape from danger	40
4. Combating evils: rackets, delinquency, sex offenses, alcoholism	37
5. Anecdotes, jokes, quips, riddles	36
6. Do-good: serving the community, living the Golden Rule, may one ever lie?	32
7. Middle-class family life: cultural activities, women's clothes, value of education	30
8. Animals: wild and tame	22
9. American strength and virtue	21
10. Popular science and technology	18
11. Value of religion and prayer	16
12. Health care	15

point: 26,000. Since then, in hundreds of cities, one newspaper has bought out all its competitors and maintains a virtual monopoly. Of 1,461 American cities and towns with daily newspapers, all but 61 are non-competitive, presenting only one editorial and political viewpoint in the particular city (Liebling, 1961). An increasing number—375 dailies in 1945—are units in a chain of papers, presenting their point of view in several different cities.

Magazines

Criticism of magazines reiterates the two charges made against newspapers. First, they exploit the sensational to attract numbers and so increase their income. Second, they are owned, run, and biased as are other big commercial enterprises. Four or five large publishers dominate the field, and the socio-economic outlook (sometimes also the religious orientation) of the publisher sets policies.

The content of popular magazines with large circulation mirrors the most widely accepted opinions—seldom does it challenge or correct prevailing views. The largest circulation for many years has been that of the *Reader's Digest*. Its prevailing themes are fairly well represented in Table 4.

A pertinent psychological comment on this inventory and on other forms of mass communication to be discussed later in this chapter is made by Berelson (1962) through one of the characters (Academicus) in an imaginary debate on cultural democracy:

What all of us most want to hear is how great and good and right we are, how justice triumphs—at least in the end—how good and evil are easily recognized, how rewarding it is to do one's duty, how pleasant and easy and full of fun life really is. To a major extent the mass media help us to indulge such global fantasies without recalling us sufficiently to the realities, the complexities, and the seriousness of life.

At the opposite end of the psychological scale from escape into Pollyanna's world is escape into a Jack-the-Giant-Killer world where villains abound. Here we find the misnomer of the comic books which, with sales of 700 million copies a year, cannot be ignored. Because they often portray crime and other violence, they have been charged (Wertham, 1954) with suggesting and sanctioning delinquent behavior. A public opinion poll (American Institute of Public Opinion, November 21, 1954) showed that 70 percent of the adult public believe that comic books are partly responsible for teen-age crime.

It is not easy to find confirmation for such fears. One study (Lewin, 1953) of 260 children aged 12 and 13 compared the 25 most interested in comic books with the 25 who had least interest and seldom or never read them. No significant differences were found in school attendance, school achievement, or school deportment. Another study of this problem, (Hoult, 1949), compared the comic books read by 235 delinquent boys and girls (aged 10–17) with the comic books read by non-delinquents. The subjects were carefully matched for age, school grade, and socio-economic status. The delinquents read significantly more of the crime, violence, and excitement-thriller type; there was no significant difference in the amount of reading of the less objectionable comics. Either delinquency creates a special appetite for these lurid comics or persons having such an appetite tend to become delinquents.

The most impressive data concern the widespread interest in comic magazines. One study (Market Research Corporation of America, January 1944) found that in 72 percent of all homes at least one member read comic books. In the age group of children 6 to 11, 93 percent regularly read comics and among the older youngsters (12 to 17), 84 percent regularly read them. The average child in this study read 12 comic books per month. Among adults, 14 percent were regular comic book readers and another 12 percent read them occasionally. In the armed forces, 44 percent of the young men were regular readers, 13 percent occasional.

The higher the level of education and of income, the less likely adults were to read comic books, but among college graduates in the highest socio-economic stratum 15 percent were regular readers and 11 percent were occasional readers. An interesting piece of data is that 95 percent of the readers passed their books on to some other reader.

A more constructive psychological role for the comic book hero has been suggested on the basis of "interviews in depth" with children (Wolf, Fiske, 1949). Well adjusted children preferred super-heroes ("Superman," "Batman") in the 11–14 age group, but they later advanced to a preference for "true" and "classic" comics. More neurotic children cherished the super-hero phantasies because they themselves failed to achieve ego-strength adequate for the stresses of their environment. The comic books seemed in this study more a symptom than a cause of emotional difficulties.

Books

Books—hardcovers and paperbacks—have served more specialized audiences and hence have less rigid conformities than is characteristic of newspapers and magazines, which reach for mass circulation. Surveys show that despite nearly universal education, only a minority of American adults are book-readers. About one in four had read a book within the past month or two. The top 10 percent of readers account for 70 percent of the books read. Americans read fewer books per person in a year than do citizens of Japan, Britain, and several other countries.

A special factor tending to maintain quality in books is the practice of serious reviewing and criticism. Book reviews are more extensive and more critical than the reviews of films, radio, television, or magazines.

In a general view of the psychological appeal of printed media, five special advantages may be noted (Schramm, 1954): (1) The reader controls his own pace; he reads when, where, and as he pleases; (2) exposure may be repeated; (3) editorial treatment may be fuller; (4) specialized appeal is possible; (5) print is the oldest of the media (except for oratory) and has the prestige of association with higher levels of education.

Motion pictures, radio, and television

The moving picture in color with full sound effects is much closer to direct experience than is radio or the printed word. To see a movie of a castle, a courtroom, or a catastrophe is not quite like being on the scene, but it can be close to first-hand experience. One picture may not always be worth a thousand words, but it is far more effective with the person of poor reading skills and may convey subtle meanings which escape a verbal report. In some instances, by slow-motion portrayal or simplified flow charts of complex processes, the picture may be more easily understood than is the event as it takes place in Nature. Pictures have a special value in our modern world because they can serve as a universal language crossing the barriers of verbal communication. But, because print is the older medium with an immense store of scholarly contributions, it has higher academic prestige. Increasingly, however, educators are building and using film libraries.

Earlier in this chapter we reviewed studies showing how certain films influenced the attitudes of children toward Negroes, Chinese, Germans, and the institution of gambling (Thurstone, Peterson, 1933). Repeated presentations have been found to strengthen the persuasive effect (Thurstone, 1931).

Numerous studies indicate that it is easier to communicate new knowledge than to bring about changes in attitude. This was true of a film on venereal disease (Lashley, Watson, 1922) and of wartime movies on "why we fight" (Hovland *et al.*, 1949).

Attitudes toward certain specific persons, objects, or behaviors presented in a film are more likely to change than are more general or basic attitudes. This was true of the war-propaganda films which had more effect on the specific issues than on the general meaning of the war for the viewers. In an earlier study, students were shown favorable or unfavorable aspects of life in the Soviet Union. The particular good and bad aspects were influential, but the general attitude toward Communism was not affected (Rosenthal, 1934).

An interesting example of the possible influence of a specific and quite peripheral item in a movie was seen in *It Happened One Night.* Clark Gable, the hero, in one scene removed his shirt and showed his chest. Sales of undershirts dropped off so noticeably that a delegation from the clothing industry went to the producers of the film to try to get that scene altered or cut (Britt, 1949, p. 260).

The impact on children of moving picture scenes of violence is controversial. One study, however, found that adults (hospital employees), after seeing a film of aggressive action (*Rebel Without a Cause*), were more willing to administer electric shock treatments to a subject who appeared to suffer from them. (No actual shocks were given.) (Walters, *et al.*, 1962).

Listening: radio and recordings. The media of radio and phonograph have extended the range of a speaker or musical performance, but have weakened the return message from the audience. Usually only numbers count: How many are listening? How many records are sold? Only a few pleased or dissatisfied listeners—usually the disgruntled—write or telephone their reactions.

A comparison (Cantril, 1937) of the reactions of listeners to a radio broadcast (*Town Meeting of the Air,* which featured discussion of current controversial issues) with the reactions of the audience actually assembled to witness the presentations and discussion showed that while the radio listeners also became somewhat involved and reacted, pro or con, to certain speakers, 72 percent of them felt thwarted, on occasion, because they were unable to answer back. Almost all felt it would be more exciting to attend the live discussion. Almost three-fourths of those who had heard the radio broadcast and who had on one or more occasions attended the actual discussion reported that they listened less critically and were less involved when the program reached them by radio.

A major factor in radio communication is the listener's work schedule. Commuters hear car radios as they drive to and from their jobs. Women listen as they do their housework. In the relaxing hours of evening, television now is usually preferred.

Before radio bowed to the greater attraction of television, the major feature was the daytime serial—the "soap opera." Several studies were made of daytime serials during their hey-day. The characters of the dramas were usually in family settings; they got into trouble; no sooner did they extricate themselves than other complications developed. Usually there was a "cliff-hanger" close: "Will Marcia decide to deceive her husband? Listen in tomorrow at 4:45 for a surprising development!" The low-cost dramas were produced by simple formulas and actors could read their lines from script. One such program followed another. The average woman devotee listened to six such programs per day.

Interviewed, the listeners said they liked the exciting emotional adventures. The stories brought some thrills into the dull routines of a housewife. Also, many women said they picked up useful pointers on dealing with their husband's moods, getting along with their in-laws, etc. More than a few housewives welcomed the excuse for a good cry over some body else's troubles. The women learned that they were not alone in having problems and crises. They welcomed the supportive assurance that the wife is the really important person in determining the fate of other family members. The crises of characters in serials also served as conversation pieces in talks with neighboring women (Herzog, 1944; Henry Warner, 1948).

A study (Henry Warner, 1948) of 62 women who regularly listened to the radio drama *Big Sister* led to the conclusion that the lives of listeners were much like that of Ruth, the heroine. They were lower middle-class housewives; their world was their house and family; their lives were rather monotonous and unrewarding; they were dependent on their husbands; they were morally rigid, self-sacrificing, and convinced of their virtues because they were controlled and not self-indulgent. They welcomed the reassurance of the serialized drama that the less upright will be punished and that virtue and self-sacrifice will be rewarded.

The real purpose of the serials was not to amuse or to elevate the audience. Like all commercial radio, it was designed to acquire listeners for the advertising message. In one hour of programing 13 minutes might be devoted to commercials. When listeners were asked: "Do you ever feel like criticizing when you listen to the radio?" two-thirds replied "Yes" and their main objection was to the commercials. The same survey revealed, however, that the average listeners would rather endure the ads than pay a modest license fee of $5.00 a year for radio programs without advertising (Opinion News, 1948).

The value of radio as a source of news first emerged clearly during the 1930's. The critical world events leading up to World War II were reported via radio. Other exciting events such as sports contests, elections, disasters, and approaching hurricanes attracted large audiences. The Orson Welles broadcast of a supposed invasion from Mars (Cantril, 1940) testifies to the faith citizens placed in radio as a source of news.

From a cultural point of view, radio music has made a vital contribution. During the 1940's when less than 3 percent of broadcasting time was was devoted to serious music, the proportion of Americans who listened to concerts and symphonies surpassed the record of any previous era. Classical music became familiar. Popular songs climbed to fame on *The Hit Parade* and its imitators. FM radio increased the number of musical programs and improved their quality. The sale of records became big business. Never before in any country at any time did citizens hear so much music. People who increased their listening became more interested in learning to play an instrument. School bands and orchestras grew into community orchestras.

A certain amount of useful information was broadcast each day. One study indicated that 6 percent of changes in farm practices were inspired by what farmers had heard by radio (Umberger, 1932). Housewives were given advice on cooking, cleaning, and home decoration; statistical analyses of rising and falling stocks enlightened the business man about economic changes. The famous "Fireside Chats" of President Franklin D. Roosevelt during the 1930's introduced an era of political reporting by broadcasts.

Before the days of FM radio, only a very limited number of channels were available. These have traditionally been allocated to private companies by the Federal Communications Commission (FCC). Some people have urged the FCC to be more aggressive in trying to raise radio and television standards, but the commission has generally acted only to bar the most offensive features.

Unlike the magazine, where the editor has responsibility for the content, the broadcasting company usually views its role as transmitting rather than preparing and selecting program features.

Concentration of ownership and control is a more serious problem in broadcasting than it is with newspapers and magazines. A study of radio at its peak—in the mid 1940's—showed 95 percent of the evening audience listening to one of the four big networks. Most of the advertising on which the radio business depended came through a few large advertising agencies. Ten national advertisers provided 60 percent of the business. Four industries—food, drugs, soap, and tobacco—accounted for 75 percent of the radio support.

We have noted earlier that newspaper publishing is big business. The same can be said for broadcasting. And the two are intertwined. In 1959 (H. J. Levin, 1961) the newspapers owned 13 percent of all radio stations and 35 percent of all television stations.

Later in this chapter we shall report a study of the blacklisting of controversial speakers, actors, and musicians, which was effective because of a solid front presented by the limited number of owners.

Television. Television has now made it possible to carry all the educational and non-educational impact of the moving picture into millions of homes simultaneously. Some studies have shown that the typical child of elementary school age watches the television screen 20 to 25 hours per week—about the same amount of time that he spends in school (Narkewicz, 1964). Others find less television viewing in the average week, but the same total time for the first 16 years of life (Schramm, Lyle, Parker, 1961). The child's television viewing, however, is voluntary and his attention is far more concentrated than it is in school. The generation that has grown up with television may actually have learned more facts and attitudes through that medium than from all their school textbooks. The audience that watched Shakespeare's *Richard III* on television could have filled the Metropolitan Opera House 3,500 times over. More significant is the probability that few of the viewers would have bought tickets to attend a performance of the play. Even in 1952, when only 40 percent of the homes had television receivers, the average citizen reported that he got more information from television about the merits of Eisenhower and Stevenson as presidential candidates than he got from his newspapers, magazines or radio broadcasts. By 1962 more homes had television sets than had indoor plumbing, and the average set was running five and one-half hours a day.

The extent to which each of the new media—movies, radio, and television—displaced other activities by adults depended on the involvement of the people before the new attraction appeared. Adults seldom gave up their most satisfying activities for the new experience. The listening or watching first filled otherwise empty or marginal time. Those persons who already enjoyed reading, music, sports, gatherings with friends, and creative work continued to do so. In a real sense, the new media added to life enjoyment; little that was good was crowded out. The usual pattern has been: first, a stage of novelty and exploration, with a sampling of a range of programs; second, a settling down to a more limited routine of viewing or listening.

The new media have not driven out the old. More books are being sold today than before radio was born. Nine of ten adults still read the newspapers. For a time, movie audiences were kept home by television, but movies have made a strong come-back. Television changed the character of radio programs, but, as reported earlier, eight of ten adults still listen to the radio occasionally, while nine of ten watch some TV.

One of the first exhaustive studies of the impact of television in the lives of children was made in England and is summarized in Abstract 33.

The first comparable study in the United States was that of Schramm, Lyle, and Parker (1961). These authors developed a typology of child television viewers. The "fantasy" type of child is devoted to television and seldom reads. The opposite type, perhaps misnamed "reality-oriented," relies heavily on printed matter and seldom watches television. The authors found that where reading skills are not well developed —in younger children and in homes with more limited cultural resources—the "fantasy" type is naturally prevalent. Among adolescents, as educational levels rise, there is more reading. This is especially true in homes of higher economic and cultural status. Reading is accompanied by more future-orientation, which motivates achievement and more socialization motivated by anxiety, which can lead to conformity. Antisocial aggressive impulses were most marked in the fantasy type. As noted earlier in this chapter, in the discussion of comic books, the violent heroes of the Superman and Wild West dramas seem to meet the special emotional needs of some disturbed youngsters. The relationship is probably circular. The crime stories are sought by the child, but they also reinforce this kind of interest.

A study comparing children (10-12 years of age) whose activities and values center mainly in their family with those whose activities and values center in their peer groups showed that the former were more apt to prefer television shows "characterized by violence, action, and aggression." Children with only limited acceptance in their peer groups preferred escapist fantasies.

A pediatric study (Narkewicz, Graven, 1964) identified a "tired child" syndrome, found in children 3-12 years of age who were spending excessive (30 hours a week or more) time watching television. Among the symptoms were fatigue, decreased appetite, headache, and vomiting.

There is general agreement that television *could* be a potent force in the education of both children and adults. Numerous comparisons of classroom instruction with what can be learned from carefully planned television courses show the latter usually more effective. One reason for the appeal of televised instruction may be novelty, but a major factor is that the telecast lesson has been prepared by a master teacher who is free to devote much more time to preparation and to developing more telling illustrations. The single lesson in science or history, recorded on film or telecast, can be used to teach millions of students.

Like radio, commercial television in the United States remains a

Abstract 33

TITLE   Television and the Child

AUTHORS   H. H. Himmelweit, A. N. Oppenheim, and Pamela Vince

PROBLEM   What are the effects of television on children?

SUBJECTS   About 4,000 children, age 10–14, in four cities in England; 1,854 matched viewers and controls. In Norwich another 370 matched viewers and controls.

PROCEDURE   Viewers and controls were matched for sex, age, intelligence, and social class. Each child answered a questionnaire and kept a diary of all activities for one week. Personality ratings were obtained from teachers. Supplementary inquiries were made with parents.

SOME FINDINGS   Average television-viewing time, 11–13 hours per week. Children with I.Q.'s below 100 watched about 14 hours, those with I.Q.'s over 115 only 11 hours.

Those who had had TV sets for three years or more watched about two hours a week less than did the newcomers.

Favorite programs were (adult) crime thrillers (75 percent of first choices). Adult political discussions had little appeal, even for more intelligent children.

Tastes in TV were similar to tastes in reading and movies.

In response to a question about the three main qualities that help a person advance in the world, more TV viewers mentioned "Being able to stand up for oneself; confidence; drive" (27 percent vs. 20 percent). More also mentioned "brains" and "being clever" (47 percent vs. 38 percent), and "not being afraid" (8 percent vs. 3 percent). Controls more often checked "Health and strength."

TV viewers expressed slightly more fear of burglars (69 percent vs. 62 percent) and of being followed (61 percent vs. 53 percent).

In response to the question, "What sort of person would you like to be when you are 25 years old?" more viewers mentioned material possessions (38 percent vs. 27 percent).

TV viewers did not differ significantly from controls on school achievement tests. A general knowledge test covering 11 areas showed viewers superior in knowledge of geography, science, sport, music, and handicrafts. In no area were controls superior. TV viewers felt themselves better informed than did controls on *Jane Eyre* (presented on a popular TV program), underwater exploring, Olympics, and penguins.

Time spent at viewing television did not reduce reading or interest in active sports; it did reduce radio listening, movie going (for younger children) and "just standing around, doing nothing special." Sleeping time was not reduced.

SOURCE: New York: Oxford University Press, 1958.

part of the advertising industry. Its real purpose is not to enlighten or to edify, but to sell the products of one manufacturer and of no other producer of similar goods. This objective is fairly well achieved. Comparison of sales of television-advertised brands to persons who own TV sets with sales to non-set owners shows higher sales to set owners. Early in this chapter evidence was cited that brands tested before and after a television advertising campaign increased in their sales to television owners, although in the control group these brands declined slightly. A study of sales of small, frequently replaced merchandise found that between February and May the average brand lost half its customers, who were replaced by other buyers. Those shoppers who, during the period had begun to view a program advertising a given brand increased purchases of that brand by 40 percent. Those who had once viewed these programs, but had stopped, showed a 43 percent decrease in the associated purchases (NBC, 1954).

In 1961 Newton Minow, newly elected chairman of the Federal Communications Commission, charged the broadcasters with creating a "vast wasteland" in their overemphasis on advertising, sex, and violence. Two years earlier the American public had been jolted by the revelation that television quiz shows, a popular form of entertainment, had been rigged, with winners and losers predetermined. A public opinion poll (American Institute of Public Opinion, December 6, 1959) showed that 75 percent (of those who had an opinion) believed television commercials used untruthful arguments. The higher the educational level of respondents, the more they supported this view. Another poll (A.I.P.O, June 14, 1961) showed 56 percent (of those committing themselves) supporting the need for stricter curbs and controls. Their main grievance was immorality and the playing up of sex and violence. A study by the National Association of Educational Broadcasters found 7,000 acts or threats of violence on a single week of commercial television in New York.

A single program *The Virginian,* on Christmas night, 1963, presented an estimated 10 million viewers with 13 killings by shooting, stabbing, or clubbing, plus eight additional assaults or fights (Amory, 1965). The average American child, watching the most popular television programs for the average period of time during his formative years will probably witness the violent destruction of some 13,000 individuals. This probably exceeds, quantitatively, the exposure to scenes of violence experienced by the youth of any other society of which we have records.

What is the result of this exposure to violence? We do not know. Most children, adolescents, and adults enjoy peaceful relations with their associates. Individual incidents of children imitating television murders can be cited. One seven-year-old boy learned from a television program how to slip ground glass into the family pot of stew. Yet in larger studies, for example, an intensive survey of 1,000 pupils in Waterbury, Connecticut (Riscuth, 1951), the psychological symptoms of fear and of destructive aggression were no more common among children who frequently watched crime, anticrime, and other adventure shows.

A sophisticated criticism of television dramas is that the characters portrayed are too often all-good or all-bad. Gradations and complexity of characterization, although the rule in life, are the exception in the world of television. All is black or white, with no grays. Motives are at the extremes of high or low—seldom as mixed as truly human motivation. Later we shall discuss the counterpart in international relations, a correlated oversimplified view of "good nations" and "bad nations."

Another criticism of most movies and television shows—perhaps applicable also to magazine stories—is that they do not give much recognition to the lives of working-class people. Heroes are seldom blue-collar workers—they are usually in business or professional fields. Families portrayed are seldom at or below the average income level. Heroines in the social climb are eventually dressed in the kind of clothes the average woman would like to be able to afford. Middle- and upper-class values are dominant. Few story-lines follow "the short and simple annals of the poor (Arnheim, 1944; Head, 1954). This unbalanced picture of life in the United States has led people in other countries to view all Americans as wealthy and has probably fostered a sense of failure and frustration in the millions who realize that they can never —short of a great gamble and payoff—aspire to what seem to be the comforts of the American Way of Life as reflected in films.

An example of the type of control exerted by advertisers is the "code" laid down by the Proctor and Gamble Soap concern, which was then spending $100 million a year on television advertising. According to statements by A. N. Halverstadt, general advertising manager of P & G, before the FCC (on September 27, 1962), no program that the firm sponsored could portray a big-business man as "cold," "ruthless," or lacking "spiritual motivation." More recently, the sponsor of a news show canceled its half-million-dollar contract because the network had carried a program on which Alger Hiss appeared. Several other sponsors also tried to cancel their programs for the same reason.

Differences between commercial and publicly operated television can be seen in the two systems as they operate in Great Britain and the United States. The BBC (British Broadcasting Corporation) is publicly owned and operated; the Independent Television (ITV) system in Britain derives its income from advertisers, although it does not go to the American extreme of permitting advertisers to create and sponsor the programs. Even so, in a typical week (April 3–9, 1960) the differences shown in Table 6 were noted.

Walter Lippmann, writing in the wake of the exposures of fraud in television quiz shows (October 27, 1959) concludes: "The great offense

TABLE 5—COMPARATIVE CONTENT OF BRITISH PUBLIC (BBC) AND COMMERCIAL (ITV) TELEVISION

	Hours	
	BBC (Public)	ITV (Commercial)
Study of current events: topical magazine articles, documentary, talks, and discussions	16½	6
Orchestral music	1¼	0
Sports	7	10
Contemporary plays	3	1
Westerns, crime, soap operas	5	17

(Williams, 1962)

of the television industry is that it is misusing a superb scientific achievement, that it is monopolizing the air at the expense of effective news reporting, good art, and civilized entertainment."

"The best line for us to take," urges Lippmann, "is to devise a way by which one network can be run as a public service with its criterion not what will be most popular, but what is good. . . . We should not, I believe, shrink from the idea that such a network would have to be subsidized and endowed. . . . Why should it not be subsidized and endowed as are the universities and the public schools and the exploration of space and modern medical research, and, indeed, the churches —and so many other institutions which are essential to a good society, yet cannot be operated for profit? . . . They are concerned with excellence and not with making money."

Another proposal, more in line with the commercial traditions of the "industry," is "pay television." An experiment under the auspices of International Telemeter in a suburb of Toronto (Etobicoke) showed that they could offer all the excellent first-run movies, some top Broadway shows, and most major sporting events for a cost of about 60 cents per week per family. Yet, in this experiment, 40 percent of the sets equipped to receive pay-as-you-go programs did not use this service, and the average family still received free commercial programs 13 hours a week and the special pay programs only about 2 hours a week. This finding supports the argument of the broadcasters that they give people what the audience wants.

Relatively few of the critics of television seem to be speaking for programs they themselves would actively support. Intellectuals, according to Steiner (1963), advocate raising standards of taste and of intellectual content for the benefit of other listeners. But they do not regard themselves as belonging to the television audience and would probably watch relatively few of the improved programs if these were offered. They prefer their libraries.

A major and highly respected function of television and radio broadcasting was vividly illustrated at the time of the assassination of President John F. Kennedy. From Friday noon, November 22, 1963, until the following Monday evening, the whole nation centered its attention on these media. People who only rarely listened to broadcasts or watched television found themselves almost transfixed by the incoming programs. This was in part hunger for the latest news. Newspapers were stale before they left the press. But more important, the ceremonies on television became a ritual of mourning. All commercial messages were suspended, at tremendous cost to the broadcasting companies. Hour after hour the solemn announcements were repeated, interspersed with requiems and other memorial music. Millions of citizens shared in the common experience of shock and bereavement. Television and radio made it possible for the whole nation—and through the Telstar satellite other parts of the world—to unite in deeply moving ceremonies. Barriers of race, religion, and region were transcended. To an unprecedented extent, the many became one.

Comparisons among media

Can legitimate comparisons be made, considering that each medium is chosen by its audience for particular reasons—as one plays a record to suit a mood or goes to a movie instead of a lecture?

When two ways of presenting the same subject matter are compared, the conclusions still have to be qualified. Are the methods equally familiar to the learners? What about the strength of attachment to whatever medium has been customary? What about the novelty effect of a previously unutilized medium? Is there an immediate interest which would wear off in time? Also the content of the subject matter may lead to preference for a medium which permits progress at ones own chosen rate—as in following the steps of a mathematical argument or reading a poem.

With all these and other reservations, we may examine the results of a few typical experiments. Do students retain better what they read or what they hear? An early study with grade-school children found that listeners recalled more (Erickson, King, 1917) than did readers, in each grade from third to ninth. Adults, tested on a 100-word prose passage, recalled it better after hearing it read than they did after reading it silently (Worcester, 1925). Oral argument, in another study (Knower, 1935, 1936), proved more potent in changing an attitude than did the same material presented in printed form.

A comparison of speeches, radio broadcasts, and printed appeals in changing attitudes (toward war, birth control, God) showed very small differences favoring the live and present speaker (Wilke, 1934).

Comparisons of motion picture presentations with words spoken or in print have usually shown the film to be more effective. In one early study with high school students (Sumstine, 1918) the subject matter presented in a moving picture was better recalled than when presented by lecture. The superiority of the picture was evident on a test given 24 hours after the instruction and was even greater after three months had elapsed. Another early study (Lacy, 1919) using pupils of junior high school age showed that learners preferred the movie to reading or hearing the story, but in this case more was recalled after hearing the story told. One of the more comprehensive comparisons (J. W. Tilton, D. C. Knowlton, 1930) was made in seventh-grade history classes using ten "Chronicles of America Photoplays." Tests credited pupils who had seen the films with learning about 19 percent more than did the controls. A pupil of average intelligence, who had seen the films, scored as well as a bright pupil who had studied in classes where the films were not used.

Protection against propaganda

Democracy cherishes the ideal of a citizen who thinks for himself. He is expected to weigh the facts and arguments and to arrive at a decision which, in the long run, will be best for society.

Many factors make this ideal difficult to realize. Earlier in the chapter it was noted that as we move away from the local area in which a citizen can base his judgments on first-hand experience, we depend more and more upon the media of mass communication. These media cannot give us the whole picture of all important events in the region, nation or world. There is no time to present, or listen to, the whole story. Someone must select and edit the bits and pieces which represent all we are likely to know about world affairs. As we discussed each of the main media, we noted how it is controlled. Almost all our newspapers, magazines, radio stations, film-studios, and television broadcasting are big business enterprises. It is very difficult for any point of view which is critical of the business system to be heard through the media of mass communication. It is difficult, also, for unpopular and unconventional views on faith, morals or patriotism to be expressed in these media. Reviewing Schramm's *The Science of Human Communication* (1963) Rosenberg writes: "The main problem is not . . . with the media as such but with their organization and with the motives and morals of at least some of those who control and use them. Perhaps in the final sense the problem is that of a social order that has gone further than most in accepting the pursuit of profit and power as imperatives possessing ultimate legitimacy" (1964).

Obstacles to presentation of deviating viewpoints in media of mass communication are found in public opinion itself, as well as in the controlling interests. There is a strong public pressure for conformity and considerable hostility among all classes against those who question traditional views.

In their study of typical teen-agers, Remmers and Radler (1957)

Abstract 34

TITLE   Communism, Conformity, and Civil Liberties

AUTHOR   Samuel A. Stouffer

PROBLEMS   Do American citizens generally support civil liberties? Is there a difference between attitudes of community leaders and the rank-and-file?

PROCEDURE   Interviews by two public opinion poll agencies, using many open-end questions.

SOME FINDINGS

Endorsing the right of persons of "deviate" opinions to speak in their community:

| | Type of Deviate | | |
	Socialist	Atheist	Communist
Average citizens	58%	37%	27%
Upper class positions			
Newspaper publishers	97%	82%	63%
President, bar association	95%	83%	63%
President, chamber of commerce	93%	58%	46%
President, school board	88%	59%	40%
President, woman's club	68%	46%	39%
President, PTA	79%	59%	43%
President, trade union	80%	59%	45%

Endorsing the "firing" of persons of deviate opinion from a position as college teacher:

| | Type of Deviate | | |
	Socialist	Atheist	Communist
Average citizens	54%	85%	91%
Community leaders	47%	71%	86%

Tolerance of deviate opinions increases with level of education:

	High tolerance
College graduates	66%
Some college	53%
High school graduates	42%
Some high school	29%
Grade school only	16%

A child should never be allowed to express disagreement to his parents or he will lose respect for them.

(age 21–40)	Disagree
College graduates	71%
Some college	54%
High school graduates	47%
Some high school	30%
Grade school only	18%

Abstract 34—*Continued*

Men seem generally to be more tolerant than women at every level of education.

Average for high school graduates	High tolerance
Males (N = 361)	48%
Females (N = 406)	36%

Church goers (who attended a service during past month) are slightly less likely to be tolerant.

	High tolerance
Attended church	28%
Did not attend	36%

Information on Communists and what is being done about them in the United States is most likely to come to community leaders via the mass media (newspapers, television, radio).

	Community leaders	National cross-section
Read or hear on air	88%	75%
Conversations with people	8%	18%
Don't know	4%	7%
	100%	100%

SOURCE: Garden City, New York: Doubleday and Company, 1955.

found 41 percent unwilling to approve real freedom of the press. About one-third were prepared to have government forbid some people from speaking in public or certain groups from meeting. Forty-two percent said: "We should firmly resist any attempts to change the American way of life." The proportion of high school pupils who would refuse to allow a Communist to speak on the radio increased from 36 percent in 1947 to 65 percent in 1951. The proportion willing to "allow newspapers and magazines to print anything they want except military secrets" surprisingly declined from 45 percent in 1951 to 29 percent in 1960 (Remmers, 1963).

A study of adult citizens, Abstract 34 shows that newspaper publishers and other opinion leaders are generally more tolerant of deviates than is the average citizen.

From time to time, a wave of special concern for orthodoxy sweeps the United States. Shortly after World War I and the emergence of the Communist regime in Russia, A. Mitchell Palmer, then attorney general, conducted a lively series of raids and deportations against "seditionists" and all "Reds." Men elected to the New York State legislature on the Socialist ticket were denied their seats. Another period of intensified hunts for subversives was led by Senators McCarran and

McCarthy in the period from World War II to 1954. A newsletter exposing suspected leftwingers was launched in 1947 under the title *Counterattack*. The same publishers (American Business Consultants) in 1950 issued a special report entitled *Red Channels, The Report of Communist Influence in Radio and Television*. An investigation of some of the effects of this attempt to purge radio and television of persons suspected of pro-Communist leanings was made by the *Fund for the Republic*. The Fund report cited cases of performers barred by all major broadcasting agencies because these persons had been charged with some "association" with left-wing causes. The reported association might involve only a paid performance or the signing of a legitimate petition. In some instances the charge of association could not be substantiated, but the performer had then become "controversial" and agents were told: "We wouldn't touch him with a ten-foot pole." Jahoda's survey of 64 television producers, directors, writers, and performers found 85 percent aware of at least one case of blacklisting by the media (Cogley, 1956).

Another approach to reducing the influence of biased propaganda is educating youth to recognize and to discount attempts at manipulation of their minds. In 1937, the Institute for Propaganda Analysis was founded by Dr. Clyde R. Miller. It publicized seven common propaganda devices:

1. Name-calling (Red, fascist, outside agitator, trouble maker)
2. Glittering generalities (free enterprise, American Way, progress, social justice)
3. Transfer (flag, church, Uncle Sam)
4. Testimonial (as for patent medicines)
5. Plain folks (common denominator, home and mother)
6. Card stacking (selecting evidence to support a view; ignoring opposing facts)
7. Band wagon (everyone believes it, buys it, supports it)

An experiment (Biddle, 1932) with high school students included nine lessons in identifying emotional appeals, including alleged support by respected authorities and the pattern of "we are good" and "they are bad." Fourteen articles on international relations were used as test material. In all the schools, the experimental group improved on the average more than did the controls in recognizing propaganda, although about 25 percent of the pupils remained unimproved. In one school where the experimenter made an assembly speech deliberately incorporating several of the propaganda devices, those students who remained critical of the speaker in their written reactions after the talk came predominantly (19 of 24) from the experimental classes.

A later study (Glaser, 1941) used a test of critical thinking with high school students before and after a ten-week course on inductive, deductive, and logical methods of thought. Experimental groups gained much more (difference six times its S.E.) than did controls. In one tenth grade class of 41 pupils, retested after six months, the instructed group maintained a score of 58 while the controls scored only 38.

Such studies indicate that it is possible to increase the disposition and ability of pupils to engage in critical evaluation of communications carried over nationwide media. As yet, these educational efforts reach only a very few American school children. It seems unlikely that the press, radio, movies, and television will give much support to an extensive program designed to decrease their power over public thought.

Conclusion

Early in this chapter we posed three questions which can now be reviewed in the light of the many studies reported.

The first concerned the extent to which the media of mass communication promote propaganda—attempting to influence opinions toward conclusions that will be accepted without thoughtful, critical consideration. In this category fall practically all the printed advertising and the broadcast commercials.

The second question dealt with the extent to which we are being manipulated toward conformity. A variety and diversity of viewpoints and sources of information do appear in some publications and programs. These safeguard some independence of thought. The great danger, however, lies in monopoly. Whenever all the papers, magazines, radio speakers, and televised programs express the same opinion on a controversial issue and the opposition has little chance to be publicly heard, democracy is endangered.

The third question turns attention to the impact of mass communication on aesthetic taste and moral standards. It is important at this point to examine one conception of how excellence is distributed in the population. Some people, including many professionals in the media of mass communication, conceive of levels of public taste as a cone. At the top are the few who are highly cultivated. As one goes down toward the base of the cone, standards become lower and numbers increase. The largest audience is said to be found at the most deprived level of culture. Actually, intelligence and many other factors of excellence are distributed in an approximately normal curve. Most fall in the middle. There are no more at very low levels than at very high levels. Perhaps the distribution of income, which is more like a cone, has contributed to the mistaken notion that the great masses are low on the scale.

Another illusion is that at one time good taste and virtue were widespread, but that this high quality has recently been pulled down to a level of mediocrity. It would be closer to the truth to say that once a small segment of the population—a kind of cultural aristocracy—read good books and ignored the state of the masses who could not qualify for this circle of elite. What the media of mass communication have done has been to bring the tastes of the common man to general attention. Edward Shils (1957) has put it cogently: "The major error of the analysts of popular culture is their belief that it has succeeded to something which was intrinsically worthy, that man has sunk into a hitherto unknown mire because of it, and that this is a necessary prelude to the further degradation, and perhaps ultimate extinction, of high culture. . . . It would be far more correct to assume that mass culture is now less damaging to the lower classes than the dismal and harsh existence of earlier centuries had ever been. The reading of good books, the enjoyment of superior music and painting, although perhaps meager, is certainly more widespread now than in previous centuries, and there is no reason to believe that it is less profound or less genuine."

There remains the clear conviction that the newer media of mass communication still fall far short of their potential contribution. If their superior techniques for attracting and holding attention could be utilized for such objectives as are fostered by liberal arts colleges and academies of fine arts, the cultural contribution would be tremendous. Occasional examples of bold and imaginative productions have shown what television, under wise guidance, can bring to mankind.

Any statement of the quality of public opinion, ethical concern, and popular taste we would like to achieve reveals immense gaps between what the media now carry and what we would most value. The following words by Berelson (1962) conclude the case:

> What values do we want a communication system to promote and, we hope, realize? That is easy: clarification of political issues, stimulation of high esthetic taste, provision of moral and ethical debate, concern with the basic and tragic ends of human existence—nothing less, in short, than furtherance of the essential dignity of man. The media do not present to us the tragic character of life, nor its glories, but only its unrealities, its superficialities, its trivialities. In short, they do not help to illuminate the human condition.

CHAPTER NINE

Culture and personality

Our central thesis—set forth in Chapter 6—is that structures lead to processes which result in certain attitudes (S-P-A). The most comprehensive and influential of these structures is what anthropologists call the *culture*. From cultural systems arise regular processes of interaction which form corresponding patterns of personality.

In his *Psychological Anthropology*, F. L. K. Hsu has proposed, more specifically, that "maintenance systems" lead to certain correlative child training practices and these to personality variables (1961, p. 356). He adds that the personality variables may then be regarded as causal for "projective systems," such as magic, myths, and rituals. Personality is thus viewed as depending on the child-rearing practices, which, in turn, are greatly influenced by the maintenance systems, that is, "the basic customs surrounding the nourishment, sheltering, and protection" of the members of the society.

Cultural relativity

Culture

Culture is the matrix that molds the main characteristics of most or all the members of a society. "Every baby," said John Dewey, "is laid in a cradle of custom." How he will view the world; how he will speak and think; how he will eat, play, work, and enjoy himself; his ethical ideals and how he will worship—all these patterns are largely predetermined by the cultural setting into which he is born. "The individual," says Linton, "is only an incident in the life history of his society" (p. 12).

"Culture" as used in the social sciences refers to the total way of life characteristic of a somewhat homogeneous society of human beings. This meaning of the term should be distinguished from the popular use of "culture" to refer to refinement of taste in intellectual and aesthetic realms. Linton (1945) defines culture as "the configuration of learned behavior whose component elements are shared and transmitted by the members of a particular society." Another anthropologist, Wissler, has outlined, as follows, nine headings under which the facts of culture may be compiled. (1923, pp. 74–5)

1. Speech
   Languages, writing systems, etc.
2. Material traits
   a. Food habits
   b. Shelter
   c. Transportation and travel
   d. Utensils, tools, etc.
   e. Weapons
   f. Dress
   g. Occupations and industries
3. Art. Carving, painting, drawing, music, etc.
4. Mythology and scientific knowledge
5. Religious practices
   a. Ritualistic forms
   b. Treatment of the sick
   c. Treatment of the dead
6. Family and social systems
   a. The forms of marriage
   b. Methods of reckoning relationships
   c. Inheritance
   d. Social control
   e. Sports and games
7. Property
   a. Real and personal
   b. Standards of value and exchange
   c. Trade
8. Government
   a. Political forms
   b. Judicial and legal procedures
9. War

The culture of a tribe, region, nation or larger society or civilization includes all its man-made objects, its customs, art, science or myths, other organized knowledge, traditions, ceremonies, economic practices, child-rearing practices, political institutions, its values, and religion. All the influences discussed in preceding chapters—the structure-process-attitude sequence and the flow of propaganda through the media of mass communication are parts of the larger complex called the *culture*.

This chapter will focus on the culture as a whole. In subsequent chapters various subcultures—those of socio-economic class, race, sex roles, etc.—will be seen as bringing variations within the general pattern formed by the overall culture.

Beginning study of culture

Comparisons of cultures began as soon as travelers encountered strange customs in the lands they visited. Marco Polo brought back to Venice, about 1300 A.D., accounts of curious manners in the court of Emperor Kublai of Cathay (China). For centuries, the level of these reports was comparable to the curious knicknacks and oddities which explorers brought home. Early missionaries added a different emphasis —they were expected to show how benighted and needy were the heathen. During the latter half of the nineteenth century, a number of German thinkers turned their attention to serious comparative study of cultures. Hegel's (1910) idea of the *objektiver Geist* referred to an embodiment of mind in such social institutions as the family, law, morals, and the political state. He saw the individual mind as a tiny and transient portion of the larger ordered mind of society, itself a manifestation of the Divine Absolute Mind. The great German psychologist, Wundt, wrote ten volumes of *Völkerpsychologie* analyzing language, myths, morals, law, art, and religion of known societies. A journal of "folk psychology" was founded in 1860. Several British psychologists (Rivers, Myers, and McDougall) joined a pioneer anthropological expedition in 1898, adding their laboratory techniques to the collection of ethnological observations.

Overthrow of instinct theory

The major impact of anthropological studies upon psychology began in the late 1920's. In 1928 Margaret Mead, in a widely discussed study, reported that emotional upheavals during adolescence which had been attributed to innate glandular changes were not apparent under the different conditions of Samoan culture. In 1924, William Graham Sumner's observations on the wide variety of practices—often irrational —reported earlier in his *Folkways*, (1906) was systematized (in collaboration with A. G. Keller) in a four-volume science of society; and in 1927 Malinowski published his criticism of Freud's view of the Oedipus Complex as universal.

During the first quarter of the twentieth century, most psychology had been founded upon instinct theories. E. L. Thorndike devoted the first and largest part of his three-volume educational psychology (1913) to an inventory of hundreds of what he regarded as inborn connections in the human make-up. McDougall (1908) preferred to relate human behavior to seven basic instincts with corresponding emotions: flight, repulsion, curiosity, pugnacity, self-abasement, self-assertion, and the parental instinct.

Backed by prevailing instinct theories, defenders of the *status quo* mocked all reformers with the argument, "you can't change human nature!" Why do we have wars? "Man is driven by unalterable instincts of hostility, aggression, and pugnacity." Why do we operate a capitalistic profit-seeking economy? "It rests soundly upon man's acquisitive instinct." Social institutions such as families, clubs or churches were simply accounted for as expressions of instincts of mating, gregariousness, and religion. Class and race discrimination were barricaded behind alleged instincts of "consciousness of kind," of "dominance and submission." A provocative study (Pastore, 1949) of the broader social attitudes of 12 prominent defenders of instinct theories showed 11 of them conservative or reactionary. The converse also held. Among 12 scientists who emphasized human plasticity and the potency of the environment, 11 could properly be called "liberal" or even "radical" in their social theories.

Quite possibly the economic depression of the 1930's, moving many intellectuals toward left-wing political views, hastened the reaction against the older instinct theories. Social change seemed required, and evidence that men could change was welcome. A pertinent example is the English biologist, J. B. S. Haldane, who served for some years as an official member of the Communist Party. His discussion of human nature (1947) emphasizes experiments like that of Kuo, who worked with kittens. Eighteen kittens which were raised in cages along with mice or white rats as playmates never, at maturity, killed the kind of rodent they had associated with in their early months. Among 20 reared in isolation from other rats and from mice, only nine showed the traditionally "instinctive" response of springing upon and killing a running mouse. In a third group of 21, which were allowed to see their cat mother kill mice, all but three later demonstrated the same kind of behavior—an impressive S-P-A sequence.

As doubt about the inevitability of instinctive behavior increased, older studies were recalled. One was Conradi's demonstration (1905) that English sparrows, brought up in a cage with canaries, did not develop their usual harsh chirp but a softer note and, after three months, actual trills. The behaviorism of John B. Watson (1919) hypothesized that proper conditioning could make any baby of adequate intelligence into "rich man, poor man, beggar man, thief; doctor, lawyer, merchant, chief."

The flood of evidence which overwhelmed traditional instinct theory came from the anthropologists. Few human actions could seem more "natural" than nodding approval, shaking one's head in negation or smiling when pleased. Yet LaBarre (1947) reports: "Among the Ainu of northern Japan, for example, our particular head noddings are unknown":

. . . . the right hand is usually used in negation, passing from right to left and back in front of the chest; and both hands are gracefully brought up to the chest and gracefully waved downwards—palms upwards—in sign of affirmation. . . .

The Semang, pygmy Negroes of interior Malaya, thrust the head sharply forward for "yes" and cast the eyes down for "no." The Abyssinians say "no" by jerking the head to the right shoulder, and "yes" by throwing the head back and raising the eyebrows. The Dyaks of Borneo raise their eyebrows to mean "yes," and contract them slightly to mean "no."

A Bengali servant in Calcutta rocks his head rapidly in an arc from shoulder to shoulder, usually four times, in assent; in Delhi a Moslem boy throws his head diagonally backward with a slight turning of the neck for the same purpose; and the Kandyan Singhalese bends the head diagonally forward toward the right, with an indescribably graceful turning in of the chin, often accompanying this with a cross-legged curtsey, arms partly crossed, palms upward—the whole performance extraordinarily beautiful and ingratiating. Indeed, did my own cultural difference not tell me it already, I would know that the Singhalese manner of receiving an object (with the right hand, the left palm supporting the right elbow) is not instinctive, for I have seen a Singhalese mother *teaching* her little boy to do this when I gave him a chunk of palm tree sugar. I only regretted, later, that my own manners must have seemed boorish and subhuman, since I handed it to him with my right hand, instead of with both, as would any courteous Singhalese.

Smiling, indeed, I have found may also be mapped after the fashion of any other culture trait; and laughter is in some senses a geographic variable. On a map of the Southwest Pacific one could perhaps even draw lines between areas of Papual hilarity and others where a Dobuan, Melanesian dourness reigned. In Africa, Gorer noted that laughter is used by the Negro to express surprise, wonder, embarrassment and even discomfiture; it is not necessarily or even often a sign of amusement; the significance given to "black laughter" is due to a mistake of supporting the idea that similar symbols have identical meanings.[1]

Hissing in Japan is a sign of courtesy and polite deference to social superiors; the Basuto applaud by hissing; but in England hissing is rude and public disapprobation of an actor or a speaker. Spitting in many parts of the world is a sign of utmost contempt; and yet among the Masai of Africa it is a sign of affection and benediction, while the spitting of an American Indian medicine man upon a patient is one of the kindly offices of the healer. Urination upon another person is a grave insult in most parts of the world, but it is part of the transfer of power from an African medicine man in initiations and curing rituals. As for other opposite meanings, Western man stands up in the presence of a superior; the Fijians and the Tongans sit down. In some contexts we put on more clothes as a sign of respect; the Friendly Islanders take them off. The Toda of South India raise the open right hand to the face,

[1] Weston LaBarre, "The Cultural Basis of Emotions and Gestures." *J. Pers.* 1947, XVI:49–56. Reprinted by permission.

with the thumb on the bridge of the nose, to express respect; a gesture almost identical among Europeans is an expression of extreme disrespect.

Patterns of sexual behavior certainly meet the criteria of "instinct" because they have a biological and physiological basis and are so nearly universal. Yet, as Ford and Beach (1951) have shown, different cultures foster widely different attitudes and behaviors. There is no agreement among human societies on the age when sex activity may begin, on the kind of partner who may be chosen, on monogamy, on the preferred time, place or positions of intercourse, or on the moral or religious significance of various forms of sexual expression. Among 18 cultures in which males have a distinct preference, five prefer the slender female, while thirteen prefer plumpness. Our culture expects male initiative, and psychoanalysts have generally assumed that this is innate and healthy. Yet Yerkes (1936, 1943) found that among our chimpanzee cousins the female was more apt to initiate intercourse. Ford and Beach tell us that among the Kwoma, the Maori, and the Mataeo, women are considered to be more highly sexed and properly signal to men by pinching them or scratching their hands. In the ceremonial dances of the Gaojiro, girls may try to trip the men, and if they succeed, the man must make love to the woman who has thus captured him. Among the Lepcha, women must not take the initiative except that aunts may seduce their nephews and most boys begin their sex life in this way.

Children were regarded, in Victorian morality, as innocent of sex interests. One of the surprising revelations associated with Freud arose from his conclusion that children's pleasure seeking normally includes stimulation of their sexual organs. Freud recognized that the "latency period" in which children are not sexually active, is not physiological but is found only in cultures which repress the sex impulses of children (Hartmann et al., 1951). Malinowski (1929) reported that, in the Trobriand Islands, children play at intercourse, under observation by adults, as acceptably as American children might play at giving dolls a party.

It seems right and natural to most members of our society that men should prize chastity in a wife, but this is by no means universal. "Among certain peoples of India, a man may compel his wife to bear him a child by another man. In some West African tribes, a girl is not considered for marriage until she has successfully borne a child" (Britt, 1949, p. 80). Wife-lending is an approved form of hospitality among the Eskimos.

Homosexual behavior is so repugnant to many in our society that it is often severely punished by law. Yet in a majority (49 of 76) of the societies on which information is available, Ford and Beach have found that homosexual activity is considered normal and acceptable for some of the members. Special roles of considerable prestige may be assigned the homosexuals, as among the Chuckchee, or the Koniaq. It was a highly esteemed relationship in Ancient Greece. Aristotle, in his *Politics*, proposed homosexual attachments as a preferred way of limiting excessive population increase. Among the Siwans and Keraki all boys are reported to enjoy some homosexual activities. In other societies (Truk; Carolinians) no boys or men were known to engage in them (Kluckhohn, 1954, p. 928).

Taboos against incest seem to be almost universal today; yet among the highly honored royalty of Egypt, Peru, and Hawaii the mating of brothers and sisters was approved. (Lowie, 1940, p. 332). Brother-and-sister twins might marry in Bali and the ancient Persians seem also to have accepted incestuous unions (Masters, 1963).

The stimuli for shame depend likewise upon the culture. Herodotus speaks with disgust of Egyptians who perform excretory processes in the privacy of their houses rather than on the public street as was done in Athens. There are numerous cultures in which neither nakedness nor excretion is a source of shame. It thus turns out that the universal "sex instinct" can tell us little or nothing about whether given individuals will be prudish or salacious; celibate or profligate; homosexual or heterosexual; monogamous, polygamous or polyandrous; whether their sentiments of shame will be connected with excretion, sex, eating, dress, or the persons with whom they converse.

Other so-called instincts have fared no better.

"Pugnacity" as a human universal does not tell us why wars are unknown to Eskimos but flourish in modern industrial nations. Neither does it explain the reluctance of many men, even in our war-oriented world, to being drafted into a wartime army. No modern nation relies for military defense on the desire of its males to engage in combat. Cultures vary in the premium they place on aggressiveness. Among the Ojibwa Indians, insults were repaid by knife wounds and trespassing on hunting grounds by murder. "War parties" arose because some man had visions of successful conquest. Yet other Indians—notably the Zuni of Southwestern North America—seem to have almost no instances of violent attack. Among the South Sea island cultures, the Mundugumor have been reported (Mead, 1928) to be aggressively violent and vengeful, while the Arapesh, on the same island, are mild and gentle.

A particularly instructive example of situational influence (S-P-A) in development of aggression may be found in the Comanche Indian culture (Kardiner, 1945). Early records describe them as humble, harmless, and placid with tolerance even for trespassing. Then came new technical instruments—horses for riding and guns for shooting. At the same time the white settlers—English, French, and Spanish—placed a premium on plunder. In this altered situation, the Comanches became fierce brigands. Later the military forces of the United States confined the Comanches to their reservation. The patterns of predatory raiding and war could no longer be enacted. These Indians under the new social structure became docile, inert, and apathetic.

Many futile arguments have been held over whether human nature is basically competitive, violent, and destructive, or cooperative, peace-loving, and constructive. The answer is that no instinct places man in either category. In some cultures, many situations call forth hostile responses; in other cultures, hostility is rare. Among the Arapesh, help-fulness and generosity are highly valued. The ideal man is not a boss but a servant of the community. Personal security is found in warm, accepting group relationships. The Kwakiutl (British Columbia) are much more competitive. Hierarchy of rank is prominent. Individuals strive competitively for noble titles which can be won by ceremonial feasts ("potlatches") during which numerous possessions are destroyed to humiliate rivals. The Ifugao (Philippines) landowners seek prestige through property. Cooperation is practiced within the kinship group, but rivalry against other families is the rule. Eskimos operate much more individually, with only a minimum of either cooperation or competition.

So we might continue to explore other traditional "instincts," which may be little more than rationalizations of our present culture. In our economy, the existence of an "acquisitive instinct" seems obvious. In the Arapesh culture, however, a man may work harder cultivating a neighbor's garden than his own. The Lesu have no scheme of owner-ship for land or other property. Among the Dakota Indians, property was valued only in order to win prestige by giving it away. Trade and bargaining were not practiced and hoarding possessions was despised. These and other examples are cited by Mead (1937). Even in America, few can be induced to work for money as hard as some will voluntarily work at recreational activities like mountain climbing or playing football or domestic duties like caring for a two-year-old child.

The alleged "parental instinct" is found in some form in most animals but there are others which attempt to destroy or consume their off-spring. Some cultures have induced parents to expose babies to die unattended or to sacrifice their first born. Even with all the pressure toward child welfare in our American culture, the Society for Preven-tion of Cruelty to Children keeps busy—and most of the offenders are parents.

If a religious instinct is posited to account for those who worship, then there must be a non-religious instinct to account for the millions who ignore or reject the religious institutions of their society.

The conclusion toward which the evidence points is that human be-ings are biologically highly adaptable and the uniformities we observe are usually produced by cultural influences rather than predetermined in the organism.

Cultural relativity: a revolution in thought

Awareness of the diversity of human mores and behavior came as a blow to the ego and as a revolutionary movement in the world of ideas. Copernicus had made men realize that our earth was not the center of the universe. A second shock came when Darwin surmised that men have evolved as a natural part of the animal kingdom. Freud struck a third great blow when his findings implied that reason has a relatively weak and subordinate voice in the control of human behavior. Yet none of these developments seem quite as disquieting as the raising of the question whether "our way of life" is necessarily the one right, wise, natural, and divinely ordained order of existence. Do others have as much right as we to claim certainty or superiority for their patriotism, their religion, their economic order, their political system, their sex attitudes, their kind of art, music or dance? It must be expected that men will react vigorously against so "subversive" a question.

One reaction, which characterized an early stage in anthropology, was the attempt to arrange a ladder of evolution with our own system at the top. Thus savages could be thought to have the lowest grade of customs; barbarians would come a little later and higher; civilization is seen moving through history to our present peak. There is an ounce of truth and a ton of appeal in this doctrine. It is satisfying to put the outsiders, the deviants, and the heretics in their inferior place. There is truth in the contention that over the millennia, since the days of the first man-like anthropoids, but particularly in recent centuries, men have increased their speed of movement, the distance over which their voices can be heard, the weights they can lift, the precision of their tools, the power of their weapons, and (since writing began) the store of accumulated knowledge. Average life expectancy has probably increased fairly steadily. It is tempting to think, by analogy, that we who have the biggest machines must also have evolved the finest families and a superior spiritual life. Lewis H. Morgan (*Ancient Society,* published in 1877) was one of the chief exponents, among ethnologists, of the idea of a unilinear evolution. His view that men have progressed from savagery to barbarism and on to civilization fits certain lines of historical development, but does not accord with more recent extensive and critical studies. We have come to respect more values in pre-industrial cultures and to recognize many important differences among them. No simple ladder of development is widely applicable.

Herskovitz (1948) for example, has called attention to some of the remarkable achievements of men in non-literate societies. Despite lack of the assistance which our technology would provide, pygmies in the Congo have built excellent suspension bridges from vines; Mayans in their early culture had achieved a calendar of extraordinary accuracy;

the pre-Spanish Peruvians constructed remarkable buildings; and the Polynesians accomplished marvels of navigation. Arts flourished in cultures which preceded Ancient Greece, and there is no evidence to prove modern man superior to many primitive peoples in the quality of his human relationships.

Another defensive reaction has been the quest for universals. Are there not some actions which all decent men approve and others which are invariably condemned? The uniformities discovered in anthropology are mainly categorical rather than substantive. Every society has some kind of language, some numerical counting, some preferred foods, some magic, some pressure toward conformity, some sort of deference paid to parents. But this does not tell us anything about the merits of the many kinds of language, arithmetic, food, magic, conformity, and deference which different cultures develop. All cultures rate some behaviors as better than others, but they do not agree to a great extent on the specific values.

There are some attitudes which are common to most cultures. Lying to members of one's own in-group is almost universally condemned. Asch writes with cogency: "We do not know of societies in which bravery is despised and cowardice held up to honor, in which generosity is considered a vice and ingratitude a virtue" (1952, p. 378). But universality is not necessary to establish ethical values. Would bravery or generosity become less desirable to any of us, if, in some corner of the globe or at some period of history, ingratitude and cowardice had been more admired?

Cultural relativity also makes it hard to define in absolute terms the normal and abnormal in mental health. Whether one who sees ghosts and treats dreams as evidence of reality is sane or sick seems to depend on his culture. In some societies not to believe in ghosts and omens would be a serious symptom of deviation. A self-effacement that would be normal for a Zuni Indian in New Mexico would seem pathological in a Kwakiutl of Vancouver Island. It was normal in many American Indian cultures to induce hallucinations by fasting and self-torture. A non-Indian American living in the same geographical region today would be sent to a mental hospital for much less. One's belief that his associates are persecuting him by black magic and the Evil Eye would be psychotic on a contemporary college campus but would have seemed sensible enough on Dobu Island near New Guinea. Not only health norms but also sickness patterns vary with the culture. Some seem to be characterized by the development of certain psychopathic syndromes; in Malaysia the insane run amuck (*amok*); only among the Ojibway and Cree Indians of Canada are men seized with the Windigo psychosis which makes them compulsive cannibals.

Later in this chapter we will return to the difficult problem of evaluating whole cultures. First, however, we must explore the way in which the various elements of a culture affect psychological processes. We may begin with language and its relation to the way minds work.

Cultural integration

Culture, language, and thought

The Marxist argues, and the anthropologist generally agrees, that in different societies "men who live differently think differently." Some anthropologists and students of language have argued also that "men who speak differently think differently." One cannot be sure whether observed differences in vocabulary are cause or effect. If Eskimos have numerous words for different kinds of snow while we have only the one inclusive term, that difference in speech arises from other experiences which have led to the distinctions. The different words, once developed, may well sharpen the subsequent perception of snow. In every field the specialist knows many terms that emphasize distinctions important for him but not for the layman. Technical words support but do not, in themselves, create the thought-habits. The Iakuti language has only one word for a color range which includes both blue and green; are those who speak it less likely to be aware of the change of color on a lake when the clouds give way to a bright blue sky? One hypothesis, proposed by Roger Brown (1958), is that the more readily codable a category is in language symbols (short, definite name) the more available it will be for general psychological use.

A more significant difference may be the categories which require different forms or endings. Are sex differences more vital to a child who has learned that every noun must be masculine, feminine or neuter? If, as a Chinese writer (Chang) has argued, Western languages lead one to ask first what an object is and later what one should do about it, while Chinese imply the "what" by giving priority to the "how," does this represent a basic difference in approach to life?

The hypothesis of linguistic determinism was suggested by Boas and then formulated by Sapir many years ago (1929). "Human beings are very much at the mercy of the particular language which has become the medium of expression for their society. The 'real' world is to a large extent unconsciously built upon the language habits of the group. The worlds in which different societies live are distinct worlds, not merely the same world with different labels attached."

Whorf (1950), after years of study of the Hopi language which differs from the "Standard Average European" languages far more than these tongues differ from one another, has noted that the Hopi do not employ our categories of past, present, and future. They distinguish rather between a realm of objective, manifested reality and a realm of subjective, to-be-manifested reality which exists in the mind or heart of men, animals, plants, rocks, and all nature. What is to come is thought of by the Hopi not as proceeding along a time dimension but as unfolding from the inner potential of things. The child learning such a language is prepared to experience a world which seems markedly different from our three-dimensional space, our three tenses, and our emphasis on distinction between the animate and inanimate. In the Hopi super-classification, a kinship is implied within a system which includes certain men, certain animals, certain birds, plants, and supernatural beings. Other men, animals, plants, and so forth, belong together in another and different category. This kind of language system results from a way of thinking but in turn the language tends to instill and to support the essentials of that system.

Another illustration may be found in Lee's analysis (1938) of the Wintu language, which emphasizes the kind of evidence for an event. If it is directly experienced, one verb form is used. If it be hearsay, another form is required. If it occurs regularly, still another form is used. A study of Navajo speech (Kluckhohn, Leighton, 1946) reports that their verbs indicate whether an act is about to start, is in progress, is about to stop, and whether the act occurs repeatedly. Verbs of manipulation, in the Navajo tongue, differ in form depending on the shape (long and rigid; long and flexible; flat; etc.) of the object handled. This suggested to Carroll and Casagrande (1958) that Navajo-speaking children might be more likely to classify objects by form than would English-speaking children of the same tribe. About 64 percent of 48 children (age 3–7) whose speech was predominantly Navajo chose on the basis of form, while only 35 percent of 30 children whose speech was predominantly English chose by form rather than by color or size. It is interesting to note, however, that the choices made by a sample of 40 children living in and around Boston resembled the Navajo-speaking children's responses more than they did those of the English-speaking Indians. The authors surmise that this may have been due to play, by the Massachusetts children, with toys of the form-board type. This observation reminds us that while language plays some part in shaping thought, other cultural experiences should also be considered.

Adults who spoke both French and English fluently, brought up in middle-class families in France but now living in the United States, were given Thematic Apperception Test pictures to respond to in one language and (six weeks later) to tell a different story in the other language. When speaking French, the subjects told stories in which characters more frequently responded to conflict situations by withdrawal and then doing as they pleased. Verbal aggression against peers was also more common when the language reinstated attitudes of French culture. In

English, the women subjects told stories which included significantly more achievement motivation. The results confirmed predictions that middle-class French culture fosters more private autonomy and pride in verbal prowess, while American culture emphasizes more need to achieve (Ervin, 1964).

Several studies have dealt with the Japanese language and its personality correlates. For example, in Japanese there are many synonyms for unhappiness but few for happiness. Many songs, poems, and maxims represent ways of coping with melancholy (Minami, 1954). An analysis of the 61 most popular songs in postwar Japan (Kato, 1959) showed the prevailing themes to be pessimism, loneliness, and resignation. The language reflects the culture, of course, but also sensitizes the child to certain values rather than others. Distinctions of hierarchical position influence pronouns in Japanese. There are several ways of saying "you" and "I," depending on relative prestige.

Arguments against the potency of language for giving structure to basic mental processes are found in the similarity of groups related in culture but different in language (the Hopi and the Hopi-Tewan; the Finns and the Swedes) or groups alike in language but quite different in culture. Holy Rollers, share-croppers, "beatniks," and bankers may all speak English!

Other mental activities

Thinking and language are both shaped by the tasks of life. Arabs have many concepts and many words which relate to camels (Thomas, 1937). Mead (1929) found that Samoan children were more likely to react aesthetically to pictures which American children "explained." Porteus (1937, p. 25) found that societies which have a labyrinth game in their culture performed better on his maze test. Nadel (1937) found that Yoruba boys in West Nigeria could not recognize drawings of persons, animals or objects on paper, but could identify these things if similar outlines were presented as wood carvings or impressed on leather in the native style. The "Draw-a-Person" test is hardly fair in cultures (Muslim, Zuni) which prohibit this act. Newman (1963) found that performance of Pakistanis on a test of technological reasoning was closely related to their contact with Western industrialism. Men did better than women; city dwellers did better than those from rural homes; those university students whose fathers had worked for the British did better than those employed only by Muslims; the more emancipated male students surpassed in technical concepts those who wanted to preserve the Purdah tradition in their wives.

Some cultures provide children with rich and varied stimulation; others are relatively more limited. Some place a premium on speed; in others, a child is free to take his own time. Some demand competence at shooting darts from a blowgun; others introduce written and numerical tasks. The performance of a child on tests is likely to depend in large measure upon his experience with the sort of activity comprising the particular test. There can be no "culture free" test.

The cultural gestalt

While language, games, occupations and other parts of a culture may each exert some influence on the psychological processes and attitudes of members, a greater effect stems from the culture as a whole. Underlying each culture is a climate of feeling, a pattern of relationships, and a system of values. Personality emerges from the matrix of the whole culture, not from a particular feature.

A school of anthropology today asserts that these factors are related. There is a consistency within a culture very much as there is in personality. A basic Gestalt principle has been carried over from general psychology to the description of a culture: Every part is what is and where it is because of its relation to the whole. Various bases for unity have been emphasized—the child-rearing practices, the economy, and the type of life are perhaps the most important.

Kardiner and Linton have contributed the unifying concept of "basic personality." Their postulates are:

1. That the individual's early experiences exert a lasting effect upon his personality, especially upon the development of his projective systems.
2. That similar experiences will tend to produce similar personality configurations in the individuals who are subjected to them.
3. That the techniques which the members of any society employ in the care and rearing of children are culturally patterned and will tend to be similar, although never identical, for various families within the society.
4. That the culturally patterned techniques for the care and rearing of children differ from one society to another.

If these postulates are correct, and they seem to be supported by a wealth of evidence, it follows:

1. That the members of any given society will have many elements of early experience in common.
2. That as a result of this they will have many elements of personality in common.
3. That since the early experience of individuals differs from one society to another, the personality norms for various societies will also differ.

The basic personality type for any society is thus that which follows from the early experiences the members have in common. It is not the whole, unique personality of any single member—it is the value-attitude system shared by all members. Especially important are such experiences as:

> Nursing and weaning
> Toilet training
> Parental discipline and affection
> Sibling relations
> Induction into play and work
> Induction into adult roles
> Mating
> Religion and folklore
> Legal definitions and sanctions
> Techniques of economic production
> Art and craft techniques

Numerous specific studies bring out correlations between the child-rearing practices of a society and the adult personality. Presumably the causation is circular. If children are taught unquestioning obedience and adult religion also emphasizes strict obedience to the laws of God (or the gods) each tends to reinforce the other. Societies in which adults permit children great freedom to indulge sex impulses turn out to be societies which also encourage sex enjoyment by adults and in which impotence or frigidity is rare. It seems plausible that the adult attitudes are partly responsible for the child-rearing practice and that the child-rearing practice makes its contribution to the adult attitude.

Abstract 35 presents the result of testing several hypotheses concerning the association of adult personality traits with the child-rearing practices normal for the culture. It seems quite clear that those societies which leave their young children with a memory of shocks and disappointments in connection with early nursing and weaning, tend to be also societies which believe adult illness most likely to be caused by something the patient *ate*. It is likewise impressive that where sex acts in childhood arouse considerable anxiety, there are (in 11 of 14 such societies) prolonged taboos on parental intercourse after the birth of a child. Some other plausible correlations do not stand up so well.

A study (Whiting, *et al.*, 1958) of 56 societies with adequate data, showed that it was usual (48 of 56) for babies to sleep with the mother until weaned, which was after they were one year old. In half of these societies both parents shared the bed with the child, but in the other 24, the father was pushed out by the infant and had to sleep in another bed, sometimes in another hut. About half of the societies permit resumption of intercourse as soon as the mother has recovered from childbirth, but half set a taboo on sex for the entire nursing period, averaging more than two years. Anthropologists hypothesized that "Societies which

Abstract 35

TITLE	Child Training and Personality
AUTHORS	J. W. M. Whiting and I. L. Child
PROBLEM	In what ways do cultures which train children differently, vary in the adult personality patterns?
SUBJECTS	Reports in Human Relations Area files covering about 75 different primitive societies. Data are reported only for those cultures about which the files contain enough information to permit confident judgments. This sometimes meant only 20 or 25 societies.
PROCEDURE	Judges read the material available and rated each culture on:

1. initial satisfaction potential (oral, anal, sexual, dependence, and aggression) and
2. anxiety generated by socialization (oral, anal, sexual, dependence and expression.)

The age at which weaning, toilet training, modesty training, training to inhibit heterosexual play, and independence training normally take place was estimated for each culture. Adult personality was studied for each culture only as expressed in customs and interpretations related to illness: oral explanations and therapy; anal explanations and therapy; dependence explanations and therapy; sexual explanations and therapy; aggression explanations and aggression-avoidance therapy.

SOME FINDINGS 1. Most societies have been more initially indulgent than were the Midwestern, American, white, middle-class mothers reported by Davis and Havighurst. The Americans weaned children earlier than any of 52 primitive societies except the Marquesans; they were less indulgent in giving babies oral nursing satisfaction than any of 51 societies again excepting the Marquesans; in severity of weaning, societies ranged from 6 (mild) to 15 (severe) with the Americans rating 13. Toilet training by American mothers began earlier than for any of 25 primitive societies, except the Tanala. Severity of toilet training in 20 societies ranged from a mild 6 to a severe 18, with Americans tied with Tanala at 18. Indulgence of masturbation ranged, in 17 societies, from a highly restrictive 10—the American score—to a very permissive attitude of 19 among the Alorese of Indonesia. Heterosexual play ratings ranged from 4, the most severe, to 20 the most indulgent, with the American attitude near the restrictive end of the scale. Age at beginning independence demands ranged from 2 to 6, with the U.S. group judged to begin at 2½. Tolerance for aggression in children ranged from 5 to 17 with the Americans a little below the median of 11.

Abstract 35—*Continued*

2. Relations to adult interpretation of illness

High anxiety in childhood socialization	Oral explanation of illness	
	Absent	Present
of oral impulses	3	17
Low anxiety	13	6

3. In 20 societies which generated high anxiety in children about eating, most (17) attributed adult illness to something eaten. This view of the cause of sickness was less common (6 of 19) in societies which did not generate childhood anxiety about eating. In societies which forbade aggression in children, illness was usually explained by adults as due to someone's hostility (12 of 16 societies). The relationships to adult interpretations were less clear in the case of childhood anxieties about sex, excretion, and dependent behavior. Recommendation of therapeutic sex gratification was more common in societies which permitted sexual play among children.

SOURCE: New Haven: Yale University Press, 1953.

have sleeping arrangements in which the mother and baby share the same bed for at least a year and those which have a taboo on resumption of intercourse for more than a year after childbirth are more likely than others to have a ceremony of transition from boyhood to manhood." The initiation ceremonies—emphasizing separation of the son from his mother and his identification with the society of adult males, usually includes painful hazing, isolation from females, and operations on the genitals. Among the 25 societies which do not exclude the father from the marital bed for a prolonged period, 23 have no such initiation ceremonies. Among the 20 which do practice the exclusion, 14 have the puberty transition ceremonies. Of the six exceptions, four societies have a kind of substitute for such initiation—a requirement that the adolescent move out of his parental house and go to a special male residence to live until married.

The McClelland and Friedman study (1952) brings out another line of consistency within cultures. Those, like the Navajos, which expect children at an early age to act independently turn out to be also cultures which cherish folk-tales emphasizing heroic achievements. Those which, like the Flathead Indians, are least concerned with getting children to assume responsibility at an early age, have folk tales which do not stress achievement.

The child-rearing pattern itself is contained within the larger context of family relations. Hsu (1961) has defined several major patterns.

The *father-son* axis is characteristic of cultures which stress the patrilineal connections. Ancient China is a prime example. Boys are brought up to honor their fathers, grandfathers, and more remote male ancestors. Sons must be, above all, obedient; they are supported and protected by their fathers; they become heirs and patriarchs. Marriage is arranged, not for love, but to produce sons and so continue the family name. A man whose wife fails to produce sons is obligated to take a concubine. A wife or concubine must please her husband's parents. These are conservative societies. Places and obligations are traditionally defined. Government is autocratic with subjects willingly submissive. Religion is ancestor worship or a derived polytheism.

The *mother-son* axis is exemplified by the Hindus. Passive dependence on maternal care persists as a world view. Although the adult culture is male-centered, children are left largely to the care of the women's side of the household. The father is a minor and often remote figure in the child's world. In religion, there are numerous female deities: Kali, Durga, Radha, Sita, Parvati, and others. Ramakrishma noted that the "God lover finds pleasure in addressing the Deity as Mother" (Hsu, 1961, p. 430). Dependence on the supernatural is like that of a baby on its mother. Rituals are forms of ingratiation to win favors. The ultimate bliss is felt to be reunion with the One.

The *husband-wife* axis is especially evident in Europe, where the husband dominates, and in the United States, where there is a closer approximation to equality. Boys and girls seek their mates largely on their own responsibility, and in the climate of romantic love. The young couple may not meet their in-law parents until after the engagement or sometimes until the marriage. Each individual man is on his own; he does not expect his family to make his way for him. Freedom and self-reliance are very important. Conflict between generations is frequent. Social change is readily advanced. Religious denominations multiply as each person asserts his right to make or adopt his own creed.

The *brother-brother* axis Hsu finds mainly in Africa, but it might well characterize also such American Indians as the Comanche. Boys at an early age leave the parental home to live with peers of about their own age. Blood-brother rites bind pairs and initiation ceremonies induct into more mature stages. Secret societies are common. Whereas the main links in the father-son pattern stretch across the generations, those of the brother-brother pattern reach out to include contemporaries. Sibling rivalry becomes competition for prestige or leadership in the gang. With less need to emphasize ties to the past or future, these cultures have been less likely to develop written languages.

It is not necessary to regard the four proposed types as "pure" or even as the best possible classification. What is evident is another application of the S-P-A formula: The structure of family obligations develops corresponding processes of interaction and consequent personality patterns.

So simple a variable as the size of the family unit has implications for attitude development. The large extended family does not put so heavy a burden of work on the one mother; more adults share in childcare; it can consequently be more indulgent (Hsu, 1961, p. 359). Children who are given this more attentive and happier childhood grow into adults who regard the universe as more benevolent. Whiting (1959) finds that societies which raise children more permissively are not afraid of ghosts at funerals. But the extended family tends also to preserve tradition. Grandparents, aunts, and uncles keep the immediate parents from radical innovation in dealing with children. Free expression of children's aggressive impulses is less tolerable in the crowded setting of the extended family. One study (Whiting, 1961) shows that in two-parent households only 25 percent were "severe" in restricting aggression by children, while 92 percent of extended families were above the median in this kind of control. Children who are inhibited in expression of aggression in childhood become adults who are unlikely to approve aggressive action within the in-group. Wright (1954) showed that this attitude is reflected in folk tales. Societies which are strict in repressing children's aggression are more apt to tell tales in which an aggressive actor is a stranger or in which the in-group hero is aggressive only toward out-group enemies.

Another reaction to over-strict control, is a sense, in children, that they have been unjustly treated. They resent the punishments and feel justified in some acts of compensation or retaliation. Societies which are severe in weaning and in punishment of children have been found to be high in frequency of theft (Hsu, 1961, p. 373). This is probably related to the fact, important particularly in understanding delinquency, that offenders often come from homes where punishment has been severe.

The extended family—as in the old Chinese culture—seems to reduce the likelihood of intense emotional relationships with any one member. The boy can pattern himself in part after several male models. The girl's frustrations within the household do not all stem from her mother. In the old Samoan society (Mead, 1928) children felt they "belonged" in the homes of aunts and uncles as well as with their own parents; hence when relationships at home became uncomfortable, they had well-accepted places of refuge. Oedipus and Electra complexes seem less likely to arise in cultures which enable children to have warm dependent relationships on a number of adults of opposite sex.

Other determinants of culture

Psychologists and psychiatrists have explored especially the child-rearing practices and their connection with cultural patterns, but other factors also exert strong influence. Geographic location affects the way men make a living and this, in turn, is intimately related to their customs, recreation, worship, and the traits they try to develop in children.

When a society depends largely on hunting and fishing, it naturally honors the successful trappers and anglers. Boys (and sometimes girls) learn the techniques for catching game. Usually the individual succeeds or fails on the basis of his own competence, courage, and cunning. The need to find new hunting grounds discourages permanent settlements.

A settled population, living by cultivation of plants and animal husbandry, is likely to develop different character ideals and social relationships. Here, children must work in the fields or tend herds. They must be obedient, reliable, and industrious. Presumably these societies will develop standards of child behavior different from those of the nomadic hunters.

A test of this hypothesis is summarized in Abstract 36.

Another indication of the way its economy influences a culture is found in the use of dreams. Hsu (1961, p. 326) has shown that hunting and fishing societies, in which men are very dependent on luck, usually (80 percent) regard dreams as communication with supernatural powers while among more settled and secure agricultural communities, only 20 percent did so.

As societies find or develop techniques of food production which raise them above a subsistence level, other activities emerge. Arts and crafts progress to a higher level than is possible when all efforts are devoted to the struggle for survival. Political relationships likewise become more elaborate when food production can sustain a larger superstructure.

The conditions of life of Bushmen on the Kalahari desert of Southwest Africa are almost unbelievably difficult (Thomas, 1959). They are always hungry, and, during most of the year, also thirsty. They get moisture only by eating plants that survive the hot drought. When nights grow cold, lacking warm clothes and having little fuel, they huddle together for comfort. They have no spare energy for fighting among themselves. They share possessions freely to avoid envy of one by others. Theft is unknown. Danger is met by escape rather than aggressive attack. Thus, moral values reflect the economic necessities.

The system of distributing whatever goods are produced also has ethical implications. In some cultures when one person kills a large animal or raises a large crop, he shares freely with other members, expecting them to do likewise when they have good fortune. Generosity is thus a virtue. In other cultures, whatever is produced goes to a chief or council, and is redistributed in some way to the consumers. Here a premium is placed on obedience by the producers and on *noblesse oblige* for the distributors. In economies where individuals bargain in a market, those persons who are most successful and admired are shrewd

Abstract 36

TITLE   Relation of Child Training to Subsistence Economy

AUTHORS   Herbert Barry III, Irvin L. Child, and Margaret K. Bacon

PROBLEM   To explore the relationship of a culture's type of subsistence economy to its emphases in child training.

SUBJECTS   The 104 societies studied were selected from categorizations by Murdock and by Bacon and Barry. Those societies categorized as *high* in accumulation of food were the predominantly pastoral, or predominantly agricultural combined with much animal husbandry; those classified as *low* were predominantly hunting and fishing; two intermediate types were mixed and tending toward either high or low.

PROCEDURE   Two judges rated the societies on strength of socialization as expressed in rewards and punishments, and the sum of the two judgments was used. They rated:
1. Obedience training
2. Responsibility training
3. Nurturance training—training child to be helpful toward siblings and other dependent people
4. Achievement training, usually on basis of competition or of standards of excellence
5. Self-reliance training—to be independent of others in supplying own needs
6. General independence training—broader than #5 to include all kinds of freedom from control.

The ratings were for childhood years from age 4 or 5 almost to puberty, and separate ratings were made for boys and girls. Ratings were ranked for each society so that relative emphasis would be shown within the society.

SOME FINDINGS   Responsibility and obedience were emphasized in the high accumulation economies, and achievement, self-reliance, and independence in the low. The relationships held true for both boys and girls. The following figures show the correlations of the six ratings with high accumulation of food:

	Boys	Girls
Responsibility	+.74	+.62
Obedience	+.50	+.59
Nurturance	−.01	+.10
Achievement	−.60	−.62
Self-reliance	−.21	−.46
Independence	−.41	−.11

Thirty-nine of the societies at the extremes showed scores in the expected direction; only seven showed high accumulation with individualistic assertion or low accumulation with compliance.

SOURCE: *American Anthropologist*, 1959, LX:51–63.

and crafty. The skills of salesmanship rate high in the marketing orientation (Fromm, 1955).

Change in the economic base of a culture brings corresponding changes in most other aspects and, of course, in the typical personality which the culture forms. History affords numerous illustrations—a British town before and after the industrial revolution; a New England community before, during, and after the dominance of whaling; a Southern town during slavery and after its end; or the emergence of a California city from frontier days to its modern patterns of life. The historian, Frederick Jackson Turner (1921) developed a famous interpretation of American culture and character, based on the influence of our frontier. Individualism, independence, egalitarianism, enterprise, expansionism, neighborly cooperation, and international isolationism were all fostered by pioneer conditions.

Anthropologists have provided a case study (Linton, Kardiner, 1939) of two cousin-tribes. They were once much alike in their dry-rice economy, their communal sharing, their family life and religion. One community remained in this state and serves as a kind of control. The other turned to cultivation of rice in the rich flooded area. With the change in economic activity and the introduction of private property the tribal unity waned; a youth problem emerged; with new insecurities, even the gods became threatening. Indeed whenever cultures become more fragmented into special-interest groups, the disintegration seems to arouse increased terror of sorcery.

A more typical instance of cultural change has been reported from Nigeria by Margaret Mead (1955). In many parts of the modern world an advanced technology impinges upon a well-organized primitive culture. The coming of the British administrators and the building of a railroad upset the old prestige hierarchy and the marriage system, destroying the morale of a people. Disputes were no longer settled by the traditional rites, and the elders lost authority. Wives were no longer acquired by the sanctioned process; consequently some children were regarded as illegitimate. Ensuing epidemics, crop failures, and other misfortunes were viewed by many as the revenge of the powerful elders.

In the preceding example, economic change was accompanied by political change. Recognition that a changed form of government may result in changed attitudes is at least as old as Herodotus who wrote: "While they were under despotic rulers the Athenians were no better in war than any of their neighbors, yet once they got quit of despots they were far and away the first of all. . . . While they were oppressed they willed to be craven, as men working for a master, but when they were freed, each one was zealous to achieve for himself." In the newly liberated colonial peoples, we see a similar psychological change.

An interesting example of the effect of political structure on character has been described by Haring (1953). Japanese have been consistently described as formal, rigid, and almost compulsive. This has not so often been related to three centuries of police tyranny. On one island —Amami Oshima—a population of Japanese descent has lived free from political dictatorship. Here one discovers the people to be more relaxed, more spontaneous, and freer in interpersonal relations.

The Gestalt of a culture is best expressed in its characteristic "style." Kardiner (1945) has described the Comanches as giving children a high degree of security which then led to little anxiety despite the actual dangers of adult life. The Comanche Indian babies were welcome; there were few taboos about birth (or disposal of the after-birth); the cradle-board kept the child close to the mother; they were fed whenever hungry; fathers tended to "spoil" children; there was no anxiety about eating, defecating or sex play in childhood. The adolescent boys banded together in a close brotherhood. Spoils of hunting were fairly divided. There was little prestige hierarchy and that for only a limited time. The adult culture included much cooperation, extending even to wife-sharing. The Comanche religion included no malevolent magic and no ingratiating procedures. There was no concept of misfortune as punishment because this was not the pattern of childhood relation to parents.

Contrast this with the culture of Alors (DuBois, 1944). Here the mother cares for her infant for only a fortnight; then returns to work in the fields. Most babies are brought up by older siblings who freely tease them. They arouse maternal solicitude only when they are sick. What does this mean for the adult culture? The basic mood of interpersonal relations is one of distrust and suspicion. Even sex relations are distorted by selfishness and disputes. Folk tales show hatred of parents. Sorcery is an important element of religion. Illness is very prominent.

We have presented earlier the integrative sequence from child-rearing toward the adult culture, but there is undoubtedly feedback from the adult folkways to the handling of children. Thus the Comanche father and mother, with their higher level of emotional security, could accept child behavior which would be intolerable to more anxious adults. Integration proceeds from child training to the adult and back again to the upbringing of the next generation.

Sometimes the integration and style of a culture enables it to resist the impact of the customs of their neighbors. The long survival of enclaves of Shakers and Mennonites within the American social scene has been due to the powerful cohesive influence of their way of life, with their religion as the most integrative force. In her *Patterns of Culture* (1934), Ruth Benedict has described the culture of the Pueblo Indians as "Apollonian," with the implication of sanity, balance, reason and moderation. All around them were neighboring tribes whose life-style was "Dionysian," built of famine and feast, hardship and orgies, dull routines and ecstatic rites. Usually, ways of living tend to spread to neighboring cultures, a process called diffusion. The Dionysian ceremonies, however, were rejected by the Pueblos. Exposure to the activities of another culture does not automatically mean incorporation of what that culture offers. Artifacts and institutions and beliefs diffuse only if they are compatible with and acceptable to the other culture. The Pueblos were insulated from influence because of the cohesive power of their different style which integrated much of their lives. Rorschach tests given to Hopi Indians (Thompson, 1950) confirmed the Benedict hypothesis of Apollonian character. The young people tested were found to be restrained, disciplined, and cautious, but still reasonably imaginative and able to enjoy pleasure in moderation.

Some cultures are generally relaxed and easy-going, with little anxiety in practical affairs or in religion. Others are tense, apprehensive, and worried over both daily troubles and the dangers of witchcraft and evil spirits. Some, like the industrialized West, are energetically innovative; others still see "nothing new under the sun."

National character

Observers who have lived for a time in England, France, Germany, and Italy have little doubt about typical differences in outlook and response among the people in those countries and see them as different again from Japanese or Americans.

A concept of "national character" is vulnerable to grave misinterpretations. One is racist. The Nazis represented this error at its worst. They taught that Germans were biologically gifted with desirable traits which other nationalities lacked. Hence they saw themselves as a "Master Race." The racist connotation of nationality can be found also in such writers as Count de Gobineau (1855), Madison Grant (1916), Houston S. Chamberlain (1925), and Lothrop Stoddard (1920), all of whom saw the Nordics, and especially the Teutons, as innately superior to all the races of darker complexion. They attributed most of the ills of social change to failure to keep the chosen racial stock pure and dominant.

Anthropology has shown many instances of peoples alike in race but different in culture. Benedict's (1934) description of Southwestern Indians is one example. The South Sea Islanders (Mead, 1928) furnish another. Biesheuvel (1950) describes two Bantu groups in Africa: the Pedi who are punitive, conformist, and warlike; the Lovendu who reject corporal punishment, love peace, and cultivate individuality. LeVine (1960) reports the Gusü as authoritarian and the Nuer as egalitarian. We commonly recognize both racial and cultural homogeneity in Denmark, Norway, and Sweden, but suicide rates are consistently much higher in Denmark and Sweden (about 22 per 100,000) and unusually low in Norway (about 8 per 100,000). Rates in the United States are about 10 per 100,000 (Hendin, 1964). We noted earlier that there has been noticeable change in attitudes from the warrior Vikings to the rather complacent life of modern Scandinavia.

The concept of national character does make sense when we recognize many forms of personality-shaping activity which do correspond to national boundaries. Insofar as members of one nation differ from members of other nations in the language they speak, the newspapers they read and trust, the literature they value, the stories they tell children, the films they see, the heroes they celebrate, their understanding of history, the goods they make and consume, the arts they cultivate, the government which they obey, and the religion they follow, they will become different kinds of persons. Not all will be alike, but their modal (most common) personality pattern will have some features arising from these shared interactions. Their generally accepted practices and ideals will show the influence of communications which affect them inside the national boundaries. The kind of person who rises to prominence and is accorded general admiration may be sharply different in two tribes or nations which otherwise have much in common.

American character

It is hard to see objectively the culture in which we ourselves are immersed. There is a saying that fish never notice water. Travelers to the United States ever since De Tocqueville have noted our peculiarities and, as many Americans have spent more time abroad in recent years, they have become more aware of factors usually taken for granted back home. Common allegations are that Americans are materialistic and that they are idealistic. We are aggressive but cordial. We are egalitrian but unusually status-conscious. We are joiners, but we cherish individualism. We have a tradition of rebellion but we foster conformity. We are competitive and we are cooperative. We are puritanical and we are dissipated.

More solid evidence would support the view that Americans, as compared with people in other nations, are distinctively prosperous, well educated, mobile (both vertically and horizontally), and likely to innovate and to accept technological changes.

Potter (1954) has developed particularly the character-consequences of our economic abundance. Because of rising prosperity, we believe that ours must be the best way of life. We ignore class differences because we like to think that there is plenty of chance for everyone to succeed. With shorter hours of work, we cultivate many ways of using leisure— sports, golf, boats, automobile travel, movies, television, and so on. We can operate a political democracy which would threaten any society in which the many are poverty-stricken and the few who rule wish to retain their privileges. We can afford to provide longer schooling. Advertising and the Man from Madison Avenue become prominent influences when production outruns the demand for necessities of life. With labor-saving devices in the home, women can participate more in vocations and in community life. We can be more permissive with children, because what they lose or break can be easily replaced.

A later chapter (14) will deal with the problem of how American prosperity keeps us from understanding the needs and attitudes of peoples with perhaps one-tenth of our per capita income. Certainly our attitude toward poverty in our own midst is colored by the notion that anyone who is willing to work can rise to at least moderate financial success. Our wealth has enabled us to transcend many of the problems which plague poorer countries. We expect that, in the future, things will be even better. As George Santayana once commented: Americans never solve any of their problems—they amiably bid them goodbye!

An economist has related American character to industrial institutions as follows: "Technology creates the attitudes of externalization, expedient rationality and quantification. The market system promotes the attitudes of acquisitiveness, the work and success-ethics, and individualistic competitiveness. The mobile society leads to unlimited striving for prestige, status, and social climbing. Mass civilization tends to foster automation, conformity, and domination-submission relationships" (Weisskopf, 1951). Such generalizations would apply to any advanced capitalist economy. Erich Fromm (1947) has likewise derived from our economic institutions the contemporary American emphasis upon "selling oneself." "The character orientation which is rooted in the experience of oneself as a commodity and of one's value as exchange value, I call the marketing orientation. . . . If one feels that one's own value is not constituted primarily by the human qualities one possesses, but by one's success in a competitive market with ever-changing conditions, one's self-esteem is bound to be shaky and in constant need of confirmation by others" (pp. 68, 72). Thus he explains a trait—the constant search for approval by others—which Riesman (1950) has attributed to societies with incipient population decline and which Gorer traces back to the dependence of the child for love upon a parent who equated the child's worth with his success in competitive achievement.

Another area in which personality traits are congruent with economic operations is that of leisure. Automation increases production from each man-hour of work and might provide a decent standard of living for workers on the basis of only a thirty-hour week. What is the human reaction to this situation? How does a culture with Puritan moral ideals and a frontier tradition of hard work react to abundant leisure? One typical reaction is "moonlighting"—the second job. Another is what has been called a kind of compulsive "fun morality" (Wolfenstein, 1951). A study of recommendations for infant care in publications of the Children's Bureau (U.S. Department of Labor) between 1914 and 1951 showed increasing acceptance of the baby's desire for pleasure. Masturbation is no longer a problem; babies who cry should be picked up and petted; play is essential to development; parenthood itself can be fun. Whereas in early period parents worried over the character of an adolescent daughter who often went out to parties and dances, today they worry over the girl who is left at home on Saturday night. A related study (Wolfenstein, Leites, 1950) identifies the popular movie heroine as a girl who can give the hero a good time and to whom he can easily give a good time. The contemporary American character seems more and more inclined to what Freud called "the pleasure principle."

The American theologian, Reinhold Niebuhr, has characterized the "woof" of American character as derived from the potential wealth of our virgin continent and its "warp" as our Messianic conviction that we have a mission to save mankind. The settlers in Massachusetts thought of their great achievement as a purified church; in Virginia they valued their new political creation; but both thought they had transcended the evils of the Old World (Dinner Meeting on the American Character, Fund for the Republic, June 1, 1961).

The two kinds of mobility—horizontal, as we move from place to place—and vertical, as we rise in the socio-economic scale—play an important part in American character. We were settled by people ready to uproot themselves from Old World culture. The effect of the advancing frontier, where men might go out West and take up free land, has been studied particularly by the historian Frederick Jackson Turner (1920). Some of the uniformity in American cities—their skyscrapers, supermarkets, filling stations, and neat school buildings—is related to the fact that people do not live all their lives in one place. Each city is made up of people who grew up in other communities. In some schools, today, teachers report a turnover of more than 100 percent of their pupils during one school year. If such mobility continues, a uniform school curriculum will seem necessary.

Our vertical mobility has been satirized by Vance Packard in *The Status Seekers* and the *Pyramid Climbers*. Everyone is and should be ambitious to rise in income, prestige, and fame. But since anyone can rise, he can also fall. In societies where each is born to a fixed station in life, those who are low have no hope of rising, but those who are set high need never feel insecure. No matter what an aristocrat did, in feudal societies, his place was established. He was not dependent on the approval of others. If Americans are very "other-directed" (Riesman, 1950), this is a consequence of the chance to rise, of which we are justly proud.

Tocqueville observed our restlessness in the early nineteenth century, as it contrasted with the more stable order of Europe.

In the United States a man builds a house to spend his latter years in it, and he sells it before the roof is on; he brings a field into tillage, and leaves other men to gather the crop; he embraces a profession and gives it up; he settles in a place which he soon afterward leaves, to carry his changeable longings elsewhere. . . . If at the end of a year of unremitting labor he finds he has a few days vacation, his eager curiosity whirls him over the vast extent of the United States, and he will travel fifteen hundred miles in a few days, to shake off his happiness (De Tocqueville, 1835–1845, p. 122–3).

If Americans are indeed more aware than most other people of "progress," this has a realistic historical basis. Within less than two centuries, typical circumstances of life changed from pioneers in log cabins to garden apartments in city suburbs. This writer recalls the first automobile to chug through the unpaved streets of his home town; the first movie to be shown as a curiosity in the auditorium of the local college.

Some of the concern which social scientists now feel over the spread of American influence to underdeveloped areas arises from what happened in North America. Like a great steam roller, the white immigrants moved across the country, crushing native Indian cultures and leaving only hopeless fragments isolated on depressing reservations.

The immigrants also changed as they came into this new geographic and cultural setting. Child (1943) studied the reactions of second generation Italians in Connecticut. The successful adapters became rebels, rejecting the old language, the old foods and customs. They fought prejudice against them by trying to become indistinguishably American. Another pattern emerged in those who gave up their loyalty to the old ways, but found themselves rejected by the other citizens of the New World. These experienced defeat and reacted with hopeless apathy. A few remained encapsulated within the transported Italian culture—enclaves in the new society which they rejected. Similar patterns could be identified in most other immigrant groups: Irish, German, Scandinavian, and Polish. The Puerto Ricans are having a more complicated adjustment, partly because of color prejudices and partly because they go back and forth more to their island homeland. Yet all of these ethnic subgroups make up part of the varied and changing tapestry of American culture.

A study of values in rural America used the interesting technique of analyzing editorials in the National 4-H Club News from its first publication in 1924 up to 1958 (Straus, Houghton, 1960). There was a statistically significant decline during the 35 years in appeals for Achievement motivation (n-Ach), which is defined as "concern for success in competition with a standard of excellence," but this remained the dominant theme, occurring about ten times as often as did appeals for cooperation or appreciation of affiliative motives (positive affective relationships with other persons).

One perceptive and intuitive observer of American character has been the British anthropologist, Geoffrey Gorer. The quotations in Abstract 37 may strike the reader as true and penetrating, or, in other instances, as superficial and false. In either case, they represent provocative comments from a European visitor who felt that in the United States he was seeing something quite different from the attitudes prevailing in other parts of the world.

One of America's most capable and distinguished anthropologists, Jules Henry, recently (1963) published a grim analysis of our contemporary culture and its psychological consequences. In *Culture Against Man,* he describes American families, schools, work, and leisure time activities, with the objectivity which anthropologists have brought to their descriptions of South Sea Island communities. He finds the prevailing *motif* to be concern for making money. This "pecuniary ethic" dehumanizes interpersonal relations. Driven by advertising, the Americans today have become "trained in heroic feats of consumption," feverish and insatiable in pursuit of material gain. He shows how such psychological characteristics as weakened sense of personal identity, pursuit of expensive pleasures, and lack of moral fibre derive from the implicit assumption that money-making and money-spending take precedence over other human values.

Empirical studies support the view that most Americans regard themselves as "happy." There are not enough studies comparing the United States with other nations and cultures to tell us how distinctive this euphoria may be. A nationwide sample of residents of small towns in the United States (Gurin *et al.,* 1960) reported 35 percent "very happy" and 54 percent "pretty happy" with only 10 percent "not too happy." The Bradburn study (1963), summarized in the next chapter, found the proportions 24 percent "very happy," 63 percent "pretty happy," and 13 per cent "not too happy" in a prosperous Illinois town. In two towns suffering economic depression, the proportions were 21 percent "very happy," 59 percent "pretty happy," and 20 percent "not too happy." Apparently 80 to 90 percent of Americans view themselves as at least moderately happy, allowing for some worries and feelings of insecurity. The Illinois data show 31 percent of adult males 25 to 49 years of age, reporting themselves as troubled by three or more of the following symptoms: nervousness, aches and pains, dizziness, headaches, muscle twitches, or rapid heart beat. In the same group, 40 percent reported three or more of the following marital problems: insufficient love, financial problems, religious differences, time with friends, child discipline, irritating personal habits, and difficulties with in-laws. Again in this same group of employed men under 50 years of age, 36 percent were scored low on job satisfaction.

Abstract 37

TITLE The American Character

AUTHOR Geoffrey Gorer

PROBLEM What can be said—in general—about American national characteristics?

PROCEDURES Generalizations based on personal observations by an English anthropologist visiting the United States for a period of several years.

SOME OBSERVATIONS "No matter how many generations separate an American from his immigrant ancestors, he rejects his father as authority and exemplar, and expects his sons to reject him."

"In their professional and political lives many American men have been forced into conformity by fear of physical violence. Violence and the threat of violence do play a significant, often a major, role in American commercial, industrial, and political life."

"The idiosyncratic feature of the American conscience is that it is predominantly feminine. Owing to the major role played by the mother in disciplining the child, in rewarding and punishing it, many more aspects of the mother than of the father become incorporated. Duty and Right Conduct become feminine figures."

"The manifestations of the female conscience in public life give rise to the peculiar behavior which Americans call 'idealism'; this is the proclaiming of moral rules of conduct which other people should follow."

"The clinging mother is the great emotional menace in American psychological life, the counterpart to the heavy domineering father in England and on the Continent."

"Relevant to this point also is the very great erotic fetishist value given to women's breasts in contemporary America; they have almost overtaken the earlier value given to legs. As a stimulating sight, well-separated and well-developed breasts under a tight-fitting over-garment are thought to surpass almost any amount of nudity. The great addiction of most American men to milk as a drink has also probably symbolic significance."

"This concept of being a sissy is a key concept for the understanding of American character; it has no exact parallel in any other society."

"Nearly all Americans have a fear of rejection, and stigmatize people who don't easily give these overt signs of friendship as 'high hat', 'snooty' or 'snobbish,' attempting to reject before they are rejected; for to be rejected, even by an overformal and unsmiling servant, suggests that one may be a failure, may be unworthy of love. In contrast, people who are prodigal with such simple signs of friendship, particularly to their economic and social inferiors, are praised as 'regular guys,' as 'truly democratic.' "

"Americans will perforce sell or lease their charm, their frankness, their warmth, their sexual appeal, their voice, to an employer to exploit for his

---

Abstract 37—*Continued*

benefit in the same way as they will sell their labor. A winning smile or a pleasant voice is nearly as marketable a business commodity as a knowledge of accountancy or skill in mining. It is a curious comment on the change in values that 'selling oneself' is a meritorious and praiseworthy act on the part of a young person setting out in life, and is a necessary preliminary to 'selling' an idea or a project, and, in most cases, to acquiring a job. A person incapable of 'selling' himself is badly handicapped."

"It can be said that, as a general rule, the acquisition of money is very important to Americans, but its retention relatively unimportant."

"The majority of Americans, at least until they near the retirement age, regard themselves as transient inhabitants of their house or apartment, ready to move to the bigger and better dwelling which will be appropriate to the greater success hoped for in the future."

"The position of minorities in America can only be understood if it is remembered that the criteria for Americanism are, in descending order of importance, appearance, clothes, food, housing amenities, ideology, and language, and that only the fully American can be considered fully human; for, be it remembered, Americanism is an act of will, and failure to achieve complete Americanism is an individual fault much more than it is a misfortune."

SOURCE: Geoffrey Gorer, *The American People*. New York: W. W. Norton and Company, 1964 (revised), pp. 26–196. Reprinted by permission.

Another interesting picture of the American self-image appears in a study (Kemler, Bennet, 1958) of a sample of citizens 15 to 64 years of age in urban portions of the northeastern United States. The four words most often chosen (from a list of 64 adjectives) to describe themselves, were: (1) anxious; (2) sincere; (3) nervous; and (4) uncertain. This is different from one foreign stereotype of the American as smug and complacent.

National character in other countries

A few reports on studies of national character in other countries will illustrate even more clearly the stamp of a distinctive culture upon typical personalities.

German. During World War II, social psychologists and anthropologists contributed studies of the characteristics of enemy peoples. Schaffner (1948) argued plausibly that the rigid training in obedience to the father which was characteristic of German family life, contributed to complete dependence on a *Führer* or national leader. An empirical study (McGranahan, Wayne, 1948) demonstrated that the 45 plays most popular in Germany during 1927 differed significantly from the 45 most popular in the United States at that time. The German plays dealt more with political problems and with idealistic sacrifices than with romance; they were more commonly historical than contemporary; the characters in German plays seemed less flexible and open to change than characters in American dramas. Women had more prominent roles in American than in German plays. Such differences accord with several characteristics of the Nazi regime: imbued with a sense of historic destiny; dedicated, ruthless, and inflexible; finding it necessary to annihilate rather than try to win over opponents; and subordinating women to their realm of kitchen, children, and church. A study of German films (Kracaver, 1947) showed the exalted role given to men of power long before Hitler became this kind of symbol.

A psychiatrist (Brickner, 1943), expressing partly the anti-German feeling of the war period, concluded that German character is fundamentally neurotic in a paranoiac direction. He noted the almost obsessive concern with control—cleanliness, neatness, order, duty, discipline, obedience, and military perfection. He related this strict upbringing to an adult pattern of repressed hostility, aggressive impulses, and suspicion of others.

Japanese. One of the earliest essays on Japanese character was written by Gorer (1943). He emphasized that customs of strict toilet training have led to a type of character which is almost compulsive in its demand for cleanliness, neatness, and order. Ruth Benedict, relying also on literature by and about the Japanese, wrote (1946) *The Chrysanthemum and the Sword.* She called attention to the concern for beauty and bravery; the veneration of traditional authority; the respect for oneself evident in self-discipline and face-saving; and the difference in sex roles, with boys brought up to be polite but dominant; girls quiet, docile, and affectionate. She worked primarily from literary and historical materials and never visited the country. A follow-up study since the war (Stoetzl, 1955) used public opinion poll techniques to show the transition as young Japanese moved away from the traditional roles to their new opportunities and responsibilities. Men and women became more nearly equal in status, and popular interest in foreign affairs had greatly increased. The pacifistic mood which followed defeat and the war-renouncing constitution was evident, but it would be rash to predict its permanence. As in many other countries at that time, young people retreated from social problems to the pursuit of personal pleasures.

An impressionistic study of the character of Japan by a Japanese writer (Minami, 1954) is based on songs, proverbs, fiction, essays, and other literary forms, as well as on extensive personal observation. He finds a pervasive mood of unhappiness. Many Japanese words express sorrow; there are few synonyms for happiness. This thesis is further supported by an analysis of the lyrics of 61 popular postwar songs (Kato, 1959). Among the prominent themes are pessimism, hopelessness, unrequited love, and loneliness.

The Human Relations Research Group at Nagoya National University has given Rorschach tests to thousands of Japanese. They find (despite regional and socio-economic differences) a general tendency for Japanese subjects to give fewer responses than do Americans, and to reject certain cards entirely. A kind of careful, guarded control is suggested by the fact that spontaneous use of color is infrequent. The emphasis on form seems to imply both realism and rigidity.

A number of empirical investigations using a variety of projective tests have been made by DeVos (1959). He notes a pervasive theme of guilt. The Japanese mother's quiet acceptance of suffering and her self-reproach if children fail in any way to meet accepted standards leaves the children with a feeling of guilt. Deriving from the basic sense of guilt is a frequent preoccupation with illness and death. Self-sacrifice for honor is another likely consequence. The Japanese child appears to have a powerful sense of obligation both to his parental family and to his nation.

Some national characteristics survive expatriation. DeVos (1955) found that Japanese-born subjects living in America (*Issei*) still reflected the characteristic rigidity in Rorschach test responses. Those of Japanese descent, born in the United States (*Nisei*), were lower in rigidity but still noticeably above usual American norms. The Nisei, in school, were reported more obedient, respectful, and docile than their classmates. They won higher grades for academic achievement and more good-conduct awards (Strong, 1934).

French. The French have always presented a special fascination and challenge to British and American observers. Andre Siegfried (1952) commented: "I don't know two peoples who are less understandable to each other than the English and the French." Differences in language, food, and clothing have been obvious, and differences in love-life assumed.

Jacques Dubourg (1958) a social psychologist who grew up in France, has interpreted his countrymen to us as follows:

> There is no French race. We are a mixture of Latins, Celts and Germans. French national unity comes from age-old adaptation to the soil, to the climate, and to historical tradition. . . . The strength of the nation lies in the family and above all in the individual. . . .
> The child is not encouraged to feed itself, but is fed by an adult until it is judged able to feed itself *neatly* (about 3 years.) By the time they eat the

same food as adults they are expected to do so quietly. 'Mange et tais toi'—eat and be quiet—is a commonly remembered admonition.

It is often amazing how long children can stay still. They are able to sit for long periods on park benches beside their parents. A typical position of a child in the park is squatting at his mother's feet, playing in the sand. His hands are busy, but his total body position remains constant. Children are often brought to the park in quite elegant (and unwashable) clothes, and they do not get dirty.

Schools in France demand rigid conformity. The child must sit quietly at his desk for 3 hours in the morning and 3 hours in the afternoon. He must not talk to other children. He can move around freely only during the 15 minute recess periods—one in the morning and one in the afternoon. Learning for the young child consists in copying and repeating whatever the teacher tells him. If the work is done bady the child is asked to do it again, after class or at home. The family cooperates wholeheartedly with the teachers. They want their children to work hard and complain if they think the teacher is not sufficiently demanding.

The first years of life in their family, vacations spent at home and boring Sundays there, have imposed on children the monotonous and reassuring style of life. In France every family is bored in its own fashion as a traditional agglomeration of people who intimidate one another. To be well brought up (*bien eleve*)—in the sense of the constantly employed terms a well-brought-up boy, a well-brought-up girl, means to be able to be bored in the family circle without protesting overtly.

France with its tradition of Gallic law does not grant women the same freedom which it gives men. Women must be protected against themselves, that is, against the sexual attraction they exercise on young men, who would court them without serious intent, just to have some fun. The reputation of young men is enhanced if they engage in sexual intercourse, while the reputation of young girls is strengthened if they resist love making. Girls phrase negatively what they want in a mate: they do not want someone lazy, someone who is a drunkard, someone who is dirty, or someone without a job. Physical qualities are passed over rapidly. The boy attaches a certain importance to physical qualities. But also he wants the girl to be serious, to run the menage economically, not to gossip too much, and not to be too proud.

First of all is a claim for independence and essentially a claim for intellectual independence. The Frenchman demands the right to think and judge for himself as an independent being. His is a critical mind, nonconformist and antitotalitarian.

Many of these observations on growing up in France are supported and confirmed by observations of children in the parks of Paris and by the report of a psychoanalyst who had worked with both French and American child patients (Mead, Wolfenstein, 1955).

English. Gorer's study (1955) of English characteristics is superior to his observations on America in at least three respects. First, as an Englishman, he had a broader and deeper basis for understanding British life. Second, he had available data from a sample of 5,000 replies to a questionnaire published in a popular magazine. Third, his study has a thesis and historical dimension, emphasizing the contrast between the violence and cruelty of the British during the seventeenth and eighteenth centuries and their orderly, calm, and peaceful life today. He credits Sir Robert Peel's introduction of the Metropolitan Police (1829) with major effectiveness in bringing about the transformation. "One of the most lawless populations in the world has turned into one of the most law-abiding; a society which uninhibitedly enjoyed public floggings and executions, dog fights and animal baiting has turned into an excessively humanitarian, even squeamish society; a fiercely and ruthlessly acquisitive society has turned into a mildly distributive society; general corruption in government has been replaced by an extraordinarily high level of honesty. What seems to have remained constant is a great resentment at being supervised or controlled, a love of freedom; fortitude; a low interest in sexual activity, compared with most of the neighboring societies; a strong belief in the value of education for the formation of character; consideration and delicacy for the feelings of other people; and a very strong attachment to marriage and the institution of the family." His thesis is that as a result of institutional changes (in accord with our S-P-A formula) nearly all potential human energy among the British is now utilized in keeping aggressive impulses under proper control; as a result, there is not much fight, not much sex, a high value on privacy, and a great deal of complaint about lack of energy.

Russian. Gorer's analysis of Russian character (1949) connects the tight swaddling of infants with the submissiveness of the Russian people to dictatorship by Czars or Commissars. A much more enlightening, although more complex, analysis is one derived from intensive examination of life histories of individual Russians, as conducted by the Harvard Project in the Soviet Social System. Adult refugees of varying social position have been studied, and it is apparent that individual Russian personalities vary widely. One published account (Bauer, 1953) presents Col. Kamen of the Red Army, an authoritarian elitist, cherishing his own independence, with very little ideological commitment, and the quite different humanitarian Chestny, who joined the Komsomols, strove for Soviet ideals, and became a member of the Communist Party. He refers to "love for mankind and some sort of an invisible, undeveloped Christianity," which, he adds, may be "invisible under the cloak of Marxism." Of course, the fact that the individuals studied have all been defectors limits the usefulness of any generalizations for understanding the more typical Soviet citizens who remain loyal.

The author, in a study not previously published, analyzed the characters and themes in six novels widely read in the Soviet Union around 1960. The heroes and heroines were predominantly innovators in science and technology. They were devoted to the popular welfare. The villains were frequently officious bureaucrats, selfish schemers, or persons like the professor who had done all his creative work many years before but who tended, by virtue of his prestige, to hamper the creative work of youth. Love interest was much less evident than it is in American novels or would have been in Russian literature of the nineteenth century. The dramatic conflicts were generally related to social change, with the reactionaries eventually vanquished and the innovators victorious. Education was seen as a major factor in changing the lives of people, and the Communist Party was usually portrayed as on the side of the angels. It is apparent that if Soviet youth are internalizing the values expressed in these novels, their national character will be quite different from that of the Russians portrayed by Chekhov and Tolstoy.

Comparative. As the new technologies increase communication and travel across the boundaries of nations and continents, more studies compare characteristics of several peoples. Gillespie and Allport (1955) gave a 50-item questionnaire to 1,800 students from 10 countries. Optimism about their future was expressed by:

Afrikaners (South Africa)	45%
Japanese	44%
Mexicans	37%
Americans (US)	35%

Least optimistic were Italians (15 percent), French (12 percent), Israelis (10 percent), and Germans (0 percent).

The view that "the world is a hazardous place in which men are basically evil and dangerous" was approved by a majority of students from Egypt (62 percent) and Bantus from South Africa (53 percent). Only 15 percent of Americans agreed.

Among areas of life found most satisfying "family life" rated high in every nation; the Japanese, however, rated "leisure" above "career." "Religion" was high for Bantus, Afrikaners, Egyptians, and Italians, but low for Israelis. "Participation in National or international affairs" was high in value for Mexicans, Japanese, and Israelis, but rated lowest by Afrikaners and Americans.

The life of children in Bali, France, and America; among East European Jews, Soviet Russians, and Germans, is described in a collection of essays (Mead, Wolfenstein, 1955). Margaret Mead, in her introduction, notes that in all cultures children must learn to eat, walk, talk, live in houses, dress themselves, and obey social rules. Yet each culture has its own distinctive way of helping children acquire the needed learning. Many possible patterns emerge for child-raising and for corresponding adult personalities and relationships.

In one paper, Dr. Wolfenstein reports on responses of parents from five different cultures on the subject of "good" and "bad" children and how they should be rewarded or punished. She speculates on whether the tendency of Czech mothers to spank children with a wooden spoon, associated with food, and the preference of American mothers for a hairbrush, reflects conflict situations in feeding little Czechs and in cleanliness for Americans. Syrian mothers and teachers pinch the ears of children to symbolize the need for children to listen more attentively. Refusal to speak to the child for a time was particularly a Jewish custom, and Wolfenstein feels that this is a way of suggesting that the child's birth and training demands are "killing" their poor mother.

In another study (Dennis, 1957) American, Lebanese, and Sudanese children were asked to associate common words (in their own language) with "mouth," "hands," "mother," "boy," "girl," etc. American children more often associated mouth with talking; the other children were more likely to mention eating. Another interesting difference appeared in the frequency of the response "play" to describe what boys and girls do. This was given by 31 percent of the American children but by only 7 percent of the Lebanese or Sudanese. Both of these differences could be related to the difference in economic level.

A thoughtful attempt to compare values in several cultures has been made by Morris (1956). Considering Canada, China, India, Japan, Norway, and the United States, he finds differences along five significant dimensions of value:

1. responsible moral outlook
2. vigorous action
3. rich inner life
4. response to Nature
5. senuous self-enjoyment

He concludes: "It is as if persons in various cultures have in common five major tones in the musical scales on which they compose different melodies" (p. 185).

Cultures change

The national character of one era cannot safely be projected into the future. We referred earlier in this chapter to the transformation of the Betsileo when a new pattern of growing rice was adopted, and to the effects of British conquest on the Tiv culture.

In a broader sense, the contemporary Greeks exemplify little of either the classic Athenian or Spartan character. The Portuguese, once intrepid explorers, have almost ceased to venture forth. Modern Italy is not organized by Roman patterns. The peaceful Scandinavians were once the militant Vikings. One must view national character as changing along the dimension of time. In the last chapter we shall discuss in more detail the processes by which cultures change and some of the resulting stresses on personality.

Evaluation of cultures

Is it possible to describe some cultures—certain ways of life—as clearly superior to others? We may have our personal preferences, usually choosing the culture in which we have spent most of our lives, but is there any objective basis for describing some cultures as "better" or "higher" than others? Do some cultures more fully develop the potential of personality?

In the last analysis, it is impossible to make any completely objective judgment about the goodness of a culture. As an extreme example, if some society should adopt universal infanticide and thus exterminate itself, would that be "bad"? Only on our assumption—not shared by the other society—that survival is valuable. Whatever we may admire in a strange culture is approved because *we* value it on the basis of *our* upbringing. The other culture may or may not agree. Whatever we condemn necessarily reflects *our* values.

Given even a slight measure of agreement on a few rather obvious values, fairly objective comparisons become possible. For example, if it is granted as desirable that human life should continue, we can then criticize policies that we believe to be mass-suicidal, like those involved in tendencies toward the spread of lethal radiation. If it is agreed that it is good to survive and better to live in harmony than to suffer conflict, a number of cross-cultural principles emerge. They are quite formal—not dependent on any particular form of economy, family life, language, education, art, government or religion. They are very nearly trans-cultural axioms.

1. *A culture is better than others if it meets more effectively the basic organic needs of most members on at least a minimum level.*

If the human organism is not given enough food, water, and oxygen it cannot survive. Deprived of sleep or subjected to intense cold or poisoned by drugs, human beings suffer and die. Needs for some self-respect, some sexual relations, for some kind of communication and companionship, and for new and zestful experiences may be less acute than the obvious physical necessities, but a culture denies them at its peril.

2. *A culture is better if it does not foster in childhood strong behavior patterns which later have to be abruptly denied and broken down.*

All cultures, to some extent, differentiate the roles of children from those of adults. Children are necessarily dependent and it would seem sensible gradually to foster the independence demanded of adults. A sharp break—fully dependent this year and completely on his own next year—severely strains human adaptability. The expectation that a child who is overindulged should suddenly become a parent capable of subordinating his own gratifications is likely to be disappointed.

3. *A culture is better if it provides most members with means to realize the ambitions it instills.*

If a culture encourages most people to believe they need and must have things which only a few can obtain, then it fosters discontent. It encourages delinquent detours to obtain what cannot be acquired legitimately. It fosters anomie and the rejection of its norms and way of life.

4. *A culture is better if it fosters compatible general attitudes in its various sectors.*

If some institutions of a culture encourage scientific ways of thinking and recommend these methods as generally valid, while other institutions urge reliance upon unquestioning acceptance of dogma, some conflict can be predicted. A culture that teaches love of fellow men but gives its major rewards to those who exploit their fellows, will find itself in trouble. If one sector is taught not to tolerate behavior which other sectors are taught to believe desirable—for example, the hostility of many communities toward certain deviate religious minorities—conflict seems inevitable. Many youngsters are attracted by gang activities which are sanctioned by their own neighborhood but punished by the representatives of the larger community.

A particularly important contradiction exists between rigidity and progress. A static society may glorify its traditional institutions, but if one sector of a culture is dedicated to research, innovation, and rapid obsolescence, while other sectors try to hold fast to the old ways, some values will have to suffer.

5. *A culture is better if it minimizes conflicts between roles.*

If a culture tells mothers they should stay at home and care for young children but makes it necessary for them to work away from the children eight hours a day, it is creating dissatisfaction. A graduate student who is "expected" to spend full time at study and likewise "expected" to earn enough to support his wife and child, feels the incompatibility of his roles. A senator who is supposed to act on the principles of his own conscience and judgment, but who must keep the support of his constituency in order to be reelected runs into another role-conflict. We noted earlier the role-conflict of sincere Christians asked to support destructive armaments.

6. *A culture is better if its members can correctly predict much of their own behavior and that of other members.*

In a strong culture, the parts must be articulated. Members must have the reassurance of knowing approximately what to expect in common situations. The quite unpredictable members are regarded as "insane," are segregated, and given special care. To the extent that collective actions bring the expected results, the culture is healthy; if action is initiated to satisfy certain desires and it does not do so, the result is frustration and resentment. Superstitions that lead members to expect that which does not happen are not very viable.

7. *A culture is better if it makes possible communication among those who must collaborate.*

The Tower of Babel remains an impressive parable of the consequences of trying to work together without a common language. Institutions which keep interdependent people from interacting—"Iron Curtains" or "Golden Curtains"—bring about actions which may disintegrate the culture and perhaps all the world around. In our world of many diverse cultures, recently brought into close proximity, that culture which can best initiate and sustain genuine communication with others, has the best chance for world leadership.

Transition

The three chapters which follow study the patterns of social interaction differentiated by socio-economic classes (Chapter 10), by race (Chapter 11), and by sex roles (Chapter 12). In accordance with our central S-P-A thesis, we shall endeavor to see how the stratification of class or race or sex role leads to distinctive processes of interaction and hence to characteristic psychological attitudes.

CHAPTER TEN

Psychological differences among socio–economic classes

Meaning of class

We have seen how perception, cognition, attitudes, and values vary from one culture to another. Within any society there usually are stratified sub-cultures which likewise affect processes of interaction and the resulting characteristics of personality. Here we shall focus on psychological differences related to social and economic status.

History

"Now in all states there are three elements: one class is very rich, another very poor, and a third in the mean." So observed Aristotle, in his *Politics*, many centuries before capitalism or socialism had taken form. Aristotle noted also that each class develops a characteristic social outlook. "Those who have too much of the goods of fortune, strength, wealth, friends, and the like are neither willing nor able to submit to authority. The evil begins at home; for when they are boys, by reason of the luxury in which they are brought up, they never learn, even at school, the habit of obedience. On the other hand, the very poor, who are in the opposite extreme, are too degraded. So that the one class cannot obey, and can only rule despotically; the other knows not how to command and must be ruled like slaves. Thus arises a city, not of free men, but of masters and slaves; the one despising, the other envying." Aristotle saw most hope for a rational outlook in the middle class.

When the Declaration of Independence was proclaimed, Adam Smith, an English economist who is sometimes regarded as the father of capitalist theory, was writing an analysis which sounds much like that made by Karl Marx some generations later. "The whole annual produce of the land and labour of every country, or what comes to the same thing, the whole price of that annual produce, naturally divides itself, it has already been observed, into three parts; the rent of the land, the wages of labour, and the profits of stock; and constitutes a revenue to three different orders of people; to those who live by rent, to those who live by wages, and to those who live by profit. These are the three great, original and constituent orders of every civilized society, from whose revenue that of every other order is ultimately derived" (1776). Adam Smith, like Aristotle, had doubts about the wisdom and virtue of the ruling class. Merchants and manufacturers, he observed, usually concentrate more on making profits for themselves than on the general welfare.

One of the Founding Fathers of our Republic, writing in *The Federalist* observed: "The most common and durable source of factions has been the various and unequal distribution of property. Those who hold and those who are without property have ever formed distinct interests in society" ("Publius").

Thus, long before Karl Marx, social philosophers were aware of class conflict. In the first section of the *Communist Manifesto*, issued in 1847, Marx and Engels gave the doctrine its classic statement:

The history of all hitherto existing society is the history of class struggles. Freeman and slave, patrician and plebeian, lord and serf, guild-master and journeyman—in a word, oppressor and oppressed—stood in constant opposition to one another, carried on an uninterrupted, now hidden, now open fight, a fight that each time ended, either in a revolutionary reconstitution of society at large, or in the common ruin of the contending classes. . . .

The modern bourgeois society that has sprouted from the ruins of feudal society has not done away with class antagonisms. It has but established new classes, new conditions of oppression, new forms of struggle in place of the old ones.

Our epoch, the epoch of the bourgeoisie, has simplified the class antagonism. Society as a whole is more and more splitting up into two great hostile camps, into two great classes directly facing each other— bourgeoisie and proletariat. . . . The executive of the modern State is but a committee for managing the common affairs of the whole bourgeoisie.

Investigations of social science support the philosophers and novelists in assigning major importance to social class. In the small California city of Ventura a social psychologist (Sargent, 1953) asked a representative sample of the population: "What would you say are the most important differences found among the people of Ventura? That is, what different groups or categories would you divide them into?" The spontaneous replies cited socio-economic class (upper, middle, or lower; rich or poor; business, farming, naval yard workers) 44 percent of the time. Other kinds of distinction, such as education (15 percent), length of residence in the town (9 percent), race (6 percent) or religion (8 percent), appeared much less prominently.

Class in other societies

The phenomenon of class is not restricted to capitalist or even to industrial societies; it is nearly universal. India has had for centuries a strict hierarchy of classes. Mead (1955) found on the South Sea Island of Palau an elite by descent who outranked the merely wealthy. In underdeveloped areas of Latin America, the Middle East, and Southeast Asia the typical pattern has been a very small upper class with wealth and power; an almost negligible middle class; and over 90 percent living in poverty. So low is the standard of living and so numerous the people barely subsisting that, at present levels of economic and population growth, a per-capita income of one dollar a day can hardly be reached within a century (Bach, 1958; Heilbroner, 1959).

The debate over class differences in Communist countries turns upon the definition. Using Marx's concept of relation to process of production, there is only one class, for all citizens are both owners and workers. But if class connotes income, power, and prestige, the differences are of the same order as in capitalist countries (Inkeles, 1953).

The classless image in the United States

While class distinctions have been recognized throughout history as among the most important differences among people in every society, many Americans feel uncomfortable about paying attention to class status. They feel that to admit class barriers is somehow un-American. The early settlers on this continent fled from feudal Europe and envisioned a society in which all men might be recognized as equal in worth.

Since the days of the first American primers, children have been taught that by their own efforts they might rise to any level—from office-boy to general manager or from a log cabin to the White House. To suggest that class distinctions still play an important part in American life seems subversive of faith in our proud democratic tradition.

Inequality is less evident in America than in many other countries because of the high and rising level of prosperity. A climate of comfort does not foster criticism or change.

Men of wealth and power in America have often affected the style of the average man. They may shun display and prefer to be spoken of as "common as an old shoe." This was particularly important in nineteenth-century politics—shirt sleeves and suspenders were symbols of trustworthiness. Even in the more recent era of millionaires in public office, Averill Harriman and Franklin D. Roosevelt omitted Groton from their *Who's Who in America* listing, but included the famous preparatory school in the English *Who's Who*.

A good illustration of the American credo on class, is Charles Gray, hero of J. P. Marquand's novel *Point of No Return*. (This novel has special interest for social psychology because its setting—Clyde—is the same small city made famous by Lloyd Warner and associates in their anthropological studies of "Yankee City".) In the novel Gray has risen to a vice presidency and is a member of a country club, but he speaks of the town of Clyde as democratic and without classes. Still, he can recall that when he first met Jessica Lovell, he was not acceptable to her family and social circle. "His aunt should have known he belonged in a different group from Jessica and that groups hardly ever mingled in Clyde."

Repression of awareness of class differences in our society has promoted optimism and faith in the *status quo*. A public opinion poll inquired, "Would you say that your children had just as good a chance, a poorer, or a better chance to rise in the world, as anybody else's?" (Centers, in Katz, *et al.*, 1955, p. 142). It is not surprising that 100 percent of the answers from business and professional men were "as good," or "better." What is impressive is the finding that 84 percent of adults in skilled labor occupations, and 79 percent of unskilled laborers answered that their children actually had as good a chance to rise as did anyone else. Their actual life opportunities will be summarized at the end of this chapter after a review of many factual studies.

Part of the disregard for socio-economic class arises from the upper class control of the media of mass communication discussed in Chapter 8. It is clearly to the advantage of the highly privileged owning class to sustain the myth that they have no special privileges and that everyone in the United States has an equal chance to succeed. Exposure of the actual advantages afforded the upper class and the handicaps imposed upon the lower class would raise disturbing questions about the *status quo*.

In contrast to the assumption of general equality is the struggle to rise to higher levels which Vance Packard has described vividly in *The*

Status Seekers (1959). Corporation job hierarchies, residential neighborhoods, and patterns in social life all reflect strong concern with the prestige and privileges of status. One theory is that in firmly stratified societies, individuals know that their place is fixed. Nothing they do is likely to enable them to rise or to cause them to fall. Since American society is viewed as open, people are eager to climb another step up the ladder and are insecure because they fear they will slip down.

Definition

Discussion of the social psychological implications of "class" is confused by the use of several different meanings of the word. Well recognized titles—serfs, knights, barons, lords, dukes, kings—served in feudal society to define sharp class lines. For most Americans, the easiest distinction to recognize is that of rich or poor. Amount of income can be used as one basis for classification.

As shown in the accompanying graph the distribution of income does not fall into sharply defined groups. Any division is arbitrary.

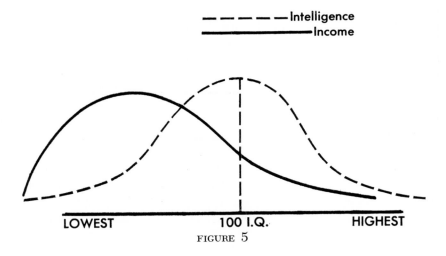

FIGURE 5

The shape of the curve of income does not fit the curve of measured intelligence. Intelligence falls into a "normal," symmetrical distribution; income is skewed with most families at lower levels and very few high. In 1965 (*Washington Post*, April 30, p. C-1) the director of the Office of Economic Opportunity proposed that the poverty level be defined as an annual income of less than $3,130 for a family of four. This would provide an average of only 23 cents per person per meal. By this definition about 18 percent of the total population is "poor."

Another definition of social class has been empirically derived from surveys which ask people how they would classify themselves. The re-

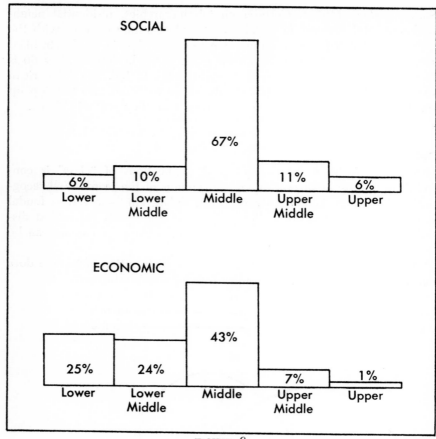

FIGURE 6

sults vary, depending upon whether "economic" class or "social" class is stressed in the question. One study based on over 3,000 interviews gave the results shown in Figure 6 (Wallace, Williams, Cantril, 1944).

In response to the question about "social class" most Americans are reluctant to claim superiority or to admit inferiority, which reflects our egalitarian ethos. But when it comes to the more apparent criterion of income, about one-half put themselves in the lower or lower middle class, and only 8 percent rank themselves above middle status.

When people are asked in which class they belong, the answers depend partly upon the names assigned. Thus, one Gallup poll found that when asked about "social class" 6 percent called themselves "upper class," 88 percent claimed "middle" status, and 6 percent said that they should be called "lower class." But, if the category "working class" were used, this became the predominant choice, yielding a distribution of the following percentages: upper class 3, middle class 33, working class 64, and lower class 12.

If, instead of asking people to classify themselves, we ask them to tell us about the classes of people who live in their community, another set of results is found. This prestige criterion has been the one most widely used by social psychologists. It was used by Davis and his associates to study a Southern town (1941), by Warner to study "Yankee City" (1941–1945) and "Jonesville" (1949), and by Hollingshead to study "Elmtown" (1949).

People seem to agree on their identification of fellow citizens who belong in upper, middle or lower strata. In "Jonesville," ten informants mentioned 340 different persons as they talked with the interviewer. There were 426 instances in which two or more informants mentioned the same individual. The informants agreed on the "class" in 95 percent of the cases. "Class" is obviously apparent to the typical citizen. The status of a family probably depends partly on their income, partly on the house and neighborhood where they live, partly on their family history in the community, partly on their dress, moral conduct, social participation, speech, and education.

Six prestige classes have been commonly discerned:

About   1% Upper-upper (wealth and distinguished lineage)
About   2% Lower-upper (wealth and prestige)
About 11% Upper-middle (important business and professional)
About 28% Lower-middle (white collar, small business, skilled workmen)
About 33% Upper-lower (semi-skilled and service employees)
About 25% Lower-lower (unskilled, drifters, unfortunates, lack respect-
                ability)
——
100%

The perspective in which these classes are viewed depends on the status of the viewer. A typical member of the upper-lower class will be conscious of a sharp gulf between himself and the destitute, shiftless lower-lowers, but will tend to telescope the more remote upper-middle, lower-upper and upper-upper, regarding them all as rich and snobbish. A typical member of the lower-upper class may not differentiate the upper-lower from the lower-lower—they are all "poor people living in run-down neighborhoods."

When Marx and Engels wrote of class conflict they employed still another definition. In Marxist theory, class is determined, not by self-identification (workers may lack class-consciousness), prestige or income, but by relationship to the processes of production. It is the nature and source of the income that is critical rather than the amount. The bourgeoisie or owning class derive their income not from what they do but from what they possess. The proletariat, or working class, derive their income only from what they do, from their labor. Between these two major groups is a middle group (independent farmers, small store keepers) who derive their income partly from what they own and partly from their labor. Marx was not interested in a description of community layers—he was seeking the dynamics of society. He focused on what people can force others to do. He observed that power, in a capitalist society, is invested in the owners. He saw that owners were able to hire or fire at their pleasure, thus determining the level at which they would allow workers to subsist. On the other hand, the owners could produce very little themselves. Only the workers produce. Once workers organize, Marx theorized, they can do all the necessary work and can eliminate the profits and dividends which go to non-workers. A society in which everyone who is able to work earns his own way and in which none receives income based solely on ownership and the exploitation of the labor of others would be "classless" in Marxist terms, even though there were wide differences among workers in income, status or privilege.

On a Marxist basis, the working class in America today would include about two-thirds of the population; the owning class who live on rents, interest, and dividends about 10 per cent; and the remaining 23 percent would derive an important part of their income from property and an important share from their own work.

Still another approach to the definition of classes is the use of attitudes as the determining factor. People whose opinions, interests, and tastes are similar are regarded as belonging to a given class. Later in this chapter, we shall present Centers' (1949) study of "attitudes, values and interests" in the upper class (3 percent), the middle class (40 percent), the working class (54 percent), and the lower class (3 percent). By this definition, members belong to a given class because they think and feel as do other members of that class.

A cross section of American male adults was asked by Centers: "In deciding whether a person belongs to your class or not, which of these things do you think it most important to know: What his family is; how much money he has; what sort of education he has; or how he believes and feels about certain things?" The most frequent response (47 percent) referred to beliefs and feelings. Education (29 percent), family (29 percent), and money (17 percent) were seen as less vital (p. 91).

Lazarsfeld (cited by Lipset, Bendix, 1951) found that in 1948 one's attitude toward the controversial Taft-Hartley Act, designed to restrict trade unions, was a better index of objective class position than was a direct question about the class in which an individual believed he should be placed.

The basis for class identification varies somewhat with the size of the community. A group of college students in Iowa wrote papers describing the stratification of their home town (T. Lasswell, 1959). Those from smaller communities (under 50,000) were inclined to refer to citizen's activities in local organizations; those from larger cities to type of housing. Occupation was a major element in all the student papers.

Popular magazines have described and listed the tastes of high-brows, middle-brows, and low-brows and the leisure-time preferences of "aristocrats," "upper bourgeois," "lower bourgeois," and "peasants." "You can always tell an Aristocrat by the way he slaves over his spare time. Results do not interest him. Being an expert does. . . . The peasant is expert only at wasting time. As for trying to make his leisure original or constructive —he couldn't care less" (Lynes, 1959). Nancy Mitford in a witty book (1956) distinguishes, by taste in things-to-do, the "U's" (Uppers) from "non-U's." The same kind of distinction is constantly being made on the campus and in the community between those who are "in" and those who are "out."

In Britain, as George Bernard Shaw neatly dramatized in *Pygmalion* (better known to many as *My Fair Lady*), speech clearly separates the upper class from the Cockney. In medieval Europe, the nobility spoke with one set of pronouns (*du, tu*) to the common people and with another, more respectful form of address (*vos, vous, sie*) to their "betters."

The importance of dress as a factor in class identification is apparent in an anecdote from modern Britain. Kingsley Martin, editor of the *New Statesman and Nation,* told in that periodical (March 22, 1958, p. 367) of a factory manager who, three times a week, after hours, changed into workmen's clothes and made political speeches on a soapbox outside the factory gates. The manager reported later that none of his fellow administrators ever recognized him. Since he was wearing overalls, they did not even see him. None of the workers who had heard his orations recognized him when he was properly dressed for his managerial tasks although one puzzled man in the shop did say to a friend, as the manager walked through: "I could swear I know his face from somewhere!"

One of the most frequent appeals to class is associated with engagement and marriage. While occasional Cinderella-and-the-Prince or heiress-and-chauffeur marriages occur outside the dream world of the movies, most weddings cement the ties of social class. The fact that the prospective mate comes from "our kind of people" seems particularly important to the upper classes. Tocqueville wrote of France after its Revolution:

> In order to ascertain whether caste, with the ideas, habits and barriers it creates amongst a nation, is definitely destroyed, look at its marriages. They alone give the decisive feature which we seek. At this very day, in France, after sixty years of democracy, we shall generally seek it in vain. The old and the new families, between which no distinction any longer appears to exist, avoid as much as possible to intermingle with each other by marriage." (1888, p. 73)

Attitudes toward the prevailing social system are employed by Goodman (1956) to identify four classes. At the top of the "Establishment" are the powerful key executives who serve on interlocking boards of directors for financial and industrial corporations; with them are the Governors, Senators, Cabinet Officers, Supreme Court Justices, chairmen of major Congressional Committees, and a few mayors or bosses of larger cities. These men—less than one one-hundredth of one percent of the population—constitute the rulers. Beneath them is the layer of "organization men"—dedicated to the "rat-race" and earning salaries of more than $10,000. Perhaps 5 percent of the population qualified in 1960 for this second class. The "masses" are at a third level down, ranging from comfortable down to poor. They are what Goodman calls "alienated operatives." They work, but they have no love for their bosses. They care for their cars, but have little concern about the working of the economic system. They usually buy major items on the installment plan and may hold a second job. They struggle to keep their heads above water. These are the millions who make up 75 percent of the population.

Lowest on Goodman's scale are the "outsiders," the "new poor." They include almost all Negroes and Puerto Ricans, sharecroppers, and migratory farm workers. They are not simply at the bottom of the ladder—they have no footing on the ladder at all. Nothing most of them can do will permit them to become "insiders." These are the most difficult to help in any national "war on poverty" because most rules for getting ahead do not apply to them. Their number has been estimated at 20 percent of the American population (Harrington, 1963).

All of these ways of stratifying an industrial society have a large measure of overlap. The large stockholder in one or more corporations would rate as "upper" by his income level, his self-ascription, his reputation, his ownership, his attitudes and interests. The wage earner in a small factory would be at working-class level in his actual earnings, his way of making his living, his status as seen by others, his view of himself, and his core of attitudes, opinions, and tastes. Correlations among five factors—prestige of occupation, average I.Q. of members of an occupation, years of schooling of those in the occupation, average income of the occupation, and restriction of size of family—range from .81 to .95, indicating that all five measure very much the same thing (Cattell, 1942). When a list of 26 occupations was rated for prestige by graduate students and by skilled and unskilled laborers, the agreement was high (correlation coefficient of .94). For both groups, physicians and bankers were high; farmers and policemen were near the middle; unskilled, casual laborers and unemployed men were at the bottom.

Using this core of agreement on what is meant by upper, middle or lower classes, we turn to exploration of ways in which the class structure affects processes of interaction and results in distinctive attitudes (S-P-A). Basic personality, as was said in the preceding chapter, is formed in childhood.

Child-rearing in different classes

In the United States, a child born into a white family of the upper class had (in 1940) a life-expectancy of 68 years as compared with only 60 years in a white family of the lower class (Mayer, Hauser, 1953). Infant survival depends, in part, upon class factors linked with housing, health facilities, and the parents' education.

The child who survives is brought up somewhat differently in different social classes. The typical middle-class parent wants his child to learn at an early age to put away his clothes, to keep his room tidy, to respect his home furnishings, and to help with certain household chores. He especially wants his child to learn to read, to get good marks in school, and to go to college. Toys bought for the middle-class children are frequently designed to help the child spell, do arithmetic, locate geographic names, or to acquire skills in science. Difference in aspiration for academic achievement is one of the outstanding factors bearing on children from homes of varying social class. Allison Davis comments:

> The middle-status way, then, with its emphasis upon respectability and morality, upon property, money and other symbols of attainment, upon organizational ties which dramatize one's adherence to group goals, upon self-improvement through education, or book clubs, or art, and music clubs, and upon community improvement through the church, the civic organizations, and the school, this way of life which is so obnoxious to the Bohemians, aristocrats, and slum dwellers, is carried on by people who are culturally motivated to suffer, to renounce, to postpone gratification in order to achieve. To propel the child along this apparently endless route of socialization so that he may attain a physician's skills, let us say, the middle-status family uses pressures and goals which build anxiety. The child is taught by a well-defined and relatively severe training to strive for the expected or allowed age, sex, or class status or to attempt to gain a higher age, or school or social class status. (1950)

Discipline by blows—direct physical punishment—remains characteristic of working-class homes. Middle-class parents more often employ praise, appeals to guilt, reasoning, or isolation of the offender. Physical violence is generally more evident in lower-class family life. Allison Davis, again, after studying lower-class families in the Middle West, the South, and New England has observed:

> Both girls and boys at adolescence may curse their father to his face or even attack him with fists, sticks or axes in free-for-all family encounters. Husbands

and wives sometimes stage pitched battles in the home. . . . Such fights with fists or weapons, and the whipping of wives, occur sooner or later in most low-class families. (1944)

A sociologist (Green, 1946) argued that middle-class boys develop a typical neurotic syndrome. Their parents, pursuing numerous interests outside the home, are ambivalent toward children who seem to bring frustration as well as satisfaction. Aware of the sacrifices they have made, these parents expect the children to compensate them by good behavior and high achievement. Green asserts that "He (the middle-class boy) can never escape his parents' norms at home, in school, or in his play groups—always he must try to live up to their high expectations of him, or he will lose their love. Thus he lives alone and afraid in a world he never made." In contrast, the working-class boy is seen as treated more harshly, as resentful and contemptuous toward the father, and hence a more successful rebel untroubled by guilt. Green's types are familiar, but he offers no impressive data on how frequent each pattern is in either class.

Most writers on social class differences have themselves come from middle-class homes and seem, in protest, to have been a little enamoured of the notion that the working-class child might have had emotional advantages. They point out that in lower-class homes, children are given more important responsibilities (Davis, Havighurst, 1946). Older children have to take care of younger ones (Kluckhohn and Kluckhohn, 1947). Children are expected to obey and respect their parents. While the working-class boy may not act aggressively toward parents, he is encouraged to use his fists to stand up for his rights or for his younger siblings in relationships with neighborhood children (Macoby, Gibbs, et al., 1954). Neighbors in working-class communities are more helpful to one another (Useem, 1942).

Abstract 38 shows that working-class parents emphasize obedience, honesty, neatness, and cleanliness; middle- and upper-class parents are concerned about the child's happiness and encourage consideration of others, self-control, and curiosity.

A study (Sewell, 1961) of 1,462 grade school children showed that healthy emotional traits, as measured by the California Test of Personality, were more common in children from homes of higher socio-economic status ($r = .25$). The differences were found especially in tendencies of children from poorer homes to reject their families, to worry over failure to achieve, and to show nervous symptoms.

In adolescence, Nye (1951) found that a poor adjustment between parents and youth characterized 42 percent of the lower-class homes, but only 15 percent of the upper-class homes. Using a picture of an older man and a younger man, an older woman and a young woman

Abstract 38

TITLE   Social Class and Parental Values

AUTHOR   Melvin L. Kohn

PROBLEM   Are child-rearing values related to social class member-ship? If so, how?

SUBJECTS   400 mothers, 100 fathers, and 100 children, half middle class, half working class. Class estimates of families were based on Hollingshead's Index (occupation and educational level of father, and rent or value of home). Classes I, II, and III were considered "Middle Class;" classes IV and V were considered "Working Class."

PROCEDURE   The sample was selected from census tract data and school enrollment lists. In home interviews mothers were asked to choose from a list of 17 characteristics the *three* most de-sirable for her 10- or 11-year old child. In every fourth family the father, separately, was asked to make this choice, and the child was also interviewed.

SOME FINDINGS

Mothers' Socio-Economic Status and Their Choice of Characteristics
"Most Desirable" in a Child of 10 or 11 Years
(in Percentages)

	Socio-Economic Stratum (Hollingshead Index)				
	I *(Highest)*	II	III	IV	V *(Lowest)*
CHARACTERISTIC					
Obedience	14%	19%	25%	35%	27%
Neatness-cleanliness	6	7	16	18	27
Consideration for others	41	37	39	25	32
Curiosity	37	12	9	7	3
Self-control	24	30	18	13	14
Happiness	61	40	40	38	30
Honesty	37	49	46	50	65
N =	51	43	80	128	37

SOURCE: *Amer. J. Soc.*, January, 1959, LXIV:337–351.

as a projective test, Neugarten (1964) found that adult respondents at upper levels (business executive and professional) differed from those at blue-collar, working-class levels in what they imagined to be the issues under discussion. The former group thought the participants in the discussions were concerned with achievement in the world. The working-class parents saw the theme of the discussion as more limited to marriage and family. More adults from the upper class than from the working class thought young people deserved respect.

Sex mores also vary with class. Kinsey (1948) reports that, as level of education—a rough index of class—rises, sexual activity among adolescent boys, age 16–20, diminishes from 3.2 "outlets" per week among those who did not go to high school to 2.7 for the boys who go on to higher education. The pattern of sexual expression is more inhibited at the higher levels. The typical kind of outlet shifts, with increasing education, from premarital intercourse (59 percent of the outlets for those who did not go beyond eighth grade but only 11 percent for the college boys) to masturbation (29 percent for the low education levels, 66 percent of outlets for the college boys). "Petting to climax" accounts for 2 percent of the sexual activity of the less educated young men, but for 5 percent in those who continue beyond high school. On the other hand, nudity within the privacy of the family is more accepted by upper levels (90 percent) than by the less educated (43 percent).

Differences in child-rearing practices are not immutable. As economic conditions have improved, interaction across class lines has increased and attitudes have converged. This is in accord with the S-P-A thesis. But another contributing factor in change has been intellectual. Recommendations based on psychoanalysis and mental hygiene have come via the mass media to the centers of influence and have diffused through schools, Parent-Teacher Association meetings, and television shows to many working-class homes. Relatively more middle-class mothers were nursing their infants in the 1950's than had done so ten years earlier (Bronfenbrenner, 1958). Similarly, early studies showed that middle class mothers began toilet training earlier and were quite strict (Davis, Havighurst, 1948). Later studies indicated that as these mothers learned more about healthy child development, they generally relaxed their over-strenuous demands. It still remains true, however, that working-class homes are more prudish about nakedness and that middle-class homes exert more pressure toward independent achievement by the child. As more and more working-class people respond to the change in employment opportunities (derived from automation—again S-P-A) they may well increase pressure on their children to prepare for college.

Children's awareness of class

Children acquire their understanding of class gradually as they learn other aspects of their culture. The study by Dr. Stendler, summarized in Abstract 39 shows that few first-graders have any clear notion of what it means to be "rich" or "poor." By the fourth grade a few—usually upper-middle class girls—show awareness of a stratified society. By the sixth grade this attitude is general. Middle-class children are convinced that their classmates who live over a tavern or down by the

Abstract 39

TITLE Children of Brasstown

AUTHOR Celia Burns Stendler

PROBLEM At what age do children become aware of differences in socio-economic class? How do they see the differences?

SUBJECTS 107 children in Grades 1, 4, 6, and 8 of an elementary school in a small New England city.

PROCEDURE Homes were classified as upper-middle (25), white-collar (37) or working class (45). Pupils responded to interviews; pictures of work, homes, recreation, and clothing; and to a 40-item "Guess Who" questionnaire.

SOME FINDINGS Stage 1–*Pre-awareness*
First graders show little recognition of socio-economic class. They categorize classmates as clean or dirty, well-behaved or bad. "Rich" is a halo word, meaning "good." Most (69%) rated themselves as "upper."

Stage 2–*Beginnings of awareness*
About fourth grade—some earlier, some later—children begin to notice that some homes are better, are located in better sections, and are better furnished. Some 56% of children in fourth grade (only 26% in first grade) use class (rich or poor) to explain why a child smokes or studies or steals or shares. Some 70% now rate themselves as "white collar" rather than as upper or working class. Friendship choice is still independent of social class.

Stage 3–*Acceptance of adult stereotypes*
Beginning before Grade 6 (especially for the upper- and middle-class children) and continuing through Grade 8, children reflect adult views. Working-class children are later in acquiring these ideas. Most pupils recognize typical upper class, white collar, or working class jobs, homes, clothes, and recreational activities.
Upper middles are regarded by sixth graders as studying hardest (82%), being best dressed (59%), going to most expensive camp (50%). Working-class youngsters are regarded as needing their clothes mended (67%), not having very nice manners (50%), being likely to work in a service station (50%), being allowed to go to the movies most often (50%). In eighth grade, pupils see upper's as having a maid (60%), going to private school (64%).
In sixth grade 93% of the choices by upper-middle class children for another child to be invited to a birthday party fell in that same class. Working class children chose their party companion in 78% of the cases from the working class. When asked to name someone with whom they would not care to associate, only 2% of the sixth graders named an upper middle-class child while 65% named a working class child.

Stage 4–*Recognition of individual worth independent of class*
Few, even in the eighth grade, reached this maturity.

SOURCE: Urbana: University of Illinois *Bulletin*, 1949, XLVI, No. 59.

railroad tracks are their social inferiors. Eighth graders believe that upper-middle class children are more likely to take riding or violin lessons, to subscribe to magazines, and to have the gang in for cocoa after skating. They believe that in general lower-class children have to work after school.

A study (Bonney, 1942) of sociometric choices of second grade children in several Texas schools showed that peer preference correlated .52 with parental occupational status. A measure of how much parents participated in community life (this is a fair index of class status except for the small number of upper-uppers who may hold aloof) correlated .62 with the popularity of their second grade children. The tendency of all children to admire and approve children from higher status homes is supported by another study (Warner, et al., 1949). Fifth and sixth grade children in Midwestern "Hometown" were asked to guess who was meant by the statement: "Here is someone who is thought to be very goodlooking" or, at another point in the questionnaire, "Here is someone whom most people think not goodlooking at all." A child from the top social class group (upper-middle) was chosen as "goodlooking" about 20 times as often, on the average, as was a child from the lowest (lower-lower) class. The "not goodlooking" child was most often from the lower-lowers; least often from the upper-middles.

Most studies show children choosing their best friends on the basis of propinquity (Chapter 2). Although a school class may include children from different neighborhoods, the out-of-school contacts usually have more influence. One investigator (Cook, 1945) found that in a junior high school about 75 percent of the seventh grade students chose friends from their own social class—upper, middle or lower. In this school the teachers tried deliberately to democratize the friendship relations. Pupils were selected across class lines to work together on committees and projects. The students were tested again when they left junior high school: About 65 percent of the choices fell within the class of the chooser. Thus a school integration policy, carried on over several years, could make only a slight impression on the social attitudes formed by out-of-school associations.

School experience and social class

The public school is a curious class hybrid. The School Board members who control its policies come largely from the upper-middle (72 percent in three cities) or lower-upper (16 percent) class. They are men (and a few energetic women) of considerable influence in the community. The principal school administrator—the Superintendent—is usually a member of the Rotary Club and associates with the leading business and professional families. The school teachers are regarded as middle class (96 percent), although some of them have risen from farm or city working-class homes. Two-thirds of the elementary school pupils come from working class or lower-lower-class homes. The school is thus controlled by the uppers, taught by the middles, and attended mainly by the lowers. Attitudes characteristic of each group may well be in conflict with the other two. According to Allison Davis, "Our public schools for the lowest third of our population, the schools in slums, are almost a complete failure. The staffs of these schools generally are aware of their basic failure and are demoralized" (Davis, 1950). This is true of the shabby rural schools for children of tenant farmers as well as of the "blackboard jungles" of the big cities.

The most impressive study of how social class operates in the public schools of a typical American community is "Elmtown's Youth." Upper-class pupils are more apt to take the college preparatory course, to get good grades, to obtain personal counsel from teachers on school work, to join music organizations, to attend athletic and social events, and to be chosen for the Student Council. The lowest group—Class 5—commonly take a trade or domestic science course; have the highest proportion of failures; get counsel mainly as discipline problems; seldom participate in athletic, musical, or social affairs or student government; are much more likely to drop out before graduation. Some 60 percent of Class 1 and 2 (Highest) belong to the Boy Scouts or Camp Fire girls; only 1 percent of Class 5. In the higher classes, 74 percent went to church; only 19 percent of Class 5 attended church. Each class chose about 75 percent of friends from the same socio-economic class. More of Class 1 and 2 went bowling; more of Class 4 and 5 went roller skating or to public dance halls.

Some of the stories make the class distinctions in Elmtown more vivid. When the principal of the high school started a campaign against tardiness by detaining late pupils after school, he was obstructed in enforcing this regulation against the upper-class pupils: they usually had excuses which would get them out of detention—Kathy getting her hair done; Frank driving up late in his father's Cadillac. "The idea is all right," said the Superintendent, "but it won't work in every case." When "Boney" Johnson, a boy of lower status (Class 4), tried to evade detention, however, the principal's anger was unrestrained. He ridiculed Boney's neat appearance ("Pretty boy!") and later engaged in a fight in which he pulled the pupil's cap over his eyes and struck the boy three times with the heel of his hand against the base of the skull. "Nothing came of it, except—Boney quit school," a report of the incident concluded.

A rather typical report is the following which comes from a New York City teacher.

For many years I taught in one of the special high schools of the city. The median IQ of the entering class was about 120; the median reading ability about eleventh year. The students took their school work very seriously.

They led very full lives outside of school—music lessons, art lessons, dancing lessons, attendance at concerts and the theatre. When I mentioned a book in class, I would find it in the hands of several students a little later. Graduates made a name for themselves in many colleges and the alumni of the school contribute much to New York.

Then I was appointed supervisor in a vocational high school where the average IQ of the entering class is about 75, the average reading ability fourth grade. The students are apathetic. School has little meaning for them. There is a high degree of truancy and cutting of classes. Parents seldom come to school when summoned, let alone when invited. Many students come from broken homes. Ten percent, at most, continue till graduation. Most are serving time till old enough to leave.

What could we teach that would make school meaningful and enrich the lives of these children? Suppose we tried to teach them how to get a job. They were not interested beyond the address of where to get it when they wanted it. When they leave school, they drift from job to job. When they have enough money and clothes, many see no point in working.

A study of experiences of more than 4,000 classroom teachers from all over the United States (National Education Association, 1956) showed that in "very good" neighborhoods 47 percent of pupils were rated as "exceptionally well behaved"; as the neighborhood grew economically poorer, the proportion of very well behaved pupils dropped to 32 percent (average neighborhood); to 21 percent (below average neighborhood) and 15 percent (slum area). Only 8–9 percent of teachers in above-average areas reported that someone had been struck physically by a pupil during the past year; in the slum areas the percent rose to 48 percent.

The fact that intelligence test scores are generally lower in the poorer neighborhoods is often used to explain the school failures. Davis contends (1950, p. 45) that at least part of the variation in test performance is due to selection of items which upper-class pupils have more chance to learn; e.g., what a "sonata" is. Conceivably, a vocabulary test might be developed which contained the argot of a slum neighborhood and which would handicap the upper-class children. Is it not arbitrary to call either examination a measure of "native intelligence"?

Several studies have shown that the conditions of lower-class life may impede normal intellectual development. A report to the American Orthopsychiatric Association (Knoblock, Pasamanick, 1960) indicated that of 300 Baltimore babies, all normal at birth, those living in lower-class homes would, on the average, be noticeably retarded by the age of three. The retarding homes had more illness; the mother was more likely to be working, and there was less stimulus to intellectual growth. A comparison of two nursery schools (Gesell, Lord, 1929) showed that the children in a lower-class neighborhood whose mothers had to go to work each day were less well developed in speech and in play initiative. Nutritional differences play some part, but cultural deprivation seems to be the major factor. Welfare and educational projects such as "Headstart" (inaugurated in some cities in 1965) help to make up for early handicaps, but age 4 may be too late.

Studies have demonstrated further that the most important single factor affecting the child's reading level in elementary school is the socio-economic class of parents (Barton, Wilder, 1964). Thirty-three percent of the teachers who taught classes in which the majority of the pupils come from lower working-class homes reported average reading retardation of one year or more. The corresponding percentages of retardation were 10 percent for upper working-class areas, 6 percent for middle-class groups, and only 3 percent in upper-class regions. Retardation in reading was found to increase over time in schools serving children from the working class. The proportion of teachers who taught pupils from lower working-class areas who reported retardation in reading of a year or more was 4 percent in first grade, 16 percent in second grade, 32 percent in third grade, 50 percent in fourth grade, and 60 percent in fifth grade. Reading advancement of a year or more was reported by 10 percent of teachers whose pupils were largely lower working class as contrasted with 41 percent of middle-class pupils and 66 percent of upper-class pupils. The differences lies not so much in what is done in the classroom as in the activities, possessions, and values of the home.

As we go up from elementary school to college, each year shows a larger proportion of children from homes of professional, proprietor, and managerial groups (Mulligan, 1951). School performance of children from what are now called "disadvantaged" homes is affected by many handicaps. Motivation is often weak; more school seems unnecessary to many parents in need of the dollars a working teen-ager might earn. Parents who have been able to earn an adequate livelihood despite limited schooling may see little use in study. Homes are not equipped with encyclopedias or dictionaries. School curricula are often remote from the urgent concerns of modern life. Neighbors and friends reinforce values which are anti-academic. Rogoff's (1960) study showed that the achievement of pupils is strongly affected by the socio-economic class of their schoolmates. "No matter how privileged or underprivileged the kind of family from which they come, high school seniors at least double their chances of scoring in the top fourth in aptitude if they attend a school where most of their classmates are from the upper strata."

Since about 1960, the large cities have awakened to the fact that they have not understood the working-class child. The author, in a preface to Frank Riessman's *The Culturally Deprived Child* wrote: "The great reservoir of undiscovered and undeveloped intellectual talent in America is not in upper-class or middle-class neighborhoods." Because there are so many more children in working-class homes than in the homes of professional men or business leaders (about 15 or 20 to 1), even if the *proportion* of intellectually gifted youngsters is lower in the less advantaged group, the actual numbers are greater. In a study (Byrns, Henmon, 1936) of seniors in Wisconsin high schools, the proportion with IQ's over 120 was 25 percent of pupils whose parents were in the professions, and 12 percent of those whose parents were unskilled laborers. Another study (Eels, 1951) shows IQ's over 120 in 40 percent of the "high status" homes and in 11 percent of the "low status" homes. If we applied this ratio to "Yankee City" (Warner, *et al.*), where 3 percent of the population were "upper class" and 58 percent "lower class," we would find 12 percent of all "gifted" children coming from upper-class homes and 64 percent from lower-class homes.

Educators have begun to revise their textbooks to depict, in pictures and words, the lives of boys and girls from slum areas. Teaching methods are being altered to give greater attention to improved techniques for teaching the slow learner.

As we shall see later in this chapter, the values of working-class youths may, in some ways, make an added contribution to those values which the school has traditionally emphasized.

Dr. James B. Conant, a former President of Harvard University, has supported the principle of "compensatory spending." Children from impoverished backgrounds should, he thinks, receive larger per-capita expenditures for their education to help make up their cultural deficit (1964). This would reverse the traditional trend in which children from the best homes and neighborhoods have attended the most beautifully equipped schools and been taught by the best teachers.

Attendance at college has become increasingly important as a prerequisite for all professional and high managerial positions. A study (Warner, *et al.*, 1944, p. 52) of high school students with IQ's of 110 or over showed that if socio-economic status were above average, 93 percent finished high school and 57 percent went on to college. If the homes were below average, only 72 percent finished high school and only 13 percent went on to college. One study (Sibley, 1942) indicated that college attendance could be much better predicted from the occupational status of the father than from the high IQ of the pupil. In Milwaukee, Helen Goetsch found among 1,023 high school graduates with IQ's over 117, if the family income was more than $8,000 (in the 1930's) *all* the graduates went on to college. Among the equally bright graduates from low income homes, only about 25 percent were able to go to college full time (Goetsch, 1939).

An opinion survey, in 1947, asked "about how much schooling do you think most young men need these days to get along well in the world?" College education was specified by 68 percent of the wealthy, 52 percent of the middle class, but only 39 percent of the lower class (Hyman, 1953). In another poll (*Fortune,* 1949) respondents were asked: "If you had a boy graduating from high school, would you personally like to have him go on to college, or would you rather have him do something else?" The choice "something else" was made by only 1 percent of adults in the professional and business executive classes, but by 15 percent of wage earners and 16 percent of farmers. When the question referred to a daughter rather than a son, 6 percent of the executive professional group rejected college, but 31 percent of wage earners did so.

Acceptance in college, success in academic pursuits and in campus social life are generally higher for the students from homes of higher socio-economic class. A study at the University of Indiana (Mueller, 1940) of 1,600 women students showed that if father was in a large business, 90 percent were in sororities; if father was a farmer or a semi-skilled worker, only 17 percent were in sororities. Social honors (Prom Queen, Homecoming Queen, etc.) were five times as likely to go to the daughter of a prominent businessman as to the daughter of a farmer or worker. The index of academic honors was 144 for students from homes of the professional class, 128 for those from the big business category, but only 94 for those from homes of farmers or semiskilled workmen.

The school and college system is for some students a ladder by which they climb to a status above that of their parents. For many more, however, the trip through high school and college is on a ticket providing first-class, second-class, or third-class accommodations, depending on the socio-economic class status of the home.

Participation in other organizations

We have examined the important influence of social class upon the kind of experience boys and girls have in school. The same kind of differences emerge in other organizations outside the school. The summary of *Elmtown's Youth* presented earlier in this chapter shows that youth organizations can fail to reach the lower-class adolescents.

Maas (1951) has called attention to differential *styles* of participation related to socio-economic class. He finds lower-class boys and girls in clubs relating, with dependence or counter-dependence, mainly to the adult leader. Middle-class youngsters are more likely to ignore the appointed leader and to pay attention mainly to their peers.

Adult participation in community organizations is also differentiated by socio-economic class. Some organizations are intended for a specific class: trade unions are for workers; exclusive country clubs are for the select. Participation in these organizations leads to interaction with others of similar outlook, intensifies in-group solidarity, and deepens the psychological cleavages which separate social classes.

TABLE 6—CLASS STATUS OF SOME RELIGIOUS DENOMINATIONS

	Upper	*Percent in* Middle	Lower	Total
Atheists, agnostics	33%	47%	20%	100%
Congregational	24%	42%	34%	100%
Episcopal	24%	34%	42%	100%
Presbyterian	22%	40%	38%	100%
Jewish	22%	32%	46%	100%
Methodist	13%	36%	51%	100%
Lutheran	11%	33%	56%	100%
Roman Catholic	9%	25%	66%	100%
Baptist	8%	24%	68%	100%

Organizations which are intended to serve the whole community some-times turn out to attract participation from certain classes rather than others. In "Yankee City," 72 percent of the upper class belonged to some organization; 64 percent of the upper middle class; 39 percent of the lower middle, and only 22 percent of the lower class belonged to one or more. Control is definitely in the hands of the upper group. In Spring-field, Massachusetts, a study of social agencies showed that while only 3 percent of the population had income (in 1951) of $10,000 or over, 55 percent of the board members of these agencies came from this top economic group. While 59 percent of the families of the city had incomes under $3,500, this large group of citizens furnished only 4 percent of the board members of the agencies organized to serve the underprivileged (Vinter, 1957).

A fairly typical relationship of social class to community participation could be outlined as follows:

Upper-upper —Exclusive clubs, private planes, polo ponies, social contacts with others of their class in other cities.

Lower-upper —Rotary Club, Chamber of Commerce, important pol-icy-making positions on community boards.

Upper-middle—Other men's luncheon clubs, women's clubs; members of church boards and school boards.

Lower-middle—Churches, parent-teacher associations.

Upper-lower —Churches, trade unions.

Lower-lower —none.

In "Jonesville," a typical small Midwestern city, 77 percent of the upper class belonged to some church; only 28 percent of the lowest class were church-affiliated (Warner, 1949). A study (Federal Council of Churches, 1948) of the class distribution of various religious denomina-tions showed that, on a nationwide basis, some draw mainly from the lower strata; in others there are relatively more middle- and upper-class members.

Within a particular community some churches are known to be favored by the local aristocracy; others, like the Pentecostal store-front churches in large city neighborhoods, draw almost entirely from the lower class.

Social and political attitudes

Few generalizations in social psychology are so well supported by many kinds of evidence as the truth that "men who live differently think differently."

Attitudes of classes on social issues derive from an historic heritage. Immediate, realistic "interests" are sometimes obscured by loyalty to honored traditions. The frightful conditions under which men, women, and children worked in the early stage of the Industrial Revolution are familiar to students of English history. It helps to understand some working-class attitudes, today, to recall that in the needle trades in New England, in the early days women working full time could earn only about $60 in an entire year. In the shoe industry in Massachusetts, 15,000 women were employed at wages from 8 cents to 50 cents a day. Debtors were still being sent to prison. In 1832, 40 percent of the workers employed in Massachusetts factories were children under 16 years of age. In those days it was a "criminal conspiracy" to organize a trade union. After the organizers had been convicted in Pittsburgh in 1814, the local newspaper triumphantly announced: "It puts an end to those associations which have been so prejudicial to the successful enterprise of the capitalists." When the Master Carpenters in Boston began their struggle to win a ten-hour day, the employers published a statement declaring: "We cannot believe this project to have originated with any of the faithful and industrious sons of New England, but are compelled to consider it an evil of foreign growth and one which we hope and trust will not take root in the favoured soil of Massachusetts." To cut the working week to 60 hours, the employers believed, would encourage idleness, dissipation, and vice.

A generation later when labor organization was gaining momentum, it was met with wage cuts, blacklisting of leaders, riots, and court injunctions. The labor movement has had its heroes, some glorified in song, like Joe Hill, many more unsung: Terence Powderly, Mother Jones, George Henry Evans, or Eugene Debs. They seldom appear in our school history texts.

The particular issues which divide the opinions of the employing class and those of the working class have changed with time, but there are underlying attitudes which persist. The right of workers to organize, maintain, and develop unions is one such issue. On the question: "Would you agree that everybody would be happier, more secure, and more prosperous if the working people were given more power and influence in government?" 31 percent of the middle-class business, professional, and white collar workers said "yes," while 64 percent of the working-class manual workers said "yes." The view that factory workers do not get enough pay was found twice as often (37 percent) among the urban workers as among the urban middle class (18 percent) (Centers, 1949). In another poll (Kornhauser, 1939) the highest of four income groups included 28 percent who "favor strong labor unions." As income went down, this proportion rose to 84 percent in the lowest income group.

In general, organizations of the working class are in favor of public support for better housing, better schools, better health, and community recreational facilities. In 1829 the establishment of public schools headed the list of reforms urged by the Workingmen's Party of Philadelphia. Five years later, the unions of The United States of America in their convention demanded an "equal, universal, republican system of education." The following year they urged free public libraries and infant schools. Social security legislation was strongly supported by labor organizations.

Opposition to taxation is greater at upper income levels. A public opinion poll (American Institute of Public Opinion, January 9, 1940) asked a sample of citizens: "Do you consider the amount of income tax which you have to pay as too high or about right?" The complaint that the tax was too high was made by 48 percent of those paying less than $50 per year; the proportion of objection increased steadily as the tax grew larger, reaching 71 percent for those paying $500 or more. Because of sales taxes, the poor may actually pay a larger proportion of their income in taxes than do most rich families (Miller, Rien, 1964).

The main target of disfavor in American society is the lower-lower class. These chronic economic failures are seen as shiftless, dirty, lazy, irresponsible, and immoral. Sensational stories about relief recipients who wear mink coats or live in comfortable hotels arouse widespread indignation; subsequent correction of misleading stories is rarely reported. Proposals that men on relief should be forced to take any kind of job, however distressing the conditions, if it pays a minimum wage, have had almost unanimous public support (American Institute of Public Opinion, Jan. 24, 1965). A majority of the people have supported the view that unwed mothers who continue to have children should be punished by withdrawal of their relief payments (A.I.P.O., Jan. 27, 1965).

Questioned on the "major cause of poverty," most Americans with incomes of $7,000 a year or more answer: "lack of effort." The poor, however (those with incomes under $3,000 a year), reply: "circumstances beyond our control" (A.I.P.O., Dec. 16, 1964).

A particularly interesting study (Jones, 1941) examined attitudes of citizens in a mid-Western manufacturing city shortly after the Congress of Industrial Organizations (CIO) had been organized during the 1930's.

TABLE 7—ATTITUDES TOWARD PROPERTY RIGHTS

Score Interval	*Percent of Responses*	
	C. of C.	CIO Leaders
24–32 (Strongest for property rights)	94%	5%
16–23 (More weight for property rights)	6%	11%
8–15 (More weight to humanitarian sympathy)	0	29%
0– 7 (Strongest for humanitarian sympathy)	0	55%
	100%	100%

The median position of several occupational groups was:

Chamber of Commerce	29
Farmers	20
Chemists	18
Teachers	16
Small merchants	12
Ministers	12
AFL leaders	8
CIO leaders	6

A series of situations—foreclosure on the mortgage of a poor farmer, eviction of impoverished unemployed tenants—was followed by a choice of whether to uphold traditional property rights or whether to disregard these in favor of humanitarian principles. Table 7 shows the distribution of answers from spokesmen of the business class (Chamber of Commerce) and of the laboring class (CIO).

It is interesting to note that labor leaders were less uniform in outlook than were the business leaders. One reason may be that the press and radio quite consistently supported the business viewpoint. Businessmen thus experienced total support; labor representatives were exposed to counter pressures from the mass media.

Political support in democratic countries tends to be organized along class lines. In Britain, Mark Abrams reports that three-quarters of the middle class vote Conservative, while two-thirds of the working class vote Labour. The New Deal of Franklin D. Roosevelt had the support, in the mid-thirties, of only about 25 percent of the upper-income groups, but of 75 percent of the union members. President Lyndon B. Johnson's War on Poverty, a generation later, has the support of people in the lower income groups. Republicans in comfortable circumstances have been likely to argue that poverty is due simply to laziness and lack of effort by the individuals so afflicted. A Gallup poll (March 22, 1964) showed two-thirds of Republicans holding this view.

Because working-class groups are strong on human sympathy and inherit a long tradition of fighting injustice, they are more prone to support drastic social reforms. Centers (1944) combined replies from questions on government ownership of industry, social security, satisfaction (or rather, dissatisfaction) with America as it is, more power for workers, and identification with workers in strikes to give an index of general "radicalism." The proportion of "radicals" among big business officials was 2 percent; among white collar workers 5 percent; among farmers 7 percent; among skilled manual workers 10 percent, and among the semiskilled or unskilled 19 percent. On issues which might admit out-groups to share in their privileges, trade unions have been divided. While some pioneered in outlawing racial discrimination, others have strongly resisted opening their ranks to Negroes. Few labor organizations have been active on behalf of women's rights, and some craft unions have restricted apprenticeships to relatives of present members.

Lipset (1959) has examined the political attitudes of socio-economic classes in several nations. In Germany, in 1953, for example, only about 10 percent of the middle classes and professionals favored a one-party system, but the lower level of the working class showed 25–30 percent in favor of a single party corresponding to their own ideas. More lower-class than upper-class citizens in almost every underprivileged nation lean toward Communism. Lipset argues that higher authoritarianism in lower-class citizens arises because the lower-class child typically gets more punishment, less love, and indulgence, is exposed to more quarreling at home, and so starts with a chip on his shoulder. The hostility is intensified by frustration in school and living under conditions clearly worse than those he sees others enjoying. "All of these characteristics combine to produce a tendency to view politics, as well as personal relationships, in black-and-white terms, a desire for immediate action without critical reflection, impatience with talk and discussion, lack of interest in organizations which have a long-range gradualistic political perspective, and a readiness to follow leaders who offer a demonological interpretation of the presumably conspiratorial forces." (P. 495–6)

The most privileged classes, used to the exercising of power to work their own will, are also inclined to be impatient with democratic processes. In the early nineteenth century, de Tocqueville saw the more affluent classes with "a hearty dislike of democratic institutions," but a need to conceal their real feelings. It was the evil genius of Hitler in the 1930's that he could mobilize the secret support of the wealthy elements and the overt impatience of the frustrated to overthrow democratic institutions. Similar patterns can be observed in right-wing authoritarianism in Latin America and Asia exploiting, as Hitler did, "anti-Communism" as a rallying cry for establishing military and financial dictatorships.

Whenever a society is stratified, members come to think of themselves as having characteristics attributed to their class. This internalizing of the norms of the culture, however prejudicial, gives kings a royal air and slaves a servile mentality. The shaping of self-concepts by the class system is one of its most serious consequences. The ruling group feel that their virtue and ability correspond to their position of power. The lower classes are often low also in self-esteem. Psychologists sometimes refer to this kind of stereotype as a "halo effect." The point we are making now is that the upper-class children come to believe that they deserve these halos; the lower-class children also accept a view of themselves as dull, dirty, and disorderly. An experiment (Harvey, 1953) in which adolescents estimated how well they would perform in throwing darts at a target showed that those who had high status with their peers were expected to do better than average; they also overestimated their own performance. The correlation was even more marked in groups of lower socio-economic status. The boys with low standing were not expected to perform well, and they thought they were doing less well than they objectively did. We shall meet this phenomenon of internalization of inferiority feelings again in the chapters that examine race prejudice and sex prejudice.

Class differences in values

David Riesman has characterized the working class as oriented to present needs and satisfactions; the middle class as centering its attention on the future and sacrificing present satisfactions for the hope of things to come; the upper class as trying to preserve its prestige and traditions out of the past. In another sense, however, the lack of contact between lower-class adults and the currents of thought expressed in colleges, serious magazines, and lectures and discussions of ideas means that these disadvantaged citizens are apt to hold fast to the views and values passed on by word of mouth from earlier generations. Thus a study in Michigan (Lehmann, 1960) showed that college students whose parents had only elementary schooling were more rigid, dogmatic, traditional, and authoritarian in attitude than were students whose parents had gone to college.

In empirical study of statements differentiating junior high school pupils by social class (Phillips, 1950) the following opinions were reported:

Differentiating upper-class youngsters
"Really nice people don't associate with just anybody."

"Marrying a person of your own social rank is very important."

"It makes a difference to your parents whether your friends come from good families or not."

"You can try a lot of things to make people respectable but you can't make up for poor family background and training."

"Some of the most popular people at school are my close friends."

Differentiating middle-class youngsters

"You should finish college because graduation from high school isn't much of a start."

"The world is all mixed up today because people are not religious enough."

"Those young people who are most popular with the opposite sex frequently are not such nice persons."

"Families need to stay in one place; moving often from one city to another is bad."

"People should take an interest in magazines which deal with community government and social problems."

Differentiating lower-class youngsters

"Almost any boy swipes a few things now and then."

"The boys and girls who like school most are usually sissies or teacher's pets."

"If you always live as you are supposed to, you lay yourself open for others to take advantage of you."

"Most people will learn more by working four years than by going to school for four years."

"Everybody should get married and have a family as soon as possible."

It is clear that the upper-class attitudes reflect exclusiveness; the middle-class values traditional Puritanism and upward-striving; the lower class places a small value on school and property rights.

A study (McArthur, 1955) of Harvard freshmen coming from select private schools (presumably upper class) as compared with those from public high schools (more middle class) was based on analysis of their made-up story responses to TAT pictures. Upper-class boys were more likely to talk of fathers, reflecting pride in lineal heritage. Middle-class boys were more inclined to envision a mother as holding up standards for her child. A picture of a boy with a violin was more likely to mean "sissy" to the middle-class students.

Rosen (1956) used the TAT pictures to differentiate responses of lower-class and middle-class high school boys. The latter more often brought out the achievement-motivation theme. They more often thought of the hero as striving for excellence or to rise or to excel.

Another study using projective techniques with a small sample showed "normal" boys from working-class homes more attached to parents, but at the same time the study showed them to be more often rejected and overprotected than in the upper classes (Lane, Singer, 1959). A further comparison of normal with schizophrenic young men showed that the psychotic differed from the normal in much the same way that the lower-class normals differed from the middle-class normals.

In another kind of study Walker (1958) asked students to select, out of a list of 112 adjectives, those which applied to the persons in each

TABLE 8—STEREOTYPES OF OCCUPATIONS

Occupation	Five terms most frequently applied
Factory owner	ambitious, practical, industrious, efficient, progressive
Doctor	intelligent, efficient, well educated, humanitarian, practical
School teacher	well educated, intelligent, fair-minded, tolerant, friendly
Factory worker	friendly, cooperative, honest, initiative, efficient
Coal miner	rough, tough, friendly, honest, industrious

of several occupations. There was considerable agreement: Twelve adjectives, on the average, covered 50 percent of the terms chosen to fit any given occupation. The top five terms describing the stereotype for several occupations are shown in Table 8.

The term most often applied to the entrepreneur was "ambitious;" the terms with highest frequency for the proletarians were "friendly" and "rough."

Most studies of delinquency show high rates in the lower-class sections. Here, as Merton (1949) has observed, people accept as desirable our material goods but see themselves as handicapped in ever attaining their ends by fair means. Yet, as Sutherland (1940) has made clear, financial losses due to upper-class crimes (embezzlement, tax evasion, collusive bidding, stock manipulation) far exceed the costs of holdups and burglaries.

One of the sentiments which seems more evident in the working class is solidarity. Poor families help their neighbors because they remember their own need and realize that misfortune may strike them next. One report (Davis, *et al.*, 1941) tells how lower-class brothers and sisters expect to turn to one another for help. Another (Useem, 1942) finds in "Prairietown" that "mutual aid is far more common among the low-status people." An interesting illustration of the same tendency is found in W. F. Whyte's 1943 comparison of two street-corner gangs in an Eastern city (Abstract 7). Chick led a group of ambitious boys who looked forward to college. They participated in the uplifting activities of the local settlement house. Doc's "corner boys" had no use for the social agency. "Everybody that goes there thinks they're a little better than the next fellow."

Doc said: "Chick would step on the neck of his best friend if he could get a better job by doing it. . . . I would never do that, Bill. I would never step on Danny even if I could get myself a $50-a-week job by doing it. None of my boys would do that."

Another time he said: "I suppose my boys have kept me from getting ahead. . . . But if I were to start over again—if God said to me, 'Look here, Doc, you can pick out your friends in advance,' still I would make sure my boys were among them—even if I could pick Rockefeller and Carnegie!"

Studies of job choices show that "a chance to rise" is very important for middle-class applicants, but congenial relations with fellow workers rate higher with factory and clerical operatives.

A study (Stephenson, 1957) of the jobs to which ninth graders aspire distinguished between their actual plans and their wishes "if things were different." For pupils from upper-class homes this distinction was not too important. About 80 percent wanted to go into Class I (highest) or Class II occupations and about 80 percent really planned to do so. Lower-class students (whose fathers worked at jobs in Class V or Class VI (lowest) did not usually aspire to continue on the same level. Less than 10 percent would choose such jobs; but about 20 percent were making plans to enter work in the Class V or Class VI category. More (about 60 percent) aspired to Class I or Class II occupations, but when they were asked to be realistic less than 20 percent felt they could make plans to do so. The results indicate that nearly half the youths from lower levels were already aware that their work would not correspond to their desires; others will be disillusioned later.

For the ordinary worker, a secure job is valued more than one with risk but chance for advancement. In Centers' study (1949) twice as many workers as middle-class adults expressed preference for "a job which you were absolutely sure of keeping;" almost twice as many middle-class as working-class adults voted for "a job where you could express your feelings, ideas, talent or skill."

Another investigation (Chant, 1932) showed that the primary reason given by white collar workers for preferring a job is "opportunity for advancement;" among factory workers this ranked in sixth place. The top demands for blue-collar workers were: (1) security; (2) comfortable working conditions; and (3) pleasant working companions.

The emphasis upon security is natural and almost inevitable in the many millions of American families who live close to the borderline of subsistence and who have no savings.

Insecurity haunts the masses of workers even in normal times, but during prolonged unemployment it is intensified and spreads through other classes. Insecurity is usually the first significant consequence of the loss of one's job. This insecurity arises and grips the individual even though he may realize that his unemployment is no fault of his own. He tends to feel guilty about his unemployment as Young (1952) points out, and to develop a sense of individual inferiority, as if his plight were due to some individual defect or limitation. The fact that it may be society's and not his fault does not extenuate his sense of inadequacy. The sense of insecurity spreads quickly to members of his family, and his fears are proportionally intensified. Not infrequently his family may blame him for the loss of his job and be impatient with his failure to find another one quickly. While he is unemployed, he still has to eat, have a coat on his back, and a roof over his head. Bills accumulate and creditors become more persistent. His fears increase and he contemplates the future fearfully. He has been deprived of one of the strongest props to security and self-esteem." (Bonner, 1953, p. 312)

Religious values find different expression in different social classes. We noted earlier (in Table 7) a greater proportion of atheists and agnostics in the upper class. At the same time, however, upper-class spokesmen strongly support religious institutions in the community. A public opinion study in Britain showed that 70 percent of the "wealthy and prosperous" advocated more religious education in the schools, while only 54 percent of the "poor" agreed with this view (*Opinion News*, 1945). If religion were, as Karl Marx once said, "the opium of the people" the privileged classes might well favor its administration to diminish agitation for change.

Class struggle

Another important class difference is reflected in attitudes toward fighting. Aggressive physical action is more common among adults in lower-class homes, and fighting is a normal peer-group activity for both boys and girls in lower-class neighborhoods. As they grow up, youths learn from their unions that labor has always had to fight against odds for every gain in wages, hours, and working conditions. An observer of the reactions of clergymen in Little Rock, Arkansas, in 1958 to the struggle over desegregation in the public high school found only eight ministers who were taking forceful, aggressive stands for the change. All were connected with small working-class churches.

Members of the upper and dominant class may be equally ruthless, but they operate in a different fashion. They do not hurl brickbats in the street; they may quietly buy up notes or mortgages which can be foreclosed; they acquire proxies to gain control; they launch powerful advertising or public relations programs; they agree to squeeze out competitors or to finance political campaigns against their opponents.

The helpless attitude of the middle class—especially the new, white-collar middle class—has been described by Mills.

The white-collar people slipped quietly into modern society. Whatever history they have had is a history without events; whatever common interests they have do not lead to unity; whatever future they have will not be of their own making. If they aspire at all, it is to a middle course, at a time when no middle course is available. . . .

The big businessman continues his big-business as usual through the normal rhythm of slump and war and boom; the big labor man, lifting his shaggy eyebrows, holds up the nation until his demands are met. . . . But not the white-collar man. He is more often pitiful than tragic . . . living out in slow misery his yearning for the quick American climb. He is pushed by forces beyond his control, pulled into movement he does not understand. . . . The white-collar man is the hero as victim, the small creature who is acted upon but does not act, who works along unnoticed in somebody's office or store, never talking aloud, never talking back, never taking a stand." (Mills, 1951 pp. 11, 12)

Life-chances vary with class

Near the beginning of this chapter we observed that while Americans like to believe that everyone in this country is given approximately equal opportunity, this belief may not fit the facts. Consider, as an extreme example, the migratory agricultural workers whom *Time* magazine (Aug. 8, 1960, p. 66) described as a "national disgrace." Their income (1958) averaged about $960 a year. They have no unions, no minimum-wage protection; they do not vote. A child of eight or nine may spend all day working in the fields; school attendance is sporadic and desultory. The probability is that the children will be malnourished and virtually illiterate.

Opportunity to be born into a family which welcomes the baby is greater in middle and upper classes which are more likely to practice family planning. The kind of house, furnishings, and neighborhood are all factors clearly related to social class. Success and popularity in school depend to a surprising extent upon social class. The vocabulary children acquire and the topics on which they are informed vary, as a rule, with the class position.

Health problems are more prevalent at lower socio-economic levels. Even within the working class, those lower in status are more likely to suffer from ulcers (Vertin, 1954). Arteriosclerosis and coronary disease were most prevalent among rank-and-file workers in industrial organizations; frequency of such illness decreased as status in the hierarchy rose (Lee, Schneider, 1958; Pell, D'Alonzo, 1961). Frequency of illness in a large public utility was consistently related to status in the organization (Kasl, French, 1962). Men who received promotions achieved better health records; those demoted had increased sickness (French, 1963).

An assessment of mental health of automobile factory workers (Kornhauser, 1962), based on intensive interviews with the men and their wives, showed large differences *within* this working-class sample. Skilled workmen were found usually (57 percent) to be in a healthy emotional condition, but among the men with repetitive, assembly-line jobs only 10–15 percent were rated as in good mental health. Problems in adjustment increased as one moved down the scale from more responsible jobs to those with low pay, little security, low status, repetitive tasks, and little chance for promotion.

The educational handicaps of lower-class children have been described earlier. The best schools have been in the best neighborhoods. Within the school the class structure of the community may be extended, with upper-class children headed for Ivy League colleges; middle-class children going to state colleges; lower-class children taking commercial or trade training or dropping out. When children leave school, the lower-class dropouts are likely to remain unemployed or to find only dead-end jobs.

Small wonder then, if strains, tensions, discouragement, and resentment become chronic in lower-class populations! The results in terms of unhappiness and personality maladjustment are apparent in the following two abstracts. Bradburn's study shows less happiness and more anxiety in the low-income group and in the economically depressed community. The Hollingshead and Redlich book is particularly striking because it reveals that the prevalence of insanity (psychoses) increases with each step down the class scale and that psychoanalytic therapy is seldom available for the lower-class patients.

Lower-class members are particularly likely to show what social psychologists call *anomie* (Durkheim, 1897; Srole, 1951), meaning a sense that they do not share in the norms of society. The mean level of anomie in a small city in New York State rose from 0.5 in the highest socio-economic class to 2.4 in the lowest (Mizruchi, 1960). A poll on "satisfaction" with income, housing, work, and education of their children showed 78 percent of whites satisfied, but only 38 percent of Negroes (American Institute of Public Opinion, 1965).

As sociological and psychological studies have focused increasing attention on the handicaps faced by youth from lower-class homes and surroundings, conditions have begun to change. Cloward (1965) has challenged what he terms the social agencies "disengagement from the poor." Harrington (1963) has written of *The Other America,* poverty off the beaten track and often invisible to the public. "I discovered this personally in a curious way. After I wrote my first article on poverty in America, I had all the statistics down on paper. I had proved to my satisfaction that there were around 50 million poor in this country. Yet, I realized I did not believe my own figures. The poor existed in the Government reports . . . . but they were not part of my experience. I could prove that the other America existed, but I had never been there." The Federally supported Anti-Poverty program, launched in 1964, has initiated projects of research and service in the interests of lower-class groups which have been long ignored. It is not over-optimistic to expect that life-chances for disadvantaged youth will improve substantially during the next ten years.

Abstract 40

TITLE In Pursuit of Happiness

AUTHOR Norman M. Bradburn

PROBLEMS How happy and well adjusted are typical Americans? Is this dependent on the economic status of the individual?

SUBJECTS About 100 men, age 25 to 49, in each of four towns in Illinois. Two towns are badly depressed economically, another has shown recent improvement, and the fourth has been consistently prosperous. A short form was administered to 516 more men and to 1,097 women.

PROCEDURE Interviews, guided by a schedule.

SOME FINDINGS
1. Of the 2,006 respondents, 24 percent reported that they were "very happy"; 59 percent said "pretty happy" and only 17 percent said "not too happy."
2. The percent of "not too happy" replies increased with age, reaching 27 percent for those over 60.
3. The percent of "not too happy" was greatest in those with least education; 25 percent for those with eighth grade or less.
4. The percent of "not too happy" was greatest in the lowest income group (31 percent for those with less than $3,000 a year) and decreased steadily as income rose (only 7 percent, for those over $8,000).
5. The percent of "not too happy" was highest for the widowed (about 40 percent); next highest for the divorced or separated (about 30 percent); lower for the single (about 25 percent) and lowest among the married (about 12 percent).
6. Among those men presently unemployed, 33 percent were "not too happy" as against 12 percent for the currently employed and 9 percent for the self-employed.
7. On an anxiety index (referring to such symptoms as nervousness, aches and pains, dizziness, headaches, twitching, and rapid heart beat), 51 percent of the low-income group (under $3,000) scored high, whereas only 34 percent of the high-income group ($10,000 or over) had similarly high anxiety scores.
8. Overall satisfaction with their job was correlated (employed men only) .80 with wage-satisfaction, .77 with liking the employer; and .70 with liking the kind of work. Those low on job satisfaction were particularly likely to wish they had chosen another line of work (32 percent of the lows; 8 percent of the others) and to feel (79 percent) that the job did not use all their abilities. Job satisfaction was more closely related to general happiness among married, employed men, than was absence of marital tension.
9. In the community which was most prosperous and in the one where conditions were improving, 13 percent rated themselves as "not too happy"; 20 percent did so in the depressed areas. Men who said they "worry

Abstract 40—*Continued*

a lot," made up 19 percent of those from the prosperous region and 29 percent of those from depressed areas. The relationship of happiness to community prosperity was *not* found in persons of higher socio-economic status. In the prosperous town, 14 percent of upper class ($5,000 or more, high school grad or more, white-collar job) people were unhappy, as compared with 11 per cent of upper-class people ratting themselves as unhappy in the depressed area.

10. Marital tension was reportedly high for 54 percent of the married men under 50 years of age in the prosperous community as compared with 41 percent of the same group in the depressed areas.

SOURCE: Chicago: University of Chicago, National Opinion Research Center, 1963

Vertical mobility

The question remains: How fixed is class position? Can individuals not rise or fall in socio-economic status? Many Americans have been brought up on the "Log-cabin to White House" or "Office boy to President of the Company" theme. Such cases occur but rarely affect the life-chances of most people.

A poll of a national sample (Natl. Opin. Res. Center, 1947) showed that about 40 percent of the business and professional men were sons of business or professional men. Only about 13 percent came from occupations ranking below skilled labor. A similar proportion had moved down in one generation from business or professional fathers to semi-skilled, service, and labor occupations. Another study (Centers, 1948) concluded that 71 percent of fathers had sons not more than one step removed on his seven-step scale of occupations. In "Jonesville" (McGuire, 1950) three of the four upper-class adults came from upper-class families and the other from an upper middle-class level. No one moved from lower-lower class to upper-middle or upper class. No one moved down from upper-middle or upper class to the lower-lower.

The route by which men rise to high positions has been altered during the twentieth century. In earlier days, a factory workman might become foreman, then supervisor, and rise eventually to a high management position. Lynd, in his studies of Middletown (1937), noted that the step up from foreman to an executive position had become harder, even by 1935. More and more often, the supervisors of production, sales, accounting, and personnel were brought in from colleges and technical schools, not from the workbench.

A study of the "Establishment" in England included cabinet ministers, directors of the big banks, prelates of the Church of England, and other elite. "Between one-quarter and one-third of the persons in the

Abstract 41

TITLE   Social Class and Mental Illness: A Community Study

AUTHORS   August B. Hollingshead and Fredrick C. Redlich

PROBLEM   Is mental illness related to class in our society? Does a patient's position in the status system affect how he is treated for his illness?

SUBJECTS   The community of New Haven, Connecticut.

PROCEDURE   New Haven residents under psychiatric care were located and sociological and psychiatric data about them were obtained. A community census (5 percent sample) was taken for comparison. Subjects were stratified according to Hollingshead's Index of Social Position (ecological area of residence, occupation and education).

SOME FINDINGS   1. Psychiatric illness increased from 553 per 100,000 in upper classes (I, II) to 1668 per 100,000 in Class V.

2. Most problems in upper-class circles were called neurotic 65 percent) rather than psychotic; in Class V they were 90 percent psychotic.

3. Psychotherapy had been given to 98 percent of the upper-class neurotic patients but to only 67 percent of those in Class V. Custodial care was the principal treatment for 23 percent of the Class V neurotics, but for none from Classes I–II.

4. Schizophrenics from the upper class received psychotherapy in 52 percent of the cases; among the lowest class only 9 percent were treated.

5. Mean expenditure per patient was $1,450 per year for patients from Class V; $3,487 for patients from Classes I–II.

SOURCE: New York: John Wiley and Sons, 1958.

Establishment went to Eton; about two-thirds attended one of the six high ranking private boarding schools. More than 70 percent went to either Oxford or Cambridge" (*New York Times*, Feb. 1, 1959, p. 8). Family relationships in the Establishment were evident in the old aristocratic names. One family linked the Prime Minister and the Duke of Devonshire. Another linked two cabinet members and the Director of the Bank of England.

Is mobility in America increasing? Has the great increase in high school and college attendance improved the chances of youth to rise to upper classes? A study (Taussig, Joslyn, 1932) of 15,000 business leaders (in the late 1920's) showed that among the older men (60 and over) 28 percent had fathers who had been laborers or farmers; among the younger men (under 40) only 17 percent had fathers from the manual labor category.

Data from Indianapolis (Rogoff, 1953) showed that 30 percent of upper- and upper-middle-class groups (professional, proprietors, managers, and officials) had sons who in 1910 had reached the same category. In 1940, the proportion was 29 percent. No increase in mobility into this favored group could be seen over a generation. At the working-class end of the scale, the proportion of skilled, semiskilled, and unskilled workers whose sons remained in one of these same categories was 75 percent in 1910 and 67 percent in 1940. The proportion of sons of workers who achieved some professional or managerial status was 16 percent in 1910 and 19 percent in 1940. Another comparison based on over 8,000 business leaders (Warner, Abegglen, 1955) showed that, in 1928, 71 percent had had fathers who were executives, owners of business, or professional men; in 1952, the comparable figure was 68 percent.

Barber (1957) after reviewing these and other comparative studies concludes: "There seems to have been no fundamental change in the amount of mobility in the United States over the last hundred years" (p. 431). Even if most young people continue schooling beyond high school, class status of the family may well determine whether the better educated youth becomes a vice president or a truck driver. The upper-class young man may well find a spot in his father's business; if not, he is well accepted by the scions of other important families, and his father knows their fathers. He may start "at the bottom of the ladder" as a token concession, but he is no ordinary workman. He usually moves quickly to top positions.

The upper-class girl has her debut at which she is introduced socially to the young men (and their families) who can offer the most in the way of social prestige and wealth. There may be an occasional elopement with a family chauffeur and a serving maid may marry the son of her millionaire employer. The Cinderella theme, however, while romantically appealing represents less than one case in a thousand. Young people from families of high privilege usually set up homes of high privilege; the sons and daughters of working-class families usually establish the kind of homes in which they themselves grew up.

Class prejudice

We turn, in the next chapter, to the dramatic changes taking place in race relations. Before concluding the discussion of socio-economic class, we need to recognize that much of what is regarded as race prejudice may actually be prejudice against a lower class. Middle-class people may object to Negro neighbors or to Negro children in their formerly all-white school, not primarily because of skin color, but because they fear that these "intruders" will bring what they envisage as lower-class habits of cleanliness, lower-class health problems, and lower-class standards of conduct. The class barrier in such cases is the real problem. Integration across class lines within one race is sometimes more difficult than is integration of different races within the same socio-economic class. The hostility—overt or hidden—of lower classes toward upper classes can be quite as virulent as that of Negroes toward whites.

CHAPTER ELEVEN

Race and ethnic barriers in psychological relationships

Introduction

Ethnocentrism

A familiar human trait is identification with some in-group and corresponding rejection of certain out-groups. Children quickly learn the difference between "our family" (or clan or tribe) and others. A parallel instinct is apparent in pets and domestic animals when they show a similar devotion to the household or farmyard in which they belong and feel at home.

As children grow older, they identify with a certain gang or clique which may stand in opposition to a well-recognized rival or enemy group. Religious affiliation may lead to a view that the people who attend our place of worship are the "right" kind—those who worship elsewhere or not at all are looked down upon. In school loyalty, manifested in pep rallies, school songs, and cheering sections, we assert that Alma Mater is better than any other school and far superior to its closest rivals. National patriotism is one of the most intense manifestations of in-group solidarity. Many people grow up to believe categorically that it would be better to die than to live under a rival government. The technical term for the feeling that the group in which we have been brought up is right and admirable while outsiders are wrong and despicable is *ethnocentrism*. In this chapter we shall be concerned with the psychology of ethnocentrism as it relates to racial and other ethnic groups. In various parts of the United States, Negroes, Jews, Mexicans, Orientals, Indians, and French-speaking groups have been targets of discrimination and prejudice. In the history of various American communities, older and better established groups have looked down upon the Irish, Swedish, Germans (Dutch), Polish, Hungarians, Puerto Ricans, or other recent immigrants. Quakers, Catholics, Jews, Mennonites, Mormons, and other religious groups have been attacked by hostile neighbors. In other parts of the world, also, majority groups have imposed limitations upon the opportunities of minorities who are rejected because of differences in physical characteristics, religion, language, or ancestry. Ethnocentrism is the principal barrier to the practice of the brotherhood of man.

Meaning of race

"Race" is a general term popularly applied to any large group of persons thought of as belonging together because of pigmentation, hairtype, shape of eyes or other physical features. Often the term is used more loosely and broadly to apply to nationalities or language or culture groups. Anthropologists, concerned with the scientific study of man, have reached no agreement on the significant dimensions of race or the number of human races. Common physical characteristics that are due to common heredity are the focus of definition. Some systems of classification emphasize dimensions of the skull; others include: hair, shape of nose or lips, stature, and skin color. Some anthropologists recognize only three or four "races;" others categorize 30 or 40. A recent consensus of experts assembled by the United Nations Educational, Scientific, and Cultural Organization (UNESCO) agreed on only three broad racial types: Mongoloid (yellow), Negroid (black), and Caucasoid (white). One of the better known classifications is that of Blumenbach, who, in 1865, wrote of the Causasian (white), Mongolian (yellow), Ethiopian (black), American (red), and Malayan (brown). Blumenbach and all later anthropologists agree, however, that no hard-and-fast lines can be drawn. With every racial trait, there is wide variation within any race and some overlap with other races. Differences are not absolute but vary in degree and in statistical probability. Human beings all belong within one species.

Mention should be made of some common misconceptions. One relates to "blood." Human blood is classified in four types, but each type is found among all races. No blood differences correspond to what is known as "race." The misunderstanding rests on a confusion of blood with the mechanism of heredity. "Pure blood" does not refer literally to blood but to genetic similarity. A "pure" strain is inbred and has many genes in common. Identical twins would be the "purest" case. Isolated Arctic or mountain tribes, long in-bred, would have much ancestry in common and should therefore be relatively "pure." Most of mankind in every race comes from a wide diversity of ancestral types, often transcending accepted lines of race. Neither science nor any great religion teaches that mankind originated as separate races.

Another misconception is the confusion of cultural with biological differences. Men who differ in language, religion, education, artistic taste, patterns of kinship, technology, and nationality are distinguished by cultural rather than innate traits. These are "ethnic," not biological differences. They relate to what has been learned rather than to what has been inherited. If a baby from a long line of Chinese ancestors were exchanged at birth with a baby from ten generations of a white New England family, and each were reared in the home of the other culture, the Chinese baby would retain his Mongolian physical appearance. However, he would speak English with a New England (not Chinese) accent, would probably attend a Congregational church, prefer the traditional foods of New England, play the games of American children, and think of himself and his nation as other American children do. The baby born in New England would grow up to share the language, dress, food, games, ways of thinking, arts, and politics of his adopted home. *Aryan* and *Semitic* are linguistic classifications and do not refer to anything racially inherited. "Jew," like "Catholic," should properly refer to a religious group, although individual members may or may not take their religion seriously. "Hebrew" is a language.

Racial differences

Whenever two races live together with important differences in economic, political, or cultural status, differences become apparent in the standard of living and intellectual and personality characteristics of the dominant and subordinate groups. The observed differences are often attributed to race. Innate superiority is attributed to the dominant race; the subordinate race is considered inferior. Thus British officials who governed colonial peoples easily assumed that their superior status was justified by their God-given virtues as Englishmen. With intelligence tests based on school achievement, one can readily determine that typical Hindu Brahmins (the highest caste) score higher than outcast Hindus; that Dutch colonialists surpass the New Guinea natives; that Mexicans who are heirs of the Spanish conquest outclass the Indian peons. Such comparisons do not show, however, what the outcastes, the New Guinea natives, or the Indian peons would have achieved if they, like our imaginary Chinese and New England babies, had been transferred at birth to a culturally privileged home. Klineberg (1935) found that Negro children who moved from the country to the city or from the South to New York made marked gains in intelligence test scores. The longer that Negro children had lived in an educationally more favorable environment, the greater was their superiority to newcomers of their own age. Intelligence score differences of this kind must be regarded as cultural rather than racial in origin.

The conclusion is also supported by later studies. A vocabulary test given to Negroes in Boston showed, at every level of schooling completed, that Negroes educated in the North scored higher than those educated in the South (Pettigrew, 1964). Negro children of lower social class in New York showed average IQ's of 91; those of higher status had IQ's averaging 103 (Deutsch, Brown, 1964).

One complicating factor in any such testing program is the attitude of Negroes toward being examined by a white person. Many feel more hostility than they are able to express. "Got one mind for white folks to see, 'nother for what I know is me"—in the words of an old Negro folksong (Ames, 1950). Even two-year-old Negro children were less responsive to a white psychologist than to a Negro (Pasamanick, Knobloch, 1955). Negro college students expressed more anger over racially derogatory stereotypes when interviewed by a Negro than when the questioner was white (Whittaker, et al., 1952). Negro adults queried in public opinion polls expressed more hostility and gave more informed answers when the interviewer was Negro (Cantril, 1944; Price, Searles, 1961; Katz et al, 1964; Pettigrew, 1964). Is there a relationship between repressed anger and poor test performance? Apparently there is. When white students were subjected to treatment which aroused hostility, those who did not express it freely suffered more decrement in performing cognitive tasks which they were assigned shortly thereafter (Goldman, et al., 1954; Rosenwald, 1961).

Ethnic groups are also seen as embodying distinctive personality traits. A study (Katz, Braly, 1933; 1935) of the adjectives applied by more than half of 100 Princeton University undergraduates, in 1932, to each of ten "races," showed that Germans were thought of as "scientifically minded" and "industrious," Italians as "artistic," English as "sportsmanlike," Jews as "shrewd," Negroes as "superstitious" and "lazy," and

Turks as "cruel." Each of these adjectives was chosen by more than half of the students tested. The date of the study is important. Another investigator (Gilbert, 1951) repeated such a rating of ethnic groups by Princeton students in 1950 and found much less readiness to generalize about the traits of ethnic groups. A number protested that there were all kinds in every nationality group or that they knew only very few persons of certain nationalities. In 1950, no group was consistently characterized by specific traits by as many as 50 percent of the students.

One reason for the change is undoubtedly that the public is becoming more sophisticated. Persons who have traveled extensively abroad know that in every country there are bright people and simpletons, thieves and honest men, ascetics and profligates, the mean and the magnanimous, the gay and the depressed. Another factor that modifies stereotypes has been assimilation of minority groups in the United States. Early in the twentieth century, immigrants lived in close-knit colonies which retained the distinctive culture patterns of their homeland. Second- and third-generation descendants, however, live scattered among other American neighbors, go to the public schools with others in the community, see the same movies, and no longer perpetuate the old language, clothing, food habits, or social behavior. One significant study (Efron, 1941) showed that Italians living in New York's "Little Italy" used wide and sweeping lateral symbolic arm gestures; Jews living in Yiddish-speaking sections of Greater New York gestured characteristically with their hands, keeping their arms close to the body, and button-holing the listener. But assimilated Americans of Italian descent or Jewish Americans, moving in cosmopolitan circles, were indistinguishable from other Americans in speech or gesture patterns. The gestures did not represent innate ethnic traits but reflected different cultures and changed as the culture changed.

Many supposedly "racial" characteristics reflect, as explained at the close of the previous chapter, differences in socio-economic class. Klineberg (1954, p. 314) reports on tests measuring personality disturbance, values, persistence, suggestibility, and one form of honesty. The tests, Klineberg reports, showed no differences among New York City college students of Nordic, Jewish, Alpine, and Mediterranean types. There were, however, marked differences within each "racial" group between students from different socio-economic backgrounds. This confirms findings from the classical study by Hartshorne and May (1928) on children's honesty. In one school, Jewish children who had low IQ's, many of whom came from broken homes, cheated on about one-half of the tests. In another school, Jewish children came from good homes and had relatively high I.Q.'s. They cheated only on one test in five. Non-Jewish children cheated on one-third of similar tests. The parent's occupational level seems to influence how much the child will cheat. Children whose parents held jobs of the lowest status cheated most on tests: Scandinavians and Italians in one school, Negroes in another.

Chapter 9 has shown how typical personality patterns in each society reflect cultural differences in adult institutions and child rearing. No racial differences have emerged from studies to date which do not seem to be better accounted for by the cultural variants. All the available research leads to the conclusion that Mongols, Caucasians, Negroes, Indians, and Malayans under the same conditions, would develop similar patterns of response. If Italians differ in behavior from Norwegians, Jews from Irish, Chinese from American Negroes, the explanation probably lies in their respective cultural milieus, not in their racial genes.

The problem of prejudice

It is one thing to establish that there is no scientific basis for attributing superiority in intelligence, physique, or personality to one race or inferiority to another. It is quite another matter to understand and to cope with the *feelings* of superiority and inferiority which are attributed to race. Barriers have been historically and traditionally erected against the free participation of certain races in voting, in property ownership, in place of residence, in restaurants and lunch counters, in schooling, in the use of public facilities, and in access to positions of prestige. Some of these obstacles are vestiges of a time when one race was enslaved by another. The same kind of barriers, however, are found against minority groups that have never been enslaved. Probably the most flagrant persecution ever suffered by one ethnic group at the hands of another was the cruel mistreatment and genocide of millions of Jews by the Nazis. Clashes between Hindus and Moslems in India and Pakistan and between Israelis and Arabs in the Middle East threaten world peace. It has become urgently important today to find ways to reduce tension across the lines of race, religion, and ethnic groups.

Although prejudices against minority races in the United States have been diminishing, the problem remains acute. In 1938, Centers found that only 18 percent of a national sample agreed that "Negroes should have the same privileges and opportunities as white people." In 1945, Cantril (1946) found 21 percent who supported equal opportunity and privileges.

In the mid-1940's, Allport and Kramer (1946) estimated that four out of five Americans showed some hostility to out-groups. Another nationwide poll (*Fortune*, February 1946) showed that only 10 percent of the sample thought that Jews should be "getting a better break in this country than they are now" and only 34 percent who approved a better lot for Negroes. Although two-thirds of white Americans believe that Negroes are treated as well as whites in their communities, only one-fourth of Negroes agree (American Institute of Public Opinion, May 5, 1965). The charge that Jews have too much political power was believed by 21 percent and the view that Jews have more economic power than is good for the country was supported by 36 percent of respondents.

More recently, a nationwide poll of high school pupils showed that 66 percent believed some races inherently less capable than others; 37 percent objected to some races living in their neighborhood; and 46 percent opposed desegregated swimming pools (Mainer, 1954). Unqualified support for racially integrated schools was expressed by 41 percent of high school students in 1956; 52 percent in 1958; and 49 percent in 1960. At least 25 percent remained firmly opposed to desegregation in education (Remmers, 1963, p. 69). On the question: "Would you vote for a (Negro) (Catholic) (Jew) for President of the United States?" the percentages of adolescents who said they would reject a minority group member as a candidate were: Negro 77; Jew 65; Catholic 42 (Polls in 1960; Remmers, 1963, p. 100).

A poll comparing attitudes of adults in the North and in the South found less difference than is sometimes assumed. White people were asked: "Would you move if colored people came to live next door?" In the South, 62 percent said "yes;" in the North, 40 percent said "yes." When the proposition was made more extreme—not just one Negro family but a neighborhood with large numbers of colored people, the replies showed that 88 percent of Southern white and 77 percent of Northern white would want to move out (American Institute of Public Opinion, Oct. 17, 1958).

Negroes, of course, are clearly aware that their problem is not yet solved. More Negroes than whites reported dissatisfaction with their family income (62 percent compared with 30 percent); their work (33 percent vs. 7 percent); their housing (54 percent vs. 21 percent); their educational opportunities (45 percent vs. 24 percent); and their future prospects (42 percent vs. 22 percent) (American Institute of Public Opinion, Oct. 11, 1963). Myrdal's classic *An American Dilemma* (1944), a study of race relations and status, showed that the typical Negro wanted primarily economic opportunity and political equality and was not, as some segregationists had charged, so much concerned with social equality. A poll of Negroes in New York City (*New York Times,* July 27, 1964) showed that they considered their biggest problem economic —lack of jobs, low pay, high cost of living. Second among their grievances was poor, overcrowded housing with exorbitant rents. During the 1960's dissatisfaction found expression in numerous protests, sit-ins, marches, and other activities of the civil rights movement.

Prejudice limits the Negro's life-chances in almost every field. Only half the white Americans in a 1944 poll (National Opinion Research

Center, Oct. 22, 1944) were willing to see a Negro with equal training do the same kind of work the whites were doing at their places of work. If the question had concerned working under the supervision of a Negro with more ability, training, and experience, fewer would have been willing to accept the situation. The Bureau on Jewish Employment Problems reported a survey in 1956–57 showing that 20 percent of some 30,000 available white collar positions in Chicago were not open to a Jew, Catholic or person of some particular nationality; 98 percent of the employers would not consider a Negro or Oriental. In the wake of World War II, more than 40 percent of Americans polled were unwilling to grant to *loyal* Japanese-Americans the same opportunity as other people would have to get any kind of job. In another poll, half of the white Americans indicated objection to being cared for in a hospital by a Negro nurse (Hyman, Sheatsley, 1950).

Political handicaps have been evident in innumerable evasions of the clear intent of the Fourteenth and Fifteenth Amendments of the Constitution. Negroes wishing to vote have been turned away from the polls by many forms of trick and threat. Orientals in California have been denied American citizenship that was easily available to Europeans. One study (Hyman, Sheatsley, 1950) reported that half of the white Christian population in a large American city believed that no Jew should be allowed to hold a high public office. The relative acceptability of several special categories of citizen for the office of President was reported in a nationwide poll (Institute of Public Opinion, Oct. 26, 1958) employing the question: "If your party nominated a generally well qualified person for President, and he happened to be a (Baptist, Catholic, Jew, woman, Negro, atheist) would you vote for him?" A Baptist was acceptable to 92 percent; a Catholic to 68 percent; a Jew to 62 percent; a woman to 52 percent; a Negro to 38 percent; an atheist to only 18 percent. By 1965, with the enactment of a Civil Rights law, a repetition of some of the questions showed 87 percent who would accept a Catholic; 80 percent a Jew; but only 59 percent who would support a well qualified Negro for President (American Institute of Public Opinion, August 25, 1965).

One of the evidences of prejudice, and a factor in its perpetuation, has been the use of stereotypes in magazine stories, films, and television programs. A study in 1946 (Berelson, Salter) of 185 short stories in eight well known magazines showed that heroes and heroines were almost always Anglo-Saxon, but that unsavory characters, crooks, and villains tended to be foreigners. In 100 movies with Negro characters, 75 were disparaging and stereotyped. Awareness of such prejudices has probably brought about considerable improvement since the 1940's. Still, some villains speak now with Russian accents.

One of the most tragic consequences of prejudice is the miscarriage of justice. For nearly a century, "lynch law" was used "to keep the Negro in his place." The sad history has been well related by Raper (1933). Lynchings have been repudiated in every section of the United States today, but, in 1965, it was still impossible to obtain a conviction in the murder of civil rights leaders in some Southern states.

The problem of justice exists in the North as well as in the South. On January 9, 1924, James Montgomery, a Negro mechanic of Waukegan, Illinois, was sentenced to life imprisonment for rape. Prior to this, the prosecuting attorney, a white man named Ashbel V. Smith, had illegally raided Montgomery's home to seek evidence of bootlegging. There was no such evidence. Mr. Montgomery, believing in our American code of justice, sued for damages and won $125 in a civil suit. The affronted prosecutor swore: "I'll get you!" He did. The police chief in Waukegan threatened Mr. Montgomery with Ku Klux Klan retaliation if he attempted any legal defense to the rape charge. The alleged victim of the rape was a demented woman of 62; the doctors who examined her found she had never been assaulted; but all this evidence was suppressed. Owing to the interest of another white Illinois attorney, Luis Kutner, the case was re-opened in 1946 and Mr. Montgomery was set free after spending much of his life—from the ages of 31 to 54—in prison.

The concern of the American public about the issue of race relations is evident in an opinion poll (American Institute of Public Opinion, July 28, 1964) showing that when a cross-section of adults were asked: "What do you think is the most important problem facing the country today?", more answered "race relations" than mentioned international tensions, economic problems or any other concern.

Where prejudice exists, it distorts the perception of the observer and damages the self-image of the victim. The observer perceives what he expects to see. The experiment, cited in an earlier chapter, in which subjects recalled having seen a razor in the hands of a Negro, although in the actual picture, it was actually a white man who held it, is a pertinent case (Allport, Postman, 1945). It is hard to preserve self-esteem when others instantly treat one as inferior.

Discrimination and prejudice are rationalized by a society through myths which mislead both the majority and minority groups. As the Group for the Advancement of Psychiatry sees it:

> In terms of racial myths, the Negro is often depicted as little better than a savage animal, intellectually and morally inferior, childish and irresponsible, and supposedly unable to control allegedly excessive sexual and aggressive impulses. . . . The Negro person (in relation to white) should be fun-loving, improvident, deferential, deeply loyal, dependent, fearful toward whites, and capable of hard physical labor with little need for rest or relaxation. (In certain versions of the myth, this entails obligations on the part of the white

person analagous to caring for beloved pets or useful farm animals.) (G.A.P., 1957, pp. 17, 19)

Another aspect of the myth portrays the Negro male as sexually highly potent and especially attracted to white females. The myth conveniently ignores the fact that, historically, white men have fathered most of the mulattoes.

People who cherish anti-Negro myths are also likely to be anti-Semitic and against the out-group generally. One study (Himelhoch, 1952) found correlations from .50 to .80 between tests of prejudice against Negroes and of prejudice against Jews among white Protestants. Both kinds of prejudices were associated with a measure of political and economic conservatism. Remmers (1963) found positive correlations between rejection of a Negro candidate for office and rejection also of a Catholic ($r = .44$) or Jew ($r = .50$).

One of the noted anecdotes of social psychology tells of an experiment performed by Hartley (1946) using a Social Distance Test given to students at Columbia, Bennington, and Harvard University. Included, along with 32 ethnic groups, were three non-existent nationalities: "Danireans," "Pireneans," and "Wallonians." One student responded in a marginal note: "I don't know anything about them; therefore, I have no prejudice against them." But one of his classmates commented, "I don't know anything about them; therefore, I would exclude them from my country." In general, the students who rejected Chinese, Jews, Italians, labor union members, Negroes, Norwegians, or Yugoslavs also rejected the non-existent groups. The correlation between attitude toward the real ethnic groups and attitude toward the imaginary ones was .80. Apparently the responses had little to do with specifically named groups, but reflected mainly a general attitude toward "foreigners," or "outsiders." Later in this chapter we shall explore the personality dynamics which underly the generalized hostility.

Effects on Negro self-evaluation

First, we must consider the effects of discrimination and disparaging stereotypes upon the victim's conception of himself.

As the Negro child, for example, internalizes the myth which underlies the restrictions imposed on him in a white-dominated culture, he comes to think of himself as unintelligent, lazy, dirty, and of small worth to his community. An extraordinary demonstration of this tendency is found in a study by Kenneth and Mamie Clark, Negro psychologists (Abstract 42). Negro children, 3–7 years of age, had already come to feel that brown skin and black hair were somehow "bad," while fair skin, light hair, and blue eyes were "nice."

Abstract 42

TITLE Racial Identification and Preference in Negro Children

AUTHORS Kenneth B. Clark and Mamie P. Clark

PROBLEM How are self-concepts of Negro children influenced by the discrimination experienced in a culture dominated by whites?

SUBJECTS 134 Negro children in segregated schools in Arkansas in 1940; 119 Negro children in integrated schools in a Massachusetts city.

PROCEDURE Subjects were shown two brown dolls with black hair and two fair-skinned dolls with blonde hair. Then they were asked to give the experimenter the doll they liked best, the doll that is nice, the doll that looks bad, etc., including "the doll that looks like you."

SOME FINDINGS 1. At age 3, 61 percent of Negro children picked the white doll as the one that looked like them; the proportion dropped to 13 percent by age 7.

2. Northern children in integrated schools usually (69 percent) regarded the white doll as "nice" and (81 percent) the Negro doll as, "looks bad." Southern children, in segregated schools, showed the same tendency in somewhat less pronounced form; 53 percent of those who made a choice offered the white doll for "nice" and 75 percent offered the Negro doll for "looks bad."

SOURCE: Prepared by the authors for inclusion in *Readings in Social Psychology;* edited by E. Macoby, T. M. Newcomb, and E. L. Hartley. New York: Holt, 1958. pp. 602–611

The conclusions from the Clark study have been confirmed in several replications and modified research projects (Clark, 1950; Goodman, 1952; Trager, Yarrow, 1952; Morland, 1958; Stevenson, Stewart, 1958). Children as young as three years of age are aware of identification as white or Negro and have been found to be a little ashamed or defensive about being Negro. For example, Morland reports a four-year-old Negro boy in Virginia who, when asked if he were white or colored, hung his head, looked away, and said in a low tone, "I guess I'se kinda colored."

James Baldwin wrote that his father was "defeated" because in his heart he really believed what white people said about him (1963).

The legal formulation of the conclusion in the Supreme Court decision of 1954 on public school desegregation was: "To separate (Negro children) from others of similar age and qualifications solely because of their race generates a feeling of inferiority as to their status in the community that may affect their hearts and minds in a way unlikely ever to be undone."

Further support for this proposition is found in data from a personality study of Southern Negro students (Brazziel, 1964). He used the Edwards Personal Preference Schedule, which registers those phrases (equal in social desirability) that subjects will choose as descriptive of themselves. Sixteen traits can be distinguished in this test. Differences emerged between the white norms and the Negro responses on three dimensions. The Negro students described themselves as less dominant, more deferential, and less interested in sex. In each comparison, Negro students from the Deep South deviated further from the white norms than did Negro students in the Upper South.

McClelland (1961) interprets the lower need for achievement in Negroes as a residue from the period of slavery. Several studies have shown that lower-class Southern Negro children demonstrate less concern for achievement and excellence of performance than do lower-class Southern white children (Mussen, 1953; Rosen, 1959; Merbaum, 1960).

Some white college students from the North who volunteered for educational work with Negroes in the South during the summer of 1964 were appalled at the extent to which Negroes had accepted prevailing white opinion. One reported: "A Negro boy told me God made the Negroes different from whites and He didn't intend for them to mix" (*New York Times*, July 3, 1964).

When the anti-Semitism of our society is internalized by Jews, it becomes "Jewish self-hatred." Some anti-Semitic Jews, not so bound to their minority by appearance as are most Negroes, discard all ties to Judaism. They may convert to Christianity, wear a cross, and sometimes alter both their names and the shape of their noses.

Hayakawa (1959) has commented on the way the internalized discrimination makes natural, spontaneous interaction difficult for both parties.

If the self-concept, "I am a Negro," is accompanied by feelings of inferiority introjected from traditional white evaluations, the Negro will act obsequiously, as if he expected to be stepped on—and he will find many white people only too willing to oblige. If it is accompanied by feelings of defensiveness, as if he expected to be treated rudely because he is Negro, he is likely to arouse a counter-defensiveness in whites. If, however, the perception "I am a Negro" is felt only as a simple statement of fact, with few or no affective components one way or the other, the Negro will act naturally, and white people will, in nine cases out of ten, act naturally too, and be happy and relieved that meeting a Negro was not the ordeal they thought it was going to be.

The secret of acting naturally is for both parties to forget about the racial classification. Both must forget that one is a Negro and the other white. Both must let the living experience absorb their awareness.

Psychodynamics of prejudice

One of the best surveys of differences between more prejudiced and less prejudiced students is that of Allport and Kramer (1946). Prejudice is sometimes equated with "narrow-mindedness" and this seems to be related to having less educated parents, being less influenced by college, being more traditionally religious, knowing less science, and looking at the world with more suspicion.

The correlates of a prejudice may not tell much about how it can be changed. For example, white persons who speak with a Southern accent may be more likely, on the average, to uphold some form of white supremacy, but changing their accent would not alter the attitude. We turn, therefore, to studies of prejudices in process of being created or eliminated. In recent years, the author has collected about 200 case histories from persons who thought they knew how they had acquired or eliminated a prejudice. The forces that increase or diminish these attitudes become evident when study is focused on the dynamics of change.

Four basic patterns have emerged from analysis of these cases: (1) conforming; (2) profiting; (3) generalizing; (4) projecting. These are pure types; in an actual person they are likely to be mixed and compounded. The learning or unlearning of a prejudice, however, will follow a different procedure depending upon its basic nature. We shall discuss each in turn, but reserve general consideration of social action against discrimination for the last section of the chapter.

Conforming

More than half of the cases of change we studied seemed to represent simple adaptation to a different set of social norms. (See Chapters 3 and 6.) For example, white or Negro students who had lived all their lives in segregated communities sometimes came to New York for graduate study. They found themselves suddenly in a new social environment where race was not considered in assigning dormitory rooms, taking seats in class, joining discussion groups, or choosing a place to eat in the cafeteria. The immediate reaction, for members of both races, was a kind of shock. This was often followed by a conscious decision to try out the behavior which other students exemplified. Frequently, contact and interaction produced friendliness and growing appreciation of an individual of the other race as a distinct person. This is the usual S-P-A pattern and incorporates the correlation between interaction and liking presented in Chapters 2 and 3.

It is probable that most prejudice arises from natural adherence to the norms of the culture in which the individual grows up. Any attitudes and behavior which are commonly practiced and approved by the group to which an individual belongs—or aspires to belong—will be adopted by him. Children acquire prejudices from one another and from adults as normally as they learn to speak the language, eat the food, wear the clothes, and play the games of their milieu. As one student put it: "In the Southern, small-town Baptist culture of my childhood, it was as proper to believe in white superiority as to believe in God or to love your mother."

A study (Horowitz, 1936) was made in New York and in small Southern towns of how white boys at various ages interpret pictures of white and Negro boys. In one test, pupils picked out, in order of rank, the faces they liked best. In another, they chose companions for certain activities, such as playing ball, a school class, a movie, and a party. In a third, they chose to join or not to join in activities pictured sometimes carried on by four white boys, in other pictures by three white boys and one Negro. Preference by white children for other white children increased gradually from kindergarten on, reaching a peak around the sixth grade. This was true in New York as well as in the South. It was true in mixed and segregated schools. It also applied to white children who had had few or no contacts with Negro children and to those who had had many. The white preference was as marked in activities that were wholly unreal and imaginary as in activities which had actually entered into the experience of the boys tested. Some prejudice was apparent in five-year-olds and even in younger children. The one marked exception was a small group of white children whose parents were Communists. These children from Communist homes showed no tendency to prefer white children as individuals or to choose to join in all-white groups. Clearly, the attitudes of these youngsters reflected what the grown-ups around them customarily said and did.

A comparison (Sims, Patrick, 1936) of changes taking place in racial attitudes of students in a northern (Ohio) college, Southern-born students in a southern (Alabama) college, and students from the North attending the same Southern college showed a conformity pattern much like that of Newcomb's Bennington study reported in Chapter 3. The tendency of students from the local region, as they progressed from freshmen to seniors in a Southern college, was to show no change in their attitudes toward Negroes. Those in the Ohio college became gradually more equalitarian and hence like the faculty of the college. Students from the North, going to a Southern college, were more equalitarian as freshmen, and gradually they conformed to the prevailing Southern norm.

A study of 93 young men from the Deep South who were enrolled in

Yale University in 1959, showed fewer seniors than freshmen still supporting a policy of elementary school segregation: 10 percent of seniors; 27 percent of freshmen. No similar difference was found between Northern freshmen and seniors, 97 percent of whom, as freshmen, favored desegregation and continued to do so as seniors (Eddy, 1964). Thus the pattern of conformity to campus norms appears in both the North and the South.

Children usually acquire the norms of their parents. Later they may modify these to accomodate peer-group norms, if the peer group attitudes differ from the home. A study at New York University (Himelhoch, 1952) analyzed race attitude tests given to students and their parents. Student scores correlated .46 with mother's score; but 95 percent of the students were more tolerant than their parents.

The *Conformity Hypothesis,* more formally stated would be:

Attitudes and behavior characteristics of a group in which an individual wants to belong and to be accepted will be adopted by that person. Change occurs when the person moves from one milieu to another with different norms, or when he rejects his former associates and aspires to acceptance in a new group.

One case in our study of change tells the experience of Jim, who brought prejudice against Negroes from his home in the South, but during the war came to like and respect Negro fighter pilots who had saved his life. But after the war, having returned to his home setting, Jim reverted to an attitude of: "Send 'em all back to Africa!" Ann's case was similar in her transition from rural Texas to New York City, but she had changed too much to be able to revert; after a few unhappy years back in Texas, she was divorced and returned to her liberal friends in New York. Roger, in New York, had a Negro boy as best friend; after some years in the South he refused to see the former pal. The case of Rose, which follows, likewise illustrates the pressure to conform to norms of groups in which one wants to be accepted.

Case 3: Rose—The Boyfriend's Friends

Rose grew up in the subculture of Irish Catholic New York. She went to parochial elementary and secondary schools and was faithful in all church obligations. One aunt is a nun. All her social and recreational life moved in this same subculture. She knew no Jews, no Negroes, and few Italians. She had accepted the stereotype of Jews as clannish, Christ killers, cheats. She heard of Negroes as over-sexed, carrying razors, and organized to push whites off the sidewalk. Italians were associated with grease and garlic. Only her own kind of Irish Catholic was felt to be trustworthy. She was passively anti-Negro, anti-Semitic, and anti-Italian.

The change in Rose took place because of a boyfriend, now her husband.

He came from Italian background, once nominally Catholic but now a free-thinker. He was a college boy and brought Rose to dances, parties, swimming, etc., with his college friends to whom Rose looked up because of their superior education. He had a liberal social outlook and friends in other ethnic groups. Several of his friends were Negroes; others were Jews. Rose's social horizon expanded with these new contacts. She is still a faithful Catholic, but she no longer judges people as good or bad by the criterion of race, creed or nationality.

Conformity to custom often leads to inconsistencies in behavior toward minority groups. A classic illustration is the acceptance by Southern whites of Negroes in their dining rooms, provided the Negroes occupy a servile status, but refusal to eat in a room in which Negroes are also eating. An investigation (Minard, 1952) of Southern white coal miners' attitudes found the majority to be quite friendly toward Negro fellow workers in the mine, but (except for union meetings) were unwilling to associate in other activities outside the mine. White motormen and conductors in Philadelphia street cars and buses had for years, been willing to serve Negro passengers on the same basis as whites, but many objected strenuously to the proposed employment of Negro co-workers.

LaPiere (1934) who planned a cross-country automobile trip with a Chinese couple was mentioned in Chapter 7. More than 90 percent of those who had accepted the patronage in fact, refused when asked, to commit themselves in writing about what they would do. In another experiment (Kutner, *et al.*, 1952), two white women and one Negro woman visited eleven restaurants in a Northern city and were served without question or delay. Written and telephone requests later to these same restaurants asking for reservations for such a party were ignored or refused. A significant observation was made when a large New York department store began to employ Negro salesladies (Saenger, 1950). An investigator interviewed sixty-one customers who had made a purchase from a Negro sales clerk and fifty-three other customers who had made their purchase from a white sales clerk. About 20 percent of each group said, on later inquiry, that they disapproved of Negro sales personnel; there was no difference in declared attitude between customers who had and those who had not made purchases from Negro sales people.

These apparent inconsistencies become psychologically consistent when it is recognized that the various behaviors all conform to prevailing norms. It seems all right to live in close, even intimate, association with Negroes who are servants and yet to object to association with Negroes as fellow church-members, because these are the accepted customs. Whether one finds it more congenial to accept Negroes as fellow workmen or as fellow travelers in a railroad car depends on what is standard practice. Proprietors who served customers without discrimination but who declined to commit themselves to this policy on paper were in both instances in accord with the usual practice in their business. Most busy shoppers in a department store are concerned with the goods they buy, not with the personal characteristics or the views on race relations of the sales people.

Conformity prejudice reflects whatever distinctions operate regularly in the society. If it is customary for people of a given ethnic group to live in a ghetto, to use distinct entrances to buildings, or to work at certain caste-correlated occupations, then it seems entirely right and proper to most citizens that such distinctions should be maintained. Sometimes it is asserted that God made these people "different" so that they would be, by nature, fitted for their special roles. The castes of India have been interpreted by Indians as a consequence of behavior in previous incarnations.

Profiting

"Personally, I have no prejudice. Why some of my best friends are _____ and _____. But in consideration of my customers_____"

So speaks the hotel owner, the restaurant keeper, the private school trustee, the real estate operator, and many others who believe that a policy of discrimination has a direct bearing on their income or property values. These business people are not conforming because of mere imitation and habit. Their interests are affected by exclusion of certain groups.

Historically, prejudice-for-profit may well be the oldest form. Slaves have been kept in many societies by owning classes which raised their own standard of living through exploitation of the labor of those regarded as inferior. It was not until the decline in cotton prices undermined the plantation economy (which employed three-fourths of all American slaves in 1850) that abolition became politically feasible. The lingering traditions of the slave era account for many of the problems faced by the Deep South in providing full citizenship and equal status for Negroes. It is still true, however, that educational and job discrimination helps to keep a supply of cheap Negro labor for household work and relatively unskilled tasks. In Western states, general acceptance of low standards of living and of community services for Mexican agricultural workers is conducive to their profitable exploitation. On the Pacific coast, Oriental immigrants were welcomed without much difficulty until they became sufficiently numerous and successful to compete with the white men economically. (Shrieke, 1936). Japanese-American personalities had not changed noticeably, but their changed economic role made them targets of hostility. Earlier, in various Mid western communities other immigrant groups aroused similar prejudices because they accepted low wages in their desperation for work. They may have been Irish or Swedish or Italian. Dollard (1938) has described the derogatory attitudes of a community toward German immigrants who were competing for jobs in the local woodenware plants. A student from Iran told the writer that in a Kurdestan village where he taught, the Moslem's hostility toward the Baha'i waxed and waned with the season, reaching its peak in the spring when competition for land and irrigation water was at its height. Later, after the harvest, when both groups had to work together in dealing with government officials, amity prevailed! The cycle is repeated year after year.

The *Profiting Hypothesis* states simply that individuals develop, maintain, and rationalize attitudes which they find expedient and profitable in some way. Change occurs when the formerly rewarding activity ceases to bring the expected gains or when it brings penalties greater than the rewards. This is a derivative of the concept of economic man.

Note that the prejudices of profit do not presuppose any personal antagonism. Individuals and groups may raise barriers in pursuing their own interests, but have only friendly relations with individuals of the group concerned. The affection of white families for Negro slaves and servants was often very great. Neither does a merchant's acceptance of customers from a minority race mean that he would be inclined to socialize with this group. The behavior is sheer expediency; "business is business."

Discrimination for profit is practiced at every socio-economic level. The big realtor or hotel or club owner may set patterns of exclusion which he finds expedient. The unskilled worker may cherish the discrimination which reduces competition for the kind of job he can get.

Sometimes a leader in a pro-segregation movement, like some American neo-Nazi Führers, makes an extra good living from capitalizing on popular fears and prejudices. But some minority group members may also find segregation expedient. Many Negroes occupy positions of high prestige in Negro churches, schools, colleges, and business establishments which they could hardly hope to preserve in free competition with whites. It is not surprising, then, to find such individuals lukewarm toward efforts at desegregation. This is not simply internalization of community mores; it is rather a vested interest in the *status quo.*

Economic considerations sometimes work for change toward integration. Some states which are financially unable to sustain one good school system are trying to operate two. Separate facilities in other community enterprises are also more costly than one.

Generalizing

A third type of prejudice arises from unjustified generalization of a specific experience. Whenever a normal organism encounters again a situation and stimulus which previously aroused distress, an effort is made to avoid or to escape the unpleasant object. The burned child dreads the fire. The same child welcomes a visitor who last time brought him a present. As a rule, these learnings are adaptive and useful. But sometimes generalization is overworked. A child frightened by one dog may shun *all* dogs. Trusting any stranger who offers candy may lead to tragedy. A popular oversimplification of psychoanalytic findings is that adults fear certain persons or are suddenly infatuated by others as a result of "transference" from childhood encounters with similar persons.

We might state our *Generalizing Hypothesis* as follows:

A single vivid experience, or several similar experiences, with persons belonging to some noticeable category forms an expectation that others in that category will behave in a like fashion.

Generalizing in this way is particularly characteristic of persons unaccustomed to disciplined, critical thought. They react quickly against Italians one day and for Italians the next, depending on their latest encounter. Sometimes the category is not very clearly perceived. Thus, newcomers to New York may regard their fellow passengers on the subway as Jews, or as Puerto Ricans, when neither is correct.

In one of our cases, people in a Midwestern community associated all New Yorkers with two men who had committed a highly publicized sex crime in their locality. In another case, Laura, a young woman from New England, ceased to be anti-Semitic because one Jewish neighbor was so sympathetic when Laura's cat was killed.

Case 4: Saturday Night Fight

Joyce and her husband own a small restaurant in the New England town where she has lived all her 33 years. Her father was a laborer, unemployed during the depression. Joyce married at 17 and she has had four children. Economic difficulties have continued, but the restaurant is succeeding better than any previous enterprise.

Although the community does not treat all citizens alike—better restaurants keep Negroes out; more Negroes live on a back road and do manual work; restrictive covenants keep Negroes from owning beach property, etc.—Joyce feels that her family did not have any prejudice. Each individual, she was taught, should prove his own worth.

Joyce says that her prejudice dates from a fight one Saturday night in the restaurant. A party of Negroes—two men and two women—protested at slow service. She had been extra busy and made a snapping retort. A Negro man hit Joyce and sent her reeling. When Joyce's 13-year-old daughter leaped in to protect her mother, she too was hit. A shelf was upset, and the general fracas was stopped by prompt entrance of a policeman.

Since that night, a year ago, Joyce has had strong antagonism to all Negroes. She regards them as undisciplined and would like them completely segregated. "Imagine, hitting a defenseless woman! And a little 13-year-old girl!"

There are cases, like that of Joyce, in which prejudice does arise from an unfortunate, first-hand encounter with a disagreeable, incompetent, or untrustworthy member of some ethnic group. In reporting the existence of this kind of prejudice, our subjects usually felt obliged to indicate that they had not generalized from one single experience. "I could tell you a lot of others," or "You just ask anyone else who's lived among them," they would add. These defenses suggest a need to show that the prejudice is widely shared and is not based on only one episode.

There is a fairly common, but mistaken, notion that most prejudice is related to actual undesirable characteristics of the rejected ethnic group. "Self-improvement programs" have been recommended to make such groups less offensive to their neighbors. Recall, however, Horowitz's (1936) finding that children usually develop race prejudice, not from unpleasant experiences with the out-group, but from the prevailing attitudes in their own families and neighborhoods.

The writer once conducted tests of attitudes, in a wide variety of American groups, toward the Chinese and Japanese (1929). Most favorable attitudes were expressed by students at Columbia University's International House, who may have generalized from favorable experiences with fellow students from the Far East. Prisoners in Bridewell, Chicago's city jail, were very hostile toward Orientals, an attitude which could hardly have arisen out of personal experience with groups conspicuously absent in Chicago's jails. Even more hostile were the prejudices expressed by some rather isolated farm groups in the Dakotas, people who had had no personal dealings with Chinese or Japanese. Is it possible that the hard conditions of life in the Chicago underworld or on Dakota farms might develop a kind of resentment which seeks a scapegoat? This possibility will be explored in our fourth type of prejudice.

Projecting

Some of the deepest, most virulent, and intense prejudices cannot be traced to conformity, profitable advantage, or traumatic experiences with members of the rejected race.

Some light on the dynamics of this rejection can be found in the Allport-Kramer study reported earlier in this chapter. Prejudiced students tended to view the whole world as hazardous and its inhabitants as untrustworthy.

The most impressive evidence on the psychology of creating scapegoats comes from studies conducted in California by a group of social scientists exiled from Germany and Austria. We reported earlier that "authoritarian" or "pro-fascist" or "antidemocratic" personalities were especially prone to hostility toward out-groups. Another of the studies in the same series is summarized in Abstract 43. Among the women students studied by Frenkel-Brunswik, the typical anti-Semite was narrowly

Abstract 43

TITLE Some Personality Factors in Anti-Semitism

AUTHORS E. Frenkel-Brunswik and R. N. Sanford

PROBLEM What personality characteristics are found in those who are most prejudiced against Jews?

SUBJECTS 216 students, mainly women, at the University of California. Analysis is based on 8 who were "high" vs. 8 who were "low" in anti-Semitism.

PROCEDURES All students were given a test of agreement with statements that Jews are offensive, clannish, apt to cheat, corrupt or threatening and that they should be avoided, excluded or suppressed. Other questionnaires described opinions on general political issues and group memberships. The 8 high and 8 low on anti-Semitism were given TAT, Rorschach, and other projective tests.

SOME FINDINGS "Subjects with high scores on anti-Semitism were found to be characterized by two major trends. First, they exhibited a kind of conservative attitude; although they showed few signs of having developed an organized social-political outlook, they tended automatically to support the *status quo*. Secondly, the approach of these subjects to social issues was found to be characterized generally by ethnocentrism, that is, a tendency to hold in high esteem one's own ethnic or social group, to keep it narrow, unmixed and pure, and to reject everything that is different. The typical anti-Semitic girl differs in her appearance very markedly from those who are against anti-Semitism. Most girls in our limited sample of high extremes were very well groomed, their appearance being in the best middle-class social tradition. The surface of most of these anti-Semitic girls appeared to be composed and untroubled. They seemed to be satisfied with themselves and with their situation generally. Their behavior was conventionally decorous. There are, however, indications that there is at the same time much doubt and feeling of insecurity beneath the surface. It was difficult in the interviews to get much material from them. They were sensitive to this encroachment from the outside, resistant to any 'prying into their affairs.' Our selected anti-Semitic girls declared without exception that they liked their parents. More of them subscribed to the statement, "No sane, normal, decent person could ever think of hurting a close friend or relative." Likewise, they tend to agree that 'He is indeed contemptible who does not feel an undying love, gratitude, and respect for his parents.' Our anti-Semitic subjects subscribe more readily to the statement "Obedience and respect for authority are the most important virtues children should learn" (Critical Ratio 4.4; n = 140).

"In the thematic apperceptions of these subjects, *aggressive* themes stand out. Not only is the preoccupation with *destruction* markedly more pronounced than in the productions of the low extremes, but it appears to be relatively

Abstract 43—*Continued*

extreme. In story No. 1, of Case 6, a murder is being committed; in story No. 3, the husband has lost both legs, and the father is mentioned only to tell us that he has been killed; in story No. 4, a man is being foiled and captured; in No. 5, a man has been killed; in story No. 6, the hero is being convicted and severely punished. Very similar are the stories of Case 4: In story No. 3, the father and son are both killed; in story No. 4, the man is a traitor; in story No. 5, he is sent to a concentration camp; in story No. 6, the hero is electrocuted; in story No. 10, the hero is burned to death and the father killed in battle. Likewise, for Case 7, in story No. 5, the 'boyfriend' is killed in an accident; in story No. 9, a man is electrocuted; and in story No. 10, the boy 'has some kind of physical handicap.'

"Thus for the group of 140 women, there is a Critical Ratio of 4.4 between the upper and lower quartile (in terms of the explicit anti-Semitism scale) on the item, 'Although many people may scoff, it may yet be shown that astrology can explain a lot of things.' Similarly, there is a significantly greater readiness to react in the affirmative to such an item as 'It is more than a remarkable coincidence that Japan had an earthquake on Pearl Harbor Day, December 7, 1941,' or to statements about the essential limitations of the natural sciences 'in understanding many important things.'

"In the stories we hear about the 'voice of suspicion' and about haunted houses, there is frequent reference to exceptional mental states like insanity, trance, being under a spell, communicating with the dead, etc. This can be seen throughout the stories but especially in the story about the picture of a hypnotist. Anti-Semites generally emphasize the complete subjugation of the hypnotized person shown in the picture, the hypnotist's misuse of his 'superhuman' powers in inducing evil or 'queer' deeds, getting vital information, etc.

"In the picture-stories of these subjects, a sharp differentiation is made between those people who are nice and have money, possessions, and power and who possess the right attitudes and standards, on the one hand, and those who are bad, sinister, morally depraved, and live in slums, on the other. Asked to list the great people they admire the most, the upper quartile name patriots and people with power and control; whereas the lower quartile list humanitarians, artists, and scientists. (The critical ratio is again 3.) It seems generally true, on the basis of the interview material, that those scoring high on the anti-Semitism scale are primarily attracted by the strong man rather than by the political program as such. Aggression in these cases is not manifested by the heroine, but is projected into the environment, or destiny, or 'lower' people such as proletarians, Jews, Mexicans, etc."

SOURCE: *J. Psychol.*, 1945, XX:271–291. Reprinted by permission.

conservative, quite conventional and proper, and apparently quite content with herself and her upbringing. Exploration of less conscious reactions brought out great turmoil beneath this mask. Concern with sex and violence fostered anxiety and almost paranoid trends. All of the evil was projected out onto acceptable targets. Denying their own sexuality, the girls projected it to the dangerous lower-classes, Negroes, or Jews. Blind to their own aggressive impulses, the conventional young women became fearful of the threatening "others." (The findings are quoted directly from the article.)

The *Projecting Hypothesis* suggests that in order to relieve anxieties the repressed personalities attribute to others the dangerous impulses they refuse to recognize in themselves; they project these forbidden traits especially onto certain out-groups which it is "proper" to despise and to reject.

Earlier we mentioned that persons who are anti-Negro are also likely to be hostile to other out-groups: Jews, Catholics, Mexicans, Chinese, Japanese, "foreigners" or even "Danireans." The common element is the need on the part of the prejudiced person to find scapegoats, and he sees that these or other "outsiders" are acceptable targets.

Correlations of an anti-Semitism scale with the F-scale (measuring the traits of an "authoritarian personality") averaged .58. The F-scale correlated even more highly (.73) with a more general scale of prejudice against Negroes and other ethnic minorities (Adorno, *et al.,* 1950). In the Purdue University poll of high school students, the correlation between their (short) measures of authoritarianism and acceptance of race discrimination was .34 (Mainer, 1954). At New York University, ethnocentrism correlated .74 with the F-scale, a result almost identical with that found in California (Himelhoch, 1952). McClintock (1958) found that college women who where high on the F-scale were unable to accept communications designed to create more favorable attitudes toward Negroes.

The case of Margery is interesting because it illustrates how psychotherapy, bringing a release of the repressed feeling about her mother, permitted friendliness to replace prejudice. In her case, the norms of the new environment were not enough to bring change without an inner emotional transformation.

Case 5: Margery and Her Mother

Margery was 20—one of the prettiest and most often dated girls in college. Several times she had been on the verge of getting engaged to one or another of her persistent and very eligible suitors, but each time she backed away from marriage. "I'm just so happy at home," she said, "and my mother is so wonderful to me, that I can't bring myself to leave her."

Margery joined a Child Care Training course and found several Negro girls in her class. Rather than sit in the only vacant chair which was next to one of the Negroes, Margery asked another white student to move over. Margery suggested to her friends that they all avoid sitting beside a Negro girl in class, in the library, or in the lunchroom. Several teachers talked to Margery. One explained that race prejudice had no scientific basis. Margery was unmoved. Another teacher laid down the law: "We can't have any discrimination on our campus." This had no effect on Margery.

When Margery came to the psychological counselor it was not because of her prejudices but because her papers always came in late. The psychologist listened quietly. "I don't know why I can't get my work in on time," said Margery, "except that I'm so mad at the teachers. They're so bossy! So different from my mother who has always been so sweet!"

When Margery's father died, she had become the center of her mother's life. Mother did everything for her. Always wonderful and unselfish. But gradually across many hours of talk, Margery's story changed. It was hard to live up to mother's image of a model girl. Mother did expect so much. Also, it was true, mother wanted Margery always near. She had threatened suicide one time when Margery talked of marriage. Maybe it wasn't so nice that mother always bought every article of Margery's clothing. "I don't like her *owning* me!" said Margery one day. Later she was able to say, "I hate her dominating me with all that sweetness and devotion!"

With this recognition, Margery no longer felt obligated to idealize her mother. She no longer projected her resentment onto women teachers.

Before long Margery became engaged. No one said anything more about race relations, but Margery worked successfully on a committee project with a Negro classmate. "I can't understand," she said one day, "how I could ever have treated those girls the way I did. They're as nice as any of my other friends."

After a period of open rebellion against her mother, Margery married and gradually was able to admit that, despite some resentment, she really loved her mother.

The materials which follow consist of excerpts from an eight-page Western Union telegram sent to the writer after a newspaper had reported some plans for research on prejudice. It was followed the next day by a six-page telegram. Both were anonymous but between the lines they reveal a pathetic story more moving than the manifest appeal. The sender clearly has serious emotional disturbances underlying much of her hostility toward certain minorities.

Case 6: Two Telegrams of Distress

New York, New York—July 4, 1949
Professor Goodwin Watson, Teachers College
Columbia University, 116 Street, New York

The *Herald Tribune* carries comments of self survey of prejudices. The heading looked very interesting. I was very hopeful at last we were going to teach the American people how to live again something they had forgotten.

I glanced eagerly down the article. I thought I was going to find that sex was a prejudice and that we did not need as much of it as we thought we did. I thought I was going to find that alcohol indulgence was a prejudice for which we should examine ourselves closely and weed it out. I thought I was going to find that to lie easily was a bad prejudice and we were going to have a survey to improve ourselves.

Imagine my chagrin to ascertain the heroic survey was propaganda for the Jewish people and perhaps the Negro. This Columbia has a flag that must have slid down the pole a little when this was published. It must have slid down the pole because sophistry is not philosophy. I understand the motive back of the Jewish organizations. It is the motive back of the labor organizations. They do not meet acceptance with the public and they expect to beat down the door instead of going quietly away and doing a little self survey themselves.

If you are a professor, bear with me in any errors and my clumsiness. I am not educated, but I am honest and fair minded; trained by philosophy and occulism and I seem to have a natural instinct for philosophy and I have an exasperating knack to adhere to logic. For these reasons bear with me.

I have moved among these people for ten years and suffered terribly by their standards which has left nothing in life desirable to me.

It is a positive fact that the Jewish and colored people in the mixture that they have given us in New York City today are an undesirable group of people. They do not need the standard of the typical American in cleanliness, physically in refinement, physically in integrity, psychologically and other qualities, I have not in mind, at the moment, I can add.

There is a heavy sensuous, almost the better word might be sexual quality to the New York Jewish type and of course to the colored people. These things alone are sufficient to account for antagonisms among people who do not reason clearly enough to find any they are antagonistic and merely group it as the Jew or Negro bias.

In case you come back at me that sex is very desirable as many Jewish doctors will tell you and plenty of Christians, I would like to refer you to an article in the Daily News, probably today's date, July fourth if not July third, stating survey in England on the subject of sex. You will be amazed at the attitude there in that report as it differs from our Hollywood and New York attitude. I raise that point because you are a professor and I am a secretary and ignorant educationally and want to win my points with you; So I need authority to support me. Do me the justice to read the article in the Daily News referred to now. If a group of people in many long generations of American and British stock are deeply opposed to sex in conspicuous amount or conspicuous intensity and you fill their community with a group to whom that is a natural quality and take that you are going to have antagonism, and in that case there is a righteous antagonism or not depending on the spiritual nature of the person.

I do not mean that for one minute that all Jewish people are undesirable. I see quite a few that I never think of as Jewish. It never enters my mind, but when I do think of a person as Jewish, it is always because some undesirable personal quality that is brought to my attention.

You can force the people into silence, into hypocrisy. You can confuse them and worry them that their heart is selfish and unAmerican. You have the position and the strength to do it and so have the Jews. They are a powerful people and they don't hesitate to use it cleverly and powerfully. I am not a very popular person socially. All my family were very beautiful women and very well received socially. Shall I insist that they be biased and prejudiced have been exerted in my behalf because I am not popular and not accepted with equal pleasure and willingness or shall I realize I do not have the qualities within myself to produce that result.

I have suffered so much from the poor morals and ethics of the heavy foreign immigrant Jewish and colored population of New York City that I go to all this trouble every time I hear this false note spoken. The Jewish and colored people that I know, as a whole, despite the fact that many individuals are very superior people, the body mass as whole, as it has been dumped on us, is objectionable and does not need our American standard. The most common complaint I hear is physical filth. The condition of the men's room in office buildings, expectorations, theatres, restaurants, and streets. The next one is sharp business practice and poor ethics. I think extreme sexiness is about the third. I have never heard a complaint against Jewish religion which is the key to whole thing. It is the characteristics of the individual that meet with opposition. I imagine this comes from the fact that they have grown up with crowded homes in their youth.

You know our Hester Street, etc. has come up now to take up Fifth Avenue or it may be the European Jew or the American I refer to, I do not know which. With the colored, of course, it is obvious they lie and steal an awful lot. They carry liquor very badly. Many are not very bright intellectually and sex is rampant. What is the use of abusing the American people and calling them bias.

This is my personal opinion by talking to patients in a professional office as a secretary and with talking with workers such as soda fountain men, waitresses, taxi men, etc. It represents a good cross section of people. The least prejudice are the better class of people of sound financial means or the college types, because naturally they do not suffer from proximity with one another when the development is relatively equal.

I hope I have not spent all this money for nothing. I hope not. I hope the message is clear. It is by telephone to Western Union and I hope you will listen to it and you will give me the greatest kindness even if you do not believe it if you will spread it among your colleagues. It is the same with labor. I believe if the individual will make himself fit and worthy one, the next 20 years there is no reason he should not run the government or share in it but if you were to force his way now it probably would destroy everything that has meant everything in this country. This forcing business is all wrong. Thank you for attention if you have given it to me.

(Signed) A New Yorker.

The dynamics of projection are apparent also in less extreme cases. People who feel they have been given a hard time in life are more likely to be harsh in condemnation of others. Campbell (1947), using a national sample poll, in 1942, related general satisfaction with the economic and political scene to expressions of attitude toward Jews. Those who were content with affairs in general included only 7 percent who disliked Jews or were hostile to them. Among those dissatisfied with both the political and the economic situation in this country, 37 percent disliked Jews and were hostile to them.

One study in the same series as those of the Authoritarian Personality focused on returning veterans of World War II. Abstract 44 shows a similar correlation between having some sense of grievance and an attitude of intolerance. Other psychologists (Miller, Bugelski, 1948) have found that when men had recently been frustrated by unwelcome tests, they were more hostile toward the Japanese and Mexicans, although neither ethnic group was connected in any way with their annoyance.

Among over 200 cases dealing with changes in prejudice we found 44 who had advanced to better jobs than they had five years ago. Of these, 31 (or 70 percent) reported getting over a prejudice they used to have. There were only 8 who had moved down in the socio-economic scale, but the changes they reported were mainly (six of eight) the acquisition of a prejudice against some group that they had formerly accepted. This fully confirms the results of Bettelheim and Janowitz: *Intolerance is a function of deprivation and anxiety. . . . The intolerant person's accusations are ways to justify his aggressions.* People who are genuinely happy have far less impulse toward prejudice.

In an interracial camp for lower-class boys, the more prejudiced were usually (r 39 and .56) those who expressed more aggression in their Thematic Apperception Test stories (Mussen, 1950).

Historically, the correlation between the number of lynchings and the price of cotton indicates that race relations improve with prosperity (Hovland, Sears, 1938; Mintz, 1946).

Introjection

A corollary of projection is introjection. Anxiety and repressed hostility may be directed either outward or inward. The inner conflicts which instigate attacks on out-groups may also feed the fires of self-hatred. Himelhoch (1952) found that anti-Catholic attitudes in students who themselves were Catholic correlated .49 with the F-scale. Authoritarian personality among Jews was even more closely ($r = .86$) related to anti-Semitic sentiments. A Cornell University study (Noel, 1964) of 515 adult Negroes in two cities showed that those who disparaged their race felt more frustrated in general than did those who identified positively with being Negro. Of course, these data could be interpreted the other way. Perhaps the self-rejection produced, or at least added to, the general sense of frustration. Moreover, among "disparagers" there were three times as many High's as Low's on the F-scale. Among Negroes with racial pride the reverse was true: there were twice as many

Abstract 44

TITLE   Dynamics of Prejudice

AUTHORS   Bruno Bettelheim and Morris Janowitz

PROBLEM   How do more prejudiced veterans differ from those without noticeable prejudice?

SUBJECTS   150 veterans of World War II living in Chicago; only enlisted men who were not Negroes, Jews, Chinese, Japanese, or Mexican.

PROCEDURE   A woman interviewer conducted an informal talk, dealing at first with current adjustments to civilian life, then with war experiences. No reference to any minority group was made by the interviewer in the first part of the poll, but questions about whether any people or groups were interfering with the subject's chances or getting better breaks than he did gave opportunity for spontaneous attacks. The last part asked specifically about Negroes and Jews in the war and in civilian life.

SOME FINDINGS   Respondents were placed in four categories:

	Toward Negroes	Toward Jews
Tolerant	8%	41%
Stereotyped	27%	28%
Outspoken prejudice	49%	27%
Intense prejudice	16%	4%
	100%	100%

Differences in prejudice were not significantly related to age, education, religious affiliation, preference toward major political parties, marital status, country of parents birth, preference among Chicago newspapers, or socioeconomic status.

Veterans who had a better job at the time of interview than they had held before the war were more tolerant (50 percent tolerant of Jews as compared with 37 percent for the no change group and only 11 percent of the downward mobile). Of 18 with a poorer job since the war, 13 or 72 percent showed outspoken or intense prejudice.

Anti-Semitism was more common among those who felt fate had been against them during their Army career; only 5 percent of the "Tolerant" group complained of getting a "bad break" on the whole, but 34 percent of the prejudiced ("Outspoken" and "Intense") did complain. Only 11 percent of the "Tolerant" were "embittered" about Army life, but 56 percent of the prejudiced were.

Lack of parental love was reported by 32 percent of the Tolerant but by 54 percent of the Outspoken and Intense anti-Semites.

An attitude of antagonism toward and dissatisfaction with the Federal government, the Veterans Administration, both political parties, and the general economic system, was expressed by 8 percent of the Tolerant, but by 48 percent of the strongly anti-Semitic.

SOURCE: New York: Harper & Bros., 1950.

low F's as high F's. Related variables are education and social class. The disparagers came largely from the lowest occupational class and had least education. Frustration in life and acceptance of the attitudes of the F-scale seem to be as clearly related to rejection of the in-group as they are to making scapegoats of an out-group.

This completes our review of the dynamics of prejudice as conforming, profit-seeking, generalizing, or projecting behavior. We turn now to a social psychological appraisal of some of the typical action programs designed to reduce the barriers between races. How appropriate are they to the real dynamics of prejudices?

Action against prejudice

Education and persuasion

Attempts to change race attitudes often begin with reasoned arguments or moral suasion. In his great pioneering study of race relations in the United States, the Swedish sociologist, Gunnar Myrdal (1944, 1962) contrasts the American creed of democratic and Christian ideals with the social, economic, and political arrangements which foster discrimination. He believes that in this *American Dilemma* the ethical ideals will eventually triumph over the practical institutional operations of segregation. What Festinger (1957) calls the effort to "reduce cognitive dissonance," certainly works toward bringing theory and practice into more consistency.

In Chapter 7 we reviewed the sources of attitudes and the effectiveness of several ways of influencing them. Most people are inclined to agree with what they believe to be the majority viewpoint, or the one upheld by persons of high prestige. One of the problems in changing attitudes on race is that prejudice is strongest in regions where both the majority and the prestige figures sustain it.

The study by Green (1952), Abstract 25, showed that pupils who received more information about Negro achievements adopted more favorable attitudes. In reviewing cases of changed attitudes, we discovered no instance in which scientific texts, factual pamphlets, or informative lectures initiated a significant reduction of prejudice. We did find, however, that many people, after they had had interpersonal experiences which opened their minds to a new outlook, made use of information to justify, to stabilize, and to reinforce their new outlook. A study (Mainer, 1963) revealed that high school pupils who reported a program of intergroup education in their school changed more in the direction of less prejudice than did the controls.

In Chapter 8 we reported experiments showing that the film *Birth of a Nation* increased anti-Negro prejudice, while the film *Sons of the Gods* had the effect of producing more favorable attitudes toward the Chinese. A fairly typical result of a film designed to improve relations with Jews is the finding (Middleton, 1960) that anti-Semitism decreased in 69 percent of the audience which had viewed *Gentleman's Agreement,* compared with a decrease in 42 percent of the control group. The effect was greatest on those who started with most prejudice.

Equal-status interaction. This principle was introduced in our study of the S-P-A sequence in Chapter 6. Reflection, in prejudice, of the status hierarchies of the social structure accounts for the fact that contact and interaction do not necessarily lead to acceptance of others as equals. Only interaction *as equals* can reduce the tendency toward discrimination. Master and slave may share many life experiences without altering the expectation of each that one is to be dominant and the other submissive.

Data illustrating the internalization of status differences in contact between races are found in the study summarized in Abstract 45. Persons who had known individuals in another ethnic group at a level of work and education equal to their own had generally favorable concepts of that ethnic group and were quite ready to associate. Those who had known only inferior-status representatives were less favorable and less ready to associate.

One of the first and most effective attempts to influence attitudes of white students toward Negroes employed the principle of interaction with Negroes of equal or superior status (Smith, 1943). Forty-six white graduate students visited Harlem, where they met Negro lawyers, actors, writers, teachers, psychologists, businessmen, and others on a level at least equal to that of the visitors at teas, dinners, and other social events. Before-and-after tests showed in forty of the participants a marked rise in favorable attitudes toward Negroes and follow-up a year later indicated that the attitudes of acceptance still persisted.

Among our case studies, 90 percent of those who changed prejudices because of the influence of some other person or persons did so in response to someone of equal or higher status. A typical instance was Dorothy's working during the summer as a counselor in an excellent camp. For the first time, she met Negro young people who were her peers. Her earlier impression had come from a lower-lower class district, not far from her middle class home. She had associated poor housing, crowding, laziness, and Saturday night brawls with Negroes. Her camp experience was followed by a Civil Service job in which she worked under a very able Negro supervisor. She now has several Negro friends, and they visit in one another's homes.

Eliminating barriers

If most prejudice arises from conformity to the prevailing mores, surely strong preference must be given to any action program which

Abstract 45

TITLE   The Importance of Contact in Determining Attitudes toward Negroes

AUTHOR   Barbara K. MacKenzie

PROBLEM   Do stereotypes break down when members of formerly segregated groups interact?

SUBJECTS   234 employees of a government agency in Washington; 1,700 college students.

PROCEDURE   Questionnaires; one part reporting "willing to associate with Negroes" (work, club, ride next to, eat with, live near); another reporting adjectives thought appropriate to Negroes; a third part reporting kinds of jobs held by Negroes the respondent had known.

SOME FINDINGS   "Willingness to associate" was expressed by 49 percent of the students who had personally known Negroes only in positions of white-collar, skilled worker or unskilled worker, but by 83 percent of students who had known Negro students or Negroes in professions.

Among Civil Service employees, where contact was more independent of preference, the corresponding proportions were 41 percent for those who knew personally only lower-status Negroes and 85 percent for those who knew equal or higher-status Negroes.

Those who considered Negroes equal or superior to whites in intelligence, ambition, carefulness, regularity of attendance and steadiness at work represented 42 percent of those who knew personally only lower-status Negroes and 74 percent of those who had known equal or higher-status Negroes.

SOURCE: *J. abnorm. soc. Psychol.* 1948, XLIII: 417–441.

has the effect of eliminating barriers based on race, creed, ethnic group, or nationality.

The Fourteenth and Fifteenth Amendments tried, in a sweeping fashion, to eliminate political barriers and to give every citizen "equal protection of the laws." The clear intent of these amendments was nullified by the folkways of the South. Not until about a century later was substantial progress evident. The progress resulted from action in limited areas to remove specific barriers in housing, education, employment, community services, voting, and life in the armed forces.

We live in an era of struggle to eliminate the barriers which have unfairly handicapped millions of our fellow human beings. There are those who counsel caution and patience. Change of custom is always resisted. Proposals for change are turned aside with the rejoinder, "The time is not yet ripe." A rising militancy is evident in the struggle for civil rights, housing, and employment opportunities. People—particularly, but not exclusively, those who have suffered long—are determined to wait no longer. Yet a public opinion poll (April 11, 1965) showed that two-thirds of white adults in the South believed that integration was being pushed too rapidly.

There is no longer any doubt about the eventual outcome. A Gallup poll in 1957 asked a sample of Southerners: "Do you think the day will ever come in the South when whites and Negroes will be going to the same schools, eating in the same restaurants, and generally sharing the same public accommodations?" At that time, 45 percent said "Yes." The figure climbed steadily to 53 percent in 1958, 76 percent in 1961, and reached 83 percent in 1963 (American Institute of Public Opinion, July 19, 1963). The significant truth is that much of the hope and heart had gone out of the resistance, and those who were fighting for integration had achieved the fresh confidence evident in the sit-in's and other mass demonstrations of the late 1950's and early 1960's. The same poll showed that by the summer of 1963, 75 percent of Southerners expected the end of segregation within ten years.

In the following sections we shall illustrate from the fields of housing, education, work, community services, and the armed forces how the elimination of barriers and the encouragement of equal-status contacts have increased acceptance of minority groups.

a. *Housing.* In Chapter 6 we referred to a study by Wilner, Walkley, and Cook showing that attitudes of white housewives toward Negro families living in the same building could be predicted more accurately from their proximity to Negro neighbors than from their initial attitudes. Living near a Negro family and making friends with them led to favorable attitudes toward Negroes in general. Note that families had no choice in this matter. They had to take whatever space was available. The arrangement was set up first and, in accord with the S-P-A sequence, the attitudes were changed.

Similar factors operated in the two kinds of housing projects compared by Deutsch and Collins (1951). Living in integrated apartment houses had far more favorable impact on attitudes than did living in neighboring but racially homogeneous buildings.

b. *Education.* Racial integration in the schools increases equal-status contacts. Twelve years before the Supreme Court decision of 1954, the proportion of white Southerners who believed Negro intelligence as high as that of whites was only 20 percent; two years after the decree, the proportion had risen to 60 percent (Hyman, Sheatsley, 1964). School desegregation was approved by only 2 percent in 1942; 14 percent in 1956; 30 percent in 1963. Although in 1963, 61 percent of white parents in the South said they would object to sending their children to school where a few of the children were colored, by 1965 the objectors had

Abstract 46

TITLE   Desegregation: Resistance and Readiness

AUTHOR   Melvin M. Tumin

PROBLEM   What kind of person is ready for desegregation? What kind is resisting?

SUBJECTS   187 white male adults rural and urban in Guilford County, North Carolina.

PROCEDURE   Interviews by graduate students with a sample representative of households with at least one employed male.

SOME FINDINGS   1. The prevailing view is that Negroes are inferior to whites in: (a) responsibility (73 percent); (b) morality (69 percent); (c) ambition (67 percent); and (d) intelligence (59 percent).

2. Persons most resistant to desegregation had the most unfavorable image of the Negro; those most amenable to desegregation held, on the average, the most favorable image.

3. The higher the socio-economic class (property, power, prestige) the more favorable is the image of the Negro and the greater is readiness for desegregation.

4. The higher the level of education—even with occupational level constant —the greater the readiness for desegregation.

5. Church attendance is not clearly correlated with attitude on desegregation.

6. Greater exposure to mass media news (frequency of listening to *news* on radio, TV, or reading newspapers or news magazines) is associated with more favorable image scores and more readiness for desegregation.

7. The group most ready for desegregation contains "respondents who have had some college education; earn upwards of $6,000 a year; are exposed to three or more mass media; have a relatively large percentage of professionals among them; and have significantly more white-collar than blue-collar workers" (p. 198). "The principal advocacy of social change, as is implied in the term desegregation, comes from those who have the widest perspective on themselves and their communities, and the deepest sense of stake in the community-in-process" (p. 199).

SOURCE: Princeton, N.J.: Princeton University Press, 1958

dropped to 37 percent. Some characteristics differentiating those who are most ready to support desegregation are brought out in Abstract 42.

Other research confirms the impression that the core of resistance is in the less educated, lower socio-economic levels. It is more rural than urban and more likely to be the older rather than the younger citizens. The pattern resembles that of the "Know-Nothings" in the Hyman Sheatsley (1947) study described in Chapter 8. Centers (1938) had already noted that while 33 percent of people in professional occupations favored giving Negroes the same privileges and opportunities given to whites, only 15 percent of manual workers and 8 percent of farm tenants agreed. Tumin (1958) has noted the remarkable fact that in North Carolina persons with no children were more resistant to school desegregation than were parents of one, two, or three children. Their resistance found full sway because they did not mind closing down the schools entirely. Parents had to think more responsibly about the on-coming generation. The greater opposition in families with four or more children was interpreted as due to the fact that the average level of education was much lower for this group of parents.

The point may well be made again that resistance is not confined to the South or to the impoverished classes. A poll (American Institute of Public Opinion, June 1963) of Northern views showed that 75 percent of whites would consider moving from their present neighborhood if large numbers of Negroes moved in. Another poll (May 23, 1965) showed that in Northern communities about one white parent in seven would object to his children's attending a school with even a few Negro children. As far as economic status is concerned, the John Birch Society, whose leaders and support have come from upper-class levels, in its March 1964 Bulletin, urged members to fight the Civil Rights Bill (in its official position, opposing the sections on public accommodations and attacking the bill as Federal encroachment on private property rights) with "the most massive protest—by mail, telegram, by advertising, by the distribution of literature, by personal conversations . . . that we have ever undertaken with regard to any legislation." The headline they suggested for 3-column advertisements was: "Every vote for the Civil Rights Act of 1963 is a Nail for the Coffin of the American Republic."

Education has an even greater task than that of bringing Negro and white children together into the same classrooms. Some ways must be found to make up for the deficits produced by pre-school deprivation and poor instruction in former years in Negro schools. The New York City Commission on Human Rights on Oct. 23, 1963, adopted the policy of being "color conscious" rather than "color blind." "The Commission," they said, "urges preferential treatment to deal with the historic and existing exclusion pattern of our society. For a limited period, until the gap is closed, we urge aggressive action in every area to accelerate the minority group's full participation in the benefits of American freedom. Society must work affirmatively for integration rather than negatively for desegregation. Color-consciousness as a concomitant of such an effort is necessary and appropriate." For schools, this means a policy like that discussed in Chapter 10 to offset the handicaps of children from homes of lower socio-economic status. It means more nursery schools, smaller classes, more exciting curricula, cultural enrichment activities, better guidance services, more scholarships, and other aids to bring deprived pupils up to the levels of which they are potentially capable. A program in Junior High School 43 in New York City, providing many such features, resulted (according to their Third Annual Progress Report) in an increase in IQ for 75 percent of the pupils after three years and an increase in the proportion failing no tenth-grade subjects from 5 percent in 1953 to about 30 percent in 1957 and 1958.

c. *Work*. During World War II, Fair Employment legislation was enacted. A poll (Sept. 24, 1945) showed that national opinion immediately after the war was almost equally divided between those who favored and those who opposed such laws. Manual workers were more ready to support such a law (52 percent) than were business groups (43 percent). Youth (under 30) were more favorable (55 percent); those over 50 less ready to reduce barriers (only 38 percent favored a Fair Employment Practices Commission).

There is evidence to support the contention that prejudices diminish when employers or unions undertake to give equal employment opportunities. A study (Brophy, 1946) of the National Maritime Union's fight for racial equality on the job showed that their pioneering insistence that members must work with competent seamen of any race had resulted in the elimination of much of the prejudice found in other union groups. In the average American craft union, 71 percent were "prejudiced" by Brophy's index; in British unions 40 percent were in the prejudiced category; in the National Maritime Union only 4 percent made the prejudiced responses during the interviews. Another significant finding was that members of any union who had never worked with Negroes were much more likely to be prejudiced against them (54 percent); those who had had five or more experiences with Negroes as fellow crew members were less likely to be prejudiced (only 10 percent).

A report by the Winchester Repeating Arms Company in New Haven states that as a result of their wartime employment and upgrading of Negro workers, "some of the chief objectors to working with Negroes became strong supporters of the new policy" (New York State War Council).

An instructive comparison has been made (Watson, 1947, pp. 71-2) between two different techniques for opening positions on public transit buses to Negroes. In Washington, D. C., a poll was taken with questions loaded against integration: "Will present operators walk out if Negro operators are employed?" "Will present operators resort to acts of violence if Negro operators are employed?" The answers indicated that it would be dangerous to attempt integration. In Philadelphia, likewise, the white drivers and conductors were asked whether they would accept Negro co-workers. They, too, answered "No" and a strike was called. In Cleveland, the integrative action was taken without fanfare. One morning a driver was introduced to his new conductor who happened to be colored. The procedure was exactly the same as it would have been with a new white employee. Very few difficulties were encountered. The change was accepted by almost everyone as routine. Apprehension is often raised in the contemplation of change, although the actual difficulties may prove to be minor. In Philadelphia, six months after the protest strike, Negro drivers were taken for granted by customers and by other employees, and one Negro had already been elected to an important union office.

Experience in introducing Negro employees in offices brought out a similar pattern. Raising issues for debate created many anxieties—about lunchrooms, washrooms, public reaction, and so forth. If the usual routines were followed, a few employees might raise their eyebrows over the skin color of their new co-workers, but no real difficulty arose. We have called this the *fait accompli* technique.

The introduction of Negro sales clerks in a New York department store (Saenger, Gilbert, 1950) was described earlier in this chapter. As long as the new employees simply sold goods over the counter, in the usual way, customers were not disturbed. But when customers were polled to discover their verbal attitudes, a substantial number of those who had not actually objected to being served by a Negro clerk reported that they thought this would be objectionable. Again, integration proceeded more effectively when it was simply a *fait accompli*.

The theories and facts presented in Chapter 6—the S-P-A sequence—fully confirm the observation that changes in practice may well precede changes in attitudes. It is more effective to attack discriminatory barriers than to try to change the prejudices while the segregated institutions remain. Living and working under segregated conditions generates prejudice faster than it can be eliminated by exhortation or education. Reliance on methods of persuasion, while life runs in segregated patterns is like bailing out a leaky boat which refills faster than the dipper can take the water out. If discrimination is institutionalized in separate facilities and buildings—in residential areas, schools, churches, eating places, playgrounds, movie houses, seats for travel, drinking fountains, waiting rooms, and lavatories—these restrictions inculcate prejudice far more effectively than the best preachers of brotherhood can eliminate it.

Acceptance of a person of another race as a co-worker does not always lead to acceptance in other relationships. As we reported, earlier in this chapter, men might work congenially in the mines but separate into different social communities in the evening. A study in a New York department store produced similar evidence. Clerks of different races worked well together and were quite willing to work in interracial settings on another job, but after working hours, a "five o'clock shadow" descended and there was little social contact (Harding, Hogrefe, 1952).

d. *Community services.* Court decisions have opened to all races such public facilities as trains, buses, waiting rooms, and parks. Occasional protests have arisen, but most of the desegregation has been maintained. Consistent with the S-P-A sequence, once the new structure has been laid down, behavior and attitude changes follow.

Experience in desegregating recreational groups is reflected in a study (Yarrow, Campbell, 1958) of attitudes and behavior of children in interracial camps. At the end of camp, white and Negro friends were about equally desired by white children. If separate cabins for Negroes and whites were maintained, few cross-racial friendships developed.

Churches vary in their readiness to provide interracial facilities, but often they have been in advance of other community agencies. This accords with Myrdal's thesis on the importance of conscience (1944). In St. Louis and New Orleans, the Catholic parochial schools were integrated before the public schools took this step. One study (Campbell, Pettigrew, 1959) is based on interviews with 29 white clergymen in Little Rock, Arkansas, which encountered problems with school desegregation in the fall of 1957. Only five supported the segregationist view, although all 29 thought their congregations were predominantly (about 75 percent) segregationist. Sixteen were "inactive integrationists." They acknowledged that desegregation is a Christian obligation, but they avoided controversy and conflict as far as possible. Most of them were seriously threatened by opposition within their churches. Several resigned, or were transferred, within a year after the incidents at the high school. Eight clergymen were really active on behalf of integration. All of them were ministers of small churches in working-class districts. Most of them were affiliated with sects more fanatical in their views than are the large denominations.

Churches have had to struggle with the obvious contradiction between Christian ideals and the practices of most white members. One study (Friedrichs, 1959) showed that in a small New Jersey city where 90 percent of those polled were church members 68 percent said: "I would not consider it fair for any white, myself included, to sell or rent a house in this neighborhood to a Negro family." Respondents seemed baffled when asked what they would do to end *de facto* segregation in the public schools. Less than 10 percent could think of a single step or act to implement their beliefs. It is not clear whether they did not feel any obligation, as Christians, to facilitate integration or whether they approved the policy but lacked any corresponding action program.

A historic event was the Inter-religious Convocation on Civil Rights, which on April 28, 1964, brought together in Washington the largest assemblage of Catholic priests, Protestant ministers, and rabbis ever congregated for a common cause. Equally notable were parades led by clergymen of several faiths in Selma, Alabama, in the spring of 1965. It is no small service to define clearly the united concern of religious conscience. We saw earlier that by 1963 most segregationists had, for the most part, lost hope of preserving racial barriers. It is even more significant that they could no longer count on the support of the spokesmen of moral and religious institutions. Good conscience was also abandoning the old order.

Community norms

Since most prejudice is the internalization of what persons growing up in the community see and hear around them, verbal expressions are also important. The advertising placards on city buses which proclaim brotherhood and acceptance of all races serve the purpose of setting a public standard. Public expression of derogatory remarks about minority groups should cause concern. If it is commonly said, and left uncontradicted, that Chinese are untrustworthy and treacherous, conformists will freely echo this opinion.

The Commission on Community Interrelations of the American Jewish Congress studied for several years the effects of antiminority remarks (Citron, Harding, 1950). Playlets in which a character on a bus, in a crowd or in a store made a disparaging remark were presented to off-the-street audiences who answered questionnaires before and after the show. In some versions a second member of the cast made a rejoinder, in others, the remark was allowed to stand. The rejoinders were systematically varied. Some were calm, others emotional. Some appealed to science, others to American democracy, still others to personal experience. The investigators concluded that *some* answer is desirable and that it is usually better to make a calm and reasonable rather than an excited reply. The real objective of the rejoinder is not to convert the bigot—this could hardly be expected—but to impress upon conformists the idea that our mores do not sanction such vilification of minorities. No clear advantage appeared for the appeal to patriotism, to personal experience, or to scientific truth. The important thing seemed to be to condemn publicly the scurrilous comment.

Having established the desirability of an answer, the investigators came up against the reluctance of most men of goodwill to become involved in a public scene. It is easier to keep quiet and to let the incident pass. Several training projects were undertaken in adult study groups using role-playing methods. Before-and-after tests, which included actual incidents staged without the trainees' knowledge, demonstrated that the likelihood of a middle-class citizen making some appropriate rejoinder could be increased tenfold by suitable training.

The armed forces

A remarkable demonstration of the power of "stateways" to change "folkways" appears in the experience of desegregation in the armed forces of the United States. An abstract in Chapter 4 shows that 93 percent of white officers who by 1945 had served in companies with Negro platoons were ready to accept desegregation. Those who had not had experience in integrated companies disliked (62 percent) the prospect. On July 26, 1948, President Truman issued the executive order demanding "equality of treatment and opportunity for all persons in the armed services without regard to race, color, religion or national origin." Air Force Secretary Symington asked the President, "Will you back me up?" "With no reservation," answered President Truman. Symington then told his generals: "We're going to end segregation. Those are my orders from the Commander-in-Chief. You've got to stop the double-talk and act" (Nichols, 1954). At that time, official testimony indicated that most white officers were skeptical or opposed to integration. Some predicted serious disturbances. Lt. Colonel Jack Marr is quoted as making what turned out to be the more accurate prediction: "Fears of social and morale difficulties are largely imaginary." Strong men at the top took strong positions. Lt. General Lawrence Kuter told his subordinates in the Military Air Transport Service: "Commanders who cannot cope with the integration of Negroes into formerly all-white units will have no place." Lt. General Idwall Edwards, Air Force personnel chief, warned officers that inaction or delay in integration would be considered "a command failure."

Of course, there were some reverberations. A mother in Tennessee sent to her congressman a letter from her son saying "They are mixing the niggers in the barracks with us. Do something quick!"

Early reports showed extraordinary success. Maj. General Harper, after two months of integrated training at Lackland Air Force Base near San Antonio, Texas, wrote that there had been "no racial disturbance in any phase, on or off duty." Elgin Air Force Base in Florida reported "only minor problems." Discipline was firm. A white airman who insulted a Negro at Goodfellow Air Base, San Angelo, Texas, was court-martialed, given 30 days' confinement, and then dismissed from the Air Force. A commander who refused to end separate clubs for Negro and white airmen at a base in South Carolina was removed; his successor integrated the clubs without disturbance. General Cannon reported, after six months of integration in European bases, that there had not been a single recorded instance of racial conflict. The Fahy committee reviewing progress concluded: "The men were more ready for equality of treatment and opportunity than the officer corps had realized."

President Truman's Committee on Equality of Treatment and Opportunity in the Armed Forces concluded that, in the Air Force and in the Navy, "Integration of the two races at work, in school, and in living quarters did not present insurmountable difficulties. As a matter of fact, integration in two of the services had brought a decrease in racial friction" (President's Committee, 1951).

The team of social scientists reported that, quite consistently, senior officers who had anticipated that integration would work well found experience confirming their expectation while those who had feared trouble were relieved to find that experience was better than they expected. A division chief of staff is quoted as saying: "My officers told me we'd have riots, murder, low standards of training, conflict with state laws, trouble with townspeople, and so forth. But we didn't. We haven't had any trouble and we won't have." The researchers found that the few instances of racial conflict reported were more apt to involve men from segregated garrisons while off the post.

Another observer reported that at an induction center, not far from Atlanta, Georgia, Negro and white young men who had spent all their lives up to the time of induction in segregated communities were, within 24 hours after entering their new and integrated army environment, sitting about in the U.S.O. recreational hall, chatting in a friendly way with one another, playing pool together, and even drinking "cokes" alongside one another at the refreshment bar.

The case study which follows describes the attitude changes at another Southern base.

Case 7: Breakthrough on the Color Front

SOME EXCERPTS

"No more significant indicator of the social import of military non-segregation could be found than at Keesler Air Force Base, whose gates opened directly into the Deep South city of Biloxi, Mississippi. Though Biloxi was once a stronghold of segregation, Negro and white airmen had lived together on the adjoining base since 1949 with little or no ripple in day-to-day operations.

"At a post rimmed by the Gulf of Mexico and brilliant with bougainvillaea and hibiscus, about 1,200 Negroes and 20,000 white airmen in May 1953 studied radar, radio and control tower operation, or cooked the food, hauled the supplies and doctored the sick of the key air force electronics training center.

"Major General James F. Powell, Virginia-born commander of Keesler, was admittedly skeptical about mixing Negroes and whites when the Air Force ordered integregration in 1949. Now, four years later, he said there was no more problem here than if the Negroes didn't exist.

"He took the author on a tour of the base, pacing rapidly from classroom to classroom where Negroes and whites rubbed shoulders leaning over complicated radar equipment or watched instructors chalk diagrams of radio circuits on blackboards. In two classrooms, Negro civilians were teaching radar operation and fundamental electronics to white airmen.

"At noon, Powell reviewed the change of classes as 9,000 airmen and Air Force women (Wafs) marched by in squadron formation. Negroes were in every squadron, scattered through the ranks, some holding the honor posts of color-bearer and line guide, a few wearing the green patch of class leader. A dozen or so Negro Wafs stepped smartly along in the Waf squadron, a tiny Negro Waf serving as line guide at the front of the column.

"Later, in the barracks of one off-duty squadron, the men were listening to radios, sleeping, writing letters. An athletic young Negro in gym shorts and T-shirt was barracks leader of one dormitory, responsible for order among its white and Negro airmen; his superiors called him a good leader, and he reported complete satisfaction with his treatment and progress in the Air Force.

"The major in charge of the squadron, a Georgian, demanded proof that the writer had been cleared to visit his squadron. Satisfied, but asking that he not be quoted by name, he said he had been surprised but found the integration plan was fine. Negroes and whites in his squadron borrowed each other's clothes with complete disregard of race.

"A Negro psychiatrist, a native of Long Island, New York, said he had successfully treated several difficult mental cases involving wives of white officers and men, and they had gratefully sent him letters of thanks and Christmas cards. Housed between white officers, he said his immediate neighbors accepted him and his wife and that they frequently played bridge at a white neighbor's home.

" 'The encouraging thing about it,' he added, 'is that so many of the younger people are free of prejudice; they've accepted integration without a struggle.'

"Regarding non-segregation at Keesler Field, the Biloxi chief of police, Earl Wetzel, remarked that the Constitution said people are equal and guessed the government had to live up to it.

"Asked if there had been objections to integration when it was begun at Keesler, he said there had been no 'official complaints, only rumors; when we'd trace them down, we'd find some damn ignoramus; now nobody says anything about it. Negroes are being treated better everywhere,' he continued. 'Maybe in two–three generations you won't know white from colored. It's what people are taught as children that makes them what they are.' "

SOURCE: Lee Nichols, *Breakthrough on the Color Front.* New York: Random House, 1954. Reprinted by permission.

The new Negro militancy

Since World War II civil rights leaders have undertaken more aggressive measures because persuasion has not been effective in attaining even modest goals. Case 8, presented in 1940 by a Negro teacher from Norfolk, Virginia, will illustrate the developing demand for more dynamic efforts.

Case 8: Persuasion Is Not Enough

Prior to 1930, Negro teachers were generally willing to accept the salaries offered in their largest white-collar occupation, although these were below what was paid to white teachers. By 1933, the Virginia Society for Research (Negro) had appointed a committee (to try) to implement the school laws of Virginia which required "separate but equal" facilities. Two methods of attack were considered by the research society. The first was the cooperative method. The facts were to be presented in an objective and friendly manner. White school officials were to be given an opportunity voluntarily to improve the situation. It was argued that "Negroes can never expect to force the majority to take any action it doesn't want to take. The best way is to make white friends who are interested in improving conditions." The second strategy considered was that of coercion. Some maintained that the best thing was to try to secure court action against school boards. They argued "No amount of persuasion would induce white school officials to risk their positions and social status to equalize Negro teachers' salaries, no matter how friendly these white officials may be."

For two and a half years the cooperative attack was tried. In no instance were we able to get even a promise from white officials that they would work toward equalization. One Negro principal who, in accord with the research society's decision, tried to publicize the facts taken from the state school report, was summarily discharged for "disturbing the good relations that had existed between the races for many years." Some white officials evaded by saying "The time is not ripe." Others were more pugnacious and announced that they would take action when they were good and ready and never in response to pressure from the Negroes.

Recognizing that the cooperative approach had got them nowhere in Virginia's cities, counties, or with the state legislature, funds were raised for a legal staff. The Virginia branch of the NAACP cooperated. A woman science teacher volunteered as a test case. She was promptly discharged by the school board and other teachers were warned that if they attempted court action they, too, would lose their jobs. Nevertheless there were other volunteers. In June 1940, the Federal Circuit Court of Appeals ruled that a citizen could not be forced to sign away his Constitutional rights and that the single salary scale must be applied. The school board attorneys accepted this ruling and drew up what they thought might be a satisfactory compromise. They got the consent of a leading Negro principal to accept this, although it was not what the Negro teachers had asked. This principal was promptly repudiated by his group as a traitor. The Negro group, through their own attorneys, eventually won a much better settlement, one which brought the 250 Negro teachers of Norfolk an additional $150,000 a year. The school board worked amiably with the committee representing the Negro teachers, showing none of the evasiveness or hostility which they had shown earlier to the cooperative approach. Their attitude was "The court has settled this, so now let's get together and make it work."

The new Negro militants in the South can be better understood through the following Case.

Case 9: John—Youth Militant

John is a Negro, one of six children of a carpenter in North Carolina. He recalls that as a boy he wondered what was wrong with him, mentally, that he had to go to a segregated school. He was 13 when his father, deeply thrilled, told him of the Supreme Court decision, with the implication that it meant a better chance for an education. He entered a newly integrated junior high school that autumn and worked hard for good grades. His father gave a dollar to the child with the best report card each term.

At the age of 15, John read the life of Gandhi and was greatly impressed. "He was an amazing guy. He goes to prison, then gets out and he does the same thing again immediately . . . I began to wonder why couldn't I be a Gandhi myself, doing something for the race." He became interested in the bus boycott in Montgomery, Ala., and Martin Luther King, Jr. became another hero of his adolescence. "I began to wonder," said John, "why my father had never done something to change conditions." John recalls that his grandmother said of segregation, "You'll never change it, it's been going on for years!"

He enrolled in A. & T. College in Greensboro in the fall of 1959. He and three friends had bull-sessions far into the night. All had been members of the NAACP but none had heard of CORE. "There were many words and few deeds; we did a good job of making each other feel bad."

On the night of January 31, 1960, one of the boys proposed that they try to buy a lunch in downtown Greensboro the next day. John agreed and dared the hesitant boys: "Are you or aren't you a man?"

They dressed carefully in coats and ties. They were determined to be gentlemanly and dignified. They expected to be arrested and feared physical violence. They sat at the counter and read school books until the store closed. A Negro woman cook came out of the kitchen and scolded them: "It is because of people like you that our race can't get ahead!" she shouted. A white woman came and sat on the stool beside John and said in a low tone: "You're doing a good job. It should have been done 100 years ago!" Outside a crowd of whites gathered and shouted epithets at them.

The first of the non-violent sit-in's, leading to freedom rides and other demonstrations had begun. John did not know at the time how big a movement he and his friends had begun. He did know that he felt great. "I used to feel kinda lousy, like I was really useless." At last he had *done* something more than talk.

SOURCE: F. Solomon, J. R. Fishman, "Youth and Social Action." *J. soc. Issues,* 1964, 20:36–46.

A survey of Negro opinion in New York (*New York Times,* July 27, 1964) showed 62 percent believing that non-violent methods like sit-in's would prove successful in achieving equal rights and better jobs for Negroes. Civil rights demonstrations, picketing, and boycotts were judged (69 percent) to have helped get better housing, jobs, and schools.

Mississippi was the center of a program of Freedom Schools taught by both Negro and white students during the summer of 1964. It is noteworthy that despite some fanatical opposition and tragic incidents, the influential sectors of the South moved steadily to accept the new relationships. The Chamber of Commerce in Jackson, Mississippi, opposed the Civil Rights Act until it had become law; then advised members to comply (*New York Times,* July 3, 1964) In McComb, Mississippi, more than 650 white citizens, including bank presidents, lawyers, ministers, and business leaders signed a statement calling for an end to racial violence and for equal treatment under the law for all citizens (*New York Times*, Nov. 18, 1964). The next day, Negroes were quietly served in previously all-white restaurants, hotels, stores, and theatres. In Chapter 15, we shall consider further the effect of law in bringing about social change.

With increasing opportunities for Negroes to obtain college education and to enter the professions and managerial levels of business, more and more whites in all sections of the nation will have an opportunity to associate with Negroes who are of equal or superior status. The rise of a Negro middle class has been well outlined by the Negro sociologist E. Franklin Frazier (1957). He notes that Negroes who have upward mobility identify with the *white middle class* and are unlikely to be crusaders. The same observation is made by Fuller (1963). A study (Hughes, Watts, 1964) of nine Negro families who moved into formerly all-white middle- or upper-class suburbs of Boston indicated that none were members of CORE or participants in demonstrations. Their values resembled those of their reference group, their white neighbors.

Cultural pluralism

The removal of barriers is not identical with forced homogeneity and amalgamation. Many members of minority groups, while concerned about having equal opportunities for employment, housing, education, political office, and recreation, are also eager to preserve their own culture and identity. The democratic objective is not to make all alike, but to give each opportunity to realize his own goals. The elimination of enforced segregation does not imply that Protestants, Catholics, Jews, Negroes, Puerto Ricans, French-Americans, Spanish-Americans, Japanese-Americans, Italian-Americans, Polish-Americans, and other ethnic minorities may not develop their own institutions and culture patterns whenever and insofar as they wish to do. American life will be richer *for its varied colors and forms.*

In the following chapter another kind of barrier—perhaps the most widespread and serious of all—will be examined.

CHAPTER TWELVE

Psychological aspects of sex roles

Following the Structure-Process-Attitude sequence, we shall look first at the social situation which defines subordinate positions for women; then note the roles associated with these positions, allowing for biological differences, and then the attitudes which are thus formed.

The tradition

Male dominance

Older, deeper, and more widespread than discrimination based on socio- economic class or race is inequality of sex roles. Hunt (1959) quotes some indignant feminist as saying that "Woman was the earliest domestic animal of man." In the mores acceptable when the early chapters of Genesis took form, woman was an after-thought, created from one of Adam's spare parts, as a companion for the man.

In primitive societies we find that such activities as fishing, handicraft, marketing, or cooking may be assigned primarily to men or primarily to women, but if the activity carries high prestige in any society, it is restricted to men. This is particularly true of religious ceremonies and the healing practiced by witchdoctors. Even in matrilineal societies political power was usually vested in a father, husband, brother, or uncle. Throughout the history of mankind, there has been a tradition of female subordination.

Older than the Ten Commandments, although expressed in them, was the tradition of Jewish tribes that a wife was a form of property like a house, an ox, ass, man-servant or maid-servant. Longer rites of purification were required if a mother gave birth to a daughter rather than a son. In synagogues women were excluded and men gave thanks that they were Jew not Gentile, free not bond, and men rather than women.

The ancient Chinese culture placed the highest value on male children. Girls might be sold as slaves or left to die. A Chinese maxim taught: "A woman married is like a pony bought—to be ridden or whipped at the master's pleasure."

Ancient Greece, according to Demosthenes, ordered matters to male convenience. "We have hetairae for the pleasures of the spirit, pallages (concubines) for sensual pleasure, and wives to bear our sons." Wives in Athens were confined to the gynaeceum, a limited area in the rear of the house; their persons and property controlled by their male guardians. Plato thanked the gods that he was free and not slave, man and not woman. Aristotle thought that femininity might be defined by "a certain lack of qualities; we should regard the female nature as afflicted with a natural defectiveness."

Christianity, despite the glorification of the Virgin, continued to symbolize the ordinary woman's lot as properly ruled by her husband even as the church is ruled by Christ. The Jewish values as expressed in Genesis were continued. "Neither was man created for the woman but the woman for the man," wrote St. Paul. St. John Chrysostom said: "Among all savage beasts none is found so harmful as woman." St. Thomas Aquinas saw man as far above woman as Christ is above man. Woman's testimony bore no weight in canon law. Hunt (1959) cites as typical a medieval statute of Villefranche in Gascony which granted husbands the right to beat their wives as they pleased, with only the limitation that it must not be so severe as to cause death.

Other major religions have been even less ready to give status and dignity to human females. Hinduism recognized goddesses, but woman's lot on earth is ruled by men. The Koran teaches that "Men are superior to women on account of the qualities in which God has given them preeminence." In the long lines of Buddhist masters and sages, stretching over twenty-five centuries, no woman is included. An old Russian proverb teaches that: "A dog is wiser than a woman; he does not bark at his master."

Virginia Woolf (1929) has called attention to the handicaps which William Shakespeare's sister would have had if she had been born with his talents. A lady in seventeenth-century England lived "protected" but immured within households. She could have received but little education, and careers in the theatre, publication, and business would all have been barred to her.

Even the iconoclasts, whose thoughts had laid the foundations of our democratic society, replacing feudalism, continued to assume that woman's place was subordinate. Jean-Jacques Rousseau wrote: "Woman was made to yield to man and to put up with his injustice." John Adams was asked in 1776 by his talented wife, Abigail, to see to it that the new government should not "put such unlimited power into the hands of the husbands."

"I long to hear that you have declared an independency and, by the way, in the new code of laws . . . I desire that you should remember the ladies and be more generous and favorable to them than your ancestors," she wrote. "If particular care and attention are not paid to the ladies we are determined to foment a rebellion and will not hold ourselves bound to obey laws in which we have no voice or representation." President Adams, in the usual male tradition, laughed at this and accused his wife of a subversive notion, probably generated by the British enemy. The women petitioned, paraded, and picketed, but the Continental Congress paid no attention.

Only about a century ago Schopenhauer (1851) expressed with vigor the prevailing view of his time as follows: "Women are big children all their life long."

We may well agree with Beauvoir (1953) that "woman has always been man's dependent if not his slave; the two sexes have never shared the world in equality."

Parallels in race and class prejudice

Statistically, women are seldom in the "minority," but when this term implies a subordinate status, it fits. The sociologist Louis Wirth defined a minority as "any group of people who because of their physical or cultural characteristics, are singled out from the others in the society in which they live, for differential and unequal treatment, and who therefore regard themselves as objects of collective discrimination." (In Linton, 1945, p. 347.)

At a press conference in 1957, a woman reporter, Mrs. May Craig, asked President Eisenhower: "Sir, you have been, and others have been, very active in trying to wipe out discriminations which are based on race, creed, religion, and color. Why have you not been as active in trying to wipe out discrimination based on sex . . .?"

Mrs. Craig was not the first to see some parallel between race discrimination, which has now become front-page controversial news, and sex discrimination, which is rarely publicized. The woman's rights movement a century ago was closely associated with the antislavery movement. The first Woman's Rights Convention was held in 1848, during the heat of the Abolitionist movement. William Lloyd Garrison's *Liberator* was supporting woman's rights as well as emancipation of Negro slaves.

In 1937, the Carnegie Corporation invited a young Swedish economist and sociologist, Gunnar Myrdal, to make an objective study of Negro-white relations in the United States. One appendix to his two volume survey (Myrdal, 1944, 1962) is entitled: "A parallel to the Negro problem." Among the similarities between the historic plight of Negroes in a white-dominated culture and that of women in a male-dominated culture, he reported the following:

1. Both have "high social visibility" owing to physical appearance or dress.
2. Originally both were forms of property, controlled by an absolute patriarch.
3. Women, minors and Negroes might not vote. (The Fifteenth Amendment came a half century before the Nineteenth!)
4. Neither wives nor Negroes, historically, had legal rights over property or guardianship of children.
5. Both were believed to have inferior mental endowment, and only limited educational opportunities were provided for them. Later a special type of education was deemed appropriate.
6. Each has been assigned to a "place" in the social system; as long as they stayed obediently in this subordinate status, they were approved; any effort to alter this scheme was abhorred.
7. "The myth of the 'contented woman' who did not want to have suffrage or other civil rights and equal opportunities had the same social function as the myth of the 'contented Negro.'"
8. It has been difficult for either to attain important public office.
9. There have been certain jobs allocated to women and others to Negroes; they are usually low in salary and in prestige.
10. It has been thought to be "unnatural" for white men to work under Negro supervisors or for males to work under female direction. Women prefer not to have woman bosses; Negroes often feel the same way about working under other Negroes.
11. A kindly paternalism as of a guardian and a ward has been thought the ideal solution (Myrdal, 1944).

It is possible to add many more parallels. For example:

12. It has been argued in the case of both Negroes and women that

God made them different and that it is His will that there should not be real equality.

13. Both Negroes and women are appreciated--even loved--in their nurturant role. The dominant group is delighted to be nursed, fed, clothed, and cared for by these servants.

14. Both women and Negroes, in studying history, discover that white males occupy most of the heroic roles. Less than 1 percent of the statues erected to great historic figures in America honor either women or Negroes. A typical school child's list of the important names in history will seldom include any woman or Negro. This probably limits aspiration for many children.

15. Women and Negroes are said to be more emotional than rational.

16. The areas in which these two "minorities" are first allowed to win distinction are music and acting.

17. They are reported to be inclined toward superstition and magic; they are supporters of traditional religion.

18. It is considered proper to pay them less for the same work than would be paid to white males; women and Negroes are said not to have such heavy responsibilities.

19. It is traditional to speak of a "Negro problem" as though the Negroes and not the whites were at the root of it; similarly the "woman problem" is really a problem created mainly by men.

20. It is convenient to ignore or deny any real problem in the relations of Negroes and whites or masculine and feminine roles. If "agitators" would only keep out, everything could be worked out harmoniously.

21. A major technique for meeting the problems the dominant groups prefer to repress is humor. Almost every joke book contains anecdotes about dominating wives or stories in Irish, Jewish, or Negro dialect. In recent issues of a popular male-oriented magazine were cartoons lampooning the woman driver, the wife carrying a rolling pin, the harried husband pushing a baby-carriage, the mother and daughter in league to spend the bread-winner's money; a marriage license was defined as one which gives a woman the right to drive a man, and bridegrooms were advised to "Let your wife know right from the start who's boss; there's no use kidding yourself!"

President Eisenhower responded to Mrs. Craig's question with a typical joking parry: "Well," he replied. "it's hard for a mere man to believe that woman doesn't have equal rights!"

22. Students of race prejudice are familiar with the expression: "But you are an exception." The same pattern appears in connection with the woman boss. A study by Patrick (1944) found that the

actual personality of women executives seldom corresponded to the stereotype, but the stereotype still persists. Both men and women are generally reluctant to work under a woman boss. When they do experience a woman administrator who is able and admirable, they regard her as an exception and preserve their prejudice.

23. There is a mystique behind the rational discussion of sex and race discrimination. The myths of Pandora and of Eve attribute to women the source of evil in life. The term "Black" applied to Arts or Magic also denotes evil and may be extended to race.

The lower-class parallel

Sex-role barriers resemble class restrictions as well as race discrimination. The factory worker, in a capitalist society, faces some of the same problems which confront Negroes in a white society or women in a male-dominated culture. It is important to note the parallels because they give unity to a socio-psychological problem larger than that of any specific prejudice.

Using Myrdal's 11 points, there are at least nine parallels between the role assigned women and that of the low-paid industrial worker.

1. Overalls distinguish the worker from the boss; dresses the woman from the man.
2. The right to vote was once linked to property; neither women nor workers were eligible.
3. Women, like workers, were thought to have inferior mental endowment; when education was offered it was of a special kind, more concerned with hands than head.
4. Both women and workers were expected to accept their ordained place.
5. There has been a myth of the "big happy family" in the factory to parallel the myth of the contented woman.
6. It has been difficult for women or working men to attain high public office.
7. Jobs allocated to women and to working men are usually low in pay and prestige.
8. Upper-class men would find it incongruous to work under the direction of either a woman or a factory worker.
9. Kindly paternalism is commended.

The role of the worker resembles that of women also in being considered assigned a subordinate place by God, living in a history made by heroes coming almost entirely from other classes; being called emotional (susceptible to agitators) rather than rational; deserving less pay than the bosses; constituting a "labor problem." Bother women and organized labor are sometimes said today to have tipped the balance of power in their own favor.

These parallels show that whenever a social system provides special privileges for some members and arbitrarily denies them to others, elaborate rationalizations will develop to defend the rightness and necessity of the discrimination.

As students of a science, it is our task to go beneath and beyond the stereotypes popularly accepted and to examine more carefully the facts. To what extent are the prevailing privileges for men the result of physical or mental superiority?

Differences scientifically established

Biological

Biologically, it is evident that males are the weaker not the stronger sex. About 135 males are conceived for every 100 females, but miscarriages and still-births are more common among male babies, leaving a ratio of 106 to 100 at birth. One study of infant mortality in the first four months after birth showed 72 percent of the deaths to be males. Life expectancy at every age is greater for the female. Differences in mortality are especially large in babyhood, before life-tasks have been differentiated, and hence cannot be correctly attributed to the strains of men's work. Census estimates for 1975 predict three million more women than men in the United States, and the disproportion increases with age. The biological handicaps of males arise from what has been called "that half-crippled" X-Y chromosome which appears in every male cell. Hemophilia is found only in males. Specific disorders like color-blindness, stuttering, epilepsy, ulcers, and gout are more common in males than in females. Probabilities of a heart attack in the age period between 30 and 62 are ten to one for men as compared with women. More women than men survive almost every serious ordeal: famine, plague, bombardment, or concentration camps. While the biological factors in behavior disorders can seldom be disentangled from learned reactions, it is noteworthy that males are more prone to school misbehavior, incorrigibility, juvenile delinquency, alcoholism, drug addiction, serious crime, and suicide.

Man's only clear advantage—the larger skeletal frame and stronger muscles—was very important in the struggle for survival under primitive conditions, when male domination probably began. A parallel development can be seen among the apes. The strong male is dominant because he can run faster, shove harder, and push others around. Under conditions of modern urban life, mere muscle-strength has become less important. Machines, easily controlled, can lift heavier weights and move things about more efficiently than can human strength.

In the reproductive process, the male role is dramatic but really minor and conceivably dispensable. In some laboratory experiments with lower animals, it has been possible to start the process of division and multiplication of the ovum by stimuli other than male sperm. There are frogs and rabbits hopping about whose only father has been a bit of chemical or the touch of an electric needle.

There are important differences between men and women related directly to their sexual functions. There is no male counterpart for menstruation, pregnancy, parturition, or lactation. Males can have intercourse only when aroused to erection; females can perform their role without desire. Men are usually more quickly ready for intercourse; in women the processes of physical stimulation take a little longer. Men commonly come to orgasm more quickly, and considerate husbands learn to time their reactions to the responses of their wives. The sex drive in human males can be easily conditioned to pictures or other stimuli. So-called perversions and fetishisms are much more commonly found in men (Ellis, 1900–1910). Exhibitionism and peeping are more frequently male activities. Ford and Beach (1951) report that in lower animals it is also true that the male sex urge can readily be conditioned to neutral signals; in female animals this is difficult.

Data on frequency of desire show great individual variation. On the average, the post-pubertal male feels the pressure of sexual desire two or three times a week. At every age from childhood to old age, average frequencies of sex outlet, reported by Kinsey, are greater for males than for females. Yet a small number—about 3 percent—of women report frequency of intercourse higher than that found in any men. More typical of physiological and psychological differences is that sex desire in the female is often related to the menstrual cycle; in men the hormones show no such pattern. About one-third of women can live comfortably with no sex activity; very few men can do so.

The Kinsey data have been criticized on several grounds which are pertinent to social psychology. One is that a statistical norm is not an ethical norm; what is now done does not govern what ought to be done. Another problem, left unsolved by the extensive record of present practice, is the relative contribution of physiological factors and of the effects of training. Apparent differences between men and women may be innate or they may be the consequences of differential upbringing, social standards, and controls. It is reasonable to suppose that periodicity related to the monthly cycle is innate; that the exploitation of lower-status females by males who hold higher economic and social positions arises in the social system. The concern of young women for a marriage which will guarantee economic security and emotional support may stem both from instinctive maternal impulses and from the arrangements, customs, and expectations of our culture.

A subtle psychological difference arises from the difference in readiness for intercourse. The male, often and quickly aroused, has a sense that his is the natural initiative. The female reaction is described by Beauvoir: "Her passive eroticism makes desire seem to her not will and aggression but an attraction akin to that which causes the divining rod to dip; the mere presence of her flesh swells and erects the male's sex; why should not hidden water make the hazel rod quiver?" (1953, p. 599) So she would explain an alleged feminine credulity for astrology, telepathy, clairvoyance, faith-healing, and bizarre religious cults.

At one time, the problems of the menopause or "change of life" were supposed to afflict women but not men. More recent research indicates that women engaged in creative professional careers may suffer little, if at all, from the glandular readjustments in middle life (Davidoff, Markewich, 1961), while the male reaction to growing old has been given increasing attention. Differences once thought to be biological seem to be largely culturally conditioned reactions. Few persons of either sex experience without some dismay the waning of vital energies.

On general energy and vitality, evidence of sex differences is meager and contradictory. Boys are reported to be more active than girls, harder to toilet-train, and generally less corrigible. They enjoy, as every parent of boys knows, more rough-house, wrestling, tumbling, and fighting than the modern living room can absorb without damage.

On the other hand, there is a kind of life-force in the typical woman as she chooses a father for her children, builds a home to provide security, gives birth, and fights against any odds for the welfare of her children, which is at least as powerful as the male achievement drive. In some career women also, there is evidence of a remarkable animation. Ernest Jones, a leading psychoanalyst, concludes: "Whatever the average may be in the two sexes, that indefinable quality called 'vitality' reaches on occasion a higher pitch of intensity, amounting to true genius, in the female sex than it ever does in the male" (1959, p. 76). Jones and George Bernard Shaw were particularly impressed by the evident "vitality" in such prominent actresses of their day as Ellen Terry and Mrs. Patrick Campbell (B. Watson, 1964, p. 75). There have been relatively few ruling queens, but the records set by Elizabeth I, Catherine the Great, the Empress Maria Theresa, and Queen Victoria can be equalled by few, if any, kings.

Intelligence and temperament

One of the first applications of intelligence tests, after they had been devised early in the twentieth century, was to discover whether boys were better endowed than girls. Gradually results established the conviction that there is no real difference in intellectual level. At a given stage of development girls may talk or read a little better than boys, but the advantage does not last; by college age no difference is found between the sexes in aptitude for higher education. The larger proportion of males in most courses in mathematics and engineering is today attributed largely to cultural factors; it is believed that, given comparable incentives, females could do about as well as males in any kind of mental work. We are so well aware of this today it may be hard to realize that the finding met considerable resistance at first. Terman and Miles (1936) further showed that as one ascends the intelligence scale, the differences in interests and personality between the sexes become less and less marked.

Personality differences, like the biological, show fairly consistent superiority for the female. More boys than girls turn out to be behavior problems and truants at school. More boys than girls are referred to child-guidance clinics (Gilbert, 1957). Under-achievement is twice as characteristic of gifted boys as of gifted girls (Gowan, 1955).

At the adult level, four times as many men as women become chronic alcoholics. The criminal population is largely male. Men automobile drivers are more likely to get into fatal road accidents than are women. Jahoda (1933) studied an Austrian village in which almost everyone had been unemployed for years. Morale broke down in the men more seriously than in the women. Durkheim (1897) found in several countries in Europe that male suicides were about four times as common as female suicides.

Perhaps the major factor in most of these personality differences is that girls are better able (by nature or training) to accommodate themselves to an unpleasant situation. A good illustration of the point is found in an experiment by Patchen (1958). Junior high school pupils were given a list of simple tasks and asked to rate "how well you think you would like doing them." Alphabetizing a list of names, for example, was rated unpleasant; modeling in clay was attractive. Later these youngsters were assigned certain tasks. Some pupils got the jobs they had chosen; others were given unattractive chores. The girls assigned unchosen tasks did more work than the boys; they did better quality work; and they expressed less resentment at the allegedly "impartial" scheme which led to their particular work assignment.

Definitive studies on sex differences in temperament in infants and young children are lacking, but parents and teachers commonly report that boys are more assertive, aggressive, and obstreperous. It may be argued that this masculine nonconformity will ultimately provide a dynamic force for progress (Lindner, 1952). Along the way, however, it seems to produce serious problems of adjustment.

Anthropological evidence

As noted in Chapter 9, many of our traditional Western stereotypes about the naturally masculine or feminine have had to be revised in the light of differences among cultures. Mead (1928) describes the "masculinity" of Tchambuli men as centered upon grace, sensitivity, and ceremony. "Every man is an artist and most men are skilled not in some art alone, but in many: dancing, carving, plaiting, painting, and so on. Each man is chiefly concerned with his role upon the stage of society, with the elaboration of his costume, the beauty of the masks that he owns, the skill of his own flute-playing, the finish and elan of his ceremonies, and upon other people's recognition of his performance."

"Femininity" in the Tchambuli culture, means productive work. Gardening and fishing are women's occupations. The manufacture of mosquito-bags is done by women, but the bargaining during their sale is an art left to men. Final decisions on most major matters, such as marriage arrangements, lie with the women. Men are believed to be timid, suspicious, and prone to gossip; women are self-reliant, competent, easygoing. Tchambuli females often take the initiative in sex relations.

Another pattern emerges among the Arapesh, different from both the Tchambuli and our own culture. It is masculine, in Arapesh culture, to be gentle and helpful and to take care of small children. It is feminine to carry very heavy loads on one's head; strong neck and shoulder muscles (a "bull neck") is a feminine characteristic.

Among the Todas, housework is sacred and reserved for men. Among the Manu it is believed that men particularly delight in playing with babies. In one Philippine tribe, tradition has it that no man can keep a secret.

It is difficult to find in biological, psychological, or anthropological science any solid justification for male dominance. Any differences in competence seem to be socially conditioned rather than inherent.

Emancipation

In Western Europe and the United States the movement for rights of women began about 1800. We quoted Abigail Adams' protest earlier in this chapter. In 1792, Mary Wollestonecraft first published her remarkable *Vindication of the Rights of Women*. Later, she married William Godwin, who shared her advanced outlook, and who described his beautiful image of her in his novel *St. Leon* (1799). Their daughter, Mary, at age 17, eloped to France with the already married poet, Shelley, putting too great a strain on her father's liberal views.

The first college for women, Mt. Holyoke, was opened in 1837.

By the middle of the nineteenth century more substantial thinkers were developing the doctrine of sex-role equality. John Stuart Mill (1869), while recognizing that women had "not yet produced any of those great and luminous new ideas which form an era in thought, nor those fundamentally new conceptions in art," attributed this not to

438

any lack of native ability in females but to differences in the education given boys and girls. Women, he noted, have to be always ready to set aside any project of their own to minister to the needs of any members of their families. Mill suspected that many of the ideas for which men have received the credit had been suggested to them by women; he admitted that this was true in his own case. He saw with special clarity the restriction imposed on wives by the expectation that they must at all times please their husbands. "I am far from pretending," he wrote, "that wives in general are no better treated than slaves; but no slave is a slave to the same lengths and in so full a sense of the word, as a wife is." (1869, 1929 ed., p. 248)

The antislavery movement, as we have said, was closely linked with the woman's rights campaign. William Lloyd Garrison was a leader in both. Lucy Stone lectured against slavery on weekends and for women's rights on weekdays. Lucretia Mott and Elizabeth Stanton, pioneer feminists, met at an antislavery convention in London. Julia Ward Howe —famous for the *Battle Hymn of the Republic*—was also active in asserting the need to emancipate women. In 1848, when the the slavery issue was dividing opinions across the nation, the first Woman's Rights Convention met at Seneca Falls, New York. They saw "man" as the enslaver:

> He has compelled her (woman) to submit to laws in the formation of which she has no voice. . . . He has taken from her all right to property, even to the wages she earns. . . . In the covenant of marriage . . . the law (gives) him power to deprive her of her liberty and to administer chastisement . . . . He closes against her all the avenues of wealth and distinction which he considers most honorable to himself. . . . He has denied her the facilities for obtaining a thorough education, all colleges being closed against her. . . . He has endeavored in every way that he could to destroy her confidence in her own powers, to lessen her self-respect, and to make her willing to lead a dependent and abject life.

In 1853, the Rev. Theodore Parker proclaimed in Boston: "The domestic function of woman does not exhaust her powers. To make one-half the human race consume its energies in the functions of housekeeper, wife and mother, is a monstrous waste of the most precious material God ever made."

Ibsen's *A Doll's House* shocked Europe in 1879. When Nora's husband, Torvald, tried to tell her to accept her sacred obligation to be a wife and mother she replies: "I believe that before all else I am a reasonable human being, just as you are—or at all events, that I must try and become one." Near the end of the nineteenth century, George Bernard Shaw wrote: "No change that has taken place in our century has been more obviously a change for the better than the change in the relations between men and women." (1895, p. 108)

During the twentieth century, opportunities for women have been extended in many directions. The first person to parachute successfully from an airplane was Tiny Broadwich (Georgia Brown) in 1913. Amelia Earhart flew across the Atlantic only a year after Lindbergh's pioneer flight. Women were granted suffrage by Constitutional Amendment—after more than 70 years of struggle—in 1920. The first woman to enter Congress, Jeanette Rankin, had been elected in 1916. During World War II, several branches of the armed forces enlisted women and gave them officer's ranks and privileges. In the 1950's, about one-third of the nation's paid jobs were filled by women. By 1960, one of every three married women was employed in a job outside the home.

Significantly, when married women take jobs, the motive is to meet *psychological* needs more than economic needs. In the lowest fifth of family incomes, only 16 percent had both husband and wife working; in the fifth with highest incomes, 41 percent had both partners employed (Miller, Rein, 1964).

Between 1940 and 1956 the number of women holding supervisory or managerial posts doubled. The number of women in the professions also doubled in those 16 years. About a million women held executive positions in business and industry by 1965. Women outnumber men as stockholders, although many are simply carrying, in name, stocks bought by their husbands. But Wall Street, in 1964, had ten times as many women brokers, as in 1946. Another 1964 report, shows about 500 women executives on Madison Avenue in New York City, all of whom earn over $10,000 a year.

The first woman to enter the cabinet of the President of the United States was Frances Perkins, appointed Secretary of Labor by President Franklin D. Roosevelt in 1932. Willingness to vote for a well-qualified woman for President is rising. In 1937 only 34 percent of a sample poll reported that they would support a woman, if nominated by their chosen party. The proportion of supporters rose to 57 percent in 1963 (American Institute of Public Opinion, Nov. 15, 1963). This may be compared with willingness to support, under the same conditions, a Catholic (84 percent), a Jew (77 percent), or a Negro (47 percent).

The progress has not been continuous. Between 1934 and 1959, there occurred a swing of the pendulum re-emphasizing home-making as the right and sufficient career for women. The Nazis insisted that a woman's responsibility was properly limited to *Kinder, Küche, Kirche* (children, cooking, church). Friedan (1963) has noted that heroines in stories published by popular magazines for women, in 1939, were adventuring into new careers. But, "in 1958 and again in 1959, I went through issue after issue of the three major women's magazines . . . without finding a single heroine who had a career, a commitment to any work, art, profession or mission in the world" (p. 44). She notes also that the proportion of women among college students was 21 percent in 1870; it rose to 47 percent by 1920; but fell off to 35 percent in 1958. Women received 16 percent of the doctoral degrees awarded in 1920; in 1961–62 only 10 percent.

Other countries have also accepted women in new roles. About three-fourths of the physicians of the Soviet Union are women, as are nearly one-third of their professional engineers. More than a quarter of the Deputies in the Supreme Soviet are women. The United Nations Commission on Status of Women reported, in 1959, new opportunities for women operating electronic data-processing machines (Austria); studying nuclear energy (Belgium); as meteorologists (India); in machine design (Switzerland); and in pharmacy (Thailand). In 1963, the first woman cosmonaut was launched by the Soviet Union.

Some new patterns seem to be emerging. In the United States today, girls are marrying on the average before they are twenty. Their last child enters school by the time the mothers are 30 or 35. Radcliffe, Vassar, Sarah Lawrence, the University of Minnesota, and other colleges are developing special programs for mothers who want to come back to finish degrees and to prepare for careers outside the home. When mothers and fathers are both employed, the men share in preparing meals, doing dishes, cleaning house, washing clothes, shopping, and child care (Blood, Hamblin, 1958).

Prejudices still persist

Despite the gains that have been made, deep-rooted prejudices with far-reaching consequences still persist.

Many interesting and rewarding jobs are open only to men. Komarovsky (1953) found that 11 percent of the occupations in our society are limited to women; 10 percent are equally accessible to both; while 79 percent usually require men. A public opinion poll (Hyman, Sheatsley, 1950) found three of every ten American men convinced that any man who can fill a job satisfactorily should be given preference over any woman for the position. Only about 2 percent of higher positions in Federal Civil Service are filled by women, despite the rules for equal treatment. Only 6 percent of our doctors, 4 percent of our lawyers, less than 2 percent of engineers, and less than 1 percent of clergyman are women. No woman has yet been chosen as pope, cardinal, bishop, or even Catholic priest; very few have been ordained as ministers or rabbis. In most business and professional fields, women have to be considerably abler than the average man to reach average status. A report of the Women's Bureau (#249, 1953) says that although 1,000 women have been certified as commercial airplane pilots, only two have been given positions by the airlines. After reviewing the filling of 215 posts in nine universities two sociologists (T. Caplow, and R. J. McGee, 1958) concluded: "Women scholars are not taken seriously and cannot look forward to a normal professional career."

The positions most likely to be available to women are dull or ill-paid or both. More than half of the employed women are occupied as clerical workers, factory operatives, domestic servants, sales girls, waitresses, or cleaning women. It is taken for granted that men direct enterprises while female aids do the routine tasks. In a large graduate class, at the beginning of the year, small groups were set up, each containing some men and some women. When they chose a group chairman, most chose a man. When they chose a recorder to take notes, most chose a woman. Even graduate students in social psychology in the 1960's un-critically operated on the traditional assumptions of male dominance and female subordination.

Top prestige jobs are reserved primarily for men. It will be many decades before a woman becomes President of the United States or Chief Justice of the Supreme Court, although many women doubtless surpass in ability our average president or justice. No woman has been president of the American Psychological Association for forty years, although a substantial part of the qualified membership is made up of women, and psychologists might be expected to be able to transcend unjustified popular prejudices. There are fewer women college presidents today than there were a generation ago. Most of the women's colleges are headed by men, and no college for men has yet dared seek a woman president. Current public opinion polls have shown that it is thought appropriate for women to run the PTA. or the Red Cross, but that men should head corporations, factories, banks, chain stores, cities, states, and the nation. In occupations primarily staffed by women, men still give the orders. The doctor directs the nurse; the school superintendent leads the teachers; men in the social work profession have a better chance for administrative positions.

When jobs are equal outside the civil services, men are likely to be paid more than women. *Business Week* (Oct. 7, 1961, p. 97) reports that an advertising agency gave a position as senior account executive to a capable woman at $9,000 although they were prepared to pay several thousand more for an equally capable man. The same article reports an estimate that women's salaries average about 86 percent of what is paid men with identical skills and experience.

While the patriarchal, male-dominated family is less common today, it still prevails in many rural areas and among recent immigrants. Yet even "modern" couples who consider their marriage status equal, retain some assumptions of feminine subordination. Only the bride is "given"

to her mate and may be asked to promise to "obey." While both partners may have jobs, the husband's usually takes priority.

The "double standard" still permits husbands more freedom than it
allows wives. A poll (*Fortune*, Aug. 1945) showed that four times as
many Americans condemned infidelity severely in a wife as would condemn similar behavior by a husband. "The counsel dispensed to dissatisfied wives in newspaper columns of advice to the lovelorn," writes
Simone de Beauvoir, "is full of the spirit of abject submission" (1953,
p. 604). *She* must be patient, tolerant, long-suffering, and hold the
family together at any cost to herself. We are still not so changed from
the days when Elizabeth Cady Stanton wrote: "A man in the full tide
of business or pleasure can marry and not change his life one iota; he
can be husband, father, and everything besides; but in marriage,
woman gives up all" (1889, p. 720). This remains particularly true in
lower-class communities where women are seen as existing to serve the
comforts of men; to cook what a man wants to eat; to keep the children from bothering him when he comes home tired from work; to give
him sexual pleasure on demand; to keep his house neat; and to flatter
his ego by submission. A professional man may be proud of his wife's
career and take satisfaction in giving her the assistance she needs. A
working-class husband is more apt to feel that his wife's working belit-
tles his capacity to support her. She may work when the wages are
needed, but must stop—whatever the outside job means in other satisfactions for her—as soon as he can become an adequate "provider." Her
idleness suits his vanity.

Even Nature is unfair: Men can become fathers for more years than
women can become mothers. If a marriage ends, by a death or divorce,
when the couple are in their forties, the man will probably find it easy
to re-marry; the woman, despite her longer life expectancy, is both physi-
ologically and emotionally "too old."

It is hardly surprising that many women are deeply discontented. All
through girlhood and adolescence, their goal has been a happy marriage.
They may have it, but being "just a burdened housewife" may not fulfill their needs. As Betty Friedan puts it: "The feminine mystique has
succeeded in burying millions of women alive. . . ." They see no way
to "break out of the housewife trap" (1963, p. 336–7).

The basic problem

Primary roles differ
The root of the discrimination is the assumption that a man's vocation is primary; his role as husband and father is secondary. For women
the reverse is true: reproductive and nurturant functions are primary

while occupation is secondary. If children are ill and require attention, father still must go to his office; mother must stay home from her job. If father's company wants to transfer him, he goes despite inconveniences to his family. If mother can get a better job elsewhere, she is not free to accept the opportunity unless she can guarantee appropriate child care.

In our society, and in most others, the boys are brought up to achieve; the girls to conform. Among 110 cultures studied (Barry *et al.*, 1951) while there was little difference between the treatment of boys and of girls in early infancy, during childhood most cultures foster self-reliance and achievement in boys; obedience, nurturance, and responsibility in girls. About 80 percent of the known societies follow this pattern; in 10 percent there is little difference; about 10 percent cultivate the traits in reverse, with the females bent on mastery and the males submissive.

The difference in primary emphasis is built into boys and girls all through their lives. The toys of boyhood are building blocks, trains, guns and punching bags; those of girlhood are dolls, doll houses, doll clothes, and tea sets.

Hartley (1961) asked 90 girls and 40 boys (age 8 and age 11) who, in their view, performed each of 150 different acts related to daily life. For example, "Who mostly fixes this kind of thing (a lamp with a broken plug)?" or "Who usually uses this (a shovel)?"

She found about 99 percent agreement that sewing, scrubbing a floor, washing or ironing clothes, dusting, or using a vacuum cleaner were woman's duties. Men were seen as putting out fires, repairing cars, teaching a boy to ride a bicycle, cutting down trees, fixing plumbing, working in a mill, driving a truck, or piloting a plane. There can be little doubt about the greater interest and excitement in the male list. Sixty-eight percent of the items assigned mainly to women were in the area of household care; for men, only 26 percent were connected with the home. Boys and girls agreed on almost all the items, and the distinctions were as well established at age 8 as they were by age 11. Further data are in Abstract 47.

When Hartley (1959) asked boys of 8 and 11 what boys need to know and to be able to do, the answers were: "They have to be able to fight in case a bully comes along; they have to be athletic; they have to be able to run fast; they must be able to play rough games; they need to know how to play many games—curb-ball, baseball, basketball, football; they need to be smart; they need to be able to take care of themselves; they should know what girls don't know—how to climb, how to make a fire, how to carry things; they should have more ability than girls; they need to know how to stay out of trouble; they need to know arithmetic and spelling more than girls do."

Boys think men are very important and able to do what they like.

Abstract 47

TITLE   Children's Concepts of Male and Female Roles.

AUTHOR   Ruth E. Hartley

PROBLEM   How do children see the male and female roles in our society today?

SUBJECTS   47 boys and 110 girls; 23 at age 5; 63 at age 8; 71 at age 11.

PROCEDURE   A battery of play, pictorial, and verbal tasks. Some data summarized here come from responses to the following questions:

1. "Suppose you met a person from Mars—or the moon— and he knew nothing about the way we live here, and he asked you to tell him about girls (your age) in this world —what would you tell him girls need to know or be able to do?

2. "What would you tell him boys need to know or be able to do?

3. "What would you tell him women need to know or be able to do?

4. "What would you tell him men need to know or be able to do?"

Other data come from analysis of responses to two in a series of pictures. One of these showed a woman with a briefcase walking away from a house, watched by a child within the house. The other showed a man leaving a watching child. The interview question for the first picture was: "This little girl is at home and her mother is going to work —how does the little girl feel about that? What makes you think so?" Other questions followed up the responses.

SOME FINDINGS   1. Children see women as functioning mainly in the home; 65 percent of responses (to the person from Mars question) fell into this category; only 6 percent referred to a work role for women.

2. Children see men as functioning also in the home (32 percent, of which 6 percent referred to activities commonly regarded as women's part of housework) but 27 percent referred to the work role. Other important categories for men were recreation and community life.

3. In the response to the picture of a woman leaving home, 64 percent of the subjects fancied that the woman was uncomfortable or unhappy about leaving. The percentage perceiving this kind of feeling rose from 53 percent at age 5 to 73 percent at age 11. In response to the picture of a man leaving, 69 percent reported him uncomfortable about it and the age trend was the same (53 percent at age 5, 83 percent at age 11).

As to whether the adult disliked the work, 45 percent of the children thought the woman did; 39 percent thought the man did. This negative attitude

Abstract 47—*Continued*

toward woman's work satisfaction was more common among children whose mothers did not work (54 percent compared with 37 percent).

4. The proportion of girls who said they planned to work after marriage was significantly ($p < .01$) larger than the proportion of boys who said they would consent to their future wife's working.

SOURCE: *Merrill-Palmer Quarterly,* 1960, VI:83–91.

They are the boss; they have the most money; they get the most comfortable chair; but they get angry a lot. They are more fun than mothers and have better ideas."

Concerning women's traditional household activities, Hartley received the following reflections: "They are always at those crazy household duties and don't have time for anything else." "Their work is just regular drudging." "Women do things like cooking and washing and sewing because that's all they can do." "If women were to try to do men's jobs the whole thing would fall apart with the women doing it." "Women haven't enough strength in the head or in the body to do most jobs." "In going to adventurous places women are pests—just a lot of bother. They die easily and they are always worried about their petticoats." "I don't know how women would get along without men doing the work."

Although most women hold a job at some time in their lives, work is not viewed as fulfilling personality needs in women as it does for men. Indeed, it is sometimes maintained that men have erected the complicated structure of civilization—its farms, factories, mines, banks, governments, arts, and services—in a strenuous effort to compensate for their obvious inability to bear a child.

Psychological studies of work satisfaction show that for both men and women, one's vocation fulfills many important needs other than providing income. Yet, a public opinion poll in the United States (1946) asking: "Do you think married women whose husbands make enough to support them should or should not be allowed to hold jobs if they want to?" brought a majority of "should not" answers from both men and women!

A study (Hartley, 1961) of working mothers showed that most of them viewed their job "as an aspect of their nurturant function. It is another way in which they can serve their families. They do not substitute work for family obligations—they *add* it to the traditional roster of womanly duties and see it as another way to help their husbands and provide for the needs of their children. Their husbands are still seen as the major and responsible breadwinners—they consider themselves merely as *helping* persons in this area."

Mary Ellen Chase, for three decades a teacher at Smith College, asked in an article in *Life* magazine: "Why is it that with their vast new freedom of opportunity, with time, talents, and encouragement, our women, with rare and notable exceptions, are not becoming great scientists, doctors, musicians, artists and writers? The best of the girls in our colleges display remarkable mental grasp and ability, do a very high grade of work and are potentially brilliant scholars and thinkers. What becomes of these abilities after those degrees are taken?"

The answer seems to lie in the subordinate place of vocation for women. Their hearts are seldom wholly in their work—not because of their hormones but because of the mores. A bachelor, unlike a spinster, is assumed to have chosen his role. An elderly woman teacher once confided to her friends: "Being an old maid isn't half bad after you quit struggling!" But that struggle, diverting a good share of attention from age 15 to 45, can irreparably damage a career.

Consequences

What are the consequences of the assumption that girls should seek their main fulfillment as wives and mothers while for men the husband-father roles are secondary to vocational achievement? We shall examine in following sections effects on the feminine ego, on male development, and the consequences for society generally.

Female role impairs her ego

Whether the growing girl accepts her prescribed role, or rejects it, or vaccilates in conflict, she is in trouble.

Suppose she embraces the "feminine mystique" as prescribed and succeeds in her efforts to attract boys, to get engaged by Christmas, to have a wonderful June wedding, to move to her own home, and to have babies soon. This was the predominant pattern among Vassar girls in 1956 (Sanford, 1956). "Strong commitment to an activity or career other than housewife is rare." "Vassar girls, by and large, do not expect to achieve fame, make an enduring contribution to society, pioneer any frontiers, or otherwise create ripples in the placid order of things. . . . Her future identity is largely encompassed by the projected role of wife-mother" (Bushnel, 1962). Another study—this one in a Midwestern university showed that the main goal of 70 percent of the freshmen women was to find a suitable husband.

For a few years, the teen-age girl, if she is attractive and popular, may have a princess role. She may live in a gratifying whirl of admiration, flattery, and servility. Meanwhile, of course, less attractive and unpopular girls may be miserable, suffering a quite unwarranted self-devaluation because they have few dates and those not with the boys of their choice. The campus queen herself, however, does not occupy her throne for more than a few years. Girls may be more eager than men for marriage as ceremony and status, but most studies show that the experience of being married proves more satisfying to husbands than to wives. Men continue their vocation; they see numerous friends of both sexes outside the home; they enjoy the comforts of home. For the wife the insistent, monotonous, confining routines of baby care, diapers, cleaning, sorting, chauffering, shopping, and money worries may be a painful contrast to her glamorous premarital visions. "Men," says one woman writer, a mother of three children, "are abashed . . . knowing that working is self-indulgent compared to keeping house and rearing children." The housewife grows inexorably older and, despite desperate efforts, less attractive to men. Her gay ascent was swift, her melancholy decline, prolonged.

Few boys, even in the exciting teen-age years, would gladly have been born girls. One study of fourth graders showed ten times as many girls wishing they could have been boys, as boys who would have chosen to be girls. A Gallup poll (July 15, 1965) showed that 16 percent of adult women wished at one time that they were men; only four percent of men had ever wished to be women.

Several studies have shown that girls do not usually find their life-role ego-gratifying. They do not identify with their mothers as readily as boys identify with their fathers (Emmerick, 1957). Both men and women see the male role as closer to what would be ideal for a human being (Eastman, 1956). A public opinion poll (*Fortune,* 1946) asked whether men or women had the more interesting life. A substantial majority of both men and women agreed that men's lives are more interesting. Distenfeld (1961) found that men generally rated themselves closer to their ideal of the masculine role than did women to the ideal feminine role. The masculine role was seen by both sexes as more socially desirable. Self-esteem was highest in women both married and employed.

The study in Abstract 48 explores whether women get more sense of worth from their roles at home or on the job.

A study of 614 wives living in or near Detroit (Wolfe, 1959), showed high satisfaction in 61 percent of the marriages in which authority was rather equally divided between husband and wife. In marriages where the husband dominated, 51 percent expressed high satisfaction. Wife domination was rare—only 19 cases—and only five of these reached high satisfaction.

Reaction to the subordinate status and less desirable role is the real root of what psychoanalysts have termed "penis envy." Alfred Adler saw more clearly than Freud that the deprivations which girls feel arise not

Abstract 48

TITLE · Social Roles of American Women: Their Contribution to a Sense of Usefulness and Importance.

AUTHORS · R. S. Weiss and N. M. Samelson

PROBLEM · How do American women feel about family, housework, job, and community life outside the home? Where do they get most sense of feeling useful and important?

SUBJECTS · 569 women over 21, selected to be a true probability sample of that population in the United States on the basis of age, marital status, education, and occupation.

PROCEDURE · Open-end interviews focused on the question: "What are some of the things you do which make you feel useful and important?"

SOME FINDINGS · 1. The depressed response, "*nothing* makes me feel useful or important" was given by none of the younger women but by about 20 percent of the older unmarried women, employed or unemployed.

2. Job activities were more frequently mentioned as a source of self-esteem than were housework, family, or informal community relations for every category of employed women except the older unmarried, who were more apt to be generally dissatisfied, but spoke of housework and job and family about equally often. Among the 93 married and employed women, 59 percent referred to job satisfactions and only 39 percent to gratifications from their housework.

3. Among women who were college graduates, housework was less often a source of self-esteem (31 percent as compared with 46 percent for less educated) and job was more often recognized (66 percent as compared with 52 percent).

4. Interpersonal relations in the family were less frequently mentioned than job or housework as a source of self-esteem, by every category in the study except young mothers with pre-school children and unmarried, unemployed, middle-aged women.

5. Informal interaction outside home or job was prominent in the responses of only one group: young unmarried women, 42 percent of whom mentioned these satisfactions. For other categories, the outside contacts were mentioned by about 28 percent of the unemployed women and 15 percent of the employed.

SOURCE: *Marriage and Family Living,* 1958 XX:358–366.

primarily from their anatomy but from their social role. Even if mother rules the household, she commonly treats the father as a prestige figure. His property, his tastes and prejudices, his decisions, are all to be respected. Often, he is the point of contact with what the child thinks of as that strange and important world beyond the home. When the wife sees that her life-chances are dependent upon her husband's success, she makes a life-project of husband management—his health, his appearance, his social contacts, his speech, his attention to business, his public relations. The daughter's Electra complex may be less a desire to go to bed with her father than to shine in reflected glory. Girls covet the freedom men enjoy more than they do the phallus.

Girls who accept the idea of male superiority build the corollary view of their own inferiority. They conclude that it is right for men to get better jobs and more pay. They shun working under a woman executive. They are bored by social gatherings exclusively female.

In a study (McKee, Sherif, 1957) of several hundred college students it was found that 61 percent of the women, but only 29 percent of the men, reported being troubled by feelings of intellectual inferiority. Girls believe women generally less able than men. Data support the conclusion that men are not intellectually superior to women.

Women who accept second-class citizenship and identify with the prescribed sex-role do not try to keep up with political issues. They echo their husband's opinions. This accounts, in part, for the disappointment of the advocates of women's suffrage, who expected that it would bring a wave of social improvement. It is interesting to note that while 58 percent of men said they would vote for a well-qualified woman if their party nominated her for President; only 51 percent of the women would support such a candidate (American Institute of Public Opinion, Nov. 15, 1963).

In a study (Remmers, Radler, 1957) of teen-agers, the differences were even more marked. Opposition to women holding high office was expressed by 31 percent of teen-age boys, but by 61 percent of teen-age girls. The prejudice against their sex seems somewhat stronger in women themselves than in men.

The damaging consequences of accepting the wife-mother role as the overriding meaning of woman's life become particularly apparent after the child-raising years. The self-concept is an internalized version of the evaluation others have given to a person. Girls who find themselves born to a subordinate status—aware at an early age that their opportunities for self-realization are more limited than those open to boys, subject for 30 years to conflict between the reproductive and more generally productive roles, under pressure to conform to a less desired social pattern, excluded from almost all positions of top prestige—almost inevitably question, as mature women, their own worth. Some may protest the social discrimination—Margaret Mead estimates that about one woman in four is outspoken about her resentment—but the more usual result is self-derogation. Pauline Wilson (1950), interviewing woman college graduates 20 years after graduation, found 90 percent of them troubled by a sense of disappointment, frustration, and futility in their lives.

The internalization of blame may result, as it does sometimes with ethnic minorities, in rejection of one's own group. Women sometimes complain that conversation with other women is superficial and silly. Men are also bored occasionally by other men, but they blame it on the individual, not the whole sex. Women are likely to prefer male doctors, dentists, lawyers, ministers, and psychotherapists. Dissatisfied with their own mothers and with themselves, they admire few women and set a discouraging model for their daughters.

Discontent usually increases in the age group of women just beyond 40. If single, they have to face the fact that they have not fulfilled woman's traditional role—marriage and motherhood. If married, their children are ready to leave the home. The average woman today marries at about 20 and has had her last child before she is 25. At 45 or 50 years of age, her period of reproductive functioning—supposed to be her primary source of self-esteem—is over. The woman, who has been taught and pressured to put her love-life and children ahead of any other interests, finds herself no longer glamorous to men, and no longer needed by her children. At about 50 years of age, when men of comparable ability are stepping into their posts of highest responsibility, women find themselves with no meaningful occupation. Restlessly, they turn increasingly to beauty parlors, community organizations, alcohol, churches, and psychotherapists, but in this society there is no really satisfying answer. George Bernard Shaw has pointed out that if most men were as cut off from intellectual and public interests as are most women, the father-in-law jokes might be as common as those that caricature mothers-in-law (B. Watson, 1964, p. 158).

Often when women try to adapt themselves to their disadvantaged status, they add to their rejection. If they show that they are sorry for themselves and seek pity, they are likely to be scorned. If they transfer their distress to somatic symptoms, they may make many visits to the doctor complaining of disorders that have no organic basis. Their pains are real enough, and the lack of diagnostic confirmation increases the woman's sense of her own worthlessness.

Often a woman puts the blame for her dissatisfaction on the decisions of her career. "I should not have dropped out of college!" "If only I hadn't been such a fool as to get married at that time!" "What a bill-of-goods that man sold me! If only I'd had enough sense to choose so-and-so instead!" "I could have made something of myself if it hadn't been for having to care for that relative." Thus the sad refrains of self-accusation continue.

Some women rebel vigorously and develop careers. As the Weiss and Samelson study, summarized earlier, has shown, such women find increased self-esteem from their success at work. But they find the path harder as they achieve more success. A woman can easily become an office manager; she is likely to encounter more prejudice against her as a vice president.

The rebellion of the active woman may lead to conscious or unconscious revenge on the dominant males in this man's world. Some women enjoy any opportunity to cut down male egoes. They are sometimes called "castrating females." Any self-assertion or self-satisfaction in boys or men, stirs up their rancor. As mothers and teachers they can inflict serious damage on young males.

The woman who tries to combine homemaking with a career not only has many practical complications, but may suffer also from a sense of guilt. Herzog (1960) reports that although children are not often really deprived by a mother who holds a job, working mothers nevertheless feel guilty when they leave house and children for their careers. They also feel they are lacking something when they are not working or earning. In suburban communities where most mothers spend the day at home, the mother who commutes daily to a job in the city is looked at with some envy and some criticism. She responds to both; she feels fortunate in not being immured in kitchen and laundry chores; she also wonders whether she is doing the right thing for her family. Sometimes she vaccilates—stays home and becomes bored; takes a job and feels "driven" and guilty; gives it up for home and restless boredom—and on through the cycle.

Small wonder that Betty Friedan can quote mothers as saying: "I feel empty somehow—incomplete;" "I feel as if I don't exist;" "I feel like crying without any reason." She quotes from *Newsweek:* The American housewife "is dissatisfied with a lot that women of other lands can only dream of. Her discontent is deep, pervasive, and impervious to the superficial remedies which are offered at every hand" (1963, p. 20; 24). A study (Davidoff, Markewich, 1961) of 50 college-educated women confirmed Wilson's observation, ten year's earlier, of a discrepancy between the values cultivated in college and the actual opportunities open to the women for achievement, success, and recognition. The volunteer jobs open to them seemed beneath the self-respect of the abler women.

Males suffer too

While women are under pressure to emulate a stereotype which stresses family life and neglects other important aspirations, males are pressed into striving for achievement which may not give full play to the potential of boys and men for tenderness, intimacy, and love. Any display of affection among males is highly suspect in our culture, although in ancient Greece and many other lands it has reached high levels. Boys are disciplined to repress tender feelings. They may not cry. They must not do anything that may label them as a "sissy." They must fight when they would rather run away, compete destructively when they might prefer cooperative friendship. A study of kindergarten boys (Hartley, 1959) showed that more distinctive and appropriate sex-role behavior was demanded from them than it was from girls their age. Boys had more anxiety about their ability to perform the required roles.

The commuter father may see very little of his family. During much of the year he is up before dawn, gulps his breakfast, departs before his family are out of bed, returns after dark for a late dinner, and may have evening meetings or a briefcase of homework before bed. Since other men take this heavy work load for granted, he, too, seldom wonders whether this prescribed occupational role really fulfills his whole self and destiny. Men are also expected to take strong initiative in courtship and sex relations; to support wives who may, if they choose, be self-indulgent and idle; to keep up with community, national, and world affairs; to serve in the armed forces; and generally to show forbearance and strength, come what may. This is no easy assignment if we recognize that, by nature, the male is no more equipped for such roles than is the female. Many men enjoy cooking; most fathers would appreciate more time with their children. A fairly typical misfortune is that of the man who intends to make friends with his sons and daughters but puts it off until it is no longer possible to achieve close understanding.

Boys, seeing less of their fathers than girls of their mothers, find it harder to identify with them. If the father is seen as a remote and punish agent (Hartley, 1959), it is difficult for the son to choose him as a life model. The demand that one become a strong, decisive, courageous, bearer-of-burdens and protector of the weak, able to cope with all difficulties from broken equipment to world affairs, is heavy indeed when there is seldom anyone around to set such an example.

Hacker, in an article with the meaningful title, "*New Burdens of Masculinity*" (1957), lists such role prescriptions as: (1) being patient, gentle, understanding yet sturdy as an oak; (2) being a person on whom a wife can rely to make decisions but who leaves her free to make her own; (3) compulsion to succeed in gainful employment; and (4) a virility which can be demonstrated only by evoking orgasm in his mate. To these are added the recent threat of competition from women in the professions, business, and industry. Some men, should women become their colleagues and share their daily routines, may find it impossible to sustain the image of the male's remarkable achievements at work.

As with every other form of discrimination, it is not only the direct victims who are injured. Boys and men suffer indirect consequences of sex discrimination against females which are almost as bad as the effects upon girls and women. Most boys today are brought up in early life surrounded by women and girls. Baby nurses in the hospital, mothers and mother-helpers at home, nursery school, kindergarten, and elementary school teachers are almost all women. In varying degrees they all suffer from their subordinate status. To some extent, they express their resentment—usually unconsciously—on the boys in their care. Or, in compensation, they become "smothering mothers," spoiling boys by overprotection.

In adult life, the man's closest and most continuous companion is his wife. Her limitations and her emotional frustrations inevitably impinge upon the man's own life. An interesting illustration is the "child wife" type, described by Greenacre (1947). The ideal wife in certain upper-class circles in Europe and in our own South was a pampered, infantile, pretty, frivolous, light-headed, extravagant, flirtatious creature who needed the protection of a big strong man.

Some men prefer women who are silly, frilly, and dependent. Charlotte Brontë wrote of one fictional character: "At heart he could not abide sense in women: he liked to see them as silly, as light-headed, as vain, as open to ridicule as possible . . . inferior toys to play with, to amuse a vacant hour and to be thrown away" (Vol. I, p. 166). However gratifying this may be to the ego of a young male, the time is likely to come when he would be happier with a helpmate who equals him in good sense, good conversation, and responsibility.

Intelligent girls who learn to act dumb on dates may flatter male vanity, but they deprive their companion of the stimulation and challenge which their ideas and viewpoints might have contributed. Without true reciprocity both partners lose the opportunity for growth in the dimensions of mature personality. Many men suffer in adolescence, in maturity, and in old age from the limited horizons our culture has imposed upon their most intimate partners. As George Bernard Shaw has said: "Men are waking up to the perception that in killing women's souls they have killed their own" (1932, p. 8).

Talents lost to society

The unused potential of women represents a loss to our civilization. "All geniuses who are born women," said Stendahl, "are lost to the public good." If we are concerned about a shortage of scientists in the United States, it may be salutary to recall that 40 percent of the members of the Academy of Sciences in the Soviet Union are women. The lives of men, too, may have been endangered and impoverished by the absence of discoveries that women might have made, the music they might have composed, the books they might have written, and the philosophic insights they might have generated.

Important occupations ill-paid

The identification of certain occupations as women's work has brought one consequence that is seldom analyzed. Why are teachers often ill-paid? The intellectual and spiritual guidance of the American child today is generally left to persons who are paid less than factory-hands. A major reason is that teaching, especially in the elementary schools, is perceived as "woman's work." For the same reason, nurses, librarians, and social workers are underpaid. An honest appraisal of the importance of education, child guidance, health care, books, and family welfare would place these functions high on the list of professional activities. The economic return is kept low by the perpetuation of a caste of cheap labor virtually excluded from high-paid occupations.

The future

Resistance

Goals, in sex role as in race relations, now lie in the direction indicated by words like democracy, equality, mutuality, reciprocity, collaboration, comradeship, freedom, liberty, and self-actualization. The obstacles are now not so much economic or political as psychological.

The first obstacle is the pretense that there is no problem. We are further along in dealing with racial or religious prejudice than we are in coping with sex prejudice because it is the fashion among men to complain, seriously or in jest, that women have everything their own way. Little research has yet been done on sex prejudice, in comparison with the great accumulation of data on racial prejudice. The first step is to affirm the problem.

A second difficulty lies in freeing men from the sense that their worth and security would be threatened by increased freedom and recognition for women. It is always hard for a dominant group to see that elimination of their special advantages would be a long-term benefit. It will be some time before the traditional-minded whites in the South recognize that Negroes as well educated, well paid, and well housed as themselves will be a positive asset to the whole society. Employers have found it difficult to accept the idea that rising wages will benefit the entire economy. As long as men feel that their masculine dignity and privilege depend upon being able to look down on women, they will resist change.

While the old-fashioned dominating male can still be found in every social class, it is particularly in the less-educated lower classes that the old stereotypes are asserted and defended. The "war between the sexes" is fought most relentlessly in lower-class circles. As noted earlier, the higher one goes on the scale of intelligence and education, the fewer distinctions there are in dignity, freedom, interests, and values between men and women. Here again is a noteworthy parallel with the civil rights movement for Negroes. It is predominantly the lower-class white who is most ardent and bitter in his opposition to increasing opportunities for other races.

Satisfaction with male dominance is highest in men who score high on the F-scale which is an indicator of authoritarian personality. One study (Nadler, Morrow, 1959) showed a correlation of .66 between the F-scale and a questionnaire devised to measure approval of "open subordination of women." The questions referred to women's inferiority, lack of judgment, narrow-mindedness, superficiality, and need for male direction. Another scale in the same study was called "chivalry." This stressed the helplessness of women, their purity, delicacy, and the demands of courtly etiquette in relations of men with women. The chivalry scale correlated .35—only a fair measure of agreement—with the open-subordination scale. Chivalry also was closely related ($r = .60$) to authoritarianism. Both chivalry ($r = .73$) and open-subordination of women ($r = .45$) were associated with ethnocentrism in attitudes toward other races and ethnic groups. Put more positively, men who have a less prejudiced, more accepting and more egalitarian attitude toward other human beings are likely to show it in their relations with minority races, unpopular religions or nationalities, and also in their relations with women.

A third difficulty connected with improvement in the opportunities given women for self-fulfillment lies in the uncertain effect upon the emotional relations of the sexes.

Will the elimination of barriers of prejudice damage in some way the masculine-feminine polarities? Does equality imply in any degree the mannish woman and the effeminate man?

When we go beyond anatomical differences to try to understand masculine and feminine temperament, we move at once into a realm structured by culture. It may be true, as psychoanalytic theory maintains, that in the sexual act men are naturally more aggressive and women naturally more receptive. Yet this is surely an oversimplification of a complicated human relationship in which both partners may feel tenderness, thoughtfulness, erotic pleasure, intense passion, vigorous activity, and quiet relaxation. In any case we cannot assume that attitudes toward all other persons, things, and ideas derive from the relationship of sexual intercourse. Neither general biology nor human physiology can tell us what it means to have a masculine or a feminine outlook on life.

If we follow Jung, we explore the unconscious archetypes of the

Animus and the *Anima*. It is true that adolescent girls fantasy masculine figures like a knight or, in modern times, a James Bond or an astronaut. Any hard-working husband, however, whose meals must be cooked, his socks washed, and who worries over the household bills must be sadly disillusioning to a wife enamored of the *Animus* figures.

Men, too, have in their psyche symbolic *Anima* figures of ineluctable woman. Woman is the morning star, the unfolding rose, the precious jewel, the cyclic moon, the tides of ocean, the fertile earth, the chattering brook, the graceful cat, the singing bird, the changeable wind. Woman is nymph, siren, the Sphinx, the alluring Venus, the enchanting Circe. This aura of *Anima* femininity seems to be expressed mainly in contemplating actual or potential sweethearts; one seldom associates it with the women that one may encounter as middle-aged scrub-women, sales clerks, bookkeepers, high school teachers, or the club ladies of the cartoonist, Helen Hokinson. Men may note very little *Anima*-enchantment in some of the finest and most wholesome mothers, aunts, and grandmothers. But the magic is in the male lover's unconscious needs and will be cast over the object of his romantic affection, however silly or sensible she may be.

We do not know what the authentic sex-differentiation in personality would be in a genuinely equalitarian society, for neither boys nor girls have ever grown up in such a world. It seems probable that to view masculine and feminine in dichotomies like agressive-receptive, active-passive, dominant-submissive, decisive-responsive, leading-following, commanding-yielding, is a culturally-induced error. Men and women are first of all human. Both must meet the basic needs of life as other animals do, but both have the higher needs to make their lives meaningful and spiritually satisfying. Both enjoy, want, and appreciate the same things—adventure, security, responsibility, being cared for, creativity, artistic achievement. Both have a practical bent and a streak of idealism; both are often rational, sometimes irrational.

Again we may quote Shaw as a prophet of the New Day for women. "What women had to do was not to repudiate their femininity but to assert its social value; not to ape masculinity but to demonstrate its insufficiency." (1920, p. 443) Or, Simone de Beauvoir in the same spirit: "To recognize in woman a human being is not to impoverish man's experience; this would lose none of its diversity, its richness, or its intensity if it were to occur between two subjectivities." (1953, p. 261)

New roles

While some other countries—notably Sweden and the Soviet Union— have moved further than has the United States toward giving women freedom and equal opportunity to order their own lives, there is no pattern in other societies that can provide the answers we seek. Changes are needed in many aspects of life, and progress cannot be measured along a single linear scale. A better quality of life for men and for women cannot be guaranteed by equal rights legislation.

An essential first step is to recognize that both men and women are human beings entitled to develop their potentialities in their own chosen way. When someone asked Shaw the secret of his remarkable understanding of women—as demonstrated in the creation of characters like Lady Cecily, Major Barbara, Ann Whitefield, Candida, and Lina Szcaepanowska—he replied: "I always assumed that a woman was a person exactly like myself, and that is how the trick is done" (B. Watson, 1964, p. 21).

If it is true, as Existentialists maintain, that self-fulfillment requires projects subjectively proposed and pursued in freedom, this self-determination is as important for women as for men. Whether life will center primarily upon love, marriage, and children, or primarily upon achievement in science, business, engineering, or the fine arts is a choice which every individual—man or woman—should feel free to make for himself or herself. For some men and women family life will come first; for others, it will not. Some men and some women may choose to keep a fairly even balance of interests in the home and outside. What is important is to keep all choices free and open, for women as well as for men.

For historic-social reasons and because of biologically connected factors, women will probably complement the masculine patterns in modifying our civilization. Because women have not been deeply involved in the world's exploitation, competition, chauvinism, and militarism, they may have remained free from some of the usual masculine assumptions and illusions.

Again, because of physiological differences and a long history of limited opportunities, we need today a policy that goes beyond simple equality. "Equal consideration," writes one wise woman, "will always dictate special privileges for women." This is analagous to the principle of compensatory expenditures on education for lower classes and for minority races, as proposed in the preceding chapter.

Increasingly, psychologists think of social change not in terms of exact design and rigid prescription but in terms of evolution, emergence, becoming, and the fuller realization of human potentialities (Allport, 1955; Murphy, 1958). Our civilization is embarked upon such a process as we give new opportunities to children from lower classes, minority races, and to women. Masculine and feminine potentialities may emerge more distinctively and more attractively in the new freedom than they have ever seemed in any historic culture. If the old barriers go down and each sex is genuinely free to affirm its own nature and to define its own goals, we may expect greater self-realization and more valuable forms of interrelationship. The essential conditions are freedom, self-discovery, and growth.

Margaret Mead has happily described the emergence of new role patterns as "a ballet in which each couple must make up their steps as they go along. When he is insistent, should she yield, and how much? When she is demanding, should he resist and how firmly? Who takes the next step forward or the next step back?" (1955, p. 14)

Transition

Here and in the preceding two chapters, we have used the resources of social psychology to aid in efforts to reduce such barriers to human development as are set up by class disadvantage, race prejudice, and sex discrimination. In the three chapters which follow, we shall show how social psychology can contribute to the improvement of business enterprise, the reduction of international tensions, and conscious direction of social change.

CHAPTER THIRTEEN

Social psychology in business and industry

American society gives its highest rewards of money and power to those who are successful in corporate leadership. Other cultures may pay their highest premiums for excellence in the fields of painting, music, dancing, athletics, or philosophy. In part of the United States during the colonial period, ministers of the church were highest in prestige. But for a century or longer, business has been the most attractive vocational field for young Americans.

We shall introduce several kinds of contributions that psychology has made to the improvement of business operations. In general, we shall follow the historic sequence in which these developments took place, but none of them has declined. Each new approach has continued its own line of development and today continues to make important contributions to effective management. Early in the twentieth century, business and industry began to apply techniques derived from research in psychology. In recent years the interaction has moved in both directions, and discoveries made in industrial psychology have enriched understanding of social psychology generally.

Psychotechnics, engineering psychology, and "scientific" management

The earliest contributions to industry from psychological laboratories were not social but dealt with visual perception, learning curves for new tasks, the waxing and waning of attention, and fatigue. More than half a century ago one investigator (Wright, 1906) demonstrated that subjects improved more rapidly when they could see how well they were doing. F. W. Taylor, founder of that "Taylorism" which came to connote efficiency experts making time and motion studies, carried over into industry the then new and exciting psychological concept of individual differences (1903). Taylor was the pioneer in social psychological analysis of industrial work. "His friends and supporters saw him as a lofty humanitarian, his critics as the creator of a morbid scheme to reduce man to a machine" (Kelly, 1965). Taylor's aim was to design systems which would appeal to and enlist the cooperative motives of workers. His techniques, however, were taken over and exploited by short-sighted operators. So thoughtful a historian as Peter Drucker has written that "scientific" management, with its implication of better design for the processes of labor and industry, made a contribution to industry as significant as that of the *Federalist* papers to political democracy.

In more recent years, other psychological ideas have made contributions to improved industrial efficiency. Studies of "readability" (Lorge, 1959) have been used to improve communications addressed to employees. Research into industrial accidents threw light on accident-prone individuals, who have also been studied in clinical psychology. Safety has been enhanced as engineers and psychologists have cooperated in identifying accident-prone personalities and situations conducive to costly errors and injuries.

A typical recent project in psychotechnology was the comparative investigation of various schemes for dialing telephone numbers. Is the rotating dial more or less efficient than numbers punched as on an adding machine? Is a horizontal row better than a vertical row? How about two rows of five each rather than one row of ten?

A review in 1958 (Fitts) of 149 studies in "engineering psychology" covered such topics as systems design, automation, machines responsive to speech and handwriting, quickening feedback signals, speed-stress, tactile discrimination, prosthetic devices for amputees, lighting problems, safety equipment, and legibility of type and of instrument scales. Psychologists invented the teaching machines which have aroused considerable interest among educators both in schools and in industry (Skinner, 1954). In contrast to the studies of single movements in the early efficiency studies, contemporary psychological research considers the whole system: the man and the machine as they operate in the productive process (F. V. Taylor, 1957).

Selection and promotion

The second phase emerged after the extensive use of intelligence tests in World War I, when business began to employ psychologists to help in the selection of employees. It is much easier to decide whether a person does or does not have the qualifications required by one certain job than to make an over-all estimate of an individual's best vocational choice. Some kinds of position require high intelligence, capacity for abstract thought, imagination, and creativity. In others more routine and dealing with concrete materials, high intelligence would mean early dissatisfaction with the job. To meet the specifications of some jobs, the psychologist looks for warmth in human relations; for others, mechanical aptitude may be required.

In preparing selection procedures for a job, the psychologist obtains from the prospective supervisor a fairly specific account of the requirements for the job. Then, a combination of tests, life-history data, analysis of responses to pictures, stories, and incomplete sentences, with intuitive interpretation of the tests and interview experiences, permits a reasonably accurate estimate of whether the individual is likely to be happy and successful in that particular job, under that particular supervision. Responses to some kinds of tests—problem check lists and emotional symptom inventories—are too easily faked to be very useful in testing eager job applicants. Test scores alone are seldom an adequate basis for recommending appointment or rejection. The usual statistical procedures (correlation) for validating a test do not indicate how accurately a critical score (or range of scores) will differentiate "successes" from "failures" (Dunnette, 1963). Nevertheless, psychological reports can identify dimensions of strength, weakness, and undeveloped potential in prospective employees. A life insurance firm, as one example among many, found that using psychological evaluations significantly reduced turnover and wasted induction and training costs among their sales agents (Ferguson, *et al.*, 1959).

One industrial psychologist (Wilson, 1964) has proposed six major areas in which differences may account for the gap in achievement between two men of similar age, one of whom finds himself still an office worker while the other has become company president. These are: (1) intellectual competence; (2) emotional maturity; (3) drive and values; (4) insight into human behavior; (5) skill in human relations; (6) competence in such administrative procedures as planning, organizing, direction, and delegation of responsibility. An interview in depth, aided by suitable tests, can lead to fairly reliable estimates along each of these dimensions.

A number of business organizations have found it helpful to have an appraisal of promising employees to assist these persons in their own development. The procedure is much like that of testing and interviewing an applicant. The aim, however, is more inclusive. It is not simply to determine whether Mr. Green meets the requirements for promotion to a given supervisory position. It is rather to determine whether Mr. Green can go far in the company, what his assets and liabilities are, and how he can develop his potentialities. This kind of study requires more scope, flexibility, and depth. It is followed by a "feedback" to the individual—Mr. Green, in this illustration—with free discussion of how he and his company can work together to increase the probability of his success. Particularly where manpower seems scarce—as in the quest for young men whose ability, energy, human relations, and drive for achievement make them good prospects for high-salaried managerial responsibilities—corporations are finding it important to use psychological consultants to search among their own employees for undiscovered talent which can be developed.

A review (Ward, 1960) of executive testing among 1,800 subscribers to the *Harvard Business Review* showed that about 60 percent of companies with 10,000 or more employees use psychological tests as aids in the selection of salaried employees. Among respondents under 40 years of age, 90 percent had themselves taken such tests; even at age 60–65, a majority of executives had taken some such tests. Among those who had been tested and given a report of findings and recommendations, 70 percent replied that it had been "very interesting!" 60 percent called it "helpful" (some made both replies); while less than 10 percent reported that they found it "of no interest."

The writer, in appraising hundreds of candidates for executive positions, has found that, at first, many applicants are tense and apprehensive—"What are these gimmicks of the psychologist? What use is a 'head shrinker' to me in business?" As the interview in depth proceeds, however, communication flows; no tricks are played on the candidate; he discovers that he is being listened to, is treated with dignity and respect, and is helped to do some serious thinking about matters of genuine concern to him.

The increased size and complexity and rate of change in business operations, together with the new technology based on automation and electronic data processing, demand managers with exceptional brain power. A company's competitive standing in the future is likely to depend largely upon two factors: the intelligence of its leadership and the use of procedures that will mobilize all the potential knowledge and insight among employees at every level. A competently administered program of psychological evaluation of executives considered for employment or promotion can do much toward achieving superior potential in management. The second factor—full use of the available brain power at every level—depends upon forms of organization and operation to be considered later in this chapter.

One way of testing whether a man is likely to obtain the maximum contribution from subordinates is to explore the attitudes of his colleagues and of those who work under his direction. A manager gets his work done by and through other people. His effectiveness depends very much on how they respond to him. One study, typical of scores of other such investigations, showed that executives rated "excellent" were more apt than other managers to be seen by their superiors in the following ways: "permits subordinates to share in decision making," "makes full use of the skills and abilities of subordinates," "regularly informs subordinates of their progress." The best way to check such qualifications is to go directly to subordinates. Do they feel that they share in decision making? Do they believe that full use is being made of their abilities? Are they regularly informed of their progress? In this particular study (Brooks, 1955) these factors were confirmed. Employees of the most successful managers agreed that they did participate in setting targets for their work, that they were regularly informed of their progress, and that they did feel challenged to give their best efforts.

Other studies have investigated the failures of executives; again it appears that the critical factors relate to the responses these executives arouse in subordinates. Among these factors in one study (Laird, 1956) were: "failure to delegate," "failure to obtain subordinate's respect," and "failure to obtain cooperation of other executives." There is still need to heed the observation of the ancient Chinese sage Mencius: "When all those about you, the ruler, say that a man is talented, do not immediately rush to promote him. Only after his subordinates say so also should you examine him more fully as a candidate for promotion. In the same way, do not rush to demote a man on the evaluation of his superiors alone." (Quoted by Bass, 1960, p. 113)

We shall return, as the chapter proceeds, to the important social psychological aspects of managing. But, following the history of the uses of psychology in business, we find the next stage to be the beginning of consumer surveys.

Consumer and marketing research

When polls of public opinion became effective, another application of psychology in business was found. It was now possible to discover what proportion of a representative sample preferred Brand A to Brands B, C, or D. The next and more interesting question was "Why?" Correlation of responses with other data might indicate differences among socio-economic classes, age groups, geographic regions, levels of education, or between the responses of men and women. Some magazines, for example, regularly analyze a sample of subscribers to determine whether each article or story was read, enjoyed, and what differences in response emerge in respect to sex, age, and other categories. A baking company compared responses of a large sample of housewives to bread wrapped in cellophane as opposed to bread wrapped in wax paper (Brown, 1958). The former seemed "fresher" to most of them. Size and price as well as style of packaging can be market-tested.

Advertisements are often pre-tested to discover the reactions of a sample of the intended audience. One technique used in testing television commercials is to assemble reviewers of defined age, sex, class, etc. Each is seated comfortably to watch the television program. Each person holds push buttons in both hands. When he enjoys what he sees, he pushes the green button in his right hand. When he dislikes it or is annoyed, he pushes the red button in his left hand. If he is indifferent, he lets the show run along without pushing either. Data can be assembled electrically and recorded for the whole audience in a curve which reveals their pleasure or displeasure at every moment. This immediate reaction record can be combined with recall tests to determine what is remembered.

Equated samples of consumers may be interviewed month after month to determine whether an advertising campaign is having a cumulative effect. The panel method, described in Chapter 7, permits reports at various time intervals of how the same people are being influenced. Sometimes, instead of opinion polls or laboratory tests, observations are made at the point of purchase. A detergent may come in three package sizes and have numerous competitors. Observers at the point of selection may ask each purchaser in a sample of markets why one choice rather than another was made.

Consumer psychology by 1965 had reached the status warranting a separate chapter in the *Annual Review of Psychology;* a *Journal of Marketing Research* was established in 1964.

A typical experiment in consumer psychology attempts to simulate the situation in which a customer chooses one brand over another. Assortments of goods are presented (actually or in photographs) with varying price tags, making it possible to measure brand-loyalty by price differential (Pessemier, 1963). Another device (Schwerin, Murphy, 1963) measures the extent to which various stimuli (e.g., pictures of cakes) cause salivation responses in the potential buyer. It can be used to pre-test advertisements.

One of the controversial newcomers in this field a few years ago was "motivational research" (Dichter, 1956), which seeks to discover unconscious factors influencing a purchase. At one time, one brand of cigarettes had a feature which many men considered effeminate. The company, discovering this, launched an advertising campaign featuring the most rugged male symbols they could devise. Advocates of motivational research contend that when a middle-aged, married man buys a racy sportscar he is not primarily interested in horsepower and gas consumption. When a young woman tries on shoes, she is usually not thinking mainly of comfort or durability. Does a typewriter have, for a secretary, an emotional as well as practical value? Evidence from psychoanalysis suggests that even such mundane items as kitchen knives or coffee cups may have hidden symbolic meaning for many people. Many people spend more freely if they can attribute moral objectives rather than pure pleasure to their purchases. To what extent these unconscious associations actually affect purchasing is still a matter of dispute and needs further research (see Packard, 1957 for a critique).

Advertising has become a prominent feature of capitalist societies. "In the Western world," says the noted historian, Arnold Toynbee, "the tempter's role is being played by everything we sum up under the name of Madison Avenue. A considerable part of our ability, energy, time and material resources is being spent today on inducing us to . . . find the money for buying material goods we should never have dreamed of wanting had we been left to ourselves" (Quoted, *Time*, Sept. 22, 1961, p. 112). Professor Toynbee concluded by predicting that the destiny of Western civilization is more dependent on "our struggle with Madison Avenue and all that it stands for," than on the issue of our contest with Communism.

It is easy to see the value of advertising in introducing a new product or service. Most advertising today, however, seeks to persuade people to buy one brand rather than another although both products might be equally satisfactory and perhaps indistinguishable to the consumer if they were not strikingly labeled. Somehow the effect of advertising, as Toynbee suggests, is to induce people to spend for items which do not really enrich their lives. The social effects are particularly damaging when they cause people to want what they cannot afford. The choice, if they cannot increase their income, may lie between the shortcuts of crime and chronic attitudes of disaffection and resentment produced by frequent frustration.

As the War on Poverty was launched, in 1964, Walter Heller, chairman of the Council of Economic Advisers, told the U.S. Congress that the total "cost of leveling up all poor families to an annual income of $3,000 would be about $11 billion a year." It seems likely that wise expenditures to eliminate poverty might do more for business and human welfare than increased sophistication of marketing or increased prodding through advertising.

Work satisfaction and morale

Another stage of development in psychology introduced concern for work enjoyment. Work is potentially one of the most satisfying of human activities. The notion that all work is a burden and should be reduced to as few hours as possible is untenable. Men who are unemployed are miserable, not only because of lack of income, but also because they miss the work and the status of a worker. Bakke (1934) in one of the earliest and best studies of the attitudes of unemployed men found many of them taking the attitude expressed by one former brewery worker in Britain: "It ain't the money any more than it is the fact that you don't have nothin' to do. Your money at the Labour (unemployment benefit) helps out a bit but it don't give you no work to do, and that's what I miss."

Other evidence that people are sustained by work is found in what has happened as the working week has grown shorter. Sociologists have predicted a great increase in leisure. Many men, however, have responded to an increase in leisure time by taking a second paid job, or by working on a project of home improvement. They keep busy. Married women whose home duties no longer require full-time attention are moving increasingly into jobs. Many retired men, for whom money is not a serious problem, are unhappy because they miss the contacts and activities of their job. In one survey the proportion of persons who found satisfaction in their work was about as high as the proportion who reported satisfaction in marriage. In what may have been the first attempt at an objective psychological study of adult happiness, the author (1930) found that satisfaction in work correlated higher (men .71; women .51) with general over-all happiness in life than did satisfaction with recreation, friends, love life, or religion. A more recent study reports a correlation of .67 between a test of job satisfaction among civil servants and their general life satisfaction (Brayfield, *et al.*, 1957). As another piece of evidence that work is more often satisfying than disliked, Morse and Weiss (1955) reported that 80 percent of a national sample of men said that they would want to continue working even if they were financially independent. Morse and Weiss found that 70 percent of professionals would continue in the same kind of work, but that only 30 percent to 40 percent of skilled or semiskilled laborers would want the same kind of job. A review of six studies, covering more than 3,000 employees, shows dissatisfaction ranging from 10 to 21 percent; in every case a large majority of workers found their jobs a source of satisfaction (Blauner, 1960).

When behavioral scientists began to study work satisfaction (Parker, 1917; Mayo, 1933) they challenged the prevailing simplistic stereotype of "economic man," who was assumed to be motivated only by desire for more money and fear of losing his job. As reported in Chapter 3, workers become part of informal groups; they come to like their companions and are strongly influenced by group norms. It would be false to assume that wages are unimportant, but other factors also play a part in motivating labor. In addition to social influences, there is the work itself. In many kinds of job, from semiskilled to highly professional, men take pride in their competence (Gellerman, 1964).

Satisfaction or dissatisfaction of workers may be measured by attitude tests, by interviews (often by exit interviews with employees who are leaving) or by departmental records of grievances, absences, tardiness, disputes, accidents, and turnover. Studies have shown that all of these indices are highly intercorrelated. One industrial psychologist, for example, found that factory accidents were three times as likely to occur on days when employees were troubled or depressed by something related to their job, their relations with other employees or supervisor, family matters or their own health, as on days when feelings were normal (Hersey, 1955).

One of the pioneer reports on work satisfaction appeared in the first yearbook published by the Society for Psychological Study of Social Issues (Watson, 1939). Although a review of research on job satisfaction published 20 years later (Herzberg, *et al.*, 1959) lists 1,500 articles, the conclusions do not significantly modify the earlier conclusions. The following statements are from the pioneer report:

> Data on the proportion of workers who today enjoy their jobs vary widely. Hoppock, (1935) for example, found more than 90 percent of 500 teachers reporting that they liked their work, whereas Bell (1937) found that 98 percent of young people working in canning factories and textile mills hated their jobs. Hoppock queried 309 adults in a small Pennsylvania town (where none were engaged in large-scale factory labor) and found 30 percent who disliked their jobs more than they liked them, but 48 percent who would remain in the same job if they had all the world to choose from. Two-thirds of these people reported getting more satisfaction from their work than from their spare time, which may be interpreted, in part, as a comment on facilities for the enjoyment of leisure in that village. In general, satisfaction was least among unskilled laborers, and rose with higher occupational levels, reaching its highest level in the professions. Older workers usually reported greater satisfaction; this may be explained, in part, by a slow shift of dissatisfied persons away from the jobs they dislike. A later review by Hoppock and Spiegler (1938) covers some 43 studies yielding 111 calculations of percent of satisfied workers. Two-thirds of the studies show two-thirds or more of the workers who are pretty well satisfied. The studies are heavily weighted toward professional and other white-collar jobs. Some weight should certainly be given to Flowers' (1927) report that 93 percent of 24,000 youth had been advised by their parents not to follow the father's occupation.

Eighty persons, some employed and some unemployed (Hoppock, 1935), were asked what they liked or disliked about their kind of work. The informal interviews made no attempt to question each person about each item, but the results, summarized in Table 9 show two outstanding factors: friendship with fellow workers and enjoyment of the work itself (merchants enjoy selling, chauffeurs enjoy driving, dentists enjoy filling

TABLE 9—FACTORS MOST OFTEN MENTIONED AS REASONS FOR LIKING
THE JOB

Factor	Number of Mentions
(1) Associates	28
(2) The work itself	24
(3) The boss	11
(4) Variety	9
(5) Freedom in work	8

teeth). An agreeable boss, variety in work, and freedom to do it in one's own way, all stood ahead of hours (6 mentions), earnings (5 mentions), or chance of promotion (4 mentions). Among reasons given for disliking some job, the work itself (20 mentions) was far more prominent than low earnings (8) or long hours (5). A great variety of other factors came out in the interviews. In general, work satisfaction seemed positively related to: respected status, pleasant relations with associates and superiors, enjoyable tasks, good earnings, reasonable hours, opportunity for advancement, variety of activities, freedom from close supervision, visible results, satisfaction in quality of achievement, opportunities to be of service to others, attractive working environment, choice of place to live, being given responsibility, vacations, excitement, chance for self-expression, success in competition, opportunity for travel, freedom from need to travel too much, freedom from fatigue, praise for one's efforts, and security for the future.

Houser (1938) has reported on the attitudes of 100,000 workers in large corporations. Among employees outside the sales force, including unskilled labor, the 12 factors which they said mattered most to them, were, in order of importance, as follows:

1. Receiving help necessary to get results expected by management.
2. Being encouraged to offer suggestions and to try out better methods.
3. Being able to find out whether work is improving.
4. Reasonable certainty of being able to get fair hearing and "square deal" in case of grievance.
5. Certainty of promotions going to best-qualified employees.
6. Encouragement to seek advice in case of real problems.
7. Being given information about important plans and results which concern the individual's work.
8. Being given reasons for changes which are ordered in work.
9. Not being actually hampered in work by superior.
10. Not getting contradictory or conflicting orders.
11. Being given to understand completely the results which are expected in a job.
12. Likelihood of pay increases from time to time.

TABLE 10—RANK ASSIGNED VARIOUS FACTORS IN MORALE
BY EMPLOYERS AND EMPLOYEES

Morale Item	Employee Ranking	Employer Ranking
Credit for all work done	1	7
Interesting work	2	3
Fair pay	3	1
Understanding and appreciation	4	5
Counsel on personal problems	5	8
Promotion on merit	6	4
Good physical working conditions	7	6
Job security	8	2

S. J. Fosdick, store manager of Boggs and Buhl, reported to the 1939 convention of the National Retail Dry Goods Association on a nation-wide poll of eight "morale items" as rated by several hundred employers and by three thousand employees. The results are summarized in Table 10.

The outstanding observation is that the workers themselves reported more concern for fair credit, appreciation, and counsel, and less for pay and security than the managers would have expected. Mr. Fosdick observed that the desire for recognition, approval, and a sense of importance was most often thwarted among these employees.

In cooperation with Jerome Seidman, the author studied persons who had had two or more full-time jobs for at least a year each, but who were unemployed in 1933–34. They had been clients of the Adjustment Service and showed no evidence of major physical defect or personality distortion. They were asked "Which of the jobs that you have held appealed to you most, or proved most interesting?" and "Why?"

A sample of 100 cases from these records was chosen by the author to be fairly representative of the 10,000 cases in distribution of age, sex (63 percent men), marital status (63 percent single), and education (65 percent high school graduates). The results are given in Table 11.

The data suggest, although the groups are not large, that congenial social contacts are even more important to women than to men, although for both sexes variations in social contacts matter more in work satisfaction than do salary or working hours. The men, even more than the women, valued positions of responsibility, initiative, and prestige, but for both sexes this satisfaction was more often a determining factor than was salary or working time. The attitude toward money must be interpreted with some care, in view of the fact that the income from the preferred job was actually greater than the earnings in four out of five of the other jobs held. (The average individual in this study has held five or six jobs.) The choices seemed to fall on the position with the greater

TABLE 11—REASONS ASSIGNED BY 100 WORKERS FOR PREFERRING
ONE JOB RATHER THAN ANOTHER

Reason	Percent Men	Women
(1) Congenial working conditions, pleasant social contacts	21%	38%
(2) Responsibility, initiative, prestige	27	23
(3) In line with vocational aspiration	15	13
(4) More variety	15	12
(5) More salary	13	6
(6) Better chance for promotion	6	2
(7) Shorter hours	3	6
	100%	100%

financial return as well as greater responsibility, variety, etc., but the report of the workers was that the difference in money was not the major consideration.

In another sample of 100 cases also from the Adjustment Service records, the writer (in cooperation with Harold Wren) found that on the Strong Vocational Interest Test, Part VII, 80 percent indicated a preference for "work which interests you, with a modest income" over "work which does not interest you, with a large income." Only 8 percent chose the latter alternative, the others answering "doubtful."

Since variety in work was often mentioned as conducive to interest, a special study was made of items on the work history and the Strong test which explored the reaction to routine. Among 159 cases, only 14 thought they could better meet the competition of others in "routine or standardized work," rather than in "meeting new and different conditions." Only seven preferred "doing the same thing" to "wide variety in work." While many of the studies just cited were made a generation ago, the coming of automation and the rising standards of living in America have not changed the psychological picture. Money is seldom a negligible factor, but in job satisfaction, it is overshadowed by intrinsic interest, social esteem, and self-esteem. When accountants and engineers described periods of feeling exceptionally good about their jobs, they stressed the challenge of their work, the recognition and responsibility (Herzberg et al., 1959). When they were unhappy on their jobs, they complained most about restrictive supervision and company policies. Gurin et al. (1960), in a national sample, found positive morale at work more related to ego factors, like interest in the job and a sense of accomplishment and recognition, than to "extrinsic" factors like wages and hours.

Other implications of these studies are as follows:

1. It seems likely that we have provided psychologically satisfactory employment for a large proportion of the people in professional and man-

agerial occupations and for a majority of the middle-class workers in small towns. We have been much less successful in the mines, factories, and unskilled trades. There seems to be a high negative correlation between the average index of work satisfaction and the amount of industrial conflict.

2. Workers generally indicate a preference for doing work their own way and resent the attempt to tell them how they must perform. Man's nature, biologically and psychologically, is better adapted to finding its own means toward a given goal than to copying some prescribed routine.

3. Respect for the worker as a person, with rights of his own, and experience which must be valued, is more emphasized by older men. This would seem to be one phase of the demand for more democracy in the administration of our economic life. Work satisfaction in some fields could be increased further, in all probability, if social attitudes were changed to accord respect to all persons who render valuable service to society, without the present odious discrimination against certain types of work.

The best known, and most often cited, study of worker morale is the project conducted in the 1930's at the Hawthorne Plant of the Western Electric Company. Engineers separated six girls, who assembled relays, from the large shop and experimented with varying the lighting, the hours, and rest periods. Every change brought increased production, even when some of the changes were returned to earlier conditions. The potent factors were not the physical conditions but the sense of being special and social cohesion developed within the small work team. Another group of workers whose rate of production had remained constant for many months had succeeded in creating the impression that their job was complicated and demanding; actually, they could have produced much more, but they took a certain pride in getting the best of their bosses.

Prior to the Hawthorne plant studies, attempts to motivate workers had relied mainly on variation in pay, hope for promotion, and the threat of being discharged. These motives continue to be important, but social psychological evidence has shown that other factors need to be taken into account. In a research group, for example, while the supervisors thought that pay was the main concern of their workers, the men themselves were more concerned about the fact that assigned jobs did not utilize their full abilities. The men also wanted more autonomy and self-direction. (Baker, 1954)

A factor analysis of morale in a much larger population of workers showed that while pay differences were correlated with satisfaction, so also were: (1) quality of organization and management; (2) quality of immediate supervision; (3) congenial relations with associates; and (4) interest in the job itself (Baehr, Renck, 1958).

Katz and Kahn (1952) found that supervisors thought men were conditioned primarily to get as much money as possible for as little work as they could get away with. Actually, the morale of the men seemed to depend more on recognition for good work, freedom in communication with supervisors, and pride in their working team.

Good mental health for workers includes both absence of grievances and the sense of significance in the work, pride in achievement, and appropriate participation in planning (Levinson, et al., 1962). Within a wide range of vocations it is evident that such occupations as those of physicians, or corporation vice presidents, U.S. senators or college professors have high morale, high prestige, and relatively high pay. At the opposite extreme, domestic servants get low pay, low prestige, and have notably low morale. In general, the professional man, who is free to set the conditions under which he will or will not work, enjoys his occupation more than does the assembly-line factory worker or the office clerk who is told where, when, and how to do his job. A national survey (Gurin, et al., 1960) showed that workers at higher status levels had better mental health.

A study of four levels of management (Rosen, 1961) found that satisfaction with the working environment increased steadily as one rose in the hierarchy. The finding is similar to the laboratory observation reported in Chapter 3, that the "central person," through whom other workers are linked, most enjoys his role. Another study of managers showed that the higher a man's position in the table of organization, the greater was his self-esteem, his autonomy, and his sense of self-actualization (Porter, 1962).

Certainly there are more satisfying aspects of higher-level jobs than those of a lower order. They offer more pay, more prestige, and usually more autonomy. On a scale of satisfactions ranging from 100 to 700 (the mean of 400 indicating indifferent or neutral feelings) professional and managerial employees in Hoppock's (1955) Pennsylvania community scored an average of 560, but manual workers scored only 440. Another study (Blauner, 1960) reports that about 90 percent of scientists and mathematicians would choose the same kind of work if they were beginning their careers over again; among skilled workers in automobile factories and steel mills, only 40 percent would again choose their line of work. Among the unskilled, the proportion drops to 20 percent or less.

In the hierarchy of personality needs proposed by Maslow (1954), needs for autonomy and self-actualization do not become prominent until the other demands have been met. While wage earners are still preoccupied with the fulfillment of their physiological needs, the security of their future, and acceptance by their fellow workers, the supervisors and higher executives have moved on up the pyramid of personality needs and are concerned mainly with success, autonomy, and self-fulfillment. Porter (1962–3) has documented these differences in studies of a nationwide sample of nearly 2,000 managers in a variety of companies. Managers in top-level positions apparently were better satisfied in large corporations than in smaller companies; those lower in authority found more needs fulfilled in smaller businesses. Line managers were, on the whole, better satisfied than were staff men; staff men expressed more need for autonomy than did line managers.

The relationship of morale to production is not simple. A factor analysis of absences, turnover, rejection of benefit programs, injuries, suggestions, disciplinary suspensions, grievances, and work stoppages yielded a general attitude (Employee Relations Index) which correlated about .40 with amount of profit in a study of seventeen plants (Merrihue, Katzell, 1955). Herzberg (1955) reviewed numerous studies on the connection between morale and productivity of workers. In a majority of studies higher morale was associated with better production, but in about one-third of them, there seemed to be no relationship. In one report in ten, the shops with better morale turned out to be less productive. A summary of studies in industrial psychology during 1956 concludes: "Gradually we are learning more of the conditions under which attitudes may or may not be related to productive performance; these include the nature of the attitudes measured, the adequacy of the performance criteria, and the extent to which behavior is regulated externally by the system" (Katzell, 1957). The skill of workers is positively related both to production and to morale. There is a "virtuous circle" in which greater competence fosters stronger interest in the work and the increased interest leads to even higher level of skilled performance. A comparative study (Katz, Hyman, 1947) of five shipbuilding yards, during World War II, identified two located near each other, one of which took nearly three times as long as the other to produce a ship. The efficient yard had a higher proportion of skilled workers. Worker satisfaction with wages, hours, working conditions, and promotional policy was consistently higher in the efficient yard. The workers were proud of their level of achievement and felt greater confidence in the management. At the inefficient yard, there was not only lower production but also more complaints about dissatisfaction with management, opportunities for promotion, working conditions, shift hours, and wages.

There is a relationship between how well a man thinks he is paid and the work he turns out. Attitude toward wages depends on reference groups, as described in Chapter 3. In one study, part-time employees who were led to believe they were being over-paid did more painstaking work (correcting errors in proof) than those, at the same wage, who thought they were getting less than the normal pay for such work

(Adams, Jacobson, 1964). This observation is in accord with the theory that people try to reduce dissonance. They adjust their efforts to fit the perceived pay level.

Productivity and morale are both likely to be greatly influenced by the climate of the group. Following the evidence from the Hawthorne plant, other companies discovered that groups of workers were establishing norms over which the management had no control. The "bogey" expressed workers' estimate of what they proposed to do in a day, and individuals were not really free to make an effort to exceed the group's norm.

A study (Gardner, 1946) of a new worker on a sand-blasting job showed that he had done this kind of work some years earlier and might easily have reached the standard output in three days. He knew, however, that new men were supposed to learn slowly and carefully controlled his production so that it took him the expected several weeks to come up to what his fellow workers were accomplishing.

Participation

In Chapter 3 the advantages of group decision were presented. A study by Coch and French (1948) has become a classic in social psychology. When management announced changes in job procedure, giving reasons, production usually dropped while absenteeism and job-quitting increased. When workers participated, through their chosen representatives, in planning the change-over, results were better. A third method— total participation—brought more rapid increase in production with no resignations. A replication of the Coch and French procedure in a factory in Norway did not affect productivity, but the group which participated in the decision gave evidence of better attitudes and morale (French, 1960).

Even when workers have no voice in decisions, they work better if they understand their work, its place in the context of the whole organization, and any changes which are likely to affect them. Employees in a plant where work groups met once a month to hear what was going on and to ask any questions showed higher morale than a similar plant where there were no such meetings (Habbe, 1952). Air crews in which men were fully informed, not only about their own duties, but also about the duties of every other man showed better coordination and group effectiveness (Hemphill, 1952). A new incentive system, in another factory, was best received by those workers whose foreman had told them of the coming changes and explained the reasons (Mahoney, 1953).

Alfred J. Marrow (1964) has described two companies, similar in size and making the same products for much the same markets but different in management style. The Harwood Manufacturing Company encouraged employee participation in planning, problem solving, goal setting, and decision making; the Weldon Company operated in a traditional hierarchy with direction from the top down. Comparing the two companies, social psychologists found Harwood superior in man-hour productivity, standards of performance, turnover, controlling of waste, and readiness to innovate. Even more decisive was what happened when Harwood acquired Weldon and introduced participative methods. A laboratory experience in sensitivity training for all levels of management was an important factor in creating the new climate. Results were evident in a 30 percent increase in earnings for piece-rate workers, while total manufacturing costs dropped 20 percent. Not a single manager or supervisor was replaced; the whole change was based on retraining of executives and increased participation by lower-level workers.

Discussion of a problem with opportunity to reach their own decision brought more change in a group of supervisors than did a talk urging the same action. The topic was the need to correct performance ratings which had been too high for workers in the upper level of jobs and too low further down in the hierarchy. Given the data, and a chance to work out their own proposals for improvement, the supervisors actually changed their way of rating. A talk by an authority figure to a control group of supervisors did not get the same results (Levine, Butler, 1952).

An experiment giving workers an opportunity to make decisions increased both production and satisfaction. A change in which decision making was taken from the workers and assigned to management brought an even larger gain in production but hurt the workers' morale (Morse, Reimer, 1956).

Experiments which encouraged clerical workers in an office and "swatchers" in a clothing factory to set their own goals increased their productivity; participation in discussion groups which did not make work decisions did not achieve the same results (Lawrence, Smith, 1955). Genuine delegation of full responsibility to workers was found to result in higher quality decisions than were achieved when only partial authority was shared (Solem, 1958).

When workers participate, they have a feeling that the resulting procedures and products are their own. The self-concept extends to cover what is "mine" or "ours." Suggestions coming from "outside our group" have the disadvantage of association with a stranger. Good projects may be postponed or done halfheartedly because the men concerned regard them as imposed or "Not Invented Here." In research-and-development divisions the initials "N.I.H." are sometimes used to disparage an idea or mechanism brought in from the outside. Men work best on projects they consider to be their own and when they feel they will be held responsible for the outcome. "Our product" is usually regarded as better than that of others (Blake, Mouton, 1962).

"The sense of participation" may be felt by all members of a cohesive group, even though only certain members have actually been active. Bias in favor of the product of "our group" was found to be as strong in a member removed from the group during its work as in those who were directly involved in the production (Ferguson, Kelley, 1964). Sills (1957) argued that loyalty of members of the National Foundation for Infantile Paralysis was based on their *belief* that the organization was democratically controlled, even though it was not. A study of the League of Women Voters showed that both loyalty and activity were higher in local units where member influence was high in comparison with the influence of the president (Tannenbaum, Smith, 1964). Their data suggest that democratic structure in this case was correctly perceived, since members differing in loyalty and activity agreed on the extent of rank-and-file influence.

A contributing factor in the improvement which comes with participation is the growth of team spirit. Walker (1950) quotes one steel worker: "There's nothing like working here in this mill. Everybody cooperates. Every man works as a member of a team and every man tries to turn out as much steel as he possibly can. We work hard and get satisfaction out of working hard." In that investigation, Walker concluded that the source of satisfaction most often expressed by the workers was pride in their crew.

While most social psychological data support the value of participation, there are some who are skeptical. Strauss (1963) points out that efforts to distribute power in industrial organizations may have serious consequences. It may be too expensive and time-consuming to acquaint workers with all the facts necessary to make a wise decision. If the rank and file are to become conversant with all the data necessary for wise policy making, the educational task may be overwhelming. A British Socialist, C. A. R. Crosland, argues that what workers want is not a voice in higher management, but rather freedom to participate in decisions about how their own work should be divided, organized, and evaluated (1959).

While there are some strong feelings on both sides, there is still very little objective evidence concerning the effects of labor participation at higher levels of management. Managers generally resist such proposals, noting that workers' representatives are seldom trained in the complex economic and engineering skills required for top-level decisions. One interesting exception was the International Ladies Garment Workers Union which had to deal with many small shops, some of them run by inexperienced managers. The union employed a highly competent industrial engineer and accountants to help the factory owners improve their financial and operating procedures. Assisting the owners enabled the shops to continue to give employment to union members. Another indication of labor's concern about having a voice in top management may be found in proposals by the United Automobile Workers' president, Walter Reuther. At the beginning of World War II he suggested ways in which the manufacturer might efficiently convert to war production; at the end of the war he offered plans for quick reconversion to the consumer's market; later he urged that the industry combat inflation and offered to forego any increase in wages and benefits if the companies would agree to reduce prices. It is not surprising that, in a democracy, workers should feel that they would like the kind of voice in the government of their corporations which they already have in the government of their cities, states, and nation.

Participation is particularly attractive to the more ambitious and intelligent workers. Others are likely to be content to let the boss do the thinking. Personality factors also make some workers more interested in having a voice in management. Vroom (1959) found that for supervisors with low authoritarian (more democratic) preferences and for those with a strong need for independence, job satisfaction was positively correlated with the amount of "influence" they had with their boss. For the workers who had little inner drive toward independence and who easily accepted a hierarchy of authority, there was no relation between participation and job satisfaction.

The amount of participation which is best depends on how much employees expect and are able to use intelligently. If they have had very little self-direction, they will probably not respond well to a great and sudden increase. But a beginning can be made with a limited amount; this is likely to be welcome. This experience increases readiness for more cooperation in showing responsibility for decisions.

Improving supervision

Since 1947, the Survey Research Center at the University of Michigan has been studying differences in morale and productivity resulting from different styles of supervision. Data have come from research in insurance companies, public utilities, railroads, machine factories, government bureaus, and many other organizations. Five characteristics of good supervisors have appeared with considerable consistency (Likert, 1961, 1963):

1. *They spend their time in supervising rather than in production work.* In a clerical operation, for example, 82 percent of the first-line supervisors of sections with high production records spent more than half their time supervising; among the corresponding supervisors in low-producing sections only 36 percent gave more than half of their time to supervisory work.

2. *They are more person-centered and more considerate.* Twice as many supervisors in high production sections were found to be "employee-centered" as were found among supervisors of low production

sections. One study (Likert, 1958) found a correlation of .64 between the production level in 32 rather similar work groups and the supervisor's thoughtful attitude toward his employees. Bass (1958) likewise found that leaders whose attitudes showed more concern for employees were more successful as supervisors. If supervisors were high on initiating procedures but low on consideration, the outcome was increased grievances, absenteeism, and turnover (Fleishman, Harris, 1962).

Studies have shown that most supervisors believe that they are closer to their subordinates than the subordinates consider them to be. Likert (1956) found in one company that 95 percent of foremen said they understood "well" or "very well" the problems of the workmen. But, only 34 percent of the workers credited foremen with understanding their problems. The same kind of disparity—not quite so large—appeared at the next higher level. Ninety percent of managers claimed to understand the problems of the supervisors under them; only 60 percent of the supervisors felt so understood.

3. *They encourage subordinates to speak their minds freely.* This is a natural consequence of paying more attention to the needs and feelings of employees. Merely exhorting subordinates to speak out does not really encourage such communication. The supervisor has to give other indications that he is ready to listen and that he can be trusted not to misuse what he is told. Indik, *et al.* (1961), report a correlation of .40 between the average number of daily deliveries made by parcel men and their sense of freedom to communicate with superiors. Another study (Smith, Knight, 1959) showed that groups who freely gave feedback to supervisors were more efficient at problem-solving. Freedom to communicate with one's superiors is partly dependent on the qualities of the subordinate; in part, however, it reflects the openness of the supervisor.

4. *They usually react supportively rather than punitively to mistakes of subordinates.* In one comparison, 60 percent of the foremen of high-producing sections reacted in a helpful, non-punitive way to a man who did a poor job; among the foremen of low-producing sections only 43 percent reacted in this way. The majority were critical and punitive. In another study, carried out in seven British factories, Argyle (1958) found non-punitive behavior of supervisors related to higher productivity. In factory work where small parts are assembled Schachter (1961) found that supervisors whose usual role was supportive rather than threatening headed units which were more productive and which adapted better to a change-over requiring new operations.

Punitive rather than educative responses are particularly characteristic of "authoritarian" personalities. In one class of 75 graduate students of business administration, 18 of the 25 highest on the F-scale (authoritarians) recommended "expiatory punishment" (coercive and intended to cause suffering) for dealing with an erring subordinate; only four of the 25 lowest on the F-scale prescribed such punishment (Sherwood, 1965).

Superiors frequently believe they are giving more support and encouragement than subordinates think they receive. When supervisors were asked, "How do you give recognition for good work done by employees in your work group?" 80 percent said they "very often" gave "sincere and thorough praise." Only 14 percent of their employees thought that such praise was "very often" given (Likert, 1958).

5. *They supervise less closely; they enlarge the area of responsibility left to subordinates.* Likert's observation on clerical sections noted that 19 of 28 low-production sections were under close supervision, but only 5 of 25 high-producing sections were given such detailed surveillance. A later report (Katz, Maccoby, Morse, 1950) again found more tight supervision in less productive units. The relationship is probably circular. Because production is unsatisfactory, the supervisor hovers over his subordinates, which then generates additional problems. Close supervision is perceived as critical, distrustful, and threatening. One study indicated that workers under such conditions not only reduced their output but also (as in the autocratically led boys clubs described in Chapter 5) were more likely to pick on a scapegoat and to express hostility toward certain fellow workers (Day, Hamblin, 1961).

When workers in an electronic manufacturing plant were given greater autonomy, they became more ego-involved in their jobs and were more productive (Vroom, 1961). When jobs for maintenance repairmen and for packaging crews were enlarged, relationships improved, quality of work improved, and costs were reduced (Davis, Werling, 1960).

In a study of two electric power plants, one of which had recently become highly automated, Mann (1964) found that in both organizations the men's satisfaction with their supervisors was highly correlated with their perception of the skill of the foreman in human relations. Worker's perception of the foreman's technical qualifications and his administrative competence were also positively correlated with their satisfaction, but not so highly as was their estimate of his way of handling people. In a hospital study, Mann found that nurse supervisors likewise valued their superiors' skills in human relations.

One important exception to the effectiveness of this kind of supervision is encountered when top management does not support supervisors and foremen in a person-centered approach. Pelz (1952) found that a supervisor's influence on subordinates depended greatly on his status with his superiors. If his friendliness toward employees runs counter to what the top administrators believe and practice, he loses their respect and also that of his own subordinates. There is often a discrepancy between the "human relations approach" taught to foremen and what higher level supervisors themselves believe and practice. Under these conditions, foremen rapidly abandon the techniques learned in their educational program (Fleishman, *et al.*, 1955). Several studies clearly support the conclusion that subordinates adopt attitudes and behavior which they observe in their superiors (Spector, Clark, Glickman, 1960; Trumbo, 1961).

As a rule middle management operates supportively or punitively depending on how the chief relates to them (Katz, Maccoby, Morse, 1950). The conscientious supervisor may find himself caught in a difficult position. To get the best from subordinates, he must be considerate. But he may get more approval and respect from his superiors if he is dominant, driving, and inconsiderate (Halpin, 1957). If he identifies with either he loses effectiveness (Brooks, 1955).

The contradictions are especially perplexing when they exist within the behavior of top management. For example (Freeman, Taylor, 1950), chief executives say they want under them men who are forceful, aggressive, and dynamic; in reality, they may more often reward those who are tactful, agreeable, and supportive. Middle managers see themselves as more successful when they are discreet, patient, practical, and modest (Porter, Ghiselli, 1957). It has become fashionable for corporation heads to decry conformity and to praise individuality; but very few organizations to date have been devised to reward the nonconformist.

The next problem is one of training. How can supervisors be aided in acquiring the desired outlook and skills? Many educational methods have been tried in efforts to train supervisors: lectures, reading, discussion, observation, demonstration, and T-group participation. Lectures are usually less effective than methods which require role-playing and experimental trial of the new ways of behaving. Sometimes written case studies, short filmed cases, or cases acted out on the spot are used to help supervisors acquire better insight. Methods which "get under the skin" of the supervisor, affecting his own feelings, are especially helpful in developing sensitivity to the feelings of those he must supervise. Later we shall describe some results of "sensitivity training" for supervisors and managers.

Periodic appraisal of performance is one of the most widely used procedures used by supervisors to help subordinates improve. French (1963) has criticized the practice because it constitutes a threat to the self-esteem of the employee. In a large industrial corporation, 92 members of management were interviewed before and after appraisal by their boss. The appraisal was observed and then improvement was rated ten weeks after the interview. Most men (82%) appraised themselves higher than did their boss. This was reflected in the high proportion who became defensive or resentful during the appraisal. Those initially low in self-esteem deteriorated in their subsequent work performance. Those who had strong pride in themselves as workers neither improved nor suffered as a result of criticism. The general effect was somewhat lower efficiency after all the appraisals.

A better procedure is to have a man's work rated by four persons— himself, his supervisor, a colleague on his own level, and an able subordinate. This would be followed by a conference in which the man's view of his own strengths and weaknesses can be compared with the view held by three outsiders who look at his work as it appears from above, a coordinate level, and from below. An atmosphere of frankness and acceptance of mutual criticism is a prerequisite to effective use of such comparative perceptions. The exploration of different views of the same worker helps everyone concerned to achieve a better understanding of differences in perception and a readiness to substitute honest, objective inquiry for the more usual defensive reactions. When this climate prevails, men improve more than they do from classes and other kinds of training (Mann, 1957; Tarnapol, 1957). Two other factors contributing to the value of appraisal interviews are: (a) ability of the subordinate to predict correctly what his superior expects from him (Rosen, 1961); and (b) obtaining company executives' approval of performance rating and the methods to be used.

The participation of social psychologists in industry has focused attention on human relations, but this is only one aspect of supervisory competence. To retain perspective, it is important to note that a man's general intelligence, his technical competence, his experience and knowledge, and his administrative skills all contribute significantly to his success as a supervisor. Indeed, Mann (1964) found that supervisors who were judged excellent in their human relations, but less competent in technical aspects of their work, worried about whether they were doing an adequate job, feared they might lose their positions, and suffered more from nervousness, insomnia, muscle stiffness, and arthritis. An interesting sidelight on periods of technological change was brought out by Mann's studies. In the pre-automation period human relation skills were seen as most vital; during the change-over the technical competence of supervisors became most salient; after the workers were adjusted to the automated plant, human relations skills again emerged as the most important ability.

Managing

A manager designs, operates, and re-designs a social vehicle. In accord with our often mentioned S-P-A principle, he must develop a structure which will foster the kind of interactions and attitudes which lead toward the goals of the organization.

Purely economic models are not sufficient to describe the full range of purposes of either the corporation or its personnel. A corporation not only makes money for stockholders, but a large part of the workers' and managers' day is devoted to the corporation; communities and consumers are affected by corporations. Responsible management must not ignore any of the impact of the social vehicle upon the lives of men. The broad influence of the corporation is exercised not only by its public relations or fringe benefits; it comes chiefly from the way its main work is organized.

The structure of a growing organization, and the processes of interaction within it, change over time.

Most organizations are small in their beginning. One man alone, or with a few associates, starts a business. As it prospers, it grows. In the early days, there can be a lot of informal, face-to-face communication by all employees. There can be flexibility of assignments. The few people involved can shift duties around to take over the work of one who is absent or to pitch in and help handle an unusual load. Everyone knows the others—usually by first name or nickname—and every part of the business is understood by all employees. New developments are talked over by everyone.

As the organization increases in size it necessarily becomes more of a bureaucracy. Job descriptions define and limit what is expected of each worker. Duties are specialized and formalized. A chain of command sets forth who may direct whom. Policies are stated in manuals of "standard operating procedures." Information moves through defined channels. A supervisor has a limited "span of control," sometimes thought of as not more than six persons over whom he exercises direct authority. A pyramid-like chart runs from the president at the top, through many levels of prestige and salary down to the numerous workers on the operating line of the factory or selling goods over the store counters. *Line* responsibilities, with direct authority, are differentiated from the *staff* functions of expert advisers. Everything is in rational order, with unity of direction coming from the top.

In every large organization, the neatly charted *formal* organization exists along side a much more vital *informal* organization. In theory, communications move through ordered channels. Actually, the grapevine may carry communications so rapidly and effectively that some subordinates may know what is coming before they are officially informed by their superiors. Relationships of executives who play golf together may be closer than for those who are tied together in the formal chart. The chart may not have a box for a certain secretary who has been a long time in the organization and who knows better than most of her superiors how to get done what she wants done and how to block what she does not want done. The friendliness or hostility of wives of some of the managerial employees may exert an influence which does not show in the formal chart. It is the informal organization—the unwritten agreements among workers—which lead to the real quotas of production, which may be kept well below what might be produced. Some rules on the books are completely unenforceable because of the defense reactions of the informal organization. Although all the workers in the bank-wiring group in the Hawthorne plant study were equals on the chart, one man had become a kind of foreign minister for the group. ("He can handle the engineers, inspectors and the supervisors. They have to come to him if they want to know anything.") Another man was virtually a secretary of the interior. He taught the men, not only how to do their jobs but also how to look busy when they were not. The appointed chief of the group—the formal leader—actually did little except supply the men with work.

Numerous experiments in industrial reorganization seek to increase consideration of human needs, satisfactions, and frustrations. More decentralization makes it possible to operate smaller units as practically autonomous. Recognizing that an organization with many hierarchical levels impedes communication, some businesses have reorganized to decrease status levels between line workers and top executives. One of the characteristics of a sharply defined status structure is that each man has to keep a careful eye on the boss above him.

An advantage of the flatter "tabernacle" type of organization, with relatively few status levels, over the "skyscraper" design, is that relationships with the "boss" on the next level are more remote and more attention can be paid to the job itself. Also, since most workers resent close supervision, some organizations have abandoned the standard "span of control" and given a supervisor so many subordinates that he must necessarily delegate most of the responsibility to the workers themselves. Other kinds of experiments involve increasing opportunity for workers to prepare themselves for other (not necessarily higher paid) jobs so they will have more variety of work experience and a broader understanding of the work of their company.

The flatter tabernacle structure promotes employee morale, initiative, self-expression, creativity, and sense of responsibility (Worthy, 1950). The satisfaction of managers seems to be influenced not only by the form of the structure but also by the size of the organization. In smaller companies (less than 5,000 employees) managers were somewhat more satisfied (security, esteem, social interaction) with flat organizational charts. But in larger companies differences were not statistically significant (735 questionnaire responses) except (at the .05 level) for a greater sense of security in the skyscraper or multilevel structure (Porter, Lawler, 1964).

The implication of the S-P-A formulation is that if there are chronic

TABLE 12—THEORIES X AND Y

Theory X		Theory Y	
Assumptions about people	Administrative policies	Assumptions about people	Administrative policies
1. Naturally inert, lazy, avoids work	1. Drive, "motivate," coerce	1. Naturally active, enterprising	1. Lead
2. Dependent	2. Direct	2. Independent	2. Use self-direction
3. Set in ways	3. Routine procedures	3. Growing	3. Open to change
4. Irresponsible	4. Check up	4. Responsible	4. Trust
5. Resistant, hostile	5. Fight, on guard	5. With you	5. Cooperation
6. Unimaginative	6. Prescribe	6. Creative	6. Encourage
7. Short-sighted	7. Plan for them	7. Capable of broad vision, long view	7. Plan with them

or recurrent problems in any phase of an organization, attention should be given to the structure. While the untrained administrator tends to seek an explanation in character traits (workers are lazy, "gold-bricking," duped by the union, etc.) the successful executive changes the situation in such a way as to bring about processes of interaction which will change the attitudes. Some desirable changes are suggested by the theories of the three social psychologists who have given special attention to industrial organizations—McGregor, Blake, and Likert.

McGregor's *Human Side of Enterprise* (1960) sets forth two contrasting theories about worker motivation and behavior which underlie the way managers think and work. The first—Theory X—corresponds to the assumptions underlying the tightly organized, top-directed bureaucracy, in which workers are seen as responding mainly, like the donkey, to the carrot in front and the stick behind. Theory Y embodies a view of worker motivation and participation more in accord with the truths of social psychology.

Table 12 emphasizes some of the contrasts.

The self-fulfilling prophecy which we have mentioned earlier in this book tends to confirm any manager in the policies he has adopted. If he operates on Theory X, his experience demonstrates that his workers are, in general, lazy, dependent, irresponsible, and hostile. He "knows" that one cannot be open with them, plan with them, or trust them. Every day's encounters support his view. The workers have behaved, in response to his treatment of them, much as he predicted. If a manager operates with Theory Y, he creates a different social structure (S) which calls forth different processes of interaction (P) and creates different attitudes (A). His experience confirms his prediction that people are active, growing, enjoy self-direction, and are capable of increasing responsibility.

A common misconception in business is that people high in position operate by Theory Y while ordinary rank-and-file workers correspond to Theory X. Again, if this is the way the organization is structured, experience will confirm the inherent assumptions.

Blake's *Managerial Grid* (1964) recognizes two important objectives of management: (1) production; (2) concern for people; these are seen as orthogonal axes.

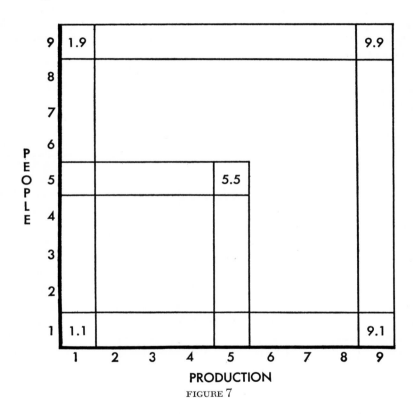

FIGURE 7

The 9.1 box represents a boss driving hard for efficient production. He plans, directs, and controls affairs to this end. People are "hands"— means to the achievement of production goals. "Produce or perish!" He runs a "tight" ship.

The opposite corner is the 1.9 box. Here people are the important concern. This manager assumes that if he can make workers contented they will take care of production requirements. He runs a relaxed ship.

The 1.1 box represents withdrawal. This manager, feeling hopeless and defeated, or ready to transfer or retire, lets things drift. He leaves others alone and is glad when they leave him alone.

The 5.5 style is full of compromises. Pressure for production is half-hearted and so is concern for people. There is mixture and balance, with considerable reliance on rules and traditions.

The most desirable manager, in this system, is at 9.9 with whole-hearted concern both for people and for production. This manager does not think in terms of either-or. He works with his subordinates to review the facts and to make plans, so that they are fully involved with him in designs which maximize efficient production. Evaluation is also a cooperative process. He creates "conditions of work where people understand the problem, have stakes in the outcome, and where their ideas make a real contribution" (p. 144).

Likert's *New Patterns of Management* (1961) attempts to incorporate four kinds of motives: (1) economic; (2) ego satisfactions; (3) security; (4) new experiences. Thus in getting men to learn, one uses the economic incentives of pay and promotion; one gives recognition,

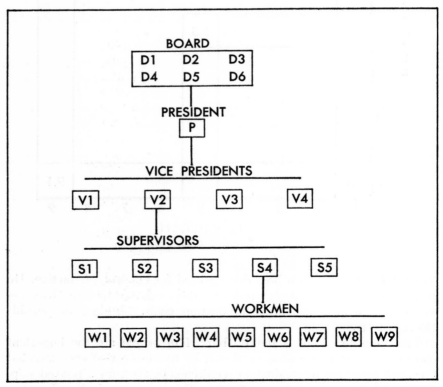

FIGURE 8

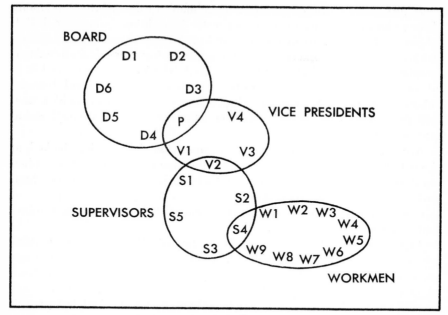

FIGURE 9

dignity, and a sense of achievement; one is careful not to threaten basic security; one stimulates originality, creativity, and the satisfactions of growth.

The traditional organization chart can be modified to recognize the fact that work by teams increases both problem-solving ability (Chapter 4) and morale (Chapter 3). Figure 8 shows the usual line relationships in a business. Figure 9 involves the same persons and positions, but is grouped to bring out the team operation. (Only those supervisors who work under the second vice president appear on this chart; each other vice president would also have subordinates. Similarly, only those workers supervised by S4 are portrayed in the diagram.)

The formal chart of Figure 8 puts each man alone in a box, with a line to his boss. The team chart of Figure 9 implies joint discussion, planning, flexibility in cooperative roles, and integrated decisions. The President is a "linking-pin" between the board and the line chiefs. Each vice president is a linking-pin between his supervisors and the top management. Each supervisor is a linking pin between his subordinates and the supervisory level of management. Relationships in the organization can be analyzed work group by work group, with a high probability that where there are problems, remedies will be devised and applied. Training procedures for team operations will be examined later in the chapter.

In discussing attitudes we wrote of Kelman's (1958) distinction among three ways of inducing men to cooperate: bargaining, belonging, belief. These apply clearly to managerial styles. The traditional boss (Blake's 9–1) manipulates workers by bargaining, offering wage incentives, and keeping men aware that they may be fired. The manager who is 1–9 in Blake's Grid tries too hard to win friends. He expects good work because subordinates like him. Neither achieves the quality of work which men will give on the basis of their own convictions about what is worth doing and how it can best be done.

Argyris, in his *Personality and Organization* (1957), has looked at the effects of organizational roles on the maturing personality. When children are very young, we expect them to be submissive, dependent, and short-sighted. As they grow older, they become more capable of initiative, independence, and self-direction with broader understanding and a longer attention span.

Argyris objects to those aspects of organization and management which—as in McGregor's Theory X—treat workers as if they were not capable of responsibility, initiative, flexible adaptation, and long-term planning. When workers are treated as if they were parts in a machine, to perform routine tasks assigned by others, to be checked by supervisors, to remain loyally obedient to any demands in the work situation, such a factory system impedes the development of mature, understanding, adaptable, and self-regulating persons. Workers respond by feeling "used," "bored," and vaguely resentful. "Job enlargement" is one attempt to treat workers as human beings capable of growth, eager to expand their knowledge and competence in mastery of new challenges.

Mutual respect between labor and management still does not eliminate conflicts of interests and struggles for power. Psychologists have helped resolve conflicts by arranging for each side to correct its perception of the opposition. It is a natural human tendency to exaggerate the evil motives and the rigidity of opponents. Blake and Mouton (1965) have described experiences in which a labor group works out its image of management and of itself; meanwhile the management group has been discussing its image of itself and of labor. Then both sides compare their view of themselves with the way they are seen by the opposition. In a frank confrontation, the evidence is examined. The conflict is not eliminated but it is made less irrelevant. When the imaginary virtues are dropped from one's perception of his side, and the imaginary malice of the opponents has been cleared away, the real issues can be faced. This technique implements a procedure for clarifying international hostility introduced by Stagner and Osgood in 1941 and applied to labor relations by Libo a few years later. A related finding emerged from another recent experiment. Bass (1963) observed graduate business students in a simulated union-management negotiation. Participants who engaged in study groups, either unilateral or bilateral, prior to the negotiation were much better able to resolve conflict and reach a satisfactory agreement than were negotiators who had had no such experience. Conflict management is one of the relatively new and promising areas for applied social psychology.

Top management

The chief executive in any organization is the key figure. We noted earlier that the men below him watch carefully for cues as to their own behavior. If he is an autocrat, they expect him to approve them when they act autocratically in relation to their subordinates. The pattern set at the top moves down through the whole organization.

Psychologists working on the improvement of human relations in industry have learned that they are more successful if they can begin at the top, that is, where the patterns are set. Trying to change the behavior of minor officials is unrewarding unless these officials believe that their bosses will look favorably on the change. The example set by the president of the company is very powerful. Subordinates have frequently been observed to imitate their bosses (E. G. Kahn, Katz, 1953; Spector, *et al.*, 1960). Their attitude toward change usually reflects their chief's attitude (Trumbo, 1961). In another study about 100 supervisors were instructed in management development. After they returned to their positions in a company in which the top management did not support their changed outlook, 85 percent regarded the training project as a failure. Within a year, 46 percent of these supervisors had already left the company or had applied for jobs elsewhere (Sykes, 1962).

What kind of men are those who hold the top positions? According to one study (Henry, 1949), leading business executives are (1) high in drive and need to achieve; (2) keenly concerned about moving upward in status; (3) able to accept guidance from their superiors without dependence or resentment; (4) able to reach firm decisions (not necessarily quickly); (5) possessed of well-defined self-identity; and (6) never quite satisfied. Another observer (Fiedler, 1957) notes that good managers do not seek gratification from warm, close personal relations. They are not "one of the boys", their objectivity depends upon keeping a certain distance. This accords with Mann's (1964) finding that as one moves up through the hierarchy of management the emphasis on skill in human relations diminishes, and administrative functions become more salient.

Selznick (1943) has emphasized a further step—from "administrative management" to "institutional leadership." The executive vice president may concern himself with efficient operations; the president must give leadership to a living institution—a responsive, adaptive organism.

The top official of a company differs from his principal assistant in the greater time the top man must give to public relations and long-range planning.

It is not easy for a man who has built up his own business—carrying a heavy burden of detail, selecting and pressing subordinates to measure up to his standards, inspecting and controlling operations—to make the transition to "institutional leadership." Efforts to decentralize large organizations often remain only a change on paper because the ingrained habits of work of the president and his staff do not shift from a supervisory role to the new role of thinking about long-range policies.

Other studies of the chief executive have emphasized his role conflicts. He is the target of pressures from within his organization, but he also symbolizes the organization to people outside. Often he cannot satisfy the contradictory demands from within and from without. Gross, Mason, and McEachern, in their *Explorations in Role Analysis* (1958), found that knowing how a top administrator felt about the rightness of pressures and the consequences of yielding or not yielding, they could predict his decision in typical role conflicts.

However complicated the equipment of a president's office (telephones, ticker tapes, dictating machines, and electronic computers), the only really important instrument at his disposal is his own personality. What he himself becomes determines the extent to which he can release and engage the potential contributions of others. Hence "managerial development" is not primarily a matter of mastering certain knowledge or principles and it is more than acquiring a bag of tricks. It is closely akin to psychotherapy. It involves helping the executive become more aware of himself so that he can be more effective in his relationships with others.

Managerial development

Managerial development takes several forms. Ferguson (1958) has called attention to a fashion in phraseology: Workers "acquire skill"; supervisors are "trained"; managers are "developed." One form of development is represented by "business games," in which managers are assigned to positions, given data and organizational problems to be solved. Their speed and wisdom in making decisions are observed and later discussed. Managing is thus learned by a complicated role-playing exercise with principles to be applied (Kepner, Tregoe, 1960).

A quite different procedure has been to provide essentially a continuation of general education in the liberal arts. The American Telephone and Telegraph Company, in cooperation with the University of Pennsylvania, at one time offered its executives the opportunity to broaden their minds by studying the humanities, sciences, and social sciences.

The summer courses at Aspen, Colorado, based on a similar program, present "great books"; it is expected that discussion of these classics will deepen an administrator's insights into himself, enhance his values, and give him a greater understanding of his times.

More closely related to social psychology is a form of laboratory training; sometimes called "human relations," "group dynamics," and "sensitivity training." It has three related goals: (1) to increase the participant's understanding of his real self; (2) to sensitize him to the feelings of others and the influence of his own behavior on other persons; and (3) to develop awareness of the processes by which groups develop open-communication, trust, consensual decisions, and cooperative action. Its basic unit is the T-Group, described in Chapter 4. (For fuller description, see L. Bradford, *et al.*, 1964.)

Because hundreds of behavioral scientists have participated in devising and developing T-Group training, it has been more carefully evaluated than have other approaches to executive education. Gibb's studies at Colorado were reviewed in Chapter 4. A study (Massarik, Carlson) using the California Psychological Inventory showed that sensitivity training enabled participants to feel freer and more spontaneous. Miles (1959) demonstrated that school principals who went through a two-week T-Group training period achieved better communication with their co-workers and were able to acheive a larger number of genuinely shared decisions. Change after eight months was reported, by associates, in 73 percent of participants and in 29 percent of controls. In one small company, five afternoons and evenings spent in T-group sessions by the key managerial groups increased the level of trust, facilitated communication, and improved team work so much that the company completed a critical job in record time. The bonus on this one job paid many times over the cost of the training (Kuriloff, Atkins, 1966).

In Chapter 4 we reported comparisons showing that participants in T-groups became better listeners, more flexible, more sensitive to the feelings of others, and more aware of their own feelings and behavior (Boyd, Ellis; Bunker, 1965).

Another study (Gibb, Allen, pending) emphasizes a different gain from sensitivity training. "The T-group-trained . . . were more vigorous in challenging the ideas of other group members, more 'hard-nosed' in their comments, more open in their criticism of persons, ideas, etc. This runs counter to a common stereotype about Bethel training." A related finding in this same research was that after training (as compared with a pre-training test), members participating in a series of group-decision tasks had fewer unexpressed reservations about the jointly made decisions.

Argyris (1962) found that a program of T-Group training within a large company increased "authenticity" which seems related to the franker and more genuine expression. Harrison (1961), reporting on the same training, noted that the participants were more aware and sensitive in their relationships with one another, but that this did not extend to relations with non-participants.

Several reports on changes in organization and ways of operating, following after fairly widespread participation of managers in T-Groups, have shown improved efficiency and profits (Buchanan, 1964; Blansfield, 1962; Blake, Mouton, 1964). Blake's experience with developing training programs that really change the functioning of an organization has led him to a four-stage operation: (1) personal application of the concepts of the managerial grid; (2) training of work teams in setting and achieving targets; (3) intergroup and interdepartmental relations: diagnosis and improvement; (4) identification of goals for the whole organization (Blake, Mouton, 1966).

The effectiveness of a managerial development program has been found to vary with (a) the "climate" of the organization (House, 1960); (b) the support and participation of top management (Hariton, 1951; Mann, 1957; Buchanan, 1958; Guetzkow, et al., 1962; Sykes, 1962); (c) the absence of threat in the program (Hariton, 1951; House, Tosi, 1963). The individuals who seem to profit most from T-Group training have been found to be those (a) of high ability (Canter, 1951; Klubeck, Bass, 1954); (b) high in adaptability (Trites, 1960); (c) well satisfied with their job and the company for which they were working (House, Tosi, 1962).

Looking ahead

As the nature of business leadership changes, insight and skill in human relations become more and more important. We seem to be approaching a time when the more progressive managers will consult their social psychology adviser at least as often as they consult their legal or financial staff. The corporations whose executives have been selected after psychological appraisal, trained in the use of social psychology concepts, and guided in their work by a social psychology "coach" will probably develop a distinct competitive advantage. The graduate schools will then face a demand for social psychologists far beyond the scope of present plans and resources.

The service of psychology to industry is shifting its emphasis. In the beginning, psychologists accepted job definitions given by business and manufacturing traditions. They then tried to find men who, like pegs, could fit into the holes designed by business. We are moving now toward reappraisal of the jobs in the light of human considerations. Perhaps, in an economy of abundance, more attention can properly be given to making work serve the ends of personal growth and satisfaction. More goods per hour of labor will come from automation. The next big problem is to make jobs more rewarding to workers in terms other than wages and fringe benefits. Work, at its best, is challenging, absorbing, creative, and socially and spiritually satisfying. Not many workers today find this kind of meaning in their jobs. More of them—perhaps all—might do so. The tremendous contribution of psychology in the years ahead may be the re-designing of jobs and organizations to fit human beings.

Several types of worker present problems which are particularly pressing. One problem, developed in Chapter 12, is the definition of jobs to fit the personality and schedules of wives and mothers who want the satisfaction of career as well as home life. It is wasteful for society to lose the talent and impoverish the lives of these women because they are not free to work daily from nine to five.

Another problem is that of men and women over 65. As life expectancy increases, more of our population survive to become senior citizens. Retirement is not a good solution for most of them. They do not want to feel pushed aside and left to amuse themselves until they die. Many of these elder citizens have valuable talents and wisdom. How should jobs be designed to use the abilities of older men and women while protecting them from injurious stress?

Another problem exists at the other end of the age range of employed persons. How soon should children and adolescents have gainful employment? The rightful protest against exploiting child labor in the early days of the Industrial Revolution may not apply to jobs that are re-designed to give maximum satisfaction and education to the young worker. It seems quite likely that many boys and girls 12-15 years of age would learn more willingly and effectively on certain jobs than they do in classrooms.

Another widespread problem is that of the adult shirker. A large part of the employable population has been taught to evade work as far as possible. Re-education will not be easy. At another extreme are the compulsive workers who may drive themselves into conditions of ulcers and exhaustion, neglecting their families and other sources of life satisfaction.

New patterns of management are emerging, also, from the growing use of high-speed computers. One social psychologist, Donald M. Michael, envisages the development of "a small, almost separate society of people in rapport with the advanced computers." He believes that men will need life-long training to achieve such competence and that few present-day managers can hope to understand fully the esoteric logic and language of cybernetics. But while no man can match the new machines in memory or in speed of complicated computation, no machine can substitute for man in imagination, creativity, and judgment. As Marks (1963) has said, "If you plan to use a computer as a substitute for tedious pencil-work, you have a good chance of making a saving; if you plan to use it as a substitute for thinking, you have a good chance of making a mess!"

Finally, there are questions of value and life-purpose related to the assumptions underlying the operations of business and industry. Automation (Mann, Hoffman, 1960) changes the nature of work, offering jobs that are more complex, with less physical demands but more need for intellect and responsibility. Corporations enlarge their concern, not only for workers but also for the communities in which they operate. The higher the level of management, the greater appears to be the focus on purposes and values. Subordinates are often fully immersed in a personal struggle to get ahead. At the peak of the enterprise, however, stand men who must answer the questions of "Whither?" and "Why?" and "For what ends?" Profit is not the only determinant.

Increasingly American corporations are active beyond our national boundaries. In 1964, corporate investments abroad increased five times as much as did investments in U.S. domestic operations. Stabilization of international order has long been sought by far-seeing statesmen. Today, this is also the goal of American business. The psychological problems of building international peace are discussed in the next chapter.

CHAPTER FOURTEEN

Social psychology of
international relations

Mankind's problem

What do the American people consider the most important problems facing the nation? Replying to this question in 1964, more referred to international affairs (44 percent) than to any other area of concern (American Institute of Public Opinion, March 1, 1964).

Worldwide problems arise from a complex of changes. Technological achievements have brought almost instantaneous international communication and have reduced to a few hours the travel time from any major city on the globe to any other. Technology has also developed weapons of unprecedented destructive power. Agrarian societies are becoming industrialized; the colonial era has ended; the common man all over the earth is demanding greater participation in decisions that affect him and a more equitable share of the material goods of life.

Wars have grown more and more disastrous. World War I killed 12 million in battle. World War II cost 21 million lives in battle and

15 million more in air raids. One B-52 bomber now carries in a normal payload more explosive power than all the shells and bombs of World War II (Hoagland, 1964). A third world war might kill all life over large areas and conceivably make the whole planet uninhabitable. Even during nominal peace, tests and experiments with nuclear weapons have already distributed in the atmosphere, in plants, and in the bodies of animals radioactive iodine, strontium 90, and plutonium, imperiling present and future generations. Motion pictures such as *On the Beach* and *Dr. Strangelove* have increased popular concern. President John F. Kennedy warned: "Today every inhabitant of this planet must contemplate the day when this planet may no longer be habitable. Every man, woman and child lives under a nuclear sword of Damocles, hanging by the slenderest of threads, capable of being cut at any moment by accident, or miscalculation or madness." In his Inaugural Address Kennedy spoke of two powerful groups of nations, "both racing to alter that uncertain balance of terror that stays the hand of mankind's final war." A similar theme was expressed by a Harvard psychologist, Henry A. Murray: "A war that no one wants, an utterly disgraceful end to man's long experiment on earth is a possibility we are facing every day. Events are hanging by a thread, depending on an accident, or some finger on a trigger, on a game of wits and tricks, of pride and saving faces" (1960, p. 12).

The psychological problem

At the heart of the problem is a curious paradox which makes international conflict especially appropriate for psychological study. We abhor the prospect of another world war but place the highest priority on programs that increase the tensions and the magnitude of potential destruction. The nuclear powers now stockpile the equivalent of tons of TNT for every inhabitant on earth, but we still spend feverishly to increase the overkill. "The grim fact is," said Lester Pearson of Canada in responding to the Nobel Peace Prize, "that we prepare for war like precocious giants and for peace like retarded pygmies." This seems to be an immense social neurosis. A psychiatrist, Jerome Frank comments: "The danger creates an emotional state which impedes problem solving and causes resort to false solutions" (1962, p. 458). One widespread maladaptation is to deny the problem; to hope wishfully that if we pay no attention to it, it will go away.

Social psychology is one of the younger sciences, but during the past 50 years it has developed a number of insights into what Sherif has called "groups in harmony and tension." The problem of building "the defenses of peace in the minds of men," as called for in the charter of UNESCO, is partly psychological. Psychology alone does not have the answer to moving mankind from the ways of war to paths of peace, but, along with statesmanship, political science, history, geography, economics, and sociology, psychology can make a valid contribution.

Since it is people who make war or peace, their perceptions, feelings, judgments, and decisions will determine the future. Lester Van Atta, after serving with the Arms Control and Disarmament Agency in Washington, told the American Psychological Association: "I conclude after a year of study in the Pentagon, that control of the arms race is not a problem of hardware design nor of technical schemes for carefully balanced disarmament, detection of weapons tests, or evaluation of war-making capabilities. It is not a problem in which technical skills can pave the way for the application of diplomatic skills, leaving us somehow more secure. It is a problem of human understanding and human control, beginning, if you like, with self control" (1962).

Our war-oriented culture

An institution which is as widespread, costly, and persistent as war must be firmly rooted in human nature, in the culture patterns, or in both. McDougall (1908) related war to man's pugnacious instinct. Freud posited a death wish in all men—murderous if turned against others and suicidal if against the self. A study in 1932 (Fletcher) showed that, by that date, well over 90 percent of competent psychologists had concluded that there is nothing in human nature which makes war inevitable. As we pointed out in Chapter 9, the concept of "instincts" to account for social institutions has proved to be unsatisfactory. Most human beings are aggressive and destructive at times, but the outlet does not have to be anything like a war system. Man has the capacity for living in relative harmony with the people who annoy him most: his own family, business associates, and neighbors. Warmaking is a stupendous, organized activity, directed for the most part against human beings that neither the soldier nor the statesman has ever personally encountered. In war, far more persons are engaged in cooperative activities than in combat.

There is no primal instinct which inevitably drives men toward war; almost no sub-human species engage in collective action against others of their own kind. The explorer, Nansen, had difficulty making Eskimos grasp the whole idea of war, and some other pre-literate societies have no war-making activities. Modern anthropologists agree with the pioneering observations of Sumner and Keller (1924) that going to war is not a biological urge but a social custom. Even among modern nations, a country like Sweden can stay at peace for many generations without experiencing the kind of frustration which would come from thwarting a basic instinct. Actually, going to war is so far from "natural" or "gratifying" that few people are inclined to volunteer to fight and extensive coercion must be employed in drafting an army.

During World War II, thirteen distinguished social psychologists prepared a *Manifesto* to help guide our nation toward permanent peace. It was circulated to about four thousand psychologists, twenty-five hundred of whom replied. More than 95 percent of those responding were in accord. The first proposition in that document declares:

> *War can be avoided: War is not born in men; it is built into men.*
> No race, nation, or social group is inevitably warlike. The frustrations and conflicting interests which lie at the root of aggressive wars can be reduced and redirected by social engineering. Men can realize their ambitions within the framework of human cooperation and can direct their aggressions against those natural obstacles that thwart them in the attainment of their goals. (Murphy, 1945, p. 455)

Since man's nature does not spontaneously produce armaments, we turn to examine the societies in which they arise.

Warfare is the most prominent feature of modern Western culture. The sociologist, Sorokin, reviewing the 902 wars in 2,500 years of recorded history concludes: "War steadily increased from the 13th to the 17th Centuries, remaining high throughout the 18th and early 19th and then soared up to an unprecedented height during the 20th Century, the bloodiest of all the 30 Centuries of Graeco-Roman and Western culture." Professor Sorokin goes on to comment that the chance that a man would die at peace rather than in war, were 6,500 in the "Dark" 13th Century to one in the "Enlightened" 20th. (1941, Vol. III) This was written before the holocaust of World War II.

Some fallacies
Before we make our constructive recommendations, let us clear the ground. One of the contributions of psychology, as illustrated above in the discussion of the "instinctive" basis of war, is to remove misconceptions which lead to efforts that are unproductive because they do not attack the real problem. Many of these turn out, on careful examination, to be half-truths which are misleading unless carefully qualified. Others are generally untrue.

The warlike peoples
It is sometimes assumed that although we want peace, some other nation is determined to drive us into war. At the moment, the most belligerent utterances are coming from the Communist Chinese, but even these usually take the form of a prediction that the capitalist nations will use any accord to try to destroy their Communist order.

In the psychologist's *Manifesto,* the first point, quoted above, denies that the people of any nation are intrinsically and inevitably committed to policies of aggression. Another point—No. 8 in the document—stresses the fact that in every country today the people want peace.

> *The root-desires of the common people of all lands are the safest guide to framing a peace.*
> Disrespect for the common man is characteristic of fascism and of all forms of tyranny. The man in the street does not claim to understand the complexities of economics and politics, but he is clear as to the general directions in which he wishes to progress. His will can be studied (by adaptations of the public-opinion poll). His expressed aspirations should even now be a major guide to policy.

A study (Richardson, 1950) on the frequency of wars engaged in by world powers between 1850 and 1950, showed Britain most war-oriented with 20 wars. The Japanese had 9, the Germans 8, the United States 7. Surely the Empire had more to do with this record than the British national character.

General Douglas MacArthur, speaking to the American Legion in 1955, warned that pressures for war were arising from "two great illusions. The one, a complete belief on the part of the Soviet world that the capitalist powers are preparing to attack it . . . And the other, a complete belief on the part of the capitalist countries that the Soviets are preparing to attack us. Both are wrong. Each side, so far as the masses are concerned, is equally desirous of peace. For either side, war with the other would mean nothing but disaster. Both equally dread it."

There have been war-directed phases in the history of many nations; it is likely that in no nation today would the people willingly start a war.

Security by detachment

Since George Washington, in his Farewell Address, warned the young nation against becoming entangled in Old World intrigues and alliances, numerous Americans have sought to preserve peace by isolation. For 150 years, the two oceans which separated the United States from Europe and Asia made the policy feasible. In the twentieth century, the technology of communication and travel narrowed our separation. The last powerful stand of isolationism was made against the League of Nations, and it shattered Woodrow Wilson's dream of a Parliament of Man. In 1937, only one American in four favored our joining the League. By the time world spokesmen were gathering in San Francisco in July of 1945, public opinion polls showed the American people, in a remarkable ratio of 20–1, in favor of participating in the United Nations. The location of its headquarters in New York symbolized the new role of the United States in world leadership.

The change in American attitudes fits into a long-term trend described as follows, in the psychologists' *Manifesto*.

The trend of human relationships is toward ever wider units of collective security.

From the caveman to the Twentieth Century, human beings have formed larger and larger working and living groups. Families merged into clans, clans into states, and states into nations. The United States are not forty-eight threats to each other's safety; they work together. At the present moment the majority of our people regard the time as ripe for regional and world organization, and believe that the initiative should be taken by the United States of America.

Repeated polls have shown that Americans continue to place hope in world organization. For example, on July 3, 1963, the American Institute of Public Opinion asked its nationwide sample: "Would it be better for the United States to keep independent in world affairs—or would it be better for the United States to work closely with other nations?" Only 10 percent voted for independent action; 8 percent had no opinion; and 82 percent wanted cooperation with other nations.

Differences in cultures make clashes inevitable

This third fallacy arises logically from the refutation of the previous ones. If war is not biologically instinctive; if no particular peoples can be held responsible for warmongering; and if we are becoming tightly knit into a one-world civilization, then the real problem must be the antagonism aroused when different cultures are brought into unprecedented proximity.

Sometimes this proposition takes the corollary form: "If we could see that other people are not really so different from us, we would avoid conflict."

In reality, wars occur mainly between nations that are very much alike. The United States has fought two wars against England and two against Germany, nations with which we have a great deal in common. We are not likely to fight the Eskimos, the Malayan nomads or the African pygmies, all of whom have cultures far different from ours. The rivalry between the United States and the Soviet Union arises because of, not in spite of, the fact that we are alike in being major world powers, highly nationalistic, with universal education, advanced technology, and a sense of world mission. China becomes more of a threat to us as it adopts more of Western technology, education, nationalism, and plays an increasing role, like America, in exporting a way of life.

No amount of cultural similarity has prevented war, and no amount of cultural difference prevents friendly alliance when national power interests coincide.

Knowledge of other nations promotes harmony

This assumption underlies many educational programs. It is partly true. By and large, as we reported in Chapter 7, knowledge and favorable international attitudes are correlated. One of the early studies, for example (Eckert, Mills, 1935), showed that the more internationally-minded students in high school were those who were both brighter and better informed. In history, the more nationalistic averaged marks of 72; the more world-minded averaged 86; a difference more than six times its standard error. The implications of correlation for causation must be carefully criticized. Perhaps the greater knowledge brings more favorable attitudes, but just as possibly the stronger interest in world affairs leads to acquisition of more knowledge. An even more probable interpretation is that certain social milieus—family, school, neighborhood, church—infuse members with both the knowledge and the attitudes.

What happens to international attitudes in experiments where new information alone is introduced without accompanying attitude influences? As shown in Chapter 7, the recipient usually ignores facts which he finds incongruent with his established attitudes, or he discounts the new information, distorts it, or finds some way of adapting it to his previously established assumptions. In Cherrington's study groups (Abstract 32) both understanding and attitude-persuasion were operative, but even then, some groups did not become world-minded. The *Monday Morning Seminar*, a discussion group of middle-aged, middleclass women, carried on their sessions for two years, without growing any less nationalistic. And the advanced group of students who spent a summer at Geneva, Switzerland, in intensive study of international diplomacy, were more disillusioned than persuaded. Dodd's (1935) observations in the Middle East showed greatest hostility between groups that were highly aware of one another. The tension between Israel and the Arab states, or that between India and Pakistan over Kashmir, is not a product of ignorance of the opposition. The civil wars in Korea, Laos, and Vietnam have taken place between people of almost identical culture with rival political leaders.

Few, if any, of the wars of the past century have been declared or conducted by officials who were ignorant of the enemy nation. Frequently the best informed people of a country are those who make the international policies which lead to war. The ignorance of the average citizen is regrettable, but there is no reason to believe that if he had as many technical data as the section chiefs in the Foreign Office or the State Department, the interests of peace would be greatly advanced.

Frustration-aggression

A hypothesis popular among psychologists since the valuable work of Dollard, Doob, Miller, Mowrer, and Sears (1939) is that most aggression arises from frustration. In international affairs, it has been argued that the low living standards in many parts of the world create intolerable frustrations and generate dangerous hostility. In one study (Miller, Bugelski, 1948) young men who felt frustrated by some boring tests expressed more hostility toward Japanese or Mexicans than did a control group who had been enjoying themselves.

Without denying the demonstrated connection between frustration and aggression in individuals, we must qualify the hypothesis when it is applied to nations. The most warlike nations are not those in which most people are poorly housed, poorly clothed, and ill-fed. The most aggressive nations have, on the whole, been fairly prosperous. Most nations of Southeast Asia, with average annual incomes corresponding to less than $100 per year are too busy fighting starvation to work out major strategies of attack and defense directed at other countries.

The hypothesis does apply to frustration of those national aspirations to glory and a place-in-the-sun, when it seems these goals can be won by conquest. We shall turn, a little later, to an examination of such nationalistic motivations.

Foreign aid can, perhaps, serve to reduce gross inequalities and to increase good will, but it cannot in itself remove the threat of war. The phenomenal rise in the standard of living in Japan during the generation preceding the attack on Pearl Harbor did not contribute to world peace.

Security through deterrence

Throughout recorded history, strong nations have been prone to assume that their impressive power would succeed in preventing others from attacking the interests of the powerful. Much of the time, for example, during the Roman Empire, this assumption has held true. It has been the most popular argument for increasing defense expenditures in the United States.

The other side of the same picture, however, is that the deterrents set up by one power are viewed as threats by another. If A has 1,000 missiles to deter any aggressive acts by B, B justifies its efforts to stockpile 1,200 missiles to deter A from aggression. Then A needs 1,500. This kind of contest has usually resulted in escalating armaments by all competitors and an eventual holocaust.

A related thesis is that the weapons of war have become so destructive and the costs of war so heavy that no nation will ever again risk going to war. The notion that threat will prove an adequate deterrent to man's resort to war has a long and disappointing history. It doubtless occurred when men first fashioned metal swords and spears and recurred with the first use of gun powder.

A former President of Columbia University, Nicholas Murray Butler, apparently believed that this kind of argument might prove effective.

In his speeches he reviewed the enormous financial cost of World War I. And he argued in speeches in the 1930's, recalling World War I, that airplane bombing would be so destructive that a new war could not be begun or pursued. Yet he was speaking only eight years before the outbreak of the far more expensive and destructive World War II.

When we were exploring attitudes (Chapter 7) and propaganda (Chapter 8) we noted experiments on reaction to threat. People seem more likely to dismiss unpleasant matters from attention than to take warnings seriously. When atomic and nuclear weapons were first introduced, there was a wave of apprehension. Further data on the ill effects of fall-out and the problem of disposing of residues from atomic energy plants have been met with concern by a few, but with apathy by most of the public. Everyone now knows that hydrogen bombs can do incalculable damage, and most people are aware that an accident or an irresponsible official might trigger disaster. But few people feel moved to take any action to eliminate such ominous possibilities. Research on methods of preserving peace still gets but a tiny fraction of the financial support given to bigger ballistic missiles and nuclear explosives.

The Federation of Atomic Scientists declares in its *Bulletin:* "With the stockpile . . . that now exists it is possible to cover the entire earth with a radiation level which for ten years would remain sufficiently intense to prove fatal to all living beings on land." Yet the efforts of the nuclear powers to stockpile more of the lethal weapons as a deterrent continue.

The psychological effects of deterrence are illustrated in several experiments that use a model called the "prisoner's dilemma." The essence of the game is that if both players trust each other, both can win moderately. If either wishes to take advantage of the other, he may succeed. If both try to get the best of the other, both lose. One of the studies (Deutsch, Krauss, 1960) demonstrated that when neither side could attack the other (disarmament), both gained; when both had weapons which could hurt each other, both lost. In striving for security, mankind, in its reliance on ways of hurting others, may be supporting its most costly illusion.

Psychologism
"Since wars begin in the minds of men, it is in the minds of men that the defenses of peace must be built."

This proposition, from the Charter of UNESCO, is partly true, but is false in some of its implications. Wars do involve the minds of men, but they are not spontaneous fantasies that can be dispelled by psychotherapy. War-readiness is not just an impulse—it is a reaction to an interpretation of circumstances and events. The pattern of S-P-A applies here.

Stagner and Osgood (1946), using an early version of the Semantic

Differential test, were able to graph the gradual change in American public opinion from April 1940 through March 1942. Before Pearl Harbor, there was a statistically significant rise in favorable attitudes toward the ideas of "Big Navy," "National Self Defense," and "Fighting;" attitudes toward "Pacifism" and "Neutrality" grew more hostile. Conceptions of "Russians" moved toward "fair" and even "noble" and those of "Germans" toward "intolerant" and "ferocious." The reaction to "Englishmen" progressed toward "strong" and to "Frenchmen" toward "weak." These changes were not engendered mainly by subjective stirrings of inner mental and emotional life; they were based on interpretations of events as reported in the news of each day.

A similar study of attitudes during this critical period was made by Cantril (1942). In the ten months from May, 1940, to March, 1941, the proportion of Americans who thought it more important to help defeat Hitler than to keep out of the war, rose from 35 to 70 percent. Between July, 1940, and September, 1941, the proportion in favor of curbing Japanese aggression, even at the risk of war, rose from 12 to 68 percent. These great changes from holding fast to peace toward readiness for war cannot be attributed to hostile psychological complexes instilled in childhood. They were directly responsive to the changing situation in the world. But the Nazi leaders and the Japanese rulers were also responding to events as they perceived them. The clear implication is that preservation of peace requires alteration in the external operating system, not merely in the hearts and perceiving mechanisms of men.

A related fallacy is that if children are intelligently brought up, they will cooperate rather than fight. Some parents are troubled by their small sons' interest in guns, tanks, and missiles. Such toys are seen as conducive to militaristic attitudes.

There are at least three important psychological fallacies implicit in this argument. One is that childhood patterns carry over unchanged into adult life. While some patterns of personality are fixed at an early age, others are altered as the young person enters college, takes a first job or marries and starts to raise a family. Many childhood activities are satisfying at one stage of development but are simply outgrown later. There is no evidence to suggest that boys who play with toy cannons are predisposed toward life in the artillery.

A second important difficulty is that adult life sets the context in which children see, desire, and act. As long as we adults channel so much of our resources into more and bigger weapons it is unrealistic to expect that we can bring up children to ignore or to minimize this phase of the culture.

The third observation is that friendly cooperation and hostile warmaking are not necessarily incompatible. When a nation is engaged in a life-or-death struggle against an external enemy, internal cooperation rises to a high level. A predatory gang may have excellent teamwork within its own group. The external threat reduces barriers to internal harmony. Insecure rulers use this mechanism, playing up the danger from without to reduce dissension within the country.

The argument has been unusually well stated by Sherif:

> In ethnological literature we find cultures which are neither quarrelsome nor bloodthirsty among themselves but most ferocious to outsiders . . . Norms toward outgroups need not correspond to the positive or negative nature of relations practiced within the in-group. Norms toward out-groups are primarily determined by the nature of relations between groups. Norms followed within the in-group may be democratic and cooperative in nature. It does not follow that norms developed toward out-groups in general will likewise be democratic and cooperative. At times, the greater solidarity and cooperativeness within the in-group may mean more effective friction with out-groups. (1953, pp. 209–10)

There is some truth in the view that an authoritarian upbringing does predispose to hostility, concern for power, and a zest for militarism. Stagner (1954) found that unusually strict home discipline produced young people who were more nationalistic, more intolerant of minorities, and more likely to endorse war as a desirable instrument of national policy.

Later in this chapter we shall suggest that "hostile personalities," inclined toward suspicion, are likely to magnify the threat from possible enemies.

Distorted perception in international relations

An experimental model

In Chapter 6 we proposed that attitudes (A) be understood as the outcome of processes of interaction (P) which grow out of structural arrangements (S). It follows that to understand international attitudes we must study the situations in which they arise. To alter attitudes, the objective situations and corresponding interaction processes may have to be changed.

A neat illustration of the way in which changed S can affect P and produce collective hostility is found in Sherif's experiment with boys in summer camp, reported in condensed form in Abstract 48. Sherif demonstrated that boys who were strangers could, after interacting in an environment set up for the purpose, forge strong links to one another. These links do not necessarily follow the line of first impression and "natural affinity" (whatever that may be) but can be built experimentally and arbitrarily. Once in-groups have been formed, they evolve

Abstract 48

TITLE — A Preliminary Study of Intergroup Relations

AUTHORS — M. Sherif and C. W. Sherif

PROBLEMS — How in-groups are formed: how hostile actions arise between such groups.

SUBJECTS — 24 12-year-old New England boys of lower middle class in a summer camp.

PROCEDURE — Stage I — Informal camp-wide activities (3 days). Sociometric choices.

Stage II — Division into two experimental cabins, with boys so assigned as to minimize the attraction of the group for each member. Activities carried on by each group separately (5 days). Repeat of sociometric choices.

Stage III — Activities bringing the two groups into competition and into situations where one group believes it is frustrated by the other (5 days).

Dr. Sherif, in the role of caretaker, was an observer throughout. Two graduate students, serving as senior counselors, assisted.

SOME FINDINGS — 1. Although each boy was arbitrarily assigned to a cabin where (on the average) only a third of the others were boys he would have chosen to be with, by the end of Stage II, 91 percent of the choices were from among their new cabin mates.

2. Each cabin developed in Stage II a strong in-group structure with norms. One cabin called itself the "Bull Dogs;" the other chose the name "Red Devils." Each group had its special nicknames, its way of going about tasks, its preferred songs. The pronouns "we," "our," and "us" were applied within each group. Leaders emerged in each group, and comparative status for each boy was established. Candy from home and comic books were invariably shared with the cabin group. The Bull Dogs devised an oath of secrecy. The colors (blue and red) become group symbols and were used in decorating the cabin.

3. In Stage III, hostility to the out-group mounted. The losing team in a tug of war accused the other cabin of unfair tactics. Name-calling emerged: "Dirty players! Cheats!" After a party where half the refreshments had been (intentionally by the leaders) mussed up, the Red Devils, first group to arrive took the attractive plates; the Bull Dogs blamed their crushed refreshments on their rivals and called them "jerks," "rotten pukes," and various unprintable names. The next morning the Bull Dogs were on kitchen police duty and the Red Devils deliberately messed up their table. The Bull Dogs not only refused to clean it up, but smeared syrup and cocoa on it to attract bees and wasps. Posters calling the Red Devils "pigs," "jackasses," "bums," and "girls" were hung in the mess hall. During lunch, food and sponges were thrown by each group at the other and each accused the other of starting the fight. When the boys began throwing saucers and table-knives, the adult leaders intervened.

Abstract 48—*Continued*

4. An effort by the counselors to call off all competition and rebuild camp solidarity proved inadequate in the remaining days. The most effective device was a softball game against an outside team. On the last night of camp, the boys refused to join in a common campfire, but insisted on separate campfires where the old names and songs could be revived.

SOURCES: I. H. Rohrer and M. Sherif (eds.) *Social psychology at the cross-roads.* New York: Harper, 1951, pp. 388–426. Also: M. Sherif and C. W. Sherif *Groups in harmony and tension.* New York: Harper, 1953, pp. 229–295.

their own hierarchy, norms, and symbols in what may be regarded as a small scale model of a club, a neighborhood, a church, a business, a community, or even a nation. Sherif was able to demonstrate further that under conditions of competition and rivalry, frustration does lead to hostile and aggressive reactions toward the opponent. Many of the features of international conflict—ethnocentrism, name-calling, recrimination, armament, and attack—could be aroused within his model. The same boys who had once been perceived as friends were later seen as malicious. The resentments aroused by the experimental manipulation persisted despite efforts to rebuild harmony.

The Sherif experiment reinforces a number of psychological principles stated earlier in the chapter. The youngsters were not bellicose by instinct nor had they become especially so by family training. They might have lived peaceably and happily all summer as they did in the first eight days. The opponents were more alike than different in culture and values. They had had a fair chance to become acquainted with, and to build a liking for, the very boys they later despised. The more weapons one side accumulated, the more their opponents gathered.

The enmity and belligerence were the product of a specific experimental manipulation. When the situation (S) was so arranged as to make the processes of group interaction (P) competitive in a win-lose contest, the attitudes of participants (A) became more and more warlike.

Now let us explore some implications when the international situation is viewed as an expansion of such a model. A simple model is never entirely adequate for a complex situation, but it provides a starting point.

Nationalism: The in-group:

The established in-groups resemble tribes or nations; the feeling of loyalty toward one's own group is patriotism. This rather arbitrary choice of what most people today regard as their major affiliation requires thoughtful reappraisal. How important is a man's nationality?

The Oxford historian, Arnold J. Toynbee, has defined nationalism as:

> . . . a state of mind in which we give our paramount political loyalty to one fraction of the human race—to the particular tribe of which we happen to be tribesmen. In so far as we are captured by this ideology, we hold that the highest political good for us is our own nation's sovereign independence; that our nation has a moral right to exercise its sovereignty according to what it believes to be its own national interests, whatever consequences this may entail for the foreign majority of the human race; and that our duty, as citizens of our country, is to support our country, right or wrong. (1963, p. 23)

In one of the first studies of the psychology of nationalism (1927) Floyd H. Allport notes that we reify (make an abstraction into a "thing") and personify nations. They are aggregates of different individuals, but we make them into some sort of Super-Being, with "interests" to be served at whatever cost to the citizen. "One of the most potent influences . . . in support of war is precisely that fallacy, which in clearer moments the average citizen will disclaim, namely, the belief that the Nation is something independent of and greater than its individuals." Reification and personification lead to sentences beginning: "Austria fears"—"Brazil believes"—"China charges"— or "Uncle Sam demands." Intellectually we know that Austria—and every nation—consists of many different human beings with varied and often conflicting opinions, interests, and feelings. All these differences are obscured by the shorthand, "Austria fears. . . ."

In the Sherif experiment, the boys built their group loyalty through direct, face-to-face relationships, as described in the relation between frequency of interaction and liking in Chapter 3 of this text. National loyalty cannot depend on direct personal contacts among all citizens. They are too numerous and scattered. So identification is fostered by symbols. The country has a name, a flag, a national anthem, a leader. Citizens are linked not through their experiences of each other, but through their shared participation in national rites and their common reverence for national symbols.

Some emotional needs of individuals are served by identification with the nation. Caspar Milquetoast may not be very forceful, but he can applaud when his Führer speaks aggressively. Weak egos have a special need to belong to strong aggregates. The individual may repress personal greed or hostility, but be gratified when his nation accumulates wealth or damns an opponent. His own hut may be mean, but the king's palace is magnificent.

Another historian, Carlton J. H. Hayes (1960), has written of "Nationalism: A Religion." "Since its advent in western Europe, modern nationalism has partaken of the nature of a religion . . . Everywhere it has a god, who is either the patron or the personification of one's *patrie,* one's fatherland, one's national state. This deity . . . is the god of a chosen people, a jealous god, preeminently a god of battles." (p. 164) The national god requires pledges of allegiance, patriotic rites of worship, and faith in his high mission and destiny. There is a national catechism, reciting the achievements and virtues of the Nation. Men bare their heads when the national symbol is raised. Hymns of praise are sung. Its holy days are national holidays. Its temples are tombs of generals, national monuments, and government buildings. The national mythology serves as theology. Any sins committed in the service of the State are transmuted to merit. Its financial levies must be paid at whatever cost to any other interests in life, and even life itself must be sacrificed when the nation-god commands.

The nation as a tribal deity is seen as perfect in virtue and omnipotent in strength. He makes no mistakes—he cannot be wrong. He can give no concessions for that would be weakness.

Blasphemy and sacrilege are heinous crimes in the national religion. It is more hazardous, in most communities, for a teacher to raise questions about the value of the national symbols and concepts than it would be to question capitalism or Christianity. If peppery old Dr. Samuel Johnson were here today and made on commercial television his statement that "Patriotism is the last refuge of a scoundrel!" he might be promptly cut off the air, and barred from future programs as "subversive" or, at least, "controversial."

In the early twentieth century, people were still free to travel whenever their inclinations and pocketbooks would permit. Elaborate systems of passports and visas have since been developed, thus making freedom of travel subject to governmental regulation. Few, if any values can take precedence over the claims of that symbol called "nation." "National interests" are somehow seen as different from and having higher priority than any other interests of persons. If national demands clash with the interests of one's family or job or leisure, then it is asserted that one owes first allegiance to the nation. At least one clergyman has been jailed in America for advising a student that in the matter of conscientious objection to a draft for military service the student's first obligation was to his God. One may not, on any logic or scruple, refuse to accede to the national demand for tax money or military service without being arrested. The nation-state is the only human institution that is permitted to engage freely in organized violence. The nation is seen as absolutely sovereign and the ultimate in social sanctions. One may be a traitor to one's family, friends, work associates, home community, or church and receive merely disapprobation, but a traitor to the nation is executed.

Nationalism is a more potent force in some nations than in others. Some of the readiness of Italy for Mussolini and of Germany for Hitler was due to the fact that these countries had been slow in achieving a national state. Some new nations of Africa and Asia exalt national symbols, partly as a protest against the old colonialism but also as a means for unifying people of diverse tribes and languages. The "melting-pot" history of the United States has placed a special emphasis on symbols of unity. Hofstadter (1955) has argued that the defensiveness of immigrants and their descendants has led to the emergence of the idea of "100 percent Americanism." In the sphere of government, our official committees on "un-American" thoughts and actions seem to have no parallel in other countries. A "Committee on Un-Swedish Activities" would be viewed as ridiculous. In the Soviet Union, nationalism was fostered, as it had been under the Czars, to unite sub-groups speaking scores of different languages, but it was further emphasized after 1917 when the U.S.S.R. stood alone as a Communist state in a world accustomed to capitalism.

The hypertrophy—excessive, unhealthy growth—of nationalism in the modern world threatens many human associations and values. Loyalty is not an unqualified virtue. Today it distorts our perception of our own nation and of others. Among high school youth (Remmers, 1963), 70 percent agree that the American way of life is superior in nearly all respects to every other. The kind of warm pride which most Americans have in their home state is no threat to the neighboring states. The problem, now, is to design the kind of social organizations and controls which will enable all the world to feel the positive kind of national pride which people in the United States feel for the home region. But nationalistic pride is another story. William Howard Taft exclaimed sadly during his campaign for a World Court: "Every attempt at world organization breaks against the dogma of the national state."

The social philosopher Thorstein Veblen once commented: "Patriotism lives on invidious comparison, and works out in mutual hindrance and jealousy between nations . . . Into this culture and technological system of the modern world, the patriotic spirit fits like dust in the eyes and sand in the bearings." Toynbee, entitles the article from which we drew his definition of nationalism: "Again nationalism threatens!" Another historian, Henry Steele Commager, has expressed concern with the impact of mounting national feeling upon scholarship. "One of the gravest perils confronting mankind today is the danger from chauvinistic, belligerent nationalism. That nationalism has extended into art and literature, scholarship and science, and has almost ended what once existed—a great universal community of learning." (1955)

Attendance at international scientific conventions and the free circulation of reports of scientific investigations have been hampered by restrictions put forth by defenders of what are supposed to be the interests of one nation or another. The collective search for truth must defer when the voice of national security is heard.

A major threat to civil rights comes from hypertrophied national-ism. The stand of two-thirds of Americans denying the constitutional right of free speech to an American Communist (Stouffer, 1955) is based in considerable measure upon the view that Communists are foreign agents and threats to the national state.

"Almost at the moment when political thinking freed itself of illusion, it fell prey to the myth of the State," writes Ernst Cassirer, Research Professor of Philosophy at Yale and author of "The Myth of the State." "The deep and ardent desire to reconstruct our cultural world from its debris is now generally felt," he says. But we are hampered by "the modern political myths (which) have intoxicated our thoughts and poisoned our feelings."

It seems clear that any effective program for improving international relations will have to come to grips with the dogma of the National State. Possible action programs will be considered later in this chapter. We now return to our model—the antipathy artificially created between the two cabins of campers.

Xenophobia: the out-group

The correlate of the good in-group is the bad out-group. Member-ship gains definition and meaning against the background of "all those others." The stranger, the foreigner, the outsider—is seen as a possible threat because he may not share the norms or respond to the sanctions of the in-group. Since he has not built into him the control and restraints of the in-group member, the foreigner is perceived as likely to do all the wild and wicked things which in-group members might wish to do but have to keep under control. The outsider is a natural target for projection of the repressed impulses of the insider.

In our model, the out-group consisted of boys very much like the in-group and so admirable that two-thirds of the best-friends choices of the average in-group member were located there. In this respect, the model is unlike the typical international situation. Only the most en-lightened and universalistic humanitarians have a peacetime concept of other nations as people much like ourselves and sometimes even more admirable. About the year 1500 Erasmus wrote: "I wish to be called a citizen of all the world, the common friend of all states." Many intellectuals today share this view, but more typical of the average citizen is the attitude revealed in Remmers' poll of teen-agers, about half of whom accepted the "super-patriot" view that foreigners have little to contribute to the American way of life and constitute a threat to us (1963).

Competition mounts

So long as the Bull Dogs and the Red Devils carried on their own busy programs independently, there was nothing in their instinctive make-up or their loyalty to the in-group which provoked hostility. When they began competitive games, track meets, tug-of-war, awarding prizes (jack knives) that were valued, the changed pattern of interaction brought attitude changes.

From day to day—almost from hour to hour of Stage III—the tension mounted in vicious circles of reinforcement. The Bull Dogs, thinking their refreshments deliberately disarranged, messed up their table for the Red Devils to clean up; the Red Devils made the mess worse. The hostile actions became cumulative. One side accumulated a store of "ammunition"; when it disappeared they retaliated with a raid. A "peace envoy" was chased off in a hail of green apples. When counselors decided matters had gone too far, it was more difficult than they had anticipated to stop the forces which had already acquired momentum. One is reminded of the sad pronouncements of statesmen at the brink of war, lamenting that the catastrophe which might perhaps have been prevented at some earlier stage has now become inevitable.

In the international situation, the number-one Power among nations is challenged by the number-two Power. They become rivals in military strength, adventures in space, industrial and agricultural production, Olympic games, propaganda, votes in the U.N., and aid to underdeveloped nations. When one wins, the other feels a sense of defeat. As with two schools that are traditional rivals in athletic and other contests, friendly competition sometimes degenerates into dangerous enmity. The competition remains a challenging game as long as it does not assume too much importance. When too much is at stake and each side becomes deeply committed to victory, the struggle becomes a cold war which leads almost inevitably to a shooting war. Given the competitive, win-lose struggle, quite healthy personalities become rabid partisans.

We referred earlier to the "Prisoner's Dilemma," which simulates the strategies of competitive struggle using "two-person, non-zero sum" games (Luce, 1957; Scodel, *et al.*, 1959; Minas, *et al.*, 1960; McClintock, *et al.*, 1963). Under the game conditions, the usual choice (by American students) is to take the risk of competition, hoping for the advantage (Minas, Scodel, 1960). Cooperative responses were few in the beginning, and, when players had once or twice had the experience of being beaten (because the opponent did not simultaneously cooperate), they became even less frequent over time. The prospect of continuous modest gains by mutual cooperation did not seem trustworthy.

In the setting of a power struggle, any gain by either side leads the opponent to strive for a greater advantage. Hence efforts at "deterrence" by threat lead to greater counter-threats, and the tension mounts. Moderates lose leadership and the fanatics gain approval. In a later camp conflict, reported by Sherif, the peacetime leader of the Eagles was displaced during raids by a more aggressive and hostile boy.

Name-calling

One of the earliest and clearest indications of the changed attitudes of participants in the boys camp model was that each group started to make derogatory remarks about the others. This is equally characteristic of international conflict. The Germans in World War I became "Huns" or "Krauts"; the Japanese were "Japs." Along with the disparaging names go unpleasant connotations. In 1935, a sample of women students rated the Japanese as "intelligent, tradition-loving, ambitious, artistic, progressive, and scientific-minded." In 1942 the leading adjectives applied by students in the same college to "Japs" were "sly, treacherous, deceitful, and cruel" (Seago, 1947). Polls in 1961 reflected a change from the 1942 image of the Japanese as "treacherous, sly, cruel, and warlike" into an image of "hard-working, artistic, intelligent, and progressive" (American Institue of Public Opinion, April 28, 1961). While the Japanese image improved, that of the Russians declined. In 1942 the allied Russians seemed "hard-working and brave, although progressive or radical." In 1961, they were seen by Americans as still "hard-working" but now "warlike" and "treacherous." Adjectives like "arrogant," "conceited," "rude," "cruel," and "sly" were used by only 5 percent of respondents in 1942, but by 18 percent in 1961. The following editorial from the *Daily Mirror* (New York) (November 14, 1951) can serve as a sample: "It ought to be made clear that if Russia stays in the United Nations, this country ought to get out of it. It makes no sense even sitting at a table with these swine—if the pig will pardon the expression!"

At its extreme, the distortion introduced by conflict leads to dehumanizing the enemy. In the model, this was carried only to "pigs" and "jackasses." In war, atrocity stories flourish, portraying the enemy as horribly bestial. In World War I the public was told of the cutting off of breasts of Belgian women by "Huns," a story that was later exposed as false propaganda. Foes become fiends and demons. Erich Fromm notes: "For the Cromwellians, the Papists were of the Devil; for the Jacobeans, the Girondists; for the Americans, the Communists. Man, in each society, seems to absolutize the way of life and the way of thought produced by his culture and to be willing to die rather than to change" (1961 p. 5). "Better dead than Red!" "The only good Indian (Hun, Jap, or Commie) is a dead one!"

A poll (American Institute of Public Opinion, Nov. 3, 1961) showed that 81 percent of Americans would prefer a nuclear war, with all its horrors, to living under Communism; only 6 percent chose to live. In Britain, only 21 percent would choose the atomic war; 31 percent would prefer to be alive under a Red regime.

While vicious motives are attributed to the enemy, he is also recognized as having a devilish cunning. Bauer, a Harvard social psychologist who for ten years studied American-Soviet relationships, reported to an International Psychological Congress that "each party attributes to the other a degree of omniscience and omnipotence that he knows is manifestly impossible in his own situation."

Even clergymen, professing belief in the brotherhood of man, and social scientists who should know better get carried along in the stream of vituperation. The story of Huns and the Belgian women was first told to the writer by a nationally known minister addressing a school assembly. In 1963, a consulting psychologist, in a letter to a New York newspaper, contended that Khrushchev and Castro were self-convicted criminal psychopaths whose words and pledges were worthless. The world could be safe from such persons, he wrote, only when they were removed from society and placed in institutions for the criminally insane.

The diabolic concept of the enemy seems to justify almost any retaliatory wickedness. "Since those beasts will stop at nothing, we are forced to do evil to them first!" The enormous malice attributed to the out-group absolves the in-group of guilt for any atrocities. This seems to be a variant of the self-fulfilling prophecy: Apprehension of evil in others generates in us, and eventually in them, the malevolence we postulate.

The Galahad syndrome

As more vice is attributed to the out-group, more virtue is seen in the in-group. "Throughout history," writes Jerome Frank, a psychiatrist, "when two groups are enemies, each becomes whiter in its own eyes, while the other becomes blacker and blacker until, finally, everything *our* side does is good and everything *their* side does is bad" (1962, p. 461). He cites observations by Dr. Urie Bronfenbrenner (which agree with our own after a number of visits in the U.S.S.R.) that the Russian image of America is the mirror image of the American picture of Russia.

1. Each believes the other an aggressor.
2. Each believes that the government of the other exploits and deludes the people.
3. The other people are out of sympathy with their own government.
4. The other power cannot be trusted in international negotiations.
5. The other power's policies verge on madness.

One is reminded of the conjugation: "I am firm; you are stubborn; he is pigheaded!"

A study of attitudes of the elite, expressed in major official and news publications, found that neither the United States in its statements, nor the U.S.S.R. in theirs, would admit that the other's goal might be self-preservation (Singer, 1963).

Bertrand Russell, commenting on letters from Premier Khrushchev and Secretary of State Dulles (*New Statesman*, April 5, 1958) wrote:

The gist of what both of them say is as follows. "There are two powerful nations in the world which we will call A and B. A is and always has been wholly virtuous; B is and always has been wholly wicked. A seeks freedom; B enforces slavery. A believes in peace; B believes in imperialistic war. A stands for justice to the weak; B stands for the tyranny of the powerful. So far, both these eminent statesmen are in agreement. There is, however, one small point of difference: namely, which is A and which is B."

In every important international conflict, the same myth recurs. The pattern is that of the knighthood legends. A fair damsel is threatened by a dragon; a knight in shining armor rides to the rescue, slays the dragon, and carries off a happy maiden.

Both the United States and the Soviet Union see themselves in the role of Galahad whose "strength is as the strength of ten because his heart is pure." Each sees the other side in the role of the monstrous dragon. Humanity—or Korea or Vietnam or Cuba or whatever land next emerges as the focus of conflict—has the role of the distressed damsel. The pattern is ancient but persistent.

At the beginning of the twentieth century, Senator Albert Beveridge introduced the doctrine of "Manifest Destiny." "And of all our race (i.e., Anglo-Saxon) He (God) has marked the American people His chosen nation to finally lead in the regeneration of the world. This is the divine mission of America, and it holds for us all the profits, all the glory, all the happiness possible to man. We are the trustees of the world's progress, guardians of its righteous peace" (Jan. 9, 1900). President Truman, a half century later, expressed similar sentiments. "The welfare of the world is now our responsibility. Whether we like it or not, we have been forced into that position by two World Wars, both of which could have been avoided if we had been willing to assume the place which God Almighty intended us to assume back in 1918."

Spokesmen for the Soviet Union attribute their divine mission not to God but to historic determinism; no less, however, do they see themselves the saviors of exploited mankind.

In this context, every move or statement of the evil ones becomes suspect. When "we" talk peace, we are sincere; when "they" talk peace, it is diabolical trickery. "They" are incapable of responding to our ideals; "they" respect nothing but brute force. So nations move from words to weapons. The boys in camp fired nothing worse than green apples; before long, many nations will have nuclear warheads on intercontinental ballistic missiles. Some may have "doomsday machines."

Two social psychologists (Leavitt, Bass, 1964, p. 382–3), reviewing studies of intergroup competition, summarize five conclusions.

1. Cohesion increases within groups as divisiveness develops between them.

2. Authoritarian leadership becomes more acceptable to members under threat.

3. Deviancy from the majority viewpoint becomes equivalent to treason as intergroup conflict grows.

4. Negotiators from groups in conflict are locked into intransigent positions.

5. Partisans over-value the achievements of their own group and under-value those of competitors.

Excitement and the mass media

International relations differ from the model of the boys camp in that each side knows the other only by report. Most Americans know what is going on in China or Chile only through what they find in newspapers or on newscasts. Newspapers and broadcasting companies, as was pointed out in Chapter 8, are run for profit from the sale of advertising. Exciting crises sell papers and draw listeners. Friendly cooperative actions make dull news. Mysteries, conflicts, and disasters call for big headlines. There is a constant temptation to dramatize international situations in the simple form of a running battle between the good people and the bad people. Thus the descent from friendly, sportsmanlike competition into bitter conflict is augmented by the crisis-oriented mass media. The propagandists are often far more extreme in their emotions than the contestants themselves. Athletic teams or research scientists of two nations may feel very little of the rivalry or hostility which broadcasters and editorial writers infuse into their news commentaries.

The craving for excitement is served by the mass media but is independently present in the population. A social psychology of war and peace must take into account the large numbers of people who would like, by some means, to escape from their humdrum existence. The prospect of war—at least up to the development of atomic weapons—carried some hint of adventure. One found escape from the tiresome routines of a job (and perhaps the home) in the promise of another kind of life in which there might be exhilarating moments of crisis and opportunity to taste forbidden pleasures.

It may well be that the boys in Sherif's camp, if questioned today, would recall Stage III (battles) as more enjoyable than the harmonious life of Stages I and II or the reconciliation attempts in Stage IV. A Norwegian psychologist, Galtung (1964), has called attention to important differences between the opinions and activities of influential persons at the "Center" of national policies and those of the great majority of citizens in the "Periphery." The Center is preoccupied with breaucratic affairs and immediate adaptations. The masses respond—if at all—in waves of feelings of good-bad, white-black, approval or rejection. Earl D. Osborn, president of the Institute for International Order, accordingly, recommends that the media of mass communication try to convey some very simple concepts: "The present situation is intolerable and government must do something about it. . . . Governments should not tax people billions for armaments while half the world is under-nourished. . . . Governments should not draft human beings and force them to kill their fellow men. . . . It is intolerable that people should be condemned to die in countless millions by a government decision in which they have no say."

Wealth and power distort perception

The extraordinary wealth and power of the United States cause a special distortion in our perception of the rest of the world and perhaps also in their perception of us. Another model may make this clear. Imagine 14 brothers. One of them makes as much money as all the others together. Because he wants most of them on his side against a hostile clique among the brothers, he doles out a limited amount of help to those who will stand by him. Meanwhile he preaches to all the others the advisability of their adopting his way of life.

When these relationships are expressed in such simple family terms, it is easier to understand some of the hard feelings in the world today. The United States, with 7 percent of the world's population has about 40 percent of the world's income. In most of the world's largest continent the per-capita income is less than $100 a year. The economist Robert Heilbroner, estimated in 1959 that a projection of the contemporary pace of economic growth, if some effective control of population is undertaken, might bring these people to a level of $200 a year, by the year 2000. Their poverty is not only abysmal, it seems perpetual. In these circumstances, their concerns must be different from those of most Americans. The average man in the world today is not what most Americans think of as "the common man." The real average is a man whose family lives in a two-room hut, with a thatched roof and a mud floor; he is barely literate, frequently hungry, often suffering from vermin and disease. He is not concerned about parliamentary procedure or the race to the moon.

The view that inequality among nations is increasing rather than being reduced by programs of foreign aid appears also in *Unequal Partners* by Thomas Balogh, an Oxford economist (1964). He contends that unplanned capitalism strengthens the already strong and cumulatively depresses the economies of the weaker nations which supply raw materials. Meanwhile the population of underdeveloped areas has been increasing faster than economic production. The world's population, according to United Nations figures, is likely to increase by 500 million during the decade of the 1960's. Most of these people will live and suffer and die in poverty.

Two nations during the past generation have risen to positions of enormous power: They can give or withhold economic aid; they can buy or refuse to purchase raw materials; they can undersell local production or subsidize it, they can erect tariffs or negotiate barter; their ships, planes, missiles, and armed forces can destroy opposition; their propaganda can flood every medium of mass communication.

Observers of human behavior have long agreed on the demoralizing effect of too much power. The most familiar maxim is Lord Acton's: "Power always corrupts, and absolute power corrupts absolutely." Less well known is another of his statements: "Among all the causes which degrade and demoralize men, power is the most constant and the most active."

Hobbes pointed out that the hunger for power is insatiable. No man can become God, and nothing less really satisfies the power-seeker. Nations, like men, seek power for "defense;" their advantage being precarious they seek more, and more, and more. Henry Adams put it succinctly: "Power is poison." If so America is taking a heavy dose.

Spain, Austria, England, France, Germany, Italy, Japan, the Soviet Union, and the United States—each in its period of dominance—all illustrate the thesis that the epoch of greatest power has been that of greatest militarism. There is a negative correlation in history between power and peace; perhaps also between power and the growth of wisdom.

Wishful thinking and vested interests

Perception is also distorted by wishful thinking. Social psychologists have frequently noted the tendency, mentioned in Chapter 7, to adjust our beliefs to what we wish were true. The tendency operates particularly in areas in which objective evidence is hard to get—for example, in predicting the future. Some of the fuzzy thinking and failure to act wisely in international relations is due to wishful distortion.

We are easily persuaded that an effective defense against the devastation of our own country has been found or is about to be found. For a short time, we were persuaded that we could keep "the secret" of atomic bombs for ourselves; many still imagine that its spread to possibly reckless little dictatorships can be prevented. We take it for granted that future generations will find some effective way to deal with the contamination of air and sea by the residue of radioactive explosions. We like to think that antithetical movements like Communism can be liquidated by force if necessary. A poll (American Institute of Public Opinion, Feb. 24, 1965) reports that one American in five believes that Russian Communism will collapse within 20 years. We fancy that the travels of our officials, ceremonially received abroad, make fast friends for us in Latin America, Asia, and Africa. We expect that—despite the obvious implications of the 14-brother model—our aid to impoverished lands will win us gratitude. The new mythology tells us that the peoples in lands ruled by our opponents and indoctrinated by total control of propaganda are all waiting eagerly for us to break through the Iron Curtain and liberate them. We may recognize that great world powers in the past have become corrupt and have declined; we think there must be something in the modern American character or democratic political procedures which will avert this fate. We hope for the best and cease to cope with uncongenial reality.

Economic interests overtly or subtly influence perception of the world. An earlier doctrine, now viewed as naïve, accused "munitions makers" of fomenting wars for profit. The situation is not that simple. But when a large part of the economy becomes involved in military production and a large part of able manpower is engaged in research and administration for the armed forces, there are dynamic tendencies not easily checked. Sumner H. Slichter, Lamont Professor of Economics at Harvard University, not long ago told a convention of the Commercial Finance Industry that the "cold war" was a good safeguard against depression. "It increases the demand for goods, helps sustain a high level of employment, accelerates technological progress and thus helps the country raise its standard of living," Dr. Slichter contended. "In the absence of the cold war, the demand for goods by the government would be many billions of dollars less than it is now and the expenditures of both industry and government on technological research would be hundreds of millions less than they are now. So we may thank the Russians for helping make capitalism in the United States work better than ever."

Disarmament which would stop the flow of orders from the Defense Department would disrupt business significantly. No doubt a changeover could eventually be made to the production of consumer goods, but it would mean a staggering readjustment which few are now ready to contemplate. Nor may one dismiss the vested interest of the military profession. A man who has chosen the armed services as his career, believing that his work is essential, may feel that talk of disarmament is subversive. In theory, he may agree with Napoleon that "there are only two powers in the world, the Sword and the Spirit, and in the long run, the Spirit will win every time." In practice he is sure that God will be on the side of the biggest bombs. Any workable program of disarmament will need to include a plan for transferring men and women from the armed forces to other careers of equal opportunity, dignity, and privilege.

Hostile personalities

Perception of world affairs is distorted by in-group loyalty and Galahadism, by out-group rejection and Satanism, by rivalry, by the crisis-hungry mass media, by gross differences in power, and by wishful thinking. Each of these social psychological factors is particularly potent for certain kinds of persons. One who is insecure and needs acceptance

TABLE 13—AUTHORITARIANISM AND APPROVAL OF ATOMIC
BOMBING OF RUSSIAN SHIPS

Authoritarianism	Number of Cases	Percent Approving Atomic Bombing
5 and above	13	62
4.5–4.9	35	54
4.0–4.4	63	25
3.5–3.9	81	22
3.0–3.4	117	19
2.5–2.9	62	15
2.0–2.4	47	2
1.5–1.9	25	8
1.0–1.4	17	0
	460	

may be a vociferous rooter for the home team. A person with a strong craving for power may find fulfillment as an officer in the police force, the armed services, or in a dictatorial government.

Some types of personality carry a "chip on the shoulder" and are particularly prone to suspect the worst of other individuals, other religions, other races, and other nations. These we have met previously, in Chapter 5, as "authoritarian personalities," identified by the F-scale (F standing for fascistic inclinations). We met these personalities again in Chapter 11, where their projection of their own conflicts onto some other ethnic group intensified racial and religious prejudice. Projectivity is a common factor in persons who have an irrational fear of the United Nations, fluoridation of drinking water, and rape of white women by darker races. It may be expected that those who score high on the F-scale will be particularly suspicious of and hostile toward foreign lands. Table 13 presents results of a study of attitudes of 460 adults—a representative sample—in Los Angeles County. The question here tabulated was: "Should atomic bombs be used, if necessary, to stop propaganda coming from Russian ships at sea?" There is a steady increase in approval for international violence as the F scores rise.

A related hypothesis is that people who cannot really accept themselves are particularly likely to be hostile toward others. Some data were reported in Chapter 2. These are the people who, in the experiment reported in Chapter 11, would exclude "Danireans" and "Pirenians" along with Jews, Turks, and Mexicans.

The attitude of hostile personalities in conflict situations has been studied in a number of research reports. In the games which permit cooperative or competitive choices, persons who have a strongly nationalistic attitude on world affairs more frequently choose the competitive approach (Lutzker, 1960; McClintock, et al., 1963). They are more suspicious of Russia and China; more in favor of "brinkmanship" in foreign policy and have more faith in the survival value of fall-out shelters (Farber, 1951; Ekman, *et al.*, 1963). High school youth who score high on "super-patriotism" score high also on "fascist ideology" ($r = .26$) and low on belief in the Bill of Rights ($r = - .22$) (Remmers, 1963). College students who accept the "cold war" interpretation of international relations have been found to be more authoritarian in personality and more conformist in tastes and interests (Rosenberg, 1964). These various opinions and attitudes fit together in a fairly consistent syndrome of intolerance, although the correlations are not high.

Constructive action

It is not the obligation of a social psychologist to direct statesmen, but responsible officials and citizens may be able to use the facts and principles of this young science in planning wise courses of action. Earlier in this chapter we have shown that psychological knowledge reveals fallacies in several naïve approaches toward achieving world peace. Are there action programs which rest upon sounder psychological insight? At least six approaches have been proposed or endorsed by some social psychologists: (1) building a world government; (2) increasing transnational interaction; (3) setting superordinate international goals; (4) graduated reciprocation; (5) education in conflict resolution; and (6) making life more satisfying. We shall describe each briefly and examine the supporting evidence.

World government

The social structure of sovereign national powers engaged in competitive struggle produces, as we have seen, the attitudes and behaviors which drive toward war. To change the attitudes we must change the structure. The idea of a world organization is at least as old as its proposal by Immanual Kant in 1795. The paramount loyalties of men cannot be attached to the human race until most of the population of the world has been incorporated in a more effective union than the present United Nations.

We know that new nations and new supra-national organizations can come into being only when certain basic psychological and social factors are present. Deutsch (1953) lists: common knowledge, common traditions, common values, communications, and the possibility of command. Each of these has become more evident as technology has given us more rapid travel and the possibility of worldwide newspapers, telephones, radio, and television programs.

Another prerequisite lies in public opinion. World leaders, differing on many policies, are nearly unanimous on the need to make the United

Nations into what President Kennedy called "a genuine world security system."

Back in the 1920's, a study of the attitudes of 1,700 students in eight nations showed overwhelming support, even then, for the proposition: "Some form of international government is inevitable." The percentages of agreement were as follows: 68 in Austria, 84 in Czechoslovakia, 83 in Denmark, 79 in England, 80 in France, 83 in Germany, 71 in Switzerland, and 74 in the United States (Harper, 1931).

Since the founding of the United Nations, a majority of adults in the United States has favored a stronger international police force. In the fall of 1950, 80 percent favored our participation in a standing U.N. army—ready for action at all times. In May of 1951, over 60 percent favored making the United Nations into a world government with power to control the armed forces of all nations, including those of the United States. Seventy percent of the Americans polled favored sending the U.N. Emergency Force into the Sinai peninsula in 1956. A proposal to build up the Emergency Force to a size great enough to deal with small wars anywhere in the world won support by a three to one ratio, in 1964 (American Institute of Public Opinion, May 28, 1964).

Once such action is taken, the probability is that support will further increase. Toynbee (1963) reminds us that when the Chinese and the Roman empires were established, the peoples united within them at first regretted the loss of their previous national sovereignty. Eventually, however, loyalty to the super-state came to take first place in the hearts of the citizens. The fears of the colonies in North America about the Articles of Confederation and later the Constitution which bound them into the United States are now recalled only by historians.

A comprehensive and technically sophisticated design for world government has been offered by Grenville Clark and Louis B. Sohn in their book *World Peace Through World Law* (1960). They propose complete and general disarmament, and an international police force, compulsory arbitration of international disputes, a reliable revenue system for the United Nations, and the development of the General Assembly into a genuine legislative body.

Several psychologists have suggested ways in which a supra-national organization might be strengthened. E. L. Thorndike proposed that, in order to gain trust, it should issue money which would be valid in every country of the world and perhaps also passports and travel insurance. He also made the suggestion that the United Nations would become more glamorous if it staged world fairs with elaborate ceremonies in every part of the globe. E. C. Tolman suggested that the U.N.'s international police force should somehow combine the romantic appeal of the Canadian Mounted Police with the humanitarian aura of the Red Cross.

A commission of psychologists from six nations, meeting at the Accra Assembly in June, 1962, recommended the establishment by a world organization of two institutes. A "World Institute for Research in Behavioral Science" would initiate and coordinate research on reducing international tensions and on building support for peace. A "World Communications Center" would develop a newspaper and broadcast programs free from the bias of all current, nationally oriented media. It would certify school textbooks in geography, history, and other social studies as factually accurate from an objective point of view, thus transcending national loyalties.

The present obstacle to implementing plans for world government is mistrust between the Communist and Western nations. Both sides agree in principle. The draft treaties submitted to the Disarmament Conference in Geneva in 1962 by Moscow and Washington were remarkably alike. Both aimed at total and permanent disarmament. Both sides accepted inspection and control by an international agency to enforce the agreement. The one key point of disagreement was that the United States wanted to set up inspection and enforcement procedures first; then to disarm. The Russians wanted disarmament first, then the operations of inspection. The United States was suspicious that false claims of disarmament would be made. The Russians suspected that the early stages of inspection would be merely espionage designed to learn Soviet military secrets and to take advantage of them. The Chinese Communists were even more suspicious and unwilling to consider disarming.

The problem now seems to be how to create enough trust so that practical steps toward disarmament and world government can be taken. A sociologist, Etzioni, in his book *The Hard Way to Peace* (1962), says that in attempting to ban nuclear weapons—the ultimate destroyers— we have begun at the wrong end of the scale. He proposes that major powers agree first to scrap the relatively useless items—old battleships and bombers and outmoded fighters. Prearranged amounts of these weapons might be delivered to some checkpoint for destruction or modification to civilian uses. Compliance could be checked absolutely. Then more tanks or planes or ships or guns might be brought in. Gradually, armament would be reduced and if all principals fulfilled the agreements, some trust would be built. Eventually it might be possible to deal with the terrible weapons of last resort. Etzioni calls this the "working-toward" effect. In 1964, a similar proposal at the Disarmament Conference was referred to as the "bomber bonfire."

Transnational interaction

In Chapters 2 and 3 we introduced the theorem that liking usually increases with frequency of interaction. In our boys camp model, interaction increased friendship up to the point where the groups became competitive. Hence the general theorem must be qualified and limited to interactions under conditions which bring shared satisfaction rather than win-lose struggles.

The term "transnational" was first used, so far as the author knows, by Laurin Zilliacus to differentiate between activities in which nations cooperate (international) and those in which people cooperate with no special reference to national identification and boundaries. His "Mail for the World" (1953) is an interesting account of the growth of one great transnational activity—the Universal Postal Union. Astronomers are transnational when they cooperate to advance their common knowledge regardless of country. For a scientist, the validity of an observation is all that matters; the nationality of the observer is irrelevant. The American philosopher, Josiah Royce, writing of "the Beloved Community" as a social ideal, used world ties of scientists as his model. Robert MacLeod reports that he was present with some American physicists when they heard the news of the first successful Sputnik: "Hurrah!" they said, "we've done it!" For the scientist in America it was "we," not "they."

There are many transnational communities of interest. Musicians are concerned mainly with the talents of the composer or performer, not with the legal body which collects his taxes. Athletes enjoy first-rate achievement and competition, which is not related to nationalities. Beauty in painting, sculpture, dance, drama, or poetry does not come in packages that bear the label of nationality. Health and education are served by contributions from many lands. The larger the role played by transnational concerns, the less people are likely to overemphasize nationalism. Religious organizations and youth-serving agencies like the Boy Scouts cross national boundaries in calling their members together for meetings. The international trade unions can serve a similar purpose.

The greatest transnational force is probably economic trade. A poll (American Institute of Public Opinion, Oct. 25, 1963) inquired of Americans: "Should the United States and Russia work out a business arrangement to buy and sell more goods to each other? While 33 percent remained opposed to such transactions, 55 per cent supported them. The proportion favoring doing business with the Soviet Union rose from 30 percent in 1948, to 40 percent in 1953, to 55 percent in 1955, 1959, and 1963. The products as well as the transactions help to build community.

In his presidential address to the Society for Psychological Study of Social Issues (1961) Morton Deutsch proposed development of international contests in many fields, following some of the procedures worked out for the Olympic Games.

Cherrington's (1934) report on sixteen American students attending a seminar on international relations in Geneva, Switzerland, in 1929 yielded mixed results. They were 90 percent international-minded before they left this country and did not appreciably change that position. They came to rate specific proposals "doubtful" or "uncertain" more often at the end of their summer study. The writer has observed similar changes in intelligent adults visiting the Soviet Union in "traveling seminars" under his leadership. The adults did not grow markedly more or less favorable in their attitudes; rather they came to appreciate the diversity and complexity of the people in the host country. They become less ready to make generalizations. Kelman (1965) found that participants in a two-month international seminar on broadcasting at Brandeis University, tested before and after the meetings and compared with back-home controls, became more favorable in attitudes toward Americans, but showed an even greater change in the complexity and differentiation of their images of this country.

Other data come from attitude studies of children in camps composed of participants from several countries (Twitchell-Allen, 1956). Bjerstedt (1958) introduced a "picture-story device" with stories written about four pictures which included children of different races; also the "four-nationality story" requiring a story that includes individuals from Russia, America, China, and France. When the picture stories were analyzed for references to cross-national friendships, it was found that 79 children of 11 years of age participating in Children's International Summer Village (C.I.S.V.) camps in Europe made 41 percent of such references at the beginning of their stay and 59 percent at the end. A reunion of children who had been in the C.I.S.V. camp two or three years earlier, scored 75 percent for cross-national friendship references. Bjerstedt found it easier to develop friendships in these camps across national lines than it was to build boy-girl friendships at this age.

Attitude changes as a result of the usual kind of tourist travel abroad have not yet been sufficiently appraised. The effects may be expected to be relatively slight since interaction is often limited to hotel clerks, railway porters, taxi drivers, waiters, and guides. Moreover, the "equal status" condition, emphasized in Chapter 11, is usually lacking. The shock-effect for travelers on their first trip, with little background and experience, may result in quite unwarranted generalizations about the foreign nation. As a tour leader, I have noted that for some travelers in my group, there was a high correlation between the comfort of hotel rooms and their estimate of the culture and attractiveness of the people of a country.

Hayakawa (1960) has made an ingenious proposal that could be applied to increasing understanding between the United States and such countries as Communist China. Discussing the Soviet Union, he made the suggestion that we invite a large number of Russian spokesmen—

perhaps thousands, of "teachers, journalists, parliamentarians, jurists and plant managers to come here and explain their way of life, their national purposes, their hopes for the future." His interest is not so much in what we might learn in such a process as in the influence that our listening would have upon the visiting spokesmen. "Whoever has the emotional strength and the courage to begin listening to the other fellow instead of shouting at him can become the psychotherapist for the other. . . . The funny thing about human beings, including you and me and the Russians, is that we tend to respect the intelligence of, and eventually to like, those who listen attentively to our ideas even if they continue to disagree with us."

As we conclude our review of the effects of available transnational experiences upon attitudes, we must recognize that the impact is usually slight. Evidence indicates that the rather superficial transnational friendships formed by athletes during Olympic games or by scientists during international conferences will not noticeably lessen inter-governmental tensions. The Nazis were able to use young Germans who had been friendly tourists in Scandinavia for their military occupation of those lands. Only if transnational interaction occurs in an atmosphere in which tensions have already become less threatening—possibly through effective world government—can the results be lasting. How can powerful tensions be reduced?

Superordinate goals

In his first camp experiment, Sherif found that a baseball game against a town team, from outside camp, helped to unify the Bull Dogs and the Red Devils. In a later experiment, the "Robber's Cave" study (1954), the competing groups called themselves the "Eagles" and the "Rattlers." The experiment replicated the earlier one on the development of intergroup hostility. But this time, more "superordinate goals" which required the cooperation of both groups, were introduced: fixing a plugged-up water line; contributing toward the cost of a feature film; pulling down a dead tree (instead of tug-of-war between groups); pushing an apparently stalled truck containing desired food supplies; planning a final campfire, etc. The boys, in the altered situation, cooperated in an effective and eventually friendly fashion.

Projects too great to be undertaken by one nation alone can bring about collaboration toward a common objective. Pioneer exploration of Antarctica has proceeded under a treaty of cooperation by the United States, Soviet Russia, and ten other nations working in reasonable harmony. The International Geophysical Year united the efforts of scientists and some government agencies as well. The United States and the Soviet Union have undertaken cooperative use of satellites to assist in weather forecasting. If the World Communications Centre, proposed at

Accra, were organized it might coordinate the use of satellites for communication. Indeed, the whole exploration of space, including rockets to the moon, could be a joint project. Other proposals have been made: cancer research, better use of solar energy, and cultivation of food resources in the oceans. Raising the standard of living of underdeveloped and poverty-stricken areas of the world is more than can be achieved by aid from any one nation, but a cooperative international effort might succeed in boosting a number of countries beyond the critical point after which the economy can grow without external assistance.

The psychological rule is that if the situation is structured competitively, one or several participants experience frustration and hostility. If groups, formerly hostile, are brought together in joint efforts to achieve a shared goal, they develop the cohesion of partners and teammates.

Graduated reciprocation: a virtuous circle

While mounting threats create a vicious circle, mounting acts of generosity may form a virtuous circle. This theme underlies a proposal made by Charles E. Osgood, then President of the American Psychological Association (1962). The pattern of behavior in relationships where tension exists has been, in the past, to seek every possible little advantage and never to give a *quid* without first getting firm hold of the *quo*. Any concession has been taken as a sign of weakness. The Osgood idea of progressively reducing international tensions is to give a little something —not so much as really to weaken security—and see whether the act of good will may not be voluntarily reciprocated, even though there was no prior agreement that it would be, and no such demands made. Any nation can begin the experiment, unilaterally. The first gesture might be giving up a threatening but not too necessary base, or reducing some significant but not essential armament. It might be an offer of needed food, medicine, machines, or services. The psychological probability is that such an act of friendliness would arouse some gift in return. If it did not—and this is an important part of the plan—another concession would be given. It may be expected that the first step will be viewed with mistrust. So another, and another must be taken. If the acts of benevolence are genuine and are seen as desirable by the recipient nation, and if they persist long enough to demonstrate a new approach, it is likely that the former opponent will venture on some reciprocal act of his own choice. In interpersonal relations this procedure is sometimes called "heaping coals of fire" on the partner's head. In Christian doctrine, it is loving an enemy and doing good to those who have mistreated us.

A timely example might be the offer of some of our food surplus to the hungry people of mainland China—an offer with no strings attached. Peking might not reciprocate immediately but might find some way to ease some of the present tensions. In any case, the act of giving helps build a reputation for moral leadership.

Education in conflict resolution

Earlier we indicated that the attempts of educators to change attitudes of children while the adult social system remains unaltered will probably fail. Yet when modifications such as stronger world government, increased transnational experiences, cooperation toward superordinate goals, and graduated benevolent reciprocation have been introduced, there remain important supplementary educational tasks.

Knowledge of other nations is no guarantee of good will toward them, but ignorance is likely to be a distinct handicap.

There are great gaps to be filled in the average American's knowledge of our world. In one poll, half of the citizens proved unable, on the outline map of Europe, to identify the location of countries as geographically conspicuous as Spain or Greece. In a book about life in a small town Hicks (1947) reports that at the beginning of a game, a player offered the ground-rule which was accepted by all: "Anything across the pond is out!" Only American cities, persons or place names were acceptable. While school curricula are now giving more attention to world geography, world history, world art and literature, many college graduates know little of the new African states, the Inca empire, Bangkok dancers or the Hindu Vedas.

Students majoring in the area of social science—or especially well-informed—are more likely to emerge as world-minded (Manry, 1928; Wrightstone, 1934; Cherrington, 1934; Smith, 1947; Grace, Neuhaus, 1952). Belief in the possibility of peaceful resolution of conflicts between the Soviet Union and the United States increases with level of education from 42 percent for those who have not finished high school to 61 percent for college graduates (American Institute of Public Opinion, Jan. 1, 1961). Willingness to recognize Communist China also increases with educational level.

Recent progress in applied behavioral science has increased our understanding of the distortions which are created by a "win-lose" orientation and of the possibility that genuinely integrative solutions can be achieved in conflict situations (Blake, Mouton, 1961; Horwitz, 1964; Walton, 1965). The first Training Laboratory in Conflict Management was held at Bethel, Maine, in 1964. Executives from many kinds of organizations are acquiring skill in the creative approach to the resolution of conflict. As this kind of education becomes more widespread and effective, it cannot but have an impact on the time-worn but fallacious assumption that the alternatives in international disputes are only dominance or submission.

Increasing life satisfaction

The greatest hostility toward others is shown by individuals suffering from conflicts and frustrations. In one of the earliest studies of attitudes toward foreign nations (1928) the author discovered that among scores of American groups tested, the ones who most despised Chinese and Japanese were farmers in drought-threatened North Dakota and prisoners in the Bridewell, Chicago's city jail. Helfant (1952) found that high school students who wanted drastic punitive action against the Soviet Union showed more symptoms of emotional difficulty than did the tolerant pupils. Earlier we noted, also, that sometimes a war seems to promise relief from tedium or chronic dissatisfaction with the conditions of peacetime living. It seems evident that whatever makes life more interesting, more challenging, and more satisfying will reduce the tendency to seek outlets in hatred and revenge. One of the handicaps of the peace movement is that the image of war is virile and dramatic; that of peace is pale and insipid. Emerson asked: "Who can blame men for seeking excitement? They are polar, and would you have them sleep in a dull eternity of equilibrium? Religion, love, ambition, money, war, brandy—some fierce antagonism must break the round . . . or no spark, no joy, no event can be. . . ."

William James used this principle in developing his famous essay *The Moral Equivalent of War.* He believed that to be satisfying, life must be strenuous, intense, vivid, effortful, and heroic. He suggested enlisting youth in difficult and hazardous crusades against the causes of disaster and in conquest of Nature and disease.

Freud symbolized the forces of love, creation, and life in the mythological figure of Eros. He symbolized by Thanatos the opposite forces of hate, destruction, and death. He saw Eros and Thanatos "locked in an eternal duel." Those who seek peace are engaged against Thanatos. They should not neglect to strengthen their ally, his eternal adversary. In every land are too many hopeless, loveless, miserable, frustrated, embittered, and vengeful people. In top posts in enterprises of government, business, and science are too many impersonal, dehumanized, bureaucratic individuals operating only as institutional mechanisms, not as persons whose lives are finding rich satisfaction and fulfillment. If our quarrelsome world is ever saved, it will have to be done by those who love life freely. In earlier chapters we have written about dyadic love and friendship, enjoyment of group membership, psychotherapy, personal autonomy, and cultures which are healthy and free from race, class or sex prejudice. These developments are pertinent to the creation of conditions which enhance satisfaction in the here-and-now, thus diminishing the strength of destructive drives.

To rely mainly on increased personal happiness to stop war would be to succumb to the fallacy we earlier termed *Psychologism.* The forces of economic and political rivalry among nations operate powerfully to condition hostile attitudes even in individuals whose personal emotional life is reasonably well-adjusted. And, in pacifist groups, there is no remarkable shortage of disturbed personalities. Yet Freud's basic insight remains true. Whatever enhances the human capacity to love, correspondingly decreases hatred and destructiveness. War is not a simple projection of personal hostility. Innumerable enterprises of worldwide cooperation are facilitated by persons easily capable of empathy, concern for others, and trustworthy friendships.

Toward an uncertain future

The half-dozen proposals just presented for reducing international tensions carry no guarantee of safe-conduct for mankind. The grave threat described at the beginning of the chapter persists. One thing we do learn from history, however, is that extrapolation from any present point is likely to be misleading. Consider, for example, the changing alliances between the United States and other nations over two centuries.

Our National Loves and Hates

1775	Loved British, hated French; French and Indian War
1776	Loved French, hated British; American Revolution
1799	Hated French; sea battles with France
1812	Loved French, hated British; War of 1812
1846	Loved Southerners, hated Mexicans; Mexican War over Texas
1861–64	North and South hated each other; North hated British; Civil War, Britain aiding South
1898	Hated Spanish; Spanish-American War
1899	Hated Chinese and Filipinos; conquest of the Philippines
1900	Loved Japanese, hated Chinese; Boxer uprising in China
1904	Loved Japanese, hated Russians; Russo-Japanese War
1914	Hated Mexicans; Marines land at Vera Cruz
1914	Loved Japanese and Russians; allies in World War I
1914	Loved British and French; hated Austrians and Germans, beginning of World War I
1915	Loved Italians; Italy joins Allies in World War I
1916	Hated Mexicans; Pershing invades Mexico
1917	Loved Japanese and Chinese; allies in World War I
1918	Loved Italians, hated Russians, our troops invade Russia
1927	Loved Japanese, hated Chinese; U.S. bombards Nanking
1935	Hated Italians; Italy invades Ethiopia
1936	Loved Chinese, hated Russians; Communists despoil China
1939	Loved British and French; hated Germans and Russians; beginning of World War II
1939	Loved Finns, hated Russians; Russia invades Finland
1941	Loved Russians, hated Finns; Russia fights Germany and Finland

1941	Loved Filipinos, hated Japanese, war with Japan
1941	Loved British, Chinese, Dutch, Russians; hated Germans, Italians and Japanese; World War II
1942	Loved some French, hated others; Vichy regime
1942	Loved Mexicans, most Latin-Americans; allies in World War II
1943	Loved Chinese; tried to love Russians, British
1947	Loved Chinese; hated Russians
1955	Loved West Germans, Japanese; hated Russians, Chinese, and East Germans

(Adapted from Mark R. Shaw)

Not only alliances but ideologies change with time. Christians and Moslems have learned to live in mutual tolerance in many parts of the world, despite the hostilities of the Crusades. Political and religious absolutists have asserted that they possessed infallible doctrine and dogma, but under changed conditions have found it possible to revise their doctrines expediently.

During the heat of the Reformation, Martin Luther proclaimed: "It is far better to be a hangman or a murderer than a priest or a monk." And on the other side, Pope Pius V wrote to Catherine de Medici: "It is only by the complete extermination of heretics that the King will be able to give back the ancient workshop of the Catholic religion to this noble kingdom. If Your Majesty continues to war openly and zealously until they are all massacred, Divine succor will not be wanting." The aroused citizens of that day would never have been able to forsee a time when Protestants and Catholics could live as good neighbors. They had to war intermittently for several centuries before admitting that neither could convert nor exterminate the other, that "peaceful coexistence" was not only a possibility but the only real possibility.

In controversy we are likely to overestimate the rigidity of our opponents. "*We* can change," we think, "but *they* will never learn!" One of the safest predictions is that the dogma of today will be revised by later generations. Most human beings learn and change. By the time we have opened our own minds to unrecognized truth, other nations will also have moved to new understanding. We shall have more to say about processes of change in the final chapter.

CHAPTER FIFTEEN

Psychology
of social change

To most of mankind, throughout history, change has come so slowly that it has passed unnoticed. "The thing that hath been, it is that which shall be, and that which is done is that which shall be done: and there is no new thing under the sun." So the world seemed in the Old Testament Book of Ecclesiastes. Food, clothing, housing, occupations, technology, rituals, illness, and hazards seemed to change as little as climate. What was, seemed always to have been. When men wanted to go somewhere they walked or rode a horse or sailed a boat. The distance of oral communication was limited to the natural range of shouts. Food was cooked over an open fire from the days of the caveman until about a century ago, and the only way of illuminating a room at night was with a flame. "The memory of man runneth not back to the contrary," said English law. Prayers and ceremonies, it was thought, would be effective only as long as every word and gesture remained unchanged. One generation passed, and another came, but ways of life continued to be constant, predictable, and dependable. Children sought to walk in parental footsteps and to live by ancient wisdom. Each child was placed in a well-worn cradle of established custom because the older generation knew best.

Accelerating change

The human organism, gifted as it is for adaptation, evolved under conditions which remained essentially stable for many centuries. *Homo sapiens* appeared only about 100,000 years ago, and what we know as civilization represents less than 10 percent of his time on earth. Julian Huxley (1942) estimates the tempo of human evolution during recorded history (the last 5,000 years) as "at least 100,000 times as rapid as that of pre-human evolution." During the past three centuries (less than one-third of 1 percent of the age of *homo sapiens*) the period allowable for assimilation of a major change has decreased from nearly a century to less than a decade.

At the beginning of this century, no one had seen a movie or an airplane, heard a radio or jazz music, shopped in supermarkets, lunched in a cafeteria, eaten an ice cream cone, paid income tax, or worried about Communist nations. At mid-century there were still no nuclear submarines, H-bombs, electronic data computers, space rockets, or tranquilizers.

Technological change has risen exponentially as shown in Figure 10.

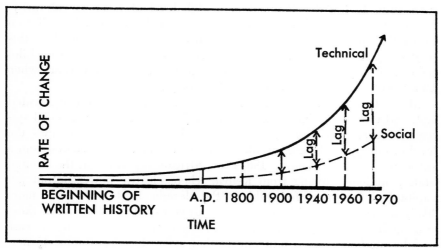

FIGURE 10

Expenditures on research and development have doubled each decade since 1930. Speed of travel increased by a factor of 10 when man moved from horses to trains and from trains to planes, but by a factor of 25 from planes to rockets. A similar curve would graph the distance over which one man's voice could be heard or the explosive power of weapons.

This unprecedented rate of technical change creates demands for individual and institutional adaptation which men in past ages have never had to meet. Youth can no longer follow the parental footsteps, nor can they be prepared by 12 or 16 years of schooling for a lifelong vocation or the understanding of the problems of their world 20 years later. Executives in government, business, education, and other fields are required to make more major decisions and to make them more quickly. Innovation is followed by obsolescence before it has been well assimilated.

The problem of adaptation is particularly severe in cultures long isolated, but now caught up in a wave of rapid industrialization. In some regions, transportation moved from primitive forms to airplanes within a decade. After World War II the average life-expectancy in the island of Mauritius in the Indian Ocean increased from 31 to 51 years during a period of only eight years, a gain which took nearly a century in Western Europe and the United States (Hoagland, 1964). Peoples with a long history of cultural stability are now thrust into processes of change for which they are psychologically and educationally unprepared.

McClelland has shown (1961) that a psychological emphasis on working hard to achieve excellence has historically appeared in cultures prior to the development of a high level of business enterprise. The contemporary cultures which are being industrialized by diffusion rather than by development from within their own institutions lack this psychological foundation. People in these cultures can drive automobiles today but they never went through a period similar to the years when Henry Ford worked at the horseless carriage.

McClelland's data support a view that the attitudes were inculcated first, and the society later came to embody the corresponding social systems—a reversal of the S-P-A sequence. Evidence that sometimes the level of energy in the culture affects individual motivation comes from a subsequent study (Veroff, 1963) of African students in the United States. Students coming from Kenya, where electric power output per capita had increased four-fold in the decade 1950–1960, were more likely to score high in drive for competitive excellence than were those coming from Ghana, where there had been only a 50 percent increase in kilowatt hours per capita during that same decade. Among 47 new arrivals in the United States, 40 percent were high on the *n ach* measure; among the 32 who had lived here for more than a year and a half, 60 percent scored high. Life in a more dynamic culture fosters achievement values, and the newly industrialized nations will probably acquire an enterprise psychology much faster than it developed in Western Europe or the United States.

Resistance to change

Men usually enjoy the excitement and challenge of new experience, but the strange and untried is also disquieting and often threatening. Ogburn long ago (1922) pointed to the phenomenon called "social lag" —the failure of institutional adaptation to keep pace with technological advance. The dotted line in Fig. 10 suggests that social systems are not changing as rapidly as the techniques of mechanical, electrical, and electronic innovation. It is easier, for example, to manufacture automobiles than to redesign cities so that these cars can easily be parked near homes, offices, shops, and places of recreation. During the period of horse-and-buggy travel a county unit of government was most practical; today there are few functions that are best carried on at the county level, but county officials persist.

Why is there reluctance to change social patterns? What psychological factors underly the lag? Some are personality characteristics—other traits of social systems.

Personality factors

A basic law of learning is that organisms repeat responses which in the past have brought satisfaction. Thus habits become drives, a process which Allport (1937) has called "functional autonomy." Responses persist for a time even when they no longer bring the satisfactions to which they once led. The earliest habits—those formed in childhood—have particular strength because they had primacy and so have had years of reenforcement. They have provided the frame for later experiences. Habits are extremely resistant to change. In Chapter 7 we noted that selective attention, selective interpretation, and retention all operate to keep early views intact. The individual ignores facts which do not fit into his framework of expectations, distorts them so they do fit, or forgets all about them.

The old, familiar ways are not only encrusted in the core of personality; they also carry a halo of virtue. The customary seems right and best. The superego defends what parents inculcated. During our childhood dependence the grownups were bigger, stronger, and wiser. Who, then, are we to question the teachings of our elders?

Resistance to change is supported by a network of interpersonal ties to individuals who represent the old patterns. We do not usually want to be "the first by whom the new is tried." After the others around us have changed, then we can go along with it, too.

We discount our own dissatisfactions because this has been the pattern of our socialization. From the first toilet-training on through school and work, we have learned that our own impulses must be brought into conformity with external demands. Self-assertion brought punishment and/or guilt. We reject our authentic rebellious responses and cripple the mainspring of humanistic innovation (Lindner, 1952).

A special problem arises from the tendency of change to evoke feelings of insecurity and anxiety. In a laboratory study, Hamblin (1958) found that when the rules of a game were suddenly changed in unexpected ways, players became more "self-oriented" (defensive, dominating, status-seeking, or dependent) and less likely to help one another in cooperative team endeavor. Praise was replaced by criticism and group morale declined. When people are disturbed, they tend to regress to the remembered or fantasied security of earlier times. It is paradoxical that just at the moment when the pressure for change is greatest, there is the strongest impulse to retreat to the comparative safety and security of the old ways.

It is interesting here to note the hypothesis that the ways of childhood persist in the inner fantasy life, while adaptation to modern changes goes on at the more superficial, rational, and instrumental level. Lee (1958) found that Zulu dreams reflected the culture that existed 50 to 75 years earlier and seldom the realities of the changed current scene. A study in rural Japan (Wagatsuma, De Vos, 1961) reached a similar conclusion: While love-marriages are approved in direct interviews, fantasy responses to T.A.T. pictures reflected the traditional Japanese preference for arranged marriages.

Resistance is often unconscious, but rationalized. Freud found that his patients who suffered from painful symptoms nevertheless tried many pretexts to keep from accepting the changes required for recovery. Analysis of the unconscious resistance which impedes adaptation and growth is a major factor in psychoanalytic therapy. It is sometimes difficult to discover the real grounds for resistance when the emotional reasons are covered by a cloak of plausible rationalizations. For example, in the Presbyterian Church in the United States, (Southern) opponents of merger with the larger (Northern) Presbyterian Church in the United States dealt only with doctrinal disputes and patterns of church law in all their published documents. Little or nothing was said of race questions, job security, status, and other issues which those familiar with the struggle believed to be the underlying concerns (Dornbusch, Irie, 1959).

Certain kinds of personality are especially threatened by change. Individuals who have not achieved genuine, wholehearted integration of their drives and impulses, but have managed by repression, suppression, and pretense to maintain a socially-acceptable facade, are likely to expect that changes will disturb their precarious equilibrium. Thus persons high on the F-scale are suspicious of social innovation and hostile to its advocates. They are susceptible, as reported in Chapter 11, to the projective form of race prejudice (McClintock, 1958). They lean to the radical right in politics (Bell, 1963; Forster, Epstein, 1964). Persons rated low in ego-defensiveness, on the other hand, have been found better able to adapt to change (Peak, Morrison, 1958; Niel, Dunn, 1960).

Some kinds of change awaken deep, irrational resentment. They arouse a mystique of the sacred. Sexual mores, religion, and national patriotism have this special quality. One may evade one's income tax without arousing much condemnation, but to refuse to salute the flag is intolerable. The campaign against adding fluoride to drinking water supplies in some communities has included a scare-story that this measure for reducing dental cavities is really a Communist plot. It is asserted that the chemical will rob American men of their virility and so facilitate the Red triumph (Davis, 1959).

Systems seek to preserve stability

By nature, social systems have evolved or been designed to operate in a fairly steady equilibrium. A change in any part disturbs the rest of the system. The interlocking functions and the feedback systems operate to continue the customary activities. Reforms such as simplified spelling or the adoption of a metric system of weights and measures or a calendar in which days and dates would correspond over the years have obvious rational advantages but are not adopted because of the many related changes which would ensue.

Sometimes after a temporary change, the old ways are resumed in a kind of social homeostasis (Cannon, 1932). The impact of World War II on the class system in England has been described as follows: "When the manor house was on fire we all lined up in the bucket brigade; when the fire was out, the servants went back to the servant's quarters!" Waves of municipal reform in most large cities have been followed by a slow drift "back to normalcy."

Another element of stability in most social systems is the correlation of power and privilege. Those who enjoy special benefits in the *status quo* are not hospitable to changes which would threaten their privileges. Their reluctance to read the portents of the times, even when change is well along, has become memorable in the proverb that "Bourbons never learn!"

Further resistance arises from the fact that most change is introduced from outside the system. Hence it bears the onus of the foreigner—the stranger—the outsider whose ways are not our ways. A typical reaction to imagined outside agents of change occurred in a Northern state where a community launched a project involving a cooperative nursery school and a softball league. Soon rumors that the whole service enterprise was really a Communist scheme began circulating in the town. The whole project was planned and financed by Moscow, it was reported (Festinger, et al., 1948).

Despite inertia, anxiety, unconscious resistance, vested interests, and suspicion of the strange, change is constantly occurring. While adaptation in social systems may not keep pace with mechanical inventions, it is proceeding at an unprecedented rate. Introducing his anthropological account of a typical Midwestern town, Warner (1949) wrote: "A dominant theme in the life of all American communities is social change." Our next interest is to review briefly some of the major historic theories men have proposed to account for change in the past and to predict its future course. Many of these still influence attitudes toward change today.

Historic theories

An ancient view, still operative in many parts of the world, is that change is unpredictable and due to the whims of the gods or of fate. Persons holding this opinion take no responsibility for planning, initiating or guiding change. They accept whatever comes. Plato offered the interesting idea that God's attention to the affairs of the universe is intermittent; He sets it in order and leaves it; if it sinks into serious disorder, then He again intervenes and corrects it.

Two rather naïve views of social change are linear. One is the familiar assumption of progress. Our society is presumed to be getting better and better. Spencer (1876) paralleled "social evolution" with biological evolution. This view seems to be supported by the curves of both technological and social advance, symbolized in Fig. 10. Comte (1830) saw altruism increasing as science advances. An opposite view, espoused by the more pessimistic (Swift, Carlyle, Malthus, Ortega y Gasset), is that a Golden Age existed sometime in the past and that every passing year brings a decline in values and increased problems and frustration. Growing population and proliferating weapons of mass destruction lend support to this view.

Cyclic theories envisage history as repeating certain recognizable sequences. Spengler's *Decline of the West* (1918) likened a civilization to an organism with stages of growth, maturity, and decline. Toynbee's celebrated analysis of 26 civilizations (1947) abandons the organic analogy, but finds a recurrent sequence: (a) response of a creative minority to some challenge; (b) degeneration into control by a merely dominant minority based on force rather than voluntary allegiance; (c) rise of an internal proletariat which, often assisted by outside enemies, ends the epoch and launches a new cycle. Another cyclic theory, propounded by Sorokin (1937–1941; 1947), describes a sequence from a "sensate" super-system, which finds reality empirically through the senses, to an "ideational" super-system in which spiritual reality is dominant. Between the two comes an "idealistic" era which combines them. The concept "super-system" is introduced because each way of understanding the world permeates many systems and areas of civilization, manifesting itself in the emphasis given within science, literature, art, law, ethics, and religion. Sorokin sees us today nearing the end of a several-century phase of emphasis on material values, with an increasing stress on scientific and technical conquests; he expects a swing toward ideational, super-sensory, and super-rational concerns. Cairns (1962) has described the cyclic view of history found in Hinduism, Taoism, Zoroastrianism, and in contemporary social scientists like Sorokin.

Dialectic theories, involving the union of opposites, are as old as philosophy, but most clearly formulated by Hegel in the famous sequence: thesis, antithesis, synthesis. Karl Marx has been the classic exponent of this view of social change (Marx, Engels, 1847). Each ruling class he saw as engaged in struggle with a rising opposition: oppressor vs. oppressed. The bourgeoisie won out against the aristocracy and created the capitalist-imperialist world. The working-class mission is to end this rule and to create a "classless" society in which everyone is both owner and worker. Marx's basic analysis is generally accepted in socialist as well as Communist nations; it is seen in capitalist countries as obsolete and seriously misleading. The value of the dialectic approach to processes of progress is not limited to its use by Marx. Teggart (1918) has emphasized that the controversies among intellectuals are often more productive than their harmonious collaboration. Many scientific and philosophic theses have been formulated in order to refute an opponent. Conflict is frequently a fertile source of new ideas.

It is true, also, that the problems of one generation are often left unsolved but become transformed or transcended. Santayana remarked that "Americans seem never to solve their problems; they amiably bid them 'Good-bye!'" Koestler has said:

"We can discern in the past a succession of levels of social awareness, like an ascending staircase. The age of religious wars ended when secular politics began to dominate human consciousness; feudal politics ended when economic factors assumed over-riding importance; the struggles of Economic Man will end by the emergence of the new ethical values of the new age. The great disputes are never settled on their own level, but on the next higher one. . . . Seen from the perspective of the next-higher historical level, the old controversies lose interest, appear drained of their meaning; and conversely, the exact properties of each succeeding period cannot be formulated from the lower level." (1945, p. 104).

The grand theories—theocratic, linear, cyclic or dialectic—are, in Allport's (1954, p. 9) phrase, too "simple and sovereign." Thus hypotheses may be illustrated by many sequences in history, but it is difficult to test them against an adequate sample of unselected data.

Cultural diffusion

The kind of social change most frequently observed in both personal experience and in social science is that which occurs when some individual or group picks up and adopts some idea or mechanism or operation which he has observed in some other person or situation. Indeed, Tarde, one of the first social psychologists (1890), made imitation his central concept. The rapid expansion in anthropology since 1920 has added a wealth of evidence on diffusion from one culture to another.

In Chapter 9, we reported the alteration of the lives of the Tiv in Nigeria with the coming of the British. In a more recent (1956) study of social change, Margaret Mead has described the changes in the Manus between her first visit in 1929 and a revisit in 1954. A major intervening variable had been occupation by the U.S. forces during World War II. The 14,000 Manus had had direct or indirect contact with about a million American soldiers. The Manus were fascinated by all the equipment, machines, and gadgets. They were impressed, in a different way, with the American respect for human values and democratic relationships. During this time, one of their own able leaders, Paliau, came back to them and his personal qualities played a part in the ensuing changes. Also a religious hope, expressed in a "Cargo Cult," had failed to arrive. By 1953, the old culture had been almost wholly repudiated. The former fishermen now tilled the soil. Cooperative enterprises such as a town council, a communal dock, and a bank had replaced the primitive barter between individuals. Many of the severe taboos of the old religion had been relaxed and Christianity was espoused. Adult quarreling had diminished. Coeducational schools had been introduced, and men no longer dominated their wives. These changes were not byproducts of the diffusion of any one particular item of culture, but rather a sweeping movement into a new, Westernized order.

Among all primitive peoples urbanization and industrialization have weakened old cultures. Biesheuvel (1959) found in South Africa that old ties which had held men in conformity to traditional norms had been discarded. This was followed by a sense of release that seemed to lead to impulsive and lawless acts. On another continent, Hallowell (1951) found that the more acculturated Ojibwa Indians of Lac du Flambeau, Wisconsin, who spoke English, sent their children to school, and listened to the radio, showed more signs (Rorschach) of personal maladjustment. Spindler (1955) also used Rorschach tests in his study of the acculturation of Menomini Indians. The traditionalists who maintained the old way of life were found to be unemotional; the Indians in transition showed more anxiety and aggression; those who were really integrated into the white civilization appeared to have achieved also a healthy emotional adjustment.

A fascinating study in cultural change is that of two adjacent villages of Pueblo Indians (Dozier, 1957). An ancient quarrel, with charges of broken promises, kept them separate, although their houses were alike and not far apart. Intermarriage was discouraged. The Hopi village, like many others around it, cultivated personalities who were passive, fatalistic, and mystical. The Tewa, descendants of rebels who had fought off the Spaniards, were proud and militant, more active than passive, more worldly than mystical. The Hopi thought they were superior to the Tewa, who were a small cultural island in the large Hopi area. The big change came with the advance of white civilization into the region. Because Tewa values were congruous with the achievement-oriented, self-reliant white man's world, they adapted easily to stock-raising, wage labor, and public schools. Suddenly the Hopi found that the despised Tewa were surpassing them. The old prejudices faded away. Hopi and Tewa learned to work together in pottery manufacture and cattle cooperatives. Intermarriage, formerly discouraged, became acceptable, and the two communities joined even in religious ceremonies. The case illustrates how diffusion from the dominant, powerful industrial civilization suppressed one set of values (Hopi) and gave support to another. Similar changes, described in Chapter 9, occurred when the diffusion of guns and horses to the Comanches developed militant raiders, but the imposed power of peaceful government later stifled that belligerency and depressed the related social vitality.

Demonstrations and Utopias

Learning new ways from observation of others underlies many projects which offer demonstrations as a technique for encouraging innovation. Model farms, model schools, model factories, and model communities have been designed to persuade observers to do likewise.

The usual outcome is that the demonstration project is a great experience for those who design and develop it, but it seldom is adopted by others (Redefer, 1950; Watson, 1964). Teachers who visit superb experimental schools and wish that they had similar buildings, equipment, pupils, and support feel incapable of transforming their own schools. The "Hawthorne effect" (referring to the high level of morale and production in the experiment reported in Chapter 11) helps to make the original project highly successful, but this does not diffuse to imitators. Sometimes, as in the experiences of the Latter Day Saints in Illinois or the Doukhabors in Canada, the surrounding world is more hostile than admiring. In Meiklejohn's experiment at the University of Wisconsin and New College at Columbia, the non-involved professors were more likely to be suspicious than converted. When the Agricultural Experiment Stations set up nearly ideal farms, these had far less influence than was later achieved by projects in which more typical farmers were persuaded to try out limited innovations in fertilizer, plowing, seed or cultivation. For most farmers, what their neighbors could do fell within their "latitude of acceptance"; what the State farms could do was not appropriate to their own powers,

The process of innovation

Introduction of change within a social system whether it is as small as a family or as large as a nation or worldwide corporation, moves through a fairly standard sequence of stages, each of which presents distinctive problems for social psychological study.

Felt dissatisfaction

Necessity proverbially leads to invention. Not all needs that are felt foster innovations, but when changes are introduced it is because some dissatisfaction has been felt. The need, however, may exist for many years before a solution is proposed. So long as a social system runs smoothly and produces about what is expected, innovation is resisted.

In Chapter 7 we noted Lewin's view that the process of social change moves in three stages: (1) unfreezing the old structure; (2) developing the new forms; and (3) re-freezing or stabilizing the change. It is as though the heat of necessity were required to break down the incrustations of custom so that it can be molded into some more appropriate pattern.

Lippitt, Watson and Westley (1958) suggest four forces for change: (1) dissatisfaction or pain in the present situation; (2) dissatisfaction with a perceived discrepancy between what is and what might be; (3) external pressures on a system to force its change; and (4) internal motivation to grow and to improve. Greening (1963) found all four factors operative behind the change of policy in a voluntary general hospital in California, when it decided to accept alcoholics as normally "sick" patients. The four motives can be seen also in the introduction of new programs of mathematics and science teaching (Miles, 1964). Schools responded to dissatisfaction with the present, to the challenge of much better achievement, to pressures of public opinion after Sputnik, and to a wholesome desire on the part of teachers and administrators to improve their services.

Mort (1941, 1960) found that, on the average, 50 years had elapsed between the first recognition of a need in education and the development of the first practical invention for meeting the need. That was prior to 1940. Later studies (Miles, 1964) have indicated that the movement from the need to a practical remedy is more rapid than it was previously.

Diagnosis

Because of urgency, there is a strong impulse to cut short any diagnostic study and to work directly for some plausible remedy. Efforts to prevent delinquency, for example, are often undertaken with very little awareness of the basic social causes. Proposals for preventing war frequently accept uncritically such fallacies as are exposed in Chapter 14.

One of the major contributions of social psychologists as consultants on change programs is that they insist on testing the diagnosis before going on to action plans.

Among the pertinent questions may be: What is the history of the alleged difficulty, when was it first noticed, and what attempts have previously been made to deal with it? Does it appear only at certain times, in certain parts of the organization, or under certain circumstances? Is it found also in certain other social systems? What is the attitude of influential persons and of the persons most directly involved?

A special difficulty often arises because managers think differently from researchers. Operators ask questions in the form: "What should I do?" Scientists seek answers to questions of truth. The answers provided by experimental inquiry yield systematic generalizations, but seldom do they prescribe the applications. The parent, teacher, or executive must cope with the concrete situation, and he is likely to be impatient with analyses of underlying forces. Merton has observed that, "Characteristically the problem is so stated (by the policy maker) as to result in the possibility of the researcher's being seriously misled as to the 'basic' aspects" (1949). Characteristically, the policy maker's complaint is that the research findings do not tell him what he ought to do.

Diagnosis is further complicated by defensiveness. The need for any change is likely to be considered a reflection on the persons who have been responsible in the past. Consciously or unconsciously, they formulate the problem to exempt themselves from possible blame. So the community leaders approach a high delinquency rate by asking what should be done to negligent parents. Each nation approaches the problem of peace in terms of how to get the other side to change. A diagnostic study which includes the change-agent as part of the problem is rarely requested.

Whole and part

Changes in any part of a social system have consequences for other parts. When a change is proposed within one subsystem of a larger organization, it is necessary to consider how other, more or less related subsystems, will react. Administrators turn down many proposals which would have favorable results in part of the system because they can see the cost of its wider application.

In a toy factory, a team of women sprayed paint on toys moving steadily along a carefully paced assembly line. A psychologist persuaded management to let the workers try regulating the speed of this moving belt to fit their preferred pace. The workers were paid on a piece-work basis. They liked the innovation because they could speed up when their energy was high and slow down when they tired. The engineers were appalled by the irregular rates, but increasing output silenced their objections. Before long, production on this worker-regulated assembly line rose to uncomfortable heights. Workers in this department were taking home more pay than were supervisors in other parts of the factory. To cut their piece-rate would, of course, have demoralized these workers. Finally, despite the less efficient production, the uniform flow of work had to be resumed. Too much efficiency in one subsystem proved too upsetting to the balance of factors in the larger system of the plant.

In their case studies of change in industrial organizations, Mann and Neff (1961) illustrated how changes in the technique of producing seamless pipe affected the social structure of work groups and the consequent satisfaction of workers with their jobs. The use of computers in billing customers of a large utility created problems in the relationships of the accounting and sales divisions which had previously operated in relative independence. Introduction of electronic data processing in handling insurance applications and claims modified the responsibilities, authority, and power of several departments, not always to the satisfaction of those concerned. A study of change in a community-service organization (Dimock, Sorenson, 1955) concluded: "No part of institutional change is an island in itself: changes in program call for changes in every other part of the institution . . . and advance in one sector cannot proceed far ahead of change in other sectors. For example, program groups cannot be changed without officer training . . . which in turn is contingent upon advisor training . . . which in turn depends upon staff re-education. Similarly, changes in staff goals and ways of working are dependent upon administrative procedures, policies and budgets which in turn require changes in Boards and Committees." A control group in one kindergarten experiment unexpectedly made more gain than did the experimental group because after the experimental group had left the room, the teacher, who taught both groups, became less burdened and more innovative.

Pressures from the more inclusive social system may nullify the progress made by subunits. In Chapter 13, we reviewed some of the evidence supporting the view that unless attitudes of top management also change, subordinates are likely to resist new practices.

Timeliness is a special case of the relationship of parts to the whole. "An idea whose time has come" is an idea that is being recognized and utilized simultaneously in many different parts of a system. A case in point is the wave of demonstrations against racial segregation beginning in 1959. The proliferation of projects to help culturally disadvantaged youth, drop-outs, and to lift standards of living in pockets of poverty after 1963 is another example. Progress which would have taken many years, at an earlier period, could be made in months because of parallel movements in other parts of the larger social system.

Because the same need may be felt in different parts of the world at a given stage in history, simultaneous inventions have been common. Ogburn (1938, pp. 90–102) lists 150 instances of parallel discoveries by inventors working independently. Barnett (1953) contends that although separated, the simultaneous inventors are really part of a large cooperative effort. They share the knowledge of their time, including its stereotypes and implicit assumptions; they share a common concern; often they have read the same materials and sometimes have been in direct or indirect communication. Perhaps both have been stimulated by rivalry. E. L. Thorndike has said: "The mother of invention is not necessity; it is the knowledge of other people's inventions."

Creative design

From the diagnosis emerge suggestions for possible remedies. The better the diagnosis, the greater the likelihood that the proposed changes will be pertinent and effective. Creative proposals may come from particularly able individuals or from group thinking as described in Chapter 4. They may arise within the organization or be brought in from outside (diffusion). Griffiths, studying change in school systems, concluded "The major impetus for change in organizations is from the outside." (1964, p. 431). Superintendents who initiated more changes were those more in touch with other schools and with other community agencies (Hemphill, *et al.*, 1962). Pressures and suggestions for innovation more commonly arose in the public and the school board, rather than coming from principals, supervisors or teachers (Brickell, 1964).

Stages in the generation of an important creative idea have been found to include:

(a) a period of preparation, immersion in the problem, time for ideas to incubate (Ghiselin, 1955);

(b) a mood of openness to associations, ideas and hunches; playing with fantasies, letting intuitions emerge from pre-conscious or unconscious levels (Kubie, 1958);

(c) sudden, spontaneous emergence of an idea or ideas; these may be, at first, only half-formed and need to be held onto and worked at until one or another becomes clear and illuminating; sometimes a series of inspirations flows and the problem is to discard the less appropriate ones;

(d) elaboration, rational testing, criticism, exploration of consequences, revision, and improvement.

Most studies of creativity have dealt with great inventors or artists, but the same phases—at many lower levels—can be found in everyday discoveries relating to more commonplace activities, such as an idea for a letter to a friend, a way of saving time during shopping, or of eliminating a rattle in the car. Spiller (1929) has estimated that about

95 percent of technological progress has been the result of the accumulation of little improvements, contributed by unknown persons, rather than of the great inventions which made someone famous.

Force field analysis

Once a target for change has been defined, the problems of strategy and persuasion become central. A significant aid in analyzing the dynamics of a change situation is the diagraming of the forces acting for and against the proposed innovation. Kurt Lewin (1951) has pointed out that what seems rigid, immobile, and unchanging in a social situation seems so only because the forces pressing upon it offset one another and result in a temporary balance. He describes this as "quasi-stationary equilibrium."

A diagram may illustrate the balance or counter-balance of forces in a system at rest. In Figure 11 below the social system is represented by the circle in the middle.

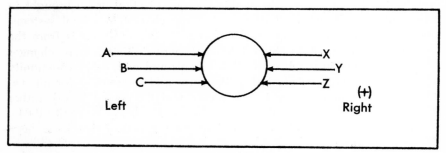

FIGURE 11

Forces A, B, and C, their relative strength indicated by the length of each arrow, are pushing toward the Right. Forces X, Y, and Z are pushing to the Left. At that moment the system does not move, for the two sets of forces are equal and opposite. Movement to the Right (toward the goal +) may be initiated either by augmenting A, B or C or by weakening X, Y or Z. In an actual situation, many more vectors operate.

The value of the force analysis depends on the accuracy with which the main forces *pro* and *con* are identified and estimated. If the system represented by the circle is an individual and the goal (+) is to change his attitude on some issue, arrows like A, B, C, etc. might represent such forces as (A) his already considerable dissatisfaction with his earlier attitude, (B) his response to the intellectual challenge of a different approach; and (C) his desire to please some proponents of the change. Arrows like X, Y, and Z would, however, identify forces within him supporting the old attitude and opposing change. Thus X might represent his preference for taking the easy way of no-change; Y, his anxiety about possible inadequacy in the new role; Z, his desire to retain ties with old associates who might resent a different outlook.

If the circle represents a larger social system—say a city school system with the right hand goal an expansion of services for disadvantaged children—the vectors toward the right (goal, +) would designate the influential groups and individuals favoring such development; vectors in the reverse direction would stand for forces in the social system opposing the new program.

During the process of charting forces and counter-forces, a planning group may find it helpful to check out the direction, strength, and saliency of some of the presumed influences. Experience in the use of this device has shown that persons interested in a change are often mistaken about the amount of support or opposition which they attribute to other persons and groups. Exploration of the dynamics of the social equilibrium may lead to modifications of the proposed action which will increase support and lessen resistance.

Examination of the gains and losses may reveal that an innovation, despite its greater efficiency, is not adequate to overcome the inevitable confusion and waste of the change-over. Barnett (1953) speaks of the "marginal value" of certain inventions and improvements as insufficient to warrant the cost of their adoption. The writer found morale in several industrial research departments depressed by the fact that the company had failed to make use of some of their well-demonstrated improvements. It was hard for the creators of a new process to accept the fact that even though their proposal was superior to present practice, it would be too wasteful to change over. A parallel is the case of a teacher who has been reasonably successful with traditional methods. Perhaps some newer techniques are usually more effective, but their superiority may not be great enough to warrant discarding the accumulated materials, habits, and skills of the teacher's customary approach.

Reducing resistance

It is possible to increase the pressures in a quasi-stationary equilibrium without bringing about the desired change. Indeed, this often happens. Advocates of a reform try by argument, persuasion, inducements, threats, and coercion to effect movement in the direction of its adoption. But their activity alerts the opposition, who bring to bear their counter-arguments, counter-inducements, and counter-coercion. After a time, as shown in Figure 12 the pressures toward the goal (+) have mounted (longer arrows), but so have the counter-pressures, and the target has not moved.

The diagonal lines in the circle indicate high tension in the system as a result of pressures and counter-pressures.

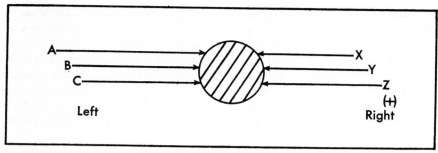

FIGURE 12

The preferable strategy is to examine the resistance and to find ways to reduce it. If a child of 12 has not learned to read, despite normal ability and all the usual pressures from school, home, and other life situations, it will not help to exhort him harder and more often. This will only increase his conflict, frustration, and resentment. Wise psychotherapy examines the impedance which has thus far prevented him from making the customary progress. In a proposed social change—for example, purifying city air—the force analysis will probably show fairly strong pressures from health departments, housewives interested in reducing soot-fall, and citizens annoyed by smoke and smog. Why, then, has the change not been made? Who is afraid of what? What are the still unsolved problems of cost and enforcement? Finding ways around the real or imagined obstacles may be more efficient than a propaganda drive.

The dynamics may be illustrated by Figure 13. Arrows A, B, and C—the pressures for change toward the goal (+)—remain unchanged from their state in Figure 11, when the situation was stable. But the length of arrow X has been a little reduced, and arrow Y is much shorter. Now the resultant of the forces makes for movement to the right, toward the goal (+).

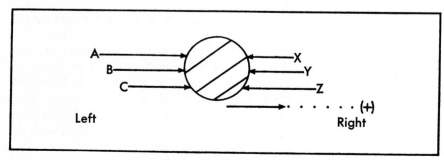

FIGURE 13

The principle that it is more rewarding to reduce resistance than to try to overcome it by greater pressure operates with almost all kinds of social change. Workers can be forced by management to accept a new pattern of production despite their feeling of insecurity, but this will increase tension and rebellious feelings. Or, as in the Coch and French experiment (Chapter 13) their insecurity about the change can be reduced by planning it themselves so they feel more confident of its success. Then the change can be made with less tension, aggression, and lowering of productivity.

On racial integration, resistance can be defeated by superior force, resulting in reluctant acquiescence and continued tension, or, in other instances, some of the apprehension may be reduced because fears of lowered academic standards, violence, sexual immorality, dirt, and disease can be relieved. In the latter case, the process will be smoother and easier. In international relations, the arms race represents lengthening of the opposing force-vectors on both sides, with increased tension in the system. Osgood's "graduated reciprocation," described in Chapter 14, follows Lewin's admonition to reduce the resistance and thus to lower the tension levels. In those historic periods when opposing groups become more urgent, strenuous, and intense in pressing for their goals there is likely to be overt conflict but no real change in position. The centuries of religious wars (Moslem-Christian; Catholic-Protestant) did not end in the triumph of either side. When both sides relaxed the pressure and counter-pressure, the positions did not change but the dangerous tension gradually diminished.

Participation

One of the most successful strategies for increasing the pressure toward a social goal, and for simultaneously reducing resistance, is to involve the persons concerned in diagnosing the difficulty and designing the innovation.

Alfred Marrow, a social psychologist with a distinguished career as head of a business and in public service, has summarized the remarkable success of change-action based on participation and involvement:

> There was an increase of 42 percent in the number of housewives who served glandular meat cuts, an improvement of 56 percent in the number of persons answering bigoted remarks, an improvement in gang behavior that resulted in a reduction of 90 percent in the number of gang fights in Seaside, an improvement of 72 percent in the skills used by community leaders after their Workshop training, an increase of 24 percent in factory production, an improvement of 40 percent in the number of gainfully employed older workers, an improvement of as much as 52 percent in favorable attitudes toward Negroes among residents of interracial housing, an increase of 75 percent in

the number of persons and organizations involved in intergroup activities in Northtown, etc.

The key words in successful introduction of innovations are *participation* and *involvement*. People enjoy and affirm the changes they make for themselves; they resist changes imposed on them by others. Even in research organizations, supposedly committed to the quest for new knowledge with no respect to source, there is a kind of provincial pride. In development and engineering shops, as we noted in an earlier chapter the "N.I.H. factor" ("not invented here") operates against proposals coming from "outsiders." It is even more important, however, that participants in the process of diagnosis and design have an opportunity to clear up misunderstandings and differences of interpretation before the changes are made. While proposals are still tentative and in flux, they can be modified so that potential opponents find some consideration given to their concerns. Participation in planning is too often limited to those already convinced and in favor of the change. This is one of the liabilities of reform movements. They set up the unproductive win-lose, dominance-submission relationship; they define their in-group as good and wise; the out-group as evil or stupid. The problem-solving orientation brings together all persons and groups concerned, so that what emerges from their thinking together is, as nearly as possible, a real integration. It is designed to incorporate the desires of all participants and to avoid or to minimize the consequences which any find undesirable. If the planning groups accept apparent resistance as justified doubts presenting still unresolved problems, a premature lineup of advocates vs. opponents can be avoided.

Temporary systems

Open exploration and creative integration are often encouraged by setting up conditions under which participants can interact with more freedom than they feel they have in their usual job and community roles. Miles (1964) refers to "temporary systems" devised to maximize opportunity for persons who are involved in working together to learn new ways of mutual understanding and collaboration. In a "training laboratory," as described in Chapter 13, a workshop, a conference, a religious retreat, or in group therapy (Chapter 4) changes are possible which would be very difficult in the customary social systems. People in families, schools, businesses, churches, and governments are very busy with their routine activities. They have relatively little time and energy to divert to the cultivation of the innovative life.

Miles has described three examples of temporary systems focused on promoting change in persons or organizations (1964, pp. 446–452). A human relations training laboratory for educators gave participants a chance to get away from the pressures of work and the patterns of personal relationship back on the job. In T-Groups, they became more aware of their own feelings and values and more sensitive to the experiences and needs of others. First, they had to "unlearn" their private conceptions of themselves, their associates, and their organization, which had become fixed with long experience. It is remarkable that after only two weeks in this special setting as many as 75 percent of the participants (as measured both by self-report and observations of associates on the job) showed noticeable improvement in ability to work with others.

A second case was an experimental summer school for children who were academically retarded. Teachers felt themselves to be part of a creative team, freed from the usual chores, to act simply as educators. More than 1,200 (of 1,500) children successfully "passed," and the participating teachers and principals gained a new confidence that they could, under suitable conditions, achieve far more than they had in the past.

Miles' third case involved a one-week conference of the managers of a British manufacturing company. Starting with the usual reserve, and defensiveness, participants learned to "open up" and "the emotional tone became one of eager involvement, extremely hard work, and a kind of equalitarian comaraderie which appeared to transcend preexisting relationships" (p. 451). A report recommending important structural changes was promptly accepted by the Board and implemented throughout the large industrial organization.

All of these experiments were characterized by: (1) time limits; (2) focus on a definite goal; (3) a defined and bounded group of participants; (4) physical and social isolation; (5) conditions facilitating better communications; (6) a norm of equalitarianism; (7) a norm of genuineness; authenticity, openness and frankness; (8) the norms of scientific thinking; and (9) an expectation of change in the persons and social systems. All of them successfully fostered such changes. Both individuals and organizations can learn to enjoy new experience and to take pride in change.

Leaders and consultants

Participation of the many does not preclude strong leadership by the most able. An important group skill, developed in training programs, is the ability to utilize the resources of all members. This includes, and with special emphasis, the resources of certain leaders. One of the most impressive demonstrations of change in a factory has been reported by Guest (1962). A new manager began by listening: he then set up regular meetings in which more men could participate more freely. Within three years, the plant changed from the poorest to the best in quality of output, low labor costs, safety record, freedom from grievances, and absenteeism. The changes—established by forceful leadership—were accepted by the workers and remained in effect after the original manager was promoted to a new position.

In their report on reorganizing a YMCA, Dimock and Sorenson described a procedure like that of Plant Y.

> At the beginning the administrative leadership provides the initiative in planning and setting the steps in motion. Staff and constituency participate in and agree to the goals and plans. But such commitment is permissive rather than propulsive in the early stages. As the project proceeds, the involvement of staff, advisors and Boards become deeper; satisfaction and confidence in new skills develop; commitment is deeper and responsibility in the branches and groups increases. As operating responsibility is distributed and initiated at more points, internal motivation is strengthened.

The people who initiate and lead in experimental and demonstration projects within communities and business organizations are usually above the average in ability and in contacts with outside groups. The school superintendents whose systems first adopted modern mathematics were above their colleagues in education, status with their peers, and frequency of friendship interaction with them (Carlson, 1964). In a study of the rate at which doctors adopt new drugs (Menzel, Katz, 1956), it appeared that the leaders more frequently learned of the innovations from journal articles and professional meetings; the followers were more apt to rely on what salesmen brought to them. Men responsible for creative social inventions in another study (De Grazia, 1961) were high in drive for achievement, ability to see relationships, tendency to express ideas through action, and in "marginality," not feeling fully identified with the dominant culture.

Schools that are innovative have teachers who attend out-of-town meetings and who read widely to discover fresh ideas. Similar results were found with farmers. The more experimental-minded go more often to metropolitan cities. Eichholz and Rogers (1964) propose the generalization that "innovativeness varies directly with cosmopolitaness."

Consultants are important leaders in processes of change because they can bring into consideration a broader range of experience than that represented by the other participants. Their success frequently depends, however, on not being persuaded to do for the other persons involved what these individuals could do for themselves.

Consultation is the strategy of change which has made most use of the skills and insights of social psychology. Individuals suffering from neurosis, groups which reach an impasse, factories which have labor problems, organizations which want to be more effective, and communities seeking to overcome conflicts have frequently sought psychological help. In trying to help a society change, a consultant uses methods similar to those of a good therapist working with an individual patient. He helps the society only at the points where the society really wants help. His strategy for dealing with resistance is to bring it into consciousness and to examine and to interpret it. He wishes to be seen as a welcome helper, not as one who imposes a change or even argues or persuades. Page (1959) has introduced the term "Socio-therapy of the enterprise."

Experience indicates that change in an organization is much more likely to be accepted if it has the support of top management. Whenever possible, consultants try to establish their contact with the president or other chief executive officer. Dimock and Sorenson (1955) caution that "because the whole agency is involved, in all of its policy making, administration, financial, building, personnel and program aspects, it is not possible for the executive officer to delegate modernization to some staff person." Griffiths (1964) states as one of his propositions: "When change in an organization does occur, it will tend to occur from the top down, not from the bottom up."

A sociologist interested in helping in a community action program found that he needed to work not only with the heads of formal organizations but also with persons who held key posts in the informal communication systems of the community. He mapped the ties of kinship and of "visiting" in the town and identified some who, although holding no office, were extremely influential. When five such persons viewed a farm demonstration, almost everyone in the community had heard about it the next day (Loomis, 1953).

Loomis experienced the initial suspicion and unwillingness to give information which we might anticipate in relationship to a stranger. One day, within a few hours, the community attitude changed to active cooperation. It developed that Mr. B., a figure of high prestige and a key man in the communications network, had gone to the county seat and talked with officials who had been informed about the Loomis project. With their approval, he could dispel the doubts of most farmers in Southtown.

Greening (1963) began his program of change in the hospital by winning the support of the President of the Board. Without this backing, the administration was reluctant to propose the program to the medical staff.

From the National Training Laboratory in 1947 came the term and concept of a "change agent," who operates usually as a consultant on a volunteer or professional basis. Lippitt, Watson, and Westley, in their book, *The Dynamics of Planned Change* (1958), pointed out the need to examine consultant-client relationships at every stage of the change action. How is the consultant seen by the various persons and groups concerned, before he enters the process? How does he see himself? What is his own motivation? If he is not successful in keeping responsibility for decisions clearly on the permanent members of the social system, he becomes the scapegoat for whatever goes wrong or proves disturbing. A good consultant helps the leadership within the organization to anticipate difficulties and to devise remedies. Yet, however well he operates, the consultant will be viewed with ambivalence by the clients. Psychotherapists are trained to expect some alternation in their patients between unwarranted rejection and equally unwarranted glorification and dependence. Experienced consultants to management are familiar with similar swings toward and against them.

In his *Helping People Change* (1963) Corey generalizes some of his experience from decades of consulting in the United States and in India. He doubts that technical competence in an area is sufficient to make an individual a good consultant. "Failures have seldom resulted, in my judgment, from a lack of knowledge about, and experience with, the specific area of activity in which change was undertaken." Corey notes that an All-American football player is not necessarily a good coach. He argues for continuing sensitivity to the subtlety of human relationships. It is not easy, particularly when working with other mature, sophisticated persons, to follow the undercurrents of feeling. "Most of us have developed many varieties of protective behavior that may keep a deterioration in human relations from coming to light. One of the characteristics of the best consultants I have worked with, however, is their ability to pick up cues of such deterioration and act to stop it" (p. 72).

The kind of empathy which enables the consultant to see the problem as the client does and to feel problems as the client feels them is closely akin to the demands on a psychotherapist. Corey notes in himself and in others a need to be vigilant against tendencies to translate the client's problems into terms more familiar to the consultant and to make an impression of brilliant competence. Corey's years of experience as an educator have left him with grave doubts about the effectiveness of most direct instruction. "I fell into the perennial trap," he reports, "of confusing an increase in knowledgeable talk about a problem with the capacity and drive to deal with it effectively." In contrast, he has found it rewarding and satisfying to become a genuine participant in a team project; to work closely with associates; and to let whatever teaching occurred be incidental to progress on the cooperative task.

The emphasis in the consultative approach tends to approve the kind of change where those who are affected are invited to participate in planning for, guiding, and evaluating what happens. This strategy enlists many different personalities, each contributing his special knowledge, his particular skills, and unique values. Group consensus is sought.

The climate is one of cooperative problem-solving rather than of a win-lose struggle. As in McGregor's "Theory Y" (Chapter 13) it is assumed that people will rise to the challenge of such expectations, will reveal unexpected resources of ability, and will want to assume responsibility. One can say of the good consultant as Lao-tze said of the good leader: "When his work is done, his goal achieved, people will say, 'We did this ourselves!'"

There is another type of leadership, especially manifest in historic movements of reform and revolution. The heroic leader may take a stand for which there is not yet much support. He may slowly win adherents, or, perhaps, achieve recognition only after his death. Monuments have often been erected to prophets who were rejected by their contemporaries. Revolutionary movements have usually been led by intellectuals and persons of some prestige who have identified with the underprivileged. Jefferson and Washington came from a class which lived far more comfortably than most American colonists. Davis (1930) found that 60 percent of the leadership of the Bolshevik Revolution in 1917, came from upper classes which comprised only 7 percent of the population in Russia at that time.

Adaptation, evaluation, and revision

A change seldom, if ever, turns out to be exactly what its advocates expected. Unanticipated difficulties appear even in such carefully designed and tested bits of machinery as new models of motor cars. Social changes rarely lend themselves to pre-testing and control. Hence, what is required is commitment to a period of adaptation and improvement. The first consequences may be so disturbing as to lead to a demand to scrap the innovation and return to the old pattern. Many a promising development has been defeated because too much was expected too quickly. Mann and Neff (1962) caution: "It is essential to set realistic expectations about what a change will mean to those directly or indirectly affected." Over-optimistic expectations are forerunners of frustration.

Participation during the processes of diagnosis, design, and introduction of a change lays the foundation for continuing activity by these participants in whatever adjustments, adaptations, and revisions emerge as the process continues. Training workers in group problem solving and decision making may enable them to deal immediately with problems which might otherwise be referred to upper levels of management.

Evaluation of changes in a business can be made rather clearly through financial controls. It is more difficult to evaluate alleged improvements in the work of educational, recreational, community, government, and religious agencies.

Johnson's report on California schools (Miles, 1964, p. 169) reveals that only 68 of 1,507 schools reported any attempt to evaluate changes they had introduced and only ten had designed what he regarded as a respectable research procedure. A $3 million investment by a Foundation in a new program of teacher preparation in Arkansas actually turned out only 194 teachers and their success, relative to teachers trained in other ways, was never clearly evaluated. Few educational activities have been researched as extensively as has been the teaching of reading. Yet Barton and Wilder (Miles, 1964, p. 375) find that the results have not been incorporated in the readers published over a subsequent 30-year period. The "Hawthorne effect" and the "placebo effect" have seldom been separated from the other consequences of experiments in schools and other community agencies. The enthusiasm of the promoters and a fair amount of acceptance by the participants seem to suffice for the proclaimed success of a substantial proportion of new enterprises.

Spread of new ideas to others

We referred earlier, in discussing demonstration projects, to the fact that the success of a new approach in one setting, does not readily lead to its adoption by others. Mort (1941; 1960) found that after an innovation in education had first been demonstrated as practical, it typically took 15 years to reach the most progressive 3 percent of the school systems. Then followed 20 years of rapid spread and 15 more years to win over the slow adapters. Hence, he found a 50-year period between first demonstration and its complete adoption.

Experience in New York State led Brickell (in Miles, 1964) to the conclusion that effective innovation requires three different kinds of people, each of which requires a different temperament and training: (1) the innovaters, who design and promote the original idea; (2) the scientific evaluators, who test the effectiveness of the new operation, and (3) the successful disseminators. Brickell sees these personality types as incompatible and believes innovation as a whole suffers when the same people try to initiate, evaluate, and disseminate the idea or invention.

Brickell also notes the need to equip people with the skills required for operating in a changed way. Much of the resistance to an innovation arises from the insecurity of those who fear that they cannot succeed well with it. Trying to win acceptance of a new philosophy without developing the appropriate habits is likely to result merely in adoption of the new-fashioned phrases while continuing the old-fashioned behavior.

Studies of other social movements generally bear out Mort's concept of three phases in the spread of an innovation—first, a phase of slow recognition; second, rapid adoption, and finally a slow absorption of the remainder. The idea is graphically presented in Figure 14.

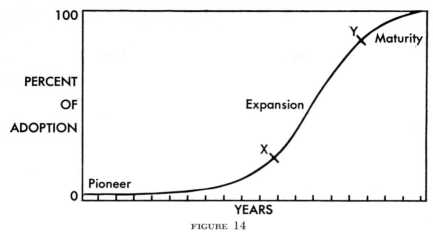

The growth cycle is made up of three phases with different psychological climates. The Pioneer phase extends from the first inception of the idea until the point of inflection (X) where the curve starts its rapid rise. The Expansion phase continues then until the second point of inflection (Y) where the curve becomes concave below and levels off in the Maturity phase.

Ideas for the improvement of an enterprise are usually adopted most readily by the organizations which have previously been most progressive. It is generally easier to sell a new idea to the best farmers, the most successful businesses, the most progressive schools and communities. Mort (1941) found innovations more quickly adopted in schools with ample financial resources; the writer found most rapid acceptance of new ideas in YMCA's where community economic indices reflected high standards of living (Watson, 1946).

As any movement spreads, it assumes new forms and attracts new leadership. At this stage the pioneers are likely to be given haloes and set on pedestals to keep them from interfering with current operations. Often they do not submit without a struggle and the movement may divide between the orthodox purists and those who defer more to expediency.

A typical outcome of the Expansion phase is the acceptance of compromises and half measures. When a controversial movement begins to look as if it might reach its goal (G), opponents begin to try to salvage something by offering something less (G-n) in the hope that this will stop the advance. Thus a number of communities in the South, aware of the growth of the movement toward racial integration in the schools, built separate schools for Negroes which were not only equal to but actually superior to the schools for white children. Similar efforts occurred with a few hospitals, housing projects, and recreation centers. The offer of (G-n) poses a problem for reform leadership. The offer represents a real advance but is less than the goal sought by the movement. The membership may divide between those who argue that half a loaf is better than none, and those who see that they would not have been offered half a loaf unless their movement had an excellent chance of winning much more.

Another issue concerns when to legislate. At what stage should advocates of a reform seek to embody their proposal in law? As William Graham Sumner (1906) expressed it, "Do stateways change folkways?" The failure and repeal of some laws—Prohibition is a noteworthy example—indicates that laws do not always prevail. Many people in the South doubted that the Supreme Court ruling on school integration could ever be enforced. On the other hand, the evidence reviewed in Chapter 11 shows that legislation has proven effective in bringing about integration in the Armed Forces, fair employment practices, and interracial housing projects. After a reform has passed the mid-point, where it has the support of a growing majority, a law or decree will greatly speed up the process of acceptance among the rest of the population.

While a movement for change remains controversial, much of the success of new legislation depends upon the commitment and firmness of responsible officials. Quick success of integration in the armed forces was produced by the unwavering stand taken by the President and the commanders (Chapter 11).

In July 1954, while the Supreme Court was deliberating on its second order, designed to implement the May 17 statement of principles on racial integration in the schools, a conference of social psychologists was assembled to discuss whether a "forthwith" or a "gradual" compliance would work better. These psychologists rejected the gradualist proposal. They argued that it would lead to such undesirable results as: (a) evasion and postponement; (b) piecemeal efforts which might be regarded as discriminating against certain communities, schools or grades which become the "guinea pigs"; (c) seizing upon minor incidents to inflame resistance and bring the program to a halt. The gradualist approach was criticized as based upon some unwarranted psychological assumptions, for example, (a) that attitude changes must precede institutional change; or (b) that it is easier to change part of a school system than it is to change the whole system. The public opinion experts contended that a "go-slow" approach would be tantamount to encouraging reluctant local authorities to adopt weak, ambiguous, self-defeating measures. The social scientists made a case for:

1. "a clear and unequivocal statement of the policy of desegregation;

2. "firm enforcement . . . persistence in the face of initial resistance

. . . . willingness on the part of responsible authorities to deal with violations, attempted violations, and incitement to violation by legal action.

3. "refusal of authorities to tolerate subterfuges, gerrymandering, or other evasions.

4. "an appeal to the public in terms of religious principles of brotherhood and American democratic traditions of equal justice."

The conference recommended only the short delay required by educational administrators to work out the details of teacher and pupil reassignment. They endorsed the idea of a prestige agency—as free as possible from political ties—to bring together leading citizens of both races for the specific purpose of implementing quickly and fully the 1954 decision.

The Supreme Court did not accept this recommendation of the social scientists. In accord with public opinion, they deemed it wiser to give more time for communities to adjust to the prospective changes. A poll (American Institute of Public Opinion, May 9, 1956) at about that time showed 71 percent in favor of giving "a long period of years" for gradual integration, and only 18 percent who agreed with the social scientists that "the government should do everything it can to see that white and Negro children in all parts of the country go to the same public schools within the coming year." It is not possible now to know whether the more drastic demand for forthright and immediate and full desegregation would have provoked more or less resistance than has arisen.

Cities like St. Louis, Louisville, and Baltimore did move with decisive speed, and desegregation in these cities was rapidly accepted. Protest movements were quashed by the authorities, who remained firmly committed. A step of considerable importance was that those who had responsibility for the success of integration—all principals, supervisors, guidance personnel, and teachers, were explicitly prepared for their new roles. Pupils and their parents were brought into the processes of preparation. Attention was directed away from the question; "Are we going to comply?" to the question, "*How* can we best achieve the prescribed integration?" Trouble has arisen mainly in communities which regarded compliance as still open and debatable. The governors of Arkansas, Alabama, and Mississippi took a stand against enforcement of the court orders, leaving citizens confused on what the law required.

After a change has won general acceptance, the drive for its adoption abates. The late stages of a reform movement usually transform the crusade into a bureaucracy. With general acceptance, effort turns to "mopping up" a few areas in which the reform has not yet been fully accepted. The memory of the pioneers is ritualistically honored, but operations are carried on by men who like the prestige and power of the established enterprise. The change becomes part of the old order, and those who pioneered for it many be resistant to their successors who would introduce new and further changes. Is it possible to cultivate commitment not to some particular innovation but to a continuing process of improvement?

Change as our way of life

The course of most civilizations, as traced by Toynbee (1933–39), has led from an initial period of enterprise to stabilization, control by a dominant minority, and the mistaken view that the prevailing institutions would endure forever. Growth and flexibility gave way to bondage to the traditions of the past and the power of rulers who were self-satisfied and blind to the need for change. Eventually the repressed energies broke through in revolution and transition to a new order.

It may be that we have now achieved emancipation from this age-old cycle of innovation, inertia, and insurrection. The United States has been described (in an issue of *Fortune* magazine) as pioneering with the new doctrine of "Continuous Revolution." If all our institutions remain open to the participation and creative contribution of their members, the steady flow of adaptive innovations will render revolutionary upheavals unnecessary.

The conditions which have brought accelerating change seem likely to continue, if they do not culminate in some all-destructive war. Education, science, invention, and wealth are cumulative. The higher the level they have reached, the more rapidly they can grow. Universal education once meant only the few years of schooling necessary for literacy. Now, in most parts of our country, it means high school education for all and college for an increasing proportion. More and more adults are involved in further education: in factories, stores, offices, and institutes, as well as on campuses (De Crow, Kolben, 1963; Clark, Sloan, 1958, 1962). Expenditures for research and development mount by billions of dollars. Communication and diffusion of knowledge increase as more and more people move about the globe. The norms of science—problem solving, search for new truth, holding hypotheses tentatively while testing them critically—increasingly pervade other areas of life.

The anchors of certainty in a world of flux are found in trustworthy and rational processes rather than in established institutions or doctrines. Faith that the answers of the past are infallible is replaced by confidence in procedures adaptable to changing conditions. In his *Human Nature and Conduct*, a social psychology written (1922) before most of the empirical data cited in this volume had become available, John Dewey wrote: (p. 323)

It sounds academic to say that substantial bettering of social relations waits upon the growth of a scientific social psychology. . . . It would have seemed absurd to say in the seventeenth century that in the end the alteration in methods of physical investigation which was then beginning would prove more important than the religious wars of that century. Yet the wars marked the end of one era; the dawn of physical science the beginning of a new one. And a trained imagination may discover that the nationalistic and economic wars which are the chief outward mark of the present are in the end to be less significant than the development of a science of human nature.

Bibliography

Adler, Alfred. *What Life Should Mean to You.* New York: Little, Brown & Co., 1931, p. 56; p. 230; p. 5.

Adorno, T. W., Frenkel-Brunswik, Else, Levinson, D. J., Sanford, R. N. *The Authoritarian Personality.* New York: Harper, 1950.

Allee, W. C. *Social Life of Animals.* New York: Norton, 1938.

Allport, F. H. "The Influence of the Group upon Association and Thought." *J. exp. Psychol.,* 1920. III:159–182.

———. "Psychological Nature of Political Structures." *Am. pol. sci. rev.,* 1927. XXI:611–618.

———. "Psychology of Nationalism." *Harpers Magazine,* 1927. CLV:291–301.

Allport, Gordon W. *Becoming.* New Haven: Yale University Press, 1955.

———. "The Historical Background of Modern Social Psychology." In Lindzey, G. (ed.). *Handbook of Social Psychology.* Cambridge, Mass.: Addison Wesley Co., 1954. Vol. I, Chapter 1.

———. *The Nature of Prejudice.* New York: Anchor Book, Doubleday & Co., 1954. Also Cambridge, Mass. Addison Wesley Press, 1954.

———. *Personality: a Psychological Interpretation.* New York: Holt, 1937.

Allport, G. W., Gillespie, J. M. and Young, J. "The Religion of the Postwar College Student." *J. Psychol.,* 1948. XXV:3–33.

Allport, G., and Kramer, B. M. "Some Roots of Prejudice." *J. Psychol.,* 1946. XXII:9–39.

564

Allport, G. W. and Postman, L. J. "The Basic Psychology of Rumor." *Trans. N.Y. Acad. Sci.*, Series II, 1945. VIII:61–81.

Almack, J. C. *Mental Efficiency of Consulting Pairs*, Ed. Res. Bull., Los Angeles City Schools, 1930. IX:2–3.

American Management Association. *Executive Personality and Job Success.* Personnel series 120, New York; 1948.

Ames, Louise. "The Sense of Self of Nursery School Children As Manifested by their Verbal Behavior." *J. genet. Psychol.*, XXCI:192–232, 1952.

Amory, Cleveland. "First of the Month." *Saturday Review.* March 6, 1965, p. 10.

Anderson, H. H. "Domination and Integration in the Social Behavior of Kindergarten Children in an Experimental Play Situation." *Genet. Psychol. Monog.*, 1939. XXI:357–385.

Anderson, W. A. and Plambeck, H. *Social Participation of Farm Families.* Ithaca, N.Y. Cornell Univ. Agric. Exper. Sta. Mimeo Bulletin No. 8, 1943.

Annis, A. D. and Meier, N. C. "The Induction of Opinion through Suggestion by Means of 'Planted Content.'" *J. soc. Psychol.*, 1934. V:65–81.

Argyle, M. "Social Pressures in Public and Private Situations." *J. abnorm. soc. Psychol.* LIV:172–75, 1957.

Argyle, M. *et al.* "Supervisory Methods Related to Productivity Absenteeism, and Labor Turnover." *Hum. Rela.*, 1958, XI:23–40.

Argyris, Chris. *Personality and Organization.* New York: Harper and Bros., 1957.

Aristotle. *Politics.* Translated by Benjamin Jowett. New York: Modern Library edition, 1943. VII, 7; also p.190.

Arnheim, Rudolf. "The World of the Daytime Serial." In Lazarsfeld, P. F. & Stanton, F. M. (eds.). *Radio Research, 1942–3.* New York: Duell, Sloan and Pearce, 1944.

Asch, S. E. "Effects of Group Pressure upon the Modification and Distortion of Judgments." In Guetzkow, H. *Groups, Leadership and Men.* Pittsburgh: Carnegie Press, 1951.

———. *Social Psychology.* New York: Prentice Hall, 1952.

Asch, S. E., Block, H., Hertzman, M. "Studies in the Principles of Judgments and Attitudes, II. Determinants of Judgment by Group and Ego Standards." *J. soc. Psychol.* 1940, XII:433–465.

Aveling, F. and Hargreaves, H. L. "Suggestibility With and Without Prestige in Children." *Brit. J. Psychol.* 1921. XVIII:362–388.

Bach, G. L. *Economics.* Englewood Cliffs, N.J.: Prentice-Hall, 1958. (2nd ed.). p. 806.

Bach, George R. *Intensive Group Psychotherapy.* New York: Ronald Press, 1954.

Back, K. W. "Influence through Social Communication." *J. abn. soc. Psychol.* 1951. XLVI:9–23.

Baehr, M. E., Renck, R. "The Definition and Measurement of Employee Morale." *Admin. sci. Quart.*, 1958. III:151–184.

Bagehot, W. *Physics and Politics.* New York: D. Appleton, 1875.

Baker, G. W. *"Recruitment, Assignment and Utilization of New Research and Development, Air Force Officers."* Randolph Field, Texas, 1954.

Bakke, E. W. *The Unemployed Man.* New York: E. P. Dutton & Co., 1934. pp. 62–3.

Baldwin, James. *The Fire Next Time.* New York: Dial Press, 1963.

Baldwin, James M. *Social and Ethical Interpretations in Mental Development.* New York: Macmillan, 1897. Abridged and reprinted in Borgatta, C. F. and Meyer, Henry J. *Sociological Theory.* New York: Knopf, 1956. p. 23.

Bales, R. F. *Effect of Size of Problem-Solving Groups on the System of Interaction.* Report to APA, 1957.

———. "The Equilibrium Problem in Small Groups." In Parsons, T. *et al. Working Papers in the Theory of Action.* Glencoe, Ill.: The Free Press, 1953, pp. 111–161.

———. *Interaction Process Analysis: A Method for the Study of Small Groups.* Cambridge, Mass.: Addison-Wesley, 1950.

———. "Some Uniformities of Behavior in Small Social Systems." In Swanson, G. E., Newcomb, T. M. and Hartley, E. L. (eds.). *Readings in Social Psychology.* New York: Holt, 1952. pp. 146–159.

Bales, R. F. and Borgatta, E. F. "Size of Group as a Factor in the Interaction Profile." In Hace, A. P., Borgatta, E. F., and Bales, R. F. (eds.). *Small groups.* New York: Knopf, 1955, pp. 396–413.

Bales, R. F., Strodtbeck, F. L., Mills, T. M., and Roseborough, M. E. "Channels of Communication in Small Groups." *Amer. social rev.,* 1951. XVI, 461–468.

Balogh, T. *Unequal Partners.* London: Blockwell, 1963.

Bandura, A. and Walters, R. H. *Adolescent Aggression.* New York: Ronald Press, 1959.

Barber, B. *Social Stratification.* New York: Harcourt Brace, 1957.

Barnard, Chester. *The Functions of the Executive.* Cambridge, Mass.: Harvard University Press, 1938.

Barnett, H. G. *Innovation, the Basis of Cultural Change.* New York: McGraw-Hill, 1953.

Barnlund, D. C. "A Comparative Study of Individual, Majority and Group Judgment." *J. abn. soc. Psychol.,* 1959. LVIII:55–60.

Barton, A. H., Wilder, D. E. "Research and Practice in the Teaching of Reading." In Miles, M. (ed.). *Innovation in Education.* New York: Teachers College, Columbia University Bur. Publ., 1964. Ch. 16.

Barton, W. A. Jr. "The Effect of Group Activity and Individual Effort in Developing Ability to Solve Problems in First-year Algebra." *J. Ed. Admin. & Supvn.,* 1926, XII:512–518.

Bass, B. M. "The Leaderless Group Discussion." *Psych. Bull.,* 1954. LI:465–492.

———. "Leadership Opinion as Forecasts of Supervisory Success." *Personnel psych.,* 1958. XI:515–518.

———. "*Leadership, Psychology, and Organizational Behavior,*" New York: Harper & Bros., 1960.

———. "Variables of the Leaderless Group Discussion." *Educ. psychol. Measmt.,* 1951. XI:196–207.

Bass, B. M. *et al.* "Personality Variables Related to Leaderless Group Discussion Behavior." *J. abn. soc. Psychol.,* 1953. XLVIII:120–28.

Bass, B. M. & Wurster, C. R. "Effects of Company Rank on LGD Performance of Oil Refinery Supervisors." *J. appl. Psychol.* 1953. XXXVII:96–104.

Bauer, R. A. "Accuracy of Perception in International Relations." *T. C. Rec.,* 1963. LXIV:291–299.

———. "The Psychology of the Soviet Middle Elite." In Kluckhohn, C. Murray,

566

H. A., and Schneider, D. A. *Personality in Nature, Society and Culture.* New York: Knopf, 1953, pp. 633–649.

Bavelas, A. "Making Leadership Effective." *Nation's Business.* March 1957, XLV:96f.

———. "Morale and the Training of Leaders." In Watson, G. (ed.). *Civilian Morale.* Boston: Houghton Mifflin Co., 1942, pp. 143–165.

———. (1947) Reported by Lewin, K. "Group Decision and Social Change." In Newcomb, T. M. and Hartley, E. L. *Readings in Social Psychology,* N.Y. Holt, 1947, p. 343. Also in 2nd and 3rd ed.

Bavelas, Alex. "Some Problems of Organizational Change." *J. soc. issues,* 1948, IV:48–52.

Beaglehole, E. and Ritchie, Jas. *Basic Personality in a New Zealand Maori Community.* In Kaplan, B. (ed.). *Studying Personality Cross-Culturally.* Evanston, Ill.: Row Peterson, 1961.

Beauvoir, Simone de. *The Second Sex.* New York: Knopf, 1953.

Bell, Howard M. *Youth Tell Their Story.* Washington, D.C.: Amer Youth Commission, 1937.

Benedict, Ruth. *The Chrysanthemum and the Sword.* Boston: Houghton Mifflin, 1946.

———. *Patterns of Culture.* Boston: Houghton Mifflin, 1934.

Bennett, Edith B. "Discussion, Decision, Commitment and Consensus in Group Decisions." *Hum. Rel.,* 1955, VII:251–274.

Bennis, W. G. and Shepard, H. A. *A Theory of Group Development.* (MS. Mimeo by the authors at MIT, 1956)

Berelson, B. "The Great Debate on Cultural Democracy." *T.C. Record,* 1962, LXIII:499–509.

Berelson, B., Lazarsfeld, P. F., and McPhee, W. N. *Voting: A Study of Opinion Formation in a Presidential Campaign.* Chicago: University of Chicago Press, 1954.

Berelson, B., Salter, P. J. "Majority and Minority Americans, an Analysis of Magazine Fiction." *Pub. opin. Quart.* 1946, X:168–190.

Berkowitz, Leonard. "Sharing Leadership in Small, Decision-Making Groups." *J. abn. soc. Psychol.* 1953. XLVIII:231–238.

Berkowitz, L., Goranson, R. E. "Motivational and Judgmental Determinants of Social Perception." *J. abn. soc. Psychol.,* 1964, LXIX:296–302.

Bettelheim, Bruno. "Individual and Mass Behavior in Extreme Situations." *J. abn. soc. Psychol.* 1943, XXXVIII:417–452.

Biddle, Wm. W. *Propaganda and Education.* New York Teachers College Bureau of Publications, No. 531, 1932.

Biderman, A. D. *March to calumny: the Story of American POW's in the Korean War.* New York: Macmillan, 1963.

Binder, A., McConnell, D. and Sjoholm, N. "Verbal Conditioning as a Function of Experimenter Characteristics." *J. abn. soc. Psychol.,* 1957. LV:309–314.

Bion, W. R. "Experiences in Groups." *Hum. rela.,* 1948. I:314–320; 487–496; 1949, II:13–22, 295–303; 1950, III:3–14; 1951, IV:221–227.

Biesheuvel, S. *Race, Culture and Personality.* Hoernte Memorial Lecture, 1959. Cited in HSV, F.L.K. *Psychological Anthropology.* Homewood, Ill.: Dorsey Press, 1961, pp. 71–2.

Bjerstedt, A. "Ego-Involved World-Mindedness." University of Leind, Sweden. (Duplicated manuscript). *See* also *Nordisk Psykologi*, 1958. X:161–178.

Blake, R. R., Hilson, H. & Mouton, J. S. "The Generality of Conformity Behavior as a Function of Factual Anchorage, Difficulty of Task, and Amount of Social Pressure. *J. pers.*, 1957. XXV:294–305.

Blake, R. R., Mouton, J., Sloma, R. L. "The union-management intergroup laboratory." *Appl. behav. Sci.*, 1965, I:25–57.

Blake, R. R. and Mouton, J. S. *The Managerial Grid.* Houston, Texas: Gulf Publishing Co., 1964.

Blansfield, M. G. "Depth Analysis or Organizational Life." *Calif. mgt, rev.*, 1962. 5:No. 2.

Blauner, Robert. *Work Satisfaction and Industrial Trends in Modern Society.* Berkeley 4, Calif.: Institute of Industrial Relations, 1960.

Blood, R. O. and Hamblin, R. L. "The Effect of the Wife's Employment in the Family Power Structure." *Social Forces,* 1958. XXXVI:347:352.

Blumenbach, J. F. *De Generis Nativa Humani Varietate.* Göttingen, 1775.

Bogardus, E. S. "Changes in Racial Distances." *International Journal of Opinion and Attitude Research,* 1947. I:58–64.

———. *Immigration and Race Attitudes.* Boston: Heath, 1928.

———. "Measuring Social Distance." *J. appl. soc. Psychol.* 1925, IX:299–308.

Bogart, Leo. *The Age of Television.* New York: Frederick Ungar, 1956.

Boldt, W. J. and Stroud, J. B. "Changes in the Attitudes of College Students." *J. educ. Psychol.*, 1934. XXV:611–619.

Bonner, Hubert. *Social Psychology.* New York: American Book Co., 1953.

Bonney, M. E. "A Study of Social Status on the Second-Grade Level." *J. genet. Psychol.*, 1942. LX:271–305.

Bovard, E. W. Jr. "Clinical Insight as a Function of Group Process. *J. abn. soc. Psychol.*, 1952. XL:534–599.

———. "The Experimental Production of Inter-Personal Effect." *J. abn. soc. Psychol.*, 1951. XLVI:521–528.

———. "Social Norms and the Individual." *J. abn. soc. Psychol.*, 1948: XLIII: 62–69.

Bowlby, J., Cantab, J. "Maternal Deprivation." *J. ment. sci.*, 1953. XCIX:265–272.

Bradburn, N. M. *In Pursuit of Happiness.* New York: John Wiley, 1958.

Bradburn, Norman M., *In Pursuit of Happiness.* Chicago: University of Chicago, National Opinion Research Center, 1963.

Bradford, L. P., Gibb, J. R., Benne, K. D. *T-Group Theory and Laboratory Method.* N.Y. Wiley & Sons, 1964.

Brayfield, A. H., Wells, R. V., and Strate, M. W. "Interrelationships among Measures of Job Satisfaction and General Satisfaction." *J. appl. Psychol.*, 1957, XLI:4.

Breslaw, B. J. *The Development of a Socio-Economic Attitude.* Arch. Psychol., N.Y. No. 226, 1938.

Brickell, H. M. *Commissioner's 1961 Catalog of Educational Change.* Albany: N.Y. State Educ. Dept., 1961.

———. "State Organization for Educational Change." In Miles, M. (ed.). *Innovation in education.* N.Y., T.C., Columbus Univ. Bur. Publ., 1964, Ch. 20.

568

Brickner, R. M. *Is Germany Incurable?* Philadelphia: J. B. Lippincott, 1943.

Britt, Stuart H. *Social Psychology of Modern Life.* New York: Rinehart, 1949.

Brodbeck, J. Nogee, P., DiMascio, A. "Two Kinds of Conformity: A Study of the Riesman Typology Applied to Standards of Parental Discipline." *J. Psychol.,* 1956. XLI:23–45.

Bronfenbrenner, U. *Socialization and Social Class through Time and Space.* In Maccoby, E. E., Newcomb, T. M., & Hartley, E. L. (ed.). *Readings in Social Psychology.* New York: Holt, 1958. pp. 400–425.

Brontë, Charlotte. *Shirley.* London: Downey, The Thornton Edition of the Novels of the Sisters Brontë. 2 Vol., 1899.

Brooks, Earl. "What Successful Executives Do." *Personnel,* 1955. XXXII:210–255.

Brophy, I. N. "The Luxury of anti-Negro Prejudice." *Public Opinion Quarterly,* 1946. IX:456–466.

Brown, R. L. "Wrapper Influence on the Perception of Freshness in Bread." *J. appl. Psychol.,* 1958. XLII:257–260.

Brown, Roger. *Words and Things: An Introduction to Language.* Glencoe: The Free Press, 1958.

Buber, Martin, *Between Man and Man.* Boston: Beacon Press, 1955. English translation first printed in England by Macmillan, 1947. pp. 19–20.

Buchanan, Paul. *Evaluating the Effectiveness of Laboratory Training in Industry,* paper presented at Amer. Mgt. Assn. (N.Y.) seminar, 1964.

——. "Evaluating the Effectiveness of Management Training in Industry." Washington, D.C.: Natl. Training Labs., N.E.A., *Explorations in Research,* 1965.

——. *Organizational Development Following Major Retrenchment.* Mimeograph, 1964.

Bunker, D. R. *The Effect of Laboratory Training upon Individual Behavior,* Prepublication draft, 1963.

——. "Individual Applications of Laboratory Training." *J. appl. behav. Sci.,* 1965, I:131–148.

Bureau of Applied Social Research. *Effects of the Movie "Naples is a Battlefield,"* Mimeo. New York: Columbia University, 1944.

Bureau of Applied Social Research. *The Effects of Oil Progress Week, 1952.* New York: Bureau of Applied Social Research, Columbia University, 1954.

Burgess, E. W. and Cottrell, L. S. Jr. *Predicting Success or Failure in Marriage.* New York: Prentice-Hall, 1939.

Burt, Cynl. *The Young Delinquent.* New York: Appleton, 1925.

Busbee, Frank A. "Social Organizations in a small city." *Am. J. Sociol.* 1945. LI:217–226.

Bushnel, John. "Student Culture at Vassar." In Sanford, N. (ed.). *The American College.* New York: Wiley, 1962.

Byrns, R., Henmon, V. A. C. "Parental Occupation and Mental Ability." *J. educ. Psychol.* 1936. XXVII:284–291.

Cairns, Grace E. *Philosophies of History: Meeting of East and West in Cycle Pattern Theories.* New York: Philosophical Library, 1962.

Campbell, A. A. "Factors Associated with Attitudes toward Jews." In Newcomb, T. M. and Hartley, E. L. (eds.). *Readings in Social Psychology.* New York: Holt, 1947, pp. 518–527.

Campbell, D. T. and McCandless, B. R. "Ethnocentrism, Xenophobia and Personality." *Hum. rela.,* 1951, IV:185–192.

Campbell, E. Q., Pettigrew, T. F. "Racial and Moral Crisis: the Role of Little Rock Ministers." *Am. J. Sociol.,* 1959. LXIV:509–516.

Campbell, J. D., Radke-Yarrow, M. "Personal and Situational Variables in Adaptation to Change." *J. soc. Issues,* 1958, XIV:3–7, 29–46.

Campbell, E. W. "Can World-Mindedness Be Influenced by Incidental Teaching?" *J. Geog.,* 1934. XXXIII:266–271.

Cannell, C. F., MacDonald, J. C. "The Impact of Health News on Attitude and Behavior." *Journalism Quart.,* 1956. 315–323.

Canning, R. R., and Baker, J. M. "Effect of the Group on Authoritarian and non-authoritarian persons." *Am. J. Sociol.,* 1959. LXIV:579–581.

Cannon, W. B. *The Wisdom of the Body.* New York: Norton, 1932.

Cantril, H. "America Faces the War." *Public Opinion Quarterly,* 1940. IV:387–407.

———. "A Comparative Study of Radio and Face-to-Face Stimulus Situations." *J. soc. Psychol.,* 1937, VIII:443–458.

———. *Gauging Public Opinion.* Princeton University Press, 1944.

———. "Identification with Social and Economic Class." *J. abn. soc. Psychol.,* 1943. XXXVIII:74–80.

———. "The Intensity of an Attitude." *J. abn. soc. Psychol.,* 1946. XLI:129–136.

———. *Invasion from Mars.* Princeton University Press, 1940.

———. "The Prediction of Social events." *J. abn. soc. Psychol.,* 1938. XXXIII:364–389.

———. "Public Opinion in Flux." *Annals Amer. acad. polit. soc. Sci.,* 1942. CCXX:136–152.

Cantril, H., and Allport, G. W. *Psychology of Radio.* New York: Harper and Bros., 1935.

Caplow, T., Forman, R. "Neighborhood Interaction in a Homogeneous Community." *Am. sociol. Rev.,* 1950. XV:357–366.

Caplow, T. and McGee, R. J. *The Academic Marketplace.* New York: Basic books, 1958.

Carlson, R. O. "School Superintendents and Adoption of Modern Math." In Miles, M. (ed.). *Innovation in Education,* New York: Teachers College, Columbia University, Bureau Publ., 1964. Ch. 14.

Carney, S. M. "A Study of Girl Gangs." *Mind and Body,* 1927. XXXIV:111–119.

Carroll, J. B. and Casagrande, J. B. "The Function of Language Classifications in Behavior." In Maccoby, Newcomb, Hartley, *Readings in Social Psychology.* New York: Holt, 3d ed., 1958, pp. 18–31.

Carter, L., Hawthorn, W., Shriver, B., Lanzetta, J. "The Behavior of Leaders and Other Group Members." *J. abn. soc. Psychol.,* 1951. XLVI:589–595.

Cassirer, Ernst. *The Myth of The State.* New Haven: Yale University Press, 1946. Reprinted, Doubleday, 1955.

Cattell, R. B. "The Concept of Social Status." *J. soc. Psychol.,* 1942, XV:293–308.

Centers, R. "Attitude and Belief in Relation to Occupational Stratification." *J. soc. Psychol.,* 1938. XXVII:159–185.

———. "Occupational Mobility of Urban Occupational Strata." *Amer. social Rev.,* 1948. XIII:197–203.

570

Centers, R. *The psychology of social classes*, Princeton, Princeton Univ. Press, 1949, pp. 244.

Chamberlain, Houston S. *Rasse und Personlichkeit*. Munich: F. Bruckmann, 1925.

Chang Tung-sun. "A Chinese Philosopher's Theory of Knowledge." *Yenching j. of Social Studies*, 1939. Reprinted in ETC, 1952. IX:203–221.

Chant, S. "Measuring Factors that Make a Job Interesting." *Personnel J.*, 1932, XI:1–4.

Chapple, E. D. and Arensberg, C. M. "Measuring Human Relations: an Introduction to the Study of the Interaction of Individuals." *Genet. Psychol. Monogr.* 1940. XXII:3–147.

Charters, W. W. Jr., Newcomb, T. M. "Some Attitudinal Effects of Experimentally Increased Patience of a Membership Group." In Swanson, G. E., Newcomb, T. M., and Hartley, E. L. *Readings in Social Psychology*. New York: Holt, 1952 (2d ed.), pp. 415–419.

Chen, W. K. C. "The Influence of Oral Propaganda Material upon Students' Attitudes." *Arch. Psychol.*, 1933. XXIII, No. 150.

———. "Retention of the Effect of Oral Propaganda." *J. soc. Psychol.*, 1936. VII:479–483.

Cherrington, B. M. *Methods of Education in International Attitudes*. New York: Teachers College, Columbia University, Bureau of Publications, 1934.

Child, Irwin L. *Italian or American? The Second Generation in Conflict*. New Haven: Yale University Press, 1943.

Chowdry, K., Newcomb, T. M. "The Relative Ability of Leaders and Non-Leaders to Estimate Opinions of Their Own Groups." *J. abn. soc. Psychol.*, 1952. XLVII:51–57.

Christie, R. and Cook, P. "A Guide to Published Literature Relating to the Authoritarian Personality through 1956." *J. Psychol.*, 1958. XLV:171–200.

Christie, R., Hanel, J., Seidenberg, B. "Is the F-Scale Irreversible?" *J. abn. soc. Psychol.*, 1958. LVI:143–159.

Citron, H. F. & Harding, J. "An Experiment in Training Volunteers to Answer Anti-Minority Remarks." *J. abn. soc. Psychol.*, 1950. XLV:310–328.

Clark, E. T. *The Small Sects in America*. New York: Abingdon Press, 1949.

Clark, Grenville and Sohn, Louis B. *World Peace Through World Law*. Cambridge: Harvard University Press, 2d Ed. Rev., 1960.

Clark, H. F. & Sloan, H. S. *Classrooms in the Factories*. Rutherford, New Jersey: Fairleigh Dickinson University, 1958.

Clark, H. F., Sloan, H. S. *Classrooms in the Stores*. Sweet Springs, Mo.: Roxbury Press, 1962.

Clark, K. B. and M. P. "Racial Identification and Preference in Negro Children." In Newcomb, T. & Hartley, E. (ed.). *Readings in Social Psychology*. New York: Holt, 1947. pp. 169–178.

Clark, R. A. *et al. Leadership in Rifle Squads on the Korean Front line*, HRRO *Technical Report* 21. Sept. 1955. Reproduced by Document Service Center, Dayton, O.

Cloward, R. A. & Ohlin, Lloyd E. *Delinquency and Opportunity.* Glencoe: Free Press, 1960.

Coch, Lester, French, J. R. P. "Overcoming Resistance to Change." *Hum. rela.,* 1948, I:512–532.

Coffin, T. E. *Television's Effect on Buying.* Hempstead, New York: Hofstra College, 1950.

Cogley, John. *Report on Blacklisting: Radio-Television.* Santa Barbara, Calif.: Fund for the Republic, 1956.

Cohen, Albert K. *Delinquent Boys: the Culture of the Gang.* Glencoe: Free Press, 1955.

Cohen, A. R. "Experimental Effects of Ego-Defense Preference in Interpersonal Relations." *J. abn. soc. Psychol.,* 1956. LII:19–27.

Commager, Henry Steele. "The New Community of Learning." *New School Bulletin,* 1955. XII, No. 34.

Commission on Freedom of the Press. *A Free and Responsible Press.* Chicago: University of Chicago Press, 1947.

Comte, August. *The Positive Philosophy.* Original edition in France, 1830. Translated, London, Trubner & Co., 1853.

Conant, J. B. *Slums and suburbs.* New York: McGraw-Hill, 1961.

Connolly, Cyril. "Palinurus". *The Unquiet Grave.* New York: Viking Press, 1945. Compass Books Edition, 1957. p. 54.

Conradi, E. "Song and Call Notes of English Sparrows When Reared by Canaries." *Amer. J. Psychol.,* 1905. XVI:190–199.

Cook, L. A. "An Experimental Sociographic Study of a Stratified 10th-grade class." *Amer. sociol. Rev.,* 1945. X:250–261.

Cooley, C. H. *Human Nature and the Social Order.* New York: Scribners, 1902.

———. *Social organization.* New York: Scribners, 1912.

Corey, S. M. *Helping Other People Change.* Columbus, Ohio: Ohio State University Press, 1963.

Council on Foreign Relations. *The United States and China in World Affairs.* New York: 1964.

Cox, C. M. *The Early Mental Traits of Three Hundred Geniuses.* Stanford University Press, 1926.

———. "Genetic Studies of Genius." Vol. II. *The Early Mental Traits of Three Hundred Geniuses.* Stanford (Cal.) University Press, 1926.

Crosland, C. A. R. "What Does the Worker Want?" *Encounter.* 1959, XII: 10–17.

Culbertson, F. M. "Modification of an Emotionally Held Attitude through Role-Playing." *J. abn. soc. Psychol.,* 1957. LIV:230–233.

Dashiell, J. F. "An Experimental Analysis of Some Group Effects." *J. abn. soc. Psychol.,* 1930. XXV:190–199.

———. "Experimental Studies of the Influence of Social Situations on the Behavior of Individual Human Adults." In Mierchison, C. (ed.). *Handbook of Social Psychology.* Worcester: Clark University Press, 1935, pp. 1097–1158.

Davidoff, I. F., Markewich, M. E. *The Post-Parental Phase in the Life-Cycle of Fifty College-Educated Women.* Unpublished Doctoral thesis. New York: Teachers College, Columbia University, 1961.

Davidson, H. & Kruglou, L. "Some Background Correlates of Personality and social attitudes." *J. soc. Psychol.,* 1953. XXXVIII:233–240.

Davis, Allison. *Adolescence.* In 43d Yearbook, Natl. Soc. Study Ed. Chicago: 1944, Ch. 11.

Davis, Allison. *Social Class Influences upon Learning.* Cambridge, Mass.: Harvard University Press, 1950. pp. 23; 34; 45.

Davis, Allison, Gardner, B. B. & Gardner, May R. *Deep South.* Chicago: University of Chicago Press, 1941.

Davis, A. & Havighurst, R. J. "Social Class and Color Differences in Child-rearing." *Amer. Sociol. Rev.,* 1948. XI:698–710.

Davis, Jerome. "Study of 163 Outstanding Communist Leaders." *Proc. Amer. Sociol. Soc.,* 1930. XXIV:42–55.

Davis, L. E., Werling, R. "Job Design Factors." *Occup. Psychol.,* 1960. XXXIV: 109–132.

Davis, Morris. "Community Attitudes Toward Fluoridation." *Pub. opin. quart.,* 1959. XXIII:474–482.

Davitz, J. R. and Davitz, L. J. "The Communication of Feelings by Content-Free Speech." *J. Communica.,* March, 1959. IX, pp. 6–13.

Day, R. C., Hamblin, R. L. *Some Effects of Close and Punitive Styles of Supervision.* St. Louis: Washington University, 1961.

DeCrow, R., Kolben, K. (eds.). *Continuing Education for Adults.* Chicago: Center for the Study of Liberal Education for Adults, No. 32. March 31, 1963.

deGrazia, A. "Elements of Social Invention." *Amer. behav. Sci.,* 1961. V:6–9.

Dennis, Wayne. "Use of Common Objects as Indicators of Cultural Orientation." *J. abn. soc. Psychol.,* 1957. LV:21–28.

de Tocqueville Alexis. C.H.M.C. *De la democratie en Amerique.* Paris: 1835–40. 4 Vol. Revised and republished, New York: Knopf, 1945. Ref. to Bk. II Ch. 5, pp. 106; 110; 122–3, 179–80.

———. *The State of Society in France before the Revolution of 1789.* 3d Ed. London: John Murray, 1868.

Deutsch, M. "An Experimental Study of the Effects of Cooperation and Competition upon Group Process." *Hum. rela.,* 1949. II:199–231.

———. "Field Theory in Social Psychology." In Lindzey, G. (ed.). *Handbook of Social Psychology.* Cambridge, Mass.: 1954. Vol. I. Ch. 5.

———. "Trust, Trustworthiness and the F-Scale." *J. abn. soc. Psychol.,* 1960. LXI:138–140.

Deutsch, M. and Collins, M. E. *Interracial Housing: a Psychological Evaluation of a Social Experiment.* Minneapolis: University of Minnesota Press, 1951.

Deutsch, M. and Gerard, H. B. "A Study of Normative and Informational Social Influences upon Individual Judgment." *J. abn. soc. Psychol.,* 1955, LI:629–636.

Deutsch, Morton, Krauss, R. M. "The Effect of Threat upon Interpersonal Bargaining." *J. abn. soc. Psychol.,* 1960. LXI:181–190.

Deutsch, M. and Solomon, L. "Reactions to Evaluations of Others as Influenced by Self-Evaluations." *Sociometry,* 1959. XXII:93–112.

DeVox, George. "A Quantitative Rorschach Assessment of Maladjustment and Rigidity in Acculturating Japanese Americans." *Genet. Psychol. Monogr.,* 1955. LII:31–87.

DeVox, Geo. and Wagatsuma, H. "Psychocultural Significance of Concern over Death and Illness among Rural Japanese." *Int. j. social Psychiatry,* 1959. V:5–19.

Dewey, John. *How We Think.* Boston: D. C. Heath, 1910.

———. *Human Nature and Conduct.* New York: Holt, 1922. p. 293.

———. "Psychology and Social Practice." *Psychol. Rev.,* 1900, VII:105–124.

Dexter, E. S. "Personality Traits Related to Conservatism and Radicalism." *Character and Personality,* 1939. VII:230–237.

Diaz, Carmen V. *A Study of the Ability of Eleventh-Grade Girls to Apply the Principles of the Moral Law to Actual and Hypothetical Life Situations.* Ph.D. dissertation. New York: Fordham University, 1952.

Dichter, Ernst. "Understanding the New Consumer." *Mgt. Rev.,* 1956. XLV: 457–9.

Dimock, Hedley S. and Sorenson, Roy. *Designing Education in Values: a Case Study in Institutional Change.* New York: Association Press, 1955.

Distenfeld, Joy. *Perceived Sex-Role Differences in Men and Women.* Ph.D. thesis, 1964.

Dodd, S. C. "A Social Distance Test in the Near East." *Amer. j. Sociol.,* 1935. XLI:194–204.

———. "Testing Message Diffusion in Controlled Experiments." *Amer. sociol. Rev.,* 1953. XVIII:410–416.

Dollard, John. *Fear in Battle.* New Haven: Yale University Press, 1943.

———. "Hostility and Fear in Social Life." *Soc. forces,* 1938. XVII:15–26.

Dollard, J., Doob, L. W., Miller, N. E., Mowrer, O. H. and Sears, R. R. *Frustration and Aggression.* New Haven: Yale University Press, 1939.

Dornbusch, S. M., Irie, R. D. "The Failure of Presbyterian Union." *Amer. J. Sociol.,* 1959. LXIV:352–5.

Douglass, Jos. H. "The Funeral of 'Sister President'," *J. abn. soc. Psychol.,* 1939. XLIV:217–223.

Dozier, Edward P. "The Hopi and the Tewa." *Sci. Amer.* 1957. CXCVI:126–136. "Resistance to Acculturation and Assimilation in an Indian Pueblo." *Am. Anthropol.,* 1951. LIII:56–66.

Driver, Helen I. and contributors. *Counseling and Learning through Small-Group Discussion.* Madison, Wis.: Monona Publications, 1958.

Droba, D. D. "Education and Negro Attitudes." *Sociol. & soc. Res.,* 1932. XVII:137–141.

Drucker, Peter. *The Practice of Management.* New York: Harper and Bros., 1954.

DuBois, Cora. *People of Alors,* Minneapolis, Minn., U. of Minn. Press, 1944.

Dubourg, Jacques. *French National Character.* Unpublished, mimeographed document. New York: Columbia University Dept. of Social Psychology, 1958.

Dunnette, M. D. "A Modified Model for Test Validation and Selection Research." *J. appl. Psychol.* 1963, XLVII:317–323.

Durkheim, E. L. *Suicide.* Paris: Alcan, 1897. English edition by Free Press of Glencoe, 1951.

Durkin, Helen E. *The Group in Depth.* New York: Internatl. University Press, 1964.

Eastman, D. *Self-Acceptance and Marital Happiness.* Unpublished doctoral dissertation. Teachers College, Columbia University, 1956.

Eckert, R. E., Mills, H. C. "International Attitudes and Related Academic and Social Factors." *J. ed. Sociol.*, 1935. IX:142–153.

Eddy, Elizabeth. *Attitudes Toward Desegregation among Southern Students on a Northern Campus.* Dissertation, Columbia University, 1961.

Edwards, A. L. and Kenney, K. C. "A Comparison of the Thurstone and Likert Techniques of Attitude Scale Instruction." *J. app. Psychol.*, 1946. XXX:72–83.

Edwards, A. L. and Kilpatrick, F. P. "A Technique for the Construction of Attitude Scales." *J. app. Psychol.*, 1948. XXXII:374–384.

Edwards, L. P. *The Natural History of Revolution.* Chicago: University of Chicago, 1927.

Efron, D. *Gesture and Environment.* New York: King's Crown Press, 1941.

Ehrlich, D., Guttman, J., Schonbach, P., and Mills, J. "Postdecision Exposure to Relevant Information." *J. Abnormal social Psychol.*, LIV, 98–102, 1957.

Eichholz, G. & Rogers, E. M. "Resistance to the Adoption of Audio-Visual aids by Elementary School Teachers." In Miles, M. (ed.). *Innovation in Education.* New York Columbia University Teachers College. Bur. Publ., 1964, Ch. 12.

Eisenhower, President Dwight. Speech quoted, *New Statesman and Nation,* April 25, 1953.

Eldersveld, S. J., Dodge, R. W. "Personal Contact or Mail Propaganda?" In Katz, D. *et al.* (eds.). *Public Opinion and Propaganda.* New York: Dryden Press, 1954. pp. 532–542.

Elkin, D. G. *Influence of Collective on Children's Ability to Reproduce Parts of their School Work.* Detski Kollective i Rebenok, 1926. 221–226.

Elliott, H. S. *The Process of Group Thinking.* New York: Association Press, 1928.

Emmerick, W. "A Study of Parental Identification in Young Children." *Amer. Psychol.*, 1954. 121–399.

Ends, E. J., Page, C. W. "A Study of Three Types of Group Psychotherapy with Hospitalized Male Inebriates." *Quart J. Studies Alcohol.* 1957. XVIII: 263–277.

Erickson, C. I., King, I. "A Comparison of Visual and Oral Presentation." *Sch. & Soc.*, Aug. 4, 1917, VI:146–8.

Escalona, S. K. "Feeding Disturbances in Very Young Children." *Amer. J. Orthopsychiat.*, 1945. XV:76–80.

Etzioni, A. *The Hard Way to Peace.* New York: Collier Books, 1962.

Ewing, T. H. "A Study of Certain Factors Involved in Changes of Opinion." *J. soc. Psychol.*, 1942. XVI:63–88.

Farnsworth, P. R. "Seat Preference in the Classroom." *J. Soc. Psychol.*, 1933. IV;373–376.

Faunce, D. & Beigle, J. A. "Cleavages in a Relatively Homogeneous Group of Rural Youths: an Experiment in the Use of Sociometry in Attaining and Measuring Integration." *Sociometry,* 1948. XI:201–216.

Fäy, Bernard. *Benjamin Franklin: the Apostle of Modern Times.* Boston: Little, Brown and Co., 1929.

Federal Council of Churches. Information Service, Dept. of Research, *Federal Council of Churches.* May 15, 1948, Vol. XXVII, No. 20, Part 2.

Feldman, H. *Problems in Labor Relations.* New York: Macmillan, 1937.

Ferguson, C. K. and Kelly, H. H. "Significant Factors in Overevaluation of Own-Group's Product." *J. abn. soc. Psychol.* 1964, LXIX:223–228.

Ferguson, L. W. "Industrial Psychology." In Farnsworth, P. R. and McNeman, Q. (eds.). *Annual Review of Psychology.* Palo Alto, Calif.: 1958, p. 253.

Ferguson, L. W., Wallace, S. R. Jr., and Zelle, R. K. "Selection and Turnover." *Personnel J.,* 1959. XXXVII:376–8.

Festinger, Leon. *A Theory of Cognitive Dissonance.* Evanston, Ill.: Row, Peterson & Co., 1957.

———. "A Theory of Social Comparison Processes." *Hum. Rela.,* 1954. VII: 117–140.

Festinger, L., Cartwright, D. *et al.* "A Study of a Rumor." *Hum. Rela.,* 1948. I:464–486.

Festinger, L., Shachter, S. and Bach, K. *Social Pressures in Informal Groups: a Study of Human Factors in Housing.* New York: Harper & Bros., 1950.

Festinger, L., Thibaut, John. "Interpersonal Communication in Groups." *J. abn. soc. Psychol.,* 1951. XLVI:92–99.

Fiedler, F. E. "A comparison of Therapeutic Relationships in Psychoanalytic, Nondirective, and Adlerian Therapy." *J. Consult. Psychol.,* 1950. XIV, 436–445.

———. "The Concept of an Ideal Therapeutic Relationship." *J. consult. Psychol.,* 1950. XVI, 237–45. also: "A Comparison of Therapeutic Relationships," *J. consult. Psychol.,* 1950. XIV:436–45.

———. "The Influences of Leader-Keyman Relations to Combat Crew Effectiveness." *J. abn. soc. Psychol.,* 1955. LI:227–235.

———. "A Note on Leadership Theory: the Effect of Social Barriers between Leaders and Followers." *Sociometry,* 1957. XX:87–94.

Fisher, C. & Paul, I. H. "The Effect of Subliminal Visual Stimulation on Imagery and Dreams." *J. Amer. Psychoanalytic Assn.,* 1959. VII:35–83.

Fitts, Paul M. "Engineering Psychology." In Farnsworth, P. R. and McNeman, Quinn (eds.). *Annual Review of Psychology,* 1958. Palo Alto, Calif.: Annual Reviews, Inc., Vol. IX, pp. 267–294.

Fleishman, E. A. "The Description of Supervisory Behavior." *J. appl. Psychol.,* 1953. XXVII:1–6.

Fleishman, E. A. *et al. Training in Human Relations.* Ann Arbor, Mich.: Foundation for Research on Human Behavior, 1954.

Fleishman, E. A., Harris, E. F. "Patterns of Leadership Behavior Related to Employee Grievances and Turnover." *Personnel Psychol.,* 1962. XV: 43–56.

Fleishman, E. A., Harris, E. F. and Burtt, H. E. *Leadership and Supervision in industry,* Columbus, O.: Ohio State University Bureau Educ. Res., 1955.

Fletcher, J. M. "The Verdict of Psychologists on War Instincts." *Sci. Monthly,* 1932. XXXV:142–145.

Flowers, M. *Young America in Revolution,* World Work, 1927. LIV:273–280.

Ford, C. S. & Beach, F. A. *Patterns of Sexual Behavior.* New York: Harper and Bros., 1951.

Foshay, A. W. "The Teacher and Children's Social Attitudes." *Teachers College Record,* 1951. Vol. LII, pp. 287–296.

Fouriezos, N. T., Hutt, M. L., Guetzkow, H. "Measurement of Self-Oriented Needs in Discussion Groups." *J. abn. soc. Psychol.,* 1950. XLV:682–690.

Fox, David. *The Effect of Increasing the Available Time for Problem-Solving on the Relative Quality of Decisions Written by Individuals and by Groups.* Ph.D. thesis. New York: Teachers College, Columbia University, 1955.

Frank, Jerome E. "World Tensions and Disarmament." *T. C. Record,* 1962. LX: 458 ff.

Freeman, G. L. & Taylor, E. K. *How to Pick Leaders.* New York: Funk & Wagnalls, 1950.

Freeman, H. E., Weeks, H. A., Wertheimer, W. I. "News Commentator Effect." *Publ. opin. quart.,* 1955, XIX:209–215.

French, J. R. P. "The Disruption and Cohesion of Groups." *J. abn. soc. Psychol.,* 1941. XXXVI:361–377.

French, J. R. P. *et al.* "An Experiment on Participation in a Norwegian Factory." *Hum, rela.,* 1960. XIII:3–19.

French, J. R. P. Jr. "Retraining an Autocratic Leader." *J. abn. soc. Psychol.,* 1944. XXXIX:1–14.

Freud, S. *The Future of an Illusion.* New York: Liveright, 1949.

———. *Group Psychology and the Analysis of the Ego.* New York: Liveright, 1951. First published 1922. Quotations from pp. 14–25; also p. 40.

Friedan, Betty. *The Feminine Mystique.* New York: W. W. Norton, 1963.

Friedrichs, R. W. "Christians and Residential Exclusion." *J. soc. Issues,* 1959. XV:14–23.

Fromm, Erich. *Escape from Freedom.* New York: Rinehart, 1941.

———. *Man for Himself.* New York: Rinehart, 1947.

———. "Man Is Not a Thing." *Saturday Review.* Mar. 16, 1957, p. 10.

———. *Psychoanalysis and Religion.* New Haven: Yale University Press, 1950.

———. *The Sane Society.* New York: Rinehart, 1955.

Galtung, Johan. "Foreign Policy as a Function of Social Position." *Journal of Peace Research.* 1964, No. 4.

Gardiner, I. C. "Effect of a Group of Social Stimuli upon Attitudes." *J. educ. Psychol.* 1935. XXVI:471–479.

Gardner, Burleigh. *Human Relations in Industry.* Chicago: R. D. Irwin, 1946.

Gardner, B. B. "What Makes Successful and Unsuccessful Executives?" *Adv. mgmt.,* 1948. XIII:116–125.

Gesell, Arnold. *Wolf Child and Human Child.* New York: Harper & Bros., 1940.

Gesell, A. & Lord, E. E. "Psychological Comparison of Nursery School Children from Homes of Low and High Economic Status." *J. Genet Psychol.,* 1929. XXIV:554–557.

Gibb, J. R. *Factors Producing Defensive Behavior within Groups.* Boulder:

Colorado: University of Colorado, Human Relations Laboratory, Technical report, Feb. 15, 1955.

Gibb, J. and Allen, J. M. *Experimental Comparison of Two Methods of Management Training,* pending publication.

Gilbert, G. M. "Stereotype Persistence and Change among College Students." *J. abn. soc. Psychol.,* 1951. XLVI:245–254.

Gilbert, G. M. "A Survey of 'Referral Problems' in Metropolitan Child Guidance Centers." *J. clin. Psychol.,* 1957. XIII:37–40.

Gilbert, W. S. *The Mikado.* New York: Modern Library, Random House, Inc., pp. 12–13.

Gold, Martin. "Power in the Classroom." *Sociometry,* 1958. XXI:50–60.

Glaser, E. M. *An Experiment in the Development of Critical Thinking.* New York: Teachers College, Columbia University, 1941.

Goetsch, Helen B. "Inequality of College Opportunity." *J. of N.E.A.,* 1939. XXVIII:271.

Goldman-Eisler, Frieda. "Breast-feeding and Character Formation." In Kluckhohn, C., Murray, H. A. & Schnerter, D. M. *Personality.* New York: Knopf, 1953. pp. 146–184.

Goodacre, Daniel M. (III) "The Use of a Sociometric Test as a Predictor of Combat Unit Effectiveness." *Sociometry,* 1951. XIV:148–152.

Goodman, Paul. *Growing Up Absurd.* New York: Random House, 1960.

Gorden, R. L. "Interaction between Attitude and the Definition of the Situation in the Expression of Opinion." *Amer. sociol. Rev.,* 1952, XVII:50–58.

Gordon, K. "Group Judgments in the Field of Lifted Weights." *J. exper. Psychol.,* 1924. 398–400.

Gorer, Geoffrey. *The American People.* New York: W. W. Norton & Co., 1964, revised.

———. *Exploring English Character.* New York: Criterion Books, 1955.

———. "Themes in Japanese Culture." New York: *Trans. N. Y. Acad. Sciences,* 1943, Ser. 2, V:106–124.

Gorer, G. and Richman, J. *The People of Great Russia.* London: Grosset Press, 1949.

Gorlow, L., Hoch, E. L., Telschow, E. F. *The Nature of Non-Directive Group Psychotherapy.* New York: Teachers College, Columbia University Bureau of Publications, 1952.

Gowan, J. C. "The Underachieving Gifted Child." *Excep. Child,* 1955. XXI:247–249, 270–271.

Gowin, E. B. *The Executive and His Control of Men.* New York: Macmillan, 1915.

Grace, Harry A., Neuhaus, J. O. "Information and Social Distance as Predictors of Hostility toward Nations." *J. abn. soc. Psychol.,* 1952. XLVII:540–545.

Graham, S. R. *The Influence of Therapist Character Structure upon Rorschach Changes in the Course of Psychotherapy.* Report to American Psychological Assn., Sept. 2, 1960.

Grant, Madison. *The Passing of the Great Race.* New York: Scribner, 1916.

Green, Arnold W. "The Middle-Class Male Child and Neurosis." *Amer. sociol. Rev.,* 1955. XX:438–442.

Green, Meredith W. *Interrelationships of Attitude and Information.* Unpublished doctoral dissertation. New York: Teachers College, Columbia University, 1952.

Greenacre, Phyllis. "Child Wife as Ideal." *Amer. j. Orthopsychiat.*, 1947, XVII: 167–171.

Greening T. C. "Planning for Change." *J. Amer. Hosp. Assn.*, 1963, XXXVII: 26–30.

Griffith, C. R. *General Introduction to Psychology.* New York: Macmillan, 1923, rev. 1928.

Griffiths, D. E. "Administrative Theory and Change in Organizations." In Miles, M. (ed.). *Innovation in Education.* New York Teachers College, Columbia University Bureau Publ., 1964, Ch. 18.

Grosser, D., Polarisky, N. & Lippitt, R. "A Laboratory Study of Behavioral Contagion." *Hum. Rela.*, 1951. IV:115–142.

Guest, Robert H. *Organizational Change: the Effect of Successful Leadership.* Homewood, Ill.: Dorsey Press, 1962.

Guetzkow, H. *Organizational Development and Restrictions in Communication.* Pittsburgh, Pa.: Carnegie Institute of Technology, 1954.

Gump, P. V. "Anti-democratic Trends and Student Reaction to President Truman's Dismissal of Gen. MacArthur." *J. soc. Psychol.*, 1953. XXXVIII: 131–135.

Gurin, G., Veroff, J., Feld, S. *Americans View Their Mental Health.* New York: Basic Books, 1960.

Gurnee, H. "A Comparison of Collective and Individual Judgment of Facts." *J. exp. Psychol.*, 1937. XXI:106–112.

––––. "Maze Learning in the Collective Situation." *J. Psychol.*, 1937. III:437–443.

Guttmann, L. "A Basis for Scaling Qualitative Data." *Amer. sociol. Rev.*, 1944. IX:139–150.

Habbe, S. "Does Communication Make a Difference?" *Mgmt. Rec.*, 1952. XIV: 414–416; 442–444.

Hacker, Helen M. "The New Burdens of Masculinity." *Marriage and Family Living*, 1957. XIX:227–233.

Haldane, J. B. S. *What Is Life?* New York: Boni and Gaer, 1947.

Halkides, G. "An Experimental Study of Four Conditions Necessary for Therapeutic Change." Cited by Rogers in Bennis, *et al., Interpersonal Dynamics.* Homewood, Ill.: Dorsey Press, 1964. pp. 317–318.

Hall, W. *The Effect of Defined Stimulus Material upon the Stability of Attitudes toward Labor Unions, Capital Punishment, Social Insurance and Negroes.* Stud. Higher Educ., Purdue University, 1938, No. 34:1–19.

Hallowell, A. I. "The Use of Projective Techniques in the Study of the Socio-Psychological Aspects of Acculturation." *J. projective techniques,* 1951, XV:27–44.

Halpin, A. W. "The Leader Behavior and Effectiveness of Aircraft Commanders. In Stogdill, R. M. & Coons, H. E. (eds.). *Leader Behavior: Its Description & Measurement.* Columbus, O.: Ohio State University Bur. Bus. Res., Monogr., 88, 1957.

––––. "The Leader Behavior and Leadership Ideology of Educational Administrators and Aircraft Commanders." *Harvard Educational Review,* 1955, XXXIX:82–84.

Halpin, A. W., Winer, B. J. "A Factorial Study of the Leader Behavior Descriptions." In Stogdill, R. M. & Coons, H. E. (eds.). *Leader Behavior,* Bur. Bus. Res. Monogr. 88. Columbus Ohio: Ohio State University, 1957.

Hamblin, Robert L. "Group Integration during a Crisis." *Human Relations,* 1958, XI:67–76.

Hamilton, G. V. *A Research in Marriage.* New York: Albert & Charles Boni, 1929.

Harding, John (ed.). "Intergroup Contact and Social Attitudes." *J. soc. Issues,* 1952. VIII:1–72.

Harding, J. & Hogrefe, R. "Attitudes of White Department Store Employees toward Negro Co-workers." *J. soc. Issues,* 1952. VIII:18–28.

Hare, A. P. "Interaction and Consensus in Different Sized Groups." *Amer. Sociol. Rev.,* 1952. XVII:261–267.

———. "Small-group Discussions with Participatory and Supervisory Leadership." *J. abn. soc. Psychol.,* 1953. XLVIII:273–275.

Haring, D. G. "Japanese National Character: Cultural Anthropology, Psychoanalysis, and History." *Yale Rev.,* 1953, XLII:375–92.

Harlow, H. F. "The Nature of Love." *Amer. Psychol.,* 1958, XIII:673–685.

Harper, H. R. *What European and American Students Think on International Problems.* New York: Teachers College, Columbia University, Bur. Publ., 1931.

Harper, M. H. *Social Beliefs and Attitudes of American Educators,* N. Y. Teach. Coll. Contrib. to Ed., 1927, No. 294.

Harris, A. J., Remmers, H. H., Ellison, C. E. "The Relation between Liberal and Conservative Attitudes in College Students and Other Factors." *J. soc. Psychol.,* 1932. III:320–336.

Harrison, Roger. "The Impact of the Laboratory on Perception of Others by the Experimental Group." In Argyris, C. *Interpersonal Competence and Organizational Effectiveness.* Homewood, Ill.: Irwin Dorsey, 1962.

Hart, Hornell. Personality and the family. *Marriage Hyg.,* 1935. I:361–370.

Hartley, E. L. *Problems in Prejudice,* N. Y. Kings Crown Press, 1946.

Hartley, E. L. and R. E. *Fundamentals of Social Psychology,* N. Y. Knopf, 1952, p. 391–2.

Hartley, Ruth E. "Children's Concepts of Male and Female Roles." *Merrill Palmer Quart.,* 1960, VI:83–91.

Hartley, Ruth E. "Sex-role Pressures and the Socialization of the Male Child." *Psych. repts.,* 1959, V:457–468.

Hartley, Ruth E. "Sex Roles and Urban Youth: Some Developmental Perspectives." *Bulletin on Family Development,* 1961. II:1–12.

Hartley, Ruth E. "Some Implications of Current Changes in Sex-Role Patterns." *Merrill Palmer Quarterly,* 1961.

Hartmann, George W. "A Field Experiment on the Comparative Effectiveness of 'Emotional' and 'Rational' Political Leaflets." *J. abn. soc. Psychol.,* 1936. XXXI:99–114.

Hartshorne, H. & May, M. *Studies in Deceit.* New York: Macmillan, 1928. pp. 248–253.

Hartshorne, H., May, M., and Shuttleworth, F. K. *Studies in the Organization of Character.* New York: Macmillan, 1930.

Hartmann, H., Kris, E. & Loewenstein, R. M. "Some Psychoanalytic Comments on 'Culture and Personality.' " In Wilbur, G. W. & Muensterberger, W. (eds.). *Psychoanalysis and Culture.* New York: International University Press, 1951. pp. 3–31.

Harvey, O. J. "An Experimental Approach to the Study of Status Relations in Informal Groups." *Amer. soc. Rev.,* 1953. XVIII:357–367.

Hayakawa, S. I. *Language in Action.* New York: Harcourt Brace, 1941.

———. "On Communication with the Soviet Union." *New York Times Magazine,* July 31, 1960.

———. *The Self-Image and Intercultural Understanding, or How to be Sane though Negro.* Address to Intl. Council of Women Psychologists, Sept. 3, 1959.

Hayes, Carlton J. H. *Nationalism: a Religion.* New York: Macmillan, 1960.

Haythorn, William. "The Influence of Individual Members on the Characteristics of Small Groups." *J. abn. soc. Psychol.,* 1953. XLVIII:276–284.

Head, S. W. "Content Analysis of TV Drama Programs." *Quart. Film, Radio, TV,* 1954. IX:175–194.

Hebb, D. D. *The Organization of Behavior.* New York: John Wiley & Sons, 1949, p. 114.

Heer, David M. "Sentiment of White Supremacy." *Amer. J. Sociol.,* 1951. LXIV: 592–8.

Hegel, G. W. F. *The Phenomenology of Mind* (first published in 1807). English translation. London: G. Allen and Unwin, 1910.

Heider, F. "Attitudes and Cognitive Organization." *J. Psychol.,* 1946. XXI:107–112.

———. *The Psychology of Interpersonal Relations.* New York: John Wiley & Sons, 1958. Ch. 7.

Heider, F. and Simmel, C. "A Study of Apparent Behavior." *Amer. J. Psychol.,* 1944. LVII:243–259.

Heilbroner, Robert L. *The Future as History.* New York: Harper, 1959, 1960.

Heise, G. A., Miller, G. A. "Problem-solving by Small Groups Using Various Communication Nets." *J. abn. soc. Psychol.,* 1951. XLVI:327–336.

Helfant, K. "Parents' Attitudes vs. Adolescent Hostility in the Determination of Adolescents' Socio-Political attitudes." *Psychol. Monogr.,* 1952. LXVI, No. 345.

Hemphill, J. K. "Aircrew Composition Research." *Eng. Exper. stat. news.* Ohio State University, 1952. XXIV:21–23.

———. "Relations between the Size of the Group and the Behavior of 'Superior' Leaders." *J. soc. Psychol.,* 1950, XXXII:11–22.

Hemphill, J. K., Pepinsky, P. N. *et al.* "An Investigation of the Relation between Possession of Task-Relevant Information and Attempts to Lead." Columbus O. *Personnel Res. Bd.,* Ohio State University, 1954.

Hemphill, J. K., Pepinsky, P. N., Shevitz, R. N., Jaynes, W. E., Christner, C. A. "The Relation Between Task-Relevant Information and Attempts to Lead." *Psychol. monogr.,* 1956, 70:1–24.

Hemphill, J., Griffiths, D. E., Frederiksen, N. *Administrative Performance and Personality.* New York: Teachers College, Columbia Univ. Bur. Publ., 1962.

Henry, W. E. "The Business Executive." *Amer. j. Sociol.*, 1949. LIV:286–291.

Herodotus. *History*. Trans. A. D. Godley, Loeb Classical Library, v. 78.

Hersey, R. *Zest for Work*. New York: Harper and Bros., 1955.

Herskovitz, M. J. *Man and His Works*. New York: Knopf, 1948.

Hertzler, J. O. "Crises and Dictatorships." *Amer. sociol. Rev.*, 1940. V:157–169.

Herzberg, F. *et al. Effects of Job Attitudes*. Psychol. Service, University of Pittsburgh, Rept. No. 3, 1955.

Herzberg, F. *et al. The Motivation to Work*. New York: Wiley, 1959.

Herzog, Elizabeth. *Children of Working Mothers*. Washington, D.C., Children's Bureau, Publ. 382, 1960.

Herzog, Herta. "What Do We Really Know about Daytime Serial Listeners?" In Lazarsfeld, P. F. & Stanton, F. N. (ed.). *Radio Research 1942–3*, New York: Duell, Sloan & Pearce, 1944.

Heyns, R. W. *Functional Analysis of Group Problems-Solving Behavior*. Ann Arbor, Mich. Psychol. Dept., University of Michigan, 1948. (Mimeographed)

Hicks, Granville. *Small Town*. New York: Macmillan, 1947.

Himelhoch, Jerome. *The Dynamics of Tolerance*. Ann Arbor, Michigan: University Microfilms, 1952.

Himmelweit, H. T. "A British Report." *J. soc. Issues*, 1962. XVIII:16–28.

———. Oppenheim, A. N., and Vince, P. *Television and the Child*. London and New York: Oxford University Press, 1958.

Hofstadter, Richard. "The Pseudo-Conservative Revolt." In Bell, D. (ed.). *The New American Right*. New York: Criterion Books, 1955, p. 46.

Hollingshead, A. B. *Elintown's Youth*. New York: John Wiley, 1949.

Hollingworth, H. L. *The Psychology of the Audience*. New York: American Book Co., 1935.

Hollingworth, L. M. *Children Above 180 I.Q.*, New York: World Book Co., 1942.

Homans, Geo. C. *The Human Group*. New York: Harcourt Brace, 1950.

Hook, Sidney. *The Hero in History*. New York: John Day, 1943.

Hoppock, R. *Job Satisfaction*. New York: Harper, 1935.

Hoppock, R., Spiegler, S. "Job Satisfaction: Researchers of 1935–7." *Occupations*, 1938. VI:636–639.

Horowitz, E. L. "Development of Attitude toward Negroes." *Arch. Psychol.*, 1936, No. 194.

Horowitz, E. L. and Horowitz, R. E. "Development of Social Attitudes in Children." *Sociometry*, 1939. pp. 301–338.

Horowitz, M. W., Lyons, J. & Perlmutter, H. V. "Induction of Forces in Discussion Groups." *Hum. Rela.*, 1951. IV:57–76.

Horowitz, M. W., Pastore, N. "Relationship of Motive to Author and Statement." *Science*, 1955. CXXI:110–111.

Hoult, T. F. *The Sociology of Religion*. New York: Dryden Press, 1958.

———. "Comic Books and Juvenile Delinquency." *Sociol. & soc. res.* 1949. XXXIII:279–284.

Houser, J. D. *What People Want from Business*. New York: McGraw-Hill, 1938.

Hovland, C. I. *et al. The Order of Presentation*. New Haven: Yale University Press, 1957.

Hovland, C. I., Janis, I. L. & Kelley, H. H. *Communication and Persuasion*. New Haven: Yale University Press, 1953.

582

Hovland, C. I., Lumsdaine, A. A. and Sheffield, F. D. "Studies in Social Psychology in World War II," Vol. III, *Experiments in Mass Communication.* Princeton, N. J.: Princeton University Press, 1949.

Hovland, C. I., & Mandell, W. "An Experimental Comparison of Conclusion-Drawing by the Communicator & by the audience." *J. abn. soc. Psychol.,* 1952, XLVII:581–588.

Hovland, C. I. & Pritzker, H. A. "Extent of Opinion Change as a Function of Amount of Change Advocated." *J. abn. soc. Psychol.,* 1957. LXIV:257–261.

Hovland, C. I., Sears, R. R. "Minor Studies of Aggression: Correlation of Lynchings with Economic Indices." *J. Psychol.,* 1938, IX:301–310.

Hovland, C. I. & Weiss, W. "The Influence of Source Credibility in Communication Effectiveness." *Pub. opin. quart.,* 1951. XV:635–650.

Hsu, F. L. K. *Clan, Caste and Club.* Princeton, New Jersey: D. Van Nostrand Co., 1963.

Hsu, F. L. K. *Psychological Anthropology.* Homewood, Illinois: Dorsey Press, 1961.

Hughes, H. M., Watts, L. G. "Portrait of the Self-Integrator." *J. soc. Issues,* 1964. XX:103–115.

Hulett, J. E. Jr. "Estimating the Net Effect of a Commercial Motion Picture upon the Trend of Local Public Opinion." *Amer. sociol. Rev.,* 1949. XIV:263–275.

Hull, C. L. *Hypnosis and Suggestibility.* New York: Appleton-Century Crofts, 1933.

Hunt, M. M. *The Natural History of Love.* New York: Knopf, 1959.

Hunt, R. G., Synnderdale, V. "Social Influences among Kindergarten Children." *Sociol. soc. res.,* 1959, 43:171–174

Hunter, F. *Community Power Structure.* Chapel Hill: University of North Carolina Press, 1953.

Hurst, J. G. *Lecture, Discussion, and Decision Teaching Methods.* Paper presented at A.P.A. meeting, 1960.

———. *Lecture, Discussion, and Decision Teaching Methods and Student Change in Elementary Educational Psychology.* Unpublished manuscript, 1960.

Husband, R. W. "Cooperative vs. Solitary Problem Solving." *J. soc. Psychol.,* 1940. XI:405–409.

Huxley, Julian. *On Living in a Revolution.* New York: Harper & Bros., 1942.

Hyman, H. *Interviewing in Social Research.* Chicago: University of Chicago Press, 1954.

———. "The Value Systems of Different Classes." In Bendix, R. and Lipset, S. M. *Class, Status and Power.* Glencoe, Ill.: Free Press, 1953, p. 430.

Hyman, H. H., Sheatsley, P. B. "Attitudes toward Desegregation." *Sci. Amer.,* Dec. 1956.

———. "The Current Status of American Public opinion." *Natl. Council for Social Studies Yearbook,* 1950, XXI:11–34.

———. "Some Reasons Why Information Campaigns Fail." *Pub. opin. quart.,* 1947. XI:413–423.

Indik, B. P. *et al.* "Superior-Subordinate Relationships and Performance." *Personnel psychol.,* 1961. XIV:347–374.

Information and Education Division, U. S. War Dept. "The Effects of Presenting 'One Side' versus 'Both Sides' in Changing Opinions on a Controversial

Subject." In Hovland, Lumsdaine, Sheffield, *Experiments on Mass Communication.* Princeton N. J.: Princeton University Press, 1949, 3:201–227.

Information and Education Division, U. S. War Dept. *Opinions about Negro Infantry Platoons in White Companies of Seven Divisions,* Washington D. C., U.S. War Dept., 1945.

Inkeles, Alex. "Social Stratification and Mobility in the Soviet Union." In Bendix, R. & Lipset, S. M. *Class, Status and Power.* Glencoe, Ill.: The Free Press, 1953. pp. 609–622.

Izard, C. E. "Personality Correlates of Sociometric Status." *J. appl. Psychol.,* 1959. XLIII:89–93.

Izard, Carroll E. "Personality Similarity and Friendship." *J. abn. soc. Psychol.,* 1960. LXI:47–51.

Jack, Lois M. "An Experimental Study of Ascendant Behavior in Preschool Children." University of Indiana: *Studies in Child Welfare,* 1934, IX, No. 3.

Jackson, Jay, M. and Saltzstein, H. D. *Group Membership and Conformity Processes.* Ann Arbor, Mich.: Research Center for Group Dynamics, Aug. 1956, (Mimeo.).

Jackson, Jay & Snock, J. D. *Effect of Invidious Exclusion from a Group on Feelings toward Self, Others, and on Tendencies to Conform.* Paper presented to American Psychological Assn., 1959.

Jacobson, Eugene. "The Growth of Groups in a Voluntary Organization." *J. soc. issues,* 1956. XII:18–23.

Jacobson, E., Kumata, H. & Gullahorn, J. E. "Cross-Cultural Contributions to Attitude Research." *Pub. opin. quart.,* 1960. XXIV:205.

Jahoda, Maria. "Conformity and Independence." *Human Rela.,* 1959. XII:99–120.

Jahoda, Maria. *Current Concepts of Positive Mental Health.* New York: Basic Books, 1958.

Jahoda, Maria. *Die Arbeitslosen von Marienthal.* Vienna: Psychological Institute, University of Vienna, 1933.

James, J. "Clique Organization in a Small Industrial Plant." *Re. stud.,* State College of Washington, Pullman, Washington, 1951. CXXV:125–130.

James, William. "Great Men, Great Thoughts and Their Environment." *Atlantic Monthly,* 1880. XLVI:441–459.

———. "The Moral Equivalent of War." In *Memories and Studies.* New York: Longmans, 1912.

———. *Principles of Psychology.* New York: Henry Holt, Inc., 1890. 2 Vol.

Janis, I. L. "Anxiety Indices Related to Susceptibility to Persuasion." *J. abn. soc. Psychol.,* 1955. LI:663–667.

———. "Personality Correlates of Susceptibility to Persuasion." *J. Pers.,* 1954. XXII:504–518.

Janis, I. L., Feshback, S. "Effects of Fear-Arousing Communications." *J. abn. soc. Psychol.,* 1953. XLVIII:78–92.

Janis, I. L., Field, P. B. "A Behavioral Assessment of Persuasibility; Consistency of Individual Differences." In Janis, I. L. *et al. Personality and Persuasibility.* New Haven: Yale University Press, 1959.

Janis, I. L. and Hovland, C. I. *et al. Personality and Persuasibility.* New Haven: Yale University Press, 1959.

584

Janis, I. L., King, B. T. "The influence of Role-Playing on Opinion Change." *J. abn. soc. Psychol.,* 1954. XLIX:211–218.

Janis, I. L. & Mulholland, W. "The Influence of Threat Appeals on Selective Learning of the Content of a Persuasive Communication." *J. Psychol.,* 1954. XXXVII:75–80.

Janis, I. *et al. Personality and Persuasibility.* New Haven: Yale University Press, 1959.

Janis, I. L., and Rife, Donald. "Persuasibility and Emotional Disorder." In Hovland, C. I. and Janis, I. L. (Ed.) *Personality and Persuasibility.* New Haven: Yale University Press, 1959. Ch. 6.

Jenkins, D., Lippitt, R. *Interpersonal Perception of Teachers, Students, and Parents.* Washington D. C.: Natl. Training Lab. Group Devel., 1951.

Jenkins, W. O. "A Review of Leadership Studies with Particular Reference to Military Problems." *Psychol. Bull.,* 1947. XLIV:54–79.

Jennings, Helen. *Leadership and isolation.* New York: Longmans Green, 1943.

Jennings, Helen H. "Leadership and Sociometric Choice." *Sociometry,* 1947, X:32–49.

Jersild, A. T. "Modes of Emphasis in Public Speaking." *J. appl. Psychol.,* 1928. XII:611–620.

Johnson, A. D. "An Attempt at Change in Interpersonal Relationships." *Sociometry,* 1939. II:43–48.

Johnson, D. M. "Confidence and the Expression of Opinion." *J. soc. Psychol.,* 1940. XII:213–220.

———. "The 'Phantom Anaesthetist' of Mattoon: a Field Study of Mass Hysteria." *J. abn. soc. Psychol.,* 1945. XL:175–186.

Jones, Alfred W. *Life, Liberty, Property.* Philadelphia: J. B. Lippincott, 1941.

Jones, Ernest. *Free Associations: Memories of a Psychoanalyst.* New York: Basic Books, 1959.

Jones, H. E. Experimental Studies of College Teaching. *Arch. Psychol.,* 1923. X: No. 68.

Jones, Mary C. "A Laboratory Study of Fear: the Case of Peter." *J. genet. Psychol.,* 1924. XXXI:308–315.

Jones, Maxwell. *The Therapeutic Community.* New York: Basic Books, 1953.

Kaplan, A. A. *Socio-Economic Circumstances and Adult Participation,* New York: Teachers College, Bureau of Publications, 1943.

Kardiner, A. *The Individual and His Society.* New York: Columbia University Press, 1939.

———. *Psychological Frontiers of Society.* New York: Columbia University Press, 1945.

———. *Sex and Morality.* Indianapolis: Bobbs-Merrill, 1954.

Kates, S. L. and Mahone, C. H. "Effective Group Participation and Group Norms." *J. soc. Psychol.,* 1958. XLVIII:211–216.

Kato, H. *Japanese Popular Culture.* Rutland, Vermont: Charles E. Tuttle, 1959.

Katz, D. & Braly, K. W. "Racial Stereotypes of 100 College Students." *J. abn. soc. Psychol.,* 1933. XXVIII:280–290; *also* 1935, XXX:175–193.

Katz, Daniel, Cartwright, Dorwin, Eldersveld, Samuel, and Lee, A. McC., eds.). *Public Opinion and Propaganda.* New York: Dryden Press, 1954.

Katz, D., Hyman, H. "Morale in War Industries." In Newcomb, T. M. and

Hartley, E. L. (eds.). *Readings in Social Psychology.* New York: Holt, 1947. pp. 437–447.

Katz, D., Maccoby, N., Morse, N. C. *Productivity, Supervision & Morale in an Office Situation.* Ann Arbor: University of Michigan Inst. Soc. Res., 1950.

Katz, David. *Animals and Men.* London: Longmans Green, 1937.

Katz, E., Lazarsfeld, P. F. *Personal Influence.* Glencoe Ill.: Free Press, 1955.

Katz, I., Goldston, J., and Benjamin, L. "Behavior and Productivity in Bi-Racial Work Groups." *Human relations,* 1958. XI:123–142.

Katz, Robert L. *Empathy: Its Nature and Uses.* New York: Free Press of Glencoe, 1963.

———. "Skills of an Effective Administrator." Harvard Business review, 1955. XXXIII–42.

Katzell, R. A. "Industrial Psychology." In *Annual Review of Psychology* (Palo Alto, Calif.), Vol. VIII, 1957, p. 247.

Keister, M. E., Updegraff, R. "A Study of Children's Reactions to Failure and an Attempt to Modify Them." *Child developm.,* 1937. VIII:241–248.

Keller, Helen. *The Story of My Life.* New York: Doubleday & Co., 1903, p. 253; pp. 353–4.

Kelley, H. H. "Communication in Experimentally Created Hierarchies." *Hum. relat.,* 1951. 39–56.

———. "Salience of Membership & Resistance to Change of Group-anchored Attitudes." *Hum. rela.,* 1955. VIII:275–289.

Kelly, Philip R. *Evolutionary Forces in U. S. Management, 1860–1932.* New York: Port of N. Y. Authority, 1965.

Kelman, H. C., Hovland, C. I. "Reinstatement of the Communicator in Delayed Measurement of Opinion Change." *J. abn. soc. Psychol.,* 1953. XLVIII:327–335.

Kemler, D. K., Bennett, E. M. *The American Personality: Urban Northeast.* Report to Amer. Psychol. Assn. Aug. 30, 1958.

Kendall, P. L. & Wolf, K. "The Analysis of Deviant Cases in Communications Research." In Lazarsfeld, P. & Stanton, F. N. (ed.). *Communication Research.* New York: Harper & Bros., 1949.

Kepner, C. H., Tregoe, B. B. "Developing Decision Makers." *Harvard Business Review,* 1960. XXXVIII:115–124.

Kerr, W. A. "Correlates of Politico-Economic Liberalism-Conservatism." *J. soc. Psychol.,* 1944. XX:61–77.

Kerstetter, L. M. & Sargent, J. "Reassignment Therapy in the Classroom." *Sociometry,* 1940. III:292–306.

King, B. T. and Janis, I. L. "Comparison of the Effectiveness of Improvised vs. Nonimprovised Role-Playing in Producing Opinion Changes." *Hum. Relat.;* 1956, IX:177–185.

Kinsey, A. C. *et al. Sexual Behavior in the Human Female.* Philadelphia: W. B. Saunders, 1953.

———. *Sexual Behavior in the Human Male.* Philadelphia: W. B. Saunders, 1948, Ch. 10.

Kipnis, D. U. "Interaction between Members of Bomber Crews as a Determinant of Sociometric Choice." *Hum. relat.,* 1957. X:263–269.

Kishler, John. "Prediction of Differential Learning from a Motion Picture." In

Penn State College, *Abstracts of Doctoral Dissertations*. State College Pa.: 1951. XIII:407–413.

Klapper, Joseph T. *Effects of Mass Communication*. Glencoe Ill.: Free Press, 1960.

Klein, E. *Relation between One's Attitude to his Father and His Social Attitudes*. M. A. essay. New York: Columbia University, 1925.

Klein, Josephine. *The Study of Groups*. London: Routledge and Kegan Paul, Ltd., 1956, p. 173.

Klineberg, Otto. *Social Psychology*. New York: Holt, 2d Ed., 1954.

Kluckhohn, Clyde. "Culture and Behavior." In Lindsey, G. (ed.). *Handbook of Social Psychology*. Cambridge, Mass.: Addison Wesley, 1954, Ch. 25.

Kluckhohn, C. & Kluckhohn, F. "American Culture: Generalized Orientations and Class Patterns." In Bryson, L. (ed.). *Conflicts of Power in Modern Culture*. New York: Jewish Theological Seminary, 1947.

Kluckhohn, C. and Leighton, D. *The Navajo*. Cambridge, Mass.: Harvard University Press, 1946.

Klugman, S. F. "Cooperative vs. Individual Efficiency in Problem solving." *J. Educ. Psychol.*, 1944. XXXV:71–100.

Knight, H. C. *A Comparison of the Reliability of Group and Individual Judgments*. Master's essay. Columbia University, 1921, 28pp.

Knoblock, H. & Pasamanick, B. Report, *N. Y. Times*, Feb. 27, 1960.

Knower, F. H. "A Study of the Effect of Oral Argument on Changes of Attitude." *J. soc. Psychol.*, 1935. VI:315–347.

———. "A Study of the Effect of Printed Argument on Changes in Attitude." *J. abn. soc. Psychol.*, 1936. XXX:522–532.

Koestler, Arthur. *The Yogi and the Commissar*. New York: Macmillan, 1945.

Kogan, N. and Tagiuri, R. "Interpersonal Preference and Cognitive Organization. *J. abnorm. soc. Psychol.*, 1958. LVI:113–116.

Kohler, W. *Gestalt Psychology*, (2d Ed.). New York: Liveright, 1947.

Kohler, W. *Zur Psychologie des Shempansen*, Psychol. Forsch., 1922, I, 1–45.

Komarovsky, Mirra. "The Voluntary Associations of Urban Dwellers." *Amer. sociol. rev.*, 1946. XI, 686–698.

———. *Women in the Modern World*. Boston: Little, Brown, 1953.

Kornhauser, Arthur W. "Psychological Basis of Class Divisions." In Hartmann, G. W. and Newcomb, T. (ed.). *Industrial Conflict*. New York: The Cordon Co., 1939. p. 236.

———. "Toward an Assessment of the Mental Health of Factory Workers." *Human org.*, 1962. XXI:43–46.

Kosofsky, S., Ellis, A. "Illegal Communications among Institutionalized Female Delinquents." *J. soc. Psychol.*, 1958. XLVIII:155–160.

Kracaver, S. *From Caligari to Hitler*. Princeton, N. J.: Princeton University Press, 1947.

Kroll, A. "The Teacher's Influence upon the Social Attitudes of Boys in the Twelfth Grade." *J. educ. Psychol.* 1934. XXV:274–280.

Kubie, L. S. *Neurotic Distortion of the Creative Process*. Lawrence, Kansas: University of Kansas Press, 1958.

Kuhlen, R. G. and Bretsch, H. S. "Sociometric Status and Personal Problems of Adolescents." *Sociometry*, 1947. X:122–130.

Kulp, D. H. II. "Prestige, As Measured by Single-Experience Changes and Their Permanency," *J. educ. res.*, 1934. XXVII:663–672.

Kunkel, F. *Eine Angstneurose und Ihre Behandlung.* Leipzig: S. Hirzel, 1931.

Kuriloff, A. H. and Atkins, Stuart. "T-Group for a Work Team." *J. appl. behav. Sci.*, 1966, II, No. 1.

Kutner, B., Wilkins, C., and Yarrow, P. R. "Verbal Attitudes and Overt Behavior Involving Racial Prejudice." *J. abn. soc. Psychol.*, 1952. XLVII:649–652.

LaBarre, Weston. "The Cultural Basis of Emotions and Gestures." *J. Pers.*, 1947. XVI:49–56.

Lacy, J. V. "Relative Value of Motion Pictures as an Educational Agency." *T.C. Record*, 1919. XX:452–65.

Laird, D. A. "Why Executives Fail." *Management Methods.* 1956. XIII:30–33.

Lane, R. C. and Singer, J. L. "Familiar Attitudes in Paranoid Schizophrenics and Normals from Two Socio-Economic Classes." *J. abn. soc. Psychol.*, 1959. LIX:328–339.

LaPiere, R. T. "Attitudes and Actions." *Social Forces*, 1934. XIII:230–237.

Lashley, K. S. & Watson, J. B. *A Psychological Study of Motion Pictures in Relation to Venereal Disease Campaigns.* Washington, D. C. U.S. Interdept. Social Hygiene Bd., 1922.

Lasswell, H. D. *Psychopathology and Politics.* Chicago: University of Chicago Press, 1930.

———. *World Politics and Personal Insecurity.* New York: McGraw-Hill, 1935.

Lasswell, H. D. & Kaplan, A. *Power and Society.* New Haven: Yale University Press, 1950.

Lawrence, L. C. & Smith, P. C. "Group Decision and Employee Participation." *J. appl. Psychol.*, 1955. XXXIX:334–37.

Lazarsfeld, P. F., Berelson, B., & Gandet, Hazel. *The People's Choice.* New York: Duell, Sloan, and Pearce, 1944.

Leavitt, Harold J. "Some Effects of Certain Communication Patterns on Group Performance." *J. abn. soc. Psychol.*, 1951. XLVI:38–50.

Leavitt, H. J. and Bass, B. M. "Organizational Psychology." In Farnsworth, P. R. (ed.). *Annual Review of Psychology.* Palo Alto, Calif.: Annual Reviews, Vol. XV, 1964.

Leavitt, H. J. & Mueller, R. A. H. "Some Effects of Feedback on Communication." *Hum. relat.*, 1951. IV:401–5.

LeBon, G. *La foule, (The Crowd),* 1895.

Lee, Dorothy D. "Conceptual Implications of an Indian Language." *Phil. of Sci.*, 1938, V:89–102.

Lee, S. G. "Social influences on Aulu dreaming." *J. soc. Psychol.*, 1958. XLVII: 265–283.

Lehmann, I. J. *Some Socio-Cultural Differences in Attitudes & Values.* Report to Amer. Psychol. Assn., 1960.

Lennard, H. L., Bernstein, A. *The Anatomy of Psychotherapy.* New York: Columbia University Press, 1960.

Lentz, T. F. "Generality and Specificity of Conservatism-Radicalism." *J. educ. Psychol.*, 1938. XXIX:540–546.

Lentz, T. F. "Personage Admiration and Other Correlates of Conservatism-Radicalism." *J. soc. Psychol.*, 1939. X:81–93.

Leuba, C. and Lucas, C. "The Effect of Attitudes on Descriptions of Pictures." *J. exp. Psychol.*, 1945. XXXV:517–524.

Levin, H. J. *Broadcast Regulation and Joint Ownership of Media.* New York: New York University Press, 1961, 219 pp.

Levine, J. and Butler, J. "Lecture vs. Group Decision in Changing Behavior." *J. appl. Psychol.*, 1952. XXXVI:29–33.

Levine, R. A. "The Internalization of Political Values in Stateless Societies." *Hum. Organ.*, 1960. XIX:51–58.

Levinger, George. "Development of Perceptions & Behavior in Newly Formed Social Power Relationships." In Cartwright, D. (ed.). *Studies in Social Power.* Ann Arbor: Institute of Social Research, University of Michigan, 1959, pp. 81–98.

Levinson, D. J., Huffman, P. E. "Traditional Family Ideology and Its Relation to Personality." *J. Pers.*, 1955. XXIII:251–273.

Levinson, D. J., Schermerhorn, R. A. "Emotional-Attitudinal Effects of an Intergroup Workshop." *J. Psychol.*, 1951. XXXI:243–256.

Lewin, K. *Field Theory in Social Science.* New York: Harper, 1951.

Lewin, Kurt. "Group Decision and Social Change." In Newcomb, T. & Hartley, E. (ed.). *Readings in Social Psychology.* New York: Holt, 1947.

———. *Principles of Topological Psychology.* New York: McGraw-Hill, 1936.

Lewin, L., Lippitt, R., White, R. K. "Patterns of Aggressive Behavior in Experimentally Created Social Climates." *J. soc. Psychol.*, 1939. X:271–299.

Lewis, H. B. "Studies in the Principles of Judgment and Attitudes, IV." "The Operation of Prestige Suggestion." *J. soc. Psychol.*, 1941. XIV:229–256.

Lieberman, S. "The Effects of Changes in Roles on the Attitudes of Role Occupants." *Hum. relat.*, 1956. IX:385–402.

Liebling, A. J. *The Press.* New York: Ballantine Books, 1961.

Likert, R. *Developing Patterns of Management.* New York: American Management Assn. 1956.

Likert, R. "Effective Supervision: an Adaptive and Relative Process." *Personnel Psychol.*, 1958. XI:317–331.

———. "Measuring Organization Performance." *Harvard Business Review,* 1958. XXXVI:41–50.

——— *Motivational Dimensions of Administration,* Chicago: Public Administration Service.

———. *New Patterns in Management.* New York: McGraw-Hill, 1961.

———. "Trends toward a Worldwide Theory of Management." *Newsletter of Inst. for Soc. Res.,* Ann Arbor, Mich.: Oct. 1963.

Linton, Harnet, and Graham, Elaine. "Personality Correlates of Persuasibility." In Hovland, C. I. and Janis, I. L. *Personality and Persuasibility.* New Haven: Yale University Press, 1959. Ch. 4.

Linton, Ralph. "The Concept of National Character." In Stanton, A. H. and Perry, S. E. (eds.). *Personality and Political Crisis.* Glencoe: Free Press, 1951.

———. *The Cultural Background of Personality.* New York Appleton-Century, 1945.

———. *The Study of Man.* New York Appleton-Century Crofts, Inc., 1936. p. 175.

Lippitt, R. "An Experimental Study of Authoritarian and Democratic group Atmospheres." In *Studies in Topological and Vector Psychology,* I. Iowa City: University of Iowa, Studies in Child Welfare, No. 16, 1940.

Lippitt, R., Polansky, N., Redl. F., Rosen, S. "The Dynamics of Power." *Hum. relat.*, 1952. V:37–64.

Lippitt, R., Watson, J., and Westley, B. *The Dynamics of Planned Change.* New York: Harcourt, Brace & Co., 1958.

Lipset, S. M. "Democracy and Working-Class Authoritarianism." *Amer. soc. Rev.*, 1959. XXIV:482–501.

———. "What Religious Revival?" *Columbia University Forum*, 1959.

Lipset. S. M., Bendix, R. "Social Status and Social Structure." *Brit. J. Sociol.*, 1951, II:150–168; 230–254.

Loeser, Lewis H. "Some Aspects of Group Dynamics." *Int. J.*, group psychotherapy, 1957, 7:10

Longstreet, R J. "An experiment with the Thurstone Attitude Scales." *Sch. Rev.*, 1935. XLIII:202–208.

Loomis, C. P. "Tapping Human Power Lines." *Adult Leadership*, 1953. I:12–14.

Loomis, C. P., & Davidson, D. M., Jr. "Measurement of the Dissolution of In-Groups in the Intergration of a Rural Resettlement Project." *Sociometry*, 1939. II, No. 2, 84–94.

———. "Sociometrics and the Study of New Rural Communities." *Sociometry*, 1939. II:56–76.

Lorenz, K. *The Companion in the Bird's World*, Auk., LIV:245–273.

———. *King Solomon's ring.* London: Methrien, 1952.

Lorge, I. *Evaluation of Instruction in Staff-Action and Decision-Making.* Maxwell Air Force Base, Alabama, 1953. Technical Res. Dept. No. 16.

Lorge, Irving. *The Lorge Formula for Estimating Difficulty of Reading Materials.* New York: Columbia University, Teachers College Bureau of Publications, 1959.

Lorge, I. and Curtiss, C. C. "Prestige, Suggestion and Attitudes." *J. soc. Psychol.*, 1936. VII:386–402.

Lowie, R. H. *An Introduction to Cultural Anthropology.* New York: Rinehart, 1940.

Lucas, F. L. Party of one. *Holiday*, March, 1960, p. 15.

Lumsdaine, A. A. "Instruments and Media of Instruction." In Gage, N.L. (ed.). *Handbook of Research on Teaching.* Chicago: Rand McNally, 1963. pp. 583–682.

Lumsdaine, A. A. & Janis, I. L. "Resistance to Counterpropaganda Produced by One-Sided and Two-Sided Propaganda Presentations." *Pub. opin. quart.*, 1953. XVII:311–318.

Lumsdaine, A. A., May, M. A. "Mass Communication and Educational Media." Palo Alto, Calif: *Ann. Rev. Psychol.*, 1965. Vol. XVI:475–534.

Lundberg, G. A. "The Demographic and Economic Basis of Political Radicalism and Conservatism." *Amer. J. Soc.*, 1927. XXXII:719–732.

———. "The Newspaper and Public Opinion." *Soc. Forces*, 1926. IV:709–715.

Lundberg, G. A., Stule, Mary. "Social Attraction Patterns in a Village." *Sociometry*, 1938. I:375–419.

Lyle, J. G. "Environmentally Produced Retardation: Institution and Pre-institution Influences." *J. abn. soc. Psychol.* 1964. LXIX:329–332.

Lynd, R. S. & Lynd, H. M. *Middletown.* New York: Harcourt Brace, 1929.

590

Lynd, R. S. and Lynd, H. M. *Middletown in Transition*. New York: Harcourt Brace, 1937.

Lynes, Russell. "How Do You Rate in the New Leisure?" *Life*, Dec. 28, 1959. Vol. XLVII No. 26, pp. 85–89.

——. *The Tastemakers*. New York: Harper, 1954.

Maas, Henry S. "Some Social Class Differences in the Family Systems and Group Relations of Pre and Early Adolescents." *Child develm.*, 1951. XXII:145–152.

MacKenzie, B. K. "The Importance of Contact in Determining Attitude toward Negroes." *J. abn. soc. Psychol.*, 1948. XLIII:417–441.

Maccoby, E., Gibbe, P. et al. Methods of child rearing in two social classes. In Martin, W. and Stendler, C. (Eds.) *Readings in child development*, N. Y. Harcourt Brace, 1954, 380–396.

Mahoney, C. M. *Supervisory & Administrative Practices Associated with Worker Attitudes toward an Incentive System*. Ann Arbor: Inst. Soc. Res., University of Michigan, 1957.

Maier, N. R. F. "The Quality of Group Decision as Influenced by the Discussion Leader." *Hum. relat.*, 1950. III:155–174.

Maier, N. R. F. & Solem, A. R. "The Contribution of a Discussion Leader to the Quality of Group Thinking: the Effective Use of Minority Opinions." *Hum. relat.*, 1950. III:155–174.

Mainer, R. E. *Attitude Change in Intergroup Education Programs*. Lafayette, Ind.: Purdue University, Division of Educational Reference, 1954.

Maisel, Richard. *A Study of Small Groups in Basic Training*. Ph. D. thesis, Columbia University, 1960.

Malinowsky, B. *Sex and Repression in Savage Society*. New York: Harcourt Brace, 1927.

Malthus, Thomas. *Essay on Population*. New York: Macmillan, 1894.

Mann, F. & Baumgartel, H. *Absences and Employee Attitudes in an Electric Power Company*. Ann Arbor, Mich.: Survey Res. Center, 1952.

Mann, Floyd S. & Hoffman, L. R. "Individual and Organizational Correlates of Automation." *J. soc. Issues*, 1956. XII:7–17.

Mann, F. L., Heff, F. W. *Managing Major Change in Organizations*. Ann Arbor, Mich.: Foundation for Research on Human Behavior, 1961.

Manry, J. C. *World Citizenship*. Iowa City: University of Iowa Dept. publ., 1928.

Marks, E. S. You Can Do It on a Computer, but Should You? *Pub. Opin. Quart.* 1963. XXVII:481–5.

Marple, C. H. The comparative susceptibility of three age levels to the suggestion of group versus expert opinion. *J. soc. psychol.*, 1933, IV:176–186.

Marquand, J. P. *Point of no return*, Boston: Little Brown, 1947.

Marquis, D., Guetzkow, H. & Heyns, K. A social psychological study of the decision-making conference. In Guezkow, H. Ed. *Groups, leadership & men*, Pittsby Carnegie Press, 1951, pp. 55–67.

Marrow, Alfred J. *Changing Patterns of Prejudice*. Philadelphia: Chilton Co., 1962.

——. *Living Without Hate*. New York: Harper & Bros., 1952.

——. *Making Management Human*. New York: McGraw-Hill, 1957.

————. Risks and Uncertainties in Action Research. *J. soc. Issues.*, 1964. XX:5–20.

Marrow, A., French, J. R. P. "Changing a Stereotype in Industry." *J. soc. Issues,* 1945. I:33–37.

Marx, K. & Engels, F. "The Communist Manifesto." In Burns E. *A Handbook of Marxism.* New York: London House, 1935. pp. 22–23; 25.

Massarik, F. and Carlson, G. *The California Psychological Inventory as an Indicator of Personality Change in Sensitivity Training.* Los Angeles: U. C. L. A., M.A. thesis.

Maslow, A. H. *Motivation and Personality.* New York: Harper, 1954.

————. "A Theory of Human Motivation." *Psychol. Rev.*, 1943. L:370–396.

Maslow, A. and Diaz-Guerrero, R. "Delinquency as a Value Disturbance." In Peatman, J. and Hartley, E. L. *Festschrift for Gardner Murphy.* New York: Harper & Bros., 1960. pp. 228–240.

Masters, R. E. L. *Patterns of Incest.* New York: Julian Press, 1963.

Mausner, B. "The Effect of Prior Reenforcement on the Interaction of Observer Pairs." *J. abn. soc. Psychol.*, 1954. XLIX:65–68.

————. "Studies in Social Interaction, III." Effect of Variation in One Partner's Prestige on the Interaction of Observer Pairs. *J. appl. Psychol.*, 1953. XXXVII:391–394.

May, Rollo (ed.) *Existential psychology.* N. Y. Random House, 1961.

May, Rollo R. *et al. Existence: a New Dimension in Psychiatry and Psychology.* New York: Basic Books, 1958.

Mayer, A. J. and Hauser, P. "Class Differentials in Expectation of Life at Birth." In Bendix, R. & Lipset, S. M. *Class, Status and Power.* Glencoe, Ill.: The Free Press, 1953, pp. 281–4.

Mayo, Elton. *Human Problems of Industrial Civilization.* Cambridge, Mass.: Harvard University Press, 1933.

McArthur, Chas. "Personality Differences between Middle and Upper Classes." *J. abn. soc. Psychol.*, 1955. L:247–254.

McCandless, B. R. "Changing Relationships between Dominance and Social Acceptibility Living Group Democratization." *Am. J. Orthopsychiat.* 1942, XII:529–535.

McClelland, David C. *The Achieving Society.* Princeton, N. J.: Van Nostrand, 1961.

McClelland, D. C., Atkinson, J. W. *et al. The Achievement Motive.* New York: Appleton-Century Crofts, 1952.

McClelland, D. C., Friedman, G. A. "A Cross-Cultural Study of the Relationship between Child-Training Practices and Achievement Motivation Appearing in Folktales." In Swanson, G. E., Newcomb, T. M., Hartley, E. L. (eds.). *Readings in Social Psychology.* New York: Holt, 1952.

McDougall, W. *Introduction to Social Psychology.* London: Methuen & Co., 1908.

McGinnies, E. "Emotionality and Perceptual Defense." *Psychol. Rev.*, 1949, LVI:244–251.

McGranahan, D. G. and Wayne, I. "German and American Traits Reflected in Popular Drama." *Hum. relat.*, 1948, I:429–455.

McGregor, Douglas. *The Human Side of Enterprise.* New York: McGraw-Hill, 1960.

McGuire, William J. "Cognitive Consistency and Attitude Change." *J. abn. soc. Psychol.*, 1960, LX:345–353.

————. "Direct and Indirect Persuasive Effects of Dissonance-Producing Messages." *J. abn. soc. Psychol.*, 1960. LX:354–358.

————. "The Effectiveness of Supportive and Refutational Defenses in Immunizing and Restoring Beliefs against Persuasion." *Sociometry*, June, 1961.

————. "Resistance to Persuasion Conferred by Active and Passive Prior Refutation of the Same and Alternative Counter Arguments." *J. abn. soc. Psychol.*, Dec. 1961.

McGuire, Wm. J. & Papageorgis, D. "The Relative Efficacy of Various Types of Prior Belief-Defense in Producing Immunity against Persuasion." *J. abn. soc. Psychol.*, 1961. LXII:338–345.

McKee, J. P. and Sheriffs, A. C. "The Differential Evaluation of Males and Females." *J. Pers.*, 1957. XXV:356–371.

Mead, G. H. *Mind, Self and Society.* University of Chicago Press, 1934. pp. 42f.

Mead, Margaret. *Coming of Age in Samoa.* New York: Morrow, 1928.

Mead, Margaret (ed.). "Cooperation and Competition among Primitive Peoples." New York: McGraw-Hill, 1937.

Mead, Margaret (ed.). *Cultural Patterns and Technical Change,* Prepared for UNESCO. A Mentor Book, 1955. p. 134–5.

————. *Growing Up in New Guinea.* New York: Morrow, 1930.

————. *Male and Female.* New York: New American Library. A Mentor Book, 1949, 1955.

————. "The Manus of the Admirality Islands." Summary in Mead, M. (ed.). *Cooperation and Competition among Primitive Peoples.* New York: McGraw-Hill, 1937. Ch. 7.

————. *New Lives for Old.* New York: Morrow, 1956.

————. "Research on Primitive Children." In Carmichael, L. (ed.). *Manual of Child Psychology.* New York: John Wiley & Sons, 1946. p. 678.

————. *Sex and Temperament.* New York: William Morrow & Co., 1928.

Mead, Margaret and Wolfenstein, M. (eds.). *Childhood in Contemporary Cultures.* Chicago, University of Chicago Press, 1955.

Menefee, S. C. "The Effect of the Stereotyped Words on Political Judgments." *Amer. soc. Rev.*, 1936. I:614–621.

Menefee, S. C. & Granneberg, A. G. "Propaganda and Opinions on Foreign Policy." *J. soc. Psychol.*, 1940. XI:393–404.

Menzel, H., Katz, E. "Social Relations and Innovation in the Medical Profession." *Publ. opin. Quart.*, 1956. XIX:337–352.

Merei, Ferenc. "Group Leadership and Institutionalization." *Hum. relat.*, 1949. II:23–39.

Merrihue, W. V. and Katzell, R. A. E. R. I. "Yardstick of Employee Relations." *Harvard Business Review*, 1955. Vol. XXXIII, No. 6, pp. 91–99.

Merton, Robert K. "Applied Social Science in Formulation of Policy." *Phil. of Sci.*, 1949. XVI: No. 3.

————. Contributions to the Theory of Reference Group Behavior. In Merton, R. K. and Lazarsfeld, P. F. (ed.). *Continuities in Social Research: Studies in the Scope and Method of the American Soldier.* Glencoe, Ill.: Free Press, 1950. pp. 40–105.

———. *Mass Persuasion.* New York: Harper, 1946.

———. *Social theory and social structure,* Glencoe, Ill. Free Press, 1949, Rev. ed. 1957.

Michael, D. M. *Effects of Audience Participation on Learning from a Factual Film.* Boston: Boston University School of Public Relations and Communications, 1952.

Michotte, A. *La perception de la Causalite.* Lovrain: L'Institut superieur de Philosophie, 1946.

Middleton, Russell. "Ethnic Prejudice and Susceptibility to Persuasion." *Amer. sociol. Rev.,* 1960. XXV:679–686.

Miles, M. (ed.). *Innovation in Education.* New York: Teachers College University. Bureau of Publications, 1964.

Miles, M. B. *Learning to Work in Groups.* New York: Teachers College University. Bureau of Publications, 1959.

Mill, John Stuart. *On Liberty.* London, 1859.

———. *On the Subjection of Women.* Everyman's Library. London: Dent., 1929 Ed. Publ. 1869.

Miller, S. M. "Poverty and Inequality in America." *Child Welfare,* 1963. pp. 442–445.

Miller, S. M., Rein, M. "Poverty and Social Change." *The American Child.* March, 1964 (National Committee on Employment of Youth, New York).

Miller, Neal, Bugelski, Richard. "Minor Studies of Aggression: II. The Influence of Frustrations Imposed by the In-group on Attitudes Expressed toward Outgroups." *J. of Psychol.* 1948. XXV:437–442.

Mills, C. Wright. *White Collar.* New York: Oxford University Press, 1951.

Minami, H. *Nihonjin no Shinoi* (Psychology of the Japanese). Tokyo: Mainichi Shimbunsha, 1954.

Minard, R. D. "Race Relationships in the Pocahontas Coal Field." *J. soc. Issues,* 1952. VIII, No. 1. pp. 29–44.

Miner, H. M. *St. Denis.* Chicago: University of Chicago Press, 1939.

Mintz, Alexander. "Nonadaptive Group Behavior." *J. abn. soc. Psychol.,* 1951. XLVI:150–159.

———. "A Re-examination of Correlations between Lynchings and Economic Indices." *J. abn. soc. Psychol.,* 1946. XLI:154–160.

Mitford, Nancy. *Noblesse Oblige: an Enquiry into the Identifiables Characteristics of the English Aristocracy.* New York: Harper, 1956.

Mitnick, L., McGinnies, E. "Influencing Ethnocentrism in Small Discussion Groups through a Film Communication." *J. abn. soc. Psychol.,* 1958. LVI:82–90.

Mizruchi, E. H. "Social Structure and Anomia in a Small City." *Amer. sociol. Rev.,* 1960. XXV:645–654.

Moede, W. *Experimentelle Massenpsychologie.* Leipzig: S. Hirzel, 1920.

———. *Der Wetteifer Zeitschr. f. pedagog. Psychol.,* 1914. XV:353–368.

Montague, Ashley. "Social Instincts." *Scientific American,* April 1950.

Moore, G. & Garrison, K. C. "A Comparative Study of Social and Political Attitudes of College Students." *J. abn. soc. Psychol.,* 1932. XXVII:195–208.

Moore, H. T. "The Attention Value of Lecturing without Notes." *J. Educ. Psychol.,* 1919. X:467–469.

594

———. "The Comparative Influence of Majority and Expert Opinion." *Amer. J. Psychol.,* 1921. XXXII:16–20.

Moore, W. E. *Social Change.* Englewood Cliffs, N. J.: Prentice-Hall, 1963.

Moreno, J. L. *Who Shall Survive.* Washington, D. C.: Nervous and Mental disease publ. Co., 1934.

Morris, C. W. *Varieties of Human Values.* Chicago: University of Chicago Press, 1956.

Morse, N. C. and Reimer, E. "The Experimental Change of a Major Organizational variable." *J. abn. soc. Psychol.,* 1956. LII:120–129.

Morse, N. C., Reimer, E. and Tannenbaum, A. "Regulation and Control in Hierarchical Organizations." *J. soc. Issues,* 1951. VII: No. 3.

Morse, N. C. and Weiss, R. S. "The Function and Meaning of Work and the Job." *Amer. sociol. Rev.,* 1955. XX:191–198.

Mort, P. R. and Cornell, F. G. *American Schools in Transition.* New York: Teachers College. Columbia University Bureau of Publications, 1941.

Mort, P. R. and Furno, O. F. *Theory and Synthesis of a Sequential Complex.* New York: Teachers College. Columbia University, Institute of Administrative Research, 1960.

Mott, F. L. "Newspapers in Presidential Campaigns." *Publ. opin. Quart.,* 1944. VIII:348–367.

Mueller, J. H. and Mueller, K. H. "Social-Economic Background and Campus Success." *Educ. & psychol. Measmt.,* 1940, III:143–150.

Mulligan, R. A. "Socio-Economic Background and College Enrollment." *Amer. soc. Rev.,* 1951. XVI:188–196.

Muraskin, J. and Iverson, M. A. "Social Expectancy as a Function of Judged Social Distance." *J. soc. Psychol.,* 1958. XLVIII:11–14.

Murphy Gardner. *Challenge of Psychical Research.* New York: Harper, 1961.

———. *Human Nature and Enduring Peace.* Boston: Houghton Mifflin, 1945.

———. *Human Potentialities.* New York: Basic Books, 1958.

Murphy, Gardner & Likert, R. *Public Opinion and the Individual.* New York: Harper, 1938.

Murphy, Gardner & Murphy, L. B. *Experimental Social Psychology.* New York: Harper & Bros., 1931. p. 174–177.

Murray, H. A. *Explorations in Personality.* New York: Oxford University Press, 1938.

———. "A Mythology for Grownups." *Saturday Review,* June 23, 1960, pp. 10–12.

Murrow, Edward R. (ed.). *This I Believe.* New York: Simon and Schuster, 1952.

Murrow, Edward R. and Lyons, L. *The Responsibilities of Television.* New York: Fund for the Republic.

Mussen, Paul H. "Some Personality and Social Factors Related to Changes in Children's Attitudes toward Negroes." *J. abn. soc. Psychol.,* 1950. XLV:423–441.

Mussen, Paul H., Kagan, J. "Group Conformity and Perceptions of Parents." *Child develpm.;* 1958. XXIX:57–60.

Myers, G. C. "Control of Conduct by Suggestion: an Experiment on Americanization." *J. appl. Psychol.,* 1921. V:26–31.

Myrdal, Gunnar. *An American Dilemma.* New York: Harper & Bros., 1962, revised.

Nadel, S. F. "Field Experiments in Racial Psychology." *Brit. j. Psychol.*, 1937. XXVIII:195–211.

Nadler, E. B. and Morrow, W. R. "Authoritarian Attitudes toward Women and Their Correlates." *J. soc. Psychol.*, 1959. XLIX:113–123.

Natl. Opin. Res. Center. "Jobs and Occupations: a Popular Evaluation." *Opinion News,* 1947. IX:3–13.

National Broadcasting Co. "Why Sales Come in Curves." New York: N.B.C., 1954.

National Education Association. Policies Commission. *Education and the People's Peace.* Washington, D.C.: N.E.A., 1943.

———. "Teacher Opinion on Pupil Behavior." Washington, D.C.: *Research Bull. N.E.A.,* 1956. XXIV:No. 2.

Neugarten, Bernice L. *Personality in Middle and Late Life.* New York: Atherton, 1964.

Newcomb, T. M. "An Approach to the Study of Communicative Acts." *Psychol. Rev.* 1953. LX:393–404.

———. "Motivation in social behavior." In *Current Theory and Research in Motivation.* University of Nebraska, 1953.

———. "Personality and Social Change." New York: Dryden Press, 1943.

———. "The Prediction of Interpersonal Attraction." *Amer. Psychologist.* XI:575–586.

Newcomb, T. M., Svehla, G. "Intra-family Relationships in Attitude." *Sociometry,* 1937. I:180–205.

Newman, H. H., Freeman, F. N., and Holzinger, K. J. *Twins—a Study of Heredity and Environment.* Chicago: University of Chicago Press, 1937.

Newman, Ruth E. *A Cross-Cultural Test of a Trait of Mental Process and Its Categorical Correlates.* Unpublished Ph.D. dissertation. New York: Columbia University, 1964.

N.Y. State War Council. *How Management Can Integrate Negroes in War Industry.* Albany, N.Y.: State Commission Against Discrimination.

Nichols, Lee. *Breakthrough on the Color Front.* New York: Random House, 1954.

Novakovsky, S. "Arctic or Siberian Hysteria as a Reflex of the Geographic Environment." *Ecology,* 1924. V:113–127.

Nunnally, J. C. and Bobren, H. M. "Variables Governing Willingness to Receive Communications on Mental Health," *J. Pers.,* 1959. XXVII:38–46.

Nye, F. Ivan. "Adolescent-Parent Adjustment—Socio-Economic Level as a Variable." *Amer. sociol. Rev.,* 1951. XVI:341–349.

———. *Family Relationships and Delinquent Behavior.* New York: John Wiley & Sons, 1958.

Ogburn, William F. *Social Change with Respect to Culture and Original Nature,* New York: B. W. Huebsch, 1922.

Ortegi y Gasset, Jose. *Revolt of the Masses.* New York: W. W. Norton, 1932.

Osborn, Earl D. *Persuading for Peace.* New York: Institute for International Order. June 7, 1965.

596

OSS (Office of Strategic Services), Assessment staff. *Assessment of Men.* New York: Rinehart, 1948. p. 98.

Opinion News. Denver, Natl. Opin. Res. Center, University of Denver.

Osgood, Charles E. *An alternative to War or Surrender.* Urbana, Ill.: University of Illinois Press, 1962.

Pace, C. R. "The Relationship between Liberalism and Knowledge of Current Affairs." *J. soc. Psychol.,* 1939. X:247–258.

Packard, Vance. *The Hidden Persuaders.* New York: David McKay, 1957.

———. *The Pyramid Climbers.* New York: McGraw-Hill, 1962.

———. *The Status-Seekers.* New York: David McKay, 1959.

Pagè, M. "The Sociotherapy of the Enterprise." *Hum. relat.,* 1959. XII:317–334.

Papageorgis, D. and McGuire, W. J. "The Generality of Immunity to Persuasion Produced by Pre-exposure to Weakened Counterarguments." *J. abn. soc. Psycho.,* June 1961.

Pareto, Vilfredo. *The Mind and Society.* 4 Vol. Translated by Livingston. New York: Harcourt Brace, 1935.

———. *Trattato di sociologia generale.* Florence, 1916.

Park, R. E. "The City: Suggestions for the Investigation of Human Behavior in the Urban Environment." *Amer. J. Sociol.* 1916, XX:577–612.

Parker, Dorothy. *Enough Rope.* New York: Boni and Liveright, 1926. p. 78.

Parten, M. B. "Social Participation among Pre-school Children. *J. abn. soc. Psychol.,* 1932. XXVII:243–269.

Partridge, E. de A. *Leadership among Adolescent Boys.* New York: Teachers College, Columbia University, 1934.

Pastore, Nicholas. "The Nature-Nurture Controversy." New York: King's Crown Press, 1949.

Patchen, Martin. "The Effect of Reference Group Standards on Job Satisfaction." *Hum. relat.,* 1958. XI:303–314.

Patrick C. "Attitudes about Women Executives in Government Positions." *J. soc. Psychol.,* 1944. XIX:3–34.

Pelz, Donald. "Influence: a Key to Effective Leadership in the First-Line Supervisor." *Personnel,* 1952. XXIX:3–11.

———. "Leadership within a Hierarchical Organization." *J. soc. Issues,* 1951. VII:49–55.

Perlmutter, H. V. and de Montmollin, G. "Group Learing." *J. abn. soc. Psychol.,* 1952. XLVII:762–769.

Pessemier, E. A. "Experimental Methods of Analyzing Demand for Branded Consumer Goods, with Application to Problems in Marketing Strategy." Pullman, Wash.: Washington State University Press, 1963.

Peterson, D. R., Quay, H. C. and Cameron, G. R. "Personality and Background Factors in Juvenile Delinquency." *J. consult. Psychol.,* 1959. XXIII:395–399.

Peterson, R. C. and Thurstone, L. L. *Motion Pictures and the Social Attitudes of Children.* New York: Macmillan, 1933.

Phillips, E. L. "Intellectual and Personality Factors Associated with Social Class Attitudes among Junior High School Children." *J. genet. Psychol.,* 1950. LXXVII:61–72.

Piaget, Jean. *The Language and Thought of the Child.* New York: Harcourt Brace and Co., 1926. pp. 76–126.

Pigors, P. *Leadership or Domination.* Boston: Houghton Mifflin, 1935.

Poincins, G. de M., Galantière, L. *Kabloona.* New York: Garden City Publishing Company, 1943.

Porter, L. W. "Job Attitudes in Management." *J. appl. Psychol.,* 1962, XLVI: 375–384.

Porter, L. W. and Lawler, E. E. "Effects of 'Tall' vs. 'Flat' Organization Structures on Managerial Job Satisfaction." *Personnel Psychol.* 1964, XVII:135–148.

Porter, L. W. and Chiselli, E. E. "The Self-Perceptions of Top and Middle Management Personnel." *Personnel Psychol.,* 1957. X:397–406.

Potter, D. M. *People of Plenty.* Chicago, University of Chicago Press, 1954.

Powdermaker, Florence B. and Frank, Jerome E. *Group Psychotherapy.* Harvard University Press, 1953.

Powdermaker, Hortense. *Life in Lesu.* New York: Norton, 1933.

President's Committee on Equality of Treatment and Opportunity in the Armed Forces. Washington: U.S. Government Printing Office, 1950, p. 44.

Preston, Malcolm G. "Note on the Reliability and Validity of Group Judgment." *J. exper. Psychol.,* 1938. XXII:462–471.

Preston, M. G. and Heintz, R. K. "Effects of Participatory vs. Supervisory Leadership on Group Judgment." *J. abn. soc. Psychol.,* 1949. XLIV:345–355.

"Publius" Quoted by Bendix, R. and Lipsett, S. M. *Class, Status and Power.* Glencoe, Ill.: The Free Press, 1953. p. 22.

Radloff, R. "Opinion Evaluation and Affiliation." *J. of Abn. Soc. Psychol.* 1961. LXII:578–85.

Rank, Otto. *The Trauma of Birth.* New York: Harcourt Brace, 1929.

Raper, Arthur. *The tragedy of lynching.* Chapel Hill, Univ. of N. C. Press, 1933.

Raths, L. and Trager, F. N. "Public Opinion and Crossfire." *J. educ. sociol.,* 1948. XXI:345–368.

Redl, F. "Groups, Emotion and Leadership." *Psychiatry,* 1942. V:573–596.

Redl, Fritz and Wineman, David. *Children Who Hate.* Glencoe, Ill.: Free Press, 1951.

Reik, Theodore. *Listening with the Third Ear.* New York: Farrar, Straus, 1948.

———. *Psychology of Sex Relations.* New York: Farrar and Rinehart, 1945.

Reilly, W. J. *Method for the Study of Retail Relationships.* Austin, Tex.: Univer. of Texas. Bull. No. 2944, 1929.

Remmers, H. H. "An Experiment on the Retention of Attitudes as Changed by Instructional Materials." *Stud. higher Educ.* Purdue University, 1938.

———. "Propaganda in the Schools: Do the Effects Last?" *Pub. opin. Quart.,* 1938. II:197–210.

Remmers, H. H. and Radler, D. H. *The American Teen-Ager.* New York: Bobbs-Merrill, 1957.

Remmers, H. H. and Whisler, L. "The Effect of the President's Speech on Pupil's Attitudes toward the Proposed Supreme Court Changes." *Sch. and Soc.,* 1937. XLVI:64.

Rheingold, H. L. "The Modification of Social Responsiveness in Institutional Babies." *Monogr. of Society for Research in Child Development,* 1956. Vol. XXI, No. 2.

Rhine, J. B. *Reach of the Mind.* New York: William Sloane Associates, 1947.

Richardson, L. F. "Statistics of Deadly Quarrels." In Peds, T. H. (ed.). *Psychological Factors of Peace and War*. New York Philosophical Library, 1950.

Riecken, H. W. "Some Problems of Consensus Development." *Rural Sociology*, 1952. XVII:245–252.

Riesman, David. *The Lonely Crowd*. New Haven: Yale University Press, 1950.

Riess, B. F. *Changes in the Attitudes of Student Political Groups towards Methods of Preventing War, as a Result of the Czechoslovakian Crisis*. Report to Eastern Psychological Assn., Mar. 31, 1939.

Robinson, D. and Rohde S. Two experiments with an anti-Semitism poll. *J. abn. soc. psychol.*, 1946, 41:136–144.

Rogers, Carl R. *"Client-Centered Psychotherapy."* Boston: Houghton Mifflin, 1951. p. 521.

———. *On Becoming a Prison*. Boston: Houghton Mifflin, 1961.

Rogers, E. M. *Diffusion of Innovations*. Glencoe, Ill.: Free Press, 1962.

Rogoff, Natalie. "American High Schools at Mid-Century." *See J. educ. Sociol.*, 1960. XXIII:252–259.

———. "Social Stratification in France and in the United States." *Amer. j. Sociol.*, 1953. XLVIII:347–357.

———. "Recent Trends in Urban Occupational Mobility." In Bendix, R. and Lipset, S. M. *Class Status and Power*, Glencoe, Ill.: Free Press, 1953, p. 445.

Rohrer, J. H., Baron, S. H., Hoffman, E. L. and Swander, D. V. "The Stability of Autokinetic Judgments." *J. abn. soc. Psychol.*, 1954. XLIX:595–597.

Rokeach, Milton. *The Open and Closed Mind*. New York: Basic Books, 1960.

———. "Political and Religious Dogmatism." *Psychol. Monogr.*, 1956. LXX, No. 18.

Roper, Elmo. *The Public's View of Television and Other Media*. (1959 + 1964.) New York: Television Information Office, 666 Fifth Avenue. March 15, 1965.

Rosen, B. C. "The Achievement Syndrome." *Amer. sociolog. rev.*, 1956, 21: 203–211.

———. "Conflicting Group Membership: a Study of Parent-Peer Group Cross Pressures." *Amer. sociol. rev.*, 1955. XX:155–161.

Rosen, H. "Desirable Attributes of Work: Four Levels of Management." *J. appl. Psychol.*, 1961. XLV:155–160.

Rosen, S. "Effects of Adjustment on the Perception and Exertion of Social Power." In Cartwright, D. (ed.). *Studies in Social Power*. Ann Arbor: Institute of Social Research, University of Michigan, 1959. pp. 69–81.

Rosenberg, M. J. "Cognitive Structure and Attitudinal Effect." *J. abn. soc. Psychol.*, 1956. LIII:367–372.

Rosenberg, M. J., et al. *Attitude Organization and Change*. New Haven: Yale University Press, 1960.

Rosenthal, S. P. "Change of Socio-Economic Attitudes under Radical Motion Picture Propaganda." *Arch. Psychol.*, 1934. No. 166.

Rougement, Denis de. "Romantic Route to Divorce." *Saturday Review of Literature*, Nov. 13, 1948. XXXI 9–10.

Rowland, L. W. "Will Hypnotized Persons Try to Harm Themselves or Others?" *J. abn. soc. Psychol.*, 1939. XXXIV:114–117.

Ruch, F. L. "Incidents of Leadership in Combat." *HRRL Res. Memo. 3*, 1953.

Rupe, J. C. "When Workers Rate the Boss." *Personnel Psychol.*, 1951. IV:271–290.

Saade, M., Farnsworth, P. R. "The Degree of Acceptance of Dogmatic Statements and Preferences for Their Supposed Maker." *J. abn. soc. Psychol.*, 1934. XXIX:143–150.

Saenger, G. and Gilbert, E. "Customer Reactions to the Integration of Negro Sales Personnel." *Int. J. opin. att. res.*, 1950. IV:57–76.

Salner, E. and Remmers, H. H. "Effective Selectivity and Liberalizing Influence of College Courses." *J. appl. Psychol.*, 1933. XVII:349–354.

Sanai, M. and Pickard, P. M. "The Relation between Politico-Economic Radicalism and Certain Traits of Personality." *J. soc. Psychol.*, 1949, XXX:217–227.

Sanchez-Hildago, E. S. *A Study of the Symbiotic Relationships between Friends.* New York: 1951. MS in library of Teachers College, Columbia University. 177 pp.

Sapir, E. "The Status of Linguistics as a Science." *Language*, 1929. V:207–214.

Sargent, S. S. "Emotional Stereotypes in the Chicago Tribune." *Sociometry*, 1939. II, No. 2, 69–75.

Sayers, Dorothy L. "The Woman Question." *Vogue.* January 15, 1947. pp. 86 ff

Schachter, S. "Deviation, rejection and communication." *J. abn. Soc. Psychol.*, 1951. XLVI:190–207.

———. "The Psychology of Affiliation: Experimental Studies of the Sources of Gregariousness." Stanford University (Calif.) Press, 1959.

Schachter, S. *et al.* "Emotional Disruption and Industrial Productivity." *J. appl. Psychol.*, 1961. XLV:201–213.

Schachter, S., Ellertson, N., McBride, D. and Gregory, D. "An Experimental Study of Cohesiveness and Productivity." *Human Relat.*, 1951. IV:229–238.

Schachter, S., Hall, K. "Group-Derived Restraints and Audience Persuasion." *Hum. relat.*, 1952, V:397–406.

Schachter, S., Singer, J. E. "Cognitive, Social and Physiological Determinants of Emotional State." *Psychol. Rev.*, 1962. LXIX:379–399.

Schaffner, Bertram. *Father Rand.* New York: Columbia University Press, 1948.

Schanck, R. L. "A Study of a Community and its Groups and Institutions Conceived of as Behaviors of Individuals." *Psychol. Monogr.*, 1932, Vol. XLIII, No. 2.

Schanck, R. L., Goodman, C. "Reactions to Propaganda on Both Sides of a Controversial Issue." *Publ. opin. quart.*, 1939. III:107–112.

Schein, E. H. "The Chinese Indoctrination Program of Prisoners of War." *Psychiatry*, 1956. XIX:149–172.

Scheler, Max. *The Nature of Sympathy.* (English translation of *Wesen und Formen der Sympathie*). London: Routledge and Kegan Paul, Ltd., 1954.

Schopenhauer, Arthur. *Parerga und Paralipomena.* Berlin, 1855.

Schramm, Wilbur (ed.). *Mass Communications.* Urbana: University of Illinois, Press, 1949.

Schramm, W. Mass Communication. *Annu. Rev. Psychol.* 1962, XIII:251–284.

Schramm, W., Lyle, J. and Parker, E. B. *Television in the Lives of Our Children.* Stanford, Calif.: Stanford University Press, 1961.

Schutz, William. *Firo: a Three-Dimensional Theory of Interpersonal Behavior.* New York: Rinehart and Co., 1959.

Schwerin, P. and Murphy, M. P. "The Development of Salivation Measurements." *Schwerin Res. Corp. Tech. Analyt. Rev.* 1963, XII:1–5.

Scott, W. A. "Correlates of International Attitudes." *Publ. opin. quart.*, 1958–9. XXII:464–472.

Seago, D. W. "Stereotypes: Before Pearl Harbor and After." *J. psychol.*, 1947. XXIII:55–63.

Seay, B., Alexander, B. K., Harlow, H. F. "Maternal Behavior of Socially Deprived Rhesus Monkeys." *J. abn. soc. Psychol.* 1964, LXIX:345–354.

Seeman, M. "Social Mobility and Administrative Behavior." *Am. sociol. rev.*, 1958, 23:633–642.

Selznick, P. "An Approach to a Theory of Bureaucracy." *Amer. sociol. Rev.*, 1943, VIII:47–54.

Sewell, W. H. "Social Class and Childhood Personality." *Sociometry*, 1961. XXIV:340–356.

Shaw, Clifford. *Brothers in Crime.* Chicago: University of Chicago Press, 1938. p. 96.

———. *Juvenile Delinquency and Urban Areas.* Chicago. University of Chicago Press, 1942.

Shaw, G. B. *Major Critical Essays: the Quintessence of Ibsenism.* London: Constable, 1932.

———. "Woman since 1860." *Time and Tide*, Oct. 8, 1920. pp. 442–445.

Shaw, Marjorie E. "A Comparison of Individuals and Small Groups in the Rational Solution of Complex Problems." *Amer. j. Psychol.*, 1932. XLIV: 491–504.

———. "A Comparison of Two Types of Leadership in Various Communication Nets." *J. abn. soc. Psychol.*, 1955. L:127–134.

———. "Some Motivational Factors in Cooperation and Competition." *J. pers.*, 1958, XXVI:155–169.

Shaw, M. E. and Gilchrist, J. C. "Intra-group Communication and Leader Choice." *J. soc. Psychol.*, 1956. XLIII:133–138.

Shaw, M. E., Rothschild, S. H. and Strickland, J. F. "Decision Processes in Communication Nets." *J. abn. soc. Psychol.*, 1957. LIV:323–330.

Sheerer, Elizabeth T. "An Analysis of the Relationship between Acceptance of and Respect for Self and Acceptance of and Respect for Others in Ten Counseling Cases." *J. consult. Psychol.*, 1949. XIII:169–175.

Sherif, M. "Needed Concepts in the Study of Social Attitudes." In Peatman, J. G. and Hartley, E. L. (ed.). *Festschrift for Gardner Murphy.* New York: Harper and Bros., 1961.

Sherif, M. "A Study of Some Social Factors in Perception." *Arch. Psychol.*, 1935. No. 187.

Sherif, M. and Sherif, C. W. *Groups in Harmony and Tension.* New York: Harper and Bros., 1953.

———. *An Outline of Social Psychology* (Revised Ed.). New York: Harper, 1956. pp. 609–610.

Sherif, M. *et al. Experimental Study of Positive and Negative Intergroup Attitudes between Experimentally Produced Groups.* Norman, Okla. Author. 1954. Multilithed.

Sherwood, John J. *Authoritarianism and Moral Realism.* Lafayette, Ind.: Purdue University School of Industrial Administration, 1965.

Shils, Edward. "Daydreams and Nightmares: Reflections on the Criticism of Mass Culture." *Sewanee Rev.,* 1957. LXV:587–608.

Shrieke, B. *Alien Americans.* New York: Viking, 1936.

Shuttleworth, F. A. "The Influence of Early Religious Home Training on College Sophomore Men." *Relig. Educ.,* 1927. XXII:57–60.

Shuval, J. T. "The Role of Ideology Is a Predisposing Frame of Reference for Immigration." *Hum. relat.,* 1959. XII:51–63.

Sibley, E. "Some Demographic Clues to Stratification." *Amer. sociol. Rev.,* 1942. VII:322–330.

Siegel, A. E., Siegel, S. "Reference Groups, Membership Groups, and Attitude Change." *J. abn. soc. Psychol.,* 1957. LV:360–364.

Simmel, George. "The Number of Members as Determining the Sociological Form of the Group." *Amer. J. Sociol.,* 1902. VIII:1–46; 158–196.

Simpson, Ray H. *A Study of Those Who Influence and of Those Who are Influenced in Discussion.* New York: Teachers College, Columbia University, Bureau of Publications, 1938.

Sims, V. M. "Factors Influencing Attitude toward the Tennessee Valley Authority (TVA)." *J. abn. soc. Psychol.,* 1938. XXXIII:34–56.

Sims, V. M. and Patrick, J. R. "Attitude toward the Negro of Northern and Southern College Students." *J. soc. Psychol.,* 1936. VII:192–204.

Sinclair, Upton. *Mental Radio.* New York: Albert and Charles Boni, 1930.

Singer, J. and Shockley, V. L. "Ability and Affiliation." *J. Pers. Soc. Psychol.* 1965. I:95–99.

Singh, J. A. L. and Zingg, R. M. *Wolf-Children and Feral Man.* New York: Harper, 1942.

Skinner, B. F. "The Science of Learning and the Art of Teaching." *Harvard Educational Review,* 1954. XXIV:86–87.

———. *Walden Two.* New York: Macmillan, 1955.

Slater, P. E. "Role Differentiation in Small Groups." *Amer. sociol. Rev.,* 1955. XX:300–310.

Smith, Adam. *An Inquiry into the Nature and Causes of the Wealth of Nations.* London, 1776. N. Y. Modern Library ed. 1937. pp. 28–29; also p. 248.

Smith, E. E. and Kight, S. S. "Effects of Feedback on Insight and Problem-Solving Efficiency in Training Groups." *J. appl. psychol.,* 1959. XLIII:209–211.

Smith, M. B. "The Personal Setting of Public Opinions." *Publ. opin. quart.,* 1947. XI:507–523.

Smith, F. Tredwell. *An Experiment in Modifying Attitude toward the Negro.* New York: Teachers College, Columbia University, 1943.

Solem, A. R. "An Evaluation of Two Attitudinal Approaches to Delegation." *J. appl. Psychol.,* 1958. XLII:36–39.

Sommer, Robert. "Leadership and group geography." *Sociometry,* 1961. XXIV:99–110.

Sorokin, P. A. *Explorations in Altruistic Love and Behavior.* Boston: Beacon Press, 1950.

――――. *Social and Cultural Dynamics*. New York: American Book Co., 1941.

――――. *Society, Cultural and Personality*. New York: Harper and Bros., 1947.

South, E. B. "Some Psychological Aspects of Committee Work." *J. appl. Psychol.*, 1927. XI:348–368, 437–464.

Spencer, Herbert. *Principles of Sociology*. First published, 1876. 2 vols. New York: D. Appleton, 1900.

Spengler, Oswald. *The Decline of the West*. Translation by Atkinson. New York: Knopf, 1926. First published *Der Untergang des Abendlandes*, 1918.

Spiller, G. "The Dynamics of Greatness." *Sociol. Rev.*, 1929. XXI:218–232.

Spindler, G. D. *Sociocultural and Psychological Processes in Menomini Acculturation*. Berkeley, Calif. University of California publications in culture and society. No. 5, 1955.

Spitz, René A. "Hospitalism: an Inquiry into the Genesis of Psychiatric Conditions in Early Childhood." In Psycholoanalytic Study of the Child, 1945. I:53–74.

Spitz, René A. and Wolf, K. M. *Anaclitic Depression*. In Psychoanalytic Study of the Child, 1946. II:313–342.

Spranger, E. *Types of Men*. Leipzig, 5th German ed., 1928.

Srole, L. *Social dysfunction, personality and social distance*. Paper read before Amer. sociolog. soc., 1951.

Staats, A. W. and Staats, C. K. Attitudes established by classical conditioning. *J. abn. soc. psycholog.*, 1958, LVII:37–40.

Stagner, Ross. Attitude toward authority. *J. soc. psychol.*, 1954, 40:197–210.

――――. "Fascist Attitudes, an Exploratory Study." *J. soc. Psychol.*, 1936. VII: 309–319.

――――. "A Note on Education and Internaional Attitudes." *J. soc. Psychol.*, 1942. XVI:341–345.

Stagner, Ross and Osgood, C. E. "Impact of War on a Nationalistic Frame of Reference." *J. soc. Psychol.*, 1946. XXIV:187–215.

Stanton, Elizabeth C., *et al. The History of Woman Suffrage*. New York: Natl. Amer. Woman Suffrage Assn., 1889–1922.

Staples, F. R., Walters, R. H. Anxiety, birth-order, and susceptibility to social influence. *J. abn. soc. psychol.*, 1961, 62:716–719.

Steinzor, Bernard. "The Spatial Factor in Face-to-Face Discussion Groups." *J. abn. soc. Psychol.*, 1950. XLV:552–555.

Stember, C. H., Hyman, H. "How Interviewer Effects Operate through Question Form." *International Journal of Opinion and Attitude Research*, 1949, III:493–512.

Stendler, Celia B. *Children of Brasstown*. University of Illinois Bull. 1949, Vol. XLVI, No. 59.

Stephan, A. S. "Population Ratios, Racial Attitudes and Desegregation." In Tumin, M. M. *Segregation and Desegregation*. New York: Anti-Defamation League of B'nai B'rith, 1957, p. 20.

Stephen, F. F., Mishler, E. G. "The Distribution of Participation in Small Groups." *Amer. sociol. Rev.*, 1952. XVII:598–608.

Stephenson, R. M. "Mobility Orientation and Stratification of 1,000 Ninth Graders." *Amer. sociol. Rev.*, 1957. XXII:204–212.

Stewart, J. B. *Repetitive Advertising in Newspapers.* Boston, Mass. Harv. Bus. Sch. 1963.

Stock, Dorothy and Thelen, H. A. "Emotional Dynamics and Group Culture." New York University Press, 1958.

Stoddard, T. Lothrop. *The Rising Tide of Color Against White World Supremacy.* New York: Scribners, 1920.

Stoetzel, Jean. *Without the Chrysanthemum and the Sword.* New York: Columbia University Press, for UNESCO, 1955.

Stogdill, R. M., Shartle, C. L. Coons, A. E., Jaynes, W. E. "A Predictive Study of Administrative Work Patterns." Columbus, O.: Ohio State Univ. Bur. Bus. Res. *Monogr. R-85,* 1956.

Stouffer, S. A. "An Analysis of Conflicting Social Norms." *Amer. sociol. Rev.,* 1949. XIV:707–717.

———. *Communism, Conformity and Civil Liberties.* New York: Doubleday, 1955, p. 41.

Stouffer, S. A. *et al. The American Soldier.* Princeton: Princeton University Press, 1949. Vol I, p. 414.

———. *Combat and Its Aftermath.* Vol. II of *The American Soldier.* Princeton: Princeton University Press, 1949. p. 136.

———. *Communism, Conformity and Civil Liberties:* A Cross-Section of the Nation Speaks Its Mind. Garden City, N. Y.: Doubleday and Co., 1955.

Strauss, G. "Some Notes on Power Equalization." In Leavitt, H. J. (ed.). *The Social Science of Organizations.* Engelwood Cliffs, N. J.: Prentice-Hall, 1963.

Strong, E. K. *The Second-Generation Japanese Problem.* Stanford University Press, 1934.

Sullivan, Harry Stack. *Conceptions of Modern Psychiatry.* Washington, D. C.: Wm. Alanson White Foundation, 1947. p. 8.

Sumner, William Graham. *Folk Ways.* New York: Ginn and Co., 1906.

Sumner, W. G. and Keller, A. G. *Science of Society.* New Haven: Yale University Press, 1924. 4 vols.

Sumstine, D. R. "Visual Instruction in High School." *School and Society,* Feb. 23, 1918. I:235–238.

Sutherland, E. H. "Is White-Collar Crime Crime?" *Amer. sociol. Rev.,* 1945. pp. 132–139.

Sutherland, E. H. (ed.). *The Professional Thief.* Chicago: University of Chicago Press, 1937.

———. "White-collar Criminality." *Amer. sociol. Rev.,* 1940, V:1–12.

———. *The Professional Thief.* Chicago: University of Chicago Press, 1937.

Survey Research Center. *The Public Impact of Science in the Mass Media.* Ann Arbor: University of Michigan, 1958.

Swanson, G. E. *The Birth of the Gods: the Origin of Primitive Beliefs.* Ann Arbor, Mich.: University of Michigan Press, 1960.

Tannenbaum, Frank. "The professional criminal." *Century,* 1925. CX:577.

Tardè, G. *The laws of imitation,* 1890.

Tarnapol, L. "Attitudes Block Communications." *Personnel Journal,* 1959, XXXVII:325–328.

Taussig, F. W. and Joslyn, C. S. *American Business Leaders.* New York: Macmillan, 1932. p. 103.

Taylor, D. W., Berry, P. C. and Bloch, C. H. "Group Participation, Brainstorming and Creative Thinking." *Admin. sci. quart.*, III:23–47.

Taylor, F. K. "Display of Dyadic Emotions." *Hum. relat.* 1957. X:257–262.

Taylor, F. W. *Principles of Scientific Management.* New York: Harper, 1911.

Teggart, Frederick. *The Processes of History.* New Haven. Yale University Press, 1918.

Terman, L. M. and Oder, M. H. *The Gifted Child Grows Up.* Stanford University, California, 1947.

Terman, L. M. *et al. Psychological Factors in Marital Happiness.* New York: McGraw-Hill, 1938.

Terman, L. M. and Miles, C. C. *Sex and Personality: Studies in Masculinity and Femininity.* New York: McGraw-Hill, 1936.

Thistlewaite, D. L. and Kamenetzky, J. "Attitude Change through Refutation and Elaboration of Audience Counterarguments." *J. abn. soc. Psychol.*, 1955. LI:3–12.

Thomas, Alan M. *A Concept of the Audience.* Unpublished. Ph.D. thesis. Teachers College, Columbia University, 1962.

Thomas, Elizabeth M. *The Harmless People.* New York: Knopf, 1959.

Thomas, W. I. *Primitive Behavior.* New York: McGraw-Hill, 1937.

Thompson, Laura. *Culture in Crisis.* New York: Harper and Bros., 1950.

Thompson, N. R. and Heron, W. "The Effects of Restricting Early Experience on the Problem Solving of Dogs." *Canad. J. Psychol.*, 1954. VIII:17–31.

Thompson, W. R. and Nishimura, R. "Some Determinants of Friendship," *J. pers.* 1951. XX:305–314.

Thorndike, E. L. *The Original Nature of Man.* New York: Teachers College, Columbia University Bureau of Publications, 1913.

Thorndike, R. L. "Effect of Discussion." *J. soc. Psychol.*, 1938a. IX:343–362.

———. "What Type of Task Do Groups Do Well?" *J. abn. soc. Psychol.*, 1938b., XXXIII:409–413.

Thrasher, Frederick M. "Social Backgrounds and Informal Education." *J. educ. Sociol.*, 1934. VII:470–484.

———. *The Gang.* Chicago: University of Chicago Press, 1927.

Thrasher, F. M. and Kerstetter, L. M. "Sociometry and an Activity Program on the University Level." *Sociometry*, 1947. X:178–185.

Thurstone, L. L. "Influence of Motion Pictures on Children's Attitudes." *J. soc. Psychol.*, 1931. II:291–305.

Thurstone, L. L. and Chave, E. J. *The Measurement of Attitude.* Chicago: University of Chicago Press, 1929.

Tilton, J. W., Knowlton, D. C. "The Contribution of Ten Chronicles of American Photoplays to Seventh-Grade History Teaching." *J. soc. Psychol.*, 1930. I:78–96.

Timmons, W. M. *Decisions and Attitudes as Outcomes of the Discussion of a Social Problem.* New York: Teachers College, Columbia University, 1939.

Torrance, E. P. *Some Consequences of Power Differences in Decision-Making in Permanent and Temporary Three-Man Groups.* Research Studies, State College of Washington, 1954. XXII:130–140.

Toynbee, Arnold, J. "Again Nationalism Threatens." *New York Times Magazine,* No. 5, 1963, p. 23.

––––. *A Study of History.* New York: Oxford University Press, 6 vol., 1934. Abridgement by D. C. Somervell, 1947.

Travis, E. L. "The Effect of a Small Audience upon Eye-Hand Coordination." *J. abn. soc. Psychol.*, 1925. XX:142–146.

Tseng, Sing-chi. *An Experimental Study of the Effect of Three Types of Distribution of Reward upon Work Efficiency and Group Dynamics.* New York: Teachers College, Columbia University, Manuscript, 1952.

Tumin, M. M. *Desegregation: Resistance and Readiness.* Princeton, N. J.: Princeton University Press, 1958.

––––. "Imaginary vs. Real Children." *Sch. and Soc.*, Oct. 11, 1958. pp. 357–360.

––––. *Segregation and Desegregation.* New York: Anti-Defamation League, B'nai B'rith, 1957.

Turner, Frederick J. *The Frontier in American History.* New York: Henry Holt and Co., 1920.

Turnure, James, Zigler, E. "Outerdirectedness in the Problem-Solving of Normal and Retarded Children." *J. abn. soc. Psychol.* 1964, LXIX:427–436.

Twitchell-Allen, Davis. "Action Research with Children of Different Nationalities." In Gilbert, G. M. (ed.). *Psychological Approaches to Intergroup and International Understanding.* Austin, Tex.: University of Texas, 1956, pp. 19–23.

Umberger, H. "The Influence of Radio Instruction upon Farm Practices." In MacLatchy, J. H. (ed.). *Education on the Air.* Columbus, O.: Ohio State University, 1932.

U. S. Department of Justice FBI. *Uniform Crime Reports.* Washington, D. C., Government Printing Office, Jan. 1953. p. 112.

Useem, John *et al.* "Stratification in a prairie town." *Amer. sociol. Rev.*, 1942, VII:331–342.

U. S. War Dept. *Opinions about Negro Infantry Platoons in White Companies of Seven Divisions. Rept. No. B-157.*, Info. and Educ. Div. Army Service Forces, 1945.

Veroff, Joseph. "African Students in the United States." *J. soc. Issues*, 1963. XIX:48–60.

Verplanck, W. S. "The Control of the Content of Conversation." *J. abn. soc. Psychol.*, 1955. LI:668–676.

Vetter, G. B. "The Measurement of Social and Political Attitudes and the Related Personality Factors." *J. abn. soc. Psychol.*, 1930. XXV:149–189.

Vinter, R. D. Unpublished doctoral thesis. Teachers College, Columbia University, 1957. Typewritten and microfilmed.

Vroom, V. H. "Ego involvement, job satisfaction, and job performance." *Personnel Psychol.*, 1962. XV:159–177.

Wagatsuma, H. and DeVos, G. "Attitudes toward Arranged Marriage in Rural Japan." *Human org.*, 1962. XXI:187–200.

Walker, C. R. *Steeltown.* New York: Harper, 1950.

Walker, K. F. "A Study of Occupational Stereotypes." *J. appl. Psychol.*, 1958. XLII:122–124.

Wallace, J. M. Williams, F. W. and Cantril, H. "Identification of Occupational groups with economic and social class." *J. abn. soc. Psychol.*, 1944. XXXIX:482–5.

Wallen, R. "Individuals' Estimates of Group Opinion." *J. soc. Psychol.*, 1943, XVII:269–274.

Walters, R. J., Thomas, E. L., Acker, C. W. "Enhancement of Punitive Behavior by Audio-Visual Displays." *Science*, 1962. CXXXVI:872–3.

Waples, D., Berelson, B., Bradshaw, F. P. *What Reading Does to People.* Chicago: University of Chicago Press, 1940.

Ward, L. B. "Problems in Review: Putting Executives to the Test." *Harvard Business Review*, 1960. XXXVIII:6–7.

Warner, W. Lloyd. *Democracy in Jonesville.* New York: Harper, 1949.

Warner, W. L., Abegglen, J. C. "Occupational Mobility in Business and Industry," 1928–1952. Minneapolis: University of Minnesota Press, 1955.

Warner, W. Lloyd *et al. Yankee City Series: 1. The Social Life of a Modern Community* (1941); 2. *The Status System of a Modern Community,* 1942; 3. *The Social Systems of American Ethnic Groups,* 1945. New Haven: Yale University Press.

Warner, W. L., Havighurst, R. J. and Loeb, M. B. *Who Shall Be Educated?* New York: Harper and Bros., 1944. p. 85.

Warner, W. Lloyd and Henry, W. E. "The Radio Daytime Serial." *Gentet. psychol. Monogr.*, 1948. XXXVII:3–71.

Washburn, M. F., *et al.* "The Moore Tests of Radical and Conservative Temperaments." *Amer. J. Psychol.*, 1927. XXXVIII:449–452.

Watson, Barbara Bellow. *A Shavian Guide to the Intelligent Woman.* New York: W. W. Norton, 1964.

Watson, Goodwin. *Action for Unity.* New York: Harper and Bros., 1947.

Watson, G. (ed.). *Civilian Morale.* Boston: Houghton Mifflin, 1942.

——.*A Comparison of "Adaptable" vs. "Laggard" Y.M.C.A.'s.* Int. Comm. of Y.M.C.A., 1946.

——. "Do Groups Think More Effectively than Individuals?" (I) *J. abn. soc. Psychol.*, 1928. XXIII:328–336.

——. "Do Groups Think More Effectively than Individuals?" (II) In Murphy, G. and Murphy, L. B. *Experimental Social Psychology.* New York: Harper and Bros., 1931. pp. 539–543.

——. "An Evaluation of Small Group Work in a Large Class." *J. educ. Psychol.*, 1953. XLIV:385–408.

——. "Happiness among Adult Students of Education." *J. educ. psy.*, 1930. XXI:79–109.

——. *The Measurement of Fair-Mindedness.* New York: Teachers College, Columbia University, Bureau of Publications, 1925.

——. *Orient and Occident.* Published by Institute of Pacific Relations, 129 E. 52 St. New York, 1928.

——. "Some Personality Differences in Children Related to Strict or Permissive Parental Discipline." *J. Psychol.*, 1957. XLIV:227–249.

——. "Utopia and Rebellion: the New College Experiment." In Miles, M. (ed.). *Innovation in Education.* New York: Teachers College, Columbia University, Bur. Publ., 1964, Ch. 4.

——. "Work Satisfaction." In Hartmann, George and Newcomb, T. (ed.). *Industrial Conflict.* New York: Cordon Co., 1939. pp. 115–122.

——. *Youth after Conflict.* N. Y. Association Press, 1947.

——. "What Makes Radicals?" *Common Sense*, 1941, 10:7–9.

Watson, Goodwin and Harris, Adeline. "Are Jewish or Gentile Children more Clannish?" *J. soc. Psychol.*, 1946. XXIV:71–76.

Watson, Jeanne. "Some Social and Psychological Situations Related to Change in Attitude." *Hum. Relat.*, 1950. III:15–56.

Watson, Jeanne, Breed, Warren and Posman, Harry. "A Study in Urban Conversation; Sample of 100 Remarks Overheard in Manhattan." *J. soc. Psychol.*, 1948. XXVIII:121–133.

Watson, Jeanne and Lippitt, R. *Learning Across Cultures*. Inst. soc. res., University of Michigan, Ann Arbor, 1955.

Watson, John B. *Psychology from the Standpoint of a Behaviorist*. Philadelphia: J. B. Lippincott, 1919.

Watson, John B. and Raynor, Rosalie. "Conditioned Emotional Reactions." *J. exper. Psychol.*, 1921. III:1–14.

Watson, W. S. and Hartmann, G. W. "The Rigidity of a Basic Attitudinal Frame." *J. abn. soc. Psychol.*, 1939. XXXIV:314–335.

Weiss, R. S. and Samelson, N. M. "Social Roles of American Women: Their Contribution to a Sense of Usefulness and Importance." *Marriage and Family Living*, 1958. XX:358–366.

Weiss, W. and Fine, B. J. "The Effect of Induced Aggressiveness on Opinion Change." *J. abn. soc. Psychol.*, 1956, LII:109–114.

Weisskopf, W. A. "Industrial Institutions and Personality." *J. soc. issues*, 1951, VII, No. 4, p. 2.

Wertham, F. C. *Seduction of the Innocent*. New York: Rinehart, 1954.

West, James. *Plainville, U.S.A.* New York: Columbia University Press, 1945.

Wheeler, D. and Jordan, H. "Change in Individual Opinion to Accord with Group Opinion." *J. abn. soc. Psychol.*, 1929. XXIV:203–206.

Wherry, R. J. and Fuyer, D. "Buddy Ratings: Popularity Contest or Leadership Criteria?" *Sociometry*, 1949. XII:179–190.

White, R. K., Lippitt, R. O. *Autocracy and Democracy*. New York: Harper and Bros., 1960.

Whiting, J. W. M. "Cultural and Sociological Influences on Development." In Maryland growth and development institute. Cited by Hsu, F. L. K. *Psychological Anthropology*. Homewood, Ill.: Dorsey Press, 1961, p. 368.

——. "Sorcery, Sin and the Superego." In *Symposium on Motivation*. Lincoln, Nebr., University of Nebraska Press, 1959.

——. *"Child training and personality."* New Haven: Yale University Press, 1953.

Whiting, J. W. M., Kluckhohn, R. and Anthony, A. "The Function of Male Initiation Ceremonies at Puberty." In Maccoby, E. E., Newcomb, T. M. and Hartley, E. L. *Readings in Social Psychology*. New York: Holt, 1958. pp. 359–370.

Whorf, B. L. "An American Indian Model of the Universe." *Int. j. Amer. Linguistics*, 1950. XVI:67–72.

Whyte, William F. *Street Corner Society*. University of Chicago Press, 1943.

Wickert, F. "Psychological Research on Problems of Redistribution." Washington: U.S. Govt. Printing Office. AAF. *Aviat. psychol. prog. res. Rept.*, No. 14, 1947.

Wilke, W H. "An Experimental Comparison of Speech, the Radio and the

Printed Page as Propaganda Devices." *Arch. Psychol.*, 1934. No. 169. (N.Y., Columbia University Press).

Willerman, B. *Group Decision and Request as a Means of Changing Food Habits.* Washington, D.C.: Committee on Food Habits, National Research Council. April 1943 (Mimeo).

Williams, Raymond. "Television in Britain." *J. soc. Issues,* 1962. XVIII:6–15.

Williams, S. B. and Leavitt, H. J. "Group opinion as a Predictor of Military Leadership." *J. consult. Psychol.,* 1947. XI:283–291.

Wilner, D. M., Walkley, R. B. and Cooh, S. W. *Residential Proximity and Intergroup Relations in Public Housing Projects.* New York: New York University, Research Center for Human Relations, 1951.

Wilson, Pauline P. "College Women Who Express Futility." New York: Teachers College, Columbia Bureau of Publications, 1950.

Winch, R. F. *Mate Selection.* New York: Harper and Bros., 1958.

Wissler, Clark. *Man and Culture.* New York: Crowell, 1923.

Wolf, K. M. and Fiske, M. "The children talk about comics." In Lazarsfeld P. F. and Stanton, F. N. (eds.). *Communications Research,* 1948–9. New York: Harper, 1949. pp. 3–50.

Wolfe, D. M. "Power and Authority in the Family." In Cartwright, D. *Studies in Social Power.* Ann Arbor: Inst. Soc. Res., University of Michigan, 1959. pp. 99–117.

Wolfenstein, Martha. "The Emergence of Fun Morality." *J. soc. Issues,* 1951. VII, No. 4, pp. 15–25.

Wolfenstein, M. and Leites, N. *Movies: a Psychological Study.* Glencoe, Ill.: The Free Press, 1950.

Wollestonecraft, Mary. *Vindication of the Rights of Women.* Everyman's Library, London, Dent, 1929 reprinting; first published 1792.

Wolman, B. "Leadership and Group Dynamics!" *J. soc. Psychol.,* 1956, XLIII: 11–25.

Woodward, H. S. "Measurement and Analysis of Audience Opinion."*Quart.J. Speech,* 1928. XIV:94–111.

Woodworth, R. S. "Review of Allport's *Social Psychology,*" *Journal of Abnormal and Social Psychology,* Vol. XX (1925), pp. 92–106.

Woolbert, C. H. "The Effects of Various Modes of Public Reading." *J. appl. Psychol.,* 1920. IV:162–185.

Woolf, Virginia. *A Room of One's Own.* New York: Harcourt Brace, 1929.

Worcester, D. A. "Memory by Visual and Auditory Presentation." *J. educ. Psychol.* 1925. XVI:18–28.

Worthy, J. C. "Organizational Structure and Employe Morale." *Amer. Sociol. Rev.* 1950, XV:169–179.

Wright, G. O. "Projection and Displacement: a Cross-Cultural Study of Folktale Aggression." *J. abn. soc. Psychol.,* 1954. XLIX:523–8.

Wright, M. Erik. "The Influence of Frustration upon Social Relations of Young Children." *Charact. and Pers.,* 1943. XII:111–122.

Wright, W. L. "Some Effects of Incentives on Work and Fatigue." *Psych. Rev.,* 1906. XIII:23–24.

Wrightsman, L. S. Jr. "Effects of Waiting with Others on Changes in Level of Felt Anxiety." *J. abn. soc. Psychol.,* 1960. LXI:216–222.

Wrightstone, J. W. "Civic Beliefs and Correlated Intellectual and Social Factors." *Sch. Rev.*, 1934. XLII:53–58.

Wundt, W. *Elements of Folk-Psychology.* New York: Macmillan, 1916. 3 vol.

Yerkes, R. M. *Chimpanzees: a Laboratory Colony.* New Haven: Yale University Press, 1943.

Yerkes, R. M. and Elder, J. H. "Oestrus, Receptivity and Mating in Chimpanzee." *Comp. psychol. Monogr.*, 1936. XIII: No. 65, pp. 1–39.

Young, Donald. *American Minority Peoples.* New York: Harper, 1932.

Young, Kimball. "The Psychology of Hymns." *J. abn. soc. psychol.*, 1925. XX: 391–406.

———. *Personality and Problems of Adjustment. New York.* Appleton, Century, Crofts, 1962.

———. *Personality and Problems of Adjustment.* New York. Appleton, Century, Crofts, 1952.

Zeaman, D. (Experiment described in Sherif, M. and Sherif, S. An Outline of Social Psychology, Rev. Ed. New York: Harper, 1956. p. 610–612.)

Zeleny, L. D. Sociometry of morale. *Amer. sociol. Rev.*, 1939: IV:799–808.

Zilliacus, L. *Mail for the World.* New York: John Day, 1953.

Ziller, R. C. "Group Size: a Determinant of the Quality and Stability of Group Decisions." *Sociometry*, 1957. XX:165–173.

Zillig, M. *Einstellung und Aussage Zeitschrift für Psychologie,* 1928. CVI:58–106.

Index of Names

Index of Subjects